Fourth Edition

Behavior Principles in Everyday Life

John D. Baldwin

Janice I. Baldwin

University of California
Santa Barbara

Prentice
Hall

Upper Saddle River, New Jersey 07458

Library of Congress Cataloging-in-Publication Data

Baldwin, John D.
  Behavior principles in everyday life / John D. Baldwin, Janice I. Baldwin.—4th ed.
    p. cm.
  Includes bibliographical references and indexes.
  ISBN 0-13-087376-4
    1. Behaviorism (Psychology)   2. Psychology, Applied.   I. Baldwin, Janice I.   II. Title.
BF199.B28 2000
150.19'43—dc21   00-033650

VP, Editorial Director: Laura Pearson
Executive Editor: Stephanie Johnson
Associate Editor: Jennifer Blackwell
Managing Editor: Mary Rottino
Production Liaison: Fran Russello
Project Manager: Pine Tree Composition
Prepress and Manufacturing Buyer: Tricia Kenny
Art Director: Jayne Conte
Cover Designer: Bruce Kenselaar
Cover Art: Donna Day
Marketing Manager: Sharon Cosgrove

This book is dedicated to
Ivan Petrovich Pavlov, B.F. Skinner,
Albert Bandura, and the many others
who have pioneered in the research on
behavior principles.

© 2001, 1998, 1986, 1981 by Prentice-Hall, Inc.
A Division of Pearson Education
Upper Saddle River, New Jersey 07458

Printed in the United States of America

ISBN 0-13-087376-4

Prentice-Hall International (UK) Limited, *London*
Prentice-Hall of Australia Pty. Limited, *Sydney*
Prentice-Hall Canada Inc., *Toronto*
Prentice-Hall Hispanoamericana, S.A., *Mexico*
Prentice-Hall of India Private Limited, *New Delhi*
Prentice-Hall of Japan, Inc., *Tokyo*
Pearson Education Asia Pte. Ltd., *Singapore*
Editora Prentice-Hall do Brasil, Ltda., *Rio de Janeiro*

Contents

Preface

It is exciting to enter the 21st century as behavioral science broadens its scope to deal ever more effectively with natural environments. We hope *Behavior Principles in Everyday Life* can, in its small way, help students and professionals learn how to apply behavioral analyses to everyday situations. This book is about people of all ages in many different kinds of settings, revealing many of the behavioral principles that produce both functional and dysfunctional patterns of behavior. Our hope is that readers will use the information to live happier, more fulfilling lives—free from pain and fear—while sharing this knowledge and behavior with others.

During the thirty years we have taught behavior principles, we have become firmly convinced that the majority of students learn the principles most rapidly and effectively when they study them with examples from everyday life. Students are more familiar with the behavior seen in natural settings than any other forms of behavior; so it takes them little effort to follow the examples, and they can focus on learning the principles of behavior and methods of behavioral analysis.

Students report having numerous "Eureka" experiences—which they describe as pleasant, positive reinforcers—as they read material that helps them understand everyday events they had never appreciated before. "So that's why I do that!" This allows readers to receive immediate positive reinforcement as they learn behavior principles and the skills for doing behavior analyses. Many of Skinner's analyses of everyday events gave us those "Eureka" experiences, and we hope to continue that tradition.

By reducing the effort of studying behavior principles—with familiar examples and frequent positive reinforcers—we can help our students learn more behavioral material in one course than if the topic were taught without these examples. This new edition contains more examples and a more carefully worded presentation of behavior principles than did prior editions. Our goal is to help students learn the behavior principles well and generalize their behavior analytic skills to numerous situations and events.

Many students are eager to understand their own behavior, and most do not accept the old psychological models that are still presented in so many of their courses. The Freudian model is so strongly focused on psychoses, neuroses, and other mental illnesses that it misses much of the fun, beauty, and positive qualities of everyday life. Sociobiology reduces so much of life to sexual imperatives that it misses much of the rest of life.

And purely cognitive psychology neglects consequences, contingencies, stimulus control, schedules of reinforcement, methods for modifying behavior, and much more.

Behavioral psychology can offer students more modern and empirically defensible theories to explain the details of everyday life than can the other psychological theories. It is time to enthusiastically advance the study of behavior into natural environments and analyze the cognitions, emotions, and behaviors that people experience in their daily lives from a behavioral perspective. The fact that behavioral science has demanded—and been rewarded for using—experimental control in laboratories and clinics should not deter us from expanding our science into less controlled environments. We firmly believe that behavior principles are far more effective than the other psychological theories in explaining behavior in natural settings.

It is important to remember that Skinner was not reluctant to generalize his science far beyond his database, and his work was an enormous catalyst for the advance of our science. In *Walden Two, Science and Human Behavior, About Behaviorism,* and other writings, Skinner (1948a, 1953, 1974) clearly showed how deeply interested he was in applying behavioral analyses and interventions to many facets of personal and social life. Skinner's writings contain insightful examples from everyday life, and they interested people from many disciplines in applying behavior principles to a broad range of topics. Modern behaviorists have vastly more empirical data than Skinner did—from laboratory, clinical and natural settings—to support analyses of everyday life; thus, we should be less reluctant than he to grapple with the fascinating details of everyday life.

Why not follow Skinner's example and allow students to discover the power of behavior principles in explaining the behavior closest to them? We believe that behavior principles help them more than the Freudian, sociobiological, or purely cognitive models do, and today's students are increasingly eager to hear behavior principles as a fresh, healthy alternative to the other theories.

Many people believe: "You only live once." In that one life, some people have years of pleasure, while others have years of pain. We can share the knowledge of behavior principles so that people gain the power and wisdom to direct their behavior toward something of beauty. In an important sense, life is an art form, and we all can create something beautiful or grotesque with our lives. Behaviorists are in a good position to help people understand: "Life is like a canvas and you are the artists. You can create a beautiful canvas or slash it to shreds. Why not learn the behavior principles that are useful in creating beautiful behaviors and relationships."

As laboratory, clinical, and field research continue to advance, behavioral science is delivering ever more powerful tools to help people be kinder, happier, and more creative. In essence, we are empowering people to analyze their lives and adjust their own behavior to attain more beautiful outcomes. In the process of improving the human condition, we are giving people greater freedom for self-creation than could any prescientific knowledge. Behavioral principles can free people from aversives and the problems of coercive control. It can free people who were once enslaved by dysfunctional habits that they did not know how to escape. Our science is strongly equated with the word "freedom": Freedom from pain and dysfunctional behavior. Freedom to create behavior that produces a beautiful "canvas of life."

Let us make our point with a less happy example. AIDS is a deadly disease that kills millions of people each year worldwide. Billions of dollars have been poured into medical research to combat the disease over the past 20 years, yet still today, the least expensive and most widely recognized solution to the AIDS problem is behavioral: Teach people to avoid risky sexual interactions, and teach a variety of risk-reducing behaviors for those who are sexually active.[1]

We can advance our discipline by making the behavior principles as accessible as possible with analyses of the behavior of everyday situations.[2] The fourth edition of *Behavior Principles in Everyday Life* continues in the path of prior editions, presenting a large number of principles about operant and Pavlovian conditioning, along with social-learning theory and cognitive behaviorism, as they apply in natural settings. Each chapter closes with both a chapter summary and a series of review questions to help students rapidly review and test themselves on their comprehension of key points. The instructor's manual for this book offers many tips for making classroom activities clearly organized and maximally rewarding for this learning.

All the behavioral principles are presented in italics and key words in bold print in order to aid readers in identifying the most central material. All sections of the book contain *abstract principles* and *concrete examples,* and both of these are worded to help readers understand and remember the other. Abstract principles foster the development of explicit and easily verbalized forms of knowledge; while familiar concrete examples draw in the tacit type of knowledge that completes our understanding (see Chapter 12).[3] Most examples used in the book are short and succinct to illustrate the behavior principles quickly and lucidly. The use of short examples allows us to cover a large range of topics, which helps students learn more of the behavior principles and apply them to a broader range of natural settings.

Much of the inspiration for writing and improving the book has come from teaching bright and inquisitive students whose intellectual curiosity has stimulated our own thought and study. We thank all those students for their questions, suggestions, and enthusiasm. For their assistance in developing the earlier editions, we sincerely thank Professors Jay Alperson, Palomar College; Thomas E. Billimek, San Antonio College; David C. Meissner, Alfred University; Kenneth N. Wildman, Ohio Northern University; Richard N. Feil, Mansfield University; Pamela E. Scott-Johnson, Spelman College; A. Robert Sherman, University of California, Santa Barbara; Frank Sparzo, Ball State University; and Perry Timmermans, San Diego City College. We are most grateful to Professors John L. Caruso, University of Massachusetts, Dartmouth; Richard N. Feil, Mansfield University; Joseph C. LaVoie, University of Nebraska, Omaha; and Margaret Vaughan, Salem State College for their suggestions in creating the recent edition.

J.D.B.
J.I.B.

[1]Coates and Collins (1998, p. 96).
[2]Heward and Malott (1995).
[3]Skinner (1969, pp. 133–171).

Chapter

1

Science and Human Behavior[1]

THE BEHAVIOR OF EVERYDAY LIFE

Why are some people so cheerful and friendly while others are so angry and nasty? Why do some people cry easily; and others, rarely? These are questions about behavior. Sometimes in movies, we become involved in the behavior of space aliens, superheros, or psychotic murderers; but most of the time we are interested in the behavior of people in our everyday lives. Our daily experience is full of fascinating behavior and it deserves our careful attention. People have always been curious about their own behavior, their relationships with others, and the countless things other people do. "Why do I feel happy one day and sad the next?" "Why are some people so creative or humorous?"

Over the past 300 years, science has proven to be the most powerful tool ever developed to answer the questions about our world; and in the past 100 years, researchers have discovered numerous valuable scientific principles that explain how learning influences almost every aspect of our behavior.[2] *This book presents the most useful of these behavior principles—also called "learning theory"—with an abundance of concrete everyday examples that help you grasp the scientific principles as easily as possible.*

Behavior science is concerned with all of human behavior—talking, thinking, eating pizzas on summer picnics, painting canvases, making love, learning new things, forgetting old things. We hope that you will see yourself, family, and friends in the numerous examples used in each chapter. *This book covers virtually every type of behavior you notice in yourself and other people,* including all the *inner thoughts* and *feelings* that we know are involved with our *external actions.* After a friend surprises us with something wonderful, we feel happy, think positive thoughts about the event, and act in ways that overtly express our excitement and appreciation. *Sequences of thoughts, feelings, and overt actions intertwine in a delicate dance as we respond to and act upon our world.* Everything that we do—even thinking and fantasizing—is behavior; and all types of behavior are open to scientific study.

This book was written with two goals in mind.[3] *First, it will help you better understand the things happening to you—inside and outside your body—in your everyday life.* Louis Pasteur, the wise French scientist who applied his knowledge of chemistry and biology to solve many important health problems, said, "In the fields of observation, chance favors only the mind that is prepared." The experiences of everyday life provide us with a constant deluge of fascinating examples of natural behavior. Yet most people are not prepared to appreciate the numerous behavior principles that are operating constantly, right before their eyes. This book can help you see more of life.

Second, an understanding of behavior principles will help you better guide and control your own thoughts, feelings, and actions toward the goals you value. We have no desire to tell you what your values should be; but we plan to explain enough behavior principles that you can learn how to modify any of your own thoughts, feelings, and actions that you wish were different. Because we all influence other people every day, you may draw upon learning theory to influence others; and we hope that you use the power of behavior principles beneficially, to help other people be the best they can be. Many examples throughout the text demonstrate the benefits of caring and generous social acts along with the painful consequences that can arise from selfish and aggressive actions.

BEHAVIORAL DEFINITIONS

What's in a word? Vagueness or detail? Vague statements about behavior are less useful than detailed ones. "See you later," is a friendly thing to say, but it is rather vague. In contrast, the words "See you outside the west tennis court at 4 this afternoon" define an expected behavior quite precisely. When it comes to meeting people and making things happen, the extra detail of precise definitions has immense value.

Throughout most of history, people have relied on vague definitions of behavior, and this limited their knowledge and behavioral effectiveness. *One of the first great advances in behavioral science, about 100 years ago, was a demand for **behavioral definitions**—which are careful, detailed, and objective descriptions of behavior.*[4] Behavioral definitions focus our attention on clear descriptions of behaviors that can be observed, measured, counted, tabulated, and analyzed.

For example, let us explore the behavioral definitions of both anger and love.[5] Rather than merely saying that someone is *angry,* behavioral scientists ask for careful descriptions of the *observable units of behavior* that would lead you to realize that a person is angry. Careful observations reveal that people can show anger in many ways: Some people express anger with fast and intense movements of their arms, body, and facial muscles; others stay calm and quietly resolve to get even the next time they can. Some raise their voices and shout; others use a "stony cold voice"—which is defined behaviorally as speaking with a firm, rigidly paced voice, not much louder than usual. Yet others become silent and pout. The observations needed to create these behavioral definitions also help us realize that we must deal with the various forms of anger in different ways: We need to respond to a loud shouter differently than to a stony cold pouter.

Love lies at the opposite end of the continuum from anger; and love is also expressed in countless ways. Some people bring flowers or send a nice card; others do not. Some express love through physical actions oriented toward sexual contact; others do not. Much of the confusion that two people can have about the meaning of love arises from their using one vaguely defined word—such as "love" or "passion"—to describe things that each defines quite differently. She may be hoping that he will bring flowers or send a card, and is disappointed if he does not. He may hope she feels the physical passion that he does, and is disappointed if she is slow to accept his moves toward greater physical intimacy.

Over the past century, we have learned that much of the confusion people have about their thoughts, feelings, and actions arises from communication based on vague and ambiguous definitions. *It is true that no one can be 100% objective and accurate in creating definitions of behavior; but efforts to improve the detail of our definitions have greatly clarified our everyday actions and experiences.* In addition, advances in creating more accurate behavioral definitions have helped scientists discover many more principles of behavior than previous generations—using cruder definitions—could identify. When people define thoughts, emotions, and activities vaguely, they can only develop simple generalizations about them. When we focus increased attention on the objective details of behavior, our understanding grows and confusions fade.

Both anger and love were mysteries before the development of modern behavioral science. However, over the past 100 years, scientists have been able to create ever more precise definitions of anger, love, creativity, street smarts, sexiness, sexism, altruism, and almost all other types of human experience; and each refinement in behavioral definitions has helped advance our knowledge about the principles of human behavior. In this book, you will learn a great deal about love, jealousy, self-discipline, art, sports, cooperation, friendship, superstition, and the many other aspects of life that can make us happy or sad, energized or depressed, close to others or lonely.

External and Internal Events

Behavioral definitions deal with both *external actions* and *their internal counterparts* (such as *thoughts* and *feelings*).[6] External acts are obvious because they are easy to observe. Internal thoughts and feelings are private and can only be observed by the person who has them. Nevertheless, behavioral definitions have greatly advanced our ability to understand both externally visible actions and inner thoughts and emotions.

External. All external behaviors can be defined behaviorally—although the task is not always easy. For example, *eating* is easy to describe behaviorally: "Leticia lifts a spoon or fork full of food to her mouth, chews, and swallows." But some external actions, such as *playing,* are difficult to define. Exactly what is it that allows us to recognize when children are playing? Close behavioral observations of children's play reveal different types of play. *Free play*—such as skipping, chasing, and clowning around—often contains exaggerated body movements that have no obvious use, other than to bring a child heightened levels of sensory experience (through any of the sense organs). Free play is often accompanied by emotional displays such as open-mouth smiles, laughs, or giggles. In contrast, *role play* often consists of imitations of adult behavior—as when a child plays at being the mother of a doll or the driver of a toy truck—and role play often includes serious facial expressions: "Bad Dolly, you shouldn't do that." "Get that dump truck out of my way."

Another type of behavior that has mystified people all through history is *creativity*. Yet careful behavioral research has allowed us to define creativity as "the production of new or novel behavior," such as creating a new painting that is not a copy of some earlier painting. Armed with this behavioral definition, trainers can now help people learn how to increase their creativity by showing them (1) how to experiment with mixing various elements from their current behavioral repertoires—in search of novel recombinations—and (2) how to reward any novel behavioral mix with positive words or thoughts, such as "That was a creative new twist!" These rewards strengthen the skills used in creating novel behavior combinations. It may take weeks or months of practice before a person notices a major rise in creativity, but there might have been *no improvement* without "behavioral mixing and rewarding."

Internal.   *Many feelings and thoughts inside our bodies can be described behaviorally— although the task is not always easy.* For example, people can learn to recognize when they are beginning to feel *angry* by noting the first sensations of their increased inner muscle tension when another person criticizes or contradicts them. People who are seeking to control their emotions of anger may learn to use these early internal feelings of increased muscle tension as internal cues to recall the thoughts: "Stay calm. I don't want to start a fight because I value this relationship too much." In contrast, other emotional feelings can be quite difficult to define—such as the differences among the emotions of boredom, lethargy, languor, melancholy, and ennui.

Not only our feelings, but also our *thoughts* can be described behaviorally. The components of our thoughts that are easiest to define are the *inner words* that we "hear" inside our heads when we are alone and think with our mouths closed. (Can you "hear" inner words in your head as you read and think about these sentences?) People can learn to control the inner words of their thoughts in ways that redirect their lives away from pain, toward more rewarding outcomes.[7] After being criticized by his girlfriend, Chazz notes the following inner words in his thoughts: "Geez, she pisses me off." This reminds him to think other, wiser thoughts: "Calm down and tell her how much you want to work through our problems in a peaceful, loving manner." If these rules for controlling himself lead Chazz to more rewarding interactions, he is on his way to learning better ways to deal with criticism.

Learning to use behavioral definitions helps us gain increased accuracy in describing our emotional feelings and the inner words of our thoughts. If we couple clear behavioral definitions plus knowledge about the behavior principles, we can learn how to design wise inner words that help us better guide our thoughts, feelings, and external actions.

The use of behavioral definitions has facilitated the discovery of numerous impor-tant **behavior principles**—*which are generalizations about the causes of our thoughts, feelings, and actions.* It is these behavior principles that we hope to share with you in this book. Your benefits are first, a better understanding of human behavior in all the forms you see in your daily lives; and second, greater power to guide your own actions. In fact, an entire academic specialty called *behavior modification* has emerged to study how be-havioral principles can be applied to almost any behavior—strengthening those thoughts, feelings, and actions that we value, and eliminating those we dislike.

BEHAVIOR MODIFICATION

Since the dawn of time, people have been modifying their own behavior and the behavior of others. History books reveal how swords, whips, and promises of gold or high office have been used for countless centuries to control people's conduct. Even dogs, cats, mon-keys, and many other animals modify each other's behavior, though they do not do this consciously. An affectionate dog that gently approaches and nudges a young child helps the child learn to love dogs. An aggressive dog could have knocked the child down and caused the child to learn to fear dogs. Behavior principles operate all the time, even when no one is aware of them.

Although humans often modify behavior without consciously planning it, we can learn to consciously plan behavioral changes. When ski instructors explain and demon-strate methods for turning and stopping, they are consciously attempting to maximize their students' learning opportunities. *Behavior modification is the systematic and scien-tific use of behavior principles to improve people's thoughts, feelings, and actions.*[8] Some ski instructors are very skillful behavior modifiers. The better we understand the princi-ples of behavior, the better the chances we have for designing effective methods of behav-ior modification.

Sometime in life, most of us learn that happiness is not to be taken for granted. Most people carry some psychological scars from the past—pains they would like to overcome. Even if their childhoods were happy, people may feel that their present con-tains more pain or unhappiness than they want. Fortunately, behavior modification allows people to assuage painful memories from the past and create happier present lives than they otherwise would have had. Learning about behavior principles and the ways to apply them via behavior modification can greatly reduce the pain and enhance the joy of living. Behavior modification is being used increasingly in therapy, child rearing, education, marital counseling, self-control, business, and government.

There are four main reasons why behavior modification is more effective than other methods of changing behavior: (1) Behavior modification utilizes carefully designed be-havioral definitions, rather than vague definitions, to describe any behavior we might wish to change. (2) Behavior modification draws on extensive scientific research to de-sign strategies that are likely to be effective. (3) Behavior principles show us how to make behavioral change easy and rewarding by arranging clearly defined changes in our exter-nal environment and inner words. (4) The scientific methods underlying behavior modifi-cation help us collect data on our behavior—to see which plans work best and which need redesign. Thoughtful people continue to observe their behavior all through life, looking for better ways to modify their behavior—and the behavior of others.

When dealing with extreme problems, early phases of behavior modification may require work in clinical or institutional environments; but after early clinical successes, the next task is to arrange behavior changes that are suited for dealing with everyday life. Knowledge of behavior principles in everyday life helps us see how to adjust our acts of behavior modification in easy steps to help people adjust smoothly in natural, nonclinical environments.[9]

Behavioral Excesses and Deficits

Two main types of problems can make life less rewarding than it could be: behavioral excesses and deficits. **Behavioral excesses**—such as overeating, overachieving, dominating conversations, getting angry too often—can create countless difficulties. Marcy is such an overachiever in her studies that she has no time to enjoy herself. Mac likes to play sports so much that he falls short in school, love relationships, and other facets of life. Both persons are hurt by their excesses and could benefit from finding better balances of activities.

Behavioral deficits—such as limited abilities for studying, exercising, or talking comfortably with others—can also create problems. Eric does not exercise enough to stay healthy. Jill was raised in an unloving home and never learned how to express friendship or love; now she is trapped in loneliness. Both people are hurt by deficits in behavior, in part because they did not have the opportunities to learn how to exercise or develop close social bonds when they were younger.

There are two central goals of behavior modification: Help people learn how to reduce behavioral excesses and gain the skills needed to overcome deficits.

Correcting for Excesses.   Some people weigh more than is healthy for them. Many foods are so tasty that it is easy to eat in excess. *When people have learned some behavior in excess, behavior modification may involve homework exercises to help them learn the skills that many other people have learned for avoiding the excess.* For example, the person who eats excessively and is overweight can learn some of the rules and guidelines that many thinner people have learned—such as following one or more of these health conscious tips: Skip snacks. Avoid fatty foods. Ask for low-calorie foods and diet drinks. Once or twice a day, eat only a salad, instead of a larger meal. Do enough strenuous activities or exercises to burn many hundreds of calories each day. And do not do any of these activities in such excess as to become underweight. *Rules need to be coupled with rewards when learning new skills.* For example, each step of progress in learning how to control weight deserves positive rewards, such as repeatedly thinking some variation on the following words of self-praise: "I'm so happy to be making progress to a healthier weight level, and I look and feel better, too." Many people also enjoy the *natural rewards* of buying new clothing in smaller sizes.

Correcting for Deficits.   Most people realize that some of their thoughts, feelings, or actions are not as good as they would like. *When people have deficits, behavior modification may involve homework exercises to help them learn the skills that people without such deficits have already learned.* A person who does not like exercise is encouraged to learn the many reasons why exercise is good for developing a healthy body and introduced to several simple but useful *rules* for creating a healthy exercise routine: Begin by doing fun, easy exercise. Exercise with a cheerful person who values health. Gradually increase your exercise levels in very small steps, but only when it feels good to do so. A lonely person learns *guidelines* for improving the social and communication skills needed to find social interactions more rewarding: Talk more to your best friend, so you learn to feel increasingly comfortable as a talker. Then gradually branch out to talk more with other people and in larger groups. *Wise rules and guidelines need to be coupled with rewards when learning new skills.* For example, people can reward themselves for each step of improvement by saying to themselves: "I'm happy to be making progress at something I hadn't learned well enough before." In addition, the behavioral gains of becoming healthier or making friends more easily make life more rewarding, and these are the *natural rewards* that prove that the rules and guidelines are wise and true.

ILLNESS OR WELLNESS?

The central goal of behavior modification is to increase our psychological wellness, personal and social adjustment, and ability to guide our lives wisely. This emphasis on wellness is a relatively new facet of the study of behavioral sciences.[10]

For the past 300 years, people have attempted to apply scientific methods to the study of human behavior. Several centuries ago, wise people began to demand that humans deserve to be free of tyranny and have the right to pursue happiness. In the 1800s, the medical sciences made progress in dealing with human suffering; and many scientists assumed that the *medical model—which specializes in dealing with illness—*could be applied to "sick" and unhappy behavior. Medical doctors, such as Krafft-Ebing and Freud, studied people with mental illness in hopes of locating the causes and progressive stages of illnesses, along with possible cures. The emphasis was much more on the causes and stages of illness than on wellness: Wellness was considered the natural state, which needed much less study than the causes of and cures for illnesses. Freud, for example, was a physician who focused his studies on people with neuroses, hysteria, and other psychological problems, attempting to extend the medical model to analyze and cure these problems.

After much research, we now know that the medical model is not as useful for understanding behavior as was first hoped in the 1800s. It is true that the medical model has had some success in treating behavioral problems, especially those with biological origins, such as genetic defects, malnutrition, and the side effects of physical diseases. However, much of the behavior we see in everyday life does not result from medical problems. In the 1900s, with the help of behavioral definitions, behavioral scientists discovered that *most of human behavior is learned and therefore better explained by behavior principles that explicate learning than by the medical model.* In addition, we have discovered that behavior modification can be extremely useful in helping people with medical problems learn to live happier lives, as you will see in examples of behavior modification related to Alzheimer's disease (p. 315) and kidney dialysis (p. 133).

When we are not sick, the medical model is far less useful than the behavior principles that explain learned behavior. Most behavior is learned with little influence from illnesses or medication. "Do you speak English?" "Habla español"? "Parlez-vous français?" The words you speak and hear in the inner conversation of your thoughts are English, Spanish, French, Chinese—or some other language—depending on your prior learning. Illness or malnutrition may slow language learning in some children, but the medical model explains only a tiny fraction of the whole story of language learning. The same is true of the learning of music, athletics, mathematics, social skills, creativity, and most other human capacities: For most of us, the influence of learning greatly overshadows the effects of illness as conceived by the medical model. One of the most important recent advances in behavior science is the shift from a narrow medical model to focus more on learning—without neglecting any relevant biomedical conditions.

Personal Adjustment

In the past century, behavioral research has discovered a large number of scientific generalizations about various types of learning related to our thoughts, feelings, and actions. If you would like to understand and guide your behavior, knowledge of these behavior principles can help you more than can knowledge of the medical model of behavior. This does not mean that the medical model is wrong when dealing with biological diseases and some psychiatric illnesses: If you notice a strange new growth or discolored area on your body, see a doctor soon! But when it comes time for you to mold your behavior, emotions, and thoughts toward the goals that you value—reducing behavioral excesses and replacing deficits with greater skills—the behavior principles of learning will help you far more than the medical model can.

The shift from a purely medical model of behavior to a greater focus on learning has led to the development of a very optimistic view of life.[11] We now realize that all of us have an enormous human potential and that most of that potential is developed through learning. The human potential encompasses beautiful, strong, creative, and caring acts, not just mental illness and abnormal behavior. Even physical strength and grace depend on learning appropriate physical exercises and training methods. As a result, modern behavioral science has made a major shift from the medical model's overemphasis on "sick" behavior: Behavior modification tends to emphasize wellness, personal and social adjustment, and the healthy development of our human potential. The principles of behavior can explain many abnormal and destructive behaviors—such as hatred, violence, and revenge; but the central goal of behavioral science is wellness: *How can we help people learn to be happy, healthy, creative, and caring? How can knowledge of behavior principles help people develop their human potentials as far as they want?*

WHERE NEXT?

The following chapters are organized to flow from the simplest and most basic behavior principles to the most subtle and private. Starting with the basics makes the material easiest to learn. Because the basic principles in the first several chapters provide the foundations on which all later chapters are constructed, you will immediately see in the early chapters some of the most powerful behavior principles along with their applications to meaningful daily events.

Starting with the basics does, however, create a small problem. The basic principles presented in the early chapters cannot explain the most subtle aspects of human behavior, and your questioning minds may correctly realize that the basic principles miss some of the more complex aspects of life. But each additional chapter will introduce more behavioral details to deal with the more nuanced facets of life—hopefully answering your early questions. By the end of the book you will have a good overview of the major behavior principles and see how they intertwine and interact.

Organizing the chapters from simple to complex roughly parallels the historical development of behavioral science. Pavlov was one of the first behaviorists to identify the principles by which reflexes and emotions undergo changes during learning (Chapter 2). Next, Thorndike, Skinner, and other behaviorists gradually worked out the principles that explain the learning of voluntary behavior in terms of instrumental or operant learning (Chapter 3). The interactions of Pavlovian and operant conditioning are discussed in Chapter 4. A variety of topics related to perception, generalization, and discrimination are explored in Chapter 5.

Once these basic behavior principles were understood, behaviorists explored ways to use the information to develop practical techniques of behavior modification (Chapter 6). Reinforcers and punishers—the prime movers of most learning—are explored in Chapters 7 and 8. There are four main ways in which learning occurs: differential reinforcement and shaping, observational learning, prompts, and rules (Chapters 9–12). The final three chapters explain how schedules of reinforcement affect our behavior (Chapter 13), the ways to replace aversive control with positive reinforcement for desirable behavior (Chapter 14), and the power of cognition and self-control in enhancing our lives (Chapter 15).[12]

To help you identify and master the key ideas, all the important concepts are accentuated by the use of bold or italic print. If you highlight them while you read, they will jump out at you all the more when you review and study them. We have attempted to make the book both scientific and sensitive, because science is one of the most useful and humanistic ways of understanding and dealing with the complexities of the world in which we live.[13]

As you read the book, do not hesitate to ask questions about the contents. Please feel free to e-mail us at baldwin@sscf.ucsb.edu or write us at University of California at Santa Barbara, Santa Barbara, CA 93106. We are always eager to learn from you. Is some point unclear? Does an example bother you? Do you want to know something about behavior that the book does not clarify? Ask and we will answer.

CONCLUSION

Over the past 100 years, numerous powerful scientific principles about behavior have been discovered. The first big step came with the demand for increasingly accurate and objective definitions of behavior. For example, what do we mean by the words *love* or *creativity?* Behavioral definitions deal with external and internal events—external actions as well as internal thoughts and feelings. All can be studied using behavioral definitions. We are making progress in applying behavior principles to the modification of human behavior in ways that correct excesses, overcome deficits, and help people actualize their human potential. This approach to behavior is much more optimistic than earlier theories that were based heavily on the medical model, with its emphasis on illness. Our present approach deals with both natural and planned learning in order to help you gain a better understanding of human behavior in all its forms and develop greater skill in planning your own future learning.

QUESTIONS

1. What are *behavioral definitions?* Why are they useful? Can you apply them to "anger" and "love"?
2. How does behavior modification apply to *behavioral excesses* and *deficits?*
3. What are the differences between the *medical model* of behavior and the *wellness orientation* of behavior modification?

NOTES

1. Skinner's (1953) book, *Science and Human Behavior,* was the first to provide extensive examples of behavior principles in everyday life.
2. Boakes (1984).
3. Fawcett (1991).
4. Boakes (1984, pp. 126–127, 136).
5. Skinner (1989a).
6. Mead (1934), Skinner (1969, 1974, 1989a, 1990), Mahoney (1974), Meichenbaum (1977), Kobes (1991), Delprato and Midgley (1992), Stemmer (1992), J. Moore (1995), Cautela (1996), and many other behaviorists include thinking as a behavior that must be analyzed in any comprehensive theory of human behavior. "An adequate science of behavior must consider events taking place within the skin of the organism, not as physiological mediators of behavior, but as part of behavior itself" (Skinner, 1969, p. 228).
7. Meichenbaum (1977); Seligman (1998).
8. Bellack, Hersen, and Kazdin (1982); Watson and Tharp (1997).
9. Cullen (1988).
10. Masters, Burish, Hollon, and Rimm (1987, pp. 5, 494–548); Follette, Bach, and Follette (1993); Seligman (1998); Baldwin and Baldwin (2000); Seligman and Csikzentmihalyi (2000).
11. Rosenbaum (1990a,b); Baldwin and Baldwin (2000).
12. Feinberg (1990).
13. Bronowski (1965, 1977); Skinner (1989b, 1990); Bernstein (1990); Heward and Malott (1995).

Pavlovian Conditioning

FORMING ASSOCIATIONS

Angela always loved to drive fast. With a good eye and quick responses, she never had an accident. But one rainy day, while driving a curve not far from home, her car slid on the freshly wetted pavement, and she spun off the road, crashing into a tree. The spin and crash were over within a couple seconds. The car was totaled, with broken glass everywhere. Luckily, Angela walked away with only wobbly knees and minor injuries, although she was emotionally shaken and frightened by her close call with death. For months thereafter she noticed a new emotion—an apprehensive uneasiness—when she drove past the scene of the accident, took other curves at high speed, or saw wet roads. *The stimuli that were related to her accident had become associated with her near-death emotions.*

In this chapter you will learn how biologically established reflexes—such as emotional responses, sexual responses, and psychosomatic symptoms—can become associated with new stimuli through Pavlovian conditioning. You will also learn when and why the effects of Pavlovian conditioning can fade over time—though they do not always fade.

Ivan Pavlov (1849–1936) studied biologically established reflexes and the processes by which new stimuli become associated with the reflexes. The type of learning he discovered is commonly called **Pavlovian conditioning;** but it is also known as **classical conditioning** and **respon-**

dent conditioning.[1] In Angela's case, the traumatic car crash elicited intense emotions—including fear, a strong adrenaline response, and quivering muscles—that lasted for almost an hour. Due to Pavlovian conditioning, several stimuli related to speed on wet, curved roads became associated with those emotions. Angela had acquired a conditioned emotional response of feeling apprehensive whenever she drove fast on wet, curved roads.

Pavlovian conditioning affects almost all reflexes,[2] including salivation, eye blinks, emotional responses, sexual responses, and psychosomatic symptoms. *Stated simply, Pavlovian conditioning occurs when some neutral stimulus is so closely associated with an existing reflex that it takes on the power to elicit the reflexive response.*[3] Before her accident, Angela never feared driving on wet, curvy roads: Such roads were neutral stimuli. But once these stimuli were linked with traumatic emotions, Angela became a different person, emotionally sensitized to fear fatal auto accidents. None of her "driver's ed" classes had taught her the emotional responses that one real life accident conditioned her to feel. Nevertheless, most people are unaware of the way Pavlovian conditioning operates in their own lives.[4]

TWO TYPES OF REFLEXES

A reflex consists of a stimulus-response sequence—in which some stimulus (S) elicits a biologically based response (R).

$$S \rightarrow R$$

The stimuli of a loud, spinning car crash elicit fear and anxiety responses. Delicious food elicits salivation. Bad food or excess alcohol in the stomach elicits stomach contractions and vomiting. Touch to the genitals elicits sexual responses, including pleasurable sensations.

The most basic and primitive type of reflex is the biologically established (or innate) reflex, which is called an **unconditioned reflex** *to indicate that no conditioning—no learning—is involved in its origin.* There are many unconditioned reflexes that operate from birth, before babies could have any chance to learn them. Each inborn reflex can only be activated by one specific type of biologically determined stimulus, which is called an **unconditioned stimulus** (US)—to indicate that *no conditioning* (no learning) is needed for this stimulus to elicit the reflexive response. The response elicited by the US is called an **unconditioned response** (UR) to indicate that *no conditioning* is necessary for this response to occur. A bee sting can elicit an unconditioned reflex. We are born with nerves that cause us to respond to a bee sting as a US that elicits the UR of pain and jerking away. The top line of Figure 2–1 shows the unconditioned reflex as the innate (or inborn) US → UR sequence. A sting is a US that elicits the UR of pain and flinching.

A second type of reflex, called a **conditioned reflex,** *can be learned through the process of Pavlovian conditioning when some new sensations become associated with an innate or unconditioned reflex.* The words "conditioned reflex" indicate that the reflex is learned, not innate. Before conditioning, only a US such as a bee sting is capable of eliciting a reflexive response (the extreme left panel in Fig. 2–1). When a young child first sees a honeybee, the child has no innate fear of the bee: The bee is a **neutral stimulus** (NS)

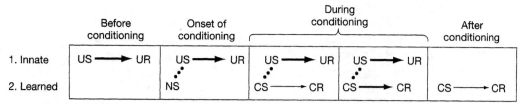

FIGURE 2–1   The process of Pavlovian conditioning, by which a neutral stimulus (NS) becomes a conditioned stimulus (CS) because it precedes a US. The width of the arrows shows the power of the S–R connection.

upon first sight. But once the child learns that touching bees can be associated with pain, the sight of a bee becomes a **conditioned stimulus** (CS) that elicits the **conditioned response** (CR) of fear.

At the onset of conditioning, a neutral stimulus (NS) precedes the US one or more times (the dotted diagonal line in Fig. 2–1). *During Pavlovian conditioning, the neutral stimulus becomes a conditioned stimulus (CS) that elicits a conditioned response (CR). The conditioned reflex is the CS → CR sequence in the bottom line of the figure.* After a conditioned reflex is established, this learned CS → CR sequence can operate even in the absence of the unconditioned reflex (as in the extreme right panel in the figure). When we see a bee nearby, the bee is a CS that elicits fear if we have been stung in the past, and we avoid touching the feared stimulus. Thus, we experience conditioned fear, without having the sting-pain reflex. When puppies or kittens initiate play with bees in the lawn, they too can learn to fear the CS of bees, even though they have no language or words to explain it.

Although a CS is capable of eliciting a reflexive response, the conditioned response (CR) is not identical to the unconditioned response (UR). After a child has been stung by bees, the sight of bees is a CS that elicits the CR of fear. This CR of fear is not as strong as the UR of pain and crying that is elicited by the US of an actual bee sting. *Although the CR resembles the UR in some ways, the CR is usually less intense and slower to appear than the UR, although other differences are possible.*[5]

Predictive Stimuli

After being stung, children respond to the sight of bees as a CS (conditioned stimulus) that can elicit reflexive responses of fear—before children make the mistake of touching the bee. Thus, *a CS contains important information about things that may come next.* In the case of bees, the CS serves as a *warning stimulus* that signals danger by eliciting fear before children carelessly touch a bee. *A CS functions as a predictive stimulus indicating that a reflex might soon be elicited.* The sight and odor of a beautifully cooked meal are CSs that can elicit salivation and pleasurable anticipation of delicious food, even before dinner comes out of the oven. In this case, the CSs are predictive stimuli for pleasurable feelings.[6]

Our brains have evolved to be quite sensitive to correlations—or contingent relations—between reflexes and the cues that precede them. *The cues that most reliably pre-*

cede and predict the onset of a reflex are usually the stimuli that become CSs. When Angela's car began to spin out of control on a wet, curvy road, her eyes were wide open and she was superaware of the car's motion, trees spinning by, and a road sign she hit before crashing into a tree. Countless stimuli were present. Did they all become CSs associated with the fear of a near-death accident? No. Trees and road signs were not the causes of the accident, and they did not become CSs for fear. *The stimuli most predictive of the accident tend to be causally—or contingently—related to the onset of the unconditioned reflex.* In Angela's case, speed, wet pavement, and curved roadway were causes of the crash, and these are the stimuli that became the CSs Angela learned to associate with anxiety.

When you are served a delicious dinner in a restaurant, you may notice the mouth-moistening salivation reflex. Which of the countless stimuli present in the room become associated with the moistening reflex? Will it be the sounds of background music and silverware clinking on plates, sights of the server and other people, words on the menu, topics of conversation, or the odor of the food? The stimuli most closely associated with a delectable meal—such as seeing it listed on the menu or smelling it at a nearby table—are most likely to become CSs that elicit the CR of happy anticipation and a moistened mouth.

The salivation reflex is the one Pavlov studied when first formulating the principles of classical conditioning. When Pavlov presented food (a US) to a hungry dog, the dog salivated (the UR). When Pavlov first preceded feeding with the sound of a bell, the sound was neutral and did not elicit salivation. However, after several feedings in which the sound of a bell preceded and predicted the presentation of food (the US), the bell became a CS, a conditioned stimulus, that could also elicit salivation (the CR).

Some people overlook the importance of S–R behavior—stimulus-response behavior—because the reflexes appear to be the simplest of all human behavior. Some neglect the importance of Pavlovian conditioning because they presume that it only involves dogs, which is incorrect. Reflexes may seem primitive when compared with actions involving higher cognitive processes, but reflexes play major roles in many aspects of our everyday lives—and the lives of other animals—hence they should not be neglected. You will see the importance of reflexes and Pavlovian conditioning throughout this book: Both are essential for survival.

COMMON CONDITIONED RESPONSES

Why do we have reflexes? Why is it essential that they can become conditioned to predictive stimuli?

First, most animals evolved to have numerous reflexes because the reflexes are crucial for basic biological functioning, survival, and reproduction. Salivation reflexes moisten our mouths for eating and mix food with the first digestive fluids. Reflexes of jerking away from sharp objects help us avoid serious injury. The reflexes underlying sexual arousal—such as vaginal lubrication, penile erection, and orgasm—are important for reproduction, which has obvious survival value. All our emotions are based on reflexes that function to add vital feelings to our inner world and communicate our feelings to others—via facial cues, sounds, and bodily movements.[7]

Second, most animals have evolved to be capable of Pavlovian conditioning, and humans are no exception. We have numerous reflexes that can be conditioned through Pavlovian conditioning (Table 2–1). Pavlovian conditioning allows us to respond not only to USs (unconditioned stimuli), but also to the numerous CSs (conditioned stimuli) that become associated with our reflexes. Through Pavlovian conditioning, each of us can learn to respond to the specific predictive stimuli we have encountered during *our* unique personal experiences, while other people learn to respond to the predictive stimuli found in *their* unique lives. For example, pictures you have associated with sex can become CSs that you find sexually arousing, even though someone from a different culture might find them unexciting.

TABLE 2–1   A partial list of unconditioned reflexes

US	UR
Voluntary muscles	
sharp or hot stimuli	jerk away and cry
blows, shock, burns	withdrawal
gentle caresses	relaxation and calm
object touches lips	sucking
food in mouth	swallowing
object touches the hand	grasping
novel stimulation	reflexive orienting
rewarding stimuli	smiles
Circulatory system	
high temperature	sweating, flushing
sudden loud noise	blanching, pounding heart
Digestive system	
good food	salivation
bad food	sickness, nausea, vomiting
Respiratory system	
irritation in nose	sneeze
throat clogged	cough
allergens	asthma attack
Reproductive system	
genital stimulation	vaginal lubrication
	penile erection
	orgasm
nipple stimulation	milk release (in lactating women)
Emotional system	
painful blows	fear
sexual stimulation	erotic feelings

Obvious Reflexes

Reflexes tend to be most conspicuous in babies, since infant behavior is based largely on unconditioned reflexes. Because adult behavior is based on reflexes and countless things learned from years of personal and social experience, the untrained eye may fail to notice reflexes in adult behavior. Nevertheless, reflexes are an important part of our biosurvival mechanisms all through life, and the attentive observer can see their importance at all ages.

Voluntary Muscles.   Babies are born with a variety of muscular reflexes of the *skeletal muscular system* that help ensure their early survival. For starters, infants have reflexes that help them respond to dangerous USs (unconditioned stimuli). Babies almost instantly jerk their arms or legs away from USs such as pokes with sharp, hot, or cold stimuli. They jolt to higher muscle tension when startled by USs of sudden, intense stimulation. They often kick at USs that irritate their feet or legs, which may push those things away. All these aversive USs can also elicit crying, which is likely to attract a caregiver to come to the baby's aid. The infant's responses can make the difference between surviving and not; hence they function as the infant's "survival kit," allowing it to respond adaptively in the months before it has a chance to learn more complex behavior. Pavlovian conditioning allows infants to learn to respond with fear to CSs associated with aversive USs.

After aversive stimuli have elicited an infant's reflexes of agitation and crying, how do we calm a disturbed infant? The stimuli of gentle caresses, soft touches, and calm rocking are USs that elicit muscle relaxation, tranquillity, and decreased crying. Most caregivers learn how to provide these USs that elicit calmness. As a result of Pavlovian conditioning, the infant learns to respond to its caregivers as CSs associated with pleasurable feelings of calmness and security. By the time an infant is several months of age, merely seeing mother or father nearby is a CS that elicits the conditioned emotions of comfort. All through life, most of us can be calmed by the US of gentle touches, and merely being in the presence of those people who have given us calming feelings in the past provides the CSs that can elicit tranquillity and reduced anxiety. Studying these reflexes helps us learn how to give unhappy children—and adults—the gentle physical USs that can calm them and help them in times of distress.

Many other reflexes help babies get started in life—functioning as their "survival kit"—before they have had a chance to learn other types of responses. From day 1, newborn infants reflexively suck when contacting a US that touches their lips, which functions to bring them milk if the US is a nipple. After several weeks, sucking responses can be elicited by CSs that regularly precede milk, such as being moved into a nursing position or held in ways associated with nursing. By 2 months of age, the sounds, odors, and patterns of touch that have been associated with nursing become CSs capable of eliciting the CRs of sucking.[8]

Although some of the infant's reflexes—such as the sucking response—disappear in childhood, many continue to function all through life. Adults jerk away from pricks with sharp objects, get startled by sudden stimuli, and calm down with gentle stroking. In infancy and all through adulthood, people tend to smile or cry when very positive or aversive things happen to them. Smiles, tears, and many other facial responses are based on reflexes, and they help communicate our emotional state to others. When we see a genuine smile on the face of another person, we often feel their pleasure, whereas another person's crying and tears can arouse vicarious feeling of sadness in us (see pp. 238–242).

Circulation. There are numerous reflexes based on the involuntary muscular responses of the *circulatory system.*[9] For example, physical exertion increases heart rate and blood flow to the entire body. Sexual stimulation also causes increased heart rate, but blood is shunted especially to the genital areas, causing vaginal lubrication and penile erection. High temperature causes the small capillaries of the skin to open and allow blood to flow close to the skin, which causes sweating, along with the cooling of the blood and body.

Circulatory system reflexes can be conditioned independently of other response systems. USs such as sudden pain or startle can elicit a strong, pounding heartbeat; and numerous CSs can be conditioned to that reflex during a person's life. The person who has associated precarious heights with painful falls may experience a pounding heart (a CR) by merely looking down from a high place into a canyon or street (the CS). Blushing is a circulatory reflex in which blood vessels in the outer layers of the facial skin open and allow blood to flow to the surface, producing a redder color. Different individuals learn to blush at different topics, thoughts, and social events, depending on their prior conditioning. People are often shocked when they suddenly find themselves blushing uncontrollably: This helps us realize that our reflexes are under the control of USs and CSs more than our conscious attempts to turn them on or off.

Digestion. Several reflexes have to do with the *digestive system,* including the salivation reflex studied by Pavlov. Food in the mouth is the US that elicits the unconditioned reflex of salivation. Through Pavlovian conditioning, we learn to salivate when exposed to cues that are predictive stimuli associated with food. Merely sitting down to a delicious dinner (a CS) can literally make a hungry person's mouth water (a CR), before food is put in the mouth.

Extreme stress, shocks, and pain are USs capable of eliciting other digestive and excretory reflexes such as butterflies in the stomach, nausea, vomiting, and even urination or defecation. If taking tests has been preceded by stressful or painful experiences in the past, a very important exam can elicit similar conditioned responses. Because many people have learned to be fearful of falling from high places, novice mountain climbers are often surprised when the mere sight of their first steep assault up a sheer mountain wall (a CS) causes them to experience anxiety defecation.

Unfortunately, cancer patients who receive chemotherapy often experience nausea and vomiting as side effects of the strong chemicals used in therapy. Chemotherapy is the unconditioned stimulus (US) that elicits unconditioned sickness (the UR). After having chemotherapy, some patients begin to experience conditioned nausea and vomiting *before* they come to therapy. Seeing that it is time to go to therapy is a predictive cue (CS) correlated with chemotherapy (the US); hence the calendar and clock provide the predictive stimuli that can elicit nausea illness before therapy actually begins.[10]

Although the brain is sensitive to correlations between predictive cues and reflexes, it does not always make the correct associations. For example, cancer patients who receive chemotherapy sometimes learn to associate the foods that they have eaten before going to therapy as CSs that elicit nausea. Patients who eat ice cream before their chemotherapy may later find that ice cream causes them to become nauseous.[11] Although evolutionary processes have prepared us to associate food tastes with nausea (as after eating rotten food and becoming sick), in this case the brain made an incorrect association. The calendar and clock are better predictive stimuli than foods. Even though wrong stimuli sometimes become CSs for reflexive responses, totally erroneous associations are not too common.

Respiration.   Reflexes of the *respiratory system* include coughing, sneezing, hiccups, and asthma attacks. Some psychosomatic illnesses result from Pavlovian conditioning. Conditioned asthmatic responses have been found to be elicited by a broad range of CSs, including perfume, the sight of dust, the national anthem, speeches by politicians, elevators, horses, police vans, caged birds, goldfish, waterfalls, and children's choirs.[12] If you heard your state's Senator give several speeches during hay fever season while you were suffering a serious asthma attack, the good senator's voice might accidentally become a CS that could trigger future asthmatic responses.

Less Obvious Reflexes

Many people do not realize that some of the most common and important human responses experienced in everyday life are based on reflexes and Pavlovian conditioning. Among these are the reproductive and emotional reflexes. Few people can recall how these less obvious reflexes were conditioned by their prior learning experiences.[13]

Reproduction.   There are a number of reflexes in the *reproductive system,* related to making babies, delivering babies, and breast-feeding them. Touch to the genitals is the US (unconditioned stimulus) that elicits the URs (unconditioned responses) of vaginal lubrication, penile erection, nipple erection, and other signs of sexual arousal, including orgasm. These sexual responses are biologically established reflexes mediated by the lower spinal cord,[14] and Pavlovian conditioning allows many stimuli that are associated with these reflexes to become "eroticized," hence capable of eliciting sexual responses. Thoughts, words, visual images, odors, and a multitude of other stimuli can become CSs (conditioned stimuli) that elicit CRs (sexual responses) after the CSs have preceded the US of the unconditioned sexual reflex. It usually takes multiple pairings before a new stimulus becomes a conditioned stimulus capable of eliciting a strong response. CSs that elicit sexual arousal are commonly called *erotic stimuli* or *sexual turn-ons.*

Many boys and girls experiment with masturbation before their midteens.[15] Touch to the genitals is the US that elicits unconditioned sexual responses of penile erection, vaginal lubrication, and pleasurable sensations. Pavlovian conditioning enters the picture when other stimuli become associated with the sexual reflex. For example, one afternoon a teen may see an attractive rock star and almost memorize the visual image. That night, if the teen masturbates, visual images of the rock star may come to mind. Because the visual images are paired with the sexual reflex, they begin to become conditioned stimuli (CSs) associated with sexual excitement. After only one pairing, the teen may not notice any sexual arousal when looking at pictures of the rock star. However, the teen who repeatedly uses visual images of famous, attractive people while masturbating will pair such images with the sexual reflex enough times to produce considerable conditioning. Eventually the images become CSs that are strong enough to elicit at least partial sexual responses—including penile erection, vaginal lubrication, and pleasurable emotional responses—even in the absence of the US (touch to the genitals).[16] No wonder that some teens have amorous feelings for their favorite stars.

Each individual learns a unique set of sexual CSs, depending on his or her unique history of Pavlovian conditioning. One woman may have had very exciting sexual interactions with a gentle lover, and the various sounds, sights, and other stimuli present when making love with this partner may become sexual CSs. Even thinking about these erotic stimuli can elicit sexual arousal. A second woman, from a different culture, might have a very different set of stimuli that triggered her sexual arousal. A third woman, who had come from a background that punished sexual interest and masturbation, might find that she had very few sexual CSs because she had few chances for the conditioning process to create these erotic stimuli. Because we all have different life experiences, it is only natural that each person learns a unique set of erotic CSs—many or few—depending on her or his unique conditioning experiences.

People with unusual histories of sexual conditioning can acquire some unique CSs for sexual arousal. Beyond a certain point, a person's unusual conditioning may strike others as "odd" or "abnormal," but the conditioning process that produces unusual sexual CSs is the same Pavlovian conditioning that produces "normal" CSs. The clinical literature demonstrates how unusual sexual CSs can be conditioned without anyone planning it. People who repeatedly masturbate or make love in the presence of objects such as panties, hose, shoes, boots, silk, leather, rubber, or other stimuli can sometimes develop sexual fetishes in which they need those CSs to become sexually aroused.

Emotional Responses. *Most unconditioned reflexes have an emotional component that is either pleasurable or aversive.* Therefore, eliciting a reflex often brings up **emotional responses.** The USs that elicit sexual responses, salivation, and reflexes associated with all the other biologically based rewards also elicit pleasurable sensations. In contrast, the USs associated with all the biologically based punishers—such as sharp, hot, and stinging stimuli—elicit aversive sensations. The pleasure and pain components of the reflexes are traced to biological survival functions:[17] We are biologically prepared to experience pleasure from stimuli that enhance our chances of surviving and reproducing, and pain from stimuli that endanger us.

When neutral stimuli precede reflexes that have an emotional component, the CSs that are created via Pavlovian conditioning can also elicit emotions. Fantasies that have been paired with masturbation or sexual relations become CSs that elicit pleasurable feelings. If a child has had several painful falls while climbing trees or standing on high places, the view from heights becomes a CS that elicits a variety of conditioned responses, such as a pounding heart, fear, and anxiety. As the child steps closer to the edge of a cliff, the number of predictive stimuli associated with painful falls increases, and the child feels even more frightened. *The emotional response elicited by a CS is called a conditioned emotional response (CER).*

Just as conditioned responses (CRs) are not identical to the URs that they predict, *CERs do not completely resemble the unconditioned emotions on which they are based.* Falling to the ground produces pain (the emotional component of the UR); whereas the view from heights—after being paired with falls—elicits fear and anxiety (the CERs). What happens if a couple regularly lights candles in their bedroom before making love? After several pairings, the candlelight may become a CS that not only elicits mild physical sexual responses, but also pleasurable CERs, even before the two people begin touching each other. However, the conditioned emotional response (CER) to candlelight is not as strong as the full sexual response elicited by touching the genitals.

Because CSs are predictive stimuli, CSs associated with USs that have emotional components can elicit pleasant or unpleasant emotions before *a US appears.* For example, seeing sexy clothing can be a CS that elicits sexual feelings before any other hint of sex arises, if seeing such apparel is a good predictor that more intense sexual pleasures lie ahead. If a child has been hurt after falling from a cliff, standing near the edge of a cliff provides the CS that is predictive of painful falls, and this CS can cause a child to cry (the CER), even if there is no repeat of the fall.

New CSs with emotional associations can be created any time that Pavlovian conditioning occurs. For example, when a mother first begins breast-feeding her new baby, the infant's sucking on her nipples is a US that elicits the milk-release reflex, which is pleasurable for the mother. Through Pavlovian conditioning, the predictive stimuli that precede breast-feeding become CSs that also elicit pleasurable feelings for the mother. Eventually, just seeing the baby tugging at her blouse and trying to reach her nipples is a CS capable of eliciting the milk-release reflex and pleasurable feelings (the CER), even *before* actual breast-feeding begins. Mothers love their infants for a variety of reasons; but many mothers who breast-feed report that the pleasures of breast-feeding enhance their positive feelings toward their babies.

New CSs are created not only by pleasure, but also by pain. When people make embarrassing blunders in social interactions, a variety of situational cues—such as the individuals or touchy topics present at the time—can become CSs that will elicit uncomfortable emotional responses (CERs) in the future. In front of his professor and whole class, Dave made a simple verbal blunder that embarrassed several people in the class. The next time Dave saw the professor, Dave noticed a change: Seeing the professor (who had now become a CS associated with the embarrassing blunder) elicited feelings of discomfort and sweaty palms even *before* the professor came near. Even when talking with a complete stranger, Dave may experience discomfort if the conversation turns to the same topic that caused embarrassment in the past, because the topic itself is now a CS for aversive feelings. Because people usually avoid CSs associated with painful CERs, it is not uncommon to see individuals steer clear of topics—or people—that have been associated with embarrassment in the past. The topics and people are predictive stimuli signaling that embarrassment could arise again.

Even cognitive stimuli can serve as CSs that elicit CERs. When a mother thinks about breast-feeding, she may experience warm and pleasant feelings. When Dave merely thinks about his embarrassment from saying something inconsiderate in front of the whole class, the thoughts are CSs that may elicit uncomfortable feelings (CERs).[18]

Due to Pavlovian conditioning, many of the stimuli that surround us in everyday life become CSs for either pleasurable or aversive CERs. Seeing a smiling face in the crowd provides a CS that elicits pleasurable feelings. Hearing someone say crass and insensitive words to a friend provides CSs that elicit bad feelings. Hearing the national anthem can elicit "goose bumps." Hearing an inspiring speech or song can cause the skin to tingle or send "chills down our spine." Criticism can elicit sweat on our face, palms of our hands, and armpits.

Understanding Emotions. As people examine the triggers for their emotional responses, they often learn to trace their feelings back to the stimuli—either USs or CSs—that elicited them. It is clear that talking about touchy topics can create CSs for embarrassment and discomfort, whereas seeing smiles and sexy clothing are CSs for pleasurable feelings. Sometimes it is easy to identify the eliciting stimuli. They can come from either outside or inside our bodies. Even thoughts, fantasies, and dreams can be CSs that elicit emotional responses: Thinking about happy or painful past experiences can elicit positive or negative emotions.

If you want to better understand your feelings and emotions, pay closer attention to the stimuli that precede and predict them. People often learn to search their memories to hunt for the stimuli that triggered a certain mood. Was it the topic of conversation? The mention of an old romance that ended painfully? Was it the sad words of a popular song that caught your attention?

It is not always easy to identify and label emotional responses.[19] A person may feel a pounding heart and a lump in the throat but not be able to determine whether the feeling is excitement or fear. For example, imagine yourself at a large Halloween masquerade party in a local hotel, where everyone is playing tricks and joking. Suddenly the fire alarm goes off and the lights go out. Everyone is laughing, and you are, too. You notice your heart pounding; but you are not certain if you are frightened or merely excited by the latest surprises of the party. Your decision to label the emotional response as fear or excitement will depend largely on environmental cues, including the responses of other people. If everyone else laughs and responds to the alarm as a fun prank, you will probably conclude that your emotional response is one of excitement. If several other people show clear signs of fear or panic, screaming and running to the exits, you may conclude that your pounding heart is a fear response. *People are often influenced by environmental cues including the emotional responses of others when labeling their own emotions.*[20] Naturally, any evidence that there is or is not a fire in the building will influence your labeling, too. *Identifying our emotions involves both internal sensations and external cues.*

As you learn to search for and locate the stimuli that elicit emotions, you can begin to use behavior modification with your emotions. You can practice *mood control* by selecting USs and CSs that elicit the emotions you want. When Sonia wants to get into a more positive mood, she plays a recording of her favorite cheerful music rather than listening to a radio station whose music makes her sad. For Sonia, and many people, cheerful music is a CS that elicits good feelings. When people have serious problems that make them unhappy, they need to solve the problems. But when only trivial problems are getting us down, turning on cheerful music that provides CSs for pleasant emotions can help us create a happier mood.

Empathy.   How is it that one person can empathize with the emotions of another? When we see other people smile with twinkling eyes, we often feel happy because years of prior Pavlovian conditioning lead us to associate genuine smiles with happy situations. Thus, smiles become CSs for our emotions of happiness. Likewise, seeing other people sobbing and shaking with grief become CSs for most of us to feel sad, too. Why? We are most likely to see people sobbing and crying when something bad has happened—such as a death or disaster, and the gravity of the event conditions us to have somber and sad emotions. Our emotions may not be identical with the emotions of those who are sobbing, shaking, and crying; but they are similar enough to allow us to feel empathy with other people. *Whenever people have had similar Pavlovian conditioning with any given emotional situation, their similar conditioning allows them to empathize with each other.*

Notice the important role that reflexes and Pavlovian conditioning play in the learning of empathy.[21] First, all humans have very similar reflexes for smiling, crying, blushing, and showing dozens of other basic emotions, hence most of us show our emotions in much the same ways—even though some people learn to inhibit or hide their inborn emotional reflexes. Second, Pavlovian conditioning tends to affect us all similarly. When people tell jokes, most listeners smile and feel happy, so most learn to associate smiles as CSs that elicit happy feelings. When people arrive at an auto accident and see the driver sobbing and shaking with fear, they can feel the fear, too, since these emotional displays are usually associated with unhappy events.

Inaccurate empathy is possible, too. When young children are standing near the edge of a steep cliff and we are standing safely below, why do we feel fear for them? If we have had painful falls from high places, we can "feel fear" as we watch them play without fear of falling. Seeing the children at risk of falling provides the CSs that are predictive of pain for us, and elicit our feelings of fear.[22] We may reflexively hold our breath as we watch the children near the top of the cliff, feeling the fears of heights that we hope they have—while worried they may not have these fears. If the children are very young and inexperienced with falls, they may not have had the Pavlovian conditioning that would make views from high places function as CSs for fear. Thus, our feelings of empathy may not be accurate if they have not yet had the relevant conditioning experiences. The best cues we have about their conditioning are behavioral: Are they smiling or are they showing facial and bodily cues of anxiety? The emotional reflexes have both internal feelings and externally visible elements: The internal feelings are linked with motivation, rewards and punishers; the external cues facilitate social communication and empathy.

People who have had unique emotional experiences may know things that only a few other people—who have had similar experiences—can empathize with. Most of us cannot empathize with a train engineer who happens to be at the controls when his train accidentally hits and kills someone standing on the tracks. This happens about a thousand times a year in the United States.[23] Even engineers cannot empathize with the feeling until they personally experience it: "I didn't know what it would be like until it did happen. The wobbly knees, the shaky voice—it was a feeling I'd never had before." Who can empathize best with this man: a therapist or another engineer who had once been in a similar unavoidable accident? The engineer.

Because no two people have had exactly the same past learning experiences, no two people have exactly the same emotional responses to daily events; hence perfect empathy is beyond our grasp. But the more that two people share important life experiences, the more empathy they can feel.

THE DYNAMICS OF CONDITIONING

For decades, people thought of Pavlovian conditioning in simple mechanistic terms. If you pair a neutral stimulus with a reflex long enough, the neutral stimulus eventually becomes a CS that can elicit a conditioned response. In recent decades, due to the work of Robert Rescorla and others, we now appreciate that Pavlovian conditioning is much more complex.

Today, we realize that the brain is a very active stimulus-processing organ. Over millions of years of natural selection, the brains of most vertebrates have evolved into active information-seeking systems. This is especially true in birds and mammals, with the human brain being one of the most advanced information-seeking organs. The brain tracks the multiple stimuli coming into it from all five external senses plus the senses that detect feelings inside the body.

Due to evolutionary processes, the brain has evolved to search for contingent relationships among stimuli, as when one stimulus causes the next. All the reflexes mediate biologically important life functions, including responses to food, sex, sharp objects, fire, allergens, and so forth (Table 2–1). When the brain detects some new stimuli that seem to be causally connected with—contingently related to—the onset of the unconditioned reflex, it builds connections that associate the new stimuli and the US → UR reflex.

Any stimulus provides an enormous amount of biologically useful information to the brain if it accurately predicts that a US is likely to appear, and this facilitates the stimulus becoming associated with the unconditioned reflex. For allergic people, the sight of spring flowers is causally linked with the onset of allergy attacks, because the flowers are shedding pollen, which is the US for the allergy response. The brain need not know that pollen is the link between flowers and allergies, but the close connection between flowers and the allergy response can be detected by the information-seeking and learning systems of the brain.

Pavlovian conditioning can occur without our being consciously aware of the processes. For example, you might pick up a piece of firewood to add to your fireplace and experience a painful sting that triggers the reflexive response of jerking away. You may not have consciously seen the spider hiding on the side of the firewood, but glimpsing the spider a mere thirtieth of a second is enough for the brain to link the sight of the spider with the pain and jerk reflex. Careful laboratory studies show that stimuli as brief as 1/30 of a second do not register in our consciousness, but they can become conditioned stimuli (CSs) for fear after the brain detects a cause-effect relationship between something like a spider and pain.[24]

Once we have developed a fear of spiders, we may not be aware how or where this phobia emerged, because the conditioning process was not consciously experienced. The active brain found the connection without our needing to consciously identify the cause-effect linkage. Many people with fears and phobias cannot recall any experiences that would explain the onset of their phobia.[25]

Of course, Pavlovian conditioning can also occur when people are conscious of things that caused them to have conditioned responses. Angela was frighteningly aware of her auto accident and can clearly explain why she now fears driving fast on wet and curvy roads. In fact, her conscious awareness facilitated the rapid conditioning of her fears, since she could relive the fearful experience over and over in her memory, allowing her brain to detect the cause-effect relationships easily. Nevertheless, the brain can do an amazing amount of cause-effect analysis (actively searching for contingent relationships among stimuli) even when we are not consciously aware of the brainwork and Pavlovian conditioning that is happening at an unconscious level. If you fear spiders, can you recall the time and events that produced this conditioning? If you cannot, you are not alone.

Much early research on Pavlovian conditioning focused on simple models with one cause and one effect. Pavlov placed food in front of hungry dogs and they salivated. Ringing a bell before presenting the food caused the bell to become a CS for salivation. The theory seemed so simple and mechanical. But today we know that the brain can detect *complex patterns* among all sorts of stimuli that can predict the onset of a reflex. For Angela, speeding on wet but straight roads is not as fear inducing as speeding on wet and curvy roads. It is the triad of speed, wet pavement and curves that fits together to spell "Danger." Because she has driven fast on wet but straight roads on many occasions without accident, these stimuli remain neutral for her (though they may not be for people who were unlucky enough to have auto accidents on straight wet roads).

The brain's sensitivity to complex stimulus patterns helps explain *conditioned inhibition,* where some special signal inhibits responses to CSs that otherwise elicit reflexes.[26] If spiders are CSs that elicit fear for you, you may jump with anxiety when seeing a spider. But if PJ—the practical joker in your crowd—drops a wiggly rubber spider in your lap, you might not jump because you have learned that stimuli from PJ are usually harmless. Likewise, if PJ gave you a check for $1000, you might not jump with joy. Since PJ has a long history of doing things while "just kidding," seeing PJ can produce conditioned inhibitions of many responses.

Our new understanding of Pavlovian conditioning reveals that the simple mechanistic model developed by early research deserves to be replaced by a much more organic model that emphasizes how the brain works as an active information-seeking system.

Biological Preparedness

The brain is not equally sensitive to all types of stimuli. Some types of stimuli are much more important for survival than others, and evolutionary processes have prepared the brain to locate some types of causal correlations more easily than others. Thus in Pavlovian conditioning, we often see a *biological preparedness* for making certain associations especially easily. *The brain is biologically structured to connect certain types of CSs with life-critical USs, even with limited learning opportunities.* Quick conditioning can sometimes make life or death differences in survival situations.

For example, various types of rich, diseased, or poisonous food can make a person sick by triggering the reflexive responses of nausea and vomiting. It may take only one experience with a certain type of food and the sickness reflex to condition a strong negative response to that particular food, even if the vomiting occurs as long as 2 to 3 hours after eating the food. Such rapid conditioning in spite of long time delays reflects considerable biological preparedness for the conditioning of the sickness reflex to new food flavors and odors.[27] Because avoiding bad food is important for survival, this biological preparedness is easily traced to evolutionary causes: Individuals have the best chances of surviving if they are biologically prepared to learn—with only one bad experience—what odors and tastes are associated with tainted food.

The rapid conditioning of negative responses to certain foods is not uncommon in everyday life. For example, if a friend invites you to a nice restaurant and coaxes you to try the seafood, you may innocently select something too rich for your stomach. When the scallops wrapped in bacon arrive, they look and smell delicious. Fried in bacon fat and smothered with a rich sour cream sauce, they are sweet and succulent. Much to your surprise, 1 or 2 hours later, your stomach starts complaining. The rich, heavy food was too much for you, and you begin to feel weak and nauseous. After another half-hour, you are burping up potent odors, and shortly thereafter everything comes up. Terrible taste! And your stomach does not calm down for another hour.

The rich food triggered the unconditioned reflex that is a part of a biological "safeguard system" which rejects bad food from the body. Pavlovian conditioning builds from this basic reflex. Each time the sickness reflex is elicited by bad food, the taste, the odor, and even the thought of the food you ate before you got sick become CSs associated with feelings of sickness. In fact, the next time you notice scallops on a menu or sit next to someone who orders scallops, you may feel weak in the stomach, perhaps a bit nauseous. Due to Pavlovian conditioning, a new stimulus—scallops—has become a CS associated with the biologically established sickness reflex. The learning experience has established a *conditioned food aversion,* in this case, a dislike for scallops.

Pavlovian conditioning allows each individual to learn the particular foods in his or her environment that trigger the sickness reflex. Someone in California may eat a rich abalone dinner that triggers an intense stomach sickness, making abalone a conditioned stimulus (CS) that later causes queasy feelings, whereas scallops cause no aversive feelings. A native in an Amazonian rain forest might become sick after eating a newly discovered red frog, and thus learn a food aversion associated with red frogs. We all begin life with the same biologically established reflexes, but Pavlovian conditioning gives us the flexibility to go beyond the biologically determined responses. Each individual's unique life experiences create patterns of conditioning that reflect that person's unique history of learning with scallops, abalone, or red frogs.

Learning allows us to benefit from experience. If you get sick once from a certain food, the conditioned nausea you feel when exposed to that food in the future will help prevent your making the same mistake twice. In some cases—as with poisonous foods—this can make a life-or-death difference. In a study of 517 undergraduates, 65% of the students had at least one food aversion.[28] Most of these developed several hours after eating a food that caused sickness. The taste of the food was more likely to become a CS for the conditioned aversion than were the appearance or odor of the food. Unfamiliar foods were more likely than common foods to become the CSs for food aversions.

The brain actively searches for causal linkages between stimuli and USs, and often makes us especially attentive to relevant stimuli.[29] For example, people become acutely aware of physical symptoms, such as a "racing heart" when it is causally linked with a medical problem. Oversensitivity to symptoms is far too common in hypochondriacs, but it is part of a functional response in normal people who attend to physical symptoms only when contingently linked with a medical problem.

Six Other Determinants of Strong Conditioning

When we do not have a strong biological preparedness for Pavlovian conditioning, several other variables determine the speed with which learning takes place and the strength of a conditioned reflex after conditioning.

First, strong USs produce stronger conditioned reflexes than do weak USs. A major car accident causes stronger emotional responses and more powerful conditioned anxiety about unsafe driving than does a minor fender bender at a slow speed. Intense orgasms cause relevant stimuli to be more strongly eroticized than are the CSs associated with mild orgasms.

Second, the more often a CS is predictive of a US, the more power the CS acquires to elicit a CR.[30] In many cases, one association between a neutral stimulus and a reflex produces only a small effect, but each additional association increases the power of the CS to elicit a CR. After ten pairings with a US, a CS has a stronger effect than after one pairing. The more often a person links a certain sexual fantasy with the USs of the sexual reflex, the more power the fantasy will take on as a CS that elicits sexual responses.

Third, when a CS is always associated with a given US, the CS takes on a greater ability to elicit the CR than if pairing is only intermittent. When a stimulus precedes a US 100% of the time, it has more predictive power and is much more likely to become a CS than if it preceded the US only 20% or 50% of the time. If a woman always wears a certain perfume before making love, and never wears it at other times, the perfume is likely to become a CS that will elicit sexual arousal for her and her partner. If she wore the perfume only 20% of the time that the couple made love, the perfume would not become as strong a CS for eliciting sexual feelings.

When several stimuli precede a US, the stimulus that is most highly correlated with and predictive of the US is most likely to become a strong CS. If gentle loving words precede love making 100% of the time, but perfumes are only associated with sexual interaction 20% of the time, the loving words are more likely than perfume to become CSs for erotic feelings. The highly correlated cues stand out most conspicuously as clear predictors of sexual pleasures, which facilitates their conditioning. Gradually, the most predictive stimuli *overshadow* the less predictive stimuli and become the strongest CSs.

Fourth, short time lags between the onset of a CS and the onset of a US facilitate Pavlovian conditioning. In the laboratory, intervals of 0 to 5 seconds between the CS and US produce stronger conditioning than do longer intervals. The optimal interval between a CS and US is often reported to be approximately 0.5 seconds.[31] A person's fantasies that are highly focused on sex just before orgasm are likely to take on greater power as CSs that elicit sexual arousal than fantasies that occurred 30 minutes before any sexual stimulation, due to the close temporal linkage of the fantasy (the CS) and sexual stimulation (the US).[32] As the time lag between a predictive stimulus and a US increases, Pavlovian conditioning usually proceeds more slowly, unless there is a strong biological preparedness to facilitate conditioning.

Fifth, cognitive processes sometimes allow people to associate a predictive stimulus and US that are normally separated by long time periods.[33] After her auto accident, Angela pondered over and over the whole series of events preceding the car crash, even thinking of things that occurred long before the car crash. The bald tires she had neglected to replace could have contributed to her sliding out of control. By repeatedly recalling predictive stimuli and the accident, Angela brings them into close temporal association, helping the predictive stimuli to become CSs. This type of Pavlovian conditioning is called **covert conditioning,** because the cognitive reliving of memories allows conditioning to take place covertly, without any overtly visible signs. Angela may even learn to fear having bald tires after rethinking her accident several dozen times.

Friends and teachers may try to facilitate covert conditioning by giving us useful words that focus our attention on relevant predictive stimuli—and minimize the number of distracting or irrelevant cues.[34] When people tell us to "Smell that delicious steak," or "Sniff the fruity quality of this wine," they help focus our attention and thoughts on odor cues that are associated with pleasant tastes, and this facilitates our learning to respond to those odors as CSs for pleasurable experiences.

Imagine the cognitive experiences of people who were badly scorched and scarred one night when their house burned to the ground: They had accidentally left the stove on before going to bed, and this caused their house to catch on fire three hours later. As these people repeatedly recall going to bed without checking the stove—along with the multiple horrors of fire and being seriously burned (the USs)—their thoughts of not checking the stove become CSs for anxiety. Even though there was a long time lag between the original act of not checking the stove and the USs of fire and bad burns, the cognitive reliving of the events brings the CSs and USs into close association and is effective in producing Pavlovian conditioning.[35] After such an accident, people sometimes develop a strong fear of going to bed or leaving the house without checking the stove several times, because not checking the stove is the CS for fears of fire.

Sixth, a predictive stimulus must occur before—not after—a US for conditioning to occur. If a neutral stimulus occurs after the US has appeared, Pavlovian conditioning rarely occurs.[36] Attempts to create "backward conditioning"—in which predictive stimuli come *after* a US—almost always fail. It makes sense that we would not have evolved a tendency to associate things in backward causal order.[37] If a person ate some bad food (the US) and became nauseous and sick (the UR), should this unconditioned sickness reflex affect the stimuli that came before or after it? The sight and odors of bad food that came before eating the bad food (US) are most likely to be the causal stimuli (CSs) we need to learn to dislike. If a nauseous person drank some warm broth to soothe the stomach after a bout of sickness, it is obvious that the broth did not cause the sickness; and it would not be functional for the soothing broth to become a CS that could elicit feelings of nausea. In

Pavlovian conditioning, stimuli that are present before a US and best predict that the US will appear are most likely to become effective CSs.

Suboptimal Conditioning

The brain is sensitive to contingent relationships among stimuli and usually associates USs with appropriate CSs; but this may not occur when two or more competing cues are possibly associated with one US. *There are two cue competition effects, called overshadowing and blocking, in which conditioning does not proceed optimally.*[38] Recall the examples where asthmatic responses have been reported to be conditioned to speeches by politicians, goldfish, waterfalls, and children's choirs. If the brain is biologically structured to find cause-effect relations between CSs and the USs that they predict, how can things such as political speeches become CSs for asthmatic responses?

In **overshadowing,** *the presence of intense, large, or conspicuous stimuli capture the brain's attention and interfere with the conditioning of the less conspicuous stimuli that better predict the onset of the US.*[39] Consider one way in which political speeches could become conditioned to asthma attacks. After a political scandal in your state, many people are concerned with the outcome of the next election. Will the dishonest scum bag get reelected or will an honest young politician be able to oust the old incumbent? A TV debate has received enormous publicity and you plan to watch, along with several of your friends. So much attention is directed to the debate that you hardly notice that it is a windy day, capable of picking up all sorts of pollen and plant matter, stirring it into the air and wafting it into your house through open doors and windows.

As you watch the political debates, hanging on every word, chatting with your friends when each politician makes a strong point or misspeaks, your attention is riveted to the TV. Hence the TV stimuli can overshadow the more subtle cues associated with wind and pollen. When your asthma attack begins half way through the political speeches, the TV stimuli are so conspicuous that they become paired with the US that triggers the asthma response.

Overshadowing helps explain many other events. If you meet someone new during a wild and festive party, the stimuli coming from the person's actual behavior may be overshadowed by all the stimuli of the exciting party. You feel euphorically happy and the new person may become a CS for wonderful feelings. Two days later the person calls and invites you out next weekend, and the CSs of their voice elicit your feelings of excitement. During the week you notice happy feelings each time you think of the person—since the person is a CS for positive emotions. Then, next Saturday arrives and you meet at a quiet cafe, with no loud music to distract you. As you listen to the person talk, you may be shocked to here words that you find insensitive or selfish. Without the positive overshadowing stimuli you would not have come to respond to this person as a CS for positive emotions!

In **blocking,** *the conditioning of a valuable predictive stimulus is hampered by the strength of CSs established by prior conditioning.*[40] Some people are afraid of snakes, due to prior fear conditioning that they may not remember. They may respond to all snakes as CSs for fear responses, and this may seem reasonable and adaptive. However, such powerful conditioning can block the conditioning of more subtle discriminations about snakes. Most people know that there are many species of snakes that are not dangerous; and some are actually beneficial—such as gopher snakes, which are not poisonous and feed on rodents.

What if we show a picture of a gopher snake to a person who fears all snakes and explain that gopher snakes are helpful in the garden? The person's first response is likely to be fear and looking away. These responses can block the Pavlovian conditioning needed to inhibit or counteract certain kinds of snake fears. There are ways that people can learn to overcome fears of harmless snakes (see Counterconditioning, pp. 36–39).

Strong positive conditioning can block the later learning of other emotional associations. Some teens have so much positive conditioning associated with a favorite movie star that they become impervious to information that the star is a drug addict. Some people fall in love with a person who later begins to use or abuse them. If the love is very strong, it can block their learning to respond to the person as hurtful and dangerous. Some battered women stay in relationships and love partners in spite of abuse.

Both overshadowing and blocking can interfere with the learning of realistic emotional responses in cases of both love and hate. Archenemies may have such a strong history of hatred that it is hard for them to make peace and learn to be friends.

EXTINCTION

Due to a process called extinction, conditioned reflexes can lose power and disappear over time. *Extinction occurs whenever a CS is present but does not precede its US.* As a child, Barbara had enough falls from high places that views from heights became conditioned into CSs for anxiety. However, once Barbara learned numerous skills for rock climbing without having any painful falls, she had many exposures to the CS of views from high places without the US of falls. Gradually, she ceased to fear heights because the CS of views from heights no longer preceded the US of painful falls. *When a CS no longer precedes a US, it gradually loses its ability to elicit conditioned responses, and the conditioned reflex (CS $\rightarrow$ CR) becomes weaker.* The more often a CS is present without a US, the weaker the conditioned reflex becomes. Eventually the stimulus ceases to elicit a conditioned response.

Extinction can occur naturally at all ages of life. The following examples illustrate the *two-phase cycle of (1) conditioning followed by (2) extinction.* Figure 2–2 shows the typical development and decline of a conditioned reflex seen during conditioning and extinction. During conditioning, the CS takes on increasing ability to elicit a CR (up to some point of maximal conditioning, marked by the "X" in Fig. 2–2), then loses that power during extinction.

During the early years of life, children are relatively small, weak, and vulnerable to numerous painful experiences. Depending on each one's unique experiences, she or he may learn to be afraid of various CSs—such as strangers, hypodermic needles, big dogs, lightning storms, large fires, being in the dark, or being alone. After enough conditioning, these CSs can elicit fear and crying. If seeing lightning precedes very loud claps of thunder, the loud noise may function as a US that conditions the child to fear lightning. Just

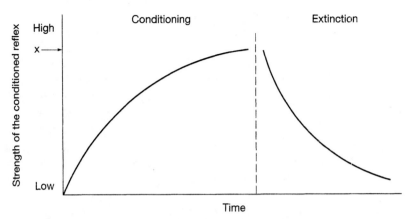

FIGURE 2–2   **The typical development and decline of a conditioned reflex seen during conditioning (left) and extinction (right). "X" on the left side shows height of maximum conditioning.**

seeing lightning in the distance can become a CS that elicits fear and crying. However, as the years pass and the child becomes familiar with many loud noises that are not predictive of pain, the childhood fears of CSs associated with loud noise gradually extinguish. As long as a person has no direct bad experiences with lightning, it is not predictive of USs for painful experiences and ceases being a CS due to extinction. Big dogs and other stimuli that elicit childhood fears may also lose their power to elicit fear as the years go by. It is this process of extinction that allows us to "outgrow" childhood fears. More accurately, extinction produces "conditioned inhibition" of the childhood fears.[41]

Extinction is not limited to fears and other negative emotional responses. Positive conditioned reflexes can also extinguish if they are no longer linked with their original USs. When a baby breast-feeds, the breasts become CSs that elicit pleasurable feelings for the baby—since they are predictive stimuli seen just before the USs of milk and soft skin contact. Merely seeing the breasts before nursing can elicit a smile and pleasurable CERs from an infant before nursing. When a mother ceases breast-feeding, the extinction process begins. At first the child may still look to mother's breasts and pull her blouse to reach them, indicating that the breasts are still CSs for positive emotions. However, after breast-feeding has ended, the breasts are no longer associated with the USs of milk, and over the next months they gradually cease to elicit pleasurable CERs, due to extinction and the conditioned inhibitions of earlier responses.

Similar cycles of conditioning and extinction occur at other times in life. When a couple's home is destroyed by fire started when they accidentally left the stove on, they become conditioned to fear making mistakes that can cause fires. Leaving the house or going to bed without checking the stove are CSs that elicit fear. After this conditioning, they may be very careful with the stove and other appliances for months or years. As time passes and *if they have no more accidents with fires,* the extinction process begins to reduce the strength of the CSs for fearing fire, because the CSs are no longer linked with accidents. Gradually, the CSs lose their ability to elicit fear, and the couple becomes less worried about fire than they were in the months immediately after their house burned. (However, occasional vivid memories of the horrors of their house burning can produce enough **reconditioning**—via cognitive means—to prevent the fear of fire from totally disappearing. Intermittent reconditioning helps explain why some conditioned reflexes never completely disappear after years without having another house fire.)

Extinction helps us understand why there is truth to the old saying "Time heals all wounds." One day we make a serious error: almost injure our best friend (by accident), embarrass ourselves in front of the whole class, or lose a pile of money in a silly investment. The CSs related to the error cause strong emotional responses. A month later, the CSs may still elicit strong feelings of guilt or embarrassment. However, extinction takes place every day that our thinking about those CSs is no longer closely linked with making similar errors again: Gradually the CSs lose their ability to elicit emotions. Several years later, we look back and realize intellectually that we made some mistakes, but no longer suffer intense emotional pain over them. So, in fact, extinction heals old wounds.

Spontaneous Recovery

Although extinction weakens conditioned reflexes, conditioned reflexes regain some of their strength during periods after extinction ends, due to a process that Pavlov called spontaneous recovery.[42] Whereas conditioning takes place when a CS precedes a US and extinction takes place when a CS appears without its US, *spontaneous recovery occurs during periods after extinction stops—when the CS is not present at all.* In the pause after extinction is over—when a person has no contact with the CS—the effects of the prior extinction weaken; and the next time the person encounters the CS, it will have a stronger effect than it did at the end of extinction. The CS shows a spontaneous recovery of *some* of its power to elicit responses (see Fig. 2–3).

By her 15th birthday in May, Barbara had noticeable fears of heights, due to prior painful falls (time 1 in the fig.). That summer, Barbara took a two-week vacation hiking safely in the mountains, without any falls; and extinction helped her overcome most of her fears of the CS of heights (time 2). However, during the pause between that summer's extinction experience and next year's vacation, some spontaneous recovery of fear will

FIGURE 2–3   Spontaneous recovery is seen after both the pause periods, which come after the end of extinction. During each pause, the conditioned stimulus regains some strength (dashed lines). The CS's strength after spontaneous recovery is marked "Spon. Recov."

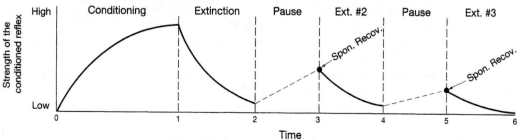

occur (by time 3). When Barbara returns to the mountains a year later, her fear of heights will be stronger than at the end of the prior vacation and extinction experiences (time 2). Spontaneous recovery requires no additional conditioning, only a pause or break since the end of the last extinction. As a result, Barbara will feel more fear on the first day of the second summer's hiking (time 3) than she felt at the end of the first summer's hiking (time 2), revealing the partial recovery of fears elicited by the CS of heights. However, Barbara will feel less fear at the beginning of the second summer than at the beginning of the first summer because spontaneous recovery does not return a conditioned reflex to the full preextinction level. During the second summer of hiking and extinction, Barbara's fears will decline again, to the low at time 4; but spontaneous recovery can partially boost those fears before the third summer's hiking begins at time 5. In essence, extinction causes the conditioned inhibition of the fear response; and after the end of extinction, the conditioned inhibitions weaken, allowing the fear response to be stronger at times 3 and 5 than times 2 and 4.

Spontaneous recovery also occurs with positive emotional reflexes. Infants who breast-feed learn to respond to their mothers' breasts as CSs for pleasurable anticipation of nursing. When a mother finally stops breast-feeding, her child's positive conditioned responses to the breasts are put on extinction. Each time the child reaches for the breasts and is not allowed to nurse, the positive conditioned responses become weaker. This is where spontaneous recovery could enter the picture. What happens if Mrs. G is called out of town for several days and her child, Camille, has a pause from extinction? If Camille has a period in which the CSs of her mother's breasts never appear, there will be some spontaneous recovery of positive conditioned responses. When Mother returns at the end of the pause, Camille will make stronger positive responses to her breasts—looking and reaching more—than she did before her mother left town. During the pause after extinction, some of Camille's conditioned inhibitions (which were created by extinction) could weaken, allowing her looking responses to regain strength due to spontaneous recovery.

Avoidance Retards Extinction

Extinction occurs whenever a CS is present but is not followed by its US. *If a person avoids contact with a CS, extinction cannot take place.* If you fear math or computers and avoid them, you deprive yourself of chances to overcome your fear of math or computers. Consider two people—M and N—who have developed a fear of skiing due to past painful falls. Next, M hires a good ski instructor to gain better skills, while N totally avoids skiing. By receiving instruction and learning to ski without falling, M finds that the fears of skiing extinguish. Good instruction hastens extinction by linking the CSs for fears of skiing with the neutral stimuli of "no falls," "no pain," and "no problems." Of course, M feels frightened the first few times the instructor requires practice on skis, because being on skis the first time after an accident is the CS that elicits fear and trembling legs. But good instruction helps M gain the skills to ski without falling, and this assures that the CSs of skiing no longer precede the USs of painful falls. As a result, M's conditioned fears extinguish, and gradually the CS of being on skis loses its capacity to elicit fear. In contrast, person N shows the effects of avoiding ski instruction. N is avoiding opportunities to have the CSs associated with the fear of skiing to occur in the *absence* of falls. Thus, extinction cannot take place. Because avoidance prevents extinction, N's CSs will retain their power to elicit fear. The avoidance response may prevent N from overcoming the fear of skiing, whereas M may eventually learn to ski well and enjoy it.

Without behavior modification, some people go to great lengths to avoid CSs that elicit fear, and their avoidance patterns can persist for years, because they never have the extinction experience needed to neutralize the CSs. For example, hearing about horrible airplane crashes causes some people to fear flying in planes. Once they are conditioned to respond to air flight as a CS for anxiety, they often suffer considerable inconvenience in making long distance trips by train, bus, or car when flying would have been much easier—and safer. But if they avoid air travel, their fears of flying cannot extinguish.

Children sometimes learn conditioned fears of authority figures—such as the police, ministers, or the principal—if these authority figures become CSs associated with punishment or threats. Those children who avoid interacting with authority figures as they grow up often retain their fears of such people well into adulthood. Twenty-five years later, when Gina had to contact the principal because her 8-year-old was having trouble in the third grade, Gina experienced emotional discomfort because her old childhood fear of principals had never had a chance to extinguish. Only after Gina was forced to interact with the feared authority figure (the CS)—and experienced no new punishment—could extinction begin to neutralize her lingering childhood conditioning. Many people carry childhood fears well into adulthood, if not all through life, even though those fears are irrational in light of their adult skills and experience.

Conditioned fears and anxieties are less likely to extinguish naturally than are conditioned pleasures. The reason for this is simple: CSs that elicit fear motivate avoidance, hence retard extinction; whereas CSs that elicit pleasure, motivate approach, which allows extinction to occur if the CSs cease to predict pleasurable USs. The person who fears flying is likely to avoid air travel, which prevents the fear from extinguishing. In contrast, CSs for pleasurable emotions are not avoided, allowing extinction to occur once these CSs no longer precede pleasurable experiences. The baby who has been breast-fed for months responds to the breasts as CSs for pleasurable emotions. Once the mother decides to stop breast-feeding, extinction can begin. Does the child show avoidance at this time? No. Nursing was pleasurable, and the child attempts to nurse. The infant's approach allows the CSs to extinguish, because the CSs of seeing and touching the breasts no longer precede the USs of milk. Thus, the extinction of pleasurable associations is not retarded by avoidance responses.

Therapeutic Extinction

Extinction can be used in behavior modification, especially when people have persistent fears that bother them for years and strong avoidance responses prevent extinction. ***Therapeutic extinction*** *involves having a person confront a fear-inducing CS in a safe environment that is free of all types of aversive stimuli.*[43] As the person experiences the feared CS in the absence of other aversive stimuli, the CS loses its power to elicit fear.

Consider the case of Mr. K who had developed a fear of opening and walking through doors after a series of traumatic conditioning experiences as a younger man during wartime.[44] While behind enemy lines, K received a tip that a group of enemy soldiers in a nearby house wanted to surrender. K suspected a trap. As he approached the doorway, which was deep in shadow under a balcony, his apprehension grew. Finally, K burst through the door to be startled by the sight of 12 enemy soldiers waking from their night's sleep. He captured them and stood guard over them for ten stressful hours, until he could take them in after dark. He was forced to kill one of the prisoners who was goading the others to attack him, and the man he shot "died horribly in the no-man's land between us." This experience and several other battle traumas caused K a great deal of anxiety and guilt associated with bursting into dangerous situations. The fright and guilt were so intense that he became fearful of opening doors. Soon he learned to avoid doors—the fear-inducing CSs—although this severely restricted his activities. His avoidance of doors prevented his fear from extinguishing naturally.

Behavior modification consisted of repeated therapeutic extinction experiences in which Mr. K stopped avoiding the fear-inducing CSs of opening doors: As he practiced his most feared behavior, bursting through a closed doorway, but in safe therapeutic settings, the conditioned fear began to extinguish. After each session, Mr. K felt less fear and guilt about opening doors, and at the end of five sessions, the extinction was complete: The old fears were now suppressed by the conditioned inhibitions produced during extinction. K's irrational fears did not reappear.

The modern technology of virtual reality (VR) allows therapists to create computer simulations of feared events so people with phobias can face their worst fears in the safety of a computer studio.[45] For example, people with acrophobia—or fear of heights—put on audiovisual headgear that allows them to enter a computer-created VR environment. As the acrophobes stand safely on a 4×4 foot platform holding on to a handrail, computer-generated visuals give them simulated experiences, such as riding an elevator to higher and higher levels of a building with an exterior elevator. Each time they decide to go to a higher floor, the computer allows them to see ever more frightening views of the VR scenery below from higher perspectives. The computer allows them to "walk" onto small construction bridges leading to small balconies on the building, all with striking views of the ground far below. At first, the acrophobes experience rubbery knees and sweaty palms in this simulated reality; but after several sessions in which there is no US for pain, most feel decreased fear of high places. Some report that they have actually stopped avoiding many high places.

HIGHER ORDER CONDITIONING

*After one stimulus is conditioned into a CS because it is predictive of a US, other stimuli that are predictive of the first CS can become conditioned into conditioned stimuli—even in the absence of the original US. The process by which new CSs are created by being associated with a CS alone (with no US present) is called **higher order conditioning**.* Seeing a bee one foot away is a CS_1 usually learned in childhood because it predicts possible pains. The words "There may be bees in here" can become a CS_2 because they predict seeing bees, even if no bees sting us after hearing those words.

In the first three sections of Figure 2–4, a first neutral stimulus (NS_1) that precedes and predicts a US (dotted diagonal lines) becomes a conditioned stimulus (CS_1). This is **first order conditioning** (the type of Pavlovian conditioning discussed in the prior pages of this chapter). The last two frames show **second order conditioning** (the simplest type of higher order conditioning), as a second stimulus (NS_2) becomes a CS_2 because it precedes and predicts the CS_1—without any US being present—in the last two frames. After the second conditioned reflex ($CS_2 \rightarrow CR_2$) is established, it can be used to condition a third neutral stimulus (NS_3) into a conditioned stimulus (CS_3). This is **third order conditioning.**

Words often become CSs with an ability to elicit conditioned emotional responses (CERs) due to higher order conditioning. If parents see that their child is about to touch a hot stove top, they might say "no-no." Young children do not understand at first and sometimes touch the hot surface anyway. Because the simple words "no-no" frequently precede USs that elicit pain, the words "no-no" become a CS_1 for fear and anxiety, due to their direct association with the US. After several such experiences, many young children immediately stop their actions as soon as they hear the words "no-no," if the parents have been consistent in using the phrase as a predictive stimulus linked with painful USs.

As children get older and learn more words, more complex phrases may be associated with the CS_1 and become CS_2s, via second order conditioning. If a parent says, "That's dangerous, Freddie," then says, "It's a no-no," the word "dangerous" can become a CS_2 that elicits fear via second order conditioning, taking on power because it precedes and predicts the CS_1 of "no-no." Note that the US of being burned by the hot stove is not present while this second order conditioning is taking place.

Pavlovian conditioning is one way that children learn the meaning, or emotional impact, of words. Both "no-no" (the CS_1) and "dangerous" (the CS_2) take their meanings from the ultimate consequences of contact with painful USs.

Higher order conditioning is not as strong as first order conditioning. As Freddie reaches to touch a hot pancake griddle, hearing the words "That's dangerous, Freddie" provides the CS_2 that elicits fear and suppresses the response to some degree. If Freddie

FIGURE 2–4 **In higher order conditioning, a CS_2 is created if it precedes and predicts a CS_1—even though the US is not present.**

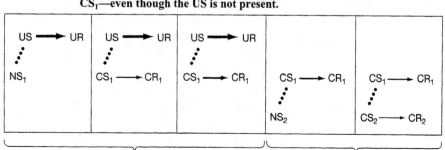

fails to respond to the CS_2, the parent may resort to the more powerful words "no-no." This CS_1 elicits a stronger fear response and strengthens the second order conditioning of the CS_2 ("dangerous").

There are two main reasons why higher order conditioning is weaker than first order conditioning. First, USs are the causes of biological reflexes and the source from which all Pavlovian conditioning takes its strength, and they are not present in higher order conditioning. Second, the higher order CSs are being conditioned from other CSs *that are on extinction during higher order conditioning*—since they are not being followed by the USs from which they take their strength. Hence, the CS_2 produces a weaker response than the CS_1, and the CS_1 is weaker than the US.

Third order conditioning is possible when a third stimulus is brought into use. If at the dinner table, parents mention "radon" several times before the word "dangerous," the child may develop a third order conditioned fear of the word "radon" without even knowing what it means. The new word "radon" becomes a CS_3 via third order conditioning, but it will not elicit as much fear and apprehension as does the CS_2, "dangerous."

Higher order conditioning is not limited to reflexes with aversive emotional components. Positive reflexes can become conditioned to higher order stimuli. The nursing mother who feels pleasure when seeing her baby reaching for the nipple (CS_1) might develop a CS_2 of talking about breast-feeding with friends, if talking and thinking about the topic are paired with the CS_1 of the infant's trying to reach the breast.

People often mix CS_1s, CS_2s, and CS_3s when trying to persuade others that a given behavior is good or bad. In order to convince someone that jogging is a great activity, a jogger may list all sorts of positive words associated with running: It is invigorating, makes you healthy, helps you lose weight, makes you feel stronger and more independent, and so on. Many of these words are CSs that elicit positive feelings in the listener, but some are CS_1s, while others are CS_2s or CS_3s. Since CS_1s tend to produce stronger effects than CS_2s, the jogger may be more successful in conditioning the word "jogging" into a CS that elicits positive feelings in the listener if the jogger uses words—such as good health or invigorating—that are CS_1s more than CS_3s.

COUNTERCONDITIONING

After a CS has been conditioned to elicit a certain response, the CS may precede a US or CS that elicits a different and incompatible response, which leads to **counterconditioning.** *Counterconditioning can reverse the effects of the original conditioning by combining extinction and new conditioning.* (1) Extinction occurs because the CS is no longer linked with the stimuli from which it was originally conditioned, and (2) new conditioning emerges as the CS is associated with the new USs or CSs that elicit new responses that are incompatible with the old ones. Counterconditioning occurs commonly in everyday life and is also a powerful tool of behavior modification.

Counterconditioning is common in everyday life: People's responses are often conditioned one way at one age, then conditioned another way at a later age. A small child may be knocked down several times by big dogs and learn to fear dogs.[46] Dogs become CSs for fear due to their association with painful falls and bites. When little Anne sees a big dog, she becomes quite fearful. What happens if Anne befriends another little girl who loves dogs, has two affectionate beagles, and often has the dogs around while the children are playing together? Anne may feel fearful at first but gradually notice her fears disappearing.[47] First, merely playing with her friend elicits positive emotions that counteract some of the fears Anne originally felt in the presence of dogs. If Anne has additional positive experiences directly associated with dogs, counterconditioning can continue even further, so dogs become CSs for pleasurable emotions. Perhaps the children take the beagles along on a picnic and have fun chasing and playing with them. Because the dogs are associated with fun and games, Anne gradually learns to respond to dogs as CSs that elicit warm, positive feelings. She may eventually ask her parents if she can have a dog for a pet. Looking back, we see that the original fear of dogs was counterconditioned by (1) the absence of aversive experiences with dogs, and (2) the presence of the positive stimuli arising from play.

Counterconditioning can work in the other direction, too, turning a once positive stimulus into something negative. Some people are socialized to respond to powerful cars and fast driving as CSs for thrills and excitement. Just seeing an ad for a sleek, fast sports car and thinking about racing it at high speeds can provide enough CSs to elicit a smile and surge of excitement. These positive associations with speed can be counterconditioned if speed becomes paired with several aversive events. After Angela's first serious auto accident, while speeding on a wet curvy road, the positive CSs of speed were partially counterconditioned by the frightening consequences. If Angela had a second major accident several months later, while driving at 80 mph on a straight, dry road, high speed would be further counterconditioned to a CS that elicits uncomfortable feelings.

The rate of counterconditioning is influenced by the number of positive and negative stimuli present during counterconditioning. A professional race driver—with fame, publicity, prize money, and a very rewarding lifestyle all centered around racing—might experience so much positive conditioning from these multiple sources that two serious accidents would not create enough counterconditioning to destroy the thrill of speeding. A teenager whose peer group lived and breathed cars, speed, racing, and thrills might also have so many positive social experiences linked with racing that two close calls with death would not change speeding from a CS for positive emotions to a CS for anxiety. However, many people would become quite apprehensive about fast driving after one serious accident and, after the second accident would experience noticeable anxiety when the speedometer pushed toward 90.

Therapeutic Counterconditioning

In behavior modification, there are two types of counterconditioning used to reverse people's conditioning to CSs that elicit unwanted emotional responses. *Systematic desensitization is a gentle procedure used to reduce people's fears and anxieties to CSs*—such as flying in airplanes, riding in elevators, or speaking in public. It is also useful in helping with post-traumatic stress syndrome, which can be caused by rape, molestation, mugging, shell shock, battle fatigue, and other horrific events. *Aversive counterconditioning is a powerful technique for reversing people's attraction to CSs that elicit troublesome posi-*

tive emotions—such as addiction to gambling, drugs or alcohol.[48] In both cases, the problematic CS is paired with stimuli that elicit emotions opposite from and incompatible with the undesired Pavlovian associations.

Systematic Desensitization.   *People can overcome fears and anxieties by pairing the CSs that elicit mild anxiety with stimuli which elicit relaxation and other pleasurable feelings. After they feel comfortable at this first mild level of CSs, they move up one step at a time to CSs that had, in the past, elicited higher and higher levels of fear and anxiety.* This process is called **systematic desensitization** to reveal the systematic step-by-step nature of working through feared CSs—from the mildest to the strongest—and reducing the person's sensitivity to them. Although this form of counterconditioning can be done by imagining the fear-inducing CSs while relaxed, systematic desensitization is more effective when people have real-life exposures to feared CSs in safe situations.[49]

One of the most common conditioned fears that people have is speaking up in a group of strangers—such as in a classroom or public gathering. People with this fear often have opinions or questions; but every time they are about to raise their hands, their hearts begin to pound or a lump comes to the throat, and they cannot bring themselves to venture a single word for fear of misspeaking or being criticized. There are many possible causes for the fear of speaking in groups of strangers. In junior high and high school, Jeanne was harshly criticized by several teachers when she gave incorrect answers to questions. When speaking to groups, Sam was embarrassed by several major blunders. During such aversive experiences, speaking up in a group can become a CS that elicits anxiety.

The systematic desensitization of public speaking begins by creating a carefully planned series of small steps for approaching this fear. A person ranks all kinds of public speaking scenarios from least threatening to most.[50] Second, the person is taught relaxation skills, because relaxation is incompatible with fear and nervousness. Lying quietly on a sofa or bed, the person listens to a relaxing tape that consists of soothing music and instructions for relaxing the feet, legs, torso, hands, arms, neck, and head. Third, imaginal counterconditioning involves a person's envisioning the least fear-inducing stimuli while relaxation brings positive emotions that are incompatible with fear. Gradually the person moves up the hierarchy, imagining more frightening scenarios while staying relaxed. Sometimes imaginal desensitization helps so much that no other steps are needed. But some people add step four and work through a hierarchical series of homework exercises in real life, starting with the least feared events. George decided to first practice relaxing and speaking to one or two of his best friends. Once he felt comfortable doing this, he tried relaxing and speaking in larger groups of friends while staying relaxed. Finally, George was ready to relax and talk in small groups of strangers, with the goal of shifting to even larger groups of strangers if needed.

Systematic desensitization exercises are done in a series of gradual steps, and people may spend weeks or months overcoming their fears of one level of CSs before going on to the next step. Real-life desensitization also helps people learn skills for avoiding blunders, embarrassing topics, or polysyllabic words they cannot pronounce.[51] After getting used to talking with small groups of strangers, George was encouraged to volunteer as a receptionist in a local charity that involved his talking with many strangers each day.

In this pleasant environment where he could feel safe and relaxed, George's fears were counterconditioned by relaxation and the positive experiences of friendly interactions. The last step was to occasionally take charge of leading large groups of people who toured the charity's facilities. As he became accustomed to speaking in front of numerous strangers, George found that public speaking—a CS that once elicited fear—eventually became a CS that made him feel pride in doing his job.

Aversive Counterconditioning.   Some people have strong attractions to activities that are self-defeating, dangerous, or socially unacceptable—such as drug abuse, child sexual abuse, or compulsive behavior. Behavior therapists can help reduce the attractiveness of these things via aversive counterconditioning. Therapists arrange to have *the CS that elicits problematic positive emotions to be followed by aversive stimuli, causing the CS to gradually lose its attractiveness and become either neutral or aversive.* This process is called **aversive counterconditioning.**

Mr. R came to a therapist because he was afraid that his habit—tying himself up tightly with black rubber bonds and masturbating—was getting out of control.[52] Because he recently had difficulty in releasing himself from his bonds, he became afraid that he might die someday if he could not untie himself. How did Mr. R ever become conditioned to find being tied in black rubber a sexual CS? When Mr. R was seventeen, a group of boys tied a rubber ground sheet over his head and masturbated him. Although the experience was somewhat frightening, it was erotically exciting. Afterward, he often tied himself in black rubber bonds while masturbating. As a consequence, being bound with black rubber became a CS capable of eliciting sexual pleasures. During the years that followed, Mr. R had not made many friends and had not established a sexual relationship. He was often alone, and his masturbatory activities were among the more pleasurable things in his life. His frequent use of rubber during masturbation eventually produced conditioning so strong that Mr. R felt powerless to restrain himself from using black rubber bonds.

The therapist used aversive counterconditioning to reverse Mr. R's unwanted conditioning to rubber bonds. In order to counteract the years of past positive conditioning, the therapist instructed Mr. R to associate black rubber objects with aversive experiences rather than the emotionally positive sexual reflex. During therapy Mr. R tied himself with rubber ground sheets and took a drug that induced nausea. After only a few sessions, Mr. R lost interest in and discarded his collection of rubber objects. For the first time in years, he began to go to dances and other social events where he might meet women.

Aversive counterconditioning is usually considered only a "stop-gap" method—with temporary benefits—that must be coupled with positive types of behavior modification to create lasting success.[53] By pairing alcohol with aversive experiences such as nausea-inducing drugs, therapists can help problem drinkers learn to find alcohol distasteful during therapy. But what happens after people leave therapy and return to their everyday lives? If aversion therapy is not linked with positive skills training, many people begin to drink again for the same reasons they drank in the past: They have unhappy marriages, depressing jobs, or buddies who like to haunt the local bars. These and a multitude of other situations can recondition alcohol to be a CS with pleasurable associations—as effectively as behavior therapists had counterconditioned it. To help former drinkers avoid becoming reconditioned to love alcohol, therapy must go beyond the stop-gap methods of aversive counterconditioning. Marriage counseling may be needed to solve family problems and make family life so enjoyable that the former drinker no longer needs to get drunk. Helping some ex-drinkers find more gratifying occupations could solve problems resulting from underpaid or monotonous jobs. Getting people into athletic groups, community activities, service clubs, or engrossing hobbies can create lifestyles that are more interesting and rewarding than using alcohol to spiral downhill from pain or boredom to booze and stupor.

CONCLUSION

Pavlovian conditioning builds from unconditioned reflexes in which an unconditioned stimulus (US) elicits an unconditioned response (UR). When a neutral stimulus precedes the US and is highly predictive of the onset of the US, this predictive stimulus becomes a conditioned stimulus (CS) that can elicit a conditioned response (CR). In everyday life, some of the most conspicuous examples of reflexes and Pavlovian conditioning involve feelings, emotions, sexual responses, and psychosomatic responses. We are biologically prepared to condition especially rapidly to life-threatening experiences. Six other determinants of strong conditioning are presented.

After a conditioned reflex is created by Pavlovian conditioning, it can be weakened during extinction, in which a CS is present without the stimuli from which it gained its strength. Fear-eliciting CSs often motivate avoidance, and extinction cannot take place if a person avoids feared CSs. Higher order conditioning occurs when a CS is created after being paired with another CS (rather than with a US). Counterconditioning reverses the conditioning of a CS by unlinking the CS from its original US and linking it with stimuli that elicit different and incompatible responses. Extinction and counterconditioning appear naturally in everyday life and are used in behavior modification.

QUESTIONS

1. Can you recall any experiences or dreams that used to make you afraid as a child but now no longer make you fearful? Explain why a child would fear those stimuli. Explain why an adult might not fear those stimuli.
2. If you had an auto accident, would all the stimuli present at the time of the accident become CSs for apprehensive emotions? Which would most likely become CSs? Why?
3. Can you think of at least one type of reflex in each of these categories: voluntary muscles, circulation, digestion, respiration, sexual responses, emotional responses?
4. Explain why we are we biologically prepared to condition especially easily to bad food and life-threatening experiences.
5. Explain the six determinants of strong Pavlovian conditioning, when there is no biological preparedness.
6. Can you explain how extinction takes place? What might you do to extinguish a child's fear of high places? What might cause the spontaneous recovery of the child's fears after extinction?
7. Can you explain how counterconditioning takes place? What would you have to do to countercondition a child's fear of dogs into a love of dogs? Explain the two processes that underlie counterconditioning.

NOTES

1. Choice of terminology varies among the various schools of behavioral science. We use the term *Pavlovian conditioning* because this label causes our students the least confusion.

2. Several reflexes—such as the knee jerk, biceps reflex, Achilles reflex—do not condition (Bijou & Baer, 1965, p. 36).

3. The research on Pavlovian conditioning is presented in greater detail by Rescorla (1967, 1969, 1980, 1988); Terrace (1971); Rescorla and Wagner (1972); Fantino and Logan (1979); Davey (1987); Gormezano, Prokasy, and Thompson (1987); Klein and Mowrer (1989); Baeyens, Hermans, and Eelen (1993); Kehoe and Macrae (1998); Papini (1998); and Honey (2000).

4. Fulcher and Cocks (1997); Taylor, Deane, and Podd (1999).

5. Bitterman and Woodard (1976); Holland (1977); Wagner and Brandon (1989).

6. Davey (1994); Martin and Levey (1994); Matute and Miller (1998).

7. Ekman (1984); Friman, Hayes and Wilson (1998); Keltner and Kring (1998); de Jong (1999); Jakobs, Manstead, and Fischer (1999); Keltner and Gross (1999).

8. Brackbill (1960).

9. Blanchard, Hickling, Taylor, Loos, and Gerardi (1994); Dworkin and Dworkin (1995).

10. The conditioned nausea and vomiting before therapy are not relieved by drugs. However, Pavlovian counterconditioning has proven effective in minimizing the conditioned nausea (Morrow & Morrell, 1982).

11. Bernstein, Webster, and Bernstein (1982).

12. Dekker and Groen (1956).

13. King, Clowes-Hollins, and Ollendick (1997); Kheriaty, Kleinknecht, and Hyman (1999).

14. Francoeur (1991); Crooks and Baur (1999).

15. Kinsey, Pomeroy, and Martin (1948); Kinsey, Pomeroy, Martin, and Gebhard (1953); Elias and Gebhard (1969); Arafat and Cotton (1974); Baldwin and Baldwin (1997a).

16. Marks, Rachman, and Gelder (1965); Mees (1966); Marks and Gelder (1967); Tollison and Adams (1979); Baldwin and Baldwin (1997b).

17. Izard (1977); Eckman (1984); Abe and Izard (1999); Keltner and Haidt (1999); Levenson (1999).

18. For data on the Pavlovian conditioning of thoughts and the ability of thoughts to produce future conditioning, see Staats (1968, 1975), Mahoney (1970, 1974), Masters et al. (1987), McNeil and Brunetti (1992), and Shafran, Booth, and Rachman (1993).

19. Leitenberg, Agras, Butz, and Wincze (1971). The discrimination and labeling of emotional feelings are learned through operant conditioning from models, rules, prompts, and differential reinforcement (see Chapters 9–12). The verbal community usually has difficulty in teaching the individual to label these internal states accurately (Baldwin, 1985; Skinner, 1974).

20. Schacter and Singer (1962); May and Hamilton (1980); White, Fishbein, and Rutstein, (1981); Istvan, Griffitt, and Weidner (1983); Baldwin (1985); Damasio (1994); Jakobs et al. (1999).

21. Cautela (1996).

22. Marshall, Bristol, and Barbaree (1992); McNeil and Brunetti (1992).

23. Gorman (1996).

24. Öhman and Soares (1998).

25. Öst and Hugdahl (1981).

26. Pavlov (1927); Rescorla (1969); Williams (1995).

27. Skinner (1969); Seligman and Hager (1972); Logue, Ophir, and Strauss (1981); Sigmundi and Bolles (1983); Elkins (1991); Jacobsen et al. (1993); Schafe, Sollars, and Bernstein (1995); Rosas and Bouton (1997); Garcia and Riley (1998). But for a critique of the theory of biological constraints on learning, see Damianopoulos (1989).

28. Logue, Ophir, and Strauss (1981).

29. Tsukamoto, Iwanaga, and Seiwa (1997).

30. Dworkin and Dworkin (1995).

31. Kimble (1961); Terrace (1971).

32. Silva and Timberlake (1997).

33. Mahoney (1974); Bandura (1977); Meichenbaum (1977); Rosenthal and Zimmerman (1978); Kent and Jambunathan (1989); Cautela (1996).

34. Barnet, Grahame, and Miller (1993).

35. This type of covert conditioning is also called covert sensitization (Barlow, Agras, Leitenberg, Callahan & Moore, 1972; Bellack & Hersen, 1977; Cautela, 1967; Rescorla, 1999a).

36. Kimble (1961); Cole and Miller (1999); Silva and Timberlake (2000).

37. Baldwin and Baldwin (1981, p. 86). There do seem to be some evolutionary reasons why backward conditioning might occur in some cases (Bevins & Ayres, 1992; Wiertelak, Watkins, & Maier, 1992).

38. Holland (1999); Rescorla (1999b).

39. Darby and Pearce (1997); Blaisdell, Denniston, and Miller (1999); Rauhut, McPhee, and Ayres (1999).

40. Kamin (1968); Arcediano, Matute, and Miller (1997); Weiss and Panlilio (1999).

41. Rescorla (1997, 1999b); Falls (1998).

42. Pavlov (1927); Goddard (1997).

43. Jansen, Broekmate, and Heymans (1992); Steketee (1994).

44. Little and James (1964).

45. Rothbaum et al. (1995); Sieder (1996); Carlin, Hoffman, and Weghorst (1997); Botella et al. (1998); Rothbaum and Hodges (1999); Smith, Rothbaum, and Hodges (1999).

46. Doogan and Thomas (1992).

47. Bandura, Grusec, and Menlove (1967); Masters et al. (1987).

48. Elkins (1991); Bujold, Ladouceur, Sylvain, and Boisvert (1994).

49. Sherman (1972); Goldstein and Kanfer (1979); Emmelkamp (1982).

50. In some cases, therapists expose people to their most feared stimuli from the start of therapy. This technique—called implosion or flooding—sometimes works well where other therapies fail (Boudewyns & Shipley, 1983).

51. Barlow, Agras, Leitenberg, and Wincze (1970); Menzies and Clarke (1993).

52. Oswald (1962).

53. Bandura (1969, p. 509); Elkins (1991); Hester (1995); Monti, Rohsenow, Colby, and Abrams (1995); Smith and Myers (1995).

Chapter

3

Operant Conditioning

OPERATING

The surgeon in O.R. 3 is operating on a teenage girl who is an innocent victim of a drive-by shooting. A bullet is lodged near her heart, and the operation requires incredible skill and caution. The surgeon is 41 years old, with years of experience in similar operations. Young medical students attending the operation marvel over the precision of the surgeon's actions. Each move of the scalpel and each suture used to sew tissue together is an operant behavior, carefully practiced over the years to repair damaged bodies.

The word **operate** means to *"perform a function"* and *"produce an effect."* Surgeons who can operate on people and save lives do both—perform a medical function and produce healing effects. People who are skillful at operating computers make them function to produce complex effects. Thoughts, words, gestures, and all other forms of action are often useful in operating on our environment. For example, thinking and planning often allow us to organize our actions to sophisticated levels and produce highly polished effects, as during surgery. When stuck in a hot auditorium, we first think of several options and then select ones that might produce good effects, perhaps asking someone, "Do you know how to operate the air conditioner—or at least open the windows?"

People actively operate on their environments in countless ways, learning from the consequences of their actions. It takes skill to operate things, and skill is acquired via learning. In this chapter, we study the basic types of operant learning that empower us to act on our world of people, places, and things in the myriad ways we do every day.

*Operant conditioning is sometimes called **instrumental conditioning** because the skills we learn are instrumental in changing things and producing specific outcomes.* Working late at the law firm may be instrumental in winning a complex case in court (the desired outcome). Adjusting the oven temperature to the right level is instrumental in cooking the turkey just right. When you see a police car, slowing down to the speed limit is instrumental in avoiding a costly traffic ticket. Planning a party carefully can be instrumental in making sure everybody has fun. Fixing the car is instrumental in being able to drive hassle free. Instrumental behavior is usually oriented toward creating rewarding outcomes and avoiding aversive ones.

Some operant behaviors are learned rapidly and others take years of practice. Children quickly learn to avoid touching the hot burners on the stove because the outcome of touching is quite painful. But surgeons need years to learn the countless skills for achieving optimal outcomes in the operating room. Children can easily learn the skills for thinking rationally, if they are raised by parents who frequently talk in rational ways and reward their children's intelligent comments. But children may be slow to learn rational cognitive skills if their parents are not very verbal—and seldom reward their children's logical observations.

In this chapter you will discover how operant behavior is learned and changes over time, depending on the types of outcomes that follow it and the types of stimuli that precede it. Operant conditioning is one of the most basic forms of learning, affecting virtually all forms of human behavior.[1] Thorndike and Skinner were among the early leaders studying and explaining the principles of operant conditioning. This chapter presents the basic features of operant conditioning that they pioneered, and subsequent chapters explain various other principles needed to understand the numerous subtleties of operant behavior.

Law of Effect

The earliest formulation of operant principles is known as the **law of effect.** This law is based on the observation that voluntary behavior is influenced by its *effects,* namely, its outcomes or consequences. If an artist is experimenting with the use of pastels and creates some nice effects, the good effects increase the chances that the artist will use pastels more in the future. If the explorative use of pastels led to bad effects on several consecutive occasions, the artist would be less likely to continue using them, perhaps turning to explore bold primary colors. *According to the early version of the law of effect, behavior that produces satisfying consequences tends to become more frequent over time; behavior that produces discomfort tends to become less frequent.*

Subsequent reformulations of the law of effect recognize the importance of relevant situational cues. *A behavior may have good effects in one situation but bad effects in another situation.* Stepping on a car's accelerator has good effects when the traffic light is green and bad effects when it is red. As a result, people become sensitive to situational cues, especially to *antecedent* cues that precede their behavior and allow them to *discrim-*

inate whether a behavior is likely to produce good effects or bad effects. *Behavior is influenced not only by the effects that follow it, but also by the situational cues that precede it.* The green and red lights on a traffic signal are important antecedent cues that help people discriminate whether stepping on the gas will produce good or bad effects. Other cues—such as the presence of pedestrian cross walks and police cars—are important, too.

Operant Conditioning

In recent decades, there has been a tendency to use the word "operant" more than "instrumental," and to talk about the "consequences" of behavior more than "effects" or "outcomes." Today, the three main components of operant conditioning are often expressed in a simple ABC formulation, where A, B, and C stand for *antecedent cues, behavior,* and *consequences.* The relationship among these three elements is symbolized as follows:

$$A: B \rightarrow C$$

Antecedent cues (A) come before a behavior (B); the consequences (C) occur after the behavior. The *arrow* between B and C indicates that *the behavior causes the consequences.* Skillful use of pastels produces pleasing consequences. Stepping on the gas at a red light can cause accidents.

The *colon* between A and B in the equation indicates that *antecedent cues do not cause behavior, they merely set the occasion for behavior.* Having a canvas on an easel does not cause an artist to create a picture; it does, however, "set the occasion" for the artist to explore various options: sit and think, mix several colors on a palette, and perhaps start brushing paint onto the canvas. Operant behavior is usually produced through the voluntary nervous and muscular systems, and antecedent stimuli cue the appropriateness of a variety of possible voluntary behaviors—rather than triggering a specific response (as occurs in a stimulus-response reflex). Although the USs and CSs discussed in Chapter 2 on Pavlovian conditioning do automatically activate S–R reflexes, the antecedent stimuli (A) in operant conditioning merely set the occasion for various thoughts and actions.

During **operant conditioning** *the consequences of a behavior do two things: They influence (1) the frequency of the behavior in the future, and (2) the ability of antecedent cues to set the occasion for that behavior in the future.* This means that consequences (the third element in the A: B $\rightarrow$ C equation), influence the future status of both of the preceding elements, A and B.[2] Therefore, the starting point for analyzing the A: B $\rightarrow$ C equation is with the consequences (C).

Consequences.   The consequences following an operant behavior are the *prime movers* of operant conditioning. The consequences (C) can be either good effects or bad effects, causing the behavior (B) to become more or less frequent in the future and influencing the way antecedent stimuli (A) set the occasion for repeating or not repeating the behavior in the future. The consequences (C) of creating beautiful effects on a canvas reward an artist for skillful behavior (B) and increase the power of antecedents (A) to cue painting rather than pausing.

Any operant behavior can be strengthened or weakened, depending on the type of consequences that follow the behavior. **Reinforcers** *are types of consequences that* *strengthen a behavior. **Punishers** are types of consequences that cause a behavior to become less frequent.* Stated in terms of the law of effect, reinforcers are good effects—or rewards—that increase the chances we repeat a behavior in the future, and punishers are bad effects that decrease the chances we repeat a behavior in the future.[3] The consequences (C) of marring a canvas with a badly placed brush stroke punish an artist for clumsy behavior (B) and empower the antecedents (A) to cue caution and concerns about artistic mistakes.

We learn from the consequences of all our actions. Driving carefully is reinforced by the enjoyable consequences of arriving at our destination safely. Driving too fast is sometimes punished by the aversive consequences of speeding tickets or accidents. In love relations, treating one's partner with consideration leads to the natural rewards of having a genuinely close relationship. Speaking harsh words that lead to uncontrollable fights is sometimes punished by the painful consequences of losing a boyfriend or girlfriend, husband or wife.

When doing any given behavior, we often respond to both reinforcers and punishers. When a musician plays at the keyboard, coordinated and sensitive hand work produces beautiful effects—rewarding consequences—and the exhilarating music serves as the reinforcer that strengthens many of the habits needed for playing well. In contrast, poor playing sounds bad—and may be criticized. These painful consequences punish the unskilled actions that caused them. When a coach tries several different strategies for improving her team's performance, she is likely to experiment mostly with strategies that, in the past, have produced good effects—reinforcers. She is also likely to abandon those strategies that produced bad effects—punishers. We all tend to be quite responsive to good and bad consequences, adjusting our behavior accordingly, even though we are often unaware of the consequences and our behavioral adjustments!

Antecedents.   Every moment of our lives, we are surrounded by countless stimuli—from outside and inside our bodies—that set the occasion for each next thought and act. Antecedent cues that preceded *behaviors that were reinforced in the past* tend to set the occasion for repeating those behaviors when the antecedents appear in the future. Antecedent cues that preceded *behaviors that were punished in the past* alert us not to repeat those behaviors at later times. If a friend says "Come on over because we're having a party," these words set the occasion for going if your friend had fun parties in the past. But the same words from Mira—who hosted the worst party you have ever been to—might be antecedent cues for not going to another one of her parties.

Sometimes a stimulus context contains both positive and negative cues, and we feel torn: Should we repeat the behavior or not? Seeing a sign that reads "Register here for your FREE GIFT" sets the occasion for some people—but not all—to fill out a registration card with their address and phone number. Who is more likely to register? People who have won free prizes in the past or people who have been "stung" by phony giveaway rackets? The past consequences of winning or being stung affect the way two people perceive the very same antecedent stimuli. People who have won in the past may think, "I might win again" and fill out a registration card. People who got stung in the past may respond differently to the same sign, thinking, "The odds of winning are miniscule" and move on to other activities. Each of us has a unique past history of experiences with "FREE GIFT" signs—and the countless other stimuli of life—hence we all may respond differently to any given antecedent stimulus.

Our thoughts and actions can be influenced by multiple and often subtle antecedent stimuli—also known as situational or contextual cues. If a 60-year-old man smiled at you, what would you think? It might depend heavily on the contextual cues. Was he a drunk in shabby clothes or an admired community leader who was commending you at an awards banquet for your stellar achievements? Our brains are always active in hunting for connections among the three parts of the A: B → C equation.[4] Seeing the unkempt drunk smiling at you might be an antecedent cue (A) that raises questions: "What behavior (B) is this guy trying to get me to do, and with what consequences (C) to me?" But a few small changes in the contextual cues could make a big difference: What if the smiling drunk was at the awards banquet, being honored for his generous and compassionate work on skid row? These contextual cues (A) might lead you to overlook some of his flaws and approach to shake his hand (B)—because you sensed benign, not threatening consequences (C).

The Operant. *The unit of behavior we study in operant conditioning is called the* **operant.** A football player who throws a successful forward pass has performed "an operant"—operating on the ball to produce desirable effects. *Operants are usually defined by their ability to produce certain consequences, not by their physical appearances.* "A successful forward pass" is an operant, but there are many possible ways to throw a ball that could result in a successful forward pass. No two quarterbacks pass quite the same, and there is even variation in the passes of any single quarterback. However, any of these behavioral variations (B) that results in rewarding consequences (C) belongs to the same category of operant behavior—"a completed forward pass."

All operants that produce similar consequences belong to the same **response class** (the shaded area in Figure 3–1). *Each response class contains many behavioral variations (1, 2, 3, 4), although not all behaviors (5, 6, 7, 8).* Thus, there are operant response classes for funny jokes and jokes that flop: Funny jokes (1, 2, 3, 4) are followed by the reinforcers of laughter and applause, whereas jokes that do not lead to laughter (5, 6, 7, 8) do not belong to the response class of funny jokes. *Each response class is defined by its consequences.*[5] All attempts at humor that fit the definition of "funny jokes" produce rewarding results; hence they are all *functionally similar,* although no two are exactly alike.

If we find any response class is too large or crude for our interests, we can always break it into smaller ones. We could subdivide "funny jokes" into "funny political jokes,"

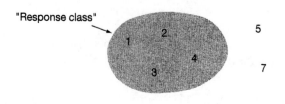

FIGURE 3–1 A response class consisting of four successful behaviors (numbered 1, 2, 3, and 4) does not include the unsuccessful behaviors (numbered 5, 6, 7, and 8).

"funny sexual jokes," "funny children's jokes," and so on. Response classes can be any size.[6] Picking up a pencil is a small response class, whereas driving a car is a large response class involving many components. There are times in which we need to look closely at small details of operant behavior and other times in which we need to stand back and examine larger chunks. A surgeon measures many behaviors in millimeters; an astronaut, in kilometers or thousands of kilometers. No matter if the response class is large or small, *any behavior patterns that produce the same consequences belong to the same response class.*

The consequences—reinforcers and punishers—are the prime movers of operant conditioning. The remainder of the chapter is organized around five fundamental ways in which consequences affect operants: (1) reinforcement, (2) extinction (i.e., the discontinuation of reinforcement), (3) punishment, (4) discontinuation of punishment, and (5) the timing and contingency of consequences.

REINFORCEMENT

A reinforcer that follows an operant increases the likelihood that the operant will occur in the future. The process by which the frequency of an operant is increased is called **reinforcement.** The word *reinforce* means "to strengthen." Reinforced concrete is strengthened by steel rods. Generals strengthen an army when they send in reinforcements. The reinforcers described in this book strengthen operant behavior and make operants more likely to occur in the future. Channel surfing to a new sitcom that makes you laugh especially hard reinforces your habit of channel surfing when bored and increases the chances you will watch the new sitcom at a later time. Receiving "A" grades on every test and paper in an art history class increases the chances you might take another course in the field. Winning race after race in high school gym classes increases the chances that a person will try out for the track team.

The word *reward* is often used as an everyday substitute for the word *reinforce,* as in this sentence: "Channel surfing may be rewarded by finding a great new show." A behavior that leads to rewarding results—or good effects—will probably recur more frequently in the future. But the word "reward" can be misleading if we use it only *in the narrow sense* of "one person intentionally rewarding another." In fact, good effects and rewarding outcomes can come from many sources. Climbing to the top of a mountain is rewarded by great views. Because the word "reward" can cause confusion, the word "reinforce" is preferred, and the word "reward" is used cautiously.

The speed with which a person learns an operant behavior depends on the complexity of the operant, the person's present level of skills, the reinforcers involved, and numerous other variables. It is usually easy to learn simple skills with even minimum reinforcement, but it can take many hours to learn operants that involve a complex set of skills. People who have already mastered many athletic skills are often quick to pick up a new activity—be it white water kayaking or playing lacrosse—but those with few athletic skills may find complex new activities difficult to learn even if a friend tries to make it easy and rewarding.

Cumulative Records

How can we measure the rate at which a person learns an operant behavior? *Cumulative records provide a convenient way of visualizing patterns of behavior by showing the total number of operants that a person has performed over a period of time.* The total number of responses performed is shown at the left of the cumulative record, as you can see in Figures 3–2 and 3–3. The lines in the cumulative record take one step upward each time a behavior is performed. A rapid series of upward steps indicates a period of frequent responses, and a long horizontal line indicates that the person is not repeating the behavior.

The activities of a freshman during the first weeks on campus illustrate the way that cumulative records track the learning of two different operants. The freshman plans to major in journalism and hopes to land a position on the campus newspaper. Thus, many facets of the campus newspaper will function as reinforcers for the student. Let us consider how two operant behaviors—one easy and one difficult—are learned due to the reinforcers associated with journalism and newspapers.

The easy behavior is that of picking up and reading the campus newspaper. The first day on campus, the freshman notices that the paper is distributed free at the dorms, takes one, and reads it. These operants are immediately rewarded by seeing the latest news, pictures, and cartoons—plus having hopes of joining the paper's staff. This immediate reinforcement increases the chances that the student will pick up and read the paper in the future.

The thin line in Figure 3–2 shows the freshman's cumulative record for picking up the daily newspaper over the first 6 weeks (42 days) at school. The first day on campus, the student picked up the paper and was rewarded by reading some well-done pieces and hoping to get a job at the paper. The cumulative record shows that the student repeated the behavior each day for the first 5 days of the week. There are no responses on the next two days because the school paper is not published on Saturday and Sunday. During each following week, there are five responses followed by the pauses on Saturday and Sunday. Because picking up the paper is an easy operant to perform and produces immediate reinforcement, the student learned to do it on the first day and never missed a single opportunity for obtaining this immediate reinforcement during the entire 6 weeks shown on the cumulative record.

The second behavior, shown by the bold line in Figure 3–2, is that of working at the campus newspaper office. This behavior requires considerably more skill and effort than simply picking up a paper at the dorms, and the cumulative record shows that the student learned this activity more slowly. On the fourth day of class, the freshman visited the newspaper office for the first time to see if there was a chance of finding a job, and the editor suggested that the freshman try writing a sample article. It was rewarding to talk with the editor and be offered a chance to write a trial piece. The student went home and worked for several days on the sample article, reworking the piece to the highest level possible. The student did not return to the newspaper office with this first piece of work until day 11 of class, indicated by the second rise of the bold line in Figure 3–2. The editor read the essay, gave the student encouraging feedback, made some useful changes, and

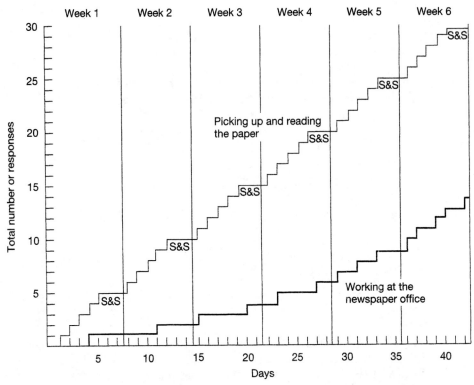

FIGURE 3–2   **A cumulative record shows the total number of times a student performed two different operants over a 42-day period. ("S & S" indicate Saturday and Sunday—the days on which the school newspaper was not published.)**

suggested a new assignment for the coming weekend. The encouragement provided reinforcement for writing more. Four days later, the student returned to the newspaper office with the next piece, which was accepted for publication with almost no changes. More rewards!

As the student learned how to write better, the average time needed to prepare each article became shorter. During the next weeks, the student returned to the news office with increasing frequency, and each visit to the office was rewarded by positive feedback on the articles and more friendly interactions with the editors, reporters, and staff—who were coming to like this gifted freshman. Although there were some 5- or 8-day pauses between visits to the office during the first weeks of class, the student came to work at the office more frequently (even on weekends) as improved writing skills yielded increasing amounts of reinforcement.

The cumulative record shows that an easy operant (such as picking up the paper) may be learned almost immediately and performed at the maximal level for long periods of time. More difficult operants (such as working for the newspaper) are usually learned more slowly. However, in the last week shown on the cumulative record, the student worked at the news office 5 days out of 7, making this difficult behavior just as frequent as the easy behavior of picking up the newspaper 5 days of each week. Once mastered, behaviors that require considerable skill may be performed as frequently as simpler activities, if they lead to ample reinforcement. By age 30 or 40, journalists often produce beautifully crafted articles day after day, enjoying the use of their highly refined writing skills.

Three Types of Stimuli

Operant conditioning is often discussed in terms of the *stimuli* that precede and follow behavior. When we do operant behaviors, our brains are sensitive to the stimuli that come both before and after our behavior. *If you do not study the next paragraphs carefully, you will have serious problems in following the logic, vocabulary, and special symbols—S^R, S^D, and S^Δ—used in the next several chapters.*

Because consequences that follow behavior are the prime movers of operant conditioning, let us begin here. *A reinforcer is called a **reinforcing stimulus** (S^R).* Because most stimuli do not have the capacity to reinforce behavior, the superscript R clarifies that this particular stimulus is a reinforcing stimulus, S^R.

S^Rs can come from inside or outside the body. The most conspicuous and easily studied reinforcers (S^Rs) come from outside the body. An athlete who wins trophies and the adulation of others is basking in S^Rs of external origin—from other people. However, inner thoughts and emotions can play important roles in the reinforcement process—as S^Rs of inner origins. Athletes often push their bodies to the limit because daily improvement is rewarded by *thoughts* that they might break a record and qualify for Olympic or professional competition. The thoughts and related positive emotions are internal S^Rs that can reinforce practicing for hours. Inner and outer stimuli are often closely intertwined, as when the athlete thinks about external rewards such as Olympic fame and lucrative commercial contracts.

*When a behavior is followed by an S^R, not only is the behavior reinforced, any relevant antecedent stimulus takes on a special quality, becoming a **discriminative stimulus.*** This type of stimulus is identified with a superscript of D to indicate that it is a stimulus for discrimination, S^D. We can now rewrite the simple ABC equation presented earlier in more precise terms. S^Ds set the occasion for operant behaviors (B) that have lead to S^Rs in the past.

$$S^D: B \to S^R$$

When a behavior (B) is followed by a reinforcing stimulus (S^R) in one context but not in other contexts, any antecedent context cue associated with reinforcement becomes a discriminative stimulus (S^D). Each S^D helps set the occasion for future responses. For example, if you travel to a foreign country where very few people speak English, signs reading ENGLISH SPOKEN HERE become S^Ds that set the occasion for your speaking English with the natives. When the signs are present, there is a good chance that speaking English will communicate and be rewarded by meaningful replies. When the signs are absent, the chances are no one will understand, and your using English will not be reinforced.

The stimuli that best predict when and where behavior is likely to be reinforced are most likely to become S^Ds. A sign reading ENGLISH SPOKEN HERE is obviously a good predictor that speaking English will produce rewarding results. But numerous other cues could become S^Ds for using English. Because the well-dressed staff at international hotels and restaurants usually speak English, seeing them may provide the S^Ds for your using English with them—especially if you have been rewarded for doing so in the past. Students at foreign universities often speak English; hence indicators that a person is a university student may become S^Ds for your speaking English with them.

When a behavior is not followed by reinforcement, the stimuli that best predict nonreinforcement become S^Δ*s,* **discriminative stimuli** *that inhibit responding.* S^Δs—pronounced as "ess deltas"—signal that the behavior is *not* likely to be reinforced in this particular context (whereas S^Ds signal that reinforcement is likely). S^Δs tend to inhibit behavior because they signal that no rewards are likely in S^Δ situations.[7] *Put simply,* S^D*s are like green lights that signal us to go ahead and do some behavior, whereas* S^Δ*s are like red lights that signal "no go."* In a foreign country, shops with signs reading ENGLISH SPOKEN HERE become S^Ds for speaking English; shops without such signs become S^Δs that inhibit the use of English. No matter what behavior interests us—speaking English or driving through a traffic signal—S^Ds signal "do it" and S^Δs signal "don't."

Just about any cue can become an S^D or S^Δ for operant behavior. Typically, there isn't just one S^D or one S^Δ for each behavior. S^Ds for speaking English may include signs in English, styles of dress, and locations (such as international restaurants or hotels). In addition, each individual may learn to respond to different cues, depending on his or her unique past history of reinforcement. A student may be especially sensitive to certain cues as S^Ds and S^Δs, whereas a banker is alert to others.

The stimuli that are S^D*s for one behavior may be* S^Δ*s that inhibit another behavior.* At a busy traffic signal, a green light is an S^D for driving ahead and an S^Δ that inhibits slamming on the brakes—since this is not the time to stop the car and risk being rearended. When a foreigner who knows no English first visits the United States and confronts doors marked PUSH and PULL, the person may not discriminate between these two cues, and randomly push or pull on doors until one of the two acts is rewarded. Gradually, PUSH signs will become S^Ds for pushing and S^Δs that inhibit pulling, because pushing is reinforced and pulling is not. Conversely, PULL signs will become S^Ds for pulling and S^Δs that inhibit pushing, because pulling is reinforced and pushing is not. Any stimulus—a person, place, or thing—can become an S^D for all the behaviors that have been reinforced in its presence and an S^Δ that inhibits behaviors that have not been reinforced in its presence. Everyone who has pushed a PULL door knows that the inhibitions are not always 100% effective.

As people learn to discriminate between the S^Ds and S^Δs for a given operant, they are more likely to perform this behavior in the presence of S^Ds than in the presence of S^Δs. However, *the* S^D*s do not cause behavior, and* S^Δ*s do not have the power to prevent a behavior from occurring.* A postcard provides S^Ds for writing on it and S^Δs that inhibit chewing and eating it. A traveler may buy ten postcards and only write six. S^D*s set the occasion for operants, they do not cause behavior.* Postcards are S^Δs that inhibit chewing and normally we do not chew them, but S^Δs do not have the power to prevent all behavior; and some people chew on postcards, perhaps when nervous or bored. *S^Δs are inhibitory*

REAL LIFE ADVENTURES By Wise & Aldrich

USE OTHER DOOR →

URF... WHY WON'T THIS OPEN?

RATTLE! RATTLE.

Yes, life *is* just one big IQ test.

The sign "USE OTHER DOOR," is an S^D for using the right-hand door and an S^Δ that signals not to use the left-hand door.

signals that reduce the likelihood of doing operant behavior; they cannot cause the behavior never to be performed.

Sometimes people learn to discriminate between two rewarding experiences merely because one provides *more reinforcers* than the other. Antecedent cues that predict *more reinforcement* become S^Ds for doing the behavior; cues that predict *less reinforcement* become S^Δs that inhibit the behavior. There may be two restaurants that both provide quite good food, but a person finds one somewhat better than the other. The better restaurant becomes an S^D for dining and the poorer one an S^Δ that signals less than optimal outcomes for dining there. *Thus antecedent cues can become S^Δs (1) because they are associated with no reinforcement, or (2) merely because they are associated with less reinforcement than is available elsewhere.*

Learning to discriminate between S^Ds and S^Δs may take place quickly or slowly. People are often quick to learn easy discriminations between *reinforcement* versus *no reinforcement* and slower to learn subtle discriminations between *more* and *less* reinforcement. When people move to a new town, they have to learn numerous new discriminations, such as the best places to eat, shop, and obtain medical care. If the new town has three chains of grocery stores—X, Y, and Z—a newcomer may learn to discriminate among the three types of stores at different rates. The first time the newcomer walks into store Z, it may be obvious that the low quality and limited choice of products would make shopping there unrewarding. Thus, store Z quickly becomes an S^Δ that inhibits shopping there.

However, the discrimination between stores X and Y may not be so easy. Several neighbors recommend store X, but other people recommend store Y. For several weeks the newcomer randomly and *indiscriminately* switches back and forth between X and Y, not noticing much difference between the food in the two stores. Both stores provide good food; hence both are S^Ds for shopping. The cumulative record presented in Figure 3–3 shows that for the first 10 weeks, the newcomer shopped 5 times at store X and 5 times at Y. However, during the next several weeks a few small incidents revealed that food at the two stores was not identical. On week 13, the meat at store Y was not very fresh. Although this alone would not be enough to make a person stop shopping at store Y, it signals a possible difference in the quality of food at the two stores. On week 15, the lettuce at store Y was wilted and bruised. The newcomer had never noticed such problems at store X. On week 19, a quart of milk from store Y was sour. Gradually the newcomer discriminates that shopping at store Y is slightly less rewarding than shopping at store X. Between weeks 10 and 20, store Y ceases to be an S^D for shopping and becomes an S^Δ that

FIGURE 3–3   **A cumulative record shows the total number of times a person shopped at two different stores, X and Y. Notice the similar frequency of responses in the first 10 weeks—before discriminations could be made. Contrast these first 10 weeks with the very different pattern of responding in the last 10 weeks—after the discriminations between the two stores were obvious.**

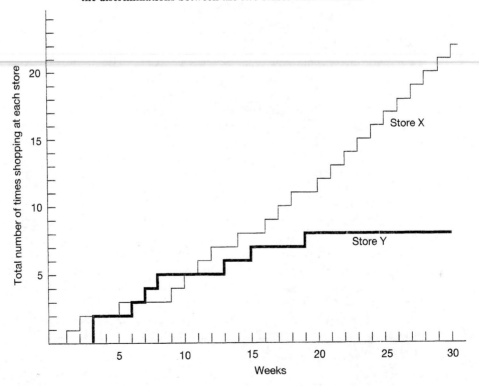

inhibits shopping there. Thus, the power of this S^Δ was not based on the total absence of rewards—because store Y had many fine products. However, *small but consistent* differences in the quality of the reinforcers are enough to cause a person to learn to discriminate subtle differences. After week 19, store X was an S^D for shopping there every week, and store Y was an S^Δ that inhibited shopping—and the newcomer never shopped there again.

Figure 3–3 shows that the person began to discriminate the differences in food quality between weeks 10 and 20, and returned less frequently to store Y during that time. By week 20, the cumulative record shows no return visits to store Y—indicated by the "flat line" of "zero new responses" after week 19. Simultaneously, the record shows increased shopping at store X because the person was shopping there every week instead of only half the time. People develop numerous subtle discriminations among situations that provide similar, but slightly different, reinforcement: We can tell the difference between good and outstanding restaurants, between so-so clubs and great clubs, between good medical service and exceptional medical service.

Positive and Negative Reinforcement

There are two kinds of reinforcement: positive and negative. To reinforce means to strengthen, and both positive and negative reinforcement strengthen behavior. Both increase the likelihood that people will repeat a behavior in the future. In terms of the law of effect, positive reinforcement consists of the *onset or addition of good effects,* and negative reinforcement consists of the *termination or subtraction of bad effects.* The onset of pleasurable music is a good effect that provides positive reinforcement for turning on the stereo. The termination of the alarm clock's aversive buzz in the morning provides negative reinforcement for turning off the alarm. The difference between positive and negative reinforcement is simple: one involves the positive (+)˙ addition of good things and the negative involves the subtraction (−) of bad things.

Learning more effective sexual techniques leads to more pleasurable feelings, which are positive reinforcers for discovering those techniques. Reducing arguments with people you love lessens the pain in life which provides negative reinforcement for learning better communication skills. Because people can have incompatible behaviors that interfere with the learning of some new skill, not all people learn to be "sexperts" or skillful in minimizing arguments.

Positive reinforcement occurs with the onset of a reinforcing stimulus, and negative reinforcement occurs with the termination of an aversive stimulus.[8] Receiving an award for breaking a track record provides positive reinforcement for regular exercise and training. Getting rid of a sore throat provides negative reinforcement for taking throat lozenges.

One way to remember the difference between positive and negative reinforcement is to think of addition and subtraction as synonymous for positive and negative. Positive reinforcement strengthens behavior when good effects *are added* to our lives. Negative reinforcement strengthens behavior when bad effects are *subtracted.* Telling jokes and funny stories at a party leads to positive reinforcement if they add to the number of smiles and laughs. Going to a marriage counselor and following the counselor's advice lead to negative reinforcement if they help a couple subtract from the number of fights they have each week.

The antecedent cues that precede any kind of reinforcement—positive or negative—become S^Ds that set the occasion for repeating the behavior. Thus, the S^Ds of darkness in the evening set the occasion for turning on the lights, because this operant produces the positive reinforcement of being able to see things at night. Several hours later, the S^Ds of yawns and sleepiness set the occasion for turning off the lights, because sleepy people find glaring lights to be painful; hence, turning them off leads to negative reinforcement, the subtraction of pain.

Both positive and negative reinforcement can strengthen any operant behavior. Consider politeness. If your being polite is followed by smiles and kind words from other people, the onset of good effects provides positive reinforcement for your politeness. If you are polite to someone who is grouchy and the person *stops* being grouchy, the cessation of grouching provides negative reinforcement for your being polite. Little children often receive both positive and negative reinforcement for running to their parents. If mother is sitting in the living room and her child climbs onto her knee and asks to play "horsy," mother may bounce the child on her knee. The *onset* of the fun game provides positive reinforcement for the child's coming to mother. If the child gets a splinter in the finger, the child may run to father for help in removing it. When father removes the splinter, the *termination* of the aversive stimulation from the splinter provides negative reinforcement for coming to father. Both mothers and fathers can become S^Ds for approach due to both positive and negative reinforcement.

Positive Reinforcement. *People usually enjoy learning via positive reinforcement because it adds to the good effects and pleasurable experiences in their lives.* Thus, positive reinforcement is an ideal method for helping people learn things in ways they will enjoy. The child who learns to help around the house via positive reinforcement—appreciative and loving comments from the parents—will learn to enjoy helping the parents (rather than doing it out of duty or fear of reprimand). Parents who show loving attention to their child as positive reinforcement for politeness, friendliness, sharing, and consideration help their child learn to take pleasure in treating others well.

Positive reinforcement is an ideal method for enhancing human creativity. All people have the potential to be either creative or uncreative. Positive social reinforcement can promote either creative or uncreative acts, as one study on childhood creativity shows.[9] While children were playing with building blocks, some were given social reinforcers for building novel, creative forms; and others received reinforcers only when they repeated old forms. The children who received rewards only when they built interesting new structures learned to become quite creative and innovative in their block play. The other children, who received rewards for repeating old patterns, became less creative because their repetitive patterns were incompatible with inventing novel, creative ones. Similar studies have shown that reinforcement will increase creativity in writing, easel painting, and other artistic endeavors.[10] Throughout life, all of us receive reinforcers for both creative and noncreative responses. The more often reinforcement follows creative rather than noncreative behavior, the more likely we are to develop the creative aspects of our human potential. Unfortunately, many people's daily lives are filled with tasks and duties that reinforce repetitious behavior rather than innovative behavior. One of the goals of the behavioral sciences is to help people increase the positive reinforcement for creative and innovative behavior.[11]

Positive reinforcement can be given in either natural or artificial ways. We have all heard adults give children clearly artificial and contrived praise: "Maria, what a *nice* doggie you have drawn." Unnatural praise and artificial rewards sometimes produce desirable effects with young children; but as children learn more about life, they can learn to be wary of highly contrived and unnatural rewards. Artificial rewards used in a manipulative manner can even *decrease* the frequency of an operant, if they arouse our fears of being conned.[12] On the other hand, natural and sincere positive remarks are usually both pleasurable to receive and effective in reinforcing behavior. Natural positive reinforcement occurs quite spontaneously when people show enthusiastic and genuinely supportive responses to things that others have done: "Wow! You're a great dancer, Sonia!" "It was so kind of you to drop by, Tom." Genuine smiles and sincerely appreciative comments for other people's behavior are the most common forms of natural positive reinforcement seen in everyday life—even though most people are not consciously aware that they are giving or receiving "positive reinforcement" when they exchange these natural forms of expression.

Some people tend to give much more positive reinforcement than others. Instead of commenting mostly on the faults and inadequacies of others, the positive person tends to focus on the good and show genuine pleasure about it: "I really like those new photos you took." This style of social interaction provides others with positive reinforcers for good things they have done rather than criticisms about their failures. As you can imagine, it is a pleasure to know positive people because they are generous with positive feedback. As a consequence, positive people tend to be well liked.[13]

Positive reinforcement is being used ever more commonly in business and industry to reward productive workers and create good rapport between employees and management. For example, increasing numbers of companies are giving their workers bonuses for reaching important production goals.[14] By giving workers a genuine stake in corporate profits, all workers are rewarded for working harder, cooperating with each other, and using their skills to improve any aspect of the company or product they can. General Electric's managers give personalized notes of praise to workers for jobs well done and offer major promotions and salary increases to any worker who improves on the business.[15] As a consequence, GE has a remarkable track record of improving goods and services. Positive reinforcement also helps the workers have good feelings about their company.

Jeanne LaMere and her coworkers (1996) studied the behavior of truck drivers and documented the value of positive reinforcement. The drivers and management of a small Kalamazoo company—Michigan Disposal Service—negotiated an incentive pay program in which improved driver performance was rewarded with bonuses. In the first phase of the experiment, the 10 drivers in Group 1 received a 2.6% bonus of their total pay if they boosted their performance; and the 12 drivers in Group 2, a 3.1% bonus. Both groups showed dramatic improvement in performance and the increased productivity was sustained over the entire study period of almost 4 years.

Because industrial productivity can be hurt significantly by worker absenteeism, efforts have been made to reduce tardiness by providing positive reinforcement for promptness. A company in Mexico devised a method of positive reinforcement to solve its problems with worker tardiness.[16] Every day that workers reported to work on time, they received slips of paper stating that their punctuality had earned a bonus worth 4% above normal wages. The workers could collect these slips and cash them in at the end of the week. Figure 3–4 shows how effective the rewards were in reinforcing punctuality. Before the start of the program, when there were no special rewards for punctuality (at A), only 80% to 90% of the workers arrived on time. During 8 weeks when positive reinforcers were given for being on time (B), punctuality improved markedly, with 97% to 99% of the people being on time. Then there was a 4-week period in which no rewards for promptness were given (C), and the promptness scores decreased to 92%. When the re-

FIGURE 3–4   **The percentage of workers who arrived punctually at work when not rewarded for punctuality (at times A, C, and E) and when rewarded (at B, D, and F).**

(Redrawn from Hermann et al. Copyright © 1973 by the Society for the Experimental Analysis of Behavior, Inc.)

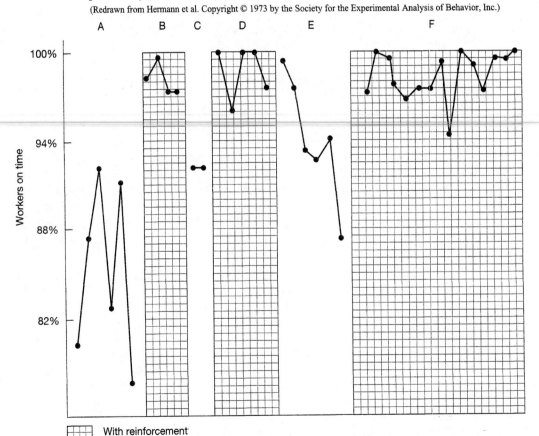

wards were reinstated for the next 9 weeks (D), the punctuality scores again increased, reaching 95% to 100%. During the next 12 weeks, reinforcement for punctuality was again removed (E), and the rates of punctuality again decreased. For the final 32 weeks of the study (F), positive reinforcement for punctuality was reinstated, increasing the frequency of the response class significantly.

Although all prior examples of positive reinforcement have involved social interactions, there are countless nonsocial examples. When you stop to smell a rose, you are often rewarded by a fragrant odor. When you drop ice cubes in a drink on a hot summer day, you are rewarded by a cooler drink. These rewards increase our chances of smelling the roses and getting ice cubes in similar S^D situations in the future.

Has anything like the following ever happened to you? While walking down the street, Jason happened to notice something green near the edge of the sidewalk. Much to his surprise, it was a five dollar bill. When he picked it up he saw a second, more hidden fiver just a few inches away. Both were dusty. No telling who had dropped them or when. So Jason put them in his pocket and continued on his way. But within a minute, he noticed a change in his own behavior. He was no longer looking at the trees or houses. Instead, his eyes kept scanning the ground, as if looking for another lucky find. The behavior of looking down had been followed by the positive reinforcement of finding money. This positive reinforcement strengthened the operants of glancing down and scanning the ground. After such a lucky find, people sometimes note that they watch the ground more than usual for several days. Because focusing attention on the ground takes little effort, two positive reinforcements can have long lasting effects.

Jason's learning experience affected his selective perception. People can pay attention to only a fraction of all the stimuli in their environment, neglecting many of the things that happen around them. One of the determinants of this selective perception is positive reinforcement. Jason's lucky find brought positive reinforcement for looking down more than usual.

Social reinforcers can affect selective attention, too. People who have had years of very rewarding experiences dealing with babies often notice babies much more than other people do. Positive reinforcement has strengthened their selective perception to focus on babies, whereas a person who had little experience with babies might not notice or spend nearly as much time focusing attention on them. Other people notice just about everything relevant to professional sports. No one can notice all the stimuli in our complex environments. It only makes sense that each of us might selectively attend to things that have been associated with positive reinforcement in the past.

Negative Reinforcement.   Whereas positive reinforcement occurs when good effects and pleasurable experiences are added to our lives, *negative reinforcement occurs when escape or avoidance allows us to subtract aversive experiences from our lives.*[17] Even though having a painful splinter removed involves some additional pain at first, we feel better afterward; we feel relief from pain. Avoiding a speeding ticket by being polite with the patrol officer is rewarding, but your palms may have been sweating before the officer let you know you were off the hook. *The rewards of negative reinforcement are based on the termination of aversive situations rather than the onset of good effects and pleasur-*

able experiences. That is why the rewards of removing splinters and avoiding traffic tickets do not feel the same as positive reinforcement. Subtracting pain does not feel like adding pleasure.

The two main classes of behavior produced by negative reinforcement are escape and avoidance. **Escape** *responses are those operants that allow a person to get away from aversive stimuli* **after** *the aversive stimuli are present.* **Avoidance** *responses are those operants that allow a person to prevent the occurrence of aversive stimuli* **before** *the aversive stimuli appear.* Pesky flies are a nuisance. Behavior that terminates them and their bothersome buzzing is strengthened through negative reinforcement. We *escape* the pesky flies by swatting them after they are already present. We *avoid* them when we put up screen doors and windows before they can get in. Unduly critical people are sometimes like pesky flies: "Why didn't you do it this way? Why can't you do that differently?" There are many escape responses that might be reinforced: For example, it might suffice to say politely, "I could get along without your comments." If this did not work, some people might say "Buzz off," "Shut up," or something even stronger. There are numerous responses people use to *avoid* excess criticism, such as avoiding interaction with overly critical people or avoiding doing those behaviors that they criticize. Some people attempt to polish their behavior beyond reproach to avoid criticism.

There are two valuable ways to learn the essence of negative reinforcement. (1) *Escape* and *avoidance* are the two main response classes learned due to negative reinforcement. (2) The word "negative" suggests the "minus sign" in subtraction math and negative reinforcement is based on the *subtraction of pain.*

Both escape and avoidance can subtract pain from our lives. Escape involves **reacting** after an aversive event is present. Avoidance involves **proacting**—taking preventative steps—before an aversive event arises. People react to splinters by pulling them out; they proact by putting on gloves before handling rough-cut wood. People react to hangovers by taking aspirin; they proact by not drinking so much that they get a hangover. Some people make multiple social blunders each day and react by making apologies. More tactful people have learned to proact and avoid making social blunders in the first place. Usually it takes more skill to proact than react—and some people never learn to be tactful.

Escape is usually learned before avoidance when dealing with any given aversive situation. First, children learn to escape wet underpants by removing them. Later, they learn to proact and avoid having wet underpants by going to the bathroom before having a urinary accident. First, children learn to escape the class bully by running away when they see him. Later, they learn to proact and avoid places the bully frequents. As people grow up and gain experience, they usually learn increasing skills for proacting and avoiding problems, and avoidance becomes more common than escape. However, when new and unexpected problems arise, even adults may return to the pattern of first learning how to escape, then how to avoid. During the first weeks after moving to a new town, a person may get stuck talking to a boring neighbor who takes an hour to escape. After living in the town several months, the person may learn to proact and avoid contact with the talkative neighbor.

Some couples allow their marriages to deteriorate into fights and arguments; then they react by trying to escape the aversive situation through marital counseling, divorce, or having affairs. Other couples who see their friends having marital troubles may proact by working on improving their communication and resolving differences before serious problems arise—thereby avoiding at least some of the fights and arguments that might undermine their love. Unfortunately, many people do not learn to proact soon enough to save their marriages. Perhaps schools should teach more about the value of proacting in all sorts of situations.

National, state, and local governments often utilize negative reinforcement in the form of tax breaks. In some states, if homeowners insulate their homes, add solar energy collectors, or install other energy-saving equipment, they qualify for tax breaks and avoid paying a portion of their taxes. Commuters may learn to form car pools if it results in their avoiding toll payments or riding in slow lanes. In suburban Virginia, cars with multiple occupants are allowed to use "high-occupancy vehicle lanes" that are less congested and allow a faster commute time. Many Washington-area employees can successfully hitch rides because drivers see the benefits of carrying passengers. This system has decreased the number of cars on the road by 10% and reduced congestion markedly.[18] The use of car pools is negatively reinforced by the avoidance of slow traffic. Many cities have some variant on these programs of negative reinforcement, and more people use car pools today than before these programs were initiated.

People who live in well-built houses may not appreciate that the technologies for building homes which stay dry in rains, warm in winter, and insect-free in summer are largely a result of negative reinforcement. Over the centuries, countless inventions have been made—then negatively reinforced—because they seal out rain, cold, winds, insects, vermin, and so forth. Much of technology consists of devices and practices that reduce unpleasant experiences and decrease aversive events.[19] To the degree that a given technology does successfully reduce or terminate aversive experiences, there will be negative reinforcement for retaining—and further refining—that technology.

In everyday conversation, negative reinforcement can condition numerous skills for sensitively guiding the course of discussion. Because certain topics can lead to embarrassment and other topics trigger anger or hostility, conversation is a potentially risky business. When people blunder into touchy topics that insult, injure, embarrass, or anger others, friendly social interaction can turn into a painful experience. Therefore, any social skills that allow the people to escape or avoid the aversive situation are negatively reinforced. As people successfully defuse dangerous topics, the avoidance of embarrassing situations negatively reinforces the skills of diplomacy, courtesy, finesse, sensitivity, and empathy.[20]

For example, religion can be a touchy topic in conversations among strangers. One person's chance derogatory comment about a certain religion may elicit anger in a listener and bring the conversation to a halt. On the brink of falling into an unwanted clash about religion, a third person may calmly let the topic slide, laugh good-naturedly, and return to an earlier, safer topic. "But as we were saying before, the important thing is to. . . ." If the other people follow suit, the three will have successfully avoided a potentially difficult situation. The skills of laughing and smoothly changing subjects are often negatively reinforced by the successful avoidance of an aversive experience.

Naturally, some people never learn the arts of tact and grace. But some people never learn how to hit pesky flies or resolve marital conflicts. Later chapters demonstrate how shaping, models, prompts, rules, and schedules combine in complex patterns to help or hinder each individual in learning the skills for coping with the multiple facets of everyday life. For example, if a person has opportunities to observe role models who are graceful and considerate in guiding conversations away from touchy topics, the models' behavior and advice (i.e., rules) can help the observer learn subtle skills more rapidly than if no models or rules were available.

EXTINCTION

Once an operant has been reinforced and become common in a given S^D context, there is no guarantee that the frequency of the response will remain the same in the future. Either *extinction* or *punishment* can cause a response to become less frequent. Hence, both of these processes work in the opposite direction from reinforcement. Let us deal with extinction first.

Extinction consists of the discontinuation of any reinforcement that had once maintained a given behavior. When reinforcement is withdrawn, the frequency of the response usually declines. When an electric drill burns out and stops producing rewarding results, we learn to stop reaching for it (until it gets fixed). When our car's engine will not start, we turn the ignition key several times, but the absence of rewarding results eventually causes this behavior to extinguish and drop to zero.

Extinction can take place because (1) no reinforcement is associated with a certain behavior, or (2) less reinforcement is associated with that behavior than with some superior alternative. We stop shopping at grocery store Y when we find it is less rewarding to shop there than in store X. We stop using the old route back and forth to home when a new expressway is completed that shortens the trip by 15 minutes. We stop voting for one politician when it is clear that another politician does a better job. Less rewarding behavior is extinguished when a superior alternative becomes available.

Antecedent stimuli that are regularly associated with nonreinforcement—or with less reinforcement than a superior alternative—become S^Δs that inhibit responding during extinction.[21] Before our car broke down, climbing in was an S^D for turning the ignition key and having the engine come to life. But afterward, it becomes an S^Δ, and we learn not to turn the key anymore. Two grocery stores are S^Ds for shopping if we like them equally; but one becomes an S^Δ after we learn that it is less rewarding to shop there than at the other store. (Shopping at store Y was put on extinction as we gradually discriminated that its products were not as good as those at store X.) When Karen first went to college, she talked about all the things that she used to love talking about with her high school friends back in Hometown. Some of these topics went over nicely, but others were of no interest to her college friends. Talking about those topics that did not interest her new friends was extinguished (because no one showed positive responses), and Karen gradually stopped mentioning them while at college. Her college friends became S^Δs that inhibited her talking about several high school topics. However, when Karen went back home on vacations, seeing her old high school friends provided S^Ds for bringing up all the old high school stories—as long as her old friends continued to show interest in them.

Extinction occurs after the discontinuation of any type of reinforcement—positive or negative—as the following examples show.

Extinction After Positive Reinforcement

When positive reinforcement for a given operant is terminated, the frequency of that operant usually declines. Several stray cats visited old Miss Meriam's house each day because she placed cat food outside each morning. When she was hospitalized for two weeks, no one put out the cat food and the cats gradually ceased visiting her house over the next several days. Dr. Ryann had been earning $51,000 a year teaching at a small private college, and he liked his work. After dramatic declines in student enrollment, his college informed him that it could no longer pay his salary, although he could continue teaching if he wanted. What would you do? Most people would stop coming to work (unless some other effective reinforcer was operating). Dr. Ryann thought about continuing as a teacher (a job he loved), but he never taught again after his last paycheck. Behavior maintained by positive reinforcement usually becomes less frequent when reinforcement is removed.

The coming and going of fads usually reflects a two-phase cycle: (1) a period of positive reinforcement followed by (2) a period of extinction. When a new style of clothing, novel slang word, or unusual toy comes on the scene, it brings novelty (which is usually a positive reinforcer). People who try the fad often receive a great deal of social attention (which is also a positive reinforcer for most people). When Furbys first appeared in toy stores, they were an instant success (phase 1). You saw them everywhere. But as the novelty wore off and reinforcement declined, the fad faded—due to extinction (phase 2). Fad diets come and go for similar reasons. When someone comes up with a novel diet that promises to take off pounds, the novelty of the method rewards people for talking about and trying the new diet. After the novelty fades, people lose interest, and the fad diet fades into oblivion.

Several years ago, a fad of light bulb eating spread across a few college campuses. Most students were surprised, a bit skeptical, but clearly interested when they first ran into someone who said he or she was going to eat a light bulb that night at 7 o'clock. "It's better than dorm food." The humor, the audience interest, and the growing excitement for the 7 o'clock show all served as reinforcers for the incipient bulb eater. Sure enough, at 7 o'clock several people came to watch, having been attracted by the positive reinforcers of novelty. The act of eating a 25-watt bulb brought generous positive reinforcement to the bulb eater as the amazed audience marveled over the feat. This positive reinforcement produced phase 1, the rise of a fad. On being coaxed to reveal the secret, the bulb muncher might have claimed, "As long as you chew it up very, very fine, it doesn't hurt much." Daredevils who imitated the feat also received the positive reinforcers of attention and novel experience. The fad spread.

Eventually the novelty of bulb eating wore off, and there was a natural shift from reinforcement to extinction (phase 2). After seeing 10 or 20 bulbs go down the hatch, most observers ceased to be surprised by the trick. Interest waned and people no longer flocked to watch the bulb munchers. Thus, there was neither novelty nor social attention for bulb eating. With the onset of extinction, bulb eating declined in frequency.

Extinction can be a powerful therapeutic tool[22] for dealing with behavior once maintained by positive reinforcement. Vivian was a 4-year-old girl who had developed an annoying cough while she had a respiratory infection. Once the infection subsided, the cough remained. Vivian's parents took her to a doctor, but there was no identifiable medical problem. Next they took her to a behavioral psychologist, who recommended that they count the occurrences of coughing in various S^D contexts over the next 3 days.[23] Coughing was most frequent when she had snacks and ate dinner; but it was infrequent at other times (see Fig. 3–5). The therapist suggested that social attention might be the reinforcer that maintained coughing, since both snack time and dinner were situations where one or both parents were present and might pay attention to her coughing. The psychologist recommended that the parents try extinction: They should not pay any attention when Vivian coughed, but they could pay attention to her when she did desirable things. Figure 3–6 shows the frequency of her coughing before treatment, during extinction, and at three follow-up periods, 1, 3, and 6 months after behavior modification. Removing the reinforcement of social attention caused the frequency of coughing to drop to zero and remain there. (Initially, an infection started Vivian's coughing. Then her parents' loving attention maintained the coughing as a psychosomatic symptom after the infection was gone. Removing the social attention allowed the cough to extinguish.)

FIGURE 3–5   **The frequency of coughing in seven different S^D situations (as observed on three different days). The S^Ds of snack time and dinner evoked the most frequent coughing.**

(Adapted from "Brief functional analysis and treatment of a vocal tic," by T.S. Watson & H.E. Sterling (1998). *Journal of Applied Behavior Analysis, 31,* pp. 471–474. Copyright by the Journal of Applied Behavior Analysis, 1998.)

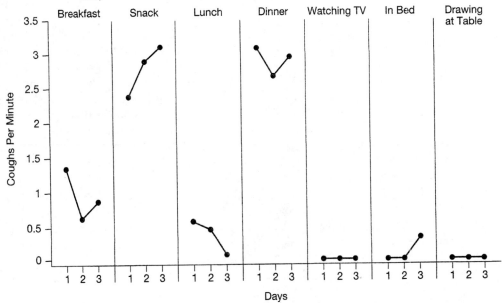

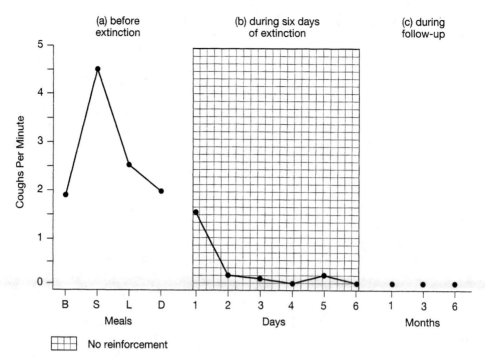

FIGURE 3–6 **The frequency of coughing (a) before extinction, (b) during 6 days of extinction, and (c) during follow-up (1, 3, and 6 months later).**

(Adapted from "Brief functional analysis and treatment of a vocal tic," by T.S. Watson & H.E. Sterling (1998). *Journal of Applied Behavior Analysis, 31,* pp. 471–474. Copyright by the Journal of Applied Behavior Analysis, 1998.)

Some children learn to whine, pout, or throw tantrums because these behaviors bring social attention. Terry whined many hours each day.[24] His parents often reinforced his behavior by paying attention to him. If whining did not attract attention, Terry usually began shouting. The whining and shouting were so aversive that his parents usually paid attention to Terry just to quiet him. Thus, Terry received the positive reinforcement of social attention for whining and shouting (and Terry's parents received negative reinforcement for paying attention to him because their attention helped them escape the aversive whining and shouting). A behavioral therapist told Terry's parents to switch their strategy and stop paying attention to Terry when he whined or shouted. They should ignore his obnoxious behavior and reward him when he behaved well. Once whining and shouting were no longer rewarded, they were on extinction. The frequency of whining and shouting fell abruptly to less than half the prior rate, and it continued to decline further. Thus, *reinforcement increases the frequency of behavior, and extinction decreases it.* During the reinforcement periods, the parents were S^Ds for Terry's whining and shouting. During extinction, the parents became S^Δs that inhibited these behaviors, because the parents no longer reinforced Terry's unpleasant activities.

Extinction After Negative Reinforcement

When an operant that was maintained by negative reinforcement ceases to be linked with negative reinforcement, the frequency of that operant usually declines.[25] The extinction of negatively reinforced behavior occurs as the second phase of a two-phase sequence: (1) a person has learned some response that helps escape or avoid an aversive stimulus, then (2) the stimulus ceases being aversive or is no longer present. During the second half of the sequence—the extinction phase—the escape or avoidance behavior becomes less frequent. This two-phase cycle often corresponds to the coming and going of problems in life. After presenting several examples of this, we examine a major exception to this general principle.

In elementary school, a bully can cause many classmates to stay vigilant and avoid the bully if possible. Thus, in phase 1, the avoidance is learned via negative reinforcement—because it can help avert painful experiences. What if a caring teacher notices the situation and resolves to stop all bullying in the classroom and on the playground? If the teacher succeeds in teaching the former bully to be nicer to his classmates and makes it clear that no one will suffer intimidation anymore, avoidance of the bully may decline. This is phase 2, the extinction of avoidance when it is clear the danger is gone.

Temporary hardships produce the same kind of two-phase cycle. Whenever a part of the nation undergoes extreme drought, water becomes scarce and costly. Due to negative reinforcement, people learn to save and recycle water: Water faucets become S^Ds for conserving water, because these frugal practices help people avoid prohibitive water bills and fines for excess usage. When the rains come and the hardship is over, what happens to the antecedent stimuli and frugal practices of conserving water? The end of negative reinforcement puts water conservation on extinction; hence water faucets gradually shift toward being S^Δs, which signal that water conservation is no longer needed because it is no longer punished with fines.

Daily problems can produce cycles of negative reinforcement and extinction. If you and a friend happen to have a bitter argument about politics, the aversive experience creates negative reinforcement for avoiding your friend or for avoiding any potentially touchy topics in subsequent conversations. The mere mention of a touchy topic becomes an S^D to avoid further words on that subject. Extinction begins as soon as you and your friend succeed in making peace. As extinction proceeds, you gradually feel less apprehensive and nervous while talking with your friend, and your cautious conversational responses decline in frequency. Eventually you are back to being your old, "natural" self around your friend, and potentially touchy topics now are S^Δs signaling that avoidance is no longer needed.

The Exception: Avoidance Retards Extinction.   There is an important exception to the general principle that behavior learned via negative reinforcement declines in frequency after the onset of extinction: *People sometimes continue doing well-learned avoidance responses long after negative reinforcement has ended—during extinction.*[26] Several decades ago, an elderly man we know was trapped in an elevator and subsequently he started avoiding elevators. Modern elevators rarely malfunction, but his fear of elevators cannot extinguish because he avoids experiences where he could learn how safe today's elevators are. *Avoidance of a once aversive situation can prevent people from learning that the situation has ceased being aversive; thus, avoidance responses may continue even when there is no longer any negative reinforcement.*

Consider people's responses to a man who is unbearably boring and self-centered. People avoid Mr. K because eluding him is negatively reinforced by their avoiding a painfully dull and arrogant monologue by Mr. K. What if Mr. K confronts his problems, works for months to overcome them, and succeeds? Will people continue to avoid him? Much to K's regret, many do. Why? In the past, many people learned to avoid Mr. K so completely that they never start a conversation with him; thus, they never have a chance to discover he is now a much more likable person. Avoidance retards extinction.

If Jennifer has some very bad experiences in her early gym classes—because her athletics instructor is strict and insensitive—she may learn to make excuses to avoid gym class. Making excuses is negatively reinforced, because it helps her avoid further aversive experiences in gym. Several years later, Jennifer enters a high school which has a kind and supportive gym teacher, yet she may have learned so many excuses for avoiding gym class that her total avoidance prevents her from learning that high school gym could be fun. At all ages in life strong avoidance responses deprive people of the opportunities to learn that things that once were aversive are no longer aversive. Thus, avoidance can produce long lasting effects on behavior. Bad experiences with gym classes in early years have caused many people to learn long lasting avoidance of sports and physical activities, even though they are rewarding to do—with important benefits for physical health, muscle tone, and positive self-concept.

One of the major goals of behavior modification is to help people overcome unneeded habits of avoidance that prevent them from exploring exciting new activities where they could learn additional skills and gain rewarding experiences. Many people avoid math, science, sports, dancing, travel—and countless other things—when they could easily stop doing so if they found positive and caring people who could teach them these new activities. Needless avoidance hurts many people, preventing them from developing numerous facets of their human potential.

PUNISHMENT

*When an operant is followed by a stimulus that suppresses the frequency of the operant in the future, the stimulus is called a **punisher**. The process by which the frequency of an operant is suppressed is called **punishment**.*[27] If you drive through a red light and receive a hefty fine for it, the punishment is likely to suppress your proclivity to run red lights in the future. Most people learn that there are certain topics they should not mention to others, because they often trigger criticism. Even though your personal learning experiences lead you to say "X is true," repeated criticism from numerous other people is likely to suppress your stating that view to strangers in the future, though you might say it with friends who have not criticized you for saying so. The response suppression seen after punishment can take place even when you are completely unaware that others' comments have caused you to stop mentioning the criticized topic.[28]

It is important to realize that punishment can come not only from people, but also from the nonsocial environment. A child touches a bee and is stung: Big ouch and tears. A college student has too many drinks at a party and is punished by a headache the next day.

Even though there has been a strong social movement to reduce the use of punishment and violence in child rearing, marriages, and many other aspects of social life, many people have not learned to do this well enough. For example, parents' poor treatment of their teen is punished by their child's joining the one million young people who run away from home each year in the U.S. In this section, we deal with punishment and its effects on behavior. After exploring more behavior principles, we return to the topic of punishment in Chapter 14 and show how people can minimize the pains of punishment in their lives.

When people do an operant behavior that is punished, any stimulus regularly correlated with the punishment may become an S$^\Delta$—discriminative stimulus—that inhibits the operant in that stimulus context. After people receive reprimands or traffic fines for driving through red lights, red lights become S$^\Delta$s that inhibit driving through the intersection. People stop trying to pet snarling dogs after being bitten by them, and snarling dogs become S$^\Delta$s that inhibit petting these dogs. Employees with nice salaries stop contradicting the boss after the boss threatens to fire them if they cannot control their tongues; and the boss becomes an S$^\Delta$ that inhibits making further contradictory comments.

Both punishment and extinction reduce the frequency of behavior; however, strong and immediate punishment usually does so more rapidly and more completely than does extinction.[29] For example, after a child has learned to pout or whine—because the parents used to respond with social attention—*the frequency of pouting or whining can be reduced by either extinction or punishment.* If the parents cease paying attention whenever the child begins to pout or whine, they have opted to use extinction. If they give the child a 30-minute "time out" from TV, phone use, electronic games, and other reinforcers each time they notice pouting or whining, they have opted to use punishment. Both methods work; however, *strong and immediate punishment usually causes a much more rapid decline in responding than does extinction.*

Figure 3–7 shows the cumulative records for behaviors that were always reinforced before time X, then switched to either extinction or potent punishment (at time X). The closer a line comes to being horizontal in a cumulative record, the fewer responses are being made. It is clear that forceful punishment (lower graph) causes much faster cessation of responding than does extinction (upper graph).

In a house with a long dark hall, people are likely to turn on the hall light whenever they walk down the hall at night. The cumulative records in Figure 3–7 show typical patterns of light switch use during evening hours. Before time X, there is a rather steady rate of responding—as people use the light switch about six or eight times an evening. At time X, the switch goes bad and no one fixes it. If flicking the switch no longer turns on the light, the behavior is on extinction (because using the switch no longer leads to rewarding results). For several days, people keep on flicking the switch—out of habit—every time they go down the hall at night. The frequency of responding gradually declines due to extinction, as is shown in the upper half of Figure 3–7. On the other hand, if the faulty light

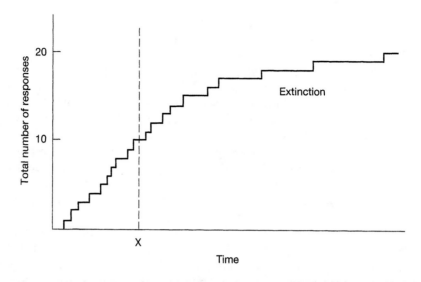

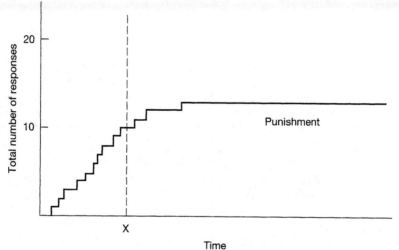

FIGURE 3-7   The cumulative records of responses that were reinforced before time X, then switched to either extinction (above) or potent punishment (below) at time X. Note that forceful
punishment produces a much faster cessation of responding
than does extinction. (A horizontal line—or "flat line"—indicates no additional responses.)

switch gave a significant shock every time people flicked it, the response of toggling the switch would be suppressed much sooner, as is shown in the bottom half of Figure 3–7. Punishment usually reduces response rates faster than does extinction.

Punishment produces the fastest suppression of behavior when it is strong, immediate, and not opposed by reinforcement. Extremely intense and immediate punishment can suppress behavior permanently.[30] After getting a serious shock from touching bare electric wires while trying to fix a faulty light switch, most people learn not to handle bare wiring without first checking to see that the electric power is off. Weak and delayed punishment is usually less effective than strong and immediate punishment. When parents see their child taking another child's toy, they may say "No-no, don't do." However, this brief, four-word reprimand alone is a weak punishment and may not be very effective in suppressing the behavior. In addition, the longer the delay between the behavior and the reprimand, the weaker the suppressive effect.

What if a behavior can be followed by both reinforcement and punishment? There is a complex mix of reinforcers strengthening behavior and punishers suppressing behavior. *When punishment is opposed by reinforcement, behavior is influenced by the relative intensity and frequency of both the punishment and reinforcement.*

The opposing effects of reinforcement and punishment are based, in part, on the *intensity* of each. If a light switch in the hall works (a reinforcer) but gives a weak shock (a mild punisher) when used, people may continue to use the switch at night because the reinforcement of light outweighs the discomfort of a weak shock. However, if the shock is more intense and painful, the punishment of shock might outweigh the reinforcement of light and suppress responding. The *cost/benefit ratio of punishment and reinforcement* helps predict how much response suppression will occur. When costs are high and benefits are low, there is more response suppression than when costs are low and benefits are high.

Also, the *frequency* of punishment and reinforcement affects the cost/benefit ratio. If a behavior is always rewarded, but punished only one time in ten, the intermittent punishment is less likely to suppress responding than would more frequent punishment. Pat believes in ESP and likes to talk about it with his roommate: It's a rewarding topic even though the roommate makes fun of Pat's more radical ravings every once in a while. However, if Pat is criticized every time he mentions ESP to strangers, he is more likely to stop talking about ESP with strangers than if he had only been criticized one time in ten by strangers. If Mike criticizes Jenny's game every time they play tennis together, his criticisms are punishers that counteract the rewards of playing. Jenny may continue to play tennis with him if the frequency of rewards is greater than the frequency of punishment; but she is likely to quit playing if the criticisms are more frequent than the rewards.

Even mild or infrequent punishment can totally suppress behavior if some alternative behavior is available—with a better cost/benefit ratio. If Jenny plays tennis with her best girlfriend and they have fun with few critical comments, Jenny may tell Mike that she is too busy to play tennis with him. People may completely stop doing a mildly punished behavior if they have access to an alternative behavior that offers a better cost/benefit ratio—more reinforcement and/or less punishment.

Two Types of Punishment

There are two kinds of punishment: one based on addition and the other on subtraction. *The onset or addition of an aversive stimulus can suppress behavior.* If you spill hot coffee on your hand while walking to a table in the cafeteria, the onset of an aversive stimulus punishes the clumsy act. You may feel pain and anger. *The second type of punishment occurs when our behavior leads to the termination or subtraction of a rewarding stimulus.* If a clumsy action results in your dropping and losing a ten-dollar bill down a roadside drain, the loss serves as punishment for the clumsy act. Thus, the loss and subtraction of a positive reinforcer can also suppress behavior, causing feelings of frustration, regret, sadness, and anger.[31]

Punishment by the addition of an aversive stimulus is called **positive punishment,** where positive means "addition." Punishment by the subtraction of a reward is called **negative punishment,** where negative indicates "subtraction." Some scientists only use the words *positive* and *negative* before the word *punishment,* but our students like the simpler vocabulary of addition and subtraction.

Punishment by Adding. *Whenever an operant leads to the onset or addition of aversive experiences, the operant is punished.* The physical environment is often a source of punishment by addition. Careless handling of fire, bees, knives, machines, and many other objects can lead to painful consequences; hence careless responses are suppressed by naturally occurring positive punishment, involving the addition of pain. Because these natural punishers continue to affect us all through life, careless responses remain suppressed to a relatively low level.

Little children sometimes fantasize that they can fly. Fairy tales entice them to dream of soaring above the house, off to a special world for kids only. With high levels of positive reinforcement awaiting the first successful flight, the child prepares a Superman or Wonderwoman cloak from a discarded sheet and climbs onto the garage roof. Ready for takeoff! The child arranges the magic cloak and steps to the edge. Looking down to the ground 10 feet below already gives the illusion of flight. Just one more step to go. Takeoff! Free flight . . . thump! Due to the laws of gravity, flying children are punished by a painful thump after each jump. How strong the punishment is depends on whether the flight ends in a haystack, in a soft garden plot, or on pavement. The haystack jumper may chalk up the failure of the first flight to a technical error and jump several more times before the mild but consistent punishment finally suppresses the behavior. The child who hit the pavement may not fly again. One powerful punishment may suffice to suppress the response once and for all. After childhood, jumping off buildings remains well suppressed throughout most people's lives.

Numerous social forms of punishment involve the addition of aversive stimuli. Some are intentional—such as reprimands, hostile criticism, and handcuffs. Others are accidental and unplanned—such as an insensitive comment that was made without anyone realizing how much it would hurt one of the listeners. Because each person has a unique history of past conditioning, social punishers often affect people differently: A cold stare or insolent answer could be very aversive to one person and hardly noticed by another.

However, most people are sensitive to many of the natural social punishers that punctuate social interactions. Imagine you are talking with people you met last week, and you know you should have already learned their names. If you accidentally call someone by the wrong name, the error may lead to an embarrassing situation. Your error has added a twinge of pain that punishes and may suppress your using other people's names until you are certain you cannot be in error. After several punishments for sloppy name use, you might not say an individual's name unless you heard someone else use the person's name a few moments ago, and hence were certain the name was safe to use.

Punishment and negative reinforcement often occur at the same time. Not only do social errors suppress wrong responses, the aversiveness of the experience can cause a person to learn—via negative reinforcement—new skills for *avoiding* social blunders. For example, you might learn to listen closely when people are first introduced, and to rehearse their name silently to yourself several times so you will be sure to remember it. *Thus, aversive situations can both (1) cause wrong responses to be punished and suppressed, via the addition of aversive stimuli, and (2) cause escape or avoidance skills to be acquired and strengthened, via negative reinforcement.*

Punishment by Subtracting.   When people drop or lose things of value, the loss produces a type of punishment that often effectively suppresses future clumsy behavior. Have you ever lost your wallet full of money and credit cards? The loss subtracts from your happiness and punishes the negligent behavior that led you to misplace it in the first place, making you less likely to misplace it in the future. *Whenever an operant leads to the loss or removal of positive reinforcers, the operant is punished by subtraction.*

We stop putting quarters in a candy machine after losing several quarters in a row and getting no candy. Clumsy, inconsiderate, or crude behavior in social interaction may result in a loss of friends and possible new acquaintances. When a person says something insensitive at a party and several of the listeners soon turn to join other conversations, the loss of social reinforcers punishes the behavior of saying insensitive things in public. The loss of positive reinforcers subtracts from happiness. The loss of a driver's license punishes fast driving and often suffices to suppress speeding in the future. The loss of love—when a good relationship goes on the rocks—punishes and may suppress some of the inconsiderate behavior that damaged the relationship. Afterward, a person may think over and over, "I'll never be inconsiderate again: A beautiful love is so rare that I never want to lose love again."

Parents can use punishment by subtraction as an effective means of behavior modification for helping children overcome problem behavior. For example, childhood aggression causes problems for many children, their parents, and teachers. Aggressive children bully their peers and disrupt their homes and classrooms. If they do not learn to control their aggression early in life, these children may grow up to be violent teens and adults. Reynolds and Kelley (1997) showed that aggressive behavior could be virtually eliminated in preschool classrooms by subtractive punishment. Figure 3–8 presents the data on Mike, one of the four aggressive children in the study. During the first part of the study, Mike's rate of aggression per hour was observed under baseline conditions, with no behavioral interventions (at time A). At time B, the teacher displayed a large Good Behavior

Chart in the classroom, and each day 5 smiley faces appeared next to each student's name. The rules were clear: Every time a child did aggressive behavior, the teacher removed a smiley face from the child's name. Any children who lost all their smiley faces would not receive special rewards—such as a prize or access to a favorite toy—so each smiley face that was subtracted from a child's name signaled risk of punishment by loss of rewards. During time period B, when aggressive behavior led to punishment by subtracting smiley faces, Mike's aggression dropped from 15 to 4 times per hour. When the teacher discontinued the use of the Good Behavior Chart for three days (the second baseline at time C), Mike's aggression became more frequent. At time D, the Good Behavior Chart and negative punishment (by subtracting rewards) were reinstated and Mike's aggression dropped to very low levels. All four aggressive children in the study showed similar reductions in belligerent behavior—and the teachers found the procedure was easy to implement in the classroom. Aggression is a serious social problem, but it can be curbed quickly when dealt with in the early years of life.

Negative punishment is used in many areas of life, including the world of business. In 1998, the clothing maker Guess cut the total pay to its top executives by 72% because they failed to meet financial goals.[32] The loss of rewards creates an incentive to do better in the coming year.

FIGURE 3–8   **The frequency of aggression declines when punished (at times B and D). The average frequency of behavior at each time period is shown by a horizontal line.**

(Adapted from "The efficacy of a response cost-based treatment package for managing aggressive behavior in preschoolers" by L.K. Reynolds & M.L. Kelley (1997). *Behavior Modification, 21*, pp. 216–230. Copyright © 1997 by Sage Publications.

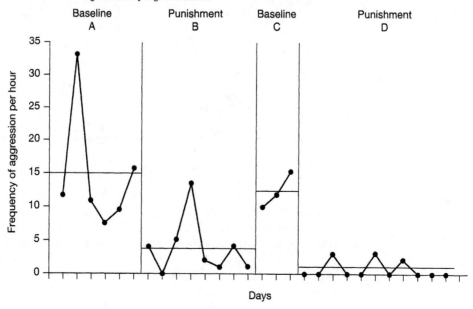

DISCONTINUATION OF PUNISHMENT

Punishment does not cause behavior to be "unlearned" or "forgotten." It merely suppresses the frequency of responding. *Often the effects of punishment are only temporary; and when punishment no longer occurs, the rate of responding usually increases.* This phenomenon is called **recovery**. In many cases, previously suppressed behavior returns to the frequency it had before punishment began, which is called full recovery. When the police begin using radar to issue speeding tickets on highway 142, speeding may be reduced. But when they stop patrolling road 142 and focus on nearby highway 152, drivers may notice that fellow motorists are speeding again on route 142 without punishment, and many former speeders return to their old practices of speeding along highway 142, though they now do not speed on route 152.

Recovery is fastest and most complete when the original punishment was mild or infrequent and it is opposed by reinforcement for doing the behavior. The milder the original punishment, the sooner a behavior is likely to recover after punishment ceases. For example, if you have a skiing accident that breaks both legs, this intense punishment may suppress skiing permanently, even after your legs are out of the casts. On the other hand, if you merely take a hard fall while skiing down a steep slope, this less intense punishment may keep you off the slope for the rest of the afternoon; but tomorrow you may be ready to hit the slopes again. In addition, reinforcement hastens recovery. The more reinforcement there is for a behavior, the sooner and faster the recovery will take place after the end of punishment. People who break both legs in skiing accidents are more likely to return to skiing if there are rewards for doing so: They really enjoy the sport, all their friends ski, they are close to winning in major competitions, or they earn their living by skiing.

Jumping off the garage roof in order to fly like a bird is a response that is usually well suppressed in childhood by the punishment of hard falls. Most people make no further attempts at free flight for the rest of their lives. However, there are special circumstances in which soaring like a bird is not followed by punishment—namely, when using a parachute or hang glider. As a parachutist steps to the airplane door for the first jump, there may be some hesitancy—seen as "approach-avoidance responses" when the novice alternates between approaching the jump point, then stepping back. However, after several successful jumps (without punishment), the parachutist jumps from the plane without any sign of hesitation or avoidance. Jumping from heights is no longer suppressed when the punishment is removed; hence there is a recovery of the response, even though it had been suppressed since childhood.

After enough years, most people notice that their mentioning any topics that lead to social embarrassment, discomfort, or other aversive consequences, become suppressed—due to punishment. Blundering into a new taboo topic leads to quick response suppression, but recovery effects are likely if the topic ceases to be punished. For example, people who live or work together often develop joking relationships to help spice up daily interaction. Normally, jokes about people dying, "kicking the bucket," or "croaking" may be part of the acceptable patterns of joking. However, when someone close dies, joking about croaking may suddenly be met with cold responses. "That's not funny now, Joe." For the period of weeks or months after the death, joking about death is punished and remains suppressed. Eventually, the death recedes so far into the past that the punishment ceases and there is a recovery in the frequency of joking about croaking.

Behavior that has been severely punished and is not closely linked with strong reinforcers can remain suppressed even after the punishers are discontinued. Many people never try skydiving or hang gliding, even though they could do these "frightening jumps" with an expert who goes with them to assure safety and no pain. Excess social punishment can make some people so shy and fearful that they avoid many social events all through life—and avoidance retards their discovery of the joys of friendly social relations.

TIMING AND CONTINGENCY OF CONSEQUENCES

Generally, operant conditioning is most likely to occur when reinforcers and punishers follow immediately after an operant.[33] The longer the delay between behavior X and its consequences, the less effect the consequences have on behavior X. In addition, any other responses Y and Z that may have occurred between behavior X and the consequences may be modified instead of behavior X. Looking down and seeing five dollar bills on the ground leads to instant reinforcement for scanning the ground, which has a strong effect on behavior. Studying hard for a test and receiving an "A" 7 days later involves delayed reinforcement—which is less effective than immediate reinforcement.

There are two exceptions to the preceding paragraph's generalization that immediate reinforcement has extra power: *Close time links between a behavior and a reinforcer or punisher do not always lead to operant conditioning; and long delays do not always prevent it.* Both depend on the **contingency of reinforcement**—*how closely the consequence is causally related to the behavior.*

First, close timing between behavior and reinforcers or punishers does not always produce operant conditioning. Humans and many other species are sensitive to the difference between reinforcers and punishers that are *consequences* of their behavior and those that only *accidentally follow* their behavior. *Reinforcers and punishers that accidentally follow—but are not actual consequences of—a behavior are not very likely to produce operant conditioning, even if they follow immediately after the behavior.*[34] If you make a joke about the rainy weather and two things happen—your friend laughs at the joke and a sudden loud thunderclap startles you—one event is a consequence of your joking, and the other is a chance event. Because your friend's laughter is a consequence of your joking, it will reinforce your jesting. However, the timing of the loud thunderclap is purely coincidental (not a consequence of your joking); and it is not likely to suppress your drollery, even though sudden loud noises serve as punishers when they are consequences of behavior. The noise may startle you, but it is unlikely to punish joke telling. In fact, you might continue joking with your friend: "I think someone up there heard us complaining about the weather." *Operant behavior is modified by contingent consequences: Reinforcers and punishers that only follow behavior by accident usually produce little operant conditioning, even if they occur immediately after a behavior.*

When reinforcers and punishers are the actual consequences of a behavior, they are called **contingent** *reinforcers and punishers—to indicate that the consequences resulted from the behavior.* The behavior produced the consequences. Contingent reinforcement strengthens behavior. Contingent punishment suppresses behavior. *Any reinforcers and punishers that only follow behavior by accident are called* **noncontingent** *reinforcers and punishers—because they are not actually related to the behavior.* Noncontingent reinforcers and punishers have little ability to produce operant conditioning, although they can under some conditions lead to unusual effects.

If Shevanda is working as a salesperson, she may learn to greet customers in a friendly manner. If customer A smiles in return, the customer's smile provides contingent reinforcement for Shevanda's cheerful greeting—because the consequence depends on Shevanda's behavior. If Shevanda gives a friendly greeting to a second customer B, then slips and sprains her ankle, the painful sprain is not likely to suppress Shevanda's making cheerful greetings, because the sprained ankle is not a consequence of giving a friendly greeting (even though pain occurred immediately after her last greeting).

Although the painful sprain does not affect behaviors that did not cause it, it can punish and suppress those behaviors that *did* produce it, such as stepping on round or slick objects lying on the floor. *Each behavior is modified most powerfully by its own consequences—but not by consequences of other behaviors (or by other accidental reinforcers and punishers).* Thus, the close timing of a behavior and a reinforcer or punisher is unlikely to produce operant conditioning if the reinforcer or punisher is not contingent on—but only accidentally follows—the behavior in question.

There is a second qualification to the generalization that operant conditioning is most likely to occur when reinforcers and punishers follow *immediately* after an operant. *Delayed consequences can produce operant conditioning if a person can detect a contingent, causal relationship between a behavior and its consequences.* What if Shevanda greets customer C in a cheerful manner before starting her regular sales routine, and 15 minutes later the customer makes a purchase? Even though the delay between the cheerful greetings and increased sales is relatively long, there *is* a contingent relationship—a causal linkage—between the behavior and its consequences, and this increases the likelihood that the delayed consequences will reinforce cheerful greetings.

Humans are more capable than any other species of detecting contingent linkages between behavior and delayed consequences. Some of this ability to respond to delayed consequences can be traced to our having large brains with many areas devoted to learning. It also depends on our ability to verbally reconstruct the events of the past hours, days, or weeks, and identify possible linkages between our behavior and delayed consequences. *The more frequently and vividly we think about a behavior and its delayed but contingent consequences, the more likely the behavior is to be modified.*[35] Even though receiving an "A" on a test that you took last week is a delayed reward, you may realize that a new study technique you tried for that test was the reason for the great grade. The more often you think about the value of the new study technique, the better the study behavior is linked with the delayed rewards. Thinking about the problems that arose after inviting some strangers to live with you during summer session at school can suppress the response of inviting strangers for such long stays in the future. *Even though there may be a long delay between a behavior and its contingent consequences, verbally reconstructing the link between a behavior and its consequences in close connection allows us to link memories of a behavior and its consequences with almost zero time delays.* Thus, cognitive reflection on past events allows behavior to be associated with contingent reinforcement or punishment with short time lags, once we identify the contingent linkages. Once people discover these causal linkages, they may go one step further and make verbal rules—"I must never invite strangers to live with me again"—and these rules further enhance the effect of delayed consequences (see Chapter 12, on the power of useful rules).

Although the earliest formulations of operant principles stated that operant conditioning is based on *immediate* reinforcement and punishment, there is more to the story. First, even immediate reinforcers and punishers must be contingent on behavior—causally related to the behavior—to produce much effect. Second, if a contingent relationship is detected between behavior and delayed reinforcers and punishers that result from it, even delayed consequences can modify operant behavior.

CONCLUSION

Operant behavior is behavior that operates on the environment and is instrumental in producing consequences. The frequency of operant behavior can be modified by (1) reinforcement, (2) the discontinuation of reinforcement (extinction), (3) punishment, (4) the discontinuation of punishment, and (5) both timing and contingency. Reinforcers and punishers are the prime movers of operant conditioning. Reinforcement increases the likelihood of a behavior, and punishment decreases the likelihood of a behavior. When a given pattern of reinforcement or punishment is discontinued, the frequency of the operant usually returns to the level it had prior to the beginning of this reinforcement or punishment.

The antecedent cues that best predict that a behavior may produce either positive or negative reinforcement become S^Ds, discriminative stimuli for responding. The antecedent cues that best predict a behavior may produce nonreinforcement or punishment become S^Δs, discriminative stimuli that inhibit responding. Although reinforcers and punishers tend to be more effective when they occur immediately after a behavior rather than after a delay, they are most powerful if they are consequences of the behavior—that is, if they are contingent on the behavior. Even delayed consequences can produce operant conditioning if they are contingent on the behavior and this causal connection is detected.

QUESTIONS

1. What is the law of effect? How does it explain the basics of operant conditioning?
2. What is an operant? How is it defined? What is a response class?
3. Can you define the words *reinforcer* and *reinforcement?* What are the two different types of reinforcers? How do they differ?
4. Can you explain discriminative stimuli (antecedents)? What is the difference between S^Ds and S^Δs? What consequences produce S^Ds and which ones produce S^Δs?
5. What is extinction? Can you give examples of extinction after positive reinforcement and examples of extinction after negative reinforcement?
6. What is punishment? What are the two types of punishment, based on addition and subtraction? What needs to be added to punish behavior? What needs to be subtracted to punish behavior?

7. What happens when a behavior that was once punished is no longer punished? How do cost/benefit ratios influence behavior?

8. How does the contingency or noncontingency of reinforcers and punishers affect behavior? Why do noncontingent reinforcers and punishers have little effect on behavior, even if they are immediate? Why can contingent consequences have major effects on behavior, even if they are delayed?

NOTES

1. Honig and Staddon (1977); Zeiler and Harzem (1979); Kalish (1981); Rescorla (1993); Lattal (1995).

2. Rescorla (1991, 1993); Lattal (1995).

3. Espinosa (1992) discusses the problematic nature of behavior change.

4. Davey (1988).

5. Haynes and O'Brien (1990).

6. Mechner (1994) argues for molecular analyses, and Nevin (1994) for an integration of both molar and molecular approaches to behavior.

7. Rescorla (1999b).

8. Donahoe (1998).

9. Goetz and Baer (1973).

10. Goetz and Salmonson (1972); Maloney and Hopkins (1973); Eisenberger and Selbst (1994).

11. Mahoney (1975); Bloom (1985); Logue (1995); Watson and Tharp (1997).

12. Deci and Ryan (1985); Bernstein (1990).

13. Thibaut and Kelley (1959); Homans (1974).

14. Hiltzik (1996).

15. Welch (1998).

16. Hermann, de Montes, Dominguez, Montes, and Hopkins (1973).

17. Iwata (1987); Crosbie (1998).

18. Stix (1995).

19. Petroski (1992).

20. Simpson, Ickes, and Blackstone (1995).

21. Rescorla (1993, 1999a).

22. Ducharme and Van Houten (1994); Lerman and Iwata (1996). However, extinction does have its limitations as a therapy (Lerman & Iwata, 1996).

23. Watson and Sterling (1998).

24. Hall et al. (1972).

25. Zarcone et al. (1993).

26. Ayres (1998); Galizio (1999).

27. Walters and Grusec (1977); Axelrod and Apsche (1983); Baron (1991); Dinsmoor (1998); Malott (1998).

28. Centers (1963); Skinner (1969).

29. Lovaas and Simmons (1969); Watson and Tharp (1997).

30. Appel (1961); Storms, Boroczi, and Broen (1962).

31. van Dijk, Zeelenberg, and van der Pligt (1999).

32. Bonuses for executives (1998).

33. White and Schlosberg (1952); Van Houten and Rolider (1988); Mazur (1995).

34. Killeen (1978); Hammond (1980); Lattal (1995); Matute and Miller (1998). But see pp. 312–314 of this book for exceptions to this generalization.

35. Mahoney (1974); Bandura (1977); Meichenbaum (1977); Rosenthal and Zimmerman (1978); Schwartz (1984, p. 450).

4

Pavlovian and Operant Conditioning Together

PAVLOVIAN AND OPERANT INTERTWINED

Operant and Pavlovian conditioning are often intertwined throughout much of everyday life. When Angela's car spun off the road and crashed into a tree, she experienced both Pavlovian and operant conditioning. Through Pavlovian conditioning, Angela began to respond to speed and wet, curved roads as CSs that could elicit emotions of apprehension and fear. Through operant conditioning, she learned to avoid driving too fast on wet, curved roads—because that behavior led to serious and contingent punishment.

When two lovers spend a beautiful evening walking in the moonlight—kissing and talking about the wonderful feelings they are sharing—they are both learning from positive experiences. Each is learning—by Pavlovian conditioning—to associate warm, loving emotions with the other's face, words, actions, and personality. Later, after parting, each finds that merely thinking about the other person provides the cognitive CSs that call up warm, loving feelings. The emotions we feel when seeing a photo of the person we love result from pleasurable Pavlovian conditioning. In addition, the positive emotions of love provide positive reinforcement for the operant behaviors of phoning or e-mailing to arrange another get-together, which is reinforced by pleasant feelings about future interactions.

TABLE 4–1   Table of symbols basic to Pavlovian and operant conditioning

US	Unconditioned Stimulus	A stimulus that elicits the unconditioned response of an inborn reflex.
UR	Unconditioned Response	The reflexive response elicited by a US.
NS	Neutral Stimulus	Any stimulus that does not elicit or evoke a response.
CS	Conditioned Stimulus	Once a neutral stimulus becomes associated with a US, it becomes a CS that can also elicit reflexes.
CR	Conditioned Response	The response elicited by a CS.
CER	Conditioned Emotional Response	The emotional part of a CR. It appears when a CS elicits a CR with emotional components.
S^D	Discriminative Stimulus	Stimuli that precede a behavior that is reinforced become S^Ds, which set the occasion for responding in the future.
S^Δ	Discriminative Stimulus	Stimuli that precede a behavior that is punished or extinguished. S^Δs are antecedent cues that inhibit operant responses.
S^R	Reinforcer	Any stimulus that can reinforce behavior.

In both Pavlovian and operant conditioning, positive learning experiences create much more pleasing effects than do aversive experiences. We hunger much more for the positive experiences of love, stimulating conversations, and exciting entertainment than for the auto accidents, bee stings, and embarrassments of life. Nevertheless, in both the positive and negative aspects of everyday life, operant and Pavlovian conditioning frequently occur together and are delicately interlaced. Before we examine the differences and similarities of Pavlovian and operant learning, you should examine Table 4–1, which brings together the definitions of all the symbols for both types of conditioning.

THE DIFFERENCES

To grasp the subtleties of learning theory, we need to contrast the main differences of Pavlovian and operant conditioning.[1] Pavlovian conditioning is seen most often in basic biological and physiological responses; whereas operant conditioning usually involves our voluntary responses. Pavlovian conditioning helps adjust many of the basic animal responses of our bodies; and operant conditioning helps adjust the behavior we often describe as "higher" than basic biological processes.

1. The Role of Reflexes.   Pavlovian conditioning builds from basic biological reflexes, whereas operant conditioning need not.[2] In Pavlovian conditioning, a conditioned reflex (CS $\rightarrow$ CR) can be established only if there is some prior reflex (conditioned or unconditioned) from which to build. Ultimately, all conditioned reflexes depend on biologically wired-in unconditioned reflexes (US $\rightarrow$ UR) for their strength. During extinction, all conditioned reflexes cease to appear once their CS ceases to precede and predict the onset of the relevant US (unconditioned stimulus).

In contrast, operant behavior does not depend on reflexes. Most operant behavior has nothing to do with reflexes (although some of the reflexes can be partially modified by operant conditioning). Some food and sex examples will show that both unconditioned and conditioned reflexes are relatively constrained by the biological makeup of the species, whereas operant behavior is much more modifiable and can be shaped into countless forms. The operant activities of cooking and dining can be performed in innumerable ways, but salivation and other digestive reflexes are relatively invariable, based on fixed biological processes. There are countless variations on the operant behaviors of sexual foreplay, but the reflexive responses of vaginal lubrication and penile erection follow fixed patterns, no matter whether elicited by USs or CSs.[3]

2. Eliciting Versus Emitting.   An important difference between reflexive and operant behavior is that reflexes are elicited whereas operants are emitted. Both USs and CSs have the power to *elicit* reflexive responses, *triggering* them as automatically as pulling the trigger of a gun fires the weapon. However, S^Ds do not automatically trigger operant behavior: They merely set the occasion for the operant—which may or may not be *emitted,* depending on prior patterns of reinforcement and other variables. Thus, reflexes look more mechanistic than do operant behaviors, which are more complex—depending on many more causal variables.

For example, the US of gentle touch to the genitals automatically elicits the sex reflex, which can be strong or weak depending on the pressure of stimulation and the pattern of movement. Instead of having this automatic effect, S^Ds have probabilistic effects. Asking a lover to provide the optimal pattern and pressure of stimulation is an S^D that sets the occasion for an operant response, but the operant that is emitted is not biologically fixed and may not be optimal.

3. The Internal-External Continuum.[4]   Our bodies do millions of things each day, and these occur on a continuum from internally oriented (such as digestion) to externally oriented (such as a wink or wave). *Reflexive responses tend to promote smooth operation of internal bodily processes, whereas operant behavior is usually instrumental in affecting the external environment.* On the continuum from internal to external, the boundaries of Pavlovian and operant conditioning overlap in the gray areas between the extreme types, but the majority of reflexive and operant responses differ in their internal or external orientations.

For the most part, reflexive responses facilitate the functioning of internal bodily processes. Bad food is regurgitated and, through conditioning, the food becomes a CS that elicits feelings of nausea. Good food becomes a CS that elicits salivation, in preparation for digestion. Parts of the sex reflex are quite visible—such as penile erection—but most are inside the body, and all evolved to initiate the internal biological processes of pregnancy. Reflexive responses are usually mediated through the involuntary (autonomic) nervous system and the smooth muscles.

Although we have voluntary control of operants such as walking and talking, most people cannot voluntarily induce blushing, sexual arousal, heart rate changes, vomiting, or other reflexive responses—except by presenting themselves with an appropriate US or

CS. In contrast, operant behavior is generally oriented to the outside environment (rather than to internal biological processes). Operant behavior is usually instrumental in coping with external events. Operants are involved in picking, purchasing, and preparing food, then moving it to the mouth and chewing. Once the food is inside the body, the salivation and other digestive reflexes do their job.

4. The Role of Reinforcers. *Although reinforcement is necessary for operant conditioning, it is not needed for Pavlovian conditioning.* The following diagrams of operant and Pavlovian conditioning show that a reinforcing stimulus (S^R) is essential for the acquisition and maintenance of operant behavior (on the top line of the diagram); but the S^R is absent in the Pavlovian model.

$$\text{Operant} \qquad S^D : \ B \to S^R$$

$$\text{Pavlovian} \left\{ \begin{array}{l} US \to UR \\ \vdots \\ CS \to CR \end{array} \right.$$

Reinforcement strengthens operant behavior and causes each relevant antecedent stimulus to become an S^D. In contrast, the reflexes that are involved in Pavlovian conditioning operate without reinforcement (on lines 2 and 3). The unconditioned reflex (line 2) is biologically wired in and does not need reinforcement to function. Pavlovian conditioning occurs when a predictive stimulus precedes the US and becomes a CS for a conditioned reflex (line 3). Reinforcement is not necessary for producing Pavlovian conditioning or for the functioning of the conditioned reflex. Therefore, the reinforcing stimulus (S^R) does not appear on either line of the diagrams of Pavlovian conditioning.

The sexual reflex can be triggered by the US of stimulation to the genitals—without any need for reinforcement. If fantasies are paired with the sexual reflex, the fantasies can become CSs that elicit sexual feelings, again without any reinforcement needed. However, reinforcement is essential for learning the operant skills needed for truly rewarding sexual activities: As people explore their sexuality, the sexual positions, techniques, and movements that produce rewarding effects are more likely to be repeated than are behaviors that lead to painful or unrewarding effects.

5. What New Thing Is Learned? *In Pavlovian conditioning, a person learns to respond to a new stimulus: At first the new stimulus is a neutral stimulus (NS), but during Pavlovian conditioning it becomes a CS that elicits a reflexive response.* Over the years, a person may become sick from eating several different kinds of unusual foods. Each time this happens, new foods—such as scallops in sour cream sauce or red frogs—become CSs for nausea and food aversions. Although the conditioned response of nausea is not new, each new food becomes a new CS capable of eliciting the conditioned response.

In operant conditioning, people learn new behavior patterns along with sensitivities to numerous S^Ds or S^Δs that cue when the new behavior may lead to reinforcement, extinction, or punishment. Thus, consequences tend to modify both the frequency of various operant behaviors and the signal value of their antecedents. This is different from Pavlovian conditioning, in which the reflexive response patterns are relatively fixed and new stimuli become associated with them. The reflexes elicited by food (such as salivation and digestion) remain relatively unchanged all through life, but the operant behaviors needed for preparing food can change in countless ways over the years—in their form, frequency, and linkage with numerous S^Ds. A brightly colored box of sugar-laden cereal may be an S^D for a child to pull the box from the grocery shelf, but years later, a dull-colored box of low-fat, high-fiber cereal may become the S^D for eating a healthy breakfast.

PAVLOVIAN AND OPERANT INTERACTIONS

Although it is possible to distinguish between operant and Pavlovian conditioning (as we have just done), the two forms of conditioning are frequently intertwined.[5] Let us examine five ways in which interactions can occur.

1. CSs for Emotions Can Serve as Reinforcers or Punishers that Produce Operant Conditioning. *Any stimulus that becomes a CS through Pavlovian conditioning can function as a reinforcer or punisher if that CS elicits pleasurable or aversive emotional responses.*[6] If your favorite radio station was playing certain popular tunes the month you fell in love, many of those songs may become CSs that elicit pleasurable emotions due to Pavlovian conditioning. When you hear one of these songs a couple of months later, you may notice its "special" ability to elicit pleasurable emotions. You may comment, "Hey, they're playing our song," as you notice the positive feelings. In addition, the song may contain enough CSs for pleasure to reinforce operants such as buying a CD with the song and playing it numerous times—because playing the CD is reinforced by the musical CSs that elicit the special, pleasant feelings.

Conversely, CSs that elicit aversive feelings can serve as punishers and negative reinforcers. Have you ever been sharply criticized and embarrassed for voicing your views on topics about which you know very little? Due to Pavlovian conditioning, talking about such topics can become CSs which elicit uneasy feelings. In the future, these CSs and bad feelings may punish and suppress the tendency to take a strong position on troublesome topics. These CSs may also serve as negative reinforcers that increase the likelihood of your tactfully avoiding touchy topics or learning to deal with them more tactfully.

The advertisement industry shows great skill in using Pavlovian conditioning to create CSs that can cause subsequent changes in operant behavior. Let us examine CSs that reward before CSs that punish.

How can you create an ad that would make people buy one type of automobile and pass up other types? Before a new advertisement for a car is placed in a magazine, it is subjected to weeks or months of testing. Because some stimuli—such as beautiful people, quaint places, magnificent landscapes—tend to be CSs that elicit positive feelings for most people, a common advertising strategy is to place a picture of an auto in the midst of a scene containing numerous pleasing images, all of which are CSs for pleasurable feelings. According to the principles of Pavlovian conditioning, the advertised auto will acquire some positive emotional power by being associated with the numerous CSs that elicit pleasant feelings. These positive associations are sometimes strong enough to influence consumers to buy the beautifully advertised product rather than a more dull-appearing competitor.

Some ads do not even have words: They merely present a collage of pleasure-eliciting CSs, such as several playful puppies jumping out of a SUV with the car's logo clearly visible. Flipping through the magazine, many people may pause to view the cute puppies, because the CSs for pleasurable emotions act as reinforcers that strengthen the operant of prolonged viewing. This in turn increases the likelihood of longer exposure to the Pavlovian conditioning that associates the SUV with CSs for pleasant feelings. After viewers have seen numerous attractive ads for a particular SUV, the experiences will tend to condition that SUV into a CS with positive associations. This positive conditioning can make a beautifully advertised SUV into a positive reinforcer. For viewers interested in purchasing an SUV, the ad may have a subtle but noticeable effect on their choice of SUVs.

Does this type of conditioning work? A multibillion-dollar advertising industry exists because it does. For every hundred people who will never buy an SUV, there are a few people who just might purchase an SUV that was beautifully advertised.[7]

The advertising industry can use CSs that elicit painful emotions to sell products or suppress certain operants. Ads that show a sad family outside their burned home have visual impact and may catch our eye. CSs that elicit fear of home fires may cause us to anxiously wonder if we have enough insurance on our own house. We may read the ad copy (an operant behavior) and tear out the advertisement as a reminder to call someone for more information (more operants) if we fear that we are underinsured.

On the other hand, advertisements and posters that are designed to suppress behavior often use CSs that elicit anxiety. Smokey the Bear and Hooty the Owl are shown standing in a burned forest, surrounded by forlorn and homeless animals, all of which are CSs that elicit sad feelings. Ads exhorting us not to drive while drunk may show a smashed car and dead body. The goal is to condition the viewer to respond to forest fires and auto accidents as CSs for anxiety or unpleasant feelings in hopes that these aversive CSs will suppress the operants which might cause forest fires or auto accidents.

Thus, CSs that elicit pleasant or unpleasant emotions can produce operant conditioning because they can serve as reinforcers or punishers. Ads for products, politicians, and public service campaigns use carefully chosen CSs that elicit positive or negative emotions to create new emotion laden CSs that in turn can serve as reinforcers or punishers.

2. Pavlovian as a By-Product of Operant. *During operant conditioning, some Pavlovian conditioning occurs as a side effect.*[8] The most common example of this operant side effect is the Pavlovian conditioning of *emotional responses.*[9]

When a child is about to stick a knife into an electric toaster to fish out a crumbling piece of raisin bread, a parent may shout, "No!" The parent has used verbal punishment to suppress the operant behavior of sticking metal objects into the toaster. In addition, there is a Pavlovian side effect: The stimulus of "knife-in-toaster" becomes a CS that elicits anxiety due to its association with the verbal punishment. In the future, the CS of "knife-in-toaster" may elicit emotions of fear or apprehension even if the parent is not present.

Because reinforcers and punishers elicit emotional responses, such as happiness or anxiety, antecedent stimuli that regularly precede reinforcers or punishers will become

CSs that can elicit emotional responses—due to Pavlovian conditioning. Thus, both the S^Ds and *behaviors* that precede reinforcers can become CSs for positive emotional responses. Seeing a gift box with your name on it is an S^D for using scissors to open it; and the gift, scissors and box opening are all CSs that elicit pleasant emotions, if these things have lead to rewards in the past. Conversely, both the S^Δs and *behaviors* that precede punishers can become CSs for aversive emotions. Seeing "knife-in-toaster" and pushing the knife into the toaster are S^Δs and behaviors that serve as CSs for anxiety.

If a person receives generous positive social reinforcement for a behavior, not only does the frequency of the operant behavior increase, doing the behavior becomes a CS that elicits pleasurable feelings, due to Pavlovian conditioning. Some people write poetry, play music, or play basketball "for the sheer joy of it." Often those people received generous social reinforcement during prior years of learning their skills, with the result that merely engaging in the behavior—even in the absence of social reinforcers—is now a CS that elicits pleasant emotional responses.[10] More of us would enjoy sports, arts, altruism, and just about anything else "for the sheer joy of it" if the behaviors had become CSs for pleasure due to generous prior positive reinforcement.

Sexual fetishes can emerge as a by-product of the operant conditioning of masturbation.[11] At his local swimming pool, Fred happened to notice how pretty the lifeguard's feet were. That evening, he recalled a vivid image of her feet while he was masturbating. The positive reinforcers of self-pleasuring not only strengthened the operant behavior of masturbation, but also conditioned the stimulus of "feet" into a CS for sexual arousal. After several evenings of self-stimulation, Fred began to find that merely thinking about Sally's feet was exciting—the signs of a mild foot fetish. At the pool next day, Fred found himself looking at female feet because the views of feet of certain shapes were rewarded by seeing CSs associated with sexual pleasure.

3. Operants Disrupted by Reflexes.

3. Operants Disrupted by Reflexes. *Operant behavior can be disrupted by reflexive responses.*[12] People who are learning new operant behavior often find that emotional responses and other reflexive responses can disrupt underlearned operant performances. For example, if you are practicing or delivering a public talk, you may notice how easily your speech is disrupted by CSs that elicit strong emotions. If you have been conditioned to fear making mistakes or being criticized in public, having a strange person walk into the room while you are doing your public talk may be a CS that elicits uncomfortable emotional responses; and these, in turn, may distract you from your speech—the underlearned operant activity—and disrupt your performance.

Being criticized repeatedly for one's poor playing of a certain passage of music can make that passage a CS that elicits anxiety. After this happens, you may begin to feel anxious as you play a piece of music and approach the problematic passage. This anxiety may cause you to make more errors, which only adds to your anxiety until eventually you fear the prospect of even starting the piece. Such emotional conditioning causes some people to develop a "psychological block" that prevents them from playing a piece and makes them fearful of practicing that piece in the future. Writer's block results from a similar type of conditioning: Failure or criticism associated with writing makes this behavior a CS that elicits fear and disrupts the operants of writing. (People who have overlearned a skill—be it playing music or writing—are less prone to develop a block, and it takes a much more intense emotional response to disrupt their operant performances. Professional pianists have overlearned their performances so well that they are not prone to experience disruption, even though they feel butterflies or other emotional responses during a concert.)

Emotions need not be aversive to disrupt operant performances. You and a friend may be engrossed in a precision task—such as fixing a delicate object with tiny tools—when one of you cracks a joke. If this leads to a funny story, more jokes, and other buffoonery, the numerous witty words serve as verbal CSs that may elicit enough laughter to disrupt your precision activities. You may try to keep working while chuckling at each other's jovialities; but after you keep dropping the tiny parts you are forced to say, "Hey, we have to cut the clowning if we're going to get this thing fixed."

4. Reflexes Disrupted by Operants.   *Reflexive responses can sometimes be interrupted or suppressed by operant activities.* Mr. R has learned to find certain kinds of tasteless jokes funny: The jokes are verbal CSs that elicit his laughter. Yet Mr. R has also learned that it is improper to laugh at such jokes in more refined company. What happens when Mr. R hears a witty but tasteless joke in a social setting where laughter would be inappropriate? Like most people, Mr. R has learned that laughter can be suppressed by tensing the stomach and diaphragm muscles. The tasteless joke is a CS that elicits definite jerks and spasms in Mr. R's diaphragm—incipient laughter responses—but his operant tensing of these muscles prevents the full-blown laughter response. Thus, Mr. R can disrupt and hide conditioned responses to tasteless jokes when needed.

The game of flinch shows how reflexive responses to an aversive CS can be interrupted or suppressed by operant activities. In this game, one person hits at, but does not quite touch, the arm of the second person. The rules of the game are simple: If the second person flinches, the first person gets to make a real hit of any strength. During childhood most people have numerous learning experiences that condition the stimulus of "object moving rapidly toward the arm" into a CS associated with pain, since that stimulus is frequently followed by the pain of being hit by the object. Being hit is a US that causes pain and a reflexive flinch response. After repeated pairings, the stimulus of "object moving rapidly toward the arm" becomes a CS that can elicit the flinch and anxious feelings. Thus, people with no experience with the flinch game are usually sitting ducks if someone talks them into playing the game: They are strongly conditioned to give a flinch response when the other person makes the first fake blow. After losing several times in a row and developing a sore arm, an initiate to the game may learn the operant skills for suppressing the flinch response—or may learn to avoid getting involved in the game. The flinch can be suppressed somewhat by tightening one's muscles or by focusing one's attention away from the fake blow, and the use of these operants is negatively reinforced by the avoidance of aversive consequences.

5. Reflexes Modified by Operant Conditioning.   *The frequency and form of many reflexes can be modified by reinforcement and punishment.*[13] For example, blushing is a reflexive response that appears during embarrassment, guilt, and a variety of other aversive experiences. If a teenager has often become very embarrassed when adults bring up the topic of sex, adults' talking about sex will become a CS that can elicit blushing (due to Pavlovian conditioning). Once the blush has been elicited, subsequent reinforcement or punishment can alter the teen's tendency to blush in the future. If a teen receives sympathy when others detect that she is blushing, the sympathy and loving concern can reinforce the blushing response and make her more prone to blush easily in the future. In contrast, if blushing is usually punished—perhaps by a curt comment, "You act like a baby, Fred"—the blushing will be suppressed. As a result of operant conditioning, some people are less likely than others to blush. Each individual's propensity to blush is influenced by his or her unique history of reinforcement and punishment for this reflexive response. Part of society's double standard is to punish males more than females for displaying emotions.

Numerous universal emotional responses—such as smiles, laughter, frowns, blushes, and tears—are seen in people all around the world.[14] These reflexive emotional responses are most invariant in early childhood, before they are modified by social learning experience. Over the years, the form and frequency of all these reflexes can be modified by reinforcement and punishment, such that some people smile and laugh much more than others, some cry more easily than others.[15]

During early infancy, smiles and laughter are purely reflexive responses elicited by moderately surprising or novel events and certain other positive stimuli. Even years later, the novelty and surprises of rides at amusement parks elicit smiles and laughter from most young people. Due to Pavlovian conditioning, various facets of amusement parks become CSs that elicit smiles and laughter, and people often smile and laugh even before they get on a ride they like. But reinforcement and punishment can enter the picture and modify the probability that these responses will occur in the future. Some people's smiles and laughter may be reinforced by frequent cheerful, positive feedback from friends. Other people's smiles and laughter may be punished more than reinforced, if their peers say that it is "childish" to get excited by the rides. After years of operant conditioning in numerous circumstances, some people will frequently show signs of enjoying themselves, while others seldom crack a smile.

CONCLUSION

In everyday life, operant and Pavlovian conditioning are frequently intertwined in complex patterns. The first part of this chapter presents five characteristics of operant and Pavlovian conditioning that allow us to distinguish between them and isolate their different effects on behavior. Then the chapter describes five ways in which the two processes interact.

The next chapter reveals still other ways that operant and reflexive responses are interwoven. Both operant and reflexive responses appear when certain antecedent stimuli (S^Ds, S^Δs, USs, or CSs) are present. The complex and ever-changing collage of multiple stimuli in everyday life produces a rich interplay of operant and reflexive responses.

QUESTIONS

1. What are the five differences between Pavlovian and operant conditioning?
2. Which form of conditioning builds on reflexes? Which one involves the eliciting of behavior, and which the emitting of behavior? Can you give examples?
3. What is the internal-external continuum? Which kinds of responses along this continuum are most involved in Pavlovian conditioning? In operant conditioning?
4. What is the role of reinforcers in operant and Pavlovian behavior?
5. What is the new thing that is learned in operant and Pavlovian conditioning?
6. How can Pavlovian conditioning be a by-product of operant conditioning? Give examples.
7. How can CSs for emotions produce operant and Pavlovian conditioning? Give examples.
8. How can reflexive responses disrupt operant behavior? Can you give examples?
9. How can operant responses disrupt reflexive responses? What are some examples?
10. How can reflexes be modified by operant conditioning? Can you give examples?

NOTES

1. Terrace (1971); Millenson and Leslie (1979); Schwartz (1984); Schoenfeld (1995).

2. Although operant conditioning need not build from reflexes, it has been shown that reflexes can be modified by operant conditioning (DiCara, 1970; Miller, 1969, 1978).

3. Masters and Johnson (1966); Masters, Johnson, and Kolodny (1995).

4. Skinner (1938, p. 112; 1953, p. 113–115); Terrace (1971).

5. Schwartz and Gamzu (1977); Teitelbaum (1977); Schwartz (1984); Weiss and Weissman (1992); Schoenfeld (1995); Allan (1998).

6. See Chapter 8 on secondary reinforcers and punishers.

7. Bem (1970, pp. 70–71); Broad (1980).

8. Staats (1975, p. 87). Pavlovian conditioning can occur, of course, without operant conditioning.

9. The Pavlovian side effects are not restricted to CERs. Other CRs—such as penile and vaginal changes, sweating, laughter, crying—may be involved.

10. Chapter 7 shows that sensory stimulation is a second major cause of internal motivation.

11. Weinberg, Williams, and Calhan (1995).

12. Crombez, Eccleston, Baeyens, and Eelen (1998).

13. Miller (1969, 1978); DiCara (1970).

14. Ekman and Keltner (1997).

15. Ekman, Roper, and Hager (1980); Ekman (1993).

Chapter

5

The Stimulus Collage

LIFE'S A 3-D STIMULUS COLLAGE

Art sometimes imitates life; and life, art. An artist creates a collage by pasting diverse fragments of pictures or materials—such as wood, cloth, paper—onto a surface. And the viewer gets the picture: Life consists of hundreds, if not thousands, of snippets of images and experiences. Even though we tend to notice and focus on only a few stimuli at a time—due to selective attention—those focal points are surrounded by a complex collage of other stimuli.

Everyday life is more complex than an artist's collage: It is three-dimensional, full of color, movement, odors, sounds, tastes, and touches. Turn your head fully to the left and focus. Are there countless things over there that are different from the things you had been focusing on one minute ago? Sometimes we are peripherally aware of them, half attentive to them—"Is that a strange person over there, watching me? And why the gun?" Sometimes we are not aware of the peripheral stimuli in our collage. We are unconscious of them. Then suddenly we glance toward them, and they instantly rise into our conscious awareness. What happens next may be trivial, or it may change our lives.

Sometimes the stimulus collage of life is very orderly and all the stimuli point to our going along one clear path in life. What a rosy picture! However, the stimulus collage can be a complex, splotchy, crazy-quilt mix of stimuli—enough to drive some people over the edge. "Where am I going in life? Everything seems so bewildering!" Much of hard rock music suggests that the vocalists find their sensory collages to be chaotic and confusing. Many adolescents can relate because they are going through so many biological and social changes so rapidly. Bryan may try to deal with his hodgepodge collage by verbally describing his life as far more orderly than it actually is. When we look at all the diverse stimuli that bombard Bryan each day—pulling him in 20 different directions—we have to wonder. Is Bryan merely trying to rationalize—with "rational lies"—that his life is more orderly than it really is? But what about us? Do we describe our stimulus collage as if it has more order than it really does? We have to take this question especially seriously when we realize that our entire sensory collage is much more complex at any point in time than our selective attention—focusing on a limited subset of inputs—allows us to see.

MULTIPLE ANTECEDENT STIMULI

In Chapter 2 on Pavlovian conditioning, we saw that USs and CSs are antecedent stimuli that appear before and elicit reflexive responses:

$$US \rightarrow UR$$
$$CS \rightarrow CR$$

This is an SR (or stimulus-response) model of behavior, in which an antecedent stimulus (US or CS) elicits a reflexive response.

In Chapter 3 on operant conditioning, we encountered an ABC model of behavior: Reinforcing consequences cause antecedent cues to become S^Ds (discriminative stimuli) that set the occasion for future behavior, since they cue that there has been prior reinforcement for that behavior in this S^D setting:

$$S^D: B \rightarrow S^R$$

When operants are extinguished or punished, the discriminative stimuli associated with extinction or punishment become S^Δs, which inhibit relevant behaviors.

This chapter focuses on all four types of antecedent stimuli: USs, CSs, S^Ds, and S^Δs. Up to this point we have discussed antecedent stimuli in a simple manner, as if most behaviors were under the control of one antecedent stimulus—or maybe a cluster of closely related stimuli. However, the situation is usually more complex. Vast numbers of different stimuli from outside and inside our bodies affect our thoughts, feelings, and actions. The world we perceive is like a collage of stimuli—an intertwined patchwork of images and scenes—that produce such a large overall picture that we can focus only on a selected portion of the whole at any point in time.

A chapter about the multiple antecedent stimuli that surround us and affect our behavior derives from the eco-behavioral approach, where *eco* refers to the complex "stimulus ecology" in which we live.[1] Multitudes of antecedent stimuli from both outside and inside the body affect our behavior. Some are orderly, others chaotic—and most lie somewhere in between. In everyday life, people are constantly surrounded by complex stimulus collages, and the eco-behavioral approach focuses special attention on the antecedent side of the equations: on the USs, CSs, S^Ds, or S^Δs. All four types of stimuli precede behavior and partially control the future appearance of the behavior. Neutral stimuli are a fifth type of stimuli in the sensory collage. Neutral stimuli have no particular influence on behavior, but they can become conditioned into CSs, S^Ds, or S^Δs during Pavlovian or operant learning.

Whereas most artists' collages are created to be looked at—and not to be tasted or felt—the stimulus collage of everyday life is a rich intermingling of sights, sounds, odors, tastes, touches, and feelings.[2] Some of the stimuli capture our attention, whereas others lie in the background or are not consciously perceived; some stimuli have strong effects on our behavior, whereas others have only weak effects. The eco-behavioral approach requires that we become sensitive to the ever changing stimulus collage and how it influences all aspects of our behavior—our thoughts, emotions, and actions. When a person looks at a beautiful painting, the stimuli from the canvas can function as both CSs and S^Ds. The CSs of the painting may elicit positive emotional responses and reinforce pausing to admire the work. The stimuli also function as S^Ds for thinking about the picture, commenting to a fellow viewer, and perhaps stepping forward to see a small detail painted in a dark corner of the canvas.

The ability of any stimulus in the stimulus collage to influence behavior depends on (1) an individual's past conditioning (or lack of conditioning) with the stimulus and similar stimuli, (2) the salience (or conspicuousness) of the stimulus in the present stimulus collage, and (3) the presence of other stimuli that evoke facilitative or competing responses.[3] These points are illustrated in the following three paragraphs.

First, *past conditioning* can cause any stimulus (even relatively small or faint ones) to have significant influences over behavior.[4] A mother who hears the faint cry of her sick baby in the next room may find her thoughts and attention instantly drawn to the child even though she is in the midst of an interesting conversation. The baby's crying functions as a CS that elicits the mother's emotional responses and an S^D for the mother to go to the aid of the sick child. (The baby's crying became an emotion-eliciting CS for the mother during past conditioning in which crying correlated with danger to the infant and problems for the mother. Crying became an S^D for the mother to help her infant because helping was negatively reinforced by termination of stressful situations.)

Second, if the infant had been in the same room with the mother, early signs of distress would have been more *salient*—more conspicuous and noticeable—to the mother. She would have noticed the infant's restlessness and early whimpers (which were not salient when the child was in the next room), and she would have helped the infant before the child began to cry. Thus, stimuli that are nearby and salient tend to affect behavior more than distant and inconspicuous stimuli.[5]

Third, the ability of any given stimulus to control behavior can be increased or decreased by *facilitative or competing responses* produced by other stimuli in the sensory collage. If the mother of a crying infant had been talking to a neighbor about her efforts to be a good mother when her baby first began to cry, the S^Ds of the conversation about being a good parent would have facilitated her operants of taking care of the child. On the other hand, if the mother had been engaged in a bitter quarrel with her husband about his neglecting the child, the S^Ds of the quarrel might have set the occasion for competing responses. She might have said, "There she is crying again. Why don't *you* go see what's

the matter this time? How come *I'm* always the one?" This turn of events makes it unlikely that the mother would be quick to respond to her baby's crying. Distracting stimuli—such as a ringing phone, someone at the door, something burning in the
kitchen—could also bring up competing responses that would decrease the chances that
the mother would respond quickly to her child crying.

Stimulus Control

*Those stimuli in the sensory collage that are effective in producing responses are said to
have **stimulus control** over the responses.*[6] The cries of a sick baby usually have stimulus
control over a mother's and father's coming to help the baby. However, stimulus control
is relative and depends on the relationship among the numerous elements of the stimulus
collage. As we have already seen, the ability of the baby's cry to control the mother's responses depends on the other stimuli in the stimulus collage.

Everyday conversations and social interactions clearly show how multiple stimuli—both verbal and nonverbal—control a large range of social responses. Sometimes the
stimuli keep the conversation on a single, logical track—sometimes not. Imagine yourself
having a conversation with three friends, trying to decide what to do over the weekend.
Erica suggests that the plans be located within a 50-mile radius of here, so driving time is
held to a minimum. Such a logical plan can serve as an S^D for Peter to offer a second rational comment: "And it's so hot outside, we should go someplace cool." Each logical
suggestion moves the stimulus collage toward a more logical plan.

But humans are not computers, robots, or logic machines, and the sensory collage
can contain stimuli that prompt digressions—sometimes causing the whole conversation
to be sidetracked. Kelly enthusiastically suggests a cool mountain area where you could
all go backpacking and hiking. Her conversation provides numerous S^Ds that control your
thoughts, memories, and "free associations"[7] about hiking and camping—the backcountry
trips you took last year, the time you got poison oak all over your arms and face, seeing
six deer, and so forth. The stimulus collage also provides CSs that elicit emotional responses: Kelly's enthusiasm, smiles, and vivid descriptions are powerful CSs that elicit
positive emotional responses that make the idea of backpacking sound appealing. However, your stimulus collage also includes your thoughts about the poison oak—which are
CSs that elicit bad feelings and partially counteract your positive feelings.

Kelly's words and your thoughts fill your sensory collage with S^Ds for your operant
habit of telling your rather humorous poison oak story. But just before you open your
mouth, Damien interjects, in response to the S^Ds of his stimulus collage: "I heard those
trails were closed due to fire hazard; and anyway there is a big show opening at the fairground that *everybody* is going to." Suddenly the stimulus collage has been radically altered by Damien's words, and a whole new set of topics occur to you. You are torn:
Should you go back and mention the poison oak experience, or blurt out a funny story
about what happened last year at the fairground? After Damien tells his story, he looks at
you and asks, "What do you think about the big show?" This is just one more S^D for the
fairground story, and out it comes. Everyone laughs. Then Kelly has another story about
last year's fair. The original conversation about hiking has been lost: The conversation

has been "sidetracked." As the S^Ds about backpacking disappear, so do the urges to tell your poison oak story—which had been so strong just a few minutes before.

Sidetracked conversations occur when one person's comments serve as S^Ds for someone else to talk about a different topic. This digression can, in turn, provide new S^Ds for other verbal responses, such as the traffic congestion near the fairgrounds; and each new digression may keep a conversation moving away from the logic of the original topic—finding a cool place to go within 50 miles. Perhaps someone eventually asks, "How did we get on this topic of traffic congestion?" Hunting for logic may not help as much as tracing back through the S^Ds that sidetracked the discussion at various points.

Stimuli from sources outside the conversation can also affect the total impact of the sensory collage. If someone turns on some loud music, the conversation will tend to become louder, due to negative reinforcement—since speakers raise their voices to escape the aversive consequences of not being able to hear what other people are saying. Next, blaring music and loud talk are often S^Ds for laughing, acting a bit sillier than normal, and moving to the beat of the music. The S^Ds of quiet music could have had very different effects, for example, setting the occasion for quieter, perhaps more gentle or serious conversation.

Clocks, magazines, ashtrays, CD covers, and other background stimuli in the room also complicate the stimulus collage. Although they may only have subtle background effects, at times they emerge from the background and have noticeable effects on behavior. Damien begins casually twirling an ashtray on the coffee table. For him, the ashtray is an S^D for twirling, even though Damien does not notice what he is doing—because his attention is focused more intently on the conversation. However, for Kelly, the twirling ashtray may be an S^D for saying, "That makes me nervous, Damien. Could you please stop?" This S^D may lead Damien to stop and say, "I wasn't trying to bug you." While glancing around the room, your eyes happen to focus on the clock. Suddenly this previously inconspicuous S^D in the background becomes a salient stimulus: "Oh no! It's four o'clock and I promised I'd be downtown at three-thirty." This comment again sidetracks the conversation and heads it in a new direction.

The stimulus collage contains multiple antecedent stimuli that affect our thoughts, words, and other behavior. Sometimes the flow of stimuli controls smooth chains of thought and action that seem completely *logical and well ordered.* But complex and jumbled stimulus inputs can easily evoke *complicated and disjointed* response patterns—such as conversations that are repeatedly sidetracked.

External and Internal Stimuli

The antecedent stimuli that influence behavior can be located either outside or inside the body.[8] The stimuli that lie *outside* the body are detected through the five senses and they can influence both Pavlovian and operant behavior. Seeing or hearing a friend coming in the front door alters your stimulus collage by adding *external* stimuli that can be (1) CSs for conditioned reflexive responses such as pleasant feelings and a smile, and (2) S^Ds for operant behaviors such as saying something congenial. Your friend's responses to this then serve as the antecedent stimuli for your next set of thoughts, feelings, and responses.

Stimuli from *inside* your body also contribute to the total stimulus collage, affecting both Pavlovian and operant behavior. A toothache is an internal US that elicits the feelings of pain. It is also an internal S^D for such operants as taking a pain reliever and calling your dentist. If a strenuous hike causes your heart to beat rapidly, the internal sensations may function as CSs, especially if you have reason to worry about the possibility of heart attacks. Likewise, feeling excess rumbling or pain in the stomach can function as a CS that elicits anxiety in a person sensitized to the possibility of getting ulcers. Either of these internal stimuli may also function as S^Ds that lead a person to call the doctor. Internal stimuli can elicit pleasurable feelings, too. When people are in good physical condition, the bodily sensations of deep breathing and strong muscle movements while jogging or climbing in the mountains are likely to be CSs of internal origin that elicit pleasurable emotional responses. The internal stimuli may also serve as S^Ds for talking to others about how good it feels to be healthy and strong.

A person's behavior can be influenced simultaneously by both external and internal stimuli. The external CSs of hearing your employer criticize your latest work may bring a lump to your throat, a quiver to your voice, strong heartbeats, and other emotional responses. These responses then serve as internal S^Ds for thoughts such as "I hope she doesn't think I'm nervous about this. She might think I'm not in control of the situation." Your thoughts that your nervousness might be visible to your employer may add to the internal CSs that elicit further emotional responses—such as sweating—and these responses might be S^Ds for additional worried thoughts. Sometimes people's anxiety escalates as each new worrisome thought is a CS that elicits strong emotional responses that serve as the S^Ds for more thoughts about the situation *not* being in control.

Fortunately, studies show that *other people are much less aware of our emotional responses than we are.* Many of our emotional responses are inside our bodies or hidden by our clothing; thus, these internal responses are less noticeable to others than they are to us.[9] This is important to know, because it helps us avoid the spiral of rising anxiety that results from fearing that others can see how worried or nervous we are in difficult situations. Feeling some internal anxiety responses now serves as an S^D to think, "She can't notice how nervous I really am if I simply talk in a steady and polite manner." People who can fake smiles that look convincing even when they are anxious are often perceived as happy and likeable by others.[10]

Many of our behaviors come under the control of both external and internal stimuli. Eating, for example, can be controlled by numerous external stimuli (such as the clock hands pointing to noon, being in the kitchen, smelling delicious food, seeing other people eating, being told to eat) and internal stimuli (such as stomach sensations that indicate hunger). Lean people and heavyset people often learn to respond to quite different S^Ds for eating.[11] Slim people tend to respond mostly to the internal S^Ds of an empty stomach as the primary cue to eat something, and they do not eat when they are not hungry. On the other hand, stocky people are likely to eat whenever they encounter any of numerous external S^Ds related to food. Thus, just walking through the kitchen can add 200 calories to an already plump person and have no effect on a lean person. Many of the S^Ds in the kitchen entice the plump person to try a piece of candy, peek into the refrigerator, and finish off the leftovers. These external S^Ds have little effect on the slender person, unless an empty stomach signals that the body needs food.

People's own behavior can influence the salience of stimuli—from both outside and inside the body—that control their next responses. For several days Linda has been intending to see her professor about a test question she thought was unfair. As she stands in front of the professor's door, ready to knock, she feels her heart pounding in her chest. Linda has had some embarrassing experiences while talking with professors: On two occasions, they have asked her questions she could not answer and then been critical of her lack of understanding. Hence approaching a professor's office to talk creates the *external CSs* that elicit anxiety and a pounding heart. The closer Linda gets to knocking on the professor's door, the more external CSs there are that elicit emotional responses, and the harder her heart pounds. She walks away from the professor's door—pretending to read something on a nearby bulletin board—and her heart ceases pounding so hard. She returns to the professor's door, again exposing herself to the external CSs that cause her heart to start pounding. As Linda wonders what she should do, her thoughts serve as *internal CSs* that also elicit emotional responses and affect her heartbeat. Her first thought is a fear-eliciting CS: "What if Professor Adams thinks I'm stupid for asking her this simple question?" Linda's heart pounds more strongly. Then Linda has a thought that is a CS for relaxation and comfort: "But she told us to come in and chat, and she seems so friendly." The pounding of her heart decreases a little. "Teachers are human after all." Another decrease in the pounding. "But what if I can't think of anything to say? She'll think I'm stupid." The pounding of her heart becomes more noticeable. Whenever Linda thinks about possible failures, her thoughts are CSs that elicit anxiety and stronger heartbeats; but thinking about good outcomes creates internal CSs for calmer emotions.

It is possible for the internal and external stimuli of the total stimulus collage to control *competing responses,* in which case one response may interfere with the expression of a second response. Studies show that many people cannot enjoy sexual relations when their sexual reflexes are disrupted by competing responses.[12] Physical stimulation of the genitals provides numerous external USs that normally elicit pleasurable sexual responses. However, negative thoughts about sex can function as CSs that elicit anxiety and guilty feelings, which are emotional responses that interfere with normal sexual functioning. Anxiety alone can stifle sexual arousal, causing a man to lose his erection, a woman to cease vaginal lubrication, and both to fall short of orgasm. During childhood some people are taught that sex is "dirty" or "sinful." This socialization can cause thoughts of sex to become CSs that elicit anxiety and guilt. Even after a person is married, the guilt-eliciting CSs often remain strong and interfere with sexual responses. Although sexual responses can be elicited by the USs of genital stimulation and any related CSs, people who think of sex as "dirty" or "sinful" are counteracting the natural sexual reflex with internal cognitive CSs that elicit negative and disruptive emotions.

Although we cannot easily observe the internal stimuli that other people experience, we can perceive and study our own internal USs, CSs, S^Ds, and S^Δs. An increased awareness of stimulus control can help us design behavior modification activities that weaken undesirable stimulus control and strengthen desirable alternatives—as when a person learns to respond to socially induced anxiety by thinking: "Keep talking in a steady and polite manner and most of my nervousness will never show to others."

OPERANT GENERALIZATION

When an operant behavior has been reinforced in the presence of certain stimuli and comes under S^D control of those stimuli, there is a tendency for similar stimuli to control the response, too. If you buy one CD by Jewel and like it, that rewards buying one Jewel CD and increases the chances you would buy a different CD with the word "Jewel" on it. *This is **stimulus generalization** as seen in operant conditioning.*[13] The more closely that some new stimulus resembles the original S^Ds associated with reinforcement, the more likely it is to control the operant, too.

For example, on first hearing the music of Bach, a person may learn to identify one piece of Bach's work. Gradually, this piece of music becomes an S^D for saying, "That's Bach's 'Toccata and Fugue.'" Generalization enters the picture when the person hears a new piece of music and responds, "That's Bach. I just know it!" Some features of the new music are sufficiently similar to those of the earlier piece that they control the verbal operant, "That's Bach." The person's generalized response may be right or wrong. The new piece may in fact be by Bach, or it may be by Vivaldi or Corelli; nevertheless, any response to stimuli that are similar to the original S^D reflects operant generalization—no matter whether it is correct or incorrect.

Operant generalization occurs all the time, when we confront new situations that resemble S^D patterns we learned to respond to in the past. *The more similar the present stimulus collage is to the stimulus settings in which a behavior was learned, the more likely that behavior is to occur.* If someone asks directions while on the street, one efficient response is to give verbal instructions and to point in the direction the person should go. When talking to people with reasonable vision, pointing is generally reinforced by hearing genuine thanks for the help. Thus, pointing is reinforced in the S^D context of "a stranger asking for directions on the street."

The operant behavior of pointing while giving directions usually generalizes to other similar stimulus settings such as S_1 and S_2 in Figure 5–1. Consider setting 1 (S_1), where a blind person stops a passerby on the street and asks directions. Many pedestrians

FIGURE 5–1   The probability of pointing in various stimulus contexts.

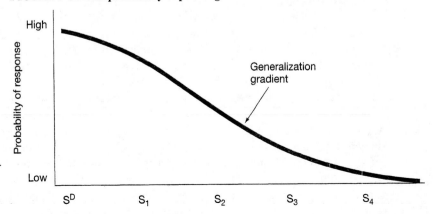

will point toward the blind person's destination while giving verbal instructions. Obviously, the pointing is of no use to the blind person and not likely to be reinforced; yet the stimuli of this situation (S_1) are so similar to those of a sighted person's asking directions on the street (the original S^D) that generalization is likely (unless the passerby had prior experience helping the blind).

If we consider another stimulus collage (S_2) that differs even more from the original learning context (S^D), the operant of pointing is somewhat less likely. Nevertheless, people sometimes do point in these circumstances. When asked for directions while standing inside a room with no windows for seeing the outside environment (S_2), a person is less likely to point than when outside; but pointing sometimes occurs inside bunker-like buildings. When a speaker cannot see the other person, such as while giving directions by phone (S_3), pointing is even less likely. When giving directions in a letter or e-mail (S_4), most people would never point while writing the directions.

The probability of responding to each of the stimuli (S^D, S_1, S_2, S_3, S_4) produces a curve called a **generalization gradient** (see Fig. 5–1). The shape of the curve—that is, the amount of generalization to new stimuli—depends on the nature and salience of the stimuli in each collage, along with a person's past history of conditioning.

Whenever a behavior comes under the control of specific S^Ds in one setting, there is a certain amount of generalization to other similar situations. *The degree of generalization depends on the number of cues in the other settings that resemble crucial S^Ds in the first stimulus collage.* Many of the salient and predictive stimuli in the contexts where a behavior is reinforced take on partial S^D control over that behavior.[14] In the original learning context—the S^D context—where several of these predictive stimuli are present, the probability of responding is high. As a person moves into situations that are *increasingly different* from the original S^D context in which the response is reinforced, *there are fewer and fewer stimuli* that resemble the original S^Ds. *As the stimulus collage becomes increasingly different from the original one, and the number of controlling S^Ds for the response declines, the probability of the response declines.* This is seen in Figure 5–1: The probability of the response declines as the stimulus context changes from S^D to S_4.

In addition, the generalized response is usually performed less quickly, less intensely, and less rapidly than the response in the original S^D context as one moves out the generalization gradient from S^D to S_4.[15] If a writer tried to point while e-mailing a friend directions for traveling some place, it might be a small finger movement associated with typing "then take a right turn." A 10-year-old girl, Reyna, did self-injurious behavior (SIB), hurting herself many times each day. Figure 5–2 shows that Reyna's SIB fits a generalization gradient that suggests her behavior was reinforced by social attention:[16] The closer other people were to her, the more SIB she did. The S^Ds of having other people closer than a half meter set the occasion for most frequent SIB, and larger distances set the occasion for less and less SIB. After Reyna received behavioral therapy—involving extinction and occasional rewards given for not hurting herself—her SIB was reduced to zero.

Benefits of Generalization.   Given the fact that life involves an ever changing series of events, we are never exposed to exactly the same stimulus collages in which our re-

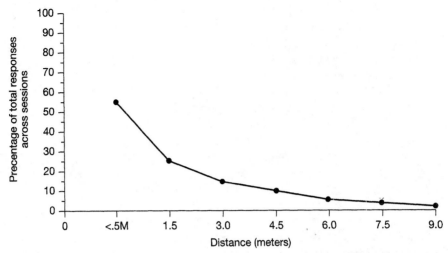

FIGURE 5–2   This generalization gradient clearly shows that Reyna did self-injurious behavior most frequently when other people were close to her (within a half meter of her). The further away from her that other people were, the less S^D control they had over her behavior, hence the behavior was less frequent with greater distances.

(Adapted from "Assessment of Stimulus Generalization Gradients in the Treatment of Self-injurious Behavior" by J.S. Lalli, F.C. Mace, K. Livezey, & K. Kates, 1998. *Journal of Applied Behavior Analysis, 31*, pp. 479–483. Copyright by the Journal of Applied Behavior Analysis, 1998.)

sponses were learned in the past. As the Greek philosopher Heraclitus observed some 2,500 years ago, "You could not step twice in the same river, for other waters are ever flowing on to you." The world is always changing. *We never experience exactly the same stimulus patterns twice; yet our world is similar enough from day to day that we can respond to our ever-changing environment with many of the same operants that worked for us yesterday.* This is the first benefit of generalization.

Second, as we gain skills, we often benefit from our ability to apply them to new situations—due to generalization. Once we learn how to drive a car with an automatic transmission in an original S^D context, our new skills may generalize such that we are moderately well prepared to drive a stick shift car, the S_1 situation—and even a big U-Haul truck, the S_2 situation. The tendency for skills that were reinforced in one context to occur in similar situations (via generalization) is often efficient and time saving: Otherwise we would have to learn how to deal with each new situation from scratch.

Extent of Generalization.   The amount of stimulus generalization that occurs in any learning situation can vary.[17] If your college helps you learn to be intellectually critical in certain courses, the topics dealt with become S^Ds for posing questions and being analytical about those topics; and your tendency to apply these critical skills may generalize extensively, moderately, or only to a small degree, depending on numerous variables. Figure 5–3 shows these three generalization gradients. In cases of *extensive generalization,* many

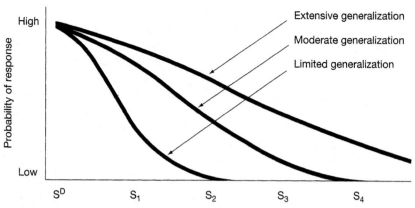

FIGURE 5–3   Three generalization gradients.

new situations (S_1, S_2, S_3, and to some degree S_4) will set the occasion for being intellec-tually critical. When there is *limited generalization,* a person may be intellectually critical in situations that are quite similar to the original learning environment (the S^D context), but never show this response in situations that differ much from the original S^D context (such as situations S_2, S_3, and S_4). Teachers who want to help people learn extensive gen-eralization try to (1) give large numbers of examples of situations where the skills they teach can be useful and (2) encourage people to apply their knowledge so the natural re-wards of having the information can strengthen their generalized responses across numer-ous situations.[18]

If generalization is too broad and causes a person to emit an operant behavior in inappropriate circumstances, the operant is said to be **overgeneralized.** If parents tell a young child to always do what the teacher says, the child may overgeneralize and uncriti-cally obey a teacher even when the teacher is requesting inappropriate behavior, such as sexual contact. Overgeneralization can occur when a person learns a "new fact" and be-gins to "explain" everything in terms of this one verbal phrasiology. When first learning about sunspots and their effects on climate, some children start using "sunspot theory" to explain daily weather, their parents' moods, bad test grades, and much more—without awareness of the limits of sunspot effects. After learning that diet can affect health, vital-ity, and mood, some people overgeneralize and begin to explain *all* types of ailments and psychological conditions in terms of diet. This type of overgeneralization is nicely sum-marized in the old saying, "Give a small boy a hammer, and he will find that everything needs hammering." Once in possession of the new tool, the child not only hammers nails (the appropriate behavior), but hammers tables, chairs, rocks, pets, and many other things (which are the inappropriate and overgeneralized behaviors).

If generalization is too narrow and fails to produce the two benefits described in the prior section, the operant is called **undergeneralized.** Students may learn a theory in the classroom or from a book and may be able to express their knowledge on a test, but often their new intellectual skills do not generalize to help them understand events in their own lives that were not included in the textbook examples. Their learning has not generalized far enough. Undergeneralization can be a problem in psychological therapies, including behavior modification.[19] In a therapeutic environment, people may overcome problems with stuttering, shyness, temper flare-ups, or alcoholism, but the new skills may not generalize enough to help them in their everyday environments.

Often special steps must be included in therapy to overcome the problems of undergeneralization. Some therapists make the therapeutic environment as similar as possible to people's everyday environments—or they carry out the therapy in natural settings—to improve generalization.[20] Sometimes friends and family are taught how to continue behavior modification practices in the home or workplace in order that newly acquired skills can be reinforced in everyday environments. And this is our next topic.

Additional Reinforcement. *No matter how much an operant has generalized, reinforcing it in new contexts can further increase the probability of the response in these new contexts.* A college student who learned to be intellectually critical of politicians (S^D) may show moderate generalization by being intellectually critical of government bureaucrats (S_1) and law enforcement officers (S_2), although not being too critical of university bureaucrats (S_3) or professors (S_4). This original generalization gradient shows a decrease in response probability as the stimulus collage becomes progressively different from the original S^D collage (see Fig. 5–4). What if a student receives reinforcers for being intellectually critical—in a polite manner—when dealing with all the situations from S_1 through S_4? Sometimes people receive reinforcement for critical thinking in a large number of contexts, if others respect and admire them for "using their brains" and making astute observations. Frequent social reinforcement for critical comments in many social contexts increases the probability of critical responses in all the situations shown by the solid line in Figure 5–5. (All the stimuli in Fig. 5–5 are now labeled S^Ds, because astute criticism has been reinforced when dealing with every stimulus.) People who have been rewarded for applying their critical skills to all types of authority figures often take great pleasure in finding fault with everyone who wields social power.

FIGURE 5–4   **The original generalization of critical skills.**

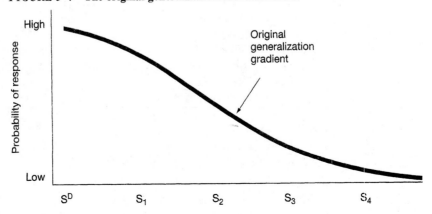

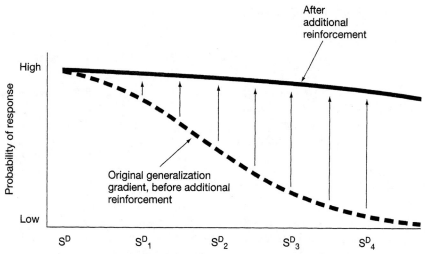

FIGURE 5–5   The probability of critical responses after reinforcement in various stimulus contexts.

Generalization helps explain why operants learned in one context are emitted in new situations. If the response works well in the new context, it will be reinforced. At first the generalized response may appear tentative, weak, or incomplete in the new context, but after being reinforced, it may become a high probability response to every new S^D context in which it is useful.

OPERANT DISCRIMINATION

In the early phases of learning any operant behavior, it is not uncommon for people to do the operant in both appropriate and inappropriate contexts. A teen who is first learning to drive a car often pushes the accelerator pedal at the correct moment and at inappropriate times, too. *As an operant is followed by reinforcement in some stimulus contexts, but not others, people learn to respond differently to different antecedent stimuli. This is the process of learning operant discriminations.* As a teen learns to drive, operant discriminations develop: Green traffic lights become S^Ds for pushing the accelerator and red lights become S^Δs that inhibit hitting the accelerator pedal. Discrimination occurs when people learn that a response which is reinforced in certain contexts is either punished or not reinforced in other contexts. As student drivers learn the effects of the accelerator pedal, they develop increasingly subtle discriminations about the multiple ways to nudge or hit the pedal.

Whereas generalization involves performing one response in various situations, discrimination involves learning to do the responses in the presence of S^Ds but not when S^Δs are present. *This is stimulus discrimination as seen in operant conditioning.*[21]

When first asked for directions by a blind person, you might answer and give your generalized response of pointing, because the current stimulus collage is so similar to all prior contexts in which pointing has been reinforced. However, pointing is not instrumental in communicating with blind people. It is wasted effort, hence not reinforced. In fact, it may be punished. Your pointing and saying, "Go that way" may be followed by a comment, "I'm blind. I can't see." This comment may serve as a punisher for pointing when giving directions to blind people: It may elicit negative emotional responses and make you feel insensitive. Due to this punishment, the special glasses or white cane used by the blind person becomes a discriminative stimulus (S^Δ) that inhibits pointing.

*The primary cause of discrimination learning is **differential reinforcement,** which occurs when any given behavior can be followed by reinforcement or punishment and there are antecedent cues that help predict when the behavior will lead to rewards or punishers. Those antecedent stimuli that precede reinforced responses and are good predictors of reinforcement become S^Ds for responding; whereas those antecedent stimuli that precede and predict punishment or nonreinforcement become S^Δs that inhibit responding.* If there is differential reinforcement for pointing—that is, reinforcement for pointing with sighted people, and punishment or nonreinforcement for pointing with blind people—the differential consequences cause predictive stimuli associated with sighted people to become S^Ds for pointing and predictive stimuli associated with blind people to become S^Δs that inhibit pointing. Receiving eye contact from another person is a predictive cue that the person is sighted, and special glasses or canes are predictive cues that the person is blind.

Figure 5–6 shows how differential reinforcement affects generalization gradients. The original generalization gradient for pointing is shown by the dashed line. (This is the same as the generalization curve for pointing shown in Fig. 5–1.) Punishment and nonreinforcement from the blind person decreases the probability of pointing in the presence of the S^Δ indicating blindness. The effects of punishment and nonreinforcement generalize to some degree, so the new response gradient (solid line in Fig. 5–6) is depressed not only in the S^Δ context but also in other contexts. The discriminating person becomes even less likely to point in rooms with no windows, in phone conversations, and while writing e-mail. If the person receives further nonreinforcement or punishment for pointing in

FIGURE 5–6   **The probability of pointing after differential reinforcement.**

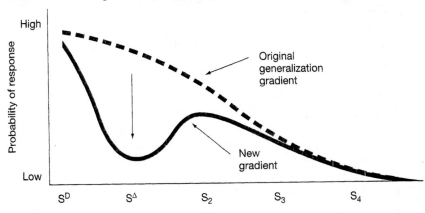

future interactions with blind people, the response curve would be suppressed even further—except in the original S^D situation of "pointing for sighted people," where pointing is still rewarded because it is useful.

Social Sensitivity.   Some people learn to discriminate subtle differences in wines, cheeses, French cooking, and other tastes. Other people do not. Some people learn to discriminate subtle differences in social cues involving facial expressions, tone of voice, body postures, and numerous other aspects of behavior. Others remain insensitive to all but the most obvious social cues. The learning of the subtle discriminations involved in *social sensitivity* is based largely on differential reinforcement.[22]

Facial expressions are important to us because they provide countless predictive stimuli that often correlate with reinforcement or punishment.[23] If everyone wore identical and unmovable masks that hid all facial cues, the masks would be useless in discriminating one person from the next or discriminating between friendly and hostile moods. However, the human face changes in ways that often correlate with a person's inclination to respond to us in a positive or negative manner. For example, when you begin joking with someone who is smiling, there is a better chance that you will experience positive reinforcement than if the person was frowning like a grouch. Thus, smiles are predictive stimuli that become S^Ds, setting the occasion for friendly joking—and many other responses that have been reinforced in this S^D context.

Note that the very same facial expression which functions as an S^D for joking can function as an S^Δ that inhibits other responses. If you try to start a serious philosophical discussion while a friend is smiling, your friend may punish your serious response: "Cut the superserious stuff and have fun for once." If the smiles of others are predictive stimuli that serious talk may be mocked, whereas joking is reinforced, smiles become S^Δs that inhibit heavy philosophizing and S^Ds for joining the joking.

Social sensitivity is also based on the combination of differential reinforcement for *noticing* other people's emotional responses and *accurately describing* those emotions—either out loud or in the inner words of our thoughts.[24] People often comment about each other's moods. "You look sad today, Julie." Julie may reply in a way that provides positive or negative feedback: "Yeah, I really feel blue today," or "No, I just lost a lot of sleep recently." Our skill at identifying the moods of other people can be modified by several types of differential reinforcement: (1) Merely being correct is a reinforcer for many people (and being incorrect is a punisher); (2) Correctly identifying another person's emotional responses often helps coordinate social interaction, hence is reinforcing (whereas errors are less helpful in producing social coordination and reinforcement); (3) People who have learned to value "social sensitivity" automatically experience reinforcement when they have succeeded in being sensitive and punishment when they have been insensitive. As the years go by, some people experience enough repeated differential reinforcement to learn numerous subtle social discriminations. Others do not.

When the social feedback is positive, it reinforces sensitive observations and verbal descriptions of other people's emotional cues; and those cues become S^Ds for making similar sensitive responses in the future. The more that people succeed at judging the moods of others, the more reinforcement they receive for paying attention to social cues, and this

in turn gives them the chance to learn even more advanced and subtle social discriminations. In contrast, people who repeatedly fail to identify social cues correctly may experience so much critical feedback that social cues become S^As that inhibit commenting about
other people's emotions in the future—and S^Ds for sticking with safer, more reinforcing
topics, such as the weather or the latest news. People who have not learned to discriminate
well among the facial expressions and tones of voice of other people are less successful in
their social relations and more depressed than people who have learned to make accurate
social discriminations.[25]

Interestingly, sensitive people may not be able to tell you exactly which stimuli are
serving as the S^Ds for their correct discriminations about the feelings of others.[26] Because
language does not provide all the words needed for describing the countless, complex patterns of facial expressions, it is difficult to learn to talk about—hence to gain "verbal
awareness" of—all the subtle cues that control advanced social discernments. In addition,
there are few reinforcers for explaining how we make accurate discriminations: As long
as we make socially sensitive responses, we receive generous social reinforcement; and
no one asks us, "Exactly what social cues help you be so sensitive?" Thus, a person can
be socially perceptive and empathetic, yet not be able to explain verbally to others which
social cues serve as S^Ds or S^As for the sensitive social distinctions.

Generalization versus Discrimination.   Generalization and discrimination are often described as opposite kinds of effects.[27] ***Generalization*** *refers to the process by which we
respond* <u>*in the same way to different stimuli*</u>*, because we recognize their similarities.* **Discrimination** *refers to the process by which we learn to respond* <u>*in different ways to different stimuli*</u>*, as we notice how they predict different consequences.*

After learning to identify several paintings by Degas, a person may be able to look
at a new picture, recognize the similarities, and say, "That's a Degas!" Generalization *increases* the number of stimuli that will control a response. Discrimination *reduces* the
number of stimuli that will control a response. When looking at a painting by Renoir, a
person may say, "That's a Degas!" If a bystander says, "The sign next to it says it's
Renoir's *Bather*," the mild punishment helps make the picture an S^A that inhibits saying
"Degas" and an S^D for saying "Renoir." Whenever behavior—such as saying "Degas" or
"You look sad today, Julie"—is followed by either reinforcers or punishers, we often
learn to discriminate between antecedent stimuli as S^Ds or S^As. But learning is not always
perfect, and many people make mistakes—by overgeneralizing, undergeneralizing, and
making erroneous discriminations. This is especially clear when we are "tricked" by the
stimulus collage. Law officers play on our imperfect discriminations when they park
empty patrol cars along high-speed roads and place cardboard cutouts that look like officers inside.[28] From a distance, we see a patrol car with two attentive officers. The S^Ds
trick us into putting on our brakes and looking closely as we pass the car. Only when we
are close do we notice that the "officers" are cardboard, not real. Speeders can even be
tricked into putting on the brakes by a full-size picture of a patrol car mounted on ply-
wood and placed next to the road.

When we watch a ventriloquist and dummy performing, we know the dummy is not
alive, yet it is so easy to be tricked into thinking we are hearing a dialogue between the

ventriloquist and lively side-kick. Why? Most of us have been rewarded for watching people's lips as they talk, because moving lips give us cues that help us understand a quiet speaker and conversations in noisy rooms. Moving lips are S^Ds that help us discriminate which person is talking when several people alternate. Hence seeing the ventriloquist's immobile mouth and the dummy's moving lips provide S^Ds to think that the dummy is talking when its lips move—and this deception is further rewarded if we enjoy the illusion that this puppet is alive.[29]

Barry Briskman is a pedophile who is spending decades in prison for tricking and sexually abusing several pubescent girls whom he talked into sexual activities with elaborate stories that they could not discriminate to be false.[30] Barry only interacted with one girl at a time, but he told them all that he was an alien from a distant planet called Cablell. He had come to earth to find exceptionally intelligent and beautiful girls to bring back to his utopian society and its Queen Hiternia. Barry flattered each girl by telling her that she was especially wonderful, and the girls came to trust him. Many were from broken and unhappy homes, and flying off to utopia was very tempting. Once hooked, the girls were told they had to be repeatedly injected with "IRFs"—immunities to ward off space diseases. They also needed to break down their "sub-cons"—subconscious barriers. Barry had each girl begin with strip poker to overcome her sub-cons. After a girl was comfortable with nudity, Barry was ready to inject her with IRFs via sexual intercourse. She knew that it would take repeated injections before she acquired 100 IRFs, the level needed for space travel.

Because most people—if not all—do not have the optimal combination of discrimination and generalization, we are open to the possibility of being tricked or conned if someone knows which stimuli will fool us. Even if no one tries to trick us, we often make imperfect judgments when dealing with the complex stimulus collages that face us each day.

PAVLOVIAN GENERALIZATION

*When a predictive stimulus precedes a reflex and becomes a CS that elicits a reflexive response, stimuli that are similar to the CS will elicit the response, too. This is **stimulus generalization** as seen in Pavlovian conditioning.*[31] New stimuli can elicit a conditioned response to the degree that they physically resemble the original CS to which the response was conditioned.

After a child has been knocked down a few times by the neighbor's big dog, Max, the dog becomes a CS that elicits fear, crying, and other negative emotional responses when the child sees the dog approaching. This fear can generalize to other dogs. Figure 5–7 shows the generalization gradient for the child's fear of various types of dogs. Because other big dogs have certain similarities to Max—large size, loud bark, and big movements—they can also elicit fear in the child, although not as much fear as Max does because these dogs do not look exactly like Max. Medium-sized dogs resemble Max to a lesser degree; hence they have even less ability to elicit the fear responses. Small dogs would be expected to elicit the least fear.

If a child is raised in a home with a very authoritarian father who frequently uses punishment for transgressions, a stern look and harsh voice from the father can become

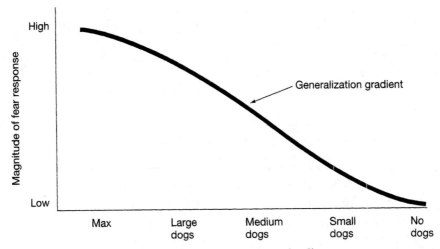

FIGURE 5–7   **The amount of fear elicited by various stimuli.**

CSs for fear because they often precede and predict punishment. This fear response may generalize to other "authority figures" who resemble the father in looks and voice. At age 16, Charlie experiences aversive conditioned emotional responses in the presence of various men in authority roles, especially those who use stern looks and a harsh voice—similar to his father. For example, the serious looks and commanding voices of male police officers elicit moderately strong aversive emotional responses, as shown in Figure 5–8. The minister at Charlie's church elicits less anxiety because he has a gentle and caring voice, though he looks a bit somber and stern. At work, Charlie's boss does not elicit

FIGURE 5–8   **The generalization of fear of "authority figures."**

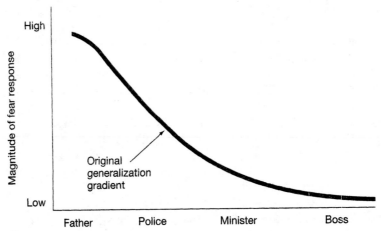

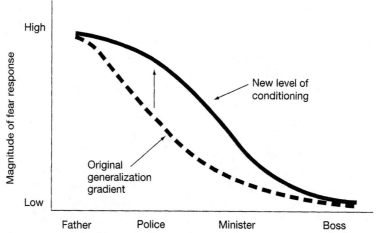

FIGURE 5–9   **The previous generalization gradient after additional conditioning.**

much anxiety because he is cheerful and friendly, almost the opposite of Charlie's authoritarian father.

Additional Conditioning.   *After a reflexive response generalizes to some new stimulus, the response to the new stimulus may become even stronger if it undergoes additional Pavlovian conditioning in the presence of that stimulus.* Charlie's original generalization gradient was based on being punished in the presence of stern looks and harsh rebukes. As Charlie gains additional experience with adults who wield punishers, the original generalization gradient may be modified. After cruising through a yellow traffic light—and seeing only a tiny glimpse of the red light—Charlie is pulled over and ticketed by a police officer. This punishment can boost Charlie's fear of police, as shown by the upward arrow in Figure 5–9. There is a definite increase in the negative conditioned emotional responses elicited by police. Also, this new conditioning generalizes to some degree to all other law officers: Uniforms and patrol cars become new fear-eliciting CSs in the stimulus collage associated with law men. Even Dad and ministers may take on additional generalized ability to elicit negative emotional responses.

PAVLOVIAN DISCRIMINATION

If two stimuli originally elicit the same reflexive response, but one of these stimuli is later paired with a different reflex (or with neutral stimuli), a person will learn to respond differently to the two stimuli. This type of learning is **stimulus discrimination** *in Pavlovian conditioning.*[32] As a result, two stimuli that once elicited similar responses come to elicit different responses.

As the son of a stern and punitive father, Charlie may have several psychological problems for which he eventually seeks counseling. Not knowing where to start, Charlie may go to the local minister for help. When he first visits the minister's office, he may feel some generalized anxiety, as shown by the height of the generalization gradient above the word "minister" in Figure 5–9. The minister looks somewhat somber and stern, though he has a gentle voice. Although these CSs cause Charlie to feel moderately fearful about sharing his problems with the minister, Charlie finds that the minister is warm and friendly. He sensitively discusses Charlie's past and shows compassion for Charlie's problems. The minister's kind and caring behavior elicits no fear. Rather it elicits comfortable feelings of relaxation that countercondition Charlie's original fears of ministers, as shown in Figure 5–10. After several visits to the minister's study, Charlie finds he no longer experiences fear as he interacts with this man. The *new conditioning* has produced a discrimination: Although certain stern-looking authority figures elicit fear, others do not. The minister's face is heavily lined and stern, like Charlie's father's, but his voice is quiet and gentle. The characteristics unique to the minister become crucial parts of the total stimulus collage because they elicit discriminated conditioned responses to otherwise stern-looking people.

Discriminations are learned when there are different patterns of conditioning associated with various stimuli that had once seemed to be similar. Although some stimuli continue to be paired with the original fear response, others are not. This differential conditioning produces discrimination.

As we proceed through life, each of us has a vast number of conditioning experiences with authority figures—and all other types of people—linking many different emotional responses with each individual. These different experiences condition a multitude of fine discriminations that no diagram can easily convey. One minister may be very kind; another, cold and aloof. One boss may be friendly, generous, and fair, and the next is a tyrant. Because we all have unique histories of Pavlovian conditioning that include complex interactions of generalized and discriminated responses, we all feel unique conditioned emotions to the multiple stimulus collages in our lives.

FIGURE 5–10　The generalization gradient after discrimination conditioning.

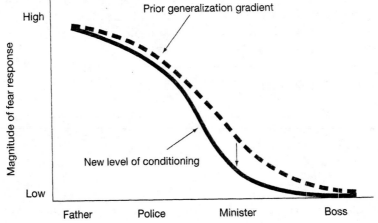

THE ROLE OF WORDS IN THE STIMULUS COLLAGE

Words can appear in either the external or internal parts of the stimulus collage. In the written or spoken form, external words often play an important role in the control of behavior. Even when alone and quiet, people tend to carry on silent internal verbal monologues with themselves.

Both external and internal words can function as CSs and S^Ds or S^Δs. The role of words as CSs is often most visible in young children.[33] A simple ghost story can frighten a young child because it contains so many words that function as fear-eliciting CSs for children. Happy fairy tales, in contrast, contain words that are CSs for pleasant emotions and thus can elicit smiles and laughter from children. Even adults can talk or think themselves into the depths of depression if they ponder too many words that are CSs for negative emotional responses. Conversely, by focusing on words that function as CSs for pleasant emotions, people can talk or think themselves into an optimistic, cheerful mood. Martin Seligman (1998) argues that most of us deserve to use more positive words in describing our lives. After all, most of us have much better lives than people of similar ages just 50 or 100 years ago!

Words can also be S^Ds or S^Δs. Words such as "What time is it?" are S^Ds that frequently set the occasion for other people to tell us the time. But the subtle effects of words are important, too. Seeing how people lived 50–100 years ago on the History Channel gives us visual S^Ds for saying or thinking positive statements about our present lives: "We have so much more freedom from disease and poverty than people in our society just several decades ago—not to mention greater freedom to travel and experience life's diversity." These positive words of appreciation are S^Δs that inhibit thoughts of self-pity or doom and gloom.

Complex or Ambiguous Situations

The countless stimuli to which you are exposed each day have complex effects on your choice of friends, career, clothing styles, and the toothpaste you use. Words that all point in the same direction can forcefully lead us in that direction. For example, hearing "thou shalt not kill" and "killing can lead to life in prison or the death sentence" successfully direct most of us away from killing other people. But much of life is more ambiguous than the issue of murder. What if we enter a stimulus situation where countless verbal and nonverbal stimuli point in different directions? We may feel torn: What to do? Our emotions may be too complex to understand.

When a situation is complex or ambiguous and people do not know how to respond to it, authoritative words can often have a powerful influence in controlling behavior. When several thirsty hikers come upon a pool of water in an otherwise dry streambed, they may find themselves in an ambiguous situation. The water functions as an S^D for drinking; but the slightly stagnant condition of the water serves as an S^Δ that inhibits drinking. As they vacillate between drinking and not drinking, a local person approaches them and says, "That water's bad." The verbal label adds crucial discriminative stimuli—verbal S^Δs—to the total stimulus collage and brings an end to the hikers' vacillation. The verbal S^Δs tip the balance in favor of not drinking.

The verbal label also functions as a CS. Prior to hearing the verbal label, the hikers were influenced by both the US of water (which is attractive when people are thirsty) and the CS of a slightly stagnant odor (which is unattractive if people have come to associate such odors with nausea and sickness). At first, the thirsty hikers were torn between the attractive and unattractive stimuli. However, the words "That water's bad" tipped the balance in favor of not drinking because they are CSs that elicit additional aversive feelings.

Much of life is ambiguous and complex, and the verbal labels that happen to be used can influence behavior significantly, especially when context cues lead us to trust the words.

Operant Behavior.   Verbal labels can serve as S^Ds that can have surprising strength in ambiguous situations. Imagine you have just met Thanatos. She is clearly unique. She enjoys making cynical jokes, but always in a friendly way with a chuckle and big smile. She always dresses in black and likes to be called "Thanatos," from a computer game she loves. At times her conversation seems disjointed and difficult to follow. Even the comprehensible things she says seem a little weird. Thanatos writes poetry; but to you, her ten-line gems sound like ten randomly constructed sentences. When you talk with Thanatos, she often breaks into laughter at the oddest times, in places that did not strike you as funny. And as you stand there looking puzzled, wondering what she found so humorous, she launches into an enthusiastic digression that catches you at a loss for words. Is Thanatos crazy? Or maybe she is a genius? Maybe she sees things you are missing, writes poetry that is above your head, and finds your conversation humorous for its simplicity? Or maybe she is zany? The stimuli are ambiguous, and you are not certain how to respond to her behavior.

One day a close friend mentions that Thanatos is truly brilliant. "She's the most creative actress in the Drama Department." You may express your uncertainty; but your friend's words, such as "brilliant," "insightful," "creative," and "gifted," are likely to have a strong effect. If a second person agrees with your friend's judgment that Thanatos is gifted, you are especially likely to be swayed. If you express some lingering doubts— "But what about that insane poetry she writes, signing it 'Thanatos'?"—your friends may explain that she has already had her work published in literary magazines, under the pen name of Thanatos. The new verbal labels are S^Ds that control new thoughts about Thanatos and may alter your future interactions with her. The next time you meet Thanatos, much of the ambiguity will be gone and you will tend to respond to her as a genius. A favorable label often serves as an S^D for thinking and saying positive things about behavior that might not have seemed so creative if displayed by a person who had been labeled as "average." It can also serve as an S^Δ that inhibits labeling Thanatos as "crazy" or "weird."

When clear labels are added to the stimulus collage by a trusted friend, or several other people simultaneously, the labels act as strong, unambiguous S^Ds for responses appropriate to the descriptive words. If everyone had labeled Thanatos as "crazy," "schizophrenic," "demented," and "delusional," those labels could have had a powerful and long-lasting influence on you, quite different from the labels of "gifted" or "genius." Labels that apply to criminals, street people, and the mentally ill are S^Ds that alert many people to expect trouble, to watch for any signs of deviance, and perhaps to shun the stigmatized person. Uncomplimentary labels also tend to be S^Δs that inhibit showing acceptance or friendliness. However, additional words can alter our responses significantly. In one home, the parents may give their children the verbal rule, "Stay away from street people. They may be dangerous." In a second home, parents may give the opposite advice, "Be nice to the street people. They appreciate people who are thoughtful and kind to them."

Once a person has acquired a label—either favorable or stigmatizing—it is often difficult for other people to respond to the person's *behavior* without being controlled by the S^Ds of the *label*.[34] For example, there have been studies in which totally normal people have had themselves committed to mental hospitals—with a fake but official-looking diagnosis of "schizophrenia"—in order to study the effects of this label.[35] At no time did these people display any abnormal behavior. However, once they were labeled as schizophrenics, all the doctors and staff responded to them as if they were like the other patients. The stigmatizing label prevented the doctors and staff from noticing that these "schizophrenics" showed no signs of abnormality.

Reflexive Responses.   Descriptive labels play an important role in determining people's emotional responses in ambiguous situations. Imagine the case of Keiko, who is taking her first airplane trip. During take off and flight, the airplane's vibrations, noises, and sudden jolts due to air turbulence are USs and CSs that may elicit mild anxiety. On the other hand, some of the stimuli in the plane are CSs that elicit relaxation and a sense of calmness: The flight attendants are friendly, and fellow passengers seem calm and comfortable. Thus, the USs and CSs of the stimulus collage—with no words yet spoken—elicit mixed emotional responses that vacillate between mild anxiety and relaxation. If Keiko now begins to listen to the person in the next seat, this person's words add new elements to the stimulus collage. "The last time I took this flight, several passengers got sick; and it feels bumpier today. And those noises. It makes you wonder if the engines will stay on! You remember that tragic accident where almost 300 people were killed when an engine broke off the plane? They spiraled out of control and crashed, nose down, killing everyone! Makes you really worry about flying." These negative verbal labels function as CSs that make Keiko more anxious than before. As Keiko listens to the noises in the plane and thinks about what her fellow passenger had said, the negative words are verbal CSs that elicit even more anxiety.

The opposite could have happened. When air turbulence first elicited mild anxiety, Keiko might have mentioned her misgivings to the person in the next seat and received an optimistic reply. "Oh, I don't think we need to worry. I've read that airplanes are 99.999% safe. Modern planes are built to withstand much more violent conditions than the strongest storm. If you want to worry, do it on the ground when you are riding in a car. Traveling by car is almost 40 times more dangerous per mile than flying. Whenever I fly, I just sit back and relax. I never let the sounds worry me." Positive statements that are based on scientific studies are verbal CSs that can alter Keiko's stimulus collage so that the noises in the plane no longer make her anxious.

In both of these examples, the new flyer may prolong the effects of the fellow passenger's words for hours after they were spoken. The airplane's noises and any turbulence serve as S^Ds for recalling the other passenger's words about the danger or safety of flying, and these words function as internal verbal CSs that elicit either fear or relaxation. Many seasoned travelers have learned to calm themselves on bumpy flights by using verbal labels that are CSs for relaxation.[36] They may begin a lengthy internal conversation with themselves, describing the safety of modern airplanes and rebutting any negative thoughts. Thereby they generate a long series of verbal CSs that elicit relaxation and counteract the potentially fear-eliciting stimuli.

Note that it is much more difficult for verbal labels to alter a person's emotional response when the stimulus collage is not ambiguous. If you are faced with a truly frightening situation—such as a harrowing automobile accident in which three other passengers die—hundreds of positive and reassuring words will have little effect in counteracting the emotions elicited by the unambiguously terrifying experience. At the other extreme, when you are enjoying one of the most positive experiences of life—such as falling in love—even a cynic may not be able to find enough negative words to destroy the beauty of your experience.

BEHAVIOR MODIFICATION

In order to practice behavior modification, people often find it useful to identify the stimuli that control behavior they want to change. If we want to gain better control of our lives, it pays to know what antecedent stimuli control important behaviors, so we can better control those stimuli. *One of the best ways to identify stimulus control of either operant or reflexive behavior is to look for the stimuli that precede and best predict the given behavior.* First, select a target behavior, and then ask which stimuli usually occur just prior to—and are highly correlated with—the behavior. These are the stimuli most likely to control that behavior.

A second way to sensitize yourself to stimulus control is to notice when you feel subjective "urges" or "pressures" to do something—before you do it. These subjective feelings are among the first signs that you are feeling stimulus control, and you can ask, "What stimuli make me feel this 'urge' or 'pressure'?"

The skills for identifying stimulus control can help people modify their own behavior. Nick has a problem that bothers both him and his friends: Every once in a while, he has temper flare-ups and he says things out of anger that he later regrets. To better understand and control the behavior, he might try to locate the *antecedent stimuli* that trigger his anger and harsh words. A good strategy is for him to keep an "anger diary," focused on all the situations in which he has temper flare-ups. The diary directs his attention to the first element of the ABCs of behavior: What are the *antecedent stimuli* that control anger behaviors? All the "who, what, when, and where" questions are useful in identifying antecedents.[37] When Nick has a temper outburst—or even feels close to having one—he may ask himself about the antecedent events. "Who was present just before I started to feel angry? What was happening? What were we doing and saying? What was I thinking? When and where did the events occur?" Usually it is best to write down all the clues revealed by these questions. Because there could be multiple possible stimuli that trigger

Nick's anger, it might take several days or weeks before he has enough self-observations to identify the CSs and S^Ds that cause anger and harsh words.

After keeping an anger diary for 10 days, Nick discovered that he was most likely to get angry with people he knew well. When he was in public or with strangers, he could remain polite and poised even in difficult situations, but with his close friends—especially his fiancée—he tended to blow up quite easily. (Sadly, this pattern is all too common: People often control their tempers and harsh words much better when they are in the presence of strangers than when they are with friends and family.[38])

After making this observation, Nick asked himself, "Why can't I be in better control with my friends and fiancée? After all, I care more about them than I do about the *strangers* I treat more politely!" Nick had all the skills needed for controlling his temper and being considerate with strangers. His self-observations revealed that strangers were the S^Ds for temper control but that there were too few S^Ds to evoke temper control when he was with his friends. To increase the number of S^Ds for controlling his temper with his friends, Nick wrote a lengthy paragraph in his anger diary about the wisdom of controlling his anger with friends. When noticing that he was beginning to get angry, he would break the response chain by verbally reminding himself of the wisdom of temper control: "My friends deserve more considerate treatment." These words are verbal S^Ds that altered his stimulus collage by reminding him to control his temper.

After using these self-reminders on various occasions, Nick noted that several potential temper outbursts were averted. It was rewarding for Nick to see his own progress in gaining control over his anger, and these rewards strengthened his resolve to continue reminding himself to use temper control with close friends. There was a second source of reinforcement to help strengthen the S^D control for considerate behavior when with close friends: His friends and fiancée commented on the nice changes they had noticed in his behavior. His fiancée told him that she enjoyed being with him more now that he did not fly into a rage so easily. She felt better about their relationship and wanted to spend more time with him. Both forms of reinforcement—seeing his own progress and getting positive feedback from people he valued—further reinforced the use of considerate behavior in the S^D context of being with his close friends and lover. After several months, Nick did not even have to remind himself to be considerate: The behavior had come under such strong S^D control of being with all types of people that it appeared naturally, without needing self-reminders.

Knowing how to identify stimulus control can help us better understand many everyday events and modify small details of our own lives. For example, some people love going to horror movies and getting frightened by the suspense, blood, and gore. Many horror movie buffs have asked themselves this question: "If some friends have seen a movie before I see it, should I let them tell me about the special effects? Will their description of the horror scenes make the movie less exciting when I see it?" Studies show that letting another person tell you about the frightening scenes in horror movies *increases* the emotional impact of the movies.[39] An analysis of stimulus control helps explain why. Movie producers and directors design horror films to contain numerous fear-eliciting CSs: rainy nights, dark passageways, eerie noises, and gruesome murders. If you let someone else tell you about a specific movie—the ax murder, the little boy's head flying off his body, and blood spurting out of his neck—the words are CSs that elicit emotions both when you hear them and later when you see the film. As you sit through the movie, your memory of your friend's words adds predictive stimuli that elicit emotional responses *before* the little boy ever gets cornered by the ax murderer. As you wait for the horrible scene, you will be thinking the words that your friend told you and already experiencing the fear-eliciting CSs *before* the ax begins to swing. As a result, you are getting an extra dose of fear-eliciting CSs because you entered the movie theater with verbal descriptions of the gore. Thus, in most cases, having someone tell you about the horrible details beforehand only increases the total number of fear-eliciting CSs in your stimulus collage. This is somewhat like riding in an airplane during a bad storm and listening to a fellow passenger tell you about the horrors of airplane accidents: The other person's words add to the number of CSs that elicit fear. If you want your next horror movie to be more frightening, let someone tell you about it in advance. (But in whodunit movies, do not ask to hear the answers to the questions that are designed to keep you eagerly guessing how things will finally be resolved.)

People can apply the principles of stimulus control for modifying their emotions outside the movie theater. For example, some people's moods swing up and down without their knowing why. When their feelings are obviously related to the stimuli of the moment—as in a horror movie—they have no trouble tracing their emotions to antecedent stimuli. But most of everyday life is far more subtle than a horror movie, and people's moods may gradually swing up and down without their noticing the relevant antecedent stimuli. Many of the CSs of our daily stimulus collage have only weak control over our emotions; hence their effect on our mood is likely to be unnoticed unless we learn to look for antecedent cues related to our emotional responses.

The large number of weak CSs in the stimulus collage can have significant cumulative effects on emotions. If you wake up in a neutral mood (neither happy nor sad), a lucky combination of CSs with weak control over positive emotions might put you in a good mood and make the day brighter, without your being able to point to any single event that was responsible. Too many CSs for aversive emotions could have had the opposite effect, causing you to have a bad day even though you could not locate any single cause. Fortunately, the more closely that people study the relationship of antecedent stimuli and emotional responses, the more alert they become to the events that affect their moods. For example, they may begin to see how important a series of pleasant morning experiences can be for setting the tone of the whole day. If you play some cheerful music from your stack of "happy morning tapes" when you wake up, think about some optimistic topics during breakfast, or have a phone call with an upbeat friend, you may start the day with a positive train of thoughts and feelings that help you focus on the good side of life all day.

All people are aware of some of the stimuli that affect their moods, and they often use this knowledge to avoid CSs for unwanted emotions and revel in CSs that elicit enjoyable emotional responses. You do this type of "mood control" when you put on a favorite tape that makes you feel good or when you avoid reading newspaper articles that depress you. The more that people learn to identify the stimuli that affect their moods, the more skillful they can be at filling their stimulus collage with CSs for the moods they want.

After years of observing correlations between their moods and antecedent stimuli, some people learn to minimize arguments and sharp words (which elicit unpleasant emotions) and to increase the use of kind comments, humor, and friendliness (all of which elicit pleasing emotions). As a result, most people notice a gradual increase in happiness from age 20 to 60—and even later if they are in good health and have good social relations.[40] People who learn to use optimistic words to describe life and predict the future tend to be happier than people who use more negative words.

We all do some behavior modification in our daily lives. Knowledge about behavior principles allows us to do it better.

CONCLUSION

In this chapter we have described the ways in which behavior is influenced by antecedent stimuli: USs, CSs, S^Ds, and S^Δs. In everyday life, behavior is affected by multitudes of stimuli from inside and outside the body. Numerous elements of the stimulus collage often control a variety of operant and reflexive responses. Generalization occurs when a behavior that is under stimulus control of one set of S^Ds, S^Δs, or CSs also appears in the presence of similar stimuli. Undergeneralization indicates that a response has not generalized as far as would be useful, and additional conditioning is needed to increase the stimulus control over the response. Overgeneralization indicates that a response has generalized to stimuli that should not control it. In this case discrimination is likely to occur as we learn that the response is reinforced in the presence of some stimuli, but not in the presence of other stimuli: This causes the cues for reinforcers to become S^Ds and CSs for positive emotions, while the cues associated with punishment and extinction become S^Δs and CSs for negative emotions.

Words and verbal thoughts are elements of the stimulus collage that often have a great deal of influence over behavior. Thinking positive thoughts and recalling wise words can help us create better days than do negative thoughts and angry, antisocial words. Verbal stimuli can be especially powerful in complex or ambiguous situations where the other stimuli in the collage are too contradictory to control any single predominant response pattern. To use the principles of stimulus control for behavior modification, people need to identify the stimuli that control a target behavior by looking for the stimuli that both precede and predict that behavior. Also, the stimuli that trigger our "urges" or make us feel "pressured" to do a behavior are likely to have stimulus control. The questions about "who, what, when, and where" help us locate relevant antecedent stimuli. Learning to identify stimulus control is useful for gaining knowledge of and control over our thoughts, emotions, and behavior.

QUESTIONS

1. Why is a mother likely to notice the faint cry of her infant in the next room? Why is an auto mechanic likely to hear problematic engine noises in our car even though we cannot?
2. What internal stimuli have you noticed? Pounding heart? Painful teeth? Butterflies in the stomach? Nausea? Bone bruises? Sore joints? How can these stimuli serve as S^Ds that control operants? How can these stimuli serve as CSs that elicit reflexes, including emotions?

3. Can you explain how operants generalize? Why do you point when giving someone directions about where to go? When does this response generalize to circumstances where it is not needed? What is a generalization gradient?

4. How do we learn to discriminate when and where operants are most useful? Is it relevant to their having good effects or bad effects? How do consequences make antecedent cues—about when, where, who, and how—into S^Ds or S^Δs?

5. Can you explain how conditioned reflexes generalize? If you learned to fear *large* space aliens, how would the principle of generalization predict your level of fear of *medium* size and *small* space aliens?

6. How does discrimination learning occur during Pavlovian conditioning? What would happen if all the next space aliens that you met were only 80% as large as the first space alien you learned to fear (in question 5)—but all the new ones were very kind and lovable? How would your emotions be affected by this Pavlovian discrimination?

7. Can you give an example that shows how words can alter the stimulus collage? Why are words especially powerful in complex and ambiguous situations? Give an example showing that effect.

8. How does knowledge about the stimulus collage help us practice behavior modification? What two techniques are useful for identifying stimulus control? Give one or two examples that show why it is rewarding to learn to identify stimulus control for modifying behavior.

NOTES

1. For a more extensive discussion of the topic, see Nevin (1971a); Rilling (1977); Rodewald (1979); Greenwood, Delquadri, and Hall (1984); Evans and Matthews (1992); Dinsmoor (1995a,b); Rescorla (1999a).

2. Although laboratory research on USs, CSs, S^Ds, and S^Δs often focuses on simple situations in which only a small number of stimuli are studied at a given time, natural settings are more complex; hence it is imperative to consider an entire collage of stimuli—including context cues—when studying behavior in natural environments (Greenwood, Delquadri & Hall, 1984; Harrison, 1990; Lynch & Green, 1991).

3. In addition to these three factors, the effectiveness of USs depends on (1) the degree to which we are biologically prepared to respond to them, and (2) in the case of USs that function as primary reinforcers, the individual's current state of deprivation or satiation.

4. Kohlenberg, Hayes, and Hayes (1991).

5. During operant and Pavlovian conditioning, a salient stimulus can overshadow less salient (but more valid) stimuli and gain an undue amount of stimulus control over the responses being conditioned (Dinsmoor, 1995b; Kamin, 1969; Mackintosh, 1975, 1977; Rescorla & Wagner, 1972; Singh & Solman, 1990; Wilkie & Willson, 1992). Even after a valid S^D or CS has gained control over an operant or reflexive response, a more salient stimulus can mask the S^D or CS control of the valid stimulus.

6. Skinner (1969); Harrison (1991); Lynch and Green (1991); Dinsmoor (1995a); J. Moore (1995); Saunders and Williams (1998); Wixted (1998).

7. Free associations are not free in the sense of being uncaused. They are evoked by S^Ds such as the thoughts, words, or other events in the current stimulus collage. They are described as free associations only because they are unexpected and surprising, that is, they are not the most logical or predictable responses to the S^Ds (see Chapter 15).

8. Although stimuli from inside the body can gain stimulus control over operants and reflexive responses much the same as can stimuli from outside the body, it is harder for society to help the individual learn to correctly identify internal stimuli than external ones (Baldwin, 1985; J. Moore, 1995; Skinner, 1974; Wulfert, Dougher, & Greenway, 1991).

9. McEwan and Devins (1983); Rapee and Hayman (1996); Wells and Papageorgiou (1998); Mansell and Clark (1999).

10. Harrigan and Taing (1997).

11. Schachter (1967); Davidson and Benoit (1998).

12. Masters and Johnson (1970); Leiblum and Rosen, (1989); Masters, Johnson, and Kolodny (1995).

13. Honig and Urcuioli (1981); Shore, Iwata, Lerman, and Shirley (1994); Young, Krantz, McClannahan, and Poulson (1994); Dinsmoor (1995a); Saunders, Drake, and Spradlin (1999). Generalization is seen with S^Δs, too: Once a person has learned not to respond in the presence of a certain S^Δ, similar stimuli will also con-

trol not responding. In order to minimize confusion in the text, the effect of S^Δs is not introduced until we reach the topic of discrimination. Response generalization is discussed in Chapter 9.

14. In the laboratory, the single best predictive stimulus becomes the dominant S^D that controls the response. Because the natural environment is often much more complex and variable than in the laboratory, some predictors may be present during some reinforcement periods but absent in others. Thus, multiple predictive stimuli may become S^Ds for a response. The more S^Ds that are present for a given behavior, the more likely the behavior will be emitted (Dinsmoor, 1995a,b; Harrison, 1990; Miller & Ackley, 1970; Weiss, 1972; Wilkie & Willson, 1992).

15. More technically, they have a longer latency, lower amplitude, and slower rate than the similar responses in the original S^D context (Nevin, 1971a, pp. 117–118).

16. Lalli, Mace, Livezey, and Kates (1998).

17. Iversen (1991); Dinsmoor (1995a).

18. Ducharme and Holborn (1997).

19. Birnbrauer (1976); Goetz, Schuler, and Sailor (1979, 1981); Goldstein and Kanfer (1979); Costello (1983); Schwartz (1984); Halle and Holt (1991); Chandler, Lubeck, and Fowler (1992) .

20. Sherman (1972); Griffiths, Feldman, and Tough (1997).

21. Saunders and Spradlin (1990); Rescorla (1991, 1993).

22. Models and rules can provide useful information that facilitates the acquisition of discriminations and sensitivity; but differential reinforcement is essential for assuring these discriminations will be utilized and refined to subtle levels (see Chapters 9, 10, and 12).

23. Ekman (1972, 1980, 1993); Keltner and Gross (1999); Keltner and Haidt (1999); Levenson (1999).

24. Simpson, Ickes, and Blackstone (1995).

25. Carton, Kessler, and Pape (1999).

26. People often learn to make a discrimination or perform a behavior without having verbal explanations for how they do the given act. Thus, "we can know more than we can tell" (Polanyi, 1966). It takes special learning experiences for people to acquire the self-descriptive skills needed for them to become "aware" of the nature of their own actions (Skinner, 1969, p. 244; 1974, p. 153). See Chapters 12 and 15.

27. Rilling (1977, p. 433).

28. Saar (1996).

29. Stein and Meredith (1993).

30. O'Neill (1995).

31. Dinsmoor (1995a); Ward-Robinson and Hall (1999).

32. Bouton and Nelson (1998).

33. Dysinger and Ruckmick (1933).

34. Although the social labels attached to a person can have an important influence on the person's future (Becker, 1963, 1964; Schur, 1965), labels are only one of many influences on social interaction (Akers, 1973; Kunkel, 1975; McCarthy & Davison, 1991).

35. Rosenhan (1973).

36. Götestam, Götestam, and Melin (1983).

37. Watson and Tharp (1997).

38. Ryder (1968); Winter, Ferreira, and Bowers (1973); Birchler, Weiss, and Vincent (1975).

39. Cantor, Ziemke, and Sparks (1984).

40. Lyubomirsky and Tucker (1998).

Behavior Modification

SONYA GETS PHYSICAL

Sonya was bothered when she read that girls and women were at greater risk of weight and health problems than males, partly because females do not exercise as much as males do. "In these days of gender equality, such an inequity is not fair," she thought. What to do? Having taken a course on behavior analysis, Sonya decided to find ways to use behavior modification to increase both her exercise and strength levels. During the first week, she went about life as usual and recorded her average daily physical activities. She bought a book about self-directed behavior modification and selected a program of behavioral change.[1] After she had enough data on her current level of physical activities, she set the goal of increasing these activities by 10%: Only after she walked 10% faster and biked 10% farther than in the past could she watch TV and talk on the phone each day.

Sonya kept two daily graphs that recorded the time she walked and the miles she biked, making it easy to determine if she reached her two goals of 10% increases. After a month of exercise, she found her new goals becoming easy to attain. She also felt stronger and more physically fit. Because she was genuinely motivated to develop her physical strength, Sonya was proud to have reached her goals; and she decided to require an additional 10% increase during the next month.

After 2 months, Sonya decided to join a gym and work on developing her upper body strength in an environment where she might meet other physically active people. She figured, correctly, that being around athletically-oriented people would increase her social contacts with those who could give her important advice and sincere social rewards for continued exercise. She might even meet an exciting new significant other! It was not long before she and Joe began training together regularly—weight lifting, biking, hiking . . . and more.

Sonya's example shows several major components of behavior modification. *Learning is central: First, we need to learn useful behavior modification techniques, then learn to apply them to the task of changing behavior. The behavior we wish to change is called the* **target behavior.** *The target behavior is given objective behavioral definitions that are designed to make it easy to measure the behavior in numerical units.* To understand the behavior at its starting point, we begin with **baseline measurements** of the target behavior before initiating behavior modification. *Behavior modification involves changing the most important antecedents and consequences that control behavior.* For Sonya, requiring 10% behavioral increases before getting access to the TV or phone changed the consequences, and joining a gym brought both new antecedent stimuli and new consequences.

If objective measures and records show that our first method of behavior modification is not completely adequate, we can experiment with adjustments that might make it better. Each new adjustment can be evaluated as we continue to collect data on the target behavior. The longer we study and analyze any given behavior, the more likely we are to have creative new ideas that help us set better goals and develop more effective behavioral interventions.

Behavior modification can be done in the home, gyms, schools, hospitals, businesses, and any other settings. Simple behavioral problems may be easy to change in everyday environments. However, severe behavior problems may need to be changed first in clinical or hospital environments, where careful environmental control and data collection are easier to arrange. After making progress in a clinical setting, it is often possible to design additional modifications that help people learn the skills needed to bridge the gap from clinical settings to increasingly natural everyday environments.

Applied behavior science has proven to be extremely valuable in helping all kinds of individuals—including children, students, athletes, business people, the elderly, and people with various disabilities and behavioral challenges. Early research on behavior modification was often done by specialists trained in helping people who had serious behavior problems. As researchers created more techniques for helping people, more programs have been developed to train counselors, therapists, nurses, hospital staff, and others to apply behavior modification to almost every type of behavior.[2] Today, increasing numbers of people in all walks of life are applying the principles of behavior modification to change behavior toward goals they value.[3]

BEHAVIOR MODIFICATION

Behavior modification *involves systematically applying behavior principles to the task of changing someone's target behavior—be it our own or someone else's behavior.* Sonya set up a basic and powerful form of behavior modification by arranging valued reinforcers to be contingent upon—dependent upon—doing 10% more exercise in both walking and biking. Researchers have developed effective methods of behavior modification for helping people increase their academic work and creativity, overcome irrational fears and panic attacks, learn social and acting skills, stop smoking or drug abuse, improve worker motivation and courteous service in business, and much more.[4] Behavior modification is extraordinarily useful in special education—helping physically and mentally challenged children and adults learn as many skills as they can for dealing effectively with everyday situations.[5]

It is important to note that the term *behavior modification* applies only to methods of changing behavior that rely on behavior principles. Surgeons who do lobotomies and other forms of brain surgery are not using behavior modification, because they are relying on surgical procedures—not behavior principles—to alter behavior. Likewise, electroconvulsive shock, drug therapies, and hormone treatments for rapists are all medical attempts to change people through biological principles, not behavior principles.

Behavior modification involves the scientific use of behavior principles to help people stop undesirable practices and learn desirable ones. It proceeds through a series of steps beginning with identifying and observing a target behavior that needs to be changed, analyzing its controlling variables, designing interventions that will produce desirable behavioral changes, and keeping scientific records of our successes and failures in order to improve on each intervention. Scientific methods help researchers hone their accuracy in describing behavior and testing hypotheses about it, and the payoffs have been enormous.[6] Never in history has useful knowledge about behavior been amassed as rapidly in the last several decades. As increasing numbers of people gain access to this knowledge, behavioral science is helping change our society by reducing problem behaviors and reinforcing more positive alternative activities.

Goal Setting

How is a behavior selected to be a target for behavior modification? How do we decide the direction in which to change it? *As mentioned in Chapter 1, there are two general classes of problems—**behavioral excesses** and **deficits.** Behavior modification is usually used to help people reduce behavioral excesses and learn desirable skills needed to overcome deficits.* In both cases the goal is to help people overcome problems and lead happier, well-adjusted lives.

First, *behavioral excesses* are often more obvious than deficits, hence more likely to be noticed and targeted for change. Excessive drug and alcohol use can create untold harm to a person and his or her family and friends. Fortunately, behavior modification programs can help people control drug abuse.[7] Even less obvious behavior—such as excessive nail biting—can cause problems, damaging and disfiguring the nails and skin—sometimes affecting a person's self-concept and social relations. Behavior modification has been successful in reducing nail biting, thumb sucking, and other related problems to noninjurious levels.[8] Behavior modification programs can help people curb excess eating and learn how to exercise at healthy levels. Students can devise behavior modification programs to reduce excess goofing off and increase effective study—if they recognize the value of obtaining a high-quality education in our knowledge-intensive society.

Second, serious *behavioral deficits* are sometimes painfully obvious. People who lack social skills often stand out in social groups—awkward, fumbling, embarrassed. People who cannot read may suddenly catch our attention due to their lack of a basic skill. However, people with behavioral deficits often learn to avoid situations where deficiencies would be noticed. People who cannot read can act as if they have no problem and we may fail to notice. In contrast, people with excesses often do not have the skill to stop or hide their excesses! If they drink too much alcohol, we quickly note the slurred speech and loss of motor control. Hence behavioral deficits are often less conspicuous than excesses. Although behavior modification can easily fill most voids, many people with behavioral deficits avoid, rather than seek out, the learning experiences needed to develop the relevant behaviors and skills.

Third is something that applies to all people, even if they have no noticeable behavioral excesses or deficits. Increasingly, people are using behavior modification as a tool for *developing their human potential*—learning skills that broaden their life experiences.[9] Behavior principles allow any of us to work on any of our behavioral goals, such as improving our verbal or social skills, physical strength, or musical proficiency. Here the goal can be stated in terms of reaching positive personal accomplishments—anywhere within the human potential—rather than overcoming problematic behavioral excesses or deficits.

Table 6–1 lists several kinds of behavioral goals based on excesses, deficits, and positive personal aspirations. Often the various goals of behavior modification blend together around the theme of "wellness" or "good personal adjustment"—helping people be as healthy, happy, and alive as they can be. Minimizing the problems of behavioral excesses and deficiencies can clearly contribute to leading a happy, healthy life, and this can help people develop their talents and skills.

BEHAVIORAL DEFINITIONS

Once a target behavior has been identified, we need to define it as accurately as possible. As explained in Chapter 1, behavioral research has benefited enormously from its focus on creating **behavioral definitions,** *which are careful, detailed and objective definitions of behavior.* Vague definitions make it difficult to identify behaviors clearly and change them effectively.

When first identifying target behaviors and goals, vague general definitions tend to be common: "I want to study better." "I want to make friends more easily." Although this is a typical starting point, it is useful to move toward more precise behavioral definitions as soon as possible. Exactly what behavioral skills are needed to study more effectively and make friends more easily? As we explained in Chapter 1, behavioral definitions focus on clear, objective descriptions of behaviors that can be easily measured, counted, tabulated, and graphed.

No behavioral definition can be 100% objective. However, the further we move along the continuum from "vague" toward "very objective," the more we can benefit from the scientific use of behavior principles. The vague behavioral goal of "I want to study better" is not as clear or objective as this statement: "For six days of every week, I want to study 30 minutes more than I used to." The vague definition can allow people to kid

TABLE 6–1   Partial list of target behaviors that deal with behavioral excesses, behavioral deficits, and the fuller actualization of the human potential

---

Problems with Behavioral Excesses

Smoking, drinking, drug abuse

Overeating

Wasting time, gossiping, excessive TV watching

Being too assertive or aggressive

Being too argumentative

Pouting, tantrums, or fighting

Excessive self-criticism or self-questioning

Problems with Behavioral Deficits

Not enough attention to study and career

Undereating

Not being able to talk through problems with family and friends

Not knowing how to interact with the other sex

Not being able to speak up in groups

Not being able to dance, sing, or join in other party activities

Not being assertive

Parts of the Human Potential Worth Developing

Gaining more skill in sports

Learning to sing or play a new musical instrument

Learning to draw, paint, dance, or perform any of the other arts

Improving intellectual skills in science, literature, mathematics, or any other field

Improving socioemotional skills of sensitivity, kindness, loving, friendship, cheerfulness, being helpful, and so forth

Being a good listener and taking serious interest in others

Caring, sharing, and helping others

Looking for the good in everyone and reinforcing it

Overcoming sexist and racist language, in both overt speech and inner thoughts

Treating all people as equals who have enormous potentials that deserve encouragement

Developing clear statements of personal goals, values, and philosophy of life

---

themselves, "Yeah, I'm studying better," when in fact they have no objective measure of that. In contrast, people who first measure their current study times then add 30 minutes a day have a reason to watch the clock and measure the time they spend studying. They may not be perfectly objective in recording their study to the minute, but they will know if the length of their studies on any given day is short of their goal by an hour, or only 5 minutes.

There are three benefits from using objective definitions. *First, objective data give us the basis for rewarding a job well done and not rewarding suboptimal behavior.* Students who reach their goal of studying 30 minutes more each day can close their books when they reach the 30-minute point and enjoy the rest of the evening, without feeling guilty about not having done their work. Tina has set the goal of studying 2 hours and 30 minutes a day for six days a week, and rewards herself by taking Saturday off—no studying required. As shown in Figure 6–1 (left), she marks an "X" onto her study graph for each 15 minutes of study. If the clock indicates that Tina is still 15 minutes short of reaching her goal, it is objectively clear that she needs to study 15 minutes more before she has earned her reward of Saturday off.

Second, objective records help us ask questions and create rules for correcting problems we may encounter during behavior modification. Some students have a hard time studying more than 1 hour a day. Corey's daily records (Fig. 6–1, right) give him objective feedback that something is keeping him from even reaching his goal of studying 1 hour and 30 minutes per day. This information can trigger questions: "Where does my time go?" "What nonstudy activities could I stop doing to free up 30 or 60 minutes a day for more study?" These questions may help Corey realize that he spends far more time watching TV and goofing off than studying. This, in turn, can help him formulate a rule that is useful in increasing his study behavior: "I can't watch TV or goof off with my friends until I have completed my 90 minutes of studying each day." This rule makes the major rewards of TV and friends contingent upon—dependent upon—his finishing 90 minutes of study. Corey writes his behavior modification rule on a piece of paper, tapes it

FIGURE 6–1 The daily records of two students provide objective data on their study behavior over a 2-week period. Both students mark an X on their graph every time they finish 15 minutes of study. Tina (on the left) studies about 2.5 hours a day, and rewards herself by taking Saturdays off (days 7 and 14). Corey (on the right) has a hard time reaching his goal of 1 hour and 30 minutes a day.

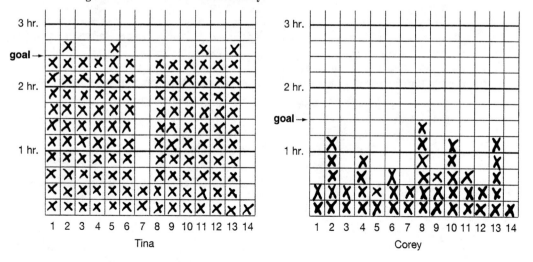

to the refrigerator and tells his friends to help him by asking: "Corey, does your turning on the tube mean you've finished your 90 study minutes?" People are especially willing to create and follow these kinds of study rules if they understand the value of education in attaining interesting and lucrative careers.

Third, objective data help people evaluate the relative merits of different behavior modification programs. Many students benefit from the behavior modification program of adding 30 minutes per day to their study time; but keeping objective data allows each individual to evaluate this strategy for improving his or her learning and grades. Maybe Sarah has such bad study techniques that boosting her study time from 60 to 90 minutes a day does not change her grades. If she keeps objective records that show she has succeeded in studying 30 minutes more each day, but failed to earn better grades, this information is useful: It orients her to look elsewhere for help. Does she need a different kind of behavioral intervention? Maybe she needs to consult one of the study counselors on campus and examine other aspects of her study habits. Does she attend class regularly and take detailed class notes? Does she type out and expand upon her class notes on a word processor as soon as possible after each lecture? Does she use colored highlighters and write marginal notes in her class notes and textbooks to emphasize the key points? Does she type out summaries of the key points of her readings? Does she create flash cards to test herself on key information? If she answers "No" to all these questions, Sarah might benefit from adding one or more of these skills each month, knowing that each one can increase the effectiveness of every hour of her study time.

Defining Chains of Behavior

Often it is useful to define a target behavior in terms of several smaller operant links that are joined together in a chain of activities. Then we can focus on the weakest links in the chain and work on improving any links needed to make the whole response chain as smooth as possible.

For example, sports psychologists use this approach to help athletes improve long chains of behavior. In order to help a pole vaulter reach new heights, trainers need to focus on many small units of operant behavior—such as how to accelerate optimally to the jump point, how to hold the pole and spring off the ground most powerfully, how to twist the body to slide over the bar without touching it, and how to land safely. If an athlete has difficulty with any one of these steps, the sports psychologist breaks that step into even smaller behavioral units to help the athlete practice and master each relevant unit of behavior.

Few things of great value are created by one unit of behavior. Many tasks that we wish to master consist of dozens, if not hundreds of small skills, and these must then be chained together to create the whole graceful act of "a successful pole vault" or "a captivating song" or "a beautiful dance." By studying all the skills needed to produce long chains of highly crafted thoughts and actions, we can help people learn all the relevant components and chain them together to create a smoothly integrated whole.

Careful behavioral observations help us attend to both the units of behavior and their place in the whole performance. After focusing too much attention on a pole vaulter's accelerating to the jump point, the sports psychologist may realize that some detail occurring a split second after the jump had been neglected. That behavior becomes the next target of attention. Much of the art of behavior modification is balancing our attention on the two complementary goals of producing a smoothly functioning behavioral whole and polishing all the links needed to create this whole, beautiful chain of behaviors.

Therefore, if you are planning to use behavior modification on your academic achievement, it is wise to visualize your broad goal of becoming a well-educated person along with a list of specific skills needed to reach that goal. Even though it may be years before you fully attain your broad objective, you can polish some of the specific skills needed to create beautifully synchronized chains of behavior every single day. Today, there may be opportunities to develop your skills of rational, logical thinking. Tomorrow, there may be chances to practice the art of public speaking. Everyday life is sometimes chaotic and we need to be flexible, ready to grab whatever opportunities there are to practice all the behavioral skills needed to attain the larger goals of creating well-crafted behavioral wholes. Two thousand years ago, the Romans captured this idea in the saying "Seize the day"—or *"Carpe diem"* in Latin.

Whether assisting children or adults, the goals of behavior modification are the same: "How can I help people learn as many useful skills as possible? Can I link them into flexible chains suited for coping with life's many challenges?"

The Coach's Trap. If a student learns quickly, behavioral chains need not be defined in the smallest units of behavior. Coaches often love it when they find a "natural" who picks up complex chains of athletic skills with the minimum of analysis or instruction: It makes their job easier. But many people need detailed assistance to master complex new activities. A person who has never surfed before can benefit from coaching about all the small units of behavior that are needed to begin successfully with easy waves, then gradually move to more difficult waves as new skills are mastered. Many people have erroneously decided that they are not cut out to be surfers, or skiers, or mathematicians because their coaches and teachers did not help them learn the skills for starting successfully. Why do coaches and teachers neglect many of their students? All too often they prefer working with the naturals, who learn quickly and attain the successes that reward both coaches and students.

Now things are changing. Behavior modification provides the tools that can help everyone—even people who are not naturals at an activity—improve their skills in any area of life.[10] With the correct training, increasing numbers of people can escape the coach's trap and become skillful at surfing, skiing, math, poetry, relationships, public speaking, finance, or anything else. We might not all acheive superstar performances, but we can learn skills that open doors to interesting experiences, which in the past were closed to us if our coaches and teachers did not define us as natural successes the first time we tried the target behavior.

FUNCTIONAL ANALYSIS

After defining and describing a target behavior as accurately as possible, we are ready to analyze the stimuli that control it. Behaviorists have discovered that the most powerful way to modify behavior is to draw upon the ABC model of behavior and locate the stimuli that precede and follow a target behavior. These are the antecedents and consequences, the A and C of the ABC model.[11] If we can correctly identify the antecedent cues that have stimulus control over a target behavior and the reinforcers that keep a behavior strong, we gain invaluable knowledge about the causes of the behavior. *Both the antecedents and consequences that explain why a person does a behavior are called the **controlling variables** of the behavior.*[12] If we can identify and alter the controlling variables of any given behavior, we can often create measurable changes in a person's behavior and quality of life.

Functional analysis is the technique used to identify the antecedents and consequences that control any given target behavior. The goal of functional analysis is to find the lawful relationships—or "functional relationships"—among a target behavior and its antecedents and consequences.[13] How does a behavior *function* in relationship to its antecedents and consequences? When we are hungry, food will function as a reinforcer and refrigerators can function as S^Ds that start a chain of behaviors for opening the fridge, taking out food, and eating. A cookie jar could also function as an S^D that sets the occasion for eating, so multiple stimuli can have S^D control over behavior that functions to obtain food reinforcers.

When we see any given behavior—be it violence, self-pity, politeness, or exemplary academic achievement—we can do a functional analysis. If Dustin is easily enraged, we ask "Why?" Might his rage bring the reinforcers of social attention? Or is it rewarded by his getting his way? Does his rage appear most frequently in the S^D contexts of work—or with his significant other? When we want to understand and change a behavior, doing functional analysis of the ABCs of behavior provides far more information than merely describing the target behavior in detail.[14]

Functional analysis involves asking questions about antecedents and consequences, then observing or experimenting to see which of many possible hypotheses might be correct. What S^Ds, USs, or CSs have stimulus control over behavior? What reinforcers or punishers are contingent on the behavior? First, we examine the entire stimulus collage in search of any *stimuli that regularly precede and predict* the target behavior, since these are most likely to be the ones that have stimulus control over the behavior. Second, we search for the *consequences that are contingent* on the target behavior, be they reinforcers or punishers, since contingent consequences have the most powerful control over behavior. Third, we experiment to see if we can change the behavior in predictable ways by altering the antecedents and consequences we have identified. Does removing the S^D we think causes excess snacking reduce calorie intake? Does removing social attention reduce whining or self-pity? We may need to ask dozens of questions and experiment with several alternative hypotheses before we find the antecedents and consequences that control a behavior.

Functional analysis does not assume that behavior is adaptive or healthy. Behavior can lie anywhere along a continuum from adaptive to maladaptive. If Zack scratches his arms until they bleed—then scratches off the scabs the next day, causing more bleeding and some infection—the behavior is maladaptive: It creates problems for Zack and his family. It would clearly be more adaptive for Zack to stop injuring himself.

Functional analysis is useful in helping create powerful behavioral interventions.[15] Consider the example of self-injurious behavior. For years psychologists were baffled by people who hit or scratched themselves until they injured themselves seriously. What causes people to inflict such pain on themselves? *Questions about the causes of behavior are the clues that a functional analysis is needed.* Iwata et al. (1994) collected data on 152 young people who engaged in self-injurious behavior (SIB) and found that over two thirds of the SIB cases resulted from social reinforcement: A child's SIB can function to attract social attention—with both positive and negative reinforcement—from parents and teachers. If Zack scratches his arm until it bleeds, adults often approach and pay a great deal of attention, which gives Zack *positive reinforcement* for self-destructive behavior. Adults often lighten their demands on children who are hurting themselves, which is *negative reinforcement.* If we ask Zack to set the dinner table and he starts scratching off scabs, causing new bleeding, we are likely to cease demanding things of him, and his escaping these task-demands provides negative reinforcement for the SIB.[16] For Zack, SIB functions to bring both positive and negative reinforcement—by attracting social attention and reducing task-demands.

Can SIB *really* have the function of attracting social attention? Daren bites his fingernails back so far that his fingers bleed. Carrie yanks out a handful of hair. Most parents and teachers direct their attention—which is a positive reinforcer—to a child who does these acts of SIB. There is a causal—or contingent—relationship between SIB and social reinforcement. This, in turn, makes the sympathetic adult an S^D for the child to do the SIB when the adult is present. Functional analyses of SIB have led behavior modifiers to develop various interventions that decrease SIB by stopping adults from giving contingent social reinforcement for SIB—while teaching them to give loving positive social attention when their child is doing more desirable alternative behaviors.[17]

In behavior modification, the goal of reducing maladaptive and undesirable behaviors is almost always coupled with the goal of reinforcing alternative behaviors that are healthier and more useful, adaptive, and prosocial.[18] Therapy for SIB could easily be coupled with a behavioral intervention developed by Mize and Ladd (1990) to increase four friendly social skills. When children with few social skills are coached in and rewarded for using friendly behaviors, they learn significant increases in these valuable social skills. "Skill-trained children doubled their use of the targeted social skills from pretest to posttest, whereas control children showed little change" (pp. 394–395). As people discover that the pivotal skills of kind, friendly, thoughtful, and prosocial behavior lead to generous social reinforcement, they do these positive behaviors more and spend less time doing old, maladaptive attention-getting behavior—be it pouting, whining, self-pity, or SIB.

Functional analysis helps us focus our observations—in both natural and experimental settings[19]—on all possible antecedents and consequences of target behaviors. If a child does maladaptive behavior—such as SIB—which functions to attract social attention, we can often find some functionally equivalent behavior that is more adaptive and helps the child learn to live a healthier life. Robert and Lynn Koegel, and their coworkers, have shown us the value of teaching *pivotal skills* that work better than maladaptive behavior in creating rewarding outcomes.[20] For example, children who learn friendly social skills often receive far more reinforcers than they did before. Social skills are pivotal in expanding a child's range of friendships, which may open opportunities to learn all sorts of athletic or artistic skills. Pivotal skills are central skills that "open doors" to many healthy and functional learning experiences.[21] Adults who still pout, whine, engage in self-pity, or throw tantrums (with anger outbursts) can develop happier adult relationships by learning the pivotal social skills needed for friendly and prosocial interactions. People can even overcome drug abuse, depression, and exhibitionism by learning the pivotal skills needed for enjoying hobbies or social interactions that occupy their time with rewarding activities that reduce their need to turn to maladaptive activities.[22]

VARIOUS OBJECTIVE MEASURES

After creating a behavioral definition of a target behavior and doing a functional analysis of its possible controlling variables, we need to devise ways of measuring and assessing all the ABCs of behavior. The more scientifically we measure a target behavior and its controlling variables, the better are our chances of reaching an accurate understanding of the behavior.

Our first observations of any given target behavior may be rather casual. Becky stands out because she teases other children. David catches our attention because he is so quiet and shy. Although behavior modification often begins with casual observations of naturally occurring behavior,[23] research in behavior science shows the value of developing objective behavioral measures as soon as possible. *Keeping objective records of the form, frequency, and timing of behavior is essential for knowing how a behavior appeared during **baseline conditions** (before behavior modification) and how it changes after starting behavioral interventions.* There are several methods for making clear and objective behavioral measures that are well suited to functional analyses and behavior modification. Sometimes one measure works so well by itself—such as measuring smoking in terms of number of cigarettes per day—that people never need any other measure. However, it is important to know several measurement methods in case the first technique we select does not work well. Palm top computers are now available for instructing people how to change their behavior at any point in time, then automatically saving a record of the behaviors involved.[24]

First, *the number of times that a behavior occurs* is a very useful measure. How many sit-ups did you do today? How many pages of your history assignment did you read? Numerical data include the number of cigarettes, beers, or cookies consumed in any given situation; number of laps at the pool or the track; approximate number of calories consumed or pounds of weight lost; pounds of weight lifted at the gym and number of repetitions. Count data can be recorded on slips of paper, file cards, graphs, or mechanical devices—such as the golf counters that can be worn like wristwatches. At the end of each hour or day, count data can be transferred to a log book, diary, or master graph that is not likely to be lost over the course of behavior analysis and modification.

Second, *frequency data* can be calculated by dividing count data by the length of the observation period. Did a child throw three tantrums per day or three per hour? Numerical data on the number of cigarettes or beers consumed often are automatically converted to frequency data when people judge them in terms of daily consumption or weekly consumption.

Third, *the time of a behavior's duration* may be a valuable measure. How many hours was I on the phone today? How many hours did I watch TV today? How many minutes or hours did I exercise this week? Many companies attempt to provide rapid service when customers need attention, and they keep data on the time lags between requests for service and the completion of service. Companies are eager to reduce the delays in providing service because reducing the time delays helps produce happier customers and repeat business.

Digital wristwatches with built-in stopwatch capacities are wonderful for keeping records of total amounts of time spent exercising, studying, working, relaxing, practicing music, or doing almost anything. Cumulative stopwatches that do not reset to zero every time we stop the clock are especially useful: They measure the total amount of time we do a given behavior, while allowing us to stop the clock during breaks or rest periods, and then resume our time recording when we return to the target behavior. If our goal is to study 2 hours a day (and we cannot watch TV until we reach that goal), we can easily rely on our watch to tell us that the cumulative study time is now 1:45—reminding us to study 15 more minutes before indulging in TV rewards.

A fourth useful measure is the *percentage of some task that is completed.* Stefan realizes that his suboptimal grades result from not getting all his reading done before each test. By keeping track of the pages he actually read and dividing that by the number of pages assigned, Stefan can calculate the percentage of pages he read. If he is only getting 60% of his assignments read, he could set the goal of reading 80% or 100% of the assignment, then keep objective records of his progress and reward each success. A drill sergeant may become very irate if a new recruit only makes his or her bed to 98% of perfection. Quality control supervisors in factories want every single step of quality control inspection completed, knowing that a success rate of 99.9% is too low when competing in modern market places.

Fifth, *rating scales* are useful in measuring some of the more subtle and elusive features of behavior. Many behaviors can be performed at different levels of quality, and we need a way to rate them so we can reward high-quality behavior more than low quality. For example, a panel of judges uses scores from 0 to 10 to rate the quality of Olympic gymnasts' performances. At first, we may wonder how the judges decide to rate different performances as 9.3 or 9.6; but the more we learn about gymnastics, the easier it becomes to tell the differences between 8-, 9- and 10-point performances.

In everyday life there are many behaviors—such as generosity, thoughtfulness, friendliness, creativity, enthusiasm, and persuasiveness—that can be evaluated with rating scales. For example, there are degrees of kindness, and some acts of kindness are more genuine and thoughtful than others. Although it is not always easy to do so, it is often desirable to assess acts of kindness on a rating scale from -10 to $+10$, where -10 is a very unkind act, zero is neutral, and $+10$ is a very kind act. Many acts of kindness fall short of $+10$, but are significantly above zero, and $+8$ acts of kindness deserve more positive attention than $+2$ acts. The more we learn about behavior, the easier it is to discriminate the differences between + 5 and + 7 acts of kindness, and added experience helps us tell the difference between a + 5 and a + 6 act.

DATA COLLECTION

Data need to be collected in ways that allow them to be recorded on graphs, checklists, notebooks, ABC diaries, computers, or other such devices. Graphs are handy because each data point can be recorded directly onto a graph as it is collected (see Fig. 6–1). Checklists are useful when observing several different behaviors, and it only takes a single check mark to note the occurrence of a target behavior in any given observation period. As shown in Figure 6–2, ABC diaries make it easy for us to record the conspicuous antecedents that precede a target behavior and the consequences that occur afterward.[25] Note the three columns that require comments on all three features of the ABCs of behavior. Golf counters, cumulative stopwatches, computers, and professional data collection equipment can all be used.

Behaviorists commonly use three methods of data collection: direct observation, indirect observation, and variations on questionnaires. In all three methods, the goal is to collect information on all aspects of the ABCs of the target behavior in order to discover how the behavior is a function of specific antecedents and consequences. This may be easy if the behavior involves a small response class, such as tantrums, successful free throws, minutes of homework done, or other easily identified behavior. However, observations on a large response class, such as courteousness, may require us to develop a checklist of all the behaviors deemed courteous in a given context, and then put a check mark next to each item on the list whenever that behavior occurs.[26]

Direct Observation.   When we can observe a behavior easily, we may be able to count or measure it by any of the five methods just described. Psychologists have long been interested in bizarre speech: "The Martians are coming. I can see Elvis now!" Helen talked

FIGURE 6–2   **This is a data page from an ABC diary on a child's tantrums. It records the antecedents that precede each tantrum (A), the length of the tantrum (B), and the consequences (C) that follow the behavior.**

Antecedents (A)	Behaviors (B)	Consequences (C)
We had just turned the TV off.	15 min tantrum	No TV. We tried to comfort him.
Started when he demanded a glass of water before bed.	24 min tantrum	We finally gave him the water.
After a bedtime story.	18 min tantrum	We left the room.
Had just turned off TV.	26 min tantrum	We sent him to his room.

for hours each day for years about an imaginary illegitimate child and several men who were pursuing her.[27] Mitch, a 46-year-old man, often said and did unusual things.[28] One day, he would slap the floor with his hands and say, "I've got to put out that fire." The next day it was something else strange. After repeated observations, it became clear that Mitch frequently engaged in bizarre speech when he was not receiving attention from others. Social attention was the reinforcer, and the lack of attention was the S^D for "crazy talk." This functional analysis led the behavioral psychologists to conduct an experiment in which other people had to stop paying attention to Mitch's bizarre talk, and soon thereafter he ceased doing it. Thus, for Mitch, the data supported the hypothesis that bizarre talk functioned to attract social attention.

Direct observations of children who have temper tantrums have revealed that children's tantrums are often reinforced by social attention. Behaviorists ask the parents to count the frequency of tantrums for several days, the baseline measurement period. Next, they tell the parents to (1) stop paying attention to their child during tantrums (putting tantrums on extinction), then (2) direct their loving attention to the child whenever they see more desirable and adaptive behavior. Behavioral measures show that tantrums usually stop within a week or two if the parents are consistent in doing these two things.[29]

Indirect Observation.   Sometimes data on behavior come from indirect observations: We observe the results of the behavior, not the behavior itself.[30] For example, we rarely catch people in the act of defacing property, but we see the results of the behavior. It costs $4 billion per year to remove graffiti from public places.[31] How can we measure and modify the behavior of graffiti writing if we never directly observe it?

On a college campus, Watson (1996) counted each single mark of graffiti in three men's bathrooms in order to see how many new marks appeared each day. After finishing baseline observations, he posted signs stating that a local doctor will "donate a set amount of money to the local chapter of the United Way for each day this wall remains free of any . . . [new] markings. Your assistance is greatly appreciated in helping to support your United Way." In all three bathrooms, new markings dropped to zero! Apparently, the negative consequences of depriving a charity of money were sufficient to punish and suppress graffiti writing completely. Behavior can be evaluated and modified without ever being directly observed.

Questionnaires and Their Variations.   Sometimes questionnaires and interviews that are given to individuals who have experience with the target behavior can yield valuable information about the ABCs of behavior. Questionnaires can be given as a series of written questions to be filled in by the person, as face-to-face interviews or phone queries, or as a structured ABC diary in which people are asked to describe the antecedents and consequences of specific target behaviors.

Severe nail biting can cause bleeding, infection, and other medical and dental complications. McClanahan (1995) gave a questionnaire and diary to a 32-year-old woman in order to collect information on the antecedents, duration, and frequency of her fingernail biting. The questionnaire and diary revealed that "anxiety was the most prevalent antecedent to nail-biting behavior" (p. 510). Because deep muscle relaxation exercises and transcendental meditation are useful in counteracting anxiety, the woman was taught to use these two techniques when confronted with anxiety. Within a month, her average rate of nail biting dropped from her baseline average of 7.3 times a day to an average of 2.4 times a day during the last week of treatment. The duration of nail biting also declined dramatically.

EXPERIMENTAL DESIGNS

There are times when we can simply implement well-researched behavior modification programs to deal with well-studied problem behavior, as Sonya did for getting fit at the beginning of the chapter. However, when working in new areas, we may need to experiment with different techniques of behavior modification to see which works best. *There are several different **experimental designs**—or scientific procedures—that are useful in testing our hypotheses about the possible controlling variables that may influence a target behavior.* There are four commonly used types of experimental design, each suited to different situations. Only data collected with carefully controlled experimental designs allow us to evaluate our hypotheses carefully and improve the techniques of behavior modification.

Reversal Designs

The most basic and important of experimental designs is called the ***reversal design**, because it allows various types of behavioral interventions to be introduced and then removed—or reversed—under the experimenter's control.*[32] Reversal designs allow us to test the effectiveness of a behavioral intervention by collecting data on a target behavior before, during, and after using it. If the behavior changes during the intervention and then returns to baseline measures when the intervention is terminated (the reversal), we have evidence that the intervention was effective and essential to behavioral change. This simple reversal design is an ABA design where A indicates baseline, B is the experimental intervention, and the second A is the reversal to baseline. If the behavioral intervention proves to be useful, we may want to reinstate the intervention (B) a second time, creating an ABAB design.

Sports psychologists recognize the need to increase the efficiency of athletes' practice sessions. Naturalistic baseline data reveal that many athletes do not practice as much as they either should or want. Hume and Crossman (1992) hypothesized that music could be used as a reward for promoting exercise. In order to determine whether contingent music could help swimmers increase their dry-land exercise, the researchers used an ABAB experimental design—where A indicates baseline observations on dry-land exercise without music, and B indicates the use of music as a reinforcer that is *contingent upon* a swimmer actually doing dry-land exercises: Music is played only when a swimmer exercises. Figure 6–3 shows the data for Kevin, one of the six competitive swimmers included in the study.

Baseline observations in the first A phase reveal that nonproductive behaviors tended to be more frequent than productive exercise. The first A phase usually lasts for several observation periods until a stable range of data points emerges. Only after we know the average and range of behavior under baseline conditions do we have enough

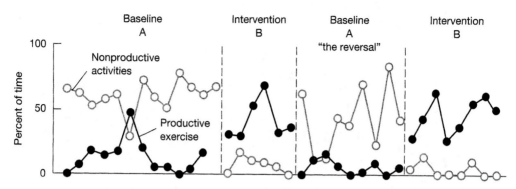

FIGURE 6–3   **These data from an ABAB reversal design show the percentage of time Kevin spent doing productive exercises and nonproductive activities during baseline and music interventions.**

(Adapted from "Musical Reinforcement of Practice Behaviors Among Competitive Swimmers," K.M. Hume & J. Crossman, 1992, *Journal of Applied Behavior Analysis, 25*, pp. 665–670. Copyright by the Journal of Applied Behavior Analysis, 1992.)

data for making comparisons with data generated in phase B, when music is played contingent upon Kevin's exercising. Observations in phase B, the behavioral intervention, reveal that contingent music did, in fact, increase the frequency of Kevin's productive exercises and reduce his nonproductive activities.

The data from the first two phases of the ABAB design are suggestive, but the next two phases are essential for reaching firmer scientific conclusions about the power of contingent music to reward exercising. Phase 3 (the second A) is called a "reversal" phase because the behavioral intervention is terminated to see if the behavioral changes seen in phase 2 disappear. And, in fact, Kevin's productive practice dropped toward baseline level in this third phase (Fig. 6–3). These data provide further support for the hypothesis that the contingent music caused the changes in the first intervention (phase 2). In the fourth phase of the ABAB design, contingent music was reintroduced and productive practice increased again, giving us even stronger evidence for the power of contingent music. When it was discovered that the other five swimmers exercised most when music was made contingent upon exercising, the findings further supported the authors' hypothesis.

Behavior modification is often used to help people adjust to difficult situations.[33] A 10-year-old boy—who we'll call Larry—has end-stage kidney disease and needs frequent dialysis treatments with "kidney machines." Unfortunately, the procedure takes 4 hours each time it is done and requires hypodermic needles to remain inserted in Larry's body the entire time, to transfer blood to the machine and return processed blood to his body. Larry hates the process and often kicks, hits, and screams at the nurses. These and other intense movements interfere with the needle insertions and successful treatment, creating potentially life-threatening medical problems—because of the severity of Larry's disease. In the first phase of an ABAB experiment, baseline observations reveal that Larry averaged 7.3 noncompliant movements during every 30 minutes of observation (Fig. 6–4).

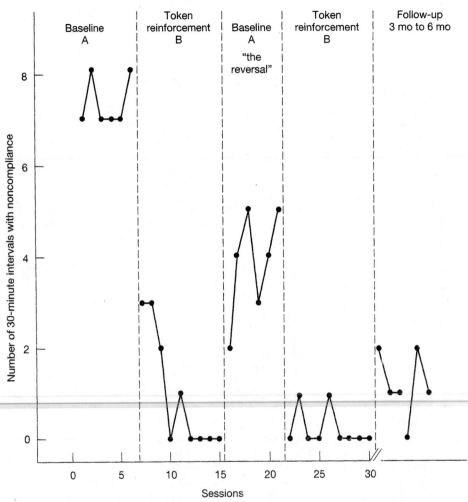

FIGURE 6–4   These data from an ABAB reversal design show the number of 30-minute intervals in which Larry did noncompliant behaviors during baseline, with a
token reinforcement economy, and during follow-ups at 3 and 6 months.

(Adapted from "Use of a Token Economy to Increase Compliance During Hemodialysis," by J.S. Carton &
J.B. Schweitzer, 1996, *Journal of Applied Behavior Analysis, 29,* pp. 111–113. Copyright by the *Journal of
Applied Behavior Analysis,* 1996.)

Before phase B, Larry ranked the attractiveness of several toys and comic books,
and he was told he could earn "tokens" that he could accumulate and exchange for these
prizes if he could remain quiet during each 30 minutes of treatment. Each 4-hour treatment was broken into eight blocks of 30 minutes each, and Larry could earn one token
during each 30-minute time period that he remained quiet. Figure 6–4 shows that Larry's
noncompliance dropped from an average of 7.3 movements per 30 minutes to one in 30
minutes during the token reinforcement period (phase B). This drop provides partial evi-

dence that the tokens—which could be exchanged for toys and other rewards—can reinforce compliance.

Stronger evidence about the power of the behavioral intervention was obtained when Larry's behavioral gains disappeared in the third phase, the reversal, or second baseline (A). Additional evidence for the power of the behavioral intervention was obtained when Larry's noncompliance dropped again in the fourth phase of the ABAB design. The ABAB data show that compliant behavior was a *function* of token reinforcement. Additional "follow-up" data were collected 3 and 6 months after the initial ABAB research, and these showed that Larry had learned to minimize problematic responses.

Sometimes behavioral changes that appear in a successful intervention do not disappear in the reversal phase (the second A of the ABAB design). What does that tell us? In the first baseline, little Dana fell off her two-wheeler several times a day when first learning to ride. During the first intervention, two extra training wheels were put on the back of her bike and Dana learned how to balance. When the training wheels were removed (the reversal phase of the ABAB experiment), Dana did not return to a high rate of falling off her bike. Why? *If an intervention helps a person learn valuable skills that yield high levels of natural reinforcement—such as riding without painful falls—that reinforcement can sustain high rates of success during the reversal (phase 3), even though the behavioral intervention has ended.* The same is true for many behaviors—such as being polite, doing arithmetic, catching baseballs, and so on. Once learned, valuable skills may never be lost. Therefore, when behavioral interventions produce changes that are not lost during the reversal phase, we know something valuable was learned during the intervention. In addition, the absence of a decline in behavior during the reversal phase indicates the intervention does not have total control over the behavior. *Natural reinforcers have taken control, making the behavioral intervention no longer necessary.* Once you can balance a bike and a checkbook, the natural rewards take over and removing the behavioral intervention does not stop the behavior. Fortunately, we have an alternative means of evaluating this kind of behavioral intervention by testing to see if our intervention can help other people learn a behavior. The more people who benefit, the more evidence we have for the power of our intervention, even if the behavior stays strong during the reversal.

The ABAB experimental design can be altered in countless ways. For example, baseline data do not have to be collected first. If a person needs behavioral help as soon as possible, we might use a BAB design and begin with an intervention (B) to see if it is helpful. If it is, we might then make phase 2 a baseline period (A) to see if the problem behavior reappears when the intervention ends. If it did, we could return to intervention B as soon as possible to see if this once again solved the problem. If Joey has a history of poking his eyes, we can skip taking baseline data and start behavior modification as soon as possible, rewarding Joey for all activities that keep his hands far from his eyes. If we stopped the behavioral intervention to see if Joey began to put his hands near his eyes—then resumed behavior modification if he did—we would have followed a BAB design.

Both ABAB and BAB designs can be followed by yet another intervention (C) or more baselines if the initial behavioral intervention (B) proves weak and we have reason to search for more effective forms of behavior modification. We could expand on the

BAB design and create a BABC design to see if method C worked better than B. If it did not, we could return to method B, creating a BABCB design.

Other variations on reversal designs are possible. For example, Cope and Allred (1991) used an ABACACA design to see how best to deter people from parking illegally in spaces reserved for the physically disabled. First, they took baseline data (A) when only vertical signs with the international wheelchair symbol were present, finding that an average of 51% of cars parked there were parked illegally. In phase B, they combined the vertical sign with a printed message that announced the possibility of surveillance for illegal parking, and illegal parking dropped to an average of 37%. In the reversal to baseline (the second A), the sign about surveillance was removed, and illegal parking rose to an average of 50%. In their second experimental procedure (C), Cope and Allred attached a message dispenser to the signpost. It contained politely worded reminder notes about the importance of showing consideration for the physically disabled, and anyone could place one of these notes on the windshield—or give to the driver—of an illegally parked car. Under this phase C illegal parking fell to an average of 25%. The last three phases of the ABACACA experiment included a reversal to baseline (A), a return to polite reminder messages (C), and a final reversal to baseline (A). The data for these last three phases were 57%, 24%, and 37%, respectively. Clearly, polite reminders worked best, reducing illegal parking to 25% and 24%.

Some ethical issues can emerge when using reversal designs. Let us assume a person has a serious behavioral problem that hurts either self or others. The first baseline would reveal the harm created by the behavior—be it wild temper tantrums, self-destructive drug use, or scratching one's hands until they bleed. What if our first behavioral intervention caused the behavioral problem to drop near zero? Would we feel compelled to follow the ABAB model and do a reversal to baseline, knowing the harmful behavior might reappear? In some cases, we might decide to stay at phase 2 and never go beyond the AB design. In other cases, after a long and successful intervention, we might try a brief reversal (the third phase of an ABA sequence) to see if the person needed continued behavior modification: Some addicts might find that being free of drugs for 9 weeks was so rewarding they could continue avoiding drugs in phase 3— much as Dana's bike riding continued even after the training wheels were removed from her bike. However, we might need to resume behavior modification (the second B in an ABAB design) for those people who were not yet skillful enough to avoid painful bike falls or drug problems.

Multiple-Baseline Designs

When there are two or more things being studied—be they people, behaviors, settings, or times—it is possible to start each one on a behavioral intervention at different times. *Multiple-baseline designs* begin baseline observations on any of the four things being studied—be they people, behaviors, settings, or times—then gradually shift each one, one at a time, to the experimental intervention. If the data points for each thing under study change *when and only when* shifted from baseline to the behavior intervention, we have evidence that the change reflects successful behavior modification. The power of multiple-baseline designs becomes clear when we examine examples of its being used with (1) several people, or (2) various behaviors, or (3) multiple settings, or (4) different times of day.

1. Kamps, Barbetta, Leonard, and Delquadri (1994) used multiple-baseline design *across different people* in studying the power of peer tutoring to help three autistic students—Michael, Adam, and Pete—who lacked social skills.[34] During baseline conditions (BL) in an integrated lower grade classroom, the teacher did traditional reading instruction, with all students participating at their seats. One at a time, Mike, Adam and Pete were shifted to the behavioral intervention in which they were paired with a nonautistic peer with whom they worked on practicing their reading fluency and comprehension. Would this behavioral intervention help the three autistic children learn better social skills? During both baseline and peer tutoring, the scientists recorded how many seconds Mike, Adam, and Pete engaged in spontaneous social interactions during the 15- to 20-minute free time after the reading period was over (Fig. 6–5). Mike was the first student shifted to peer tutoring (PT) and he was the first to show an increase in spontaneous social interactions at time 1 (t_1 in the fig.). Adam did not show much increase in spontaneous social interactions until time 2 (t_2), when he was shifted to the behavioral intervention (PT). Pete was the last to be shifted to PT and the last to show improvements in spontaneous socializing at time 3 (t_3). Because each student showed behavioral gains *when and only when* he was shifted to the behavioral intervention, we have evidence that all the behavioral change was caused by the peer tutoring program.

Kamps and her colleagues combined their multiple-baseline design with an ABAB design. In phase 3, they had each student return—at different times—to baseline (BL, with no peer tutoring) for a short period. During this reversal (the second BL period), each autistic child showed a partial decline in reading and socializing—but this happened only when the behavioral intervention was stopped! Finally, each of the autistic children was shifted back to peer tutoring (the fourth phase of the ABAB design): Then and only then did each child show increased spontaneous socializing—even though this occurred at different times for each student. Multiple-baseline design is a powerful tool because it allows us to see if each person's behavior changes when and only when the behavioral intervention begins or ends.

2. Multiple-baseline design can be used *across different behaviors,* when different behaviors are shifted to a behavioral intervention at different times. Bay-Hinitz, Peterson, and Quilitch (1994) wanted to see how cooperation and competition games affected children's aggressive behavior. They made baseline observations on the frequency of aggression of 70 preschool children in four classes, before teaching either cooperation or competition games. Next, the children in one classroom (group A) were taught to play competitive games (the first behavior) while the other children remained on baseline. At that time, the frequency of aggression increased and cooperation declined in this first classroom (A), and only there. Whenever competition games were introduced to a new classroom (B or C or D), aggression increased and cooperation declined in that particular classroom. When cooperation games (the second behavior) were introduced in classroom A, cooperation activities increased and aggressive behavior declined. Each time cooperation games were introduced to class B, C or D, aggression declined and cooperation increased. This

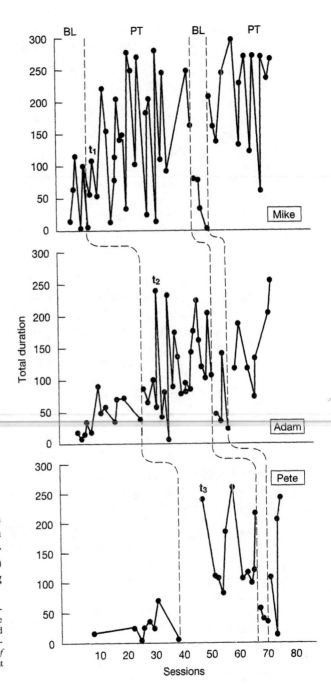

FIGURE 6–5 These data are from a study using a **multiple-baseline design** *across subjects*. They show the total duration of social interactions (in seconds) during baseline (BL) and peer tutoring (PT) conditions.

(Adapted from "Classwide Peer Tutoring: An Integration Strategy to Improve Reading Skills and Promote Peer Interactions Among Students with Autism and General Education Peers," by D.M. Kamps, P.M. Barbetta, B.R. Leonard, & J. Delquardi, 1994, *Journal of Applied Behavior Analysis, 27,* pp. 49–61. Copyright by the Journal of Applied Behavior Analysis, 1994.)

research adds to the literature showing that competitive activities tend to increase aggression and reduce cooperation.[35] Fortunately, the aggression trained by competitive games can be minimized when competition games include training for good sportsmanship.[36]

3. Multiple-baseline design can be used to study one behavioral intervention *across different settings.* Bay-Hinitz and her colleagues did this when looking at two behaviors (competition and cooperation) in four different classrooms (four different settings). Similarly, we could observe the changes in one behavior—such as cooperation—in six different elementary schools by introducing cooperation games to each school on a different Monday over a 6-week period. If the target behavior of cooperation changed in each of the six settings when and only when behavior modification went into place in that setting, we could be confident that the behavior change was due to the intervention, and not some extraneous factors.

4. Finally, multiple-baseline design can be used *across different times,* for example, at different times of day. Jill was 12 years old, had multiple handicaps, and "frequently displayed high-intensity disruptive behavior characterized by aggression, yelling and cursing, . . . and delusional speech, spitting, tipping over desks, and property destruction."[37] A behavioral intervention was designed to reduce her disruptive behavior and increase appropriate behavior, and it was tested with a multiple-baseline design across morning and afternoon time periods. As Figure 6–6 shows, Jill's disruptive behavior declined dramatically and her on-task responding increased substantially in her afternoon classes when behavior intervention was begun in those PM classes. Nine days later, her behavior changed in her morning classes when the behavior intervention was begun in the AM classes. The close association between the onset of behavioral intervention and declines in disruptive behavior in two different time periods shows that the behavioral intervention was effective.

   A major advantage of multiple-baseline design is that it allows us to study behaviors that we may not want to put on reversal. If we help a child such as Jill learn to behave better, it is more humanistic to test our behavioral interventions first in the afternoon then in the morning rather than see if Jill's good behavior extinguishes during phase 3 of an ABAB design. Once any valuable behavior has been learned, we can advance our research on the variables which control that behavior by seeing if we can extend the behavior to new time periods, settings or people.

   In all types of multiple-baseline designs—for different people, behaviors, settings, or times—the strongest proof of having a successful form of behavior modification comes from seeing the behavioral data points change when and only when any person, behavior, setting, or time is shifted from baseline to the behavioral intervention. Usually two or three successful changes are the minimum number for scientific confidence.[38]

   However, multiple-baseline design is not without its problems. Studies are not always as neat and clear-cut as those just presented. Take the example of teaching 5 families the value of using democratic communication skills, politeness, and compromise—shifting one new family from baseline to intervention each Monday for 5 weeks. During the first intervention, the data points for family 1 may be the only ones that change, as predicted. But week 2 might produce some unexpected results: When family 2—and only

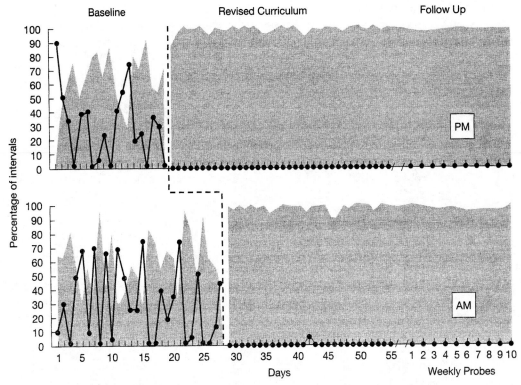

FIGURE 6–6   Jill's disruptive behavior is shown by the black circles connected by solid lines; and her "on-task responding" is shown by the height of the grey zone. Both behaviors are influenced when and only when the behavioral intervention was introduced in the afternoon (PM) and morning (AM) phases of a multiple-baseline design.

(Adapted from "Function Assessment, Curricular Revision, and Severe Behavior Problems," by G. Dunlap, L. Kern-Dunlap, S. Clarke, & F.R. Robbins, 1991, *Journal of Applied Behavior Analysis, 24,* pp. 387–397. Copyright by the Journal of Applied Behavior Analysis, 1991.)

that family—was shifted to the behavioral intervention, all five families might show behavioral improvements. What could cause this effect? It is often difficult to know. Perhaps the increase in prosocial behavior in families 3, 4, and 5 resulted from some cause external to our behavioral experiment. Nothing in the experimental records would show that in week 2, several TV talk-show hosts interviewed the author of a new book on the value of politeness and compromise. Because numerous extraneous events can affect the behaviors we study, it is often difficult to locate the external variables that produce complex and unpredicted results.

Alternating-Treatment Designs[39]

When we want to experiment with two or more different behavioral interventions, we can alternate among them to see how each one affects behavior. *Alternating-treatment de-*

signs test the efficacy of two or more different treatments by alternating among them in clearly different stimulus situations.

David does disruptive behavior in high school math, English, and gym classes. We could use an alternating-treatment design in order to evaluate three different behavioral interventions. We take baseline measures on David's problem behavior in all three classes to evaluate the initial frequencies of the target behavior. Next, we could instruct each of the three teachers—for math, English, and gym—in one of the three methods and let David alternate among the three behavioral interventions in the three different classes. The math teacher may be taught to use extinction, paying no attention to David's disruptive behavior. The English teacher may be taught to do positive reasoning, explaining sensitively and caringly to David why prosocial actions are far more admirable and desirable than is disruptive behavior. The physical education teacher may be taught to reward David generously when he is doing nondisruptive behavior.

After several days of baseline observation in all three classes, we ask the 3 teachers to introduce their different behavioral interventions and count the number of disruptive acts in each class. At this time (phase 1) David *alternates* across all three behavioral techniques each day that he has math, English, and gym classes. Once we have enough data to know which method works best with David, we can advance to phase 2 of analysis by having all of David's teachers use the method that was best in the first intervention. Will all teachers get the best results with the behavioral intervention that worked best in phase 1? If they all do, we feel secure that we have found a good solution for David's problem. But the math teacher may not do well with the method that the gym teacher executed so successfully. More work may be needed.

Will Kathleen's classroom disruptions be changed most effectively by the behavioral intervention that worked best with David? Perhaps, but perhaps not. Therefore, it might be desirable to repeat all three of the interventions with Kathleen to evaluate the best method for helping her, without assuming she will respond the same as David did. Each individual is unique, and programs of behavioral modification are often customized to serve each person's needs.

Group Experimental Designs

It is possible to experiment on a whole group of people to see if their behavior changes more than the behavior of a control group. *Group experimental designs allow us to evaluate the effectiveness of a behavioral intervention with an experimental group by comparing that group with a similar group of people—called the control group—that does not receive the intervention.* First, people are randomly assigned to either the experimental group or the control group. The experimental group may be treated as a group or one person at a time. If the behavior of the experimental group changes and becomes significantly different from that of the control group, we have evidence that the intervention affected behavior.

For example, Telch et al. (1993) used a group experimental design to study ways to help people with panic disorder. Some people are especially prone to experience sudden bursts of intense fear, panic, or discomfort. Telch and his associates identified a group of people with panic disorder and randomly assigned about half of their subjects to an experimental group, in which they could learn cognitive-behavioral skills for controlling panic attacks in a group setting. The other half of the subjects served as the control group—not given behavior modification. After the treatment, over 85% of the experimental group no longer experienced panic attacks, whereas only 30% of people in the control group had overcome their panic responses.

Decades ago, people realized that it was unfair for control group members to be unable to benefit from the scientific knowledge derived from the research project in which they participated. For years behaviorists have solved this problem by using a technique called *the **delayed treatment control group**, in which the control group is seen as waiting in line to be the next experimental group if the first experiment yields beneficial results.* A careful scientist repeats the experiment, allowing the first control group to be the next experimental group. After repeating the study enough times, the last control group is given the best behavioral intervention that was discovered.

It is possible to study two or more experimental groups at a time, with each group receiving different experimental interventions, and all being compared with one control group. For example, Silber and Haynes (1992) compared two experimental methods for helping people stop excessive fingernail biting. Over a 4-week period, 7 people painted a bitter substance on their fingernails, 7 other people were instructed to perform a "competing response" that involved clenching the hand for 3 minutes when they bit or were tempted to bite their nails, and 7 other people composed the control group. All 21 people recorded the severity of their nail biting. Figure 6–7 shows the degree of damage they inflicted before and after the experiment. The people in the control group showed little change. The people who painted a bitter substance on their nails made a small amount of progress, due to the mild aversiveness of the bitter taste. The people who learned to do a competing response—that interfered with and prevented nail biting—made dramatic progress!

Group experimental designs differ in several ways from all the preceding designs, which are called **single-subject designs.** Both group and single-subject designs are valuable, though for different reasons. Group designs reveal average scores, which can be very useful in predicting how the average person would respond to various interventions. In contrast, single-subject designs allow us to assess the behavior of each unique individual, by himself or herself, to see what kind of behavioral interventions help that individual attain desirable behavioral changes. Group designs have been used in many branches of science, and they are invaluable when we need to see how an intervention will affect large numbers or special types of people. However, studying data on group averages can obscure the fact that a given behavioral intervention may not help certain individuals change, even though it helped many. Single-subject design allows us to study how each individual responds to an intervention and work to bring the best results to each person.[40] It also requires fewer participants. On the other hand, group therapy sometimes works as well as individual therapy and is more cost-effective since a therapist can help a whole group at once;[41] hence group experimental design is needed to evaluate which group therapies work well.

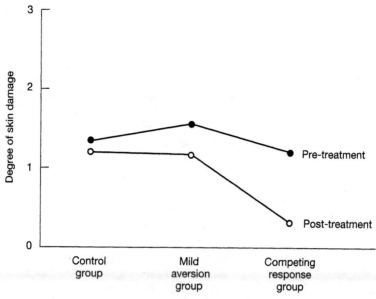

FIGURE 6–7   **These data show the average skin damage scores before and after treatment for all three groups in the experiment. Skin damage was recorded as 3 for severe, 2 for moderate, 1 for mild, and 0 for none.**

(Adapted from "Treating Nailbiting: A Comparative Analysis of Mild Aversion and Competing Response Therapies," by K.P. Silber & C.E. Haynes, 1992, *Behaviour Research and Therapy, 30*, pp. 15–22. Copyright 1992, with permission from Elsevier Science Ltd, The Boulevard, Langford Lane, Kidlington 0X5, UK.)

EVALUATION

Research on behavior modification benefits from constant examination and evaluation of all its components. Have we correctly identified the controlling variables—antecedents and consequences—that determine the target behavior? Have we created a behavioral intervention that produces the best results? Have the original goals been attained? Has the person benefited? Do we have enough objective data to document our answers to all these questions? Do we have enough data to understand interventions that resulted in only partial successes or failures, so we can learn from our shortfalls? We need data before, during, and after each behavioral intervention to evaluate all such questions. The data are valuable for improving earlier forms of behavior modification—and recognizing areas in which we have not yet been successful.[42]

   The core question in behavioral evaluations is this: Did any given behavioral intervention produce adequate changes in behavior? The absence of notable behavioral change indicates that we have not successfully identified and altered the controlling variables needed to modify behavior.[43]

A primary goal of behavior modification is to produce such obvious behavioral changes that there is simply no question about the effectiveness of the procedures used. If a behavioral intervention reliably produces the desired behavioral change almost every time it is used, it is deemed successful. Men who have sexual problems such as premature ejaculation take heart when they learn that behavioral sex therapy has a 94% success rate! Women who cannot have sexual intercourse due to vaginismus—a spastic contraction of the muscles surrounding the vagina that makes intercourse painful or impossible—are happy to learn that behavioral sex therapy has a 99% success rate in dealing with this problem.[44] If you ever need to have therapy, shop around and ask several therapists about their success rates. Many therapists do not have data on the success rates of the methods they use; but there are enough scientifically proven methods that you have a right to ask for treatments that are proven successes.[45]

The visual inspection of behavioral graphs offers us three ways to identify which behavioral changes are meaningful or not.[46] First, when every response during intervention is higher (or lower) than all the baseline responses, a major change has occurred. Figure 6–4 shows that Larry was much less noncompliant during his kidney treatments after behavior modification than before (during baseline). Second, when dealing with behaviors that change slowly, behavior modification is considered effective if there is a clear trend for the behavior to improve during the behavioral intervention. The third and weakest test is to see if the frequency of the target behavior at the end of behavior modification is clearly different from baseline. Any of these three findings is especially impressive if the behavioral change is still substantial when measured 2 or 12 months later—by a follow-up study.[47]

Practical criteria are essential, too. What if 5-year-old Tyler likes to play with fire? He often lights several books of matches a day, starting several fires each week. He almost burned down the house last month. We might design a behavior modification program that successfully reduced both match and fire lighting by 70%. On a graph, the results look impressive. A mathematician might find the data statistically significant. Nevertheless, if Tyler still comes close to torching the house once or twice a year on the new intervention, his parents might not be satisfied with the 70% improvement. In final analysis, practical criteria are often the bottom line. We need to find some method that brings Tyler's fire play close to zero, or only allows it in the safest of conditions—such as allowing Tyler to be "Designated Fire Starter" on camping trips and cookouts.

Normalcy is sometimes the criterion of choice. Shy people might want to attain normal social skills so they could interact and talk like their peers without feeling anxious. People who are quick to show anger and rage might wish to learn how to bring their aggressive outbreaks down to such a low level that others saw them as normal. This might involve their learning how to deal with difficult situations with poise, a calm voice, reason, constructive suggestions, and gracious compromises. Once formerly shy people or previously pugnacious people are close enough to normalcy that they can have reasonable lives, they may be satisfied. There is evidence that behavior modification that is done in natural settings creates more "normal" behavior than similar training in clinical settings.[48] Training in natural environments helps behavior come under the control of everyday life S^Ds, USs, CSs, and the natural consequences of behavior, hence the behavioral results look more natural and normal. If clinical training is needed at the start, a shift to naturalistic settings helps improve generalization of adaptive behavior to everyday life.

Health and personal adjustment can provide another set of criteria. People who are overweight or underweight might set their behavioral goal as reaching the "optimal weight zone," using medical charts that show the healthiest weights for people their height. Many people set personal goals of learning to exercise and eat correctly in order to attain optimal physical health. Some individuals set high goals for developing their human potential, and they evaluate their progress in terms of those criteria. Others seek to learn enough altruistic, academic, work, or business skills to create a personally fulfilling and economically stable lifestyle.

Consumer satisfaction can also be a very important element of our definition of significant change. What if Daniel discovers he can improve his grades by a half a letter score by merely graphing his study time and requiring that he works 25% more than baseline before he can play sports or watch TV each day? He may be quite happy with the change, even though it is not a radical one. An outside observer might agree if Daniel's grades improved from B to A–, but not be so impressed if they changed from D to C–. Some scholars argue that a consumer's subjective satisfaction with behavior modification is a weak measure and should not be ranked higher than objective measures and expert judgments.[49] Nevertheless, consumer satisfaction is important and needs to be assessed along with objective measures in an interactive process where consumers and researchers learn from each other.[50] One way to earn consumer satisfaction is to explain that behavioral interventions have been empirically demonstrated to be more effective than nonbehavioral therapies.[51] Arnold Lazarus (1997, p. 369) suggests that "it may soon be unethical, unprofessional, and perhaps illegal to by-pass scientifically established treatments of choice for specific disorders."

CONCLUSION

Behavior modification is the systematic application of behavior principles to produce behavioral change. Traditionally, behavior modification has been used to deal with behavioral excesses and deficits, but it can also be used to help people actualize greater portions of their human potential. First, a target behavior is identified and defined behaviorally—in objective terms that are easily measured. Long chains of behavior may need to be broken into smaller units that are clearly defined and measured. Second, each target behavior is subjected to a functional analysis, in search of all its possible antecedents and consequences—which are called the "controlling variables" of the target behavior. The data generated from functional analyses are used to create multiple hypotheses about the behavior and possible ways to alter its controlling variables in order to create behavioral changes. As the hypotheses and possible study techniques begin to take shape, appropriate units of measurement can be selected—be they numerical counts, frequencies, cumulative times, percentages, numbers of people, or rating scales. Data can be collected and then recorded on graphs, checklists, tape recorders, notebooks, ABC diaries, computers, or other such tools.

Four types of experimental designs are commonly used in behavioral research. Reversal designs—in such formats as ABAB—allow us to see if behavioral changes appear during the behavioral intervention and then disappear in the reversal phase (the second A). Multiple-baseline designs start different treatments at different times to see if behavior changes when and only when it is shifted to the behavioral intervention. Alternating-treatment designs allow us to watch for behavioral changes as a person alternates among two or more different behavioral treatments. Group experimental designs apply a behavioral intervention to an experimental group to see if it creates behavioral changes that make them different from the control group. Evaluation is the process used to determine whether or not behavioral changes are large enough to be considered meaningful. All aspects of behavioral research are open to evaluation and improvement.

QUESTIONS

1. What is a good basic definition of behavior modification? Can you apply your definition to one or more examples of behavior modification given in this chapter?
2. How does one identify target behaviors and create behavioral definitions of them? Can you demonstrate how these two tasks are done by using examples from this chapter?
3. What is the definition of functional analysis? How does one do a functional analysis of a target behavior? Can you demonstrate your answers with one or more examples of behavior modification given in this chapter?
4. How can the ABC model be used to understand how behavior functions in specific contexts or environments? How does a functional analysis of the ABCs of a target behavior help us understand ways we can change it and create plans for behavior modification?
5. Can you explain several ways to make objective measures of behavior? When is a stopwatch or digital chronograph useful? Why? How can one use a small golf-score counter in keeping behavioral data?
6. What are baseline measures? Why are they important?
7. Can you name the four research designs used in studies of behavior modification?
8. Explain ABAB reversal designs. Why are these useful? What does the word reversal mean in this type of design?
9. Can you explain how multiple-baseline designs are used? When are these useful?
10. How are alternating-treatment designs used?
11. What are group experimental designs? Give an example.
12. What is the difference between group experimental design and single-subject design?
13. What are the main points of the section on evaluation?

NOTES

1. Cohen, DeJames, Nocera, and Ramberger (1980); Craighead, Stunkard, and O'Brien (1981); Katahn, Pleas, Thackrey, and Wallston (1982); Foreyt and Goodrick (1984); De Luca and Holborn (1992); Janzen and Cousins (1995); Watson and Tharp (1997).
2. Sloan and Mizes (1996); Freiheit and Overholser (1997); Matson, Bamburg, Smalls, and Smiroldo (1998); Matson, Smalls, Hampff, Smiroldo, and Anderson (1998).
3. Skinner (1988); Logue (1995); Martin and Pear (1996); Watson and Tharp (1997).
4. Bandura (1969); Sherman (1972); Glover and Gary (1975); Walen, Hauserman, and Lavin (1977); Hersen and Bellack (1985); Mersch, Emmelkamp, Bögels, and van der Sleen (1989); Mize and Ladd (1990); Axelrod (1991); Bannerman, Sheldon, and Sherman (1991); Budney, Higgins, Delaney, Kent, and Bickel

(1991); Halle and Holt (1991); Horner, Day, Sprague, O'Brien, and Heathfield (1991); Antonuccio, Boutilier, Ward, Morrill, and Graybar (1992); Booth and Rachman (1992); Hill, Rigdon, and Johnson (1993); Telch et al. (1993); Beck and Zebb (1994); Johnson and Fawcett (1994); Kern, Childs, Dunlap, Clarke, and Falk (1994); Gould and Clum (1995); Jason et al. (1995); Mental Health (1995); Green and Reid (1996); Marshall (1999).

5. Horner et. al. (1990); Werts, Caldwell, and Wolery (1996); Huang and Cuvo (1997); Koegel, Camarata, Valdez-Menchaca, and Koegel (1998).

6. Staats (1999) reminds us that behavior modification most benefits from drawing on its scientific foundation in behaviorism.

7. Grabowski, Stitzer, and Henningfield (1984); Budney et al. (1991); Brigham, Meier, and Goodner (1995).

8. Baer (1962); McClanahan (1995).

9. Martin and Pear (1996); Watson and Tharp (1997); Baldwin and Baldwin (2000).

10. Theeboom, De Knop, and Weiss (1995).

11. Reflexes do not need consequences (reinforcers or punishers) to appear; but they can be shaped by consequences (see Chapter 4).

12. The controlling variables are sometimes called "causal variables" (Delprato & Midgley, 1992).

13. Correa and Sutker (1986); Spaulding (1986); Day, Horner, and O'Neill (1994); Horner (1994); Ishaq (1996); Hagopian et al. (1997); Smith and Iwata (1997); Lalli and Kates (1998); Kahng and Iwata (1999).

14. O'Neill et al. (1990); Harding et al. (1999).

15. O'Neill et al. (1990); Axelrod (1991); Fawcett (1991); Ishaq (1996). But it is not always possible to identify the functional role of behavior.

16. Smith, Iwata, Goh, and Shore (1995).

17. Vollmer, Iwata, Zarcone, Smith, and Mazaleski (1993); Iwata et al. (1994); Derby, Fisher, and Piazza (1996).

18. Bandura (1969); Mahoney (1974); Bellack and Hersen (1977); Horner and Day (1991); Kazdin (1994); Martin and Pear (1996).

19. Spaulding (1986); Carr (1994).

20. Koegel, Koegel, and Schreibman (1991); Koegel, Koegel, Hurley, and Frea (1992); Koegel and Frea (1993); Koegel, Bimbela, and Schreibman (1996).

21. Derby et al. (1997); Rosales-Ruiz and Baer (1997).

22. Schneier, Martin, Liebowitz, Gorman, and Fyer (1989); Donohue, Acierno, Van Hasselt, and Hersen (1995); Crolley, Roys, Thyer, and Bordnick (1998); Paul, Marx, and Orsillo (1999).

23. Spaulding (1986).

24. Newman, Consoli, and Taylor (1999).

25. Watson and Tharp (1997).

26. Miller and Kelley (1994).

27. Ayllon and Michael (1959); Ayllon and Haughton (1964).

28. Mace and Lalli (1991).

29. Williams (1959); Zimmerman and Zimmerman (1962); Bandura (1973).

30. Webb (1966).

31. Brewer (1992).

32. Kazdin (1980); Perone (1991, p. 154).

33. Bandura (1969); Kazdin (1980); Carton and Schweitzer (1996).

34. See Goldstein, Kaczmarek, Pennington, and Shafer (1992) for an alternative approach to increasing social interaction.

35. Bandura (1973); Kohn (1992).

36. Sharpe, Brown, and Crider (1995).

37. Dunlap, Kern-Dunlap, Clarke, and Robbins (1991, p. 388).

38. Kazdin (1994, pp. 110–111).

39. Barlow and Hersen (1984); McGonigle, Rojahn, Dixon, and Strain (1987). Alternating-treatment designs are sometimes called **simultaneous-treatment designs.**

40. Hersen and Barlow (1976); Kazdin (1980).

41. Bandura (1969); Peterson and Halstead (1998).

42. Kazdin (1993).

43. Bellack and Hersen (1977); Vollmer, Marcus, Ringdahl, and Roane (1995).

44. Masters and Johnson (1966); Masters, Johnson, and Kolodny (1995).

45. Thyer (1995).

46. Scruggs and Mastropieri (1998).

47. Eight-year follow-ups are especially impressive (Welsh, Miller, & Altus, 1994).

48. Koegel, Camarata, Koegel, Ben-Tall, and Smith (1998); Koegel, et al. (1998); Eifert, Forsyth, Zvolensky, and Lejuez (1999).

49. Hawkins (1991).

50. Finney (1991); Schwartz and Baer (1991).

51. Montgomery and Ayllon (1995).

Primary Reinforcers and Punishers

NO PAIN, NO GAIN

If asked if you would like to go through the rest of life without ever feeling any pain again, would you say "yes"? Many people would. It sounds like pain-free bliss. Tanya is one of several hundred people who are incapable of feeling pain.[1] A bee stings her, and she feels no pain. She stubs her toe—and feels no pain. She falls down a flight of stairs—still no pain.

Actually, Tanya's story is a tragic one, and it teaches us what an important signal pain can be. Tanya's parents thought their baby was healthy and normal until her mother found her 18-month-old daughter fingerpainting with blood on the sheets of her playpen. Tanya had bitten off the end of her finger and was using her own blood as fingerpaint. Her parents tried to punish her for doing this self-damage, but she felt no pain. When Tanya began to walk, things got worse: She could not feel pain if she stepped on thumbtacks, broken glass, or other sharp objects, and her feet became a mass of wounds and open sores.

Tanya was born with a rare disorder known as "congenital indifference to pain." From birth she could not feel pain. She could feel reinforcers and pleasure, but no punishers or pain. When she cut herself or fell, she experienced no pain and no punishment. As a result, she had a hard time learning not to fall, cut, or burn herself. By age 4, her body was covered with bruises and open sores. She had dislocated her foot so badly that her left ankle hung loosely in its

149

socket. By age 11, her fingers had been worn to stubs and both her legs amputated.[2] Most people with Tanya's condition die of wounds, injuries, or fatal accidents before age 20.

Tanya was deprived of the pain feedback that punishes most of us when we do something that injures our bodies. We feel pain for a reason. It is an important signal. Our bodies are filled with sensory nerves that connect to pain centers in the brain and punish those behaviors that bring us bodily harm. Pain is not the greatest of all feelings, but it is important to our health and survival. And we have evolved to be able to tolerate mild and moderate levels of pain and benefit from it. Better to feel some pain than lose our fingers and legs, as Tanya did.

Most of us are born with the capacity to feel pleasure and pain—primary reinforcers and punishers—and they help keep us alive, healthy, and out of harm's way. Yet most people are not very aware of the full importance of the primary reinforcers and punishers in their lives, even though they enjoy food, drink, and other primary reinforcers—and dislike the pain of the primary punishers. This chapter will heighten your awareness of the amazing ways that pleasure and pain function as reinforcers and punishers. This knowledge can help us heighten the pleasures we have a right to enjoy in life and avoid some unwanted pains—while respecting the importance of the pain signals that our body sends us when we endanger it.

BIOLOGICALLY IMPORTANT STIMULI

Reinforcers and punishers can be divided into two general types, primary and secondary. *The word "primary" implies a primitive, biological origin. We are biologically prepared to respond to **primary reinforcers** and **primary punishers** without having to learn to do so.* Our survival depends on them, and most of us are born with the ability to feel their pleasures and pains. Tanya shows us some of the perils of being unresponsive to such primitive signals.

*Stimuli that regularly precede and predict primary reinforcers and punishers often become **secondary reinforcers** and **secondary punishers**.* These can vary considerably among individuals because they depend on our unique personal learning experiences. Rap and hard rock music can be secondary reinforcers to a teen and secondary punishers to a grandparent raised in a different generation. Chapter 8 shows how secondary reinforcers and punishers take on their power if they are associated with primary reinforcers and punishers. The present chapter deals with the primary reinforcers and punishers.

All the primary reinforcers and primary punishers are biologically important stimuli, essential to survival.[3] Our ability to respond to them allows us to be rewarded for locating food, water, optimal temperature, sex, and other primary reinforcers, and punished when we cut, burn, or otherwise harm our bodies. *Primary reinforcers and primary punishers are also called **unconditioned reinforcers** and **unconditioned punishers** to indicate that they are USs that derive their power from primitive biological sources and do not need conditioning to be effective.*

As Skinner observed, "The capacity to be reinforced . . . must be traced to natural selection."[4] Our ability to respond to food and water as primary reinforcers—and cuts and burns as primary punishers—is crucial for survival; hence these biological capacities have been favored and established through evolutionary processes. Individuals who are biologically inclined to respond to food, water, and sex as primary reinforcers (USs) are more likely to survive and reproduce than are individuals without these inclinations. People who are biologically predisposed to respond to cuts, burns, falls, and other hazards as primary punishers (USs) are also more likely to survive than individuals—such as Tanya— without these predispositions.

Although the primary reinforcers and punishers established during millions of years of evolution help us learn many adaptive behaviors, we should not assume they are perfectly tuned for dealing with modern life. We have evolved with a strong tendency to respond to sugar as a positive reinforcer, perhaps because sugar was scarce in our evolutionary past. But in our modern world, refined sugar can be produced cheaply and many people consume far more calories from sugar than is healthy for them. The primary reinforcers and punishers established by past evolutionary conditions do not always serve us well today. The ease with which people can become addicted to cocaine, heroin, and other drugs shows that the body can respond to harmful substances as positive reinforcers. Nothing in our evolutionary past could have prepared us to deal with these potent drugs.

Fixed But Flexible

Primary reinforcers and punishers are biologically rooted—as USs—thus they are somewhat fixed and reliable. But, they are also flexible and vary across times and situations: They are relative, not absolute or unchangeable.

To understand the fixed but flexible nature of primary reinforcers and punishers, it is helpful to place all reinforcers and punishers on a continuum (see Fig. 7–1), with powerful reinforcers (at the left end) having the ability to raise the probability of behavior, and powerful punishers (at the right end) having the ability to suppress behavior.[5] In the middle of the continuum, the stimuli are called neutral because they have no measurable capacity to reinforce or punish behavior. Adjacent to the neutral stimuli, the reinforcers and punishers are weaker than at the ends of the continuum.

Most primary reinforcers and punishers do not occupy a single location on the continuum. A given stimulus, such as food or sex, can take various positions on the continuum at different times and in different situations.[6] When we are hungry, a delicious meal serves as a strong positive reinforcer (near the left end of Fig. 7–1); but after we have eaten our fill, the food ceases to be a strong positive reinforcer and becomes more neutral (near the center of the continuum). Same for sex. Thus, one cannot make a fixed classification of a given stimulus as having one and only one location on the continuum of reinforcers and punishers.

The ability to reinforce or punish behavior is not a fixed or intrinsic quality of a stimulus. Even though the physical properties of a stimulus may be fixed, its ability to function as a primary reinforcer or punisher depends on the state of our bodies and our prior learning. A dark, quiet room provides reinforcement for entering and staying when we are tired and sleepy, but staying there is boring when we are awake and well rested.

Thus, the effects of reinforcers and punishers are relative. Their effects are not fixed and unchangeable, even when their visible stimulus properties are stable and unchanging.

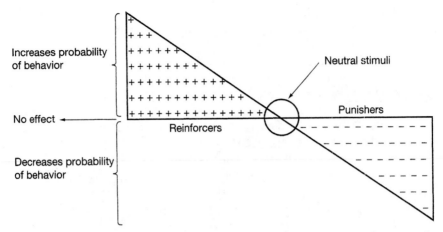

FIGURE 7–1 The continuum of consequences, with the strongest reinforcers at the left end and the strongest punishers at the right end.

In addition, having determined that a stimulus is a reinforcer or a punisher in one context does not mean the stimulus will have the same function at other times or in other contexts. Grade school children often hold onto their parents while being hugged and kissed at home with the family; yet they may pull away if a parent hugs or kisses them in front of their friends. This response pattern shows that the children respond to hugs at home as reinforcers for making physical contact, and hugs in public as punishers that motivate avoidance. *Stimuli that function as reinforcers or punishers in one situation can have different effects in different contexts.* During childhood a person may consistently avoid eating brussels sprouts; yet in adulthood, the person may love eating them. Thus, brussels sprouts functioned as a punisher in childhood and serve as a reinforcer in adulthood. *A given stimulus can function as a reinforcer, neutral stimulus, or punisher in different situations.* Marge had enjoyed sexual relations for years, but after being raped, she came to fear and avoid any behavior that might lead to a sexual interaction. Sex was a positive reinforcer before Marge was raped; afterward it became a punisher. After a year with a very caring and loving partner, Marge found that sex slowly shifted across the continuum to neutral and then became a positive reinforcer.

UNCONDITIONED STIMULI

The primary reinforcers and punishers take their power from their connection with the unconditioned stimuli (USs) that trigger biologically based reflexes. *Unconditioned stimuli (USs) have two separate functions: (1) They elicit unconditioned reflexes (which makes Pavlovian conditioning possible), and (2) most function as primary reinforcers or primary punishers (which makes operant conditioning possible).*[7] When we are hungry, food is an effective US that (1) elicits salivation and positive emotional responses, and (2) reinforces operant behaviors that help us find and ingest food. Scalding hot water is a US that

(1) elicits a withdrawal reflex and negative emotional responses, and (2) punishes operant behaviors that lead to being burned by boiling water.

The following sections describe several of the major primary reinforcers and punishers, showing why they are often stable and fixed. But we will also see why they sometimes vary in power from moment to moment, day to day, and year to year.

Primary Reinforcers

Table 7–1 lists some of the primary reinforcers that commonly influence behavior in everyday life. If you compare this list with Table 2–1, you will see that some of the primary reinforcers in Table 7–1 are also USs that elicit unconditioned reflexes: Food elicits salivation and genital stimulation elicits sexual responses. Food, water, comfortable temperatures, rest, caresses, and body massages all are socially acceptable in our society; genital stimulation and drugs, however, can raise eyebrows. Not all societies are equally accepting of the use of primary reinforcers. When Captain Cook first discovered Tahiti, he reported that public displays of sex were acceptable, but people were unwilling to eat with others—because filling one's mouth with food was unacceptable in social settings and caused embarrassment![8]

Primary reinforcers can have strong or weak effects at different points in time. They often take on especially strong powers to reinforce when we have not had access to them for a while, then lose their reinforcement power after we have had considerable recent exposure to them. Two important processes, *satiation* and *deprivation,* help explain why primary reinforcers lose or gain power.[9]

Satiation.   *Satiation occurs when a person has had so much of a certain primary reinforcer that the stimulus loses its ability to function as a reinforcer.* Generally, the more satiated a person is with any primary reinforcer, the less power that US will have to reinforce behavior. When a person is satiated with food, it ceases to function as a rein-

---

TABLE 7–1   A partial list of primary reinforcers

Food

Water

Normal body temperature

Optimal levels of sensory stimulation*

Rest after exertion

Sleep

Caresses, rubbing, itching, scratching

Genital stimulation

Nipple and breast stimulation (especially during lactation)

Nicotine, alcohol, various other drugs

---

*Optimal sensory stimulation is one of the least noticed of the primary reinforcers, yet it is one of the most important primary reinforcers in everyday life, as explained in the text.

forcer. The fifth Hershey bar you eat in a row will not taste as good as the first one. After working hard on a hot day, a swallow of cool spring water is a refreshing and pleasurable experience, but the water ceases to function as a reinforcer after you have drunk several glasses. Being itched, scratched, or rubbed for several minutes is pleasurable and rewarding; but itching and rubbing cease to be reinforcers after a given part of the body has been stimulated for an extended period of time. Genital stimulation also loses its positive reinforcement qualities when partners engage in prolonged sexual stimulation without pauses. Inserting pauses between the Hershey bars—or other positive reinforcers—slows the satiation process.

Deprivation.   *Deprivation is the opposite of satiation: The longer a person has been deprived of a given primary reinforcer, the more power that US acquires for reinforcing behavior.* For example, when a person is deprived of food for many hours, food becomes increasingly reinforcing. In everyday life, deprivation can result from a variety of causes: natural, deliberate, and compulsory.

1. Natural Deprivation.   While engaging in long chains of activities that are reinforced by one type of reinforcer, people often do not notice that they are being deprived of other reinforcers. But when they satiate on the first reinforcer, they may notice some of their other states of deprivation. While playing basketball all afternoon, the players may not detect the increasing food deprivation. During an exciting afternoon at the stock exchange, a broker may forget to eat and not notice any signs of hunger. But when the broker leaves the office and the basketball players finish their game, they may be surprised how hungry they have become and how strongly their attention is directed to food. Because active and busy people are usually very intent on the activities of the moment, they often do not notice levels of deprivation that others might consider aversive.

2. Deliberate Deprivation.   People often deliberately abstain from eating before a big Thanksgiving meal because it makes the food seem more delicious and allows them to eat more of it. People sometimes deliberately stay up until they are very tired before going to bed, because the deprivation makes them sleep more deeply, and they find this more pleasurable than light, fitful sleep after minimal sleep deprivation.

3. Compulsory Deprivation.   Sometimes husbands and wives have to live in different cities because of the location of their schools or jobs. When they do get a chance to see each other, they often find that the days of deprivation have enhanced the degree to which touching, caressing, and making love are positive reinforcers. Poor people in undeveloped countries often experience compulsory food deprivation from which there is little relief. Hundreds of millions of the world's poorest people are almost always in a state of food deprivation. Although people in wealthy nations sometimes complain about their food deprivation when they cannot find anything in the refrigerator they really want to eat, their hunger pains are minimal compared with the chronic hunger of the world's truly hungry people.

Extreme deprivation can lead people to do things they would never otherwise do. In the winter of 1846, a group of American pioneers—the Donner Party—was trapped high in the California mountains, just north of Lake Tahoe, while heading west. Thirty-four people died of cold and hunger. Many of the 45 survivors kept from starving by eating their dead companions.[10] In China, during the great famine of 1943, people stripped the bark off trees in order to have something to put in their stomachs—even though bark is of minimal nutritive value.[11] There were reports that children were sometimes killed and eaten, in spite of the cultural and moral sanctions against such behavior. In World War II, the Germans blockaded Leningrad (now St. Petersburg) for 900 days, causing over a million people, mostly civilians, to die from hunger and cold. Historical records reveal that

> [c]annibalism was so much a fact of everyday life that parents feared their children would be eaten if allowed out after dark. . . . [T]he city police created an entire division to fight cannibals, and some 260 Leningraders were convicted of the crime and jailed for the crime. . . .
>
> They [citizens] scraped wallpaper down and ate the paste, which was supposedly made from potatoes. They extracted the same paste from bookbindings, or drank it straight from the glue jar. They boiled leather belts and briefcases to make an edible jelly, and plucked and pickled grasses and weeds.
>
> They ate cats and dogs, petroleum jelly and lipstick, spices and medicines, fur coats and leather caps.[12]

In October, 1972, an airplane with 45 people aboard crashed in the snow-covered Andes at nearly 12,000 feet altitude, and 32 passengers survived the crash.[13] Rather than die of starvation, the survivors decided after weeks had passed to cut the bodies of their dead companions into small pieces and eat them. Sixteen people survived the 73 days of cold and hardship until rescue came. Under extreme food deprivation, people sometimes turn to behaviors they would never normally do, even if the behavior seems odd or revolting.

Primary Punishers

Table 7–2 lists some of the primary punishers that are common in everyday life. *Primary punishers are those things that can hurt our bodies and endanger our survival, and we are biologically primed to find them painful.* Bee stings, dog bites, and falls from high places are among the painful stimuli we feel as primary punishers. You will find some of the USs that are primary punishers in Table 2–1, which lists several unconditioned reflexes: Burns elicit the withdrawal reflex, tainted foods elicit nausea.

Primary punishers do not show the rapid changes in strength seen with the satiation and deprivation of primary reinforcers. However, primary punishers can change over time, due to **adaptation.** *We sometimes adapt to punishers that we experience over and over during life, finding them somewhat less painful over time.* If you are not a carpenter and you get 2 or 3 splinters while working with wood, each splinter hurts. However, if you are a carpenter and have multiple experiences with splinters, you may find that you cease to notice them as much as the years go by. You have adapted to a pain you encounter often and find it less of a pain. People who often get burned at work get "toughened up," and adapt to the minor burns as "no big deal."

Usually there is a **threshold effect** with punishers. *The total amount of primary punishers we experience must exceed some crucial level—called a threshold—before we*

TABLE 7–2   **A partial list of primary punishers**

Extreme cold and extreme heat

Cuts, strong blows, sharp scratches

Shock, stings, burns

Sore skin

Overly full stomach or bladder

Effortful or strenuous work

Certain odors and tastes

Loud noise

Extinction

Lack of air

Water in the lungs

Poisons, diseases, tainted foods that cause nausea or sickness

find them aversive. Many people are happy to do easy tasks but when the effort needed to do the task is raised above their personal threshold of acceptability, they begin to avoid the effortful tasks.[14] Being scratched must surpass a certain limit before scratches are aversive. Once above the threshold, increasing the intensity of the sharp scratches increases the strength of the pain and punishment effects. If your neighbor's cat gave you a superficial scratch every once in a while, this mild punisher might slightly suppress your tendency to pick up the cat. However, if the cat regularly gave you quite painful scratches, the intense punishment might completely suppress your reaching toward the cat.

Some cats, dogs, and people learn to strike out at others with sharp and punitive behavior. *There are two reasons why the use of strong primary punishers can be learned very quickly and easily.* If we want to create a more caring and humane society, we need to know these two in order to resist their influences and help others avoid them, too.

First, the individual who uses strong punishment on others often receives immediate rewards for doing so. If Uncle Ed wants to stop his niece from pestering him, strong punishment usually produces immediate effects. Threats of punishment can also create instant effects: "If you don't stop pestering me right this minute, I'll give you a spanking you'll never forget." If such threats have been followed by strong punishment in the past, the niece may stop pestering and avoid being near Uncle Ed. The instant effectiveness of both punishment and threats thereof provides immediate rewards for the person who wants to stop a behavior and does not think about the bad effects it can have.

Second, strong primary punishers are almost always effective: Even after several uses, they do not lose much power to punish behavior or negatively reinforce escape or avoidance. In contrast, primary reinforcers lose their effectiveness after a person reaches satiation: Food ceases to be a reinforcer after a person is full. Strong punishment usually remains aversive; thus, some people come to rely heavily on aversive control because strong punishment almost always produces effects.

People who have not learned friendly cooperative ways of interacting with others—based on positive reinforcement—are most likely to be drawn into heavy reliance on strong punishment. When their limited positive skills fail, they can always fall back on threats or punishers—with their immediate effects and persistent power.

Physical punishment is used far more commonly in everyday life than many people realize. For example, there are about 3 million cases of child physical abuse per year in the United States.[15] Because small children cannot escape or fight back, parents meet little resistance in using corporal punishment in child rearing, and some escalate the intensity of punishment to dangerous, bone-breaking levels. Although small, dependent children cannot escape the parent who punishes so hard that bones are broken, older children frequently run away from home when staying is too aversive. Over a million children run away from home each year.

Violence can beget violence: By observing their parents' behavior, children from violent homes often learn habits of using violence on others. They may not strike back at their parents for fear of getting a physical blow in return, but on the playground they may fight and bully other children, imitating social patterns they see at home.[16] Once they reach adulthood, people from violent homes are more likely to be child abusers than are people from nonviolent homes.[17] They are also more likely to expect and to use physical violence in interactions with their spouse.[18] An aggressive husband may strike his wife when she refuses to comply with some wish, and she may accept this as normal, if that is the way she saw her father treat her mother. Severe physical abuse—involving biting, kicking, hitting, beating, or using a weapon—occurs at least once, and often more than once in over 6% of marriages.[19] Each year 1,500 women are murdered by their husbands or boyfriends. The use of primary punishers is not restricted to the home. Throughout history, people have used flogging, torture, branding, lynching, crucifixions, inquisitions, witch-hunts, concentration camps, and war in the attempt to control others by inflicting pain.

In the long run, aversive techniques of social control produce numerous problems. Punishment can condition a variety of responses ranging from fear, anxiety, and avoidance to hatred, violence, and revolution. All of these responses undermine stable, cooperative, and constructive social relationships. Modern behavioral science has demonstrated that most behavior can be learned, or prevented, via positive reinforcement—without the bad side effects produced by punishment (Chapter 14). In addition, positive reinforcement makes learning much more pleasant than learning via punishment or negative reinforcement. One of the greatest challenges to modern society is to phase out the heavy reliance on punishment that has been so common in the past and to help people learn the power and pleasure of using positive reinforcement.[20]

MODIFYING PRIMARY CONSEQUENCES

Because primary reinforcers and punishers play important biological roles in survival and reproduction, it might seem logical to assume they would be biologically fixed and resistant to change (except for the short-term fluctuations due to deprivation, satiation, or adaptation). One might expect that food would always be a reinforcer for a hungry person, whereas being beaten would always be a punisher. But this is not the case.

Any US that serves as a primary reinforcer or primary punisher can be modified to a different location on the continuum from strong reinforcers to strong punishers (Fig. 7–2).[21] As a result, some people learn to find food or sex to be more powerful reinforcers than is normally the case (shifting from "a" to "A" in the fig.). Other people learn to dislike food and become dangerously underweight (shifting from "a" to "b"). There are people who assiduously avoid sex, indicating that it functions as a punisher for them. On the other hand, some people learn to find primary punishers less painful than others, and a minority respond to them as positive reinforcers (a shift from "b" to "a" or "A"). Some children engage in hours of head banging and self-mutilation each day, and some adults are drawn to masochistic sexual practices that others would find aversive.

Any US that is a primary reinforcer or primary punisher can be shifted to a new location on the continuum from strong reinforcers to strong punishers. This modification occurs through Pavlovian conditioning when a US is predictive of and frequently followed by other reinforcers or punishers.[22] Pavlov's original experiments with dogs illustrate how a US can be a predictive stimulus and be influenced much as a CS would be.[23] For a moderately hungry dog, food is normally a US that elicits salivation and reinforces relevant operants. However, if food is regularly presented before a powerful punisher, such as a strong electric shock, food also becomes a CS that elicits aversive emotional responses. After repeated presentations of food before strong shock, the dog will show signs of fear when food is presented. It may whine and yelp, cower, and pull its tail between its legs. Food can become so powerful a punisher that it suppresses eating. Food has been shifted from position "a" to position "b" in Figure 7–2.

The opposite modification can occur, too. If a dog is made hungry by food deprivation and shock precedes the presentation of food, shock can be conditioned into a positive reinforcer, even though shock is normally a US that elicits pain. After repeated pairings, the shock becomes a CS that elicits smacking of the lips and salivation, and it also functions as a positive reinforcer. As long as the shocks reliably signal that food is forthcoming, they will serve as positive reinforcers. Shock has been shifted from position "b" to position "a" in Figure 7–2.

The Modification of Primary Reinforcers

Numerous examples from everyday life show how primary reinforcers and primary punishers are modified by learning. Some people learn to have little interest in food, whereas others become overly responsive to food as a reinforcer. The same is true of alcohol, sex,

FIGURE 7–2 **The modification of primary reinforcers and primary punishers.**

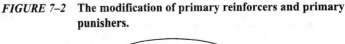
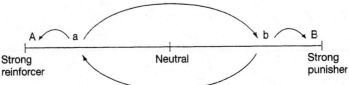

and other primary reinforcers. A variety of conditioning events can be responsible for decreasing or increasing a person's responsiveness to primary reinforcers—shifting them from "a" to "b," or to "B," or to "A" in Figure 7–2.

When a primary reinforcer regularly precedes aversive stimuli, the primary reinforcer becomes a weaker reinforcer, and may—with sufficient conditioning—even become a punisher. Some children grow up in families where fights occur frequently at the dinner table. Dinner is commonly paired with nasty arguments and ugly criticisms, all of which elicit negative emotional responses in the children. Eventually, food becomes a CS that elicits aversive responses, which makes eating less reinforcing and weight loss likely.

Some people have been made so fearful of gaining weight or getting fat—because the super models and "beautiful people" in the media are not "fat"—that food can become a CS for aversive feelings. As food loses its strength as a reinforcer and begins to function as a punisher, some people eat less and lose weight. Sometimes people can become dangerously thin and close to death by starvation, as in extreme cases of anorexia.[24]

Even though Hollywood splashes sexy images in most of its movies (making it seem like sex is ubiquitous in our society), many people do not respond to sex as a positive reinforcer.[25] When sex is continually paired with aversive circumstances, it ceases being a positive reinforcer and becomes aversive, a source of anxiety, worry, guilt, doubt, or fear. Many different kinds of experiences can condition sex into a punisher. In some homes, the parents repeatedly stress that sex is dirty or sinful. Some parents punish masturbation with fear-eliciting threats about impending mental illness, acne, or damnation: "It will cause you to go blind and hair to grow on the palms of your hands." None of this is true, but it can frighten a child.

When children ask questions about sex out of innocent curiosity, they may be chastised for thinking such "filthy thoughts." When heavy doses of punishment and fear-eliciting threats are paired with sex, the aversive experiences can be stronger than the biologically reinforcing aspects of sex, hence modifying sex to be a punisher. While children are growing up, they may not know they are being conditioned to find sex aversive. A boy may realize he does not like to talk about sex even though his friends do, but his prior conditioning would make it aversive for him to indulge in such "dirty, base, and animalistic thoughts." A girl may be aware she does not like to be kissed and avoids it, but she may feel proud she has a good reputation. By their late teens, the boy and girl know that they are not engaging in heavy petting, even though some of their peers do, but again they find that their abstinence shows higher values. Perhaps it is not until they are married and free to have sexual relations that they discover how anxious they actually feel when confronted with sex. Even after marriage, some of these people cannot find pleasure in something that has been described as "dirty" for so many years. Sometimes the negative conditioning leads to erectile problems and the inability to have orgasm. After years of marriage some men and women admit they have never enjoyed sex, and their rare lovemaking was done only to have children or satisfy one partner's desires.

People can develop conditioned anxieties about sex in a very short time. After a man fails to have a full sexual response with his wife on several consecutive occasions, he may begin to fear that he is "impotent." This fear can then interfere with his further sexual functioning and increase the chances of additional sexual failures. Each time sexual activity is paired with failure, the aversive conditioning modifies sex toward the punishment end of the continuum of reinforcers and punishers (Fig. 7–2). Eventually, hearing his partner ask to make love raises his fears of failure and elicits performance anxiety. Sex has now become a punisher that functions as a negative reinforcer for avoiding situations that could lead to sexual interaction.

Sex need not remain a punisher forever. With the appropriate counterconditioning, sex can be modified to again be a positive reinforcer. Numerous forms of sex therapy are very effective in establishing pleasurable sexual functioning even in people who have had years of sex-related anxieties—or who *never* have had any sexual success.[26]

When a primary reinforcer regularly precedes other reinforcers, the primary reinforcer gains even greater reinforcement value. For example, when food is paired with numerous other reinforcers—or the avoidance of aversive events—it can become an unusually powerful positive reinforcer, making it hard for people to stop eating even when they should. Many people regularly eat food in the presence of other positive reinforcers. The process can begin in infancy or later in life. Many well-intentioned mothers think that pudgy children are healthy children. When the child stops eating, the mother coaxes the child to have another helping of food. When dinner is over, mother scoops out a big serving of the child's favorite dessert. If the child is not seduced by the sweetness and flavor, the mother may encourage the child to eat by acting hurt: "I made it especially for you and now you won't eat it." When the child eats the extra food, the mother responds with warmth and affection. These multiple conditioning influences make food a more positive reinforcer than is biologically adaptive.

All through life, people are exposed to numerous types of social conditioning that can increase the reinforcement value of food. When college students eat together in cafeterias or restaurants, food is often paired with rewarding social interactions, jokes, laughter, fun—and perhaps the avoidance of studying. These positive experiences help condition food further toward the left end of the continuum of reinforcers (Fig. 7–2). All through adulthood, people frequently have chips, dips, ribs, niblets, and other enticing foods available while socializing, which often pairs food with social reinforcers. In addition, people can become excessively attracted to food when eating is regularly paired with an escape from anxiety, boredom, or other aversive experiences. People who are bored look for something to do. Eating is something to do. Escaping boredom is a reinforcer. Eating gradually becomes an unusually powerful reinforcer, because it is followed by escape from boredom. The round bellies that become increasingly prevalent as Americans enter their 30s and 40s reflect, in part, the cumulative results of years of conditioning of food into an increasingly powerful positive reinforcer.

The Modification of Primary Punishers

Primary punishers can lose some of their aversiveness—and even become positive reinforcers—if they are paired with numerous other reinforcers.[27] Athletes often become conditioned to find the rigors of their sport less aversive than the ordinary individual would. During the socialization of football players, giving and receiving painful blows is associated with positive reinforcers—such as praise, team support, the excitement of the game, promotions to first string, comradeship with the "top players," and social status. After having violent blows paired with these positive reinforcers for years, many football players cannot only tolerate higher levels of painful stimuli, but actually find these stimuli less punishing.

When unathletic people take up jogging for the first time, they often find the physical exertion sheer torture. They find it difficult to believe the experienced runner who says the aversiveness will go away after a while. Many joggers quit before they discover that pain-inducing stimuli can be modified. However, the joggers who receive enough reinforcement to keep running begin to discover that it is an exhilarating experience. If there are enough rewards for running, the sensations from the straining legs and pounding heart begin to function as well-earned rewards.

Certain aspects of masochism can be traced to experiences in which primary punishers were often paired with positive reinforcers. For example, a person who enjoys masochistic sexual practices usually has a history of conditioning that began when mild punishers were paired with exciting sexual experiences. After an exhilarating rock concert, Abby tied Michael loosely to the bed and spanked him gently on the derrière. This led to some playful imitations of a B&D scene (bondage and discipline) they had seen in a video and ended with a great time in bed. The sexual excitement plus the novelty of the experience counterconditioned fears of being tied loosely and swatted gently, which shifted B&D swatting slightly toward the reinforcer zone in Fig. 7–2. The next time, Michael allowed the ropes to be tied tighter without fearing any real danger, allowing him and Abby to explore the next steps of their newfound "dangerous" game. Over several months, being tied tightly and spanked became conditioned into a reinforcer by the positive reinforcers of sex, fun, and games. Eventually Michael came to enjoy B&D stimuli that would be experienced as painful or frightening by most people.

Social conditioning can cause some people to become more sensitive to pain and suffering over time.[28] People who experience back pain or other painful medical conditions often receive considerable social attention for their maladies, especially if they have a very caring and solicitous spouse. Studies show that the more solicitous the spouse, the higher the patient's pain perception. Parents of depressed teens often become very concerned for their child: Some may inadvertently reinforce depressive behavior by showering sympathy on the child (positive reinforcement) or reducing demands and hassles (negative reinforcement). Gradually, people who receive generous reinforcers for noticing the pain, suffering, or misery in life can become hypersensitive to negative feelings.

THE PREMACK PRINCIPLE

Because all reinforcers and punishers can be modified by conditioning, we cannot assume that any primary reinforcer or punisher is fixed and unchangeable. Knowledge about a person's past conditioning helps explain how any given primary reinforcer or punisher may have been modified by experience. However, we do not always have access to the information we would need to determine a person's past history of conditioning. Did Terri's parents make her find food to be aversive or overly rewarding? Is there any way—other than knowing a person's prior conditioning—that can allow us to determine whether a given stimulus is a reinforcer or punisher?

The **Premack principle**[29] provides a quick and useful method for determining whether a behavior is associated with strong reinforcers, strong punishers, or any other consequences on the continuum between these two (Fig. 7–2). The Premack principle focuses on the frequency of behavior rather than on stimuli—such as "reinforcing stimuli" (S^Rs). High frequency behaviors are called high probability behaviors (HPBs) and low frequency behaviors are called low probability behaviors (LPBs). In simplified form, the Premack principle states: *Access to any frequent behavior (HPB) will serve as a reinforcer for any infrequent behavior (LPB). On the other hand, doing an LPB will punish any HPB that comes before it.* For example, if we note that eating is a HPB within the first hour after waking, the Premack principle indicates that eating is a HPB that can reinforce prior behaviors, such as making breakfast. If watching a favorite TV show is an HPB (because we do it often), it will reward the behaviors of getting home on time, finishing dinner and switching the TV to the favorite show.

Parents frequently apply the Premack principle without knowing it. When a parent sees children playing frequently and for hours in their sandbox, the parent may use sandbox play (the HPB) to reinforce some low frequency behavior (LPB), such as taking out the garbage. "You can play in the sandbox if you take out the garbage first." The HPB of sandbox play is used to reinforce the LPB of garbage disposal. If cleaning up after the dog is a low probability event in a child's daily activities, the parents may use this LPB to punish undesired HPBs, such as coming home late from school too frequently. "If you get home late one more time this week, you'll have to clean up after the dog for the next five nights."

The Premack principle can be used to understand all types of behavior in people of any age. The next two examples show the power of HPBs (such as favorite activities) to serve as reinforcers for LPBs (infrequent behaviors). If we observe that a woman spends a great deal of time talking about her children, it is clear that talking about the children is an HPB. The chance to talk about children should function as a reinforcer for any behavior that allows a conversation to turn to children. If the woman is listening to a conversation about real estate and only by chance interjects, "Do you have any children?" her chance question (which is an LPB) may sidetrack the conversation from real estate to children (her HPB). The opportunity to engage in her HPB will reinforce her asking the sidetracking question. In the future, she will be more likely to digress conversations with the question, "Do you have any children?" If a man never misses the big game on TV every weekend, watching sports is clearly an HPB. If the TV picture dies on Wednesday night, the man may either procrastinate about getting it fixed or promptly take it in for repairs. Because procrastinating may make him miss a game, this behavior will be punished by the loss of access to the HPB. Getting the TV fixed will be reinforced by the HPB of watching the game. Not surprisingly, most TV addicts learn some behaviors—getting the old set fixed, buying a new set, going to a friend's house—because these behaviors are reinforced by the HPB of watching their favorite programs.

The next two examples show the power of LPBs, low probability behaviors, to serve as punishers. If we observe that Letifia sees many movies, but never movies with violence, we can conclude that seeing violent movies is a LPB and hence a punisher for her. We would expect that the LPB would cause Letifia to avoid any social obligation that would get her involved in seeing a violent movie. And if she actually got stuck going to one, she might try to escape it and its punishing qualities—perhaps by going out for popcorn and being slow to return. At a law firm, we may notice that one of the new attorneys never goes to talk with the senior partner—even though most of the other lawyers do. We recognize that talking with the senior partner is an LPB for the new attorney, hence a punisher. This LPB should function to suppress any behavior that would cause the new lawyer to have to talk with the senior partner. For example, making serious mistakes in legal documents would cause the senior partner to call in the new attorney for consultation. We would expect the new lawyer to be very cautious about such mistakes: The frequency of such mistakes would be suppressed by the consequences of having to do the LPB of talking with the senior partner.

The Premack principle sidesteps the problem of determining whether a given consequence is a primary or secondary reinforcer or punisher. The principle works equally well in dealing with any combination of primary and secondary reinforcers or punishers.[30]

SENSORY STIMULATION

Sensory stimulation might well be called "the unknown reinforcer." Of all the primary reinforcers, sensory stimulation is the one that people understand the least. Yet sensory stimulation is one of the most important reinforcers in everyday life.[31] It influences our behavior 24 hours a day, whether we are asleep or awake, alone or with other people. The remainder of this chapter describes the basic properties of "the unknown reinforcer," sensory stimulation.

Sensory stimulation *refers to the total amount of stimulation coming to us from all parts of the stimulus collage—both from outside and inside the body.* We continually receive stimuli from the external world via the five senses: seeing, hearing, smelling, tasting, and feeling. The more things happening in our environment, the more sensory stimulation enters the five senses. There are also internal sense organs that detect sensations from many sources inside the body, including the brain. These sensors allow us to feel many internal responses, such as butterflies in the stomach, flutters of the heart, and contractions of our muscles when we move our arms, legs, or other body parts. We can also sense when our brain is alive with exciting thoughts or dropping into an inactive state. Thought, fantasy, and daydreams can provide so much interesting sensory stimulation inside the brain that people may neglect external sensory stimulation for the pleasure of cognitive stimulation.

Sensory stimulation can be either a reinforcer or punisher, depending on the quantity of stimulation entering the sensory systems. The total amount of sensory inputs from the entire stimulus collage—from outside and inside the body—can range anywhere from very low, to medium, to very high. *Under normal waking conditions, both low and high levels of sensory inputs function as primary punishers. Between the extremes, there is an optimal, intermediate level of sensory stimulation that functions as a primary reinforcer.* When we receive too little stimulation from external and internal sources, we experience the aversive feelings of boredom—and often do not do our best behavioral performance. Too much sensory stimulation, on the other hand, causes the aversive feelings of nervousness, anxiety, or hypertension—which also can interfere with doing our best. Between too little and too much—between boredom and anxiety[32]—there is an *optimal zone* where the sensory input is pleasurable—and our behavioral and cognitive skills shine most beautifully.[33] People can learn to find different levels of sensory stimulation to be optimal, with some loving more sensory stimulation than others.

If you were at home alone one afternoon with nothing to do, you might become bored. Having nothing to do leaves you with low levels of sensory input, which cause boredom. Turning on the stereo might help relieve the boredom because the music provides increased amounts of sensory stimulation. Turning on the stereo is reinforced by the escape from boredom and the onset of musical sensory stimulation. If you have a powerful stereo system, you might turn it up full blast just to feel the impressive power of the 200-watt amplifier, but the volume would probably come down to a more comfortable level after a few minutes. Overly loud sounds produce aversively high levels of sensory stimulation, and hence provide negative reinforcement for turning down the volume. However, you do not turn down the volume to the point where you can hardly hear the music. Between the extremes of too little and too much sensory stimulation is the optimal zone, where the volume brings pleasure. Because all primary reinforcers are relative, it is not surprising that some people find the optimal level of loudness higher than others like. For each individual, adjusting the volume to their personal optimal zone is reinforced by sensory inputs that are neither over- or understimulating. Note that the optimal zone is fairly broad: There is a range of volume settings that people find rewarding, depending on the type of music, time of day, and activities of the moment.

People sometimes describe the subjective experience of sensory stimulation in terms of "energy" they feel inside their bodies. Optimal sensory stimulation makes them feel "excited about life" and "energized." Too little sensory stimulation makes them feel lethargic and devoid of energy; overstimulation can make a person feel "hyper," or overly excited, with too much energy. In fact, the "energy" is more accurately understood as their general level of physiological arousal—induced by high, medium or low levels of sensory stimulation. Inside the zone of optimal stimulation, people often feel a state called "flow," since their behavior comes out so beautifully and is linked with optimal sensory rewards.[34]

People frequently adjust the quantity of their sensory inputs to keep them inside their optimal stimulation zone, as in adjusting the volume on the stereo. When we squint on a bright day, we are reducing the amount of light entering the eyes to a more rewarding level. When we turn on the lights at night, we are increasing the light to optimal levels. If our heads are so busy with thoughts that we cannot go to sleep at night, a sleeping pill may help turn off the excessive mental stimulation. If we have nothing to think about and feel bored, we may pick up a magazine or turn on the TV to get inputs that stimulate our senses. When some people want more stimulation, they use stimulant drugs—such as caffeine, nicotine, amphetamines, or cocaine—which produce a quick "high" by activating the brain. Other people learn that leading an exciting life and doing invigorating physical activities produce a natural high. Actively seeking the sensory wonders of life is the natural way to fill the brain with exciting stimulation.

Fixed But Flexible

All primary reinforcers and punishers are relative—fixed but flexible—and sensory stimulation is no exception. The ability of any given sensory input to serve as a sensory reinforcer or punisher depends on several factors.

First, the ability of one source of stimuli to function as a reinforcer or a punisher is influenced by the other stimuli present in the stimulus collage. Doing daily exercises can be boring because it is so repetitious, but exercising to music—or with friends—can be fun, because exercising is now part of a more stimulating total sensory experience. A noisy, action-packed TV show may provide optimal levels of sensory input and reinforce our full attention if there is nothing else going on in the house. However, we may find a blaring TV nerve-racking if the kids are screaming, the washing machine is overflowing with sudsy water, the toaster is belching black smoke, and the phone has been ringing every couple of minutes. The noisy TV may push the total amount of sensory stimulation so high that it is aversive, which provides negative reinforcement for turning off the TV to escape an aversive experience.

Second, novel stimuli provide more sensory stimulation than familiar stimuli— which often produce boredom. A stimulus is most novel the first time a person experiences it. The first time we see a movie, we find it most novel and exciting. The second and third viewings are less novel because the ability of a given stimulus to provide novel experience declines with repeated exposure.[35] *Repeated experience with any given stimulus causes it to "lose its novelty," through a process called* **habituation.** The first time a teenager drives a car, the experience is novel, stimulating, and exciting. With repeated experience, the novelty "wears off," due to habituation. By age 25, driving is often less exciting than it was at first. The first time we do anything, the behavior seems especially exciting, because it is novel. Novelty is an important contributor to sensory stimulation, and each stimulus we experience loses its novelty and ability to provide optimal levels of sensory stimulation as we have repeated experiences with it.

Figure 7–3 shows how habituation reduces the total sensory stimulation of a stimulus as the novelty wears off. When you buy a new CD, the music is most novel during the first several times you listen to it. Novelty adds to the total sensory stimulation obtained from playing the music, producing the optimal levels of sensory input that reinforce playing the CD several times during the first week. After hearing the CD 10 or 15 times, you notice the novelty is already wearing off. As the novelty declines, there are fewer sensory reinforcers for playing the CD, and you play it less frequently each week. Eventually, there is so little novelty that the CD becomes boring, and soon you stop playing it.

A new house going up in the neighborhood provides more novel visual stimuli than older houses (because the old ones have already lost their novelty). Therefore heads turn much more to look at the new house—with its novel sensory stimulation—than to look at the older houses when driving past. However, over the months and years, the newest house will also lose its novelty, and looking at it will provide no more sensory rewards than looking at the other houses. It eventually "blends in," even though it "stood out" when it was new.

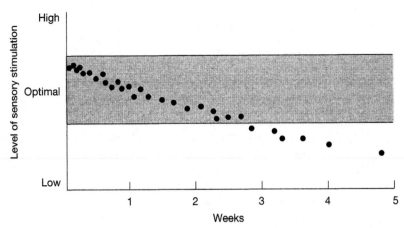

FIGURE 7–3   A CD loses its novelty and ability to provide optimal sensory stimulation after repeated playing. Each dot in the figure represents one playing of a CD. As the novelty declines, the time gap between each playing of the CD increases.

The speed of the habituation process can vary. Some stimuli lose their novelty quickly; others, slowly. *Habituation is usually slowest when a stimulus is complex, variable, and quite different from stimuli that are already familiar.* Some fast-paced movies with complex special effects provide so much novel stimulation that people go back several times before getting bored. Other movies, with less novel and complex content, may get boring before we sit through the first viewing, and we would never pay to see them a second time. When a child receives several toys as birthday presents, the simple ones—and the ones most similar to old familiar toys—tend to lose their novelty faster than complex and totally new toys. The sooner a toy loses its novelty, the sooner the child stops playing with it (due to the lack of sensory reinforcement).

Novel sensory stimulation is only one of the many reinforcers that affect our behavior; thus, we may continue doing a behavior long after the novelty is gone if the behavior is maintained by other reinforcers. Driving was novel and exciting when we were teens, but people keep driving long after the novelty has worn off because cars are so useful in getting to places where other rewards are found—be they family, friends, movies, malls, parties, or concerts.

Third, after a person ceases to find a stimulus novel (due to habituation), the stimulus can regain a fraction of its novelty if there is a period of time in which a person does not encounter the stimulus.[36] *The process by which a stimulus regains novelty is called* **recovery.** Figure 7–4 shows the original habituation to a stimulus (from time A to B), followed by a period of no contact (from time B to C), then the recovery of interest (at time C). If you are flipping through your audio cassette collection and see a tape that you have not played for a long time, you may get it out and listen to it. Because it has been several months since you listened to the cassette last, the stimuli will have regained some of their novelty (at C). The cassette will not sound as novel as it did when you first played it (at

A), but it will seem fresher and more interesting than the last time you listened to it (at B). Because the tape has recovered enough novelty to again provide optimal levels of sensory stimulation, there are sensory reinforcers for playing it several times. During each replay, habituation again robs the tape of its novelty. The decline of interest (from time C to D) tends to be faster than the original habituation (from time A to B). After the novelty has worn off this second time, the cassette again fails to provide enough sensory stimulation to reinforce playing it.

Some children saw *Dinosaur* several times when the movie hit the big screen. After seeing the movie five times, a child might eventually lose interest because habituation has removed the novelty that reinforced prior viewings. Several years later, the child might watch *Dinosaur* on video and show renewed interest in it because the film seemed novel again due to recovery effects, but it might only take one or two video viewings before the novelty wore off the second time.

Behavior that is reinforced by novelty sometimes appears in repeated cycles of habituation and recovery. Every June when a family goes to a favorite lake for summer vacation, the novelty and excitement are especially strong during the first week because there has been a whole year for the boating, water skiing, and picnicking to recover their novelty. However, the lake activities lose their novelty as the vacation progresses, and the family is ready to leave the lake and return home after a couple of weeks. One year later, the cycle of recovery and habituation will occur again: Love the lake, then hunger for home. People may go through periods of visiting Chinese restaurants several nights a week (until the novelty wears off), then go for months without eating Chinese food. During the pause, recovery effects make Chinese food novel again. The cycle of dining at Chinese restaurants then stopping may be repeated a couple times each year.

When parents buy roller blades for their child, they may initiate cycles of habituation and recovery. First, the child goes roller blading every day for several weeks because there is abundant novelty to reinforce frequent skating. Gradually, the novelty wears off, the sensory experiences drop below the optimal zone, skates become boring, and the child

FIGURE 7–4   **The first habituation period is between A and B. Recovery of novelty is seen at time C, after a period of no contact with the stimulus. The second habituation period occurs between C and D. Each dot in the figure represents one playing of the cassette as it loses its novelty and boredom eventually punishes further playing of the cassette.**

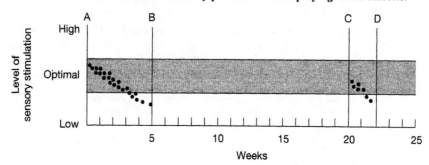

stops skating as frequently. Eventually, the roller blades end up in the back of the child's closet. The parents ask, "How come we never see you on your blades anymore?" "Aw, skating is boring," the child responds. Once the novelty is gone, there are few sensory reinforcers for roller blading. After the child goes for months without skating, there is a partial recovery of novelty for skating. The child may rediscover the roller blades one day and return to skating for two or three days before the novelty—and sensory reinforcers—again decline. This cycle of skating and not skating may repeat several times before recovery can no longer bounce roller blades into the optimal zone of sensory stimulation.

Fourth, there are individual differences in people's preferred types of sensory inputs. Some children grow up in active homes where the parents participate in several sports or clubs, have frequent house guests, have noisy parties, and encourage their children to have their friends over at any time. If there is generous positive reinforcement for participating in this high level of social activity, the children will grow up loving constant social activity, and solitude may be boring for them because it is below their preferred level of sensory stimulation.

Other children grow up in homes that are much quieter. Some may find that their happiest hours are spent daydreaming or playing quietly with favorite toys. Ralf's parents read in the evening instead of having people over, and Ralf learns to enjoy reading because his parents show sincere interest in the books he is reading. In this type of home, a child may grow up loving quiet surroundings with the minimum of intrusive, high-intensity sensory inputs. An outsider's first impression might be that Ralf loves low levels of sensory stimulation. More careful observation would reveal that Ralf is actually enjoying high levels of novel intellectual stimulation, even though loud and intense stimuli are absent.

People's personal preferences for different types of stimulation often influence their social interactions.[37] Two people who have learned to be highly social—talking and joking all day long with dozens of different people—are likely to get along well with each other, but neither will find it very exciting to interact for long periods with Ralf—a quiet, reflective person who prefers serious, in-depth conversations. In contrast, two very quiet and serious conversationalists may get along perfectly with each other, even though neither finds much pleasure in interacting with people who capriciously jump from topic to topic.

Sensory stimulation preferences can be situation specific. A professor may love to teach in a very active manner—moving around and writing on the board all the time—because stimulating lectures make many students excited about the course. Yet the professor may prefer very quiet and gentle forms of face-to-face interaction because calmness is conducive to serious and meaningful conversations.

Fifth, there are individual differences in people's "taste" for different types of sensory stimulation. For example, most people enjoy listening to music because it can provide optimal levels of sensory stimulation. However, people have quite different tastes in music. Some people love rock, and others hate rock. Some love Baroque music; others find it too mechanical. Taste preferences are at least partly learned. Many teenagers receive social reinforcers from peers for liking rock music, but some learn to love classical music. People usually develop a taste for types of music that are common in their culture—especially the music that their peers enjoy— because there are social rewards for playing and talking about those types of music. People develop different tastes in art, literature, humor, conversational topics, and many other forms of sensory stimulation. Books provide sensory stimulation via words; but some like biographies, while others like mysteries, and yet others prefer love stories.

Risky behaviors—such as speeding and sky diving—are sources of high sensory stimulation. Some people love these behaviors and find them exhilarating, while others respond with fear, due to past rewards or punishers associated with each behavior. When given a chance to do a risky behavior, people who can "taste the excitement" of the behavior seek it out while those who "sniff fear" avoid it.[38]

Sixth, daily cycles of sleep and wakefulness alter the height of the optimal stimulation zone.[39] When we are sleepy, we often seek out a dark, quiet room because low levels of sensory stimulation are most conducive to sleeping. But when we have had enough sleep, such low levels of sensory stimulation are understimulating, boring, and aversive. Well-rested people typically like more stimulating sensory inputs than those they seek when sleepy.

Biological regulatory systems in our brains automatically adjust our optimal zone up and down to produce the daily wake-sleep cycle.[40] Figure 7–5 shows the typical daily cycle of stimulus preferences, from noon one day to noon the next. During the afternoon and early evening, people usually find intermediate levels of sensory stimulation to be optimal and reinforcing. Thus, being active and busy are reinforced by optimal sensory stimulation, and passivity is punished by boredom. However, as bedtime approaches, the body's optimal zone begins to descend, making it rewarding to seek out dark, quiet surroundings—which are, of course, well suited to sleep. All during the night, the low levels of sensory input most conducive to sleeping well are rewarding. If we are awakened by unusual noises in the house that trigger a long chain of thoughts, the cognitive activity may provide so much internal sensory stimulation that we cannot go back to sleep. Cognitive activity that lies above the low optimal zone for sleep prevents us from sleeping and

FIGURE 7–5 **A typical wake-sleep cycle, showing how the optimal zone for sensory stimulation descends when people are tired and rises after they are well rested.**

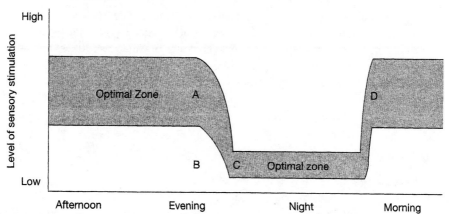

is aversive; we are tired and eager to sleep. We may try to stop thinking about the strange noises by thinking reassuring thoughts, counting sheep (a monotonous, low-stimulation activity), or taking a sleeping pill.

When children are put to bed before they are tired, their optimal zones are still high (at A in Fig. 7–5) and the bed is boringly understimulating (at B). Thus, children who are put to bed early often discover ways of boosting their sensory inputs above the boredom zone until sleep overtakes them. Some fantasize in bed. Others smuggle toys or books into the bed. Many talk with their brother or sister or make a few trips to the bathroom. When genuine tiredness finally lowers their optimal zone (at C in Fig. 7–5), they find low levels of sensory stimulation rewarding, snuggle in quietly, and go to sleep.

After a night's sleep, the brain adjusts the optimal zone to the higher daytime levels (D in Fig. 7–5). At this time, the low levels of sensory stimulation that are optimal for sleep become boring, and people need higher levels of sensory input for optimally rewarding daytime experiences. It is time to open the curtains, let the light flood into the bedroom, and head out for a day of stimulating activities.

Some "early birds" wake up and reach their full daytime activity level faster than others. Their optimal zone shoots up to the full daytime level immediately upon awakening. In contrast, "slow risers" may need several hours—and perhaps several cups of coffee—before their eyes are completely open and they are ready for the day. These differences often reflect a person's prior conditioning. If there are highly rewarding activities that occur when a person gets up each morning, these reinforce the response of waking up quickly. On the other hand, if the morning is associated with few reinforcers or with aversive experiences, a person learns to wake up slowly.

Sensory stimulation is one of the most important reinforcers in everyday life because it influences our behavior 24 hours a day, whether we are awake or asleep. Even though people prefer different levels of sensory stimulation while sleeping than when awake, stimuli are always impinging on the sense organs and there is always an optimal level of sensory input—be it low or high—that provides positive reinforcement.

Seventh, there are brain mechanisms that depress the zone of optimal sensory stimulation when we are sick or fatigued. When we are ill or exhausted, we find it is rewarding to seek out dark, quiet places. A sick person finds the bright sunshine of a clear summer day painful to the eyes. The aversiveness of bright daylight provides negative reinforcement for putting on sunglasses or going inside. Socializing at a noisy party also provides too much sensory input for the person who is sick or exhausted. Illness and fatigue cause a person to avoid stimulating activities that would be optimal for a healthy person. When we are sick or exhausted, snuggling into a soft bed in a dark room is reinforced by the pleasures of low sensory input. This is, of course, a biologically adaptive response to illness or exhaustion, since quiet and relaxation are conducive to rest and recuperation.

Staying Optimal

Because optimal levels of sensory stimulation are rewarding, there are positive reinforcers for seeking optimal levels of sensory stimulation. Since both under- and overstimulation are aversive, there are negative reinforcers for avoiding both boredom and anxiety. However, *most people cannot stay optimally stimulated all the time.* Few people lead lives that are totally free of boredom, and many people go through periods in which overly high levels of sensory input cause them to become nervous, tense, stressed, and anxious. The following examples show the different kinds of problems that children and adults face in staying optimally stimulated.

Childhood Problems.   Children tend to experience the extremes of under- and overstimulation more often than adults. These extreme experiences occur because children have less power and skill than adults for controlling their surroundings and the activities of others. It usually takes years to gain the skill and control needed to avoid the situations that induce under- and overstimulation.

Children are often caught in situations that cause understimulation. Being trapped in the house on a rainy day can cause boredom if a child has not learned a repertoire of activities for self-entertainment. A child may turn on the TV set and be rewarded by a barrage of sensory stimulation. After a couple of hours, watching TV becomes boring. The child has habituated to the types of sensory stimulation it presents. The child begins wandering around the house, looking out the windows, opening all the closet doors, and looking through dresser drawers. Nothing novel is found in any of those places. The child wanders listlessly around the house and then goes up to the attic. Looking at the old clothes and antique toys may provide some novelty if the child has not been in the attic for a couple of months (due to recovery); however, habituation may soon rob these stimuli of their novelty, and the child is back to boredom again.

Fidgeting is a common childhood behavior that is learned as a partial escape from boredom. Many a child has had to sit and listen while parents, relatives, or other adults linger at the dinner table to talk about abstract topics—the stock market, Roth IRA plans, the boss's duodenal ulcer—using words that are frequently incomprehensible to children. Clearly, there is rewarding sensory stimulation for the adults who enthusiastically talk and talk and talk, but the child has not had the learning experience needed to make the topics comprehensible and interesting. The unlucky child trapped in this environment fidgets, rocks back and forth in the chair, looks around the room, and shakes or kicks a leg or two. All of these operants produce some sensory input, and hence are reinforced by the partial escape from boredom. For example, leg kicking produces reinforcing sensory input from the movement of the leg muscles, from the leg hitting against the furniture, and from the wobbling of the chair. These may not seem like the most exciting types of sensory input possible, but they do provide more sensory stimulation than sitting passively.[41]

At the other extreme, children are sometimes thrown into situations that are totally novel for them, in which they are bombarded with high levels of sensory stimulation that can overstimulate them to the point of panic and crying. This is due, in part, to the fact that so much of the world is novel for children, who have not habituated to as many stimuli as adults have. Consider 2-year-old Billy's plight when taken for his first haircut. If Billy has never been inside a barbershop, he will be deluged with novel stimuli the first time he enters one. He may be surrounded by shiny white walls with big mirrors reflecting in all directions. He hears the whir of high-pitched motors and watches oddly dressed men in white uniforms doing weird things to the heads and faces of strangers who are sitting in unusual-looking white chairs. Billy has never seen anything as bizarre as this place. He stands next to his father, holds his leg, and looks around. Suddenly, a white-clad stranger picks him up and carries him to an odd-looking chair. Billy is positioned, then wrapped in strange smelling, stiff, and rough materials. If Billy has not started to cry by now, just wait until the cold steel tools are laid against his tender skin or the electric shears with ozone odor begin to cut and pull at his hitherto unshorn locks. The child is being exposed to a very high level of novel stimuli all jammed together into one small room and in one short period of time. Overstimulated, he cries with fear and anxiety. These panic and crying responses are inborn reflexes that can be elicited by a variety of aversive situations, including excess sensory stimulation. If Billy cries loudly enough, his father may come to comfort him. If he picks up Billy, hugs him gently, and says soothing things to him, the father may help Billy escape overstimulation, but many young children are not easily calmed in such novel and frightening situations.

As a child grows older and becomes familiar with a large number of different environments, fewer and fewer novel situations will produce extreme overstimulation. When Billy is 4 years old and first goes to preschool, he is again exposed to a new set of environmental stimuli, but he will probably be less severely affected than he was in the barbershop 2 years before. By 4 years of age, he has become habituated to a large number of different types of places, playgrounds, buildings, adults, and other children. The first time he goes to school and is surrounded with 20 new classmates, Billy will be exposed to a level of novelty and strange stimuli that exceeds his normal daily experience, but with 4 years of learning behind him, the situation will not be totally strange. On the first day of preschool, he may feel a little anxious and somewhat afraid to approach the unknown children for play. He is likely to avoid the strangest stimuli (the sources of greatest overstimulation) by staying near more familiar stimuli. If he knows a neighbor child, he may play with this child on the first day. If his mother does not leave, he may remain near her at first. This mild overstimulation may not produce crying or severe disruption of behavior, but it is aversive and negatively reinforces those activities that escape or avoid the overstimulation.

Adult Problems. By adulthood, many people have learned to avoid both under- and overstimulation fairly well. However, not all adults are equally lucky. Some are trapped in boring jobs and repetitive daily routines. People are most likely to experience boredom if they have routine lives coupled with few social contacts, few friends, few interests in life, or few hobbies. The problems of boredom can increase with advancing years, especially when people lose their spouse and close friends die or move out of the neighborhood. If people do not keep expanding their range of friends and activities, the loss of old companions and earlier interests can leave them with too few things to do.

Overstimulation usually becomes less of a problem as people get older. As the years pass and people habituate to most normal everyday events, fewer and fewer things are novel enough to induce sufficient overstimulation to cause panic and hysteria. Nevertheless, highly unusual situations—such as being caught in a falling airplane, sinking ship, or war-torn city—can swamp even an adult's senses with so much novel, intense, and frightening stimuli that the person is overstimulated to the point of panic and hysteria.[42]

Milder forms of overstimulation are, of course, more common. Many adults feel some degree of nervousness and anxiety about taking new jobs, moving to new states, or joining new groups. When people from small towns visit New York City or any other large city for the first time, they are barraged with much more sensory stimulation than they are used to: The high density of cars, people, signs, and fast business transactions can generate a level of overstimulation that is nerve-racking. After several days in the big city, some find the overstimulation has made them nervous, anxious, snappy with their family, and eager to leave for a more quiet vacation spot. (After living in a big city for a while, people usually habituate to much of the sensory stimulation, learn lifestyles that minimize overstimulation, and enjoy the varied opportunities that a big city offers.[43])

Some fast-lane workaholics and upwardly aspiring people are busy many hours a day, loading themselves down with numerous responsibilities until they are swamped with work. At first, the challenge of keeping up with countless projects may seem quite exciting, but the constant high level of sensory stimulation often leads to tension and nervousness. People in stressful jobs can eventually suffer from stimulus overload if they do not set aside enough time for rest and relaxation. *Overstimulation can be wearing on the body, especially if the overstimulation persists for prolonged periods.* Air traffic controllers in the control towers of large airports are constantly inundated by sensory input as they handle the complex, ever-changing patterns of planes on the ground and in the air; and they have unusually high rates of insomnia and heart disease.[44]

Reacting and Proacting.   Young children tend to react to under- and overstimulation. *To react means to respond after the onset of these aversive events.* Aversive sensations are the S^Ds for reacting. As children gain skills, they gradually learn to *proact* in increasing numbers of situations. *To **proact** means to respond before an event, rather than after it.* The cues indicating that over- or understimulation is about to arise become S^Ds which allow people to act in advance to avoid aversive levels of sensory stimulation. By adulthood, some people are able to arrange their lives in ways that prevent most cases of under- and overstimulation.

Figure 7–6 shows how reacting and proacting differ in the case of sensory stimulation. Typical patterns of reacting are shown in the top half of the figure. For example, on a gray Saturday morning a young child might wander around the house aimlessly, until totally bored (time A). After suffering from boredom for a while, the child reacts and looks for something exciting to do. If the child went outside and joined several children in play, their active games would create the sensory inputs needed for optimal stimulation (time B in the figure). If several older children joined the games, their rough play might produce overstimulation for the younger children (time C). After being overstimulated, a young child might run inside where a parent's soothing words and physical contact would help reduce the child's sensory input levels into the optimal zone (time D). The child reacted to aversive levels of stimulation at A and C, *after* experiencing the aversive situation of being out of the optimal zone.

An older child might have proacted by going out to play *before* getting bored and by leaving play *before* it got too rough. Typical patterns of proacting are shown in the bottom half of Figure 7–6. When a person recognizes that current activities are not very ex-

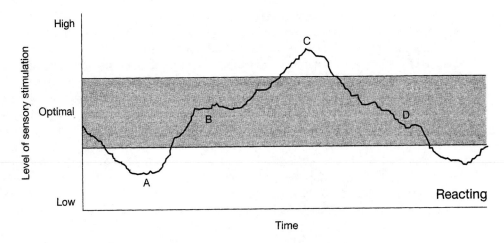

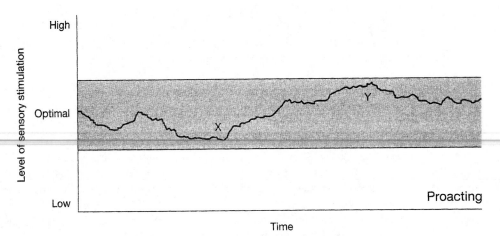

FIGURE 7–6   Typical patterns of reacting (above) and proacting (below).

citing (time X), the person switches to more stimulating activities before boredom begins. If the person notices that events are becoming too stimulating and stressful (time Y), the person switches to a quieter, more relaxing activity before becoming aversively overstimulated.

It is possible to proact in numerous situations. If all your roommates have said they are going to leave town for the weekend, their statements can function as S^Ds for proacting, if proacting in similar situations has been rewarding in the past. You might say to yourself, "Think ahead. What stimulating activities can I plan for the weekend to assure I won't be bored?" Successfully avoiding boredom and having a stimulating weekend reinforces your skills for proacting. If your supervisor gives you a demanding job that could easily produce overstimulation, such as meeting several deadlines for your work on the campus newspaper, your boss's words can be S^{D}s for proacting to minimize hectic events that could produce overstimulation. Early in your job, you could delegate responsibilities to other people, give each of them deadlines, ask everyone to give early warnings if they have difficulties, and help them solve their problems before disasters can happen.

Naturally, not everyone becomes equally skillful at proacting, nor does the ability to proact in some situations guarantee the ability to proact in others. However, as people gain skill at proacting, they can stay optimally stimulated more hours each day. A good understanding of sensory stimulation—the unknown reinforcer—is useful in helping people learn to proact and regulate their sensory inputs successfully.

Social Reinforcers

There are numerous reasons why most people find social interaction to be reinforcing, and two of these involve sensory stimulation: *Some types of social activity are rewarding because they are exciting and boost our sensory inputs. Other social activities are rewarding because they calm us when we need reduced levels of sensory stimulation.*

Exciting Stimuli. When we are bored or hungry for sensory stimulation, interesting and exciting social interactions often provide the sensory input required to give us the optimal levels of sensory stimulation needed for positive reinforcement. When bored, it is possible to obtain sensory inputs from a game of solitaire or watching TV alone, but many people prefer social interaction as a source of stimulating input. Getting on the phone and talking with a friend is often more stimulating and rewarding than staying home alone. People who work at dull jobs frequently spice up their boring hours with friendly banter, jokes, and other interaction.

All through life, humor and jokes can bring exciting jolts of sensory stimulation that make us happy—if done tastefully. And what makes jokes funny? Something novel in the wording creates surprise, as in these gems from children who were asked to share their wisdom: Jared said, "Don't pick on your sister when she's holding a baseball bat." Danielle said, "When your dad is mad and asks you, 'Do I look stupid?' don't answer him." Unexpected and novel words serve as positive sensory inputs that may elicit a smile or chuckle.

People tend to evaluate others along a continuum from being boring to being hyper. The boring person brings too little sensory stimulation to social interaction. The hyper person may talk so fast and skip from topic to topic so often that the interaction is too hectic. Between the extremes of boring and hyper are intermediate levels of stimulating interaction that many people find most rewarding. People who bring optimal levels of sensory stimulation to social interactions are sometimes described as "vivacious," "dynamic," "full of life," or "full of energy" because they generate stimulating experiences. But even more subdued levels of stimulation—just talking about people and the things they have been doing—can also be optimally stimulating and rewarding. Much depends on our personal tastes for sensory stimulation.

Calming Stimuli. *When a person is overstimulated and stressed, soothing and calming social interactions can provide rewarding levels of sensory input.* When anxious, nervous, or panicked by overstimulation, people need sources of gentle, soothing stimuli to reduce their total sensory load to a tolerable level. Because children can easily be overstimulated, they often need someone to turn to for stimulus reduction. Mother, father, and other caregivers can reduce their sensory load by holding, caressing, hugging, and talking gently to the child. These soft, soothing, gentle stimuli—along with shelter from whatever highly stimulating inputs caused the overstimulation—help lower the child's stimulation levels into the optimal zone. Part of children's love for their parents is based on the parents' ability to provide calm, comforting social contact in times of overstimulation.[45] (Teddy bears and security blankets can also provide calming stimuli, but not nearly as effectively as loving parents can.)

People never outgrow their need for calming stimuli, especially when they are overstimulated and stressed. Any hectic experience or major life transition can produce overstimulation and motivate the search for gentle, soothing contact. When a student first leaves Hometown and goes off to college in a strange city, there are so many novel stimuli to deal with during the first weeks that overstimulation is not uncommon. A student may seek out old acquaintances from Hometown or make new friends in order to have reassuring interactions with supportive friends. Telephone calls to family or close friends may help bring comfort, too. Although there are nonsocial sources of stimulus reduction—meditation, relaxation exercises, tranquilizers—many people prefer to have comforting social contact when they are overly stimulated.

Internal Motivation

Sensory reinforcers help explain behavior that is often described as resulting from "intrinsic motivation"—or "internal motivation."[46] For example, the creative work of artists who paint merely for the joy of painting—never even trying to show or sell a single piece of their work—is usually attributed to intrinsic motivation. There does not appear to be any external source of reinforcement for their creative behavior, so it is easy to infer internal motivation.

Knowledge of sensory reinforcers helps clarify that there are both *external* and *internal* sources of sensory rewards for creativity. The artist who is working on a new canvas watches the visual effect of every new brush stroke on the ever-changing canvas. Each change in the emerging picture provides visual sensory stimulation that reinforces attention to detail, careful brush strokes, and tasteful selection of colors. There is also internal sensory stimulation from mental activity as the artist plans the piece, evaluates each step of progress, and decides what brush strokes and color to use next. At times the artist may step back, gaze at the work, and take pleasure from the total sensory effect. However, there are more sensory reinforcers for painting than pausing: Going back to work on an ever-changing picture provides more sensory stimulation than does viewing a static picture—until the piece is completed and additional brush strokes could harm the finalized work. In addition, sensory stimulation is the natural reinforcer for developing increasing skills for creativity. The more creative the artist's work is, the more sensory reinforcers it produces in the form of novel and interesting sensory stimulation.

Creative behavior is rewarded by the novel sensory stimulation it produces, even if it never leads to social recognition, monetary profit, fame, or other conspicuous external rewards.[47] By definition, creativity involves producing new things, and novelty is a key component of sensory stimulation. The creative scientist develops new theories. The creative sales manager develops new ways of marketing products. Creative behavior always produces novelty; hence it is always followed by the sensory reinforcers based on variety and novelty. *Novel sensory stimulation is the natural reinforcer for creativity.* Even if there are no social rewards—such as praise, fame, or money—creative behavior produces some rewards via novel stimulation.

Exploration and play are two other behaviors (besides creativity) that are frequently attributed to internal motivation, and they too are reinforced by optimal levels of sensory stimulation. *Exploration* is sometimes described as being motivated by curiosity or inquisitiveness, two closely related types of internal motivation. Yet exploration is actually oriented to and reinforced by novel sensory stimulation. An inquisitive child opens drawer after drawer in the parents' bedroom because this explorative behavior is reinforced by seeing new things in each drawer. An explorer-adventurer travels to distant lands in search of new experiences. *Explorative behavior is reinforced every time it produces optimal levels of novel experience.* A novel and surprising sensory event—if in the optimal zone—often produces a sudden rush of pleasurable emotions, such as joy, excitement, or enthusiasm. When scientific exploration leads to a new discovery, the novel instant sensory experience gives the scientist a rush of excitement which is sometimes called a "Eureka" experience.

Because children's *play* looks so spontaneous, it is often attributed to the internal motivation of playfulness. But researchers are not satisfied to hear someone say that "Playfulness causes play." Careful studies reveal a deeper analysis. *Play is reinforced by optimal levels of sensory stimulation.* This is most conspicuous when play is very active. When children run around the yard, chasing each other and tumbling in the grass, their play is producing continuous sensory stimulation from *external* and *internal* sources. Their physical movements, shouting, and laughter produce ever changing external sensations—sights, sounds, tactile feelings, and meaningful communications. There is internal stimulation, too, from the mental activity and muscular movement needed to produce fast-paced actions. The children's smiles and laughter let us see how pleasurable play is for them.

Playing a game of chess is also reinforced by sensory stimulation, but both the behavior and the reinforcers are less conspicuous than in active and giggly play. A chess player may sit quietly, scanning the chessboard, thinking of strategies, rehearsing dozens of possible offenses and defenses. Each new game creates continuous novel mental stimulation for the person who knows the game and has opponents who play at a similar level. The sensory stimulation of internal mental activities provides sensory reinforcers for play. Winning is a reinforcer that may come at the end of the game, but all those people who play "for the joy of the game" are enjoying the sensory stimulation of each move.

Many people love to "play with ideas," and this form of play is also reinforced by sensory stimulation. A step away are the forms of mental play called fantasies and daydreams. Scientists and mathematicians play with hypotheses and theories, deriving much internal sensory stimulation and sensory reinforcement from the process. Einstein once commented, "When I have no special problem to occupy my mind, I love to reconstruct proofs of mathematical and physical theorems that have long been known to me. There is no *goal* in this, merely an opportunity to indulge in the pleasant occupation of thinking."[48] Business managers may play with ideas for changing their companies, developing new products, promoting old ones.

Although exploration, play, and creativity are often attributed to "internal motivation," all three are learned and maintained by the reinforcers of optimal sensory stimulation from both external and internal sources.[49]

On Growing Old

As the years pass, some people find that life becomes increasingly monotonous and boring. After having experienced countless things in life, many adults find less novelty and variety per day than does a child—who finds newness in many sensory experiences. By the age of 20, 30 or 40, some people notice that fewer and fewer experiences elicit feelings of excitement and enthusiasm for life. This can become an especially serious problem in the later years of life, when truly novel experiences are rare.

There are several reasons why life loses its novelty over the years. As people age, they often settle into routines, and the deeper they get into ruts, the more they deprive themselves of variety—which is the spice of life. Also, most everyday experiences gradually lose their novelty due to habituation: The longer a person lives, the fewer stimuli there are that still provide novel and stimulating inputs. It is very easy for children to find fresh and novel experience in life. After all, everywhere they look, children find new stimuli. Playing with a bar of soap in the bathtub is novel for a child, but not for adults. As the years pass and fewer stimuli seem novel, people sometimes find it harder to stay optimally stimulated. They find that many things no longer seem as interesting and exciting as they were earlier in life.

Fortunately, there is no reason for life to become less stimulating and exciting as the years pass. Some people—for example, Eleanor Roosevelt, Pablo Picasso, Margaret Mead, George Burns—remained alive, inquisitive, and creative well into their advanced years. Many other people who are less well known have also led dynamic and stimulating lives well into old age.[50] *What can we do to keep our lives full of novel, stimulating experience, rather than settling into unstimulating ruts?*

First, it is wise to avoid tedious routines and repetitious behavior. Monotonous activities are boring. The more hours of the day that people devote to repetitious behavior, the duller their lives become. After 8 hours at a tedious and repetitious job, a tired worker may not be able to think of anything but going home and sinking into a chair in front of the TV. In addition, monotonous tasks are *competing responses* that prevent people from doing more novel and stimulating alternatives. Each hour of routine, repetitious behavior represents one less hour available for more exciting possibilities. By minimizing repetitious routines, we can reduce boredom and open up time for more challenging and stimulating activities.

Second, people need to continually expand their range of interests and activities to counteract the effects of habituation. People who are not growing and learning—people with unchanging interests and activities—find that the novelty eventually disappears from their lives, due to habituation. To stay ahead of habituation, we need to keep expanding our interests and activities, perhaps learning new sports or hobbies, joining new groups, volunteering for good causes. New activities infuse life with the excitement derived from novel experience. Sometimes old activities can continue to provide novelty if we explore numerous new variations on them. For example, music can provide endless novel experiences for a musician who continually explores new types of music, plays with different groups to learn new styles and techniques, or experiments with music from different cultures or historical periods. As habituation kills the novelty of last month's musical variations, the musician turns to yet untried variations to find fresh sources of novelty.

Third, people need to develop mental and physical skills to continue to find novel experiences as the years pass. Young children—who have only limited skills—can find novelty almost anywhere they turn. Because so many things are new for them, even simple behavior such as opening all the kitchen drawers can bring novel sights and sounds. However, after several decades of experience, people cease to find novelty in the simple things that interest young children. As habituation robs simple stimuli of their novelty, increasing skill is needed to continue to discover new and stimulating experiences. It takes physical and mental skills to obtain the multiple sensory experiences of skiing, scuba diving, or playing a fast game of tennis. It takes intellectual skills to unlock the stimulating worlds of literature, computing, science, or chess. It takes artistic skills to enjoy the challenge and stimulation of creating art and music. The more skills that people have, the less likely they are to run out of novel and stimulating experiences. Actually, the world contains more sensory stimulation than any one person could discover in one life time.

Fourth, it is wise to choose friends and companions who live stimulating lives and value that lifestyle. People who lead exciting lives serve as models (Chapter 10) and sources of information (Chapter 12) from which we can learn skills for attaining stimulating experience. People with large repertoires of stimulating activities often provide opportunities for us to join them, share in exciting activities, and learn from them.

Fifth, it is wise to interact with people who provide reinforcement—not punishment—for seeking stimulating experience. Supportive friends and people who lead stimulating lives can be wonderful sources of social reinforcers, if they show spontaneous enthusiasm, offer sincere encouragement, and give us useful positive feedback for learning stimulating behavior. In contrast, people who belittle or criticize efforts to learn stimulating activities are, in fact, punishing those behaviors. The higher the ratio of reinforcement to punishment, the easier it is to maintain a stimulating life and expand one's range of activities and skills well into old age.

Sixth, health and physical fitness are important prerequisites for engaging in many forms of stimulating behavior. People who remain healthy and fit are able to lead active lives well into the advanced years. Although some people remain mentally active, alert, and alive long after they lose physical health and vigor, most people find their sphere of sensory stimulation shrinking when their health and physical fitness begin to decline. People who learn good health and exercise habits increase the chances that they can lead active and stimulating lives for a long time.

More than any other species, humans have the mental and physical potential for locating and creating novel experience even during the senior years. The world contains an inexhaustible supply of sensory stimulation for those with the time, skill, and health to locate it. The earlier in life that we learn the skills and good health practices for leading a physically and mentally stimulating life, the better prepared we will be for continuing that lifestyle well into old age.

CONCLUSION

Primary reinforcers and punishers are biologically based. We find food a reinforcer and a wasp sting a punisher because such biologically established responses favor survival. However, there are two ways in which primary reinforcers and primary punishers are relative—having different strengths at different times. First, primary reinforcers gain or lose power to control behavior due to an individual's level of deprivation from or satiation with the reinforcer. Primary punishers hurt most when we are first stung by one, but we adapt and find the thirtieth less painful than the first one. Second, Pavlovian conditioning can cause primary reinforcers and punishers to become more reinforcing or more punishing, due to pairing with other reinforcers or punishers: Anorexics cease to find food as rewarding as other people do, and some athletes learn to enjoy pain. After all, "No pain, no gain." The Premack principle provides an efficient way to evaluate reinforcers and punishers without need for knowledge about prior deprivation, satiation, or conditioning.

An optimal level of sensory stimulation is one of the more important primary reinforcers in everyday life. Because people are always in one of the three levels of sensory stimulation—under-, over-, or optimal stimulation—the reinforcers and punishers of sensory stimulation affect behavior at all times. As is true of all reinforcers and punishers, sensory reinforcers are relative, both fixed and flexible. People who learn skills for proacting can avoid the extremes of under- and overstimulation and stay optimally stimulated much of the time. Sensory stimulation is a key component of social reinforcers, because other people can help bring exciting sensory stimulation into our lives or calm and comfort us when we are overstimulated. Many activities, such as exploration, play, and creativity—that appear to reflect "internal motivation"—are maintained largely by sensory stimulation reinforcers. Although some adults cease finding their lives novel and stimulating as the years pass, many people learn to be among those who enjoy optimally stimulating experiences all through their lives.

QUESTIONS

1. Why did Tanya suffer because she was born with "congenital indifference to pain"?
2. What are *primary* reinforcers and *primary* punishers? What are *secondary* reinforcers and *secondary* punishers? How do they differ?
3. How are primary reinforcers and punishers traced to natural selection and evolutionary causes?
4. What does it mean to say that primary reinforcers and punishers are fixed but flexible?
5. Can you list at least five primary reinforcers?
6. What is satiation? How does it affect primary reinforcers?
7. What is deprivation? How does it affect primary reinforcers?
8. What are three different ways in which deprivation can occur?

9. Are primary punishers influenced by satiation and deprivation effects? Why?
10. Can you explain how the strength of primary punishers is affected by adaptation?
11. Can you list at least five primary punishers? Do primary punishers show a threshold effect? Explain your answer clearly.
12. How does Pavlovian conditioning explain how primary reinforcers can become more rewarding? How does Pavlovian conditioning explain how primary reinforcers become punishers?
13. How does Pavlovian conditioning explain how primary punishers can become rewarding? How does Pavlovian conditioning explain how primary punishers become extra-aversive?
14. Can you explain the Premack principle? What are HPBs and LPBs? How do they influence each other?
15. What is sensory stimulation? How does the quantity of sensory stimulation affect whether it is a primary reinforcer or punisher?
16. What seven factors cause sensory stimulation reinforcers to vary across time and situation (rather than being unchangeable)?
17. Why do children and adults face different problems in staying optimally stimulated?
18. What two ways does sensory stimulation play a role in making social interactions rewarding?
19. How do exploration, play, and creativity show the role of sensory stimulation reinforcers in explaining "internal motivation"?
20. What six pieces of advice are given to help people continue to enjoy optimally stimulating experiences all through life?

NOTES

1. Brand and Yancey (1993).
2. Maybe these sad consequences could have been averted if someone had developed a behavior modification program for her, but that was not the case.
3. Skinner (1966, 1969); Baldwin and Baldwin (1981); Zeiler (1992); Werle, Murphy, and Budd (1993); Carr (1994).
4. Skinner (1969, p. 206).
5. See Catania (1971) for further details.
6. Morse and Kelleher (1970, 1977); Barrett and Glowa (1977).
7. Not all USs are reinforcers or punishers. Some lie in the neutral zone on the continuum shown in Figure 7–1. For example, changes in light intensity between low and moderate levels elicit reflexive changes in pupil size without being either reinforcers or punishers (Staats, 1963, p. 53; 1975, p. 36; Terrace, 1971, p. 77). Only at higher intensities does light both elicit reflexive pupillary restriction and serve as a punisher.
8. Ellis (1942, pp. 10–11).
9. Several decades ago, it was common to describe motivation in terms of "drives" or "needs." Because drives and needs could only be inferred from behavior and were not directly measurable, many behaviorists ceased using the terms and now describe motivation in terms of hours of deprivation from reinforcers or exposure to aversive stimuli (see Skinner, 1953, p. 141f.).
10. Rhodes (1973).
11. White (1978).
12. Bivens (1994, p. A6).
13. Read (1974).
14. Horner and Day (1991); Alling and Poling (1995); Friman and Poling (1995); Mathis, Johnson, and Collier (1995); Zhou, Goff, and Iwata (2000).
15. Hull (1994); D.W. Moore (1995).
16. Bandura and Walters (1959, 1963); Hoffman (1960).
17. Egeland (1993).
18. Barnett, Miller-Perrin, and Perrin (1997).
19. Strauss and Gelles (1990); Dutton (1995).
20. Skinner (1971); Seligman (1998); Baldwin and Baldwin (2000).
21. Garcia, Brett, and Rusiniak (1989).
22. Schedule effects (Chapter 13) provide a second, compatible explanation for the modification of primary reinforcers and punishers (Morse & Kelleher, 1970, 1977).

23. Pavlov (1927).

24. Walen, Hauserman, and Lavin (1977); Hersen and Bellack (1985); Thompson (1992); Davidson and Benoit (1998). Anorexia can also result from positive reinforcement for not eating.

25. Kinsey et al. (1948, 1953), Masters and Johnson (1970), and Laumann, Gagnon, Michael, and Michaels (1994) have shown that there is an enormous variation in people's sexual behavior. Much of this can be traced to people's history of conditioning.

26. Heiman and LoPiccolo (1988); Leiblum and Rosen (1988, 1989); Zilbergeld (1992).

27. Green (1972).

28. Flor, Breitenstein, Birbaumer, and Fürst (1995); Gil et al. (1995); Sheeber, Hops, Andrews, Alpert and Davis (1998).

29. Premack (1965, 1971). There is considerable empirical evidence to support the Premack principle. The strengths and weaknesses of the Premack principle are reviewed by Eisenberger, Karpman, and Trattner (1967), Danaher (1974), Dunham (1977), and others.

30. One behavioral approach to increasing people's happiness and quality of life is to increase their participation in rewarding activities (Green & Reid, 1996).

31. Schultz (1965), Ellis (1973), and Zuckerman (1974, 1984, 1994) present some of the best integrated analyses of the reinforcement properties of sensory stimulation. Baldwin and Baldwin (1981) and Baldwin (1986a) present a summary of the literature on sensory stimulation reinforcement.

32. Csikszentmihalyi (1975, 1993); Csikszentmihalyi and Csikszentmihalyi (1988).

33. Yerkes and Dodson (1908). Although there may be some genetic predisposition for some children to prefer more sensory stimulation than others (Kagan, 1997), these preferences are not stable or fixed and can change over time (Kagan, Snidman, & Arcus, 1998).

34. Csikszentmihalyi (1975).

35. Welker (1961, 1971); Csikszentmihalyi (1975, 1993).

36. Welker (1961); Csikszentmihalyi (1975, 1993).

37. Maddi (1980).

38. Cook, Peterson, and DiLillo (1999).

39. Kleitman (1949); Maddi (1980).

40. Steriade (1996).

41. Weisberg and Rovee-Collier (1998).

42. Hebb (1972, p. 199).

43. Fischer (1981a,b).

44. Cobb and Rose (1973) report that hypertension in airport traffic controllers is four times higher than in pilots. Selye (1956), Martindale (1977), and Kawachi, Sparrow, Vokonas, and Weiss (1994) have related insomnia, nightmares, headaches, hypertension, sudden cardiac arrest, and other diseased conditions to chronic overstimulation.

45. Korner (1974); Stern (1977); Ainsworth, Blehar, Waters, and Wall (1978).

46. Secondary reinforcers provide a second major source of the reinforcers for "internally motivated behavior" (Chapter 8).

47. Baldwin and Baldwin (1981, pp. 209–210, 230–231); Gottfried (1985); Balsam, Deich, Ohyama, and Stokes (1998); Gottfried, Fleming, and Gottfried. (1998).

48. Dukas and Hoffmann (1979).

49. Baldwin and Baldwin (1981). Aberrant behavior can also be automatically rewarded by the sensory consequences it produces (Piazza, Adelinis, Hanley, Goh & Delia, 2000).

50. Comfort (1976); Montagu (1981).

Chapter

8

Secondary Reinforcers and Punishers

RALPH LAUREN AND HARA-KIRI

During our years of learning, all kinds of neutral stimuli can become conditioned into secondary reinforcers or punishers. These secondary reinforcers and punishers can have powerful effects on behavior. *There are cases in which secondary reinforcers and punishers have stronger effects on behavior than primary reinforcers and punishers!*[1]

Some fashion models love the social reinforcers of being looked at and photographed. Social attention is such a strong secondary reinforcer that some models will starve themselves—and resist the primary reinforcers of eating delicious food—in order to have the small waists and lean figures that attract social attention and photographers. They pose for us wearing the latest styles of Ralph Lauren, Versace, and Gucci clothing. Looking good on each job increases their chances of capturing attention—the powerful secondary reinforcer—and landing more modeling jobs. Some models earn $10,000 a day for photographs where they are at their leanest, even though they are painfully hungry. *The secondary reinforcers for being lean, based on cultural values and social conditioning, can be more powerful than the biologically based primary reinforcers of food.* Each year, millions of girls and women look at photos of these models, photographed at their leanest, and try to imitate their behavior.

In many cultures, "losing face" is a social disgrace associated with enormous pain. It is a secondary punisher based on cultural values and social conditioning, yet it can be more painful than committing suicide, which usually involves the primary punishers of physical pain. In 1996, a military leader in the United States committed suicide rather than be disgraced in a minor public scandal.[2] He wore more medals on his uniform than he actually deserved to wear, and the painful consequences of losing face in social disgrace were more painful to him than taking his own life by shooting himself. In Japan, men sometimes follow the old cultural practice of hara-kiri to dignify their suicide. After his company lost a major contract and he had to dismiss 40% of its employees, Mr. Masamura went home, opened his precious family heirlooms, removed a gleaming sword from its scabbard, placed the handle on the floor and its tip against his stomach, then fell forward onto the sharp blade. *Losing face, a culturally based secondary punisher, can be more painful than the primary punishers of running a sword through the gut.*

Secondary reinforcers and punishers do not always play such spectacular roles in motivating our behavior. However, they are almost always present and important in everyday life. First, most people respond to a multitude of stimuli as secondary reinforcers and punishers. Second, many of these stimuli are major determinants of behavior—especially in long chains of operants where primary reinforcers come only at the end of the entire chain.

THE CONDITIONING PROCESS

*When neutral stimuli repeatedly precede and predict reinforcers, they become **secondary reinforcers**. When neutral stimuli repeatedly precede and predict punishers, they become **secondary punishers**.*[3] A $20 bill and a parking ticket are merely pieces of paper, and young children respond to them no differently than they do to other colorful printed paper. However, after a few years of having money and parking tickets paired with a broad range of other rewards and punishers, most young people learn to respond to $20 bills as strong secondary reinforcers and traffic tickets as secondary punishers.

Secondary reinforcers and secondary punishers are acquired through learning rather than being biologically established. Therefore, they are different from the primary reinforcers and punishers discussed in Chapter 7, which take their power from biologically primitive reflexes—and not learning. *Secondary reinforcers and secondary punishers are also called **conditioned reinforcers** and **conditioned punishers** to indicate that they are CSs that derive their power from conditioning, rather than from biological sources.* Primary reinforcers and primary punishers are USs that elicit positive or negative emotional responses, based on primitive biological mechanisms; whereas secondary reinforcers and punishers are CSs that take on their power to reinforce or punish via Pavlovian conditioning.

Social cues—such as smiles and frowns—often become secondary reinforcers and punishers.[4] Because social attention, smiles, approval, sincere praise, and signs of affection often precede and predict other rewarding social events, most of us find them to be secondary social reinforcers. Because frowns, scowls, criticism, insults, and signs of dislike often precede or predict painful experiences, we tend to respond to them as secondary social punishers.

Secondary reinforcers and punishers can lie anywhere along a continuum from strong reinforcers to strong punishers, with the weakest stimuli near the center of the continuum (similar to Fig. 7–1). Because each individual has a unique history of conditioning, the same stimulus can function as a secondary reinforcer, neutral stimulus, or secondary punisher for different individuals. One person may find sarcastic humor very reinforcing and learn a range of skills for weaving such dark humor into conversations. Another person may find sarcasm to be very aversive and avoid people who use it. A third person may be quite indifferent to it, responding to it as a neutral stimulus. Almost all people are born responding the same way to primary reinforcers and punishers, because of their biological primacy. But we all can have different responses to the secondary reinforcers and punishers, since we all have years of unique learning experiences with them. As Confucius said, "By nature, men are nearly alike; by practice, they get to be wide apart."[5] Nature is the primary biological basis that makes us much alike; learning is the secondary process that allows us to be unique.

PREDICTIVE STIMULI

Secondary reinforcers and punishers are stimuli that were once neutral stimuli, but have acquired reinforcing or punishing properties because they *precede* and *predict* other reinforcers and punishers.[6] *The stimuli most likely to become secondary reinforcers or punishers are those that are the best predictors that other reinforcers or punishers are likely to come.* The sight of your bowling ball rolling down the alley toward a perfect strike is a good predictor of a rewarding experience; hence that visual image provides secondary reinforcement for skillful bowling *before* the ball actually hits the pins. Note that the secondary reinforcer follows the behavior closely, helping provide more immediate reinforcement of behavior than if you had to wait until all the pins fell. As we saw in Chapter 3, immediate reinforcement is more effective than delayed reinforcement, so secondary reinforcers play an important role in bringing early feedback about our behavior.

The sight of an angry dog approaching is a secondary punisher because it is a predictor that there is a danger of being bitten. The sight of the dog punishes and suppresses approach to the dog *before* being bitten, and negatively reinforces avoidance or self-protection. In this way, secondary punishers help us proact and avoid primary punishers— because they precede and predict the primary punishers, giving us extra time for proacting.

Three Functions

Because secondary reinforcers and punishers are predictive stimuli, they usually have the properties of both CSs and S^Ds, which are also predictive stimuli.[7] Secondary reinforcers and punishers can have three separate functions. Two functions are based on the properties of CSs and one is based on the properties of S^Ds. As CSs, they function as (1) *elicitors* of reflexive responses with emotional components, and (2) *consequences* that modify the prior operant behavior. As S^Ds, they (3) *set the occasion* for subsequent operant behaviors.[8] Both secondary reinforcers and punishers have all three functions, as you can see in the following examples.

Secondary Reinforcers.   As a person gains experience with predictive stimuli that precede reinforcement, those stimuli become secondary reinforcers with the properties of both CSs and S^Ds. As such, they can (1) *elicit pleasurable emotional responses,* (2) *reinforce behavior,*[9] and (3) *set the occasion for future operants.* When a 4-year-old girl sees a gift-wrapped box with her name on it, the box is a predictive stimulus that something nice will happen if she opens the box. By age 4, she has received enough presents to have learned that gift-wrapped boxes usually contain new clothes, toys, or dolls, all of which are reinforcers. Thus, nicely wrapped boxes become secondary reinforcers because they are predictive stimuli that regularly precede reinforcement. As a secondary reinforcer, a gift-wrapped box provides CSs that *elicit* pleasurable emotional responses and *reinforce* the child's looking at the box. Because secondary reinforcers also serve as S^Ds, they *set the occasion* for operants such as opening the box. (If the box contains a new toy, the operant of "box opening" will be rewarded by the primary reinforcer of novel sensory stimulation and the power of the secondary reinforcers further strengthened.)

$$\text{Gift boxes are} \begin{cases} \text{CSs that (1) elicit pleasurable emotional responses} \\ \text{CSs that (2) reinforce looking at the box} \\ \text{S}^D\text{s that (3) set the occasion for opening the box} \end{cases}$$

Secondary Punishers.   As a person gains experience with predictive stimuli that precede punishment, those stimuli become secondary punishers with the properties of both CSs and S^Ds. As such, they can (1) *elicit unpleasant emotional responses,* (2) *punish prior behaviors,* and (3) *set the occasion for operants that help avoid punishment.* If you have had prior experience with wasps, the sight of several wasps trapped, agitated, and flying around wildly in your kitchen provides predictive stimuli that you could get stung if you are not careful. The predictive stimuli are secondary punishers, with the properties of both CSs and S^Ds. As CSs, they can *elicit* uneasy feelings or fear and *punish* and suppress responses of moving too close to the wasps. As S^Ds, they *set the occasion* for subsequent operants, such as leaving the room or opening a window so the wasps can leave.[10]

$$\text{Wasps are} \begin{cases} \text{CSs that (1) elicit unpleasant emotional responses} \\ \text{CSs that (2) punish moving too close} \\ \text{S}^D\text{s that (3) set the occasion for opening the window} \end{cases}$$

Information

Information is a key determinant of the power of secondary reinforcers and punishers.[11] Seeing a gift box with your name on it is informative: It is a secondary reinforcer because the information predicts that your operants of box opening will have rewarding results. Seeing wasps in the house is informative: It is a secondary punisher because the information predicts that approaching them could lead to painful stings.

The amount of information we obtain from a stimulus depends on two things: (1) how reliably the stimulus predicts reinforcement or punishment, and (2) how well we have learned to recognize and respond to this predictive information. First, if a stimulus always precedes reinforcement or punishment, it is a much better predictor than stimuli that only occasionally precede and predict reinforcement or punishment. *The more reliably a stimulus is predictive of subsequent reinforcers or punishers, the more informative it can be, and the more power it can have as a secondary reinforcer or punisher.* The sight of a gift box with your name on it—or a room buzzing with agitated wasps—would be highly informative to most of us.

On the other hand, the potential information available from highly predictive stimuli is useless to people who have little or no experience with the stimuli and the reinforcers or punishers they predict. Thus, *learning* is the second determinant of the amount of information we can find in a stimulus. *People must have had adequate experience with predictive stimuli and related consequences to learn to find them informative as secondary reinforcers and punishers.* A young child who has no experience with gift boxes or wasps does not respond to the sight of them as predictive and informative stimuli the way that more experienced children do. Only when a child has adequate experience with the consequences predicted by gift boxes and wasps do these stimuli become secondary reinforcers or punishers. It may take several gift boxes before a child learns to respond to them as secondary reinforcers; but once stung, the child will respond to the sight of wasps in a new way. Again we see that the ability of stimuli to serve as secondary reinforcers and punishers is based on learning (whereas primary reinforcers and punishers are based on our basic biology).

Good News or Bad News

In essence, secondary reinforcers convey information that is "good news" (for those with relevant experience). A gift-wrapped box conveys the good news that a nice present is inside. The more good news information is present, the more rewarding the box is. For most people, a very large gift box, wrapped in shiny gold paper with elaborate ribbons, conveys more good news than does a simple white package the size and shape of a handkerchief box. Of course, we can be misled: Maybe the small box contains tickets for a two-week all-expense-paid vacation in Paris!

Secondary reinforcers take on especially great power when numerous elements of the stimulus collage contain information predicting subsequent reinforcement. People do not always respond to gift-wrapped boxes as secondary reinforcers. A nicely wrapped box will not be a secondary reinforcer for you if it is not your birthday and someone else's name is on the box. If it is not your birthday, but your first name is clearly on the gift box, there is more predictive information that it might be a gift for you—but you look around to see if anyone else in the room has your first name. If it is your birthday, but no name is on the box, you may feel happy but cautious, hoping the box is for you. Finally, if it is your birthday *and* your name is on the box, the box would be a strong secondary reinforcer for you, eliciting good thoughts and feelings, without fears that the gift belongs to someone else. Various elements in the stimulus collage—the box, name tag, day of year, and context cues—contribute to the predictive information that determines how strong a secondary reinforcer the gift box will be.

The information conveyed by secondary punishers serves as "bad news" (for those with relevant experience). Seeing that a police car has pulled out and started to follow your car is bad news, and you may have a noticeable emotional response and slow down even if the police car does not turn on its flashing lights and stop you. However, if the police car's red lights begin flashing, the extra information is extra bad news. The more information there is that serious punishment could follow, the worse the bad news is and the greater impact it has on your behavior and emotions.

Secondary punishers also become especially powerful when numerous elements of the stimulus collage carry information predicting subsequent punishment. If you are driving 10 miles per hour above the speed limit, the sight of a police car sitting in a side street just ahead might be a predictive stimulus that signals the danger of receiving a speeding ticket. However, the strength of the secondary punisher depends on the total information contained in the stimulus collage. If you live in a city where it is common knowledge that the police arrest every violator they find, the sight of the police car is an excellent predictor that speeding will be punished. Hence it is a secondary punisher that elicits noticeable emotional responses, punishes speeding, and sets the occasion for reducing speed. However, if the police in your town only stop out-of-state cars and rarely bother local drivers, the sight of the police car signals quite different information, and the car is less likely to serve as a secondary punisher.

Observing Responses

Because secondary reinforcers and punishers are informative—containing good news or bad news—it is not surprising that people learn to pay attention to these stimuli. After all, the information is useless if the predictive cues go unobserved. *The operants that are reinforced by information are called **observing responses**.*[12] Many of the secondary reinforcers and punishers relevant to our current behavior are S^Ds for us to pay attention—and direct our observing responses—to them.[13] We observe the names on letters and gifts, because the information tells us whether it is OK to open them or not. It is rewarding to open things with our name on them, but embarrassing to open things addressed to others.

When we get in the car on a cold winter morning, we listen to hear if the engine will start. Hearing the electric starter bring the engine to life is good news. Hearing the electric starter crank and crank without activating the engine is bad news. We listen attentively for both kinds of news, although the good news is much more pleasing to hear than bad news. *Observing responses* could be called "attentiveness behavior" to emphasize that we do not merely "observe" with our eyes. We pay attention to information via any of our five external senses and our internal senses. After hearing that your next-door neighbor has a painful ulcer, you may become especially attentive to your internal digestive feelings, wondering if a stomach growl or inner twinge is a sign that you have an ulcer.

Informative cues from any sense modality can serve as CSs and S^Ds that elicit emotional responses, reinforce or punish prior behavior, and set the occasion for subsequent actions. Hearing the engine start is good news that reinforces our having had the engine tuned recently. It also elicits good feelings about our reliable car and sets the occasion for backing out of the driveway. Feeling strange sensations in our stomach can elicit fearful feelings about our health, punish our eating foods that irritate ulcers, and set the occasion for phoning the doctor.

Uncertainty.   *Observing responses are most likely to be performed in times of uncertainty.* This is because information is most valuable—hence most reinforcing—when people are not certain how to behave. Consider three alternative situations. If a behavior is *always* reinforced whenever it is emitted, there is no uncertainty about the chances of reinforcement, and there is no need to look for cues that predict reinforcement is forthcoming. If a behavior is *never* reinforced, again there is no uncertainty and no need for observing responses. However, if a behavior is *sometimes* reinforced and sometimes punished on an unpredictable schedule, there is uncertainty about when to perform the behavior and when not. In such cases of uncertainty, any cues that predict if reinforcement or punishment might be forthcoming can be most informative, hence quite valuable. We learn to look for them, with observing responses. We can be attentive via all sense modalities.

The green and red lights of a traffic signal are secondary reinforcers and punishers for driving through the intersection. Green predicts that one can drive through safely; red predicts risk or danger for driving into the intersection. The information provided by both red and green lights reinforces observing responses, and people usually glance at the lights often enough to keep track of current traffic conditions. When the traffic lights go out at a busy intersection (and there is no traffic officer to give hand signals), there is increased uncertainty about who should drive through next and who should wait. When the traffic lights begin working again, people resume looking to them for information that decreases uncertainty and reduces accidents.

When people play tennis, baseball, or other sports, they frequently glance at teammates and opponents for information predictive of subsequent actions. Fast games are filled with uncertainty about the next possible turn of events, and good players learn to observe each other for relevant predictive information. When the batter sees a fielder miss the ball, it elicits good feelings, it is a secondary reinforcer for a well-placed hit, and it reduces any uncertainty about running for an extra base.

In conversations, we often glance at people's faces to see if they are smiling, frowning, or giving off any other emotional cues.[14] Signs of pleasure are usually "good news," and signs of unhappiness are usually "bad news." These social cues are especially valuable when we are uncertain how an interaction is progressing. Studies show that when people interact with a stranger, they spend more time looking at the other person than when they interact with a friend.[15] There is more uncertainty when interacting with a stranger, thus more reinforcement for watching for informative cues.

While walking across campus, we glance quickly at the people walking toward us, to see if they will nod and say "Hi" or walk past without recognizing us. If we are uncertain about when and where we might run into someone we know, observing responses reduce the uncertainty. *Informative cues increase the chances of reinforcement.* They increase the chances of noticing people we know and starting rewarding interactions with them. *Informative cues also decrease the chances of punishment.* They help us avoid the embarrassment of saying "Hi" to a complete stranger who stares back at us in disbelief—and the embarrassment of not saying "Hi" to someone we like and who feels hurt by our lack of friendliness.

Positive or Negative Reinforcement.   *Observing responses can be reinforced by either positive or negative reinforcement, depending on whether they bring information that helps us attain rewards or avoid punishers.* People enjoy making observation responses that bring the good news about positive reinforcers. It is good news to receive a letter that reads "We are happy to announce that your application for a scholarship has been approved." These words are secondary reinforcers that elicit pleasurable emotional responses, provide positive reinforcement for being attentive, and they serve as S^Ds for the next behavior, such as returning the form that confirms that you accept the financial support. When playing checkers, it is good news to see your opponent move a piece onto a square that will allow you to jump three of his pieces in one play. No wonder all eyes are on the checkerboard when a person begins to make a move.

Although people enjoy observing informative stimuli that predict reinforcement, they are usually not so happy to observe secondary stimuli that predict punishment. Watching your opponent move a checker or chess piece into a position that defeats your plans is bad news that elicits unhappy feelings and punishes you for relying on simple strategies. The unexpected move also carries information that is an S^D indicating you have more work ahead if you are to win the game.

Secondary punishers—those "bad news" events—can serve as either punishers or negative reinforcers for observing responses. People sometimes stop observing secondary punishers, an effect of punishment: They look away and hope the wasps will just go away, by themselves, with no hassle.[16] However, secondary punishers can also provide negative reinforcement for observing the wasps, keeping an eye on their locations and activities. Are they still in the house or have they left? Bad news is something better than no news![17]

What determines whether people observe secondary punishers or not? It is frightening to hear strange noises in the house at night, especially if you walk out into the hall and see a burglar pointing a gun at your gut. Seeing the burglar is a secondary punisher that elicits fear and punishes negligent acts (such as leaving the back door unlocked). Will the aversive sight of the armed intruder punish and suppress your observing him, or will it negatively reinforce your watching him to see what he does? What determines whether you will observe or not? If the burglar cocks the hammer, aims for your heart, and prepares to shoot, you may look away. However, if the burglar is 15 years old, uncertain about what he is doing, and somewhat inattentive, you might watch him for informative cues about possible opportunities to escape or disarm him.

Whether people observe or avoid observing secondary punishers depends largely on whether escape or avoidance is possible.[18] If you are absolutely certain that there is no way to escape or avoid an aversive situation, watching for extra information has no positive value—it is not rewarding. In fact, the information is aversive. If an angry burglar points his gun at your heart and cocks the hammer, there may be nothing you can do to avoid being shot. The situation is ugly and the predictive stimuli elicit emotions of extreme fear and anxiety. The predictive stimuli are secondary punishers that punish and suppress looking. They are S^Ds that may lead you to close your eyes or turn away in horror.

Things would be different, however, if escape were possible. If the burglar was not pointing his gun at you and there was a possibility of escape or avoidance, you might watch him closely, searching for informative cues that might help you escape. Might you have a chance to knock the gun out of his hand or dash for the door? Cues that indicate the possibility of escape would be S^Ds for observing closely, especially if your being observant during difficult situations in the past had been negatively reinforced by successful escapes. Because there is uncertainty about the best way to cope with aversive situations, the information is quite valuable—since escape would bring negative reinforcers—even though you are very frightened by the possible risk of being shot.

Observing secondary punishers can be aversive, but there is negative reinforcement for paying attention to them if they convey information that helps you escape or avoid additional punishment. Luz cringes when she sees a D on her test, but she adds the points to see if an error was made. She might discover information that could help her escape or avoid an aversive situation. If the information indicates she was graded unfairly, she may ask for a regrade and perhaps get a better score (an escape from a bad grade). If the information makes her aware the course is going to be difficult, she may decide to drop the class or ask the teacher for help in mastering the material.

Extinction of Secondary Reinforcers and Punishers

*When secondary reinforcers and punishers no longer precede and predict other reinforcers and punishers, **extinction** takes place, and the secondary stimuli lose their power.* They cease being informative and we cease paying much attention to them.

Secondary reinforcers are on extinction when they no longer predict other reinforcers. If you have a new roommate who invites you to go sailing this weekend, the invitation is good news—a secondary reinforcer—if similar invitations have often been followed by rewarding experiences in the past. However, when the weekend comes, your roommate is too busy to go sailing. The roommate may make similar invitations over the next several months. If all the invitations lead to cancellations, invitations from your roommate will lose their power as secondary reinforcers, due to extinction. Because the invitations are not followed by rewarding experiences, they cease being good news. (However, invitations to do things with more reliable friends will retain their power as secondary reinforcers, if those invitations are followed by rewarding experiences.)

Secondary punishers also lose their power during extinction. If you move into a new apartment and a cranky neighbor threatens to call the police every time you play your stereo, the threats are bad news. Because they are secondary punishers, they elicit aversive emotional responses and may stop your playing the stereo for a while. However, if you turn on the stereo later that week, hear more threats, and the threats are not followed by any other form of punishment, the threats will begin to lose their power as secondary punishers. After hearing empty threats for two months, the vacuous verbiage may no longer elicit aversive feelings or suppress your behavior in the least.

SOCIAL REINFORCERS AND PUNISHERS

Most of us find that smiles, compliments, friendly words, and merely being near other people are reinforcers; whereas frowns, criticisms, and insults are punishers.[19] *These social cues are secondary reinforcers and punishers, not primary ones.* Newborn infants do not respond to compliments, humor, frowns, or criticisms as reinforcers or punishers. Infants do respond to some conspicuous social stimuli: Their attention is reinforced by the sensory stimulation of seeing animated faces and hands, as when the parents try to elicit smiles with playful gestures and peekaboos. But it takes months before infants learn to respond to the more subtle social stimuli that we experience as secondary reinforcers and punishers. The fact that most infants are raised in social environments guarantees most will learn to respond to smiles, compliments, and humor as secondary reinforcers—while frowns and criticisms become secondary punishers.

On rare occasions children are found who have been raised in closets or social isolation, and it is striking how unresponsive they are to many social stimuli that function as secondary reinforcers or punishers for other children of their own age.[20] Their limited social contacts deprived them of the chances to learn to respond to social cues that are powerful secondary reinforcers and punishers for most children.

During the early years of life, infants are highly dependent on their parents and other caregivers for access to positive reinforcers and escape from punishers. In most homes, mother, father, or some other caregivers bring food, fluids, warmth, sensory stimulation, and so forth, and they remove dirty diapers, sharp objects, and other sources of irritation. If a child becomes frightened by overly novel stimuli, the familiarity of the caregivers and their gentle, soothing behavior help the child escape aversive overstimulation. In loving homes, all these rewarding childhood experiences are preceded and predicted by the caregivers' approaching and directing attention to the child. Thus, receiving *social attention* becomes a powerful secondary reinforcer in childhood, because it frequently predicts the onset of important reinforcers or the termination of punishers. In contrast, children raised in social isolation are deprived of these learning experiences that would condition social attention into a secondary reinforcer. Fortunately, most children have loving caregivers and they learn to respond to social attention as a secondary reinforcer that has been established across a large number of motivational states based on a variety of reinforcers.[21]

Because social attention is a powerful secondary reinforcer, it is not surprising that many children learn behaviors in the response class known as "attention-getting behavior." If a child says, "Look at me, Daddy; look what I did," the attention-getting response is likely to attract the father's gaze and hence reinforce the child's behavior. Some forms of children's attention-getting behavior are so cute, darling, and irresistible that parents cannot help but smile as they look at their child. Their attention then reinforces the child's cute behavior.

Other forms of childhood attention-getting behavior—such as fighting, acting out, throwing tantrums, being a nuisance or doing self-pity—can make parents unhappy, yet many parents give attention and secondary reinforcers to the child when these behaviors occur. As a result, it is not uncommon for children to learn one or more bothersome attention-getting activities; and after years of attention reinforcement, some young people find it hard to stop doing overlearned childhood behaviors during their teens and twenties. Juan often slips into doing self-pity at age 20, and hours of self-pity tend to make him very sad. Parents who know how to use behavior principles learn to be careful in giving their social attention—focusing it mostly as a reward for their child's creative, prosocial behaviors and keeping negative behaviors on extinction. Their child learns how rewarding it is to be creative and considerate and may never learn to be obnoxious.

Unfortunately, some parents and teachers fail to understand that social attention is a reinforcer that can maintain problematic behavior. Rachel has been squirming in her seat at school, talking to herself, and banging furniture around for 10 minutes. Finally, the teacher says, "Rachel, sit still or else!" The whole class turns to look at Rachel. All this social attention can reinforce Rachel's undesirable behaviors so much that the teacher's mild threat—"or else"—is ineffective. Some teachers report that whenever they say "Sit down," many children jump up. Social attention from adults is reinforcing the children's behavior that is causing problems for the adults. In addition, the children who have not learned many prosocial behaviors are most at risk for learning to be "class pests," since they get so much social attention for this.

Both adults and children benefit when social attention is given to young people who do considerate, friendly, and creative behavior—and not when they do negative and obnoxious behavior. Children who draw well or are kind to others often attract attention and reinforcers from both peers and teachers. These children both receive the pleasures of attention and have their desirable skills further reinforced. Unfortunately, many children who have no especially noteworthy skills may learn unruly behaviors as the only activities that bring them social attention in a class of 20 or 30 other children. Thus, while Kara is receiving reinforcers for her creative artistic behavior and Nate for his kindness to others, Rachel is learning to be a nuisance because this is the only one of her behaviors that attracts attention to her.

Behavioral research is helping parents and teachers learn to treat their Rachels differently.[22] If adults (1) give generous attention to any of the desirable and appropriate things that Rachel does, and (2) ignore her undesirable attention-getting behavior, they can help Rachel learn better ways to get attention. To speed the learning process, they can coach Rachel in prosocial habits and pair Rachel with a more skillful peer—such as Kara or Nate—for valuable peer learning experiences.

Discrimination Learning

Children learn that their parents' smiles are often followed by other reinforcers—such as affection, joking, play—and this conditions smiles into secondary reinforcers. In contrast, their parents' frowns are often followed by punishment, which conditions the frowns into secondary punishers. *Due to this differential conditioning, children learn to discriminate that certain stimuli are secondary reinforcers and others are secondary punishers.*

Because young infants have not learned these discriminations, they often do not appear to "understand" when Mommy or Daddy is angry. But as the months go by, the child will learn more discriminations. As Daddy's smile turns into a penetrating stare, the child ceases playing with the food on the coffee table, indicating the child has "understood" the parent's nonverbal signals: The child now discriminates between smiles and penetrating stares, responding to one as a secondary reinforcer and the other as a secondary punisher.

Over the years, children usually learn that smiles, nods, signs of interest, gentle tones of voice, compliments, and praise are secondary reinforcers—if they are often followed by hugs, caresses, play, and other reinforcers. Frowns, pursed lips, wagging fingers, harsh tones of voice, and criticism usually become secondary punishers—if they are often followed by punishment. Dad's smile while saying "It's a sunny day" may not be very rewarding to a child if Dad leaves to play golf on sunny days.[23]

With years of social experience, each of us learns to be sensitive to countless social stimuli as secondary reinforcers and punishers. *Because we all have unique histories of conditioning, we often respond to different social cues as positive or negative stimuli.* Some people find obscene language very aversive and a secondary punisher, if they have been—or have seen others be—criticized for using it in the past. In contrast, other people respond to obscenities as secondary reinforcers because "four-letter words" are common and accepted in their social circles, often useful in having fun, making jokes, and putting down rivals. Some boys learn that pushing hard to get sex is a fun game (because it is full of secondary reinforcers that precede having sex); the girls they push may experience the same sexual interaction to be secondary punishers associated with date rape.

Subtle Social Discriminations.   By adulthood, most of us learn that some social signals, such as compliments and attention, can function as secondary reinforcers in some contexts and secondary punishers in other contexts. For example, compliments can be *sincere* or they can be *manipulative,* and people often learn to discriminate the differences between them as they gain experience with them.

Young children often learn to respond to most compliments as secondary reinforcers, because praise from adults is often predictive of various other rewards. Yet as the years go by, most of us have experiences in which other people manipulate us with insincere compliments and fake flattery—which results in our being stuck doing something aversive. Have you ever been conned by a manipulative compliment, such as, "Gee, Jim, you're so good with the kids, why don't you take care of them for the afternoon"? After Jim hears the compliment, he may agree to help out, only to be burdened with a difficult 3 hours of work. After a couple of such experiences, Jim may learn to discriminate the differences between sincere and manipulative compliments. *Over the years, most people learn that manipulative compliments and overly generous praise are actually secondary punishers.* When someone tries to manipulate Jim with insincere praise in the future, the manipulative compliments may now be visible to Jim as "bad news." They are CSs that make him feel negative emotions and punish his volunteering to help the manipulative person. They are also S^Ds for avoiding the situation: "Sorry, I have to meet a friend in a few minutes."

Even in situations where fake compliments and false praise are used to manipulate other people (and not us), we may feel bad because those stimuli are secondary punishers—if we have been manipulated in the past. As we hear Jeffrey give fake compliments to Wendy, we sense the possible deception and hope that she will not be abused. We hope

Wendy can make the discrimination we have learned. Later, when Jeffrey says something nice to us, we may also wonder if we can trust him. If he uses fake compliments with Wendy, does he manipulate everyone? As we notice more and more people use manipulative praise and fake compliments, we may increasingly distrust them—which in turn causes us to appreciate and trust the people who do not manipulate others, an important social discrimination.

For similar reasons, most people learn that not all forms of social attention are rewarding. *Although social attention is often a reinforcer, being watched carefully is not: Surveillance often functions as a secondary punisher.* When people are engaged in enjoyable activities, such as playing games that produce reinforcing levels of sensory stimulation, no one has to watch to make sure they continue playing. However, when people have to do aversive tasks, it is often necessary to have some type of surveillance to make certain they do not stop or slow down—making surveillance associated with aversive experiences. Thus, the parents check to see if the children have mowed the lawn; the boss checks to see if the workers produce items that meet the standards of quality; the IRS checks to see if people's income tax forms are filled out correctly.

Any cues that our behavior is being monitored often become secondary punishers, because being under surveillance and checked up on are good predictors that the behavior is not as rewarding as we were led to believe. This is one reason people prefer jobs where there is no surveillance—and they can be their own boss—even though they might work equally hard at either job.[24] Experiments have shown that when adults begin to watch children's play as if monitoring an aversive task, the adults' surveillance alone suppresses the frequency of the children's play.[25] Being watched makes many people nervous and makes them feel uncomfortable, indicating that surveillance is a CS that elicits negative emotional responses and serves as a secondary punisher. It also is an S^D for saying, "Stop watching me; it makes me nervous," as we attempt to escape the aversive effects of surveillance.

TOKENS AS REINFORCERS AND PUNISHERS

*People often use physical objects as secondary reinforcers or secondary punishers. These objects are called **tokens** because they stand for other kinds of reinforcement or punishment.*[26] Prizes, plaques, medals, high grades, diplomas, and other honors are tokens of social esteem given to people who excel. Many people have learned to find these tokens so rewarding that they will work long and hard to earn them.[27] The conditioning begins early in life when parents shower attention on their children for earning good grades and awards. Because high grades, awards, honors, and diplomas often open doors to better colleges, more stimulating jobs, faster promotions, and other rewards, they can acquire additional reinforcement power over the years. Of course, the students who always earned low grades (and were deprived of the reinforcers given to the A student) may learn to find the whole grading system to be aversive! For these students, grades are paired with surveillance, failure, criticism, and lost opportunities.

Tokens are sometimes used in behavior modification as a quick and easy way to reward target behaviors. Almost any object—be it poker chips, pennies, gold stars, buttons, or check marks on a graph—can be called a token. Tokens take on value when they can be traded in for snacks, gum, recess time, toys, comic books, or any other reinforcers. Once the trade-in value of the tokens is established, we have created a "token economy," and earning tokens can be made contingent on target behaviors. We may promise 7-year-old Serena that every 5 minutes she spends studying quietly is worth one token. Serena benefits from seeing immediate reinforcement of her behavior as the poker chips pile up— even though the ultimate reinforcement may not come until an hour later when she trades her tokens for her chosen reward.

Token economies can be used for both secondary reinforcement and punishment. If Serena has a tendency to chew her fingernails, we can tell her that each new sign of fingernail damage will cost her 5 tokens!

Eisenberger and Selbst (1994) studied 504 children in fifth and sixth grades, making tokens contingent on their being creative. When the children's creativity was rewarded with pennies as tokens, it increased significantly as the pennies piled up in front of the children. Interestingly, when dimes were used as tokens, the results became more complex. Receiving shiny, silvery dimes (with ten times more monetary value than pennies) caused enough distraction that the children's creativity did not improve; but receiving hidden dimes—nondistracting rewards—increased their creativity as much as the visible penny tokens did. This and other research shows that receiving glitzy and distracting tokens can disrupt behavior. Large corporations give their employees tokens—or chits—for submitting creative ideas or shepherding new products through development and into production.[28]

Tokens are sometimes used as secondary punishers. Traffic and parking tickets are used as tokens that precede the loss of reinforcers. A parking ticket under the windshield wiper is an informative stimulus: Bad news! It is a CS that makes most people feel bad as soon as they see it, and it can also punish and suppress illegal parking. In addition, it functions as an S^D for paying the specified fine, because paying is negatively reinforced by escaping the more severe punishment given to those who fail to pay their parking tickets.

As immortalized in Hawthorne's novel *The Scarlet Letter,* the red letter *A* was a punitive token worn by adulteresses in Puritan New England. When tokens of social disapproval are affixed to people's clothing or belongings, they may be eager to remove them. Hence stigmatized people may need to be kept under surveillance and threatened with punishment if they do not display the tokens. In years past, when a child was punished by having to wear a dunce cap, the teacher had to watch the child to ensure that the child did not take off the negative token. The Jews in Hitler's Germany were liable for arrest if they did not wear the Star of David that identified and stigmatized them in Nazi society. Few took the risk of not wearing it.[29]

GENERALIZED REINFORCERS AND PUNISHERS

When people learn that certain stimuli are predictive of a variety of different kinds of reinforcement across a broad range of circumstances, these secondary reinforcers become **generalized reinforcers.** Money is an excellent example of a generalized reinforcer. Because money can be used to obtain many kinds of positive reinforcers or avoid many punishers in countless different situations, most people learn to respond to money as a generalized reinforcer. If you are bored, money can buy entertainment. If you like the latest fashions, money can buy new clothes. If you get a traffic ticket, money can help you avoid the heavier penalties you would face if you did not pay. Most people learn to respond to money as a secondary reinforcer in many contexts and deprivation states.

Although money is a generalized secondary reinforcer for most people, it is not universal. Some societies utilize shells, arrowheads, necklaces, and other items for trade and barter. People from those societies might look at a $20 bill or £10 note and be surprised it could have any value, other than as colored paper. And we might be surprised at the great value they place on their exchange objects. However, any object can become a generalized secondary reinforcer when a group of people uses it in exchange for numerous other reinforcers.

Even though money is a generalized reinforcer for most people in our society, we may learn discriminations that prevent *all* money from being a reinforcer in *all* circumstances. For example, the possession and use of counterfeit money and marked, stolen bills can get us into trouble with the law. Hence any clues that a piece of money is counterfeit or stolen will usually suffice to make us respond to the money as a secondary punisher, which elicits aversive feelings and motivates avoidance. In addition, most people learn to discriminate that certain situations should not be associated with money. When you help someone because you love them, receiving money in payment can make it look like your behavior was mercenary, rather than an act of love. Others may then criticize: "You didn't help your grandmother because you loved her. You were just doing it for the money." This kind of social conditioning makes most people discriminate that they should not take money in situations where social criticisms will deprive them of the rewards of being recognized as doing the behavior for love, friendship, patriotism, or other noble reasons. Thus, even strong generalized reinforcers such as money may not be effective in *all* situations.

Because money can be exchanged for almost anything people want, this generalized reinforcer has become a "market signal" on which the entire modern global economy is built. In recent years, many consumers have fallen in love with sport utility vehicles (SUVs): The large amount of money flowing toward SUVs has served as a market signal that has oriented many auto makers to build and advertise their SUVs. In all sectors of the economy, monetary profits reward companies for finding better ways to produce goods and services that consumers like enough to endorse with their money.[30]

Many people respond to social attention, talking with others, and socializing as generalized reinforcers.[31] Children who grow up in loving and supportive social environments have countless learning experiences in which social attention precedes and predicts the onset of reinforcement and escape from pain. The more generalized these positive experiences with social interaction are, the more likely children are to find social attention to be a generalized reinforcer. Over the years, merely being in the company of others reinforces some people for walking up to strangers and striking up a conversation. Although some people sit alone in restaurants, bars, theaters, and parks, most prefer to sit and talk with others. The generalized reinforcers people obtain from being together facilitate the formation of groups—though people do not form groups indiscriminately. We often form groups with certain types of individuals but not others. Teenagers often prefer to interact with other teens—and adults with adults—because people with similar age, interests, and habits often find many rewarding things to do together. Much of the time, people voluntarily divide themselves into groups based on common interests and behaviors, since this produces more rewards and fewer costs than interactions with people with whom they have little in common.

Most of us respond to certain reinforcers that are not as universally valued as money and social attention. Some people have learned to find music a generalized reinforcer, and they like to hum, play, or sing music for hours each day—because music is such a strong generalized reinforcer for them. Other people have learned to find knowledge a generalized reinforcer, and they love to read, go to lectures, surf the Web, and visit museums— because of the knowledge that these activities bring. Some find beauty a generalized reinforcer, and they dedicate an unusual amount of time to art, decorating, and flower gardening under the influence of this reinforcer. But even in these cases, discriminating people respond to counterfeit art or pseudo knowledge as aversive, as secondary punishers.

When people learn that certain stimuli are predictive of a variety of different kinds of punishment across a broad range of circumstances, these secondary punishers become **generalized punishers.** Generalized punishers are aversive in a large number of contexts. Frowns, cold stares, harsh tones of voice, criticisms, and other related social cues tend to be generalized punishers for most people. As a consequence, people usually learn to avoid topics that cause others to respond with these social cues. Most of us respond to traffic tickets, fines, and other legal devices as generalized secondary punishers, because the legal system enforces them across as many situations as it can.

Many facial and vocal expressions—such as smiles, laughter, frowns, and cries of pain—are based on reflexes and their high correlation with happiness or sadness helps most of us learn to respond to them as generalized reinforcers and punishers. Because of their biological origins, smiles, laughter, frowns, and crying tend to have similar looks and sounds across many different contexts; hence they tend to be predictive cues about people's emotions that are reliable across much of the generalization gradient. If smiles were only correlated with food reinforcers—when people sat down to enjoy a meal—they would be very specific to dining pleasures and not serve as generalized reinforcers. However, people experience smiles in association with a wide range of reinforcing situations in everyday life, and smiles become generalized reinforcers in many contexts. Frowns tend to become generalized punishers due to their association with aversive experiences in a broad range of social situations.

As explained in Chapter 4, some people gain operant control over reflexive gestures, learning to fake smiles and grimaces without effort. And those of us who observe fake signals often learn to discriminate between fake smiles and genuine smiles, theatrical frowns and real frowns, along with other related expressions. As we learn these discriminations, not all smiles are generalized reinforcers, nor are all frowns generalized punishers.

CHAINS OF OPERANTS

Many of our everyday activities actually consist of long chains of operants. To grill a steak you begin by arranging the charcoal, applying lighter fluid, igniting the fire, waiting until the coals are hot, then grilling the meat for just the right amount of time. Changing the batteries in a flashlight takes several steps: Open the flashlight, pop out the dead batteries, take the new batteries out of their package, drop them into place, and reassemble the flashlight. A shoe salesperson may spend 20 minutes with a customer, answer a dozen questions, and show five different pairs of shoes before making a sale. *Each of these sequences of operants is called an* **operant behavior chain.** Secondary reinforcers and punishers play important roles in explaining the long sequences of behavior that are typical of everyday life.

In well-polished chains of behavior, each behavior is usually joined to the next behavior by secondary reinforcers, although primary reinforcers may be involved, too. Each

$$\text{Operant} \rightarrow \boxed{\begin{array}{c}\text{secondary}\\\text{reinforcer}\end{array}} \rightarrow \text{operant} \rightarrow \boxed{\begin{array}{c}\text{secondary}\\\text{reinforcer}\end{array}} \rightarrow \text{operant} \rightarrow \text{etc.}$$

secondary reinforcer links two operants together, acting as the "glue" that holds these links together. Each reinforcer between the behavioral links does three things: (1) elicits positive emotions, (2) strengthens the prior operant, and (3) sets the occasion for the next operant. When punishers appear in a "behavioral chain," they signal "bad news"—that some behavioral blunder endangers the smooth flow of the behavioral chain. Such punishers usually do three things: (1) elicit unpleasant emotions, (2) decrease the probability of the punished operant, and (3) set the occasion for taking some corrective action to keep the chain going as smoothly as possible.

The most commonly researched type of operant chain consists of a series of several operants that end with the acquisition of a primary reinforcer. For example, a person may

$$\text{Start grill} \rightarrow \boxed{\begin{array}{c}\text{secondary}\\\text{reinforcer}\end{array}} \rightarrow \text{grill steak} \rightarrow \boxed{\begin{array}{c}\text{secondary}\\\text{reinforcer}\end{array}} \rightarrow \text{eat} \rightarrow \boxed{\begin{array}{c}\text{primary}\\\text{reinforcer}\end{array}}$$

do this three-link operant chain: Start a charcoal grill, grill a steak to the desired point, then eat the meat. The last behavior in the chain—eating—is followed by the primary reinforcer. The earlier responses in the chain are followed by secondary reinforcers that take their reinforcement power from their ability to precede and predict the primary reinforcer, eating the charcoal-grilled steak. Starting the charcoal grill is the first operant, and it produces the secondary reinforcers of seeing the white coals that will make the steak taste so good. Grilling the steak is the second operant, and it produces the secondary reinforcers of smelling delicious steak odors. Next comes the behavior of eating, which produces the primary reinforcer of food. Both of the secondary reinforcers early in the chain take on their positive powers because they precede and predict the arrival of the primary reinforcer, which follows the third operant, eating the steak.

The secondary reinforcers early in a chain help bridge the time gap between early responses in the chain and the eventual primary reinforcer at the end. A person may spend 30 minutes preparing a charcoal-grilled steak. Hundreds of separate small steps may be performed in careful sequences before the dinner is finally served. The primary reinforcer of food is very effective in reinforcing responses that occur immediately before the primary reinforcer, such as putting food in the mouth; but it cannot directly reinforce responses that occurred 30 minutes before. It is the secondary reinforcers that precede and predict the eventual delicious food that bridge the time gap between early operants in the behavioral chain and the primary reinforcer at the end.

Two-Link Operant Chains

In order to better understand operant chains, let us first examine the simplest of operant chains, in which two operants are connected by one secondary reinforcer and followed by one primary reinforcer. After Julie played basketball for 2 hours, her back felt tired and she wanted her boyfriend to give her a back massage. The tight and tired muscles in her back were the S^Ds that set the occasion for a two-link behavioral chain: Ask her boyfriend for a back massage, then lie down to enjoy it. The first S^D that starts the response chain is the feeling of a sore back. This S^D sets the occasion for the first operant, asking for a back rub. When her boyfriend says "Yes," his positive answer is a secondary reinforcer for the first operant, and it has three functions. As a CS, the secondary reinforcer gives Julie pleasant feelings, and it strengthens her habit of asking for back rubs (operant number one). The word "Yes" also functions as an S^D for the second operant in the chain, lying down to be massaged. Finally, receiving a massage on sore muscles brings the primary reinforcers that are experienced as pleasurable physical feelings.

S^D:	1st operant	$\rightarrow$	secondary reinforcer (CS and S^D)	$\rightarrow$	2nd operant	$\rightarrow$	primary reinforcers
Sore back	$\rightarrow$ Ask for massage	$\rightarrow$	Boyfriend says "yes"	$\rightarrow$	Lie down on stomach	$\rightarrow$	Receive back massage

Now let's see the value of working backward through the preceding figure. The primary reinforcer of a massage directly reinforces the second operant in the chain, when Julie lies down on her stomach to receive the massage. Because the words "Yes, I'll give you a massage" regularly precede this second operant and predict the massage reinforcers, they become secondary reinforcers for Julie. These secondary reinforcers are responsible for reinforcing the first operant of asking for a massage, and they also make a sore back serve as an S^D for asking for a massage.

*The secondary reinforcers in operant chains are usually **response-produced stimuli;** namely, they are stimuli that are produced by the prior response.* The first operant of asking for a massage helped produce the boyfriend's answer of "Yes," which is the *response-produced stimulus* that both reinforces the first operant and sets the occasion for the second operant. As S^Ds, response-produced stimuli control the timing and coordinate the linking of responses in the chain: Julie does not lie down for a massage until she hears the S^D of "Yes."

Multiple-Link Operant Chains

Most operant chains contain more than two links. An Olympic gymnast links hundreds of behavioral movements to create an award winning performance, while the judges watch each unit of behavior and the way it flows into the next to evaluate the entire performance. It takes thousands of behavioral units to write a term paper, long letter, or beefy e-mail.

Many long chains of behavior are linked in the same manner as two-link chains. Between each operant is a secondary reinforcer which serves as a CS and an S^D: As a CS, it elicits emotions and reinforces the prior operant, while also being an S^D for the next operant. Driving a car involves a long chain of behaviors—getting in the car, putting on the seatbelt, starting the engine, putting the car in gear, accelerating, and steering. Many of these behavioral units are linked by response-produced stimuli: Getting in the car creates the S^Ds for starting the engine. Hearing the engine is the S^D for putting the car in gear, and so on. Many of these secondary reinforcers involve response-produced stimuli, but other features of the stimulus collage can "steer" the behavioral chain one way or another. Once our car is on the road, many outside cues—such as traffic lights, a slow car ahead of us, or a stop sign (which are not response-produced stimuli)—have major influences on the details of the behavior chain we call "driving."

To illustrate the role of secondary reinforcers and punishers in multiple-link operant chains, let us consider the five-link chain of starting a video. When you are bored or want some sensory stimulation, you may do this five-link chain almost without thinking. You push the VCR's "power" button (behavior 1), pop in a video (behavior 2), press "play" (behavior 3), turn on the TV (behavior 4), and begin watching the video (behavior 5). Such chains are quite common in everyday life. Figure 8–1 shows how these five behaviors lead to the primary reinforcer of entertainment—optimal levels of sensory stimulation. The first four behaviors produce stimuli: Pressing the "power" button makes the VCR's green light come on, putting in the video-cassette makes the motor spin to load the tape, pressing "play" causes another motor to start, and the TV begins to hum when you turn it on. All four of these response-produced stimuli are secondary reinforcers because they precede and predict the last behavior, watching the sensory stimulation of the video, which is the primary reinforcer at the end of the chain. The final reinforcer causes each

FIGURE 8–1 The top line shows a chain of behaviors. The bottom line shows the secondary reinforcers and the final primary reinforcer. Dark arrows show how each behavior leads to a response-produced stimulus that functions as a secondary reinforcer. Light arrows show that each secondary reinforcer is a CS which reinforces the previous operant and an S^D that sets the occasion for the next operant.

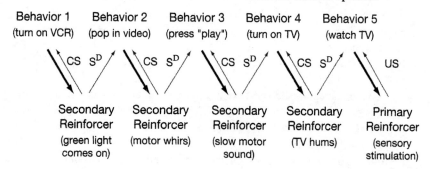

response-produced stimulus in the chain to become a CS that elicits positive emotions and rewards the preceding operant links. Each response-produced stimulus also serves as an S^D for the next behavior.

You might think that the secondary reinforcers are not very important: "I never feel any big reward when I hear the hum of VCR motors or TV sounds." But you may become appreciative of these response-produced sounds if the motors in your VCR break. "Geez, I bet this will cost me $100 to get fixed." After the time, effort, hassle, and expense of getting your VCR fixed, you will probably be more appreciative of the sounds of a smoothly functioning VCR. Sometimes we do not consciously appreciate secondary reinforcers until we lose them. A grinding sound in the VCR is a secondary punisher because it predicts both hassles and costs, which are punishers for most of us.

Bridging Long Time Gaps.   In long multiple-link behavior chains, secondary reinforcers and punishers help *bridge long time gaps between early behaviors in a chain and the terminal consequences (located at the end of the chain).*[32] In Chapter 3, we saw that reinforcers and punishers are most effective when they occur *immediately* after a behavior (p. 75). Although long chains may take many minutes or hours before reaching a primary reinforcer at the end, each behavior in the chain is followed immediately by a secondary reinforcer—even though the final primary reinforcer is too distant from the early behaviors in the chain to have much direct effect on them. In such chains, secondary reinforcers and punishers bridge the time gap between early operants and final primary reinforcers. *The secondary reinforcers and punishers that occur right after each operant in a chain provide immediate consequences for each behavioral link, if the chain is effective in reaching a valuable terminal reinforcer.*

Reinforcers show this effect nicely. The first links in the chain for preparing a delicious omelet occur when a person buys the ingredients at the grocery store—hours or days before eating the food. Purchasing the food is not followed immediately by food reinforcers, but the secondary reinforcers appear immediately, because owning the ingredients produces stimuli that predict that food reinforcement will occur later in the chain. After the person gets home and starts to make an omelet, there are additional secondary reinforcers, because preparing the ingredients is also predictive of food reinforcement. Although acts that put food in the mouth are immediately reinforced by food, all the preceding operant links are reinforced by the secondary reinforcers that are predictive of reaching the terminal reinforcer. *Thus, the secondary reinforcers bridge the time gap by providing immediate reinforcement for each behavior that advances a person through a chain toward terminal reinforcers.* Many good cooks talk to themselves as they work, saying inner words such as "Keep the final goal in the forefront if you want each step to blend together well." This keeps a person alert to the importance of doing each step as well as possible.

Secondary punishers can occur anywhere in a behavior chain and bridge time gaps of seconds, minutes, hours, or days. Whenever a behavior produces slipups, goofs, blunders, and other mistakes that endanger the completion of the chain, the error is "bad news": It signals a risk that we may not reach the terminal, delayed reinforcers. While performing any long chain—such as interviewing for a job, training for an athletic event, or preparing a dinner—one or two mistakes can endanger the success of the entire chain of behavior. *The stimuli produced by mistakes become secondary punishers that can bridge long time gaps by providing immediate punishment for actions which could endanger the completion of the behavior chain.* During a job interview, Jedd may think about making a silly joke, then feel an immediate twinge of apprehension. Just thinking about making the joke generates response-produced stimuli that are secondary punishers: "Telling one dumb joke could ruin the whole job interview." The secondary punishers serve as CSs that elicit apprehension and suppress the thought of making the joke. They also serve as S^Ds for talking about something else. Secondary punishers function as "warning signals" that bridge the time gap between the current behavior and the eventual aversive consequence, such as a failed job interview. When it is important to reach a desirable final outcome at the end of the chain, people will sometimes skip the happy moods during the chain (as in skipping over a joke) and accept the negative moods (induced by warning signals).[33]

Other Types of Chains

So far, we have discussed two of the simplest types of operant chains: two-link chains leading to a primary reinforcer, and multiple-link chains leading to a primary reinforcer. Other types of operant chains are also seen in everyday life.

First, some chains contain not only secondary reinforcers but also have primary reinforcers mixed in at various points along the chain. For example, eating dinner is a chain of operants that includes taking another helping of rice, taking a bite of rice, cutting a piece of meat, putting the meat in the mouth, passing the salad, and so forth. All along the chain, some of the operants are followed by mouthfuls of food (primary reinforcers), whereas others are only followed by secondary reinforcers associated with food. After Julie's boyfriend massages her sore back for 15 minutes and her sports bra is gone, the primary reinforcers of sexual intimacy may be among the next links of their interaction chains.

Many common behavior chains contain mixtures of primary and secondary reinforcers. The primary reinforcers of sensory stimulation are often present—along with secondary reinforcers—at various points throughout operant chains.[34] Playing music, talking with a friend, exploring a new city, and playing a game all involve long chains of behavior in which novel and stimulating sensory experiences appear at various points in the chains and make the behavior more rewarding than it would be if it were only maintained by secondary reinforcers and one primary reinforcer at the end of the chain.

Second, in some chains, terminal reinforcers that end the chain are not primary reinforcers. The terminal reinforcer can be one of the more powerful secondary reinforcers, such as social attention or money. Paychecks are terminal reinforcers that will maintain long chains of work for days at a time. An outstanding pole vault may be rewarded by a prize or trophy, which is a token given for success, not a primary reinforcer. Children who whine or pout may generate long behavior chains lasting an hour or more before receiving the terminal secondary reinforcer of social attention.

Third, the terminal reinforcer need not be very powerful if many of the earlier reinforcers in the chain are relatively powerful. For example, a telephone conversation ends with "Good-bye" and hanging up the phone. The final acts of the phone conversation do not produce terminal reinforcers that are sufficiently rewarding to maintain the entire chain of conversational behaviors leading to the terminal act. In most conversations, the terminal reinforcers are of trivial importance compared with the reinforcers of social interaction, meaty gossip, and the other forms of sensory stimulation that occur during many links of the conversational chain.

Learning Long Operant Chains

Some people's greatest acts of creativity derive from long chains of operants.[35] In order to reach the Olympics, athletes have to train and compete for many years, sometimes practicing 10,000 hours or more. They have learned to create long chains of practice with no assurance of winning a gold medal. In order to complete novels, authors must produce long chains of writing for hours at a time over many months. How can they do that? Most people could not perform all the long behavior chains needed to qualify for the Olympics or complete a novel. We find clues about the learning of long chains by studying the years of earlier learning.[36] Many athletes did well in sports early in childhood and received such abundant social reinforcement that they learned to spend hours at a time doing sports. Many successful writers came from homes or schools where they received generous assistance and reinforcement for writing short pieces in childhood. After multiple rewards for those productions, they gradually learned to write longer and longer works, creating ever-longer chains of writing activities.

A child who will someday write novels begins by acquiring the skills of forming letters of the alphabet, then linking these letters together to create one word at a time. Perhaps the child draws a picture of a house and labels it, "My HOuSe." Teachers and parents reward these early skills with loving attention, displaying the "masterpiece" for all to see and admire. After the child can write words, the child is given practice in creating sentences, then paragraphs, and finally short essays. The early essays are not of literary quality, but children in loving homes often receive generous social reinforcement for each step in learning longer chains of behavior. If mother or father enjoys using the subtleties of the language, a child may hear beautifully worded phrases and gems of humor every day. Knowing how nicely words can be strung together helps a budding writer create more interesting sentences than most other classmates can, which draws high levels of social attention and praise for the work. By high school, the writer has mastered the long chains of writing needed for crafting lengthy essays, and a caring teacher may help the writer learn how to insert extra links in the writing chain to increase creative word use, literary allusion, and character development. Over the years, the student may continue to receive social reinforcers for adding more links to the behavior chains that will be involved in the eventual production of novels.

Whereas the first grader received social reinforcers after completing each phrase or sentence, the college-age writer can link together thousands of words without external social reinforcers for each link. This is because many links in long writing chains are followed by response-produced secondary reinforcers that owe their strength to years of social reinforcement. There are also the reinforcers of novel sensory stimulation as the writer toys with variations in plot development, imagines how each character would speak, and ponders all the other details of a well-crafted novel.[37] Good novelists are also rewarded by the societal reinforcers of book sales and national recognition.

It is not uncommon to hear people attribute the work of creative people to "internal motivation," because it seems like a mystery that they can write for hours each day without any conspicuous rewards. But understanding the novelist's long history of reinforcement helps us see that the novelist's internal motivation results from two main sources—the secondary reinforcers which are based on generous social rewards for earlier writing and from the primary reinforcers of novel sensory stimulation that arise from doing creative writing (see Chapter 7).[38] Without help from others, most children do not grow up to produce great novels, Olympic records, musical compositions, scientific discoveries, or other peaks of human accomplishment. Role models and wise advice from others help young people acquire the skills needed to produce ever-more-creative work; and generous amounts of social reinforcement help young people discover how rewarding long chains of creative behavior can be. Over the months and years, a budding novelist or scientist learns to find secondary reinforcers scattered all through long chains of creative behavior. As the links lead to novel and creative work, the sensory stimulation of novelty adds primary reinforcers all along the behavior chains and adds credibility to the belief that "I may have the talent to do something special." People who have been raised to value success and find it a secondary reinforcer also enjoy working on projects they see as leading to success.[39]

Most creative art works are built from long chains of behavior learned via primary and secondary reinforcers from several different sources. First, beautiful art is a secondary reinforcer for many people, especially art students. Thus, the mere act of creating a beautiful drawing automatically provides the student with secondary reinforcers for skillful drawing. Second, self-evaluation and self-reinforcement consist of thinking positive words, such as "Mmm. I like that effect." These words—whether spoken out loud or silently to oneself—are also secondary reinforcers. In addition, artistic behavior is shaped by the primary reinforcers of sensory stimulation—as the picture changes with each new line and novel effects emerge (Chapter 7). Art students may receive social rewards in the form of compliments, admiring comments, prizes, or offers to purchase the work. Finally, some artists are motivated by the cognitive reinforcers of imagining great future successes.

Long-Term Relationships

Long-term friendships, love relationships, and family bonds depend on our being able to create chains of social interactions that are rewarding year after year—while also minimizing destructive fights and tendencies to drift apart (because there is not enough reinforcement to keep us together). How do people create highly positive chains of social interactions that are rewarding for many years?

All social relationships involve two or more people linking their behavior chains together. The long-term survival of relationships depends on the ratio of reinforcers to punishers that people bring to each other.[40] When two people create chains of social interactions that are rewarding to both, the social rewards elicit the emotional feelings of liking or love; in contrast, social exchanges filled with anger and ugliness often lead to disliking or hatred. Therefore, it follows that people who wish to build long-term bonds of friendship or love need to bring as many reinforcers—primary and secondary—as possible to their chains of social interaction, while minimizing the punishers.[41] When social exchanges contain few rewards and many painful experiences—such as harsh criticism, insults, cheating, anger, fights—they make people feel so many unhappy emotions that feelings of friendship or love can be diminished or destroyed. People who value long-term relationships try to keep fights and ugly exchanges to a minimum while building long chains of rewarding behavior.

Both good friendships and love relationships become especially rewarding when people create behavior chains full of *many* different positive reinforcers, such as generosity, fun times, honest communication, kindness, and sincerity. Lovers may want to expand on that list by adding romance, passion, and sex. Of course, each individual may want different mixes of these and other items, so each pair of people needs to discuss the things they find most rewarding if they seek to create chains of social behavior that bring abundant rewards to them both. There are numerous examples of successful relations between humorous people, between serious people—between extroverts who love to party together, between introverts who love to share quiet times together. The better that two people understand the things that make them happy—both the primary and secondary rewards—the more wisely they can select a good partner and make sure their chains of social interactions are rewarding and gratifying for both persons.

In the beginning weeks and months, love relationships often provide novelty and sensory excitement that makes them seem especially rewarding. As the novelty "wears off," over time (due to habituation) love relationships may seem less spicy and exciting, but this need not happen. Successful couples learn how to build ever-longer chains of activities that both find so rewarding that their growing love feels more profound than the novelty of first meeting. People can keep love strong for a lifetime if they build many chains of behavior that they both enjoy and continue to explore novel experiences together.[42]

Chains of social interaction must be rewarding for *both* partners to build long-lasting relationships based on friendship or love. Most couples benefit from creating a list of shared activities—such as going to restaurants, dances, sport events, movies, picnics—that chain together activities that *both* find to be rewarding. Each couple needs to create their own list of pleasurable activities that best enhance the pleasures they chain together in order to build their mutual feelings of love. This often requires many democratic discussions about all the behaviors two people could link together. If each person is careful in assuring that they have equal roles in discussing their favorite activities, both are likely to find their chains of interactions quite rewarding. People who wish to keep the novelty and zest in their shared lives need to continue exploring new activities together. Democratic conversations help them imagine many possible futures they could explore in the process of continually growing—together.

One of the nicest things two people can share is psychological intimacy. This begins with their both appreciating the specialness of having a close, intimate relationship.

Psychological intimacy grows ever stronger with the thoughtful communication and sensitive listening fostered by democratic conversations—as two people explore all the behaviors they might chain together—along with their feelings about the consequences they anticipate from each plan. Intimacy involves the wonderful emotions we have when we can share our most honest thoughts, feelings, and behaviors with a caring and loving partner—while being caring and loving when our partner shares with us. The frequent exchange of honest, heartfelt words creates a very special relationship. It involves a chain of intimate communication that can bring two people close together and build a strong love provided the two people live up to their words—showing through their behavior that their words were honest. Over time each person feels increasingly fortunate to share in a relationship that is being constructed so carefully, lovingly, and honestly.

CONCLUSION

Neutral stimuli can become either secondary reinforcers or secondary punishers if they precede and predict other reinforcers or punishers. Due to our individual history of learning experiences, each of us learns to respond to a unique set of secondary reinforcers and punishers. These secondary consequences serve as CSs that reward or punish prior behaviors and elicit emotional responses. They also serve as S^Ds that set the occasion for our next behavior. Secondary reinforcers and punishers carry information for the person who learned to use it: Secondary reinforcers are good news, and secondary punishers are bad news. All secondary consequences draw their strength from the consequences they predict, and they can extinguish if they cease to be linked with and predictive of those consequences.

Some of the most common secondary reinforcers and punishers seen in everyday life are social cues (such as smiles, attention, frowns, surveillance), tokens (including money, prizes, grades), and the response-produced stimuli from our own actions as we carry out chains of operants. Generalized secondary reinforcers (such as money and social attention) are secondary reinforcers that can have power across many different situations. The same is true of generalized punishers (such as surveillance by police). Secondary reinforcers are the good news signals that reward us for staying on course as we move through a long chain of operants toward some terminal reinforcer. They serve to bridge the time gap between early links in the chain and a delayed terminal reinforcer. Secondary punishers are the bad news signals that provide early punishment if we begin to drift off course during a behavioral chain; hence they often suppress sloppy behavior before a careless response brings a punisher or endangers our reaching a terminal reinforcer at the end of a chain. When people interact, they create chains of social behavior. People who learn how to make social chains full of reinforcement and low on punishment have the best chances of creating long-lasting relationships, such as friendships, love, and family bonds.

QUESTIONS

1. What are secondary reinforcers and punishers? Can you define them?
2. How do secondary reinforcers and punishers come into existence? What kind of learning experiences produce them?

3. In what sense are secondary reinforcers and punishers predictive stimuli? What do they predict? Why?
4. Because secondary reinforcers and punishers are both CSs and S^{D}s, what three functions do they have?
5. In what sense are secondary reinforcers and punishers informative? When are they "good news" or "bad news"?
6. What causes the extinction of a secondary reinforcer or punisher?
7. Give four examples of social stimuli that are secondary reinforcers or punishers.
8. What kinds of learning experiences cause us to discriminate that certain social reinforcers and punishers are faked in certain circumstances?
9. Can you give some examples of tokens as secondary reinforcers and punishers? How did they become secondary reinforcers and punishers?
10. What are generalized reinforcers and punishers? Give some examples. How did they gain their generalized power?
11. Can you give an example of a simple two-link operant chain? What is the "glue" that holds the two links together? How does it relate to the terminal reinforcer (at the end of the chain)?
12. Give an example of a multiple-link operant chain. What roles do secondary reinforcers and punishers play in multiple-link operant chains?
13. How do secondary reinforcers and punishers bridge long time gaps between the early operants in a chain and terminal reinforcers?
14. Can you explain how novelists learn the long chains of behavior needed to write a novel?
15. How do you explain socially interlocking chains?
16. What facts about reinforcers and punishers should people know if they want to create long-lasting friendships, love relationships, or family bonds?

NOTES

1. Hursh (1977).

2. Lance (1996).

3. For further information on secondary reinforcers and punishers, see Nevin (1971b); Fantino (1977); Gollub (1977); Millenson and Leslie (1979); Schwartz (1984); Mazur (1993); Williams (1994).

4. Keltner and Gross (1999); Keltner and Haidt (1999).

5. Bartlett (1980, p. 69, n. 18).

6. These other reinforcers and punishers can be either primary reinforcers and punishers or secondary reinforcers and punishers.

7. Staats (1975, pp. 37–38). They can also be S$^\Delta$s that set the occasion for not performing previously punished operants. For simplicity, S^{D}s are the main focus of our examples.

8. Although secondary reinforcers and punishers often have this third function—serving as discriminative stimuli—they need not (Stein, 1958).

9. Generally, an individual must be deprived of a primary reinforcer (a US) before secondary reinforcers based on that US will begin to function to reinforce behavior. However, there are cases in which deprivation from one US will cause secondary reinforcers based on other USs to become effective (Nevin, 1971b).

10. They are also S$^\Delta$s for not doing things that are likely to lead to stings, such as approaching or swatting at the wasps.

11. Egger and Miller (1962, 1963); Seligman (1966); Williams (1994).

12. Wyckoff (1969); Fantino (1977); Fantino and Moore (1980); Case, Ploog, and Fantino (1990); Dinsmoor (1995a).

13. Haider and Frensch (1999).

14. Keltner and Gross (1999); Keltner and Haidt (1999).

15. Rutter and Stephenson (1979).

16. Tolin, Lohr, Lee, and Sawchuk (1999).

17. Lieberman, Cathro, Nichol, and Watson (1997); Thorpe and Salkovskis (1998).

18. Whether a person will attempt to escape depends on several factors: how difficult it is to escape the current situation; how many skills the person has for escaping the situation; and the person's prior history of re-

inforcement for attempting to escape difficult situations. People who have often failed to escape in the past may develop learned helplessness and not attempt escape in situations where escape is possible (Peterson, Maier, & Seligman, 1993; Seligman, 1975; Veljaca & Rapee, 1998; Zvolensky, Lejuez, and Eifert, 2000).

19. Guerin (1992); Ervin, Miller, and Friman (1996).

20. Davis (1940, 1947); Curtiss (1977); Candland (1993).

21. As is explained later, this makes it a generalized reinforcer (Skinner, 1953, p. 77).

22. O'Leary, Kaufman, Kass, and Drabman (1970); Hall et al. (1972); Sulzer and Mayer (1972); Axelrod (1977); Ginsburg (1990); Webster-Stratton and Herbert (1994); Nathanson (1996).

23. Fisher, Ninness, Piazza, and Owen-DeSchryver (1996).

24. Wolko, Hrycaiko, and Martin (1993).

25. Although Lepper and Greene (1975) and Deci and Ryan (1985) used attribution theory to interpret these results, the data clearly indicate that surveillance functioned as a social punisher. See Bandura (1977, 1986) and Bernstein (1990) for criticisms of the use of attribution theory in cases such as this.

26. Kazdin (1988); Sharpe, Brown, and Crider (1995); Fisher, Grace, and Murphy (1996); Grace, Thompson, and Fisher (1996).

27. Cavanaugh (1998). King and Logue (1990) point out that the reinforcement value of a token depends in part on the way it is delivered.

28. Stepanek (1999).

29. Hilberg (1961, pp. 121–122).

30. Hayek (1988).

31. As we noted in Chapter 7, sensory stimulation is an important part of social reinforcers, too.

32. Williams (1994).

33. Martin and Davies (1998).

34. Houston (1976, p. 173) notes that even in the laboratory, sensory stimulation may appear at various points along a chain.

35. Balsam et al. (1998).

36. Bloom (1985); Gottfried et al. (1998).

37. Larson (1988).

38. Carton and Nowicki (1998); Reitman (1998).

39. Puca and Schmalt (1999).

40. Burgess and Huston (1979); Hendrick and Hendrick (1992).

41. Gottman (1999).

42. Hendrick and Hendrick (1992).

Differential Reinforcement and Shaping

A BALL OF CLAY

We watch a child play with a ball of clay. The shape of the clay is always changing. Ted's thumbs go squish and two dents appear. Will they be eye sockets in a sculpted head, two cylinders in an engine block, or merely two random changes? Alyssa is clearly shaping her ball of clay into a statuette: Is that Barbie again?

Our own behavior is also molded and shaped, every day, as if it were a piece of clay. As the ancient Greek philosopher, Heraclitus, said 2,500 years ago: "All is flux, nothing stays still."[1] Sometimes our behavior changes dramatically in a brief span of time, but most of the time behavioral changes are small and subtle. A big lottery win or traumatic event may produce large and noticeable behavioral changes, but these are rare in everyday life. Most of the shaping seen in everyday life involves small and subtle forms of behavior modification, although thousands of minor shifts can add up to produce a big change over time. Because most behavioral shifts are small and subtle, most people are unaware of how behavior is shaped. But even if we are not conscious of the shaping process, reinforcers and punishers are molding our behavior every day, increasing the frequency of some behaviors and decreasing the frequency of others.

A child shapes a ball of clay—creating a face, or a car, or a surreal art form which the child titles "Freedom." But who shapes the child? Why the word *freedom?* Does the child's word choice reflect an influence from the child's parents? Teachers? Culture? Debbie, a first grader, proudly displays her color drawing of an American flag, without ever once wondering why it is an American flag and not an Egyptian flag or Chinese flag. Most people do not analyze their own actions and ask how their thoughts, emotions, and behaviors have been molded to be what they are.

If we knew more about the ways behavior is shaped, the knowledge could increase our awareness of learning processes and help us gain more personal control over the molding process. If we are not in control of shaping our own behavior, then who is in control? Our parents? Teachers? Peers? Mass media? The government? At what age can a child begin to do self-shaping? What must we learn to increase our ability to shape our own behavior?

Increased knowledge about shaping helps us gain increased power to guide the shaping processes rather than taking the passive role of a ball of clay under a sculptor's hands. People have pondered their role as clay or sculptor for thousands of years. In the Old Testament, the Lord asks, "Shall the clay say to him that fashioneth it, 'What makest thou?'" (Isaiah 45:9). Today, increasing numbers of people want to have control over the way their own behavior is shaped.

Chapters 9 through 12 deal with the five main ways in which people learn new behavior patterns. This chapter discusses *differential reinforcement* and *shaping*. The following three chapters examine *observational learning, rules,* and *prompting*. In everyday life and behavior modification, these five processes often intertwine in various combinations.[2] We discuss each process separately in order to clarify its unique contribution to behavior modification, but pure examples of each process are less common than mixed examples. Although the major emphasis of these chapters is on operant behavior, these five modes of learning also influence Pavlovian conditioning.

In this chapter you will learn first how consequences can gradually modify any operant and second how repeated steps of change can shape behavior into new patterns.

DIFFERENTIAL REINFORCEMENT

Variability is a natural part of human behavior. Each time we greet a friend or say our names, there are usually variations in pitch, loudness, tone of voice, inflections, and other speech elements. We rarely repeat any behavior exactly the same way on two different occasions. *Whenever people's behavior is variable and some of these variations lead to reinforcement but others do not, the behavior is under **differential reinforcement**.*[3] As you would expect, the reinforced variations become more frequent while the nonreinforced or punished variations become less frequent. This is the simplest way that behavior is molded.

When little Jessie is first given a spoon while eating, she may stick the spoon into the applesauce in any of a variety of different ways. If the spoon is upside down, it fails to pick up much applesauce and fails to produce much reinforcement. If the spoon is right side up, the child may succeed in loading it with a spoonful of applesauce. The parents wait somewhat nervously for the next event: Will the applesauce reach Jessie's mouth or end up on the bib, the floor, or them? Sometimes, the spoon flies across the room. Only when it moves into Jessie's mouth and brings food reinforcers does Jessie learn how to eat with a spoon. Differential reinforcement occurs when useful behavior leads to rewards and other behavior leads to no rewards—or punishers.

A young child who is sitting in a high chair with a spoon in hand is in an S^D context that sets the occasion for several behaviors (B_1 through B_7): pushing, hitting, eating, throwing, dropping, patting, and mashing.

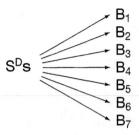

The figure shows that the S^Ds of the stimulus collage can lead to any of these seven different responses. The child's behavior may show considerable variability, as the child alternates somewhat randomly among the seven activities.

As Jessie plays around with the seven behaviors, the consequences that follow each behavior begin to modify its frequency, via differential reinforcement. If behavior B_1 causes food to fall on the floor, Jessie receives no food reinforcement (indicated by a zero), and the behavior begins to extinguish.[4] If behavior B_2 causes food to be splattered all over the high chair, again there is no food reinforcement (another zero), and behavior B_2 is also on extinction. If behavior B_3 brings food into the mouth, it is followed by food reinforcement (a positive effect). As a result, behavior B_3 begins to become more frequent. If the remaining responses (B_4 through B_7) dump food on the bib, the dog, the parents' clothes, or other places, they also are followed by nonreinforcement (the other zeros). As Jessie has repeated experiences with the consequences of each behavior, gradually behavior B_3 becomes the most frequent response to the S^Ds of sitting in the high chair with spoon in hand, and the other responses decline in frequency. Eventually Jessie learns to direct almost all food to her mouth and none onto the floor.

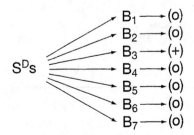

Whenever one or more responses to a given S^D context lead to reinforcement but others do not, differential reinforcement can occur. The different amounts of reinforcement produce two effects: Reinforced behaviors become more frequent while less reinforcing responses decline in frequency. Eventually the S^D context sets the occasion for those behaviors that are rewarded (B_3 in the example). The same context stimuli become S^Δs that inhibit all the other behaviors (B_1, B_2, B_4, B_5, B_6, B_7) that are not reinforced.[5]

$$S^\Delta s \;\text{----}\; \text{inhibit } B_1$$
$$S^\Delta s \;\text{----}\; \text{inhibit } B_2$$
$$S^D s \;\text{----}\; \text{set the occasion for } B_3 \longrightarrow (+)$$
$$S^\Delta s \;\text{----}\; \text{inhibit } B_4$$
$$S^\Delta s \;\text{----}\; \text{inhibit } B_5$$
$$S^\Delta s \;\text{----}\; \text{inhibit } B_6$$
$$S^\Delta s \;\text{----}\; \text{inhibit } B_7$$

Differential reinforcement is often in effect when there is a "right way" and a "wrong way" to do something. When a teenager first learns to drive a car, just getting the key to start the car takes learning. Turning the ignition key forward is rewarded by the car's starting. Turning it the other way is not rewarded. The right way leads to reinforcement; the wrong way results in either no reinforcement (extinction) or punishment. In everyday language, this type of learning is often called "trial and error learning."[6] A more accurate, nontechnical label might be "success and failure learning" because appropriate behavior leads to successes and inappropriate behavior leads to failures.

Because children have so much to learn, numerous examples of differential reinforcement can be found in childhood. When young children attempt to open screw-top bottles, they often pull, twist, push, and pry the tops in a variety of ways. Many of their actions have no effect on the bottle tops; however, a counterclockwise twist often succeeds in opening a bottle. Opening a bottle is usually more rewarding than manipulating a top that will not budge—especially when an open bottle provides reinforcers such as food or novel objects. Thus, children's early responses to bottles are influenced by differential reinforcement: Those responses that succeed in opening bottles are reinforced, and those that fail to open bottles are extinguished. After repeated experiences with bottles, children learn to open them quickly and efficiently by twisting the top counterclockwise and not wasting time with other types of manipulations. Bottle tops become S^Ds for counterclockwise twists and S^Δs that inhibit using other techniques.

Continuous Variations in Behavior

So far we have described differential reinforcement as it affects several separate behaviors (labeled B_1–B_7 in the first example). There is a second way to analyze differential reinforcement: Here we focus on the *continuous variability* in behavior, rather than on several separate response classes. To do this, it is useful to graph behavioral variability as shown in Figure 9–1. All the variations in a given behavior are represented by locations along the horizontal axis in the figure. For example, if a behavior can be performed at different levels of physical strength, we might graph the weakest responses at the left of the figure, the strongest responses at the right, and all intermediate cases in between these extremes. The frequency of each variation is indicated by the height of the curve above it. For example, those behavioral variations near the left end of the continuum (in the zone marked A in Fig. 9–1) are less frequent than those behaviors in the middle zones (marked B and C).

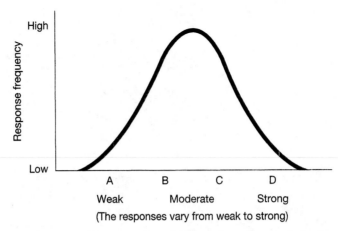

FIGURE 9–1   The natural variability of an operant behavior before differential reinforcement.

Continuous variations in behavior can be molded by differential reinforcement if some behavioral variations are reinforced and others are not. When children first learn to tie their shoes, they create a variety of different knots: some with more loops than others; some pulled more tightly than others. Some of these knots *succeed* in keeping the shoes on, and others *fail* to do so. Due to this differential reinforcement, children eventually learn the effective way to tie shoes—and ineffectual variations disappear due to extinction. The operant skill of tying laces comes under such strong S^D control that older children and adults can perform the task without paying attention.

For simplicity, let us only focus on the tying of shoelaces with pulls ranging from weak to strong. The loosest ties are shown at the left end of Figure 9–1, and the tightest ties are at the right end. Ties of intermediate tightness are the most frequent (in zones B and C). What happens as children tie knots of different strengths and experience the consequences associated with different types of knots? Because the weaker ties (in zones A and B) often come undone and cause stumbling on the loose laces, they fail to produce high levels of reinforcement. As a result, they gradually become less frequent. Because tighter ties (in zones C and D) are usually successful in keeping shoes on and producing reinforcement, they gradually become more frequent. After repeated differential reinforcement, the frequencies of the various responses are modified as shown in Figure 9–2. The responses that are reinforced (indicated by + signs) become more frequent, whereas the responses followed by nonreinforcement (indicated by zeros) become less frequent, due to extinction. The original response pattern is thereby shifted to the right. Due to differential reinforcement, children learn to tie their laces tightly enough to keep the shoes on and produce reinforcing results.

Response Differentiation

The changes in behavior produced by differential reinforcement are called **response differentiation.** An early, undifferentiated, and unspecialized response pattern becomes differentiated into two separate response classes. Early childhood shoelace tying (the before

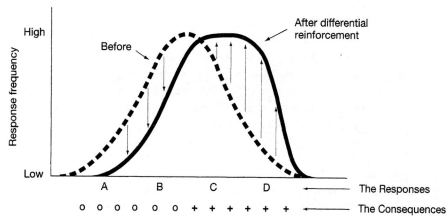

FIGURE 9-2 **The pattern of operant responses shifts to the right after differential reinforcement. Zero indicates no reinforcement, which causes behavior to extinguish (downward arrows); and + indicates positive reinforcement,
which strengthens behavior (upward arrows).**

in Fig. 9-2) becomes differentiated into the unreinforced responses (in zones A and B of
Fig. 9-2) and the reinforced responses (in zones C and D). During response differentiation, the unreinforced responses become inhibited, under S^Δ control; the reinforced responses become stronger, under S^D control.

The process of response differentiation can be seen in many everyday situations.[7]
For example, when children are first learning to play baseball, outfielders are often less
than outstanding in throwing the ball from the outfield to home plate. Their long throws
reveal a high level of response variability, which is typical of untrained, undifferentiated
behavior. Some throws come close to home plate, but others fall far from the mark. This
leads to differential reinforcement and response differentiation. The poor throws are not
reinforced; they may even be punished by criticisms from the coach or other players. The
good throws are reinforced by holding a runner at third base, producing an out at home
plate, and maybe facilitating a spectacular double play. As the outfielder repeatedly hurls
the ball toward home plate, the differential reinforcement conditions improved accuracy.
Gradually, the early, uncontrolled, and undifferentiated behavior is split into two response
classes: accurate throws and inaccurate throws. The more often an outfielder practices
long throws under differential reinforcement, the sooner the ball player will gain the skills
needed for accuracy.[8]

In many social situations a person's opening lines can make or break a social interaction. A good approach is reinforced; a poor one is punished. People who are frequently
thrown into social approach situations will have their behavior modified by differential
reinforcement. For example, a door-to-door saleswoman may depend heavily on her introductory few sentences to get her foot in the door. Something catchy, surprising, cheerful,
or disarming may succeed better than a dull or straight pitch. An inexperienced saleswoman may employ a variety of lines, but the successes of some lines and failures of others will differentially reinforce the use of the more effective openers.

Society's Variabilities

Differential reinforcement from the social environment tends to be more variable and unpredictable than differential reinforcement from the nonsocial environment. Bottle tops reinforce counterclockwise twists—though extra force may be needed if the top is on too tight. Patterns of differential reinforcement from the physical environment tend to be stable. Counterclockwise turns succeed in opening most bottles, while other manipulations lead to failure. Most shoes stay tied if the knot is somewhat tight, but loose laces can cause problems. The social environment tends to be more variable. A saleswoman may have been learning to be more cheerful and witty—due to several recent successes with this opening performance—only to have the door slammed in her face at the next house. Inconsistent patterns of reinforcement generally complicate the acquisition of social behaviors and discriminations, making the process of response differentiation slower than it would have been with more consistent feedback. Thus, the learning of many social skills is often more difficult than the learning of skills for coping with the nonsocial environment—opening bottles and tying shoes.

Because differential reinforcement brings operants under S^D or S^Δ control, complex learning experiences may result in subtle discriminations about the appropriate context for each differentiated operant. It may take our saleswoman many months of experience to learn to use witty opening lines with people who are smiling, friendly lines with people who are not smiling, and sympathetic lines with people who look sad.

Although many social situations are complex and variable—making it difficult to learn social skills—there are exceptions to the rule. This is easy to see in situations that produce social conformity. In a street gang where membership is marked by leather jackets, torn jeans, and old shirts, a nonconformist who dares to wear "straight" clothes is crying out to be heckled. In corporate main offices, an executive who comes to work in jeans and a sweatshirt may raise eyebrows as the "nonconformist." In many social groups, there is at least some degree of differential reinforcement for clothing styles, manners of speech, and topics of conversation when conformity is rewarded more than nonconformity. A student who dressed sloppily all through college may shift quickly to a very different dress code when beginning an internship at a law firm. The person may feel odd at first when adjusting to the new dress code, but the rewards of "fitting in" at the law firm tend to produce more positive feelings in short order.

A person who deviates from their peer group may feel pressures to conform. In behavioral terms, feeling "pressures to conform" is merely the subjective experience of feeling the punishment or nonreinforcement that follows nonconformist behavior. Subjectively, it feels aversive when other people avoid you, or snicker when you walk by, or cancel their contracts with your company. In contrast, conformity feels good when it is reinforced by friendliness and acceptance into one's group. This differential reinforcement for conforming and punishment for deviating tends to bring most people into synchrony with actions their group especially values.

When discussing conformity—and most other topics—behaviorists focus on "conformity behaviors" and their ABC contingencies, not "conformity as a personality trait."[9] If you dress like your peers, your choice of clothing may conform, but this is not enough to argue that you have a "personality trait" called "conformity." After all, you may do many other behaviors that do not conform with your peers. A person who conforms to traffic laws may be very creative and nonconforming in art and music. Instead of assuming that people have some deep down trait for conforming or not, we need to look to society's patterns of differential reinforcement. Most of us conform to traffic laws and social standards of civility due to differential reinforcement, and society runs more smoothly as a result. But you can select the friends, career, and lifestyle of your choice. You do not have to conform to some "master plan" dictated by "Big Brother" or any other tyrant. Modern democracies give us more freedom for personal choices and nonconformity than most prior societies ever did.

Behavior Therapy

Differential reinforcement can be used as a means of behavior modification to help people acquire valuable social skills. For example, Keith had a difficult time meeting women and seldom got a date. After years of frustration, he went to a behavior therapist for help. During the initial interview, the therapist noted that Keith talked too much, rarely asked questions, and did not listen well. No wonder Keith had little success with women. To help Keith learn better skills for interacting with women, the therapist arranged for Keith to have a series of practice dates. Three times a week a woman would go to lunch with Keith, listen to his conversation, and provide differential reinforcement for the good and bad variations in his social behavior. The woman was instructed to provide differential feedback by (1) making normal conversation when Keith interacted in any manner that women might enjoy, and (2) raising her hand and saying "Boring" when Keith began rambling about topics of little interest to women.

On Monday, the first practice lunch date, Katla had to give the "Boring" signal over 25 times as Keith kept talking about his latest engine repair project, the difficulty of getting precision dune buggy parts, and the problems caused by overheating at high speeds. However, Keith did come up with several good topics: He wondered if Katla would like to take a ride in his dune buggy. He asked her about her plans for the future. In these cases, it was easy for Katla to respond with genuinely sincere conversation. Nevertheless, when Keith returned to discussing the new camshaft he installed in his dune buggy engine and the effects of RPM on horsepower, Katla would raise her hand and say, "Boring."

Two days later, Keith had a lunch date with Latanya, and he again found that technical details about his vehicles were boring but that a variety of other topics led to mutually rewarding conversations. On Friday, Alycee showed more interest in cars and engines than the other two women, but she too let Keith know when his overly specialized interests were boring. Alycee was a law student, and she and Keith became engrossed in an absorbing discussion about women moving into the professions. Keith was interested in Alycee's opinions about the career choices available for modern women, and his sincere questions helped him learn a lot about the thoughts and feelings of a career-oriented woman.

As Keith continued with his practice lunch dates the following week, he bored his partners less and received less negative feedback. As he developed a more serious concern for the issues of interest to women, he asked more meaningful and relevant questions. These questions helped him learn even more about women his age and ways to interact with them in mutually rewarding manners. Several weeks later, Keith told his behavior counselor that he and Alycee—the law student he met on date 3—were getting serious, and he suggested that he no longer needed the practice lunch dates. Seven months later, Keith again contacted his counselor with the good news that Alycee and he were engaged to be married.

Differential reinforcement had successfully changed Keith's interaction style. An early response pattern underwent response differentiation as Keith learned to avoid topics boring to women and focus more on topics of mutual interest. Both he and the women he knew found the new style more rewarding. Differential reinforcement can also be used to increase empathy with others.[10]

RESPONSE GENERALIZATION[11]

The simplest cases of differential reinforcement do not lead to the creation of new behavior. During differential reinforcement, some variations of a person's existing behavior are being made more frequent, and other variations are being made less frequent. At the end of differential reinforcement, no new variations have been created. As shown in Figure 9–2, all the response variability lies in zones A, B, C, and D—both *before* and *after* differential reinforcement. Only the distribution of the responses was changed, being shifted to the right.

However, behavioral processes that often accompany differential reinforcement can produce new and innovative behavior. These creative processes are *response generalization* and *shaping*, both of which allow people to develop completely new behavior patterns that lie outside the range of their old responses.

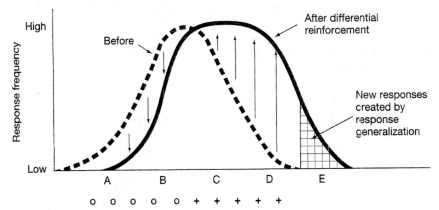

FIGURE 9–3   New behavior emerges due to response generalization (in the shaded area, above E). Zero indicates no reinforcement, and + indicates positive reinforcement.

When an operant is reinforced and increases in frequency, reinforcement not only strengthens the operant, it has generalized effects that strengthen closely related responses. Through this process, called **response generalization,** *variations on an operant may also appear and increase in frequency, even though they have not been reinforced.* When behavioral variations in zones C and D are reinforced—but other variations in zones A and B are not reinforced—all the responses in zones C and D increase in frequency. In addition, other changes occur due to response generalization: Completely new behaviors appear as generalized variations of the responses that were reinforced. The process of reinforcing behaviors of type C and D increases the frequency of those behaviors *and* some completely new responses that had never been seen before (in the shaded area above E in Fig. 9–3). Thus, response generalization sometimes causes novel and creative variations on old behavior to appear.[12] The new behaviors in zone E are natural variations on the reinforced operants of type D, but they add novel and creative responses to a person's behavior repertoire.

For example, when Gina first learned to high jump, there was a broad range of variation in the height of her early jumps. Some were only 5 feet, the majority were around 5 1/2 feet, and the highest reached was 6 feet (the "before" curve in Fig. 9–4). When differential reinforcement was initiated, reinforcement was given for all jumps of 5 1/2 to 6 feet, but not for other heights. Gina soon learned to make more of the higher jumps and fewer jumps below 5 1/2 feet. In the process, Gina learned many skills for approaching the crossbar from the best angle, selecting the best spot for jumping, tensing her muscles more, thrusting harder with her takeoff leg, turning more smoothly in midair to avoid hitting the bar, and so forth. All these skills and coordinations were reinforced when they resulted in higher jumps—above 5 1/2 feet. Not only does Gina's average jump increase from 5 1/2 to 5 3/4 feet (the solid curve in Fig. 9–4), her improved skills allow her to

FIGURE 9–4   **Even without special reinforcement for new behavior, response generalization allows new kinds of operants to appear (in the shaded area above 6 feet). Zero indicates no reinforcement; + indicates positive reinforcement.**

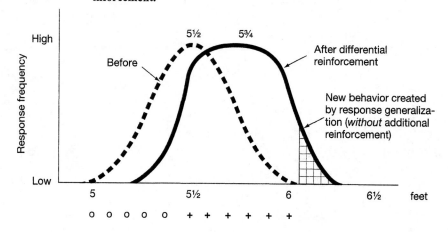

make some especially strong and coordinated jumps that actually surpass her original best jumps of 6 feet. These new behaviors (the shaded area in Fig. 9–4) have emerged via response generalization: They appear as a natural consequence of learning the numerous skills needed for higher jumps—even if no one ever provided any reinforcement for jumps above 6 feet.

Typically, newly produced behavior *is* reinforced—after it appears—if it is better than most prior responses. The athlete and coach who have been reinforcing 6-foot jumps are very likely to give even more reinforcement for jumps higher than 6 feet. Because these new jumps over 6 feet are also reinforced, they soon become more common than is shown in Figure 9–4 (where only jumps between 5 1/2 and 6 feet were reinforced). Thus, response generalization *plus* extra reinforcement increases the total amount of new behavior created, which is easily seen by comparing the shaded areas in Figure 9–4 and Figure 9–5.

In everyday life, newly created behavior resulting from response generalization is often reinforced. If a real estate agent increased the average number of home sales from 6 houses a quarter to 6 1/2 per quarter, the higher level of productivity would be something to celebrate. If a newspaper journalist increased average output from 6 quality articles per month to 6 1/2 quality articles per month, doors might open to promotions and more exciting stories. If a person who enjoyed improvising at the piano gained extra skills for creating new melodies, the extra novelty would provide sensory stimulation reinforcers for learning the new skills. Listeners might also appreciate the more interesting new music and provide a second source of reinforcement—social reinforcement—for the pianist's more creative skills.

Response generalization plus reinforcement can be used as teaching tools. Comedians and stage performers are often given special training to help them be more spontaneous and say more whacky and hilarious things on stage. One method that directors use

FIGURE 9–5   **When response generalization is coupled with additional reinforcement for new behavior, the new behavior (in the shaded area above 6 feet) is more frequent than in Fig. 9-4. Zero indicates no reinforcement; + indicates positive reinforcement.**

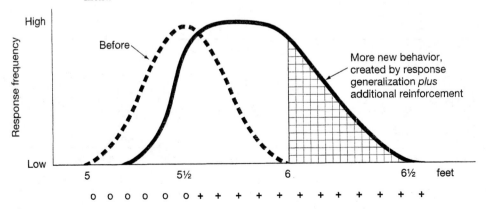

requires the performer to free-associate aloud and rapidly.[13] Once the performer starts spilling out words and phrases, the director gives positive feedback for the funny, silly, weird, or playful statements: "That's it!" "You're hot!" "Keep it up." "Another one like that." All of us can invent playful phrases, but generous reinforcement is needed to help a person to spew them out at a high rate. Differential reinforcement for funny phrases and extinction for prosaic phrases strengthens a performer's skills for creating funny lines and skipping dull ones. Response generalization is a common side effect of this exercise: As a performer's comedy skills improve, it becomes easier and easier to create entirely new forms of humorous banter.

SHAPING

When differential reinforcement and response generalization are repeated over and over, behavior can be "shaped" far from its original form. *Shaping is a process by which operants are changed in a series of steps from their initial condition to a later—and usually more sophisticated—level.* It may take months of practice for a high jumper to move up the 5 steps shown below as the coach sets progressively higher criteria for jumps that will be rewarded as outstanding. *Each step results from the application of a new and higher criterion for differential reinforcement. Each step produces both response differentiation (seen as improved skills) and response generalization (the new behavioral variations that eventually make possible the next creative step of behavior change).*[14]

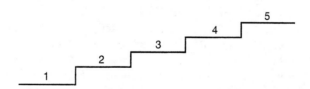

Ed wants to improve his skills for comedy, so he and his trainer start at step 1 with differential reinforcement for making funny free associations out loud. As this skill is reinforced to a high frequency, a variety of novel responses—including humorous little stories—appear due to response generalization. After a period of time, Ed and his trainer decide to move to step 2, now reinforcing witty stories, but not the simpler types of humorous free associations that had been reinforced during step 1.

Differential reinforcement for witty stories at step 2 will improve Ed's skills for telling funny stories and will cause new responses to appear (due to response generalization). Perhaps some of the stories at step 2 will involve a dialogue between two fictitious characters, and Ed may use two different styles of voice to make it clear which character is talking. Ed and his trainer may decide to use these new responses (that appeared due to response generalization) as the raw material for step 3 of shaping, and require the acting out of different humorous characters as the criterion for reinforcement. At step 3, the trainer gives reinforcement, "That's great," only when Ed creates funny stories with impersonations of the characters. This new pattern of differential reinforcement increases the frequency of good impersonations, and opens even more possibilities. At step 4 Ed might learn to act out the various impersonations while ad-libbing with another performer. At step 5 Ed might devise entire scripts for interweaving multiple impersonations with lines for several other performers. Eventually, Ed might be ready to create a full-length stage performance that incorporates the skills learned during all five steps.

In everyday life, shaping appears in a range of different forms, from systematic to unsystematic. Systematic shaping is most likely to produce rapid and effective behavioral changes—with the minimum of failure and aversive consequences—whereas unsystematic shaping tends to create slow and disorganized changes in behavior, with a greater risk of failure and aversive consequences. In order to clarify the mechanisms of shaping, we first turn to examples of systematic shaping. Later we consider less systematic, less efficient forms of shaping.

Systematic Shaping

The type of shaping studied in the laboratory and in behavior modification is systematically and carefully executed. *Systematic shaping involves changing behavior in carefully designed steps of successive approximation toward a preestablished final performance. At each step, reinforcement is given for behaviors that best approximate the desired final performance.* Step 1 always begins with the behavior a person is currently capable of performing well. The next steps are made small enough to allow the person to make easy progress and receive generous reinforcement all during the shaping process. No new step is taken until the prior step is well learned and enough desirable, new responses appear (due to response generalization) to allow an easy transition to the next step of differential reinforcement.

At each step, the behavioral variations that best approximate the final performance are reinforced, and the poorest approximations are allowed to extinguish due to nonreinforcement. As response generalization continues to produce new variations, all desirable variations that approximate the final performance are also reinforced. As a result the person learns ever-more advanced skills without failure—and without needing to experience punishment.

Figure 9–6 shows how behavior changes during the first step of shaping. Darcia's first reading was slow and full of pauses, consisting of behavioral variations that lie in zones A, B, C, and D of Figure 9–6. If we wanted to shape her reading into a faster and more fluent pace (at zones E, F, G, and H in the same figure), we would start precisely as described in the first part of the chapter—using differential reinforcement that rewards responses in zones C and D, but does not reward responses in zones A and B. We would reinforce the best half of Darcia's reading and let the rest be on extinction. This would cause her behavior to change as shown in Figure 9–6. Less skillful behaviors A and B become less frequent, and more skillful behaviors C and D become more frequent. New responses begin to appear in zone E (due to response generalization), and we would reinforce these variations in reading because they best approximate the goal of having all behavior lie in zones E, F, G, and H.

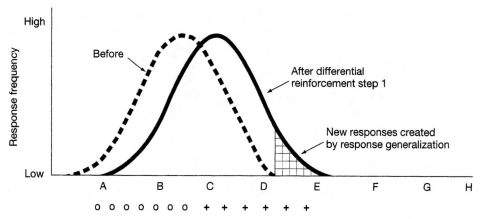

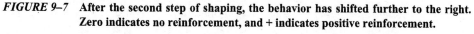

FIGURE 9–6   After the first step of shaping, the behavior has shifted to the right. Zero indicates no reinforcement, and + indicates positive reinforcement.

Once Darcia learns enough skills in zone E (due to reinforcement), we can shift her to a second step of differential reinforcement: Only responses in zones D, E, and F are reinforced (but responses in zones A, B, and C are not). As shown in Figure 9–7, smoother and faster patterns of reading—in zones D and E—become more frequent, and new, more fluent responses appear in zone F, due to response generalization. Darcia's overall reading skills have changed considerably from the earliest undifferentiated pattern (marked "before" in Fig. 9–7).

After mastering enough skills, Darcia is ready to progress to the third and fourth steps of successive approximation, with more demanding criteria of differential reinforcement. She must read smoothly and naturally, without pauses. The criteria for reinforce-

FIGURE 9–7   After the second step of shaping, the behavior has shifted further to the right. Zero indicates no reinforcement, and + indicates positive reinforcement.

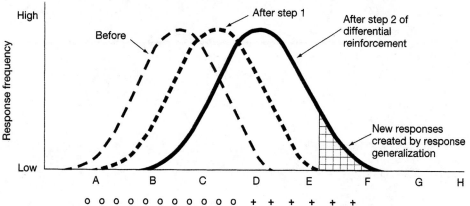

ment are not raised at such a rapid rate that Darcia cannot keep up. The goal is to make sure she will continue to receive generous reinforcement and feel successful about learning to read. The absence of failure and punishment reduces the chances that she will give up or avoid further learning opportunities. Although behavior is modified in a series of small and gradual steps, the steps eventually add up to yield major overall changes in behavior.

After the fourth step of differential reinforcement, Darcia's overall response pattern is *entirely new* compared with her earliest performance: Step 4 in Figure 9–8 is far more advanced than the "before" curve. At each step Darcia's best performances have been rewarded, and this has created new responses via response generalization. Gradually, the series of steps of differential reinforcement shaped these into a totally new and more advanced level of performance.[15]

There are major benefits from using systematic shaping. It provides generous positive reinforcement for learning new behavior. It minimizes the risks of failure and aversive feelings associated with learning. As people move up the series of steps—with generous positive reinforcement and few failures—they develop a strong sense of *perceived self-efficacy:*[16] "I can learn things without failures, and it feels great!" People learn the self-perception that they are in charge of their lives and will be successful in approaching new challenges. The multiple successes and reinforcers experienced during shaping boost people's self-confidence about being able to learn many other things in the future.

Everyday life examples of systematic shaping are usually found in situations where a person is being taught a new skill in a well-organized manner. You can tell a person how to shoot a bow and arrow or how to play the piano, but it takes years of practice—success and failure learning, coupled with shaping—for a person to learn advanced skills.[17] Although models, rules, and prompts can facilitate learning, many skills can only be learned through prolonged practice and shaping.

FIGURE 9–8   **After the third and fourth steps of shaping, the behavior has shifted quite far from its original form (marked "before"). Zero indicates no reinforcement, and + indicates positive reinforcement.**

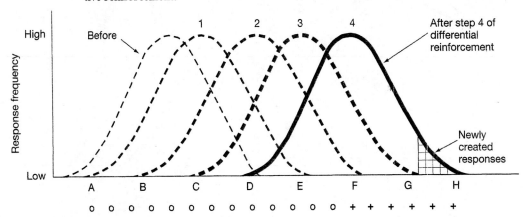

Scott, Scott, and Goldwater (1997) used systematic shaping to help an international-level pole vaulter (who we will call Paulo) improve his performance. Close behavioral observations indicated that 21-year-old Paulo did not extend his arms as far up the pole as possible before pushing off at the moment of his jump. Paulo knew this was a problem, but felt it was a habit he could not break. The behavior modifiers set up a photoelectric beam at a height of 2.30 meters, which Paulo could reach easily, and each arm extension that reached this height triggered a beeper when the photo beam was broken. As Paulo practiced, each long arm extension was rewarded with a beep. After he learned to reach to 2.30 meters often (with beeps to reinforce his efforts), the photo beam was raised to 2.35 m. After enough practice with this new criterion, Paulo began to hear the beep reinforcers more often. Gradually, in easy steps, the photo beam was raised to 2.40 m, then 2.45 m and 2.50 m. During each step of successive approximation, Paulo improved his pole vault records from 5.15 m to 5.37 m. Smith, Smoll, and Christensen (1996) observed that "the sport environment is an ideal naturalistic laboratory for behavioral research and interventions."

Naturally Occurring Efficient Shaping

Carefully conducted systematic shaping is not too common in everyday life. Most people do not know how to use behavior principles for shaping behavior. There are, however, some cases that approach systematic shaping, and these are most likely to occur when someone acts as a teacher, trainer, or coach to help another person (the student) learn a specific behavior. Many teachers do not discover how to shape behavior effectively, but some do.[18] If students have the chance to see a teacher use shaping effectively to train increasing skills, the students may learn to apply similar methods to their own behavior, hence learn to be self-shapers.

People who play the teacher role sometimes become effective shapers, whether they are parents, teachers, roommates, or anyone else you might turn to for help in learning a new skill. Let us consider some best case examples of teachers who demonstrate considerable skill at shaping.

The teacher who is effective at shaping behavior watches the variations in each student's behavior, gives positive feedback for the desirable parts of the variation, and changes the criteria for reinforcement in small steps as behavior shows successive approximations toward the desired behavioral goals. In the beginning, the effective teacher-shaper studies each student's initial behavioral skills so that shaping begins at the correct place—where the student is currently. Among the behaviors the student *can do at present,* the better variations are reinforced and the poorer variations are not. New and better variations will emerge via response generalization, and these deserve special attention. An art teacher might comment on the better aspects of a student's latest sketches: "Your use of shading has improved nicely in the past several days." By always focusing on the better features of the student's work, the teacher provides differential reinforcement that automatically includes any new responses which emerge via response generalization. Focusing on the best behavior the student can do at present also helps the teacher adjust the criteria for reinforcement at the same rate that the student's work improves: As the student gains skill, the teacher always looks for the better features of behavior and rewards them.

Shaping is an ideal way to assure that students enjoy developing new skills, because students are rewarded at every step for doing what they do well at that step. Shaping does not demand that a person do better than he or she can already do: That is unnecessary because improved performances will appear naturally and automatically (due to response generalization) as the better variations in behavior are repeatedly reinforced.

Parents sometimes use shaping when they help their children learn to walk, talk, throw balls, swim, and master other skills. When parents first hear their child babbling and making sounds that resemble words—"meh-meh," "deh-deh"—they may shower the child with loving attention, smiles, and other reinforcers that they do not give so abundantly when the child makes sounds like "glakagraga." This is differential reinforcement, and after a few more steps, the child will be saying "Mama" and "Dada." There is variation in verbal behavior, walking responses, and school performance; and parents usually reward the better performances and adjust their criteria for reinforcement each time their child reaches a new level of skill. This sets up natural steps of successive approximation oriented toward the goal of full competence.

Shaping does not have to include punishment: The shaper merely rewards the better behavioral variations and allows the others to extinguish. However, some students benefit when mild punishers—in the form of constructive criticisms—are added to the shaping process. In a drawing class an art teacher might say, "That's a good facial expression. I love the way you are learning to capture eye expressions with so few lines. But the lips aren't as good as the ones you did in your charcoal drawing yesterday." The teacher is noticing variations in drawing skill, then reinforcing improvements and critiquing behavior that does not live up to past achievement. Some students can deal with criticisms better than others, and teachers need to be sensitive to the effects of critiques. Some students are so sensitive to criticism that even a constructive criticism can cause a setback: Scott may become so obsessed with drawing lips as well as he did yesterday that his whole drawing suffers.

Sometimes other people ask us to be behavioral shapers. This is most clear when people ask for feedback about skills they are trying to learn. For example, Janet may ask her tennis partner, "Please tell me how my serves are this week, OK?" If the partner provides feedback (saying which serves are good and bad), the partner is providing differential reinforcement. If the partner also sets higher criteria for good serving every time Janet's serve improves, Janet's behavior will be shaped up a series of steps toward greater sophistication.

Self-Shaping.   *Most people learn at least some skills for shaping their own behavior toward desired goals.* When our parents, teachers, and friends give differential reinforcement and use steps of successive approximation, they serve as models that we can imitate for shaping our own behavior. Some people become quite skillful in shaping at least portions of their own behavior repertoire.

Self-shaping can produce rapid effects. Often the person who knows best when a behavior was done well or poorly is the person who did the behavior. An art teacher who checks a student's drawings every 15 or 20 minutes sees only the end product of many small units of behavior. The teacher's reinforcers are infrequent and often distant from the actual behavior that produced the desirable effects. However, when a teacher helps shape a student's skills, the teacher is also serving as a model the student can imitate. If the teacher says, "The eyes are sensitively done in this picture," the student may learn to evaluate and reinforce future artwork according to similar criteria.[19] If the teacher keeps raising the criteria for reinforcement as the student's skills improve, the student may also learn to impose higher criteria for self-reinforcement with each step of progress. As the student acquires these self-shaping skills via observational learning (Chapter 10), the student gains increased power to shape subsequent improvements in drawing without total reliance on the teacher.

The student can watch each pencil stroke and give instant self-reinforcement for quality behavior: "Hey, I got it just right that time." The reinforcement is both immediate and directly related to the relevant behavior, so it can have more impact than a teacher's comment that might come 15 minutes later. Likewise, if there is a slip of the pencil and part of the sketch is marred by a clumsy line, the student spots the error instantly and gives a gentle but immediate punitive evaluation: "Darn! How clumsy!" Each time the student sees new developments in artistic skills (due to response generalization), the student is likely to give especially generous self-reinforcement: "Wow, that's the best face I've ever drawn. I never thought I'd be this good." After several repeated successes at this new level of performance, the student is likely to raise the criterion for giving self-reinforcement. A series of such adjustments in reinforcement criteria creates natural steps of successive approximation that shapes continued development of artistic skills.

Why do people learn skills for doing self-shaping? *There are several sources of reinforcement for learning to do self-shaping.* If a student has observed people who are effective shapers and has imitated their methods, the student's self-shaping will be rewarded by (1) faster learning, because self-reinforcement is immediate and efficient, (2) positive reinforcers from people who are impressed by the student's rapid progress, (3) escape from the aversive consequences of errors and criticisms that come from making mistakes, and (4) the positive consequences of having greater independence and autonomy in guiding one's own development. Related to point 4, people who dislike being balls of clay that are molded by others find that autonomy and independence can be especially strong reinforcers for learning how to shape their own behavior.

Why is self-shaping rarely discussed in public? The reason is simple: Behavior that clearly results from a long period of practice often seems less impressive than behavior that seems to come effortlessly and "naturally." Hence practiced and shaped behavior receives less attention and praise than does similar looking behavior that seems to have required no effort or practice. If an artist told you that it took 10 to 15 practice canvases and many failures to refine each artistic project into a completed work, the artist's painting might seem less impressive than if the artist told you it only took a few hours to develop an artistic concept into a fully finished canvas. Just before his death at age 88, Michelangelo, the famous Renaissance artist, burned nearly all the drawings he still owned so that people would not know how hard he had struggled to perfect his art.[20] *Because people often hide the fact that considerable self-shaping was involved in developing advanced skills, many young people do not see how important self-shaping is in producing quality behavior; hence they fail to learn and use this powerful technique for improving their own skills.* They may wish they could shape their own ball of clay, but not know how it is done.

Haphazard Shaping

In everyday life, many people reinforce each other's behavior in inconsistent ways that produce **haphazard shaping.** *Individuals who have little skill at systematic shaping often reinforce behavior without setting specific goals, without paying careful attention to which behavior they are reinforcing, and without using orderly steps of successive approximation.* Although haphazard shaping can produce considerable behavior change, the change is often sporadic, chaotic, fraught with failures, and suboptimally rewarding.

A *good* teacher-shaper uses small steps of successive approximation in order to make each step easy and minimally aversive (see Fig. 9–9). The student is not forced to progress up the steps any faster than is comfortable. The use of small, easy steps reduces the risk that the student will experience failures and be motivated to avoid further steps of shaping.

Haphazard shaping is often not conducted in small, gradual steps. Often an inappropriately large step is introduced or a person is rushed to the next step before mastering prior steps. Both rushing and taking big steps can be aversive and increase the risk of failure. For example, when someone with advanced skills at any activity introduces a friend to the activity, the skilled person may be eager to have the friend progress rapidly to high levels of skill—in order that both of them can share the activity at the same advanced level. As a result, the skilled person may rush the friend up the steps too quickly or encourage the friend to make a big step before the friend has all the needed skills. A professional dirt track motorcyclist is overjoyed to discover that a close friend wants to learn dirt track skills. The pro may carefully show the friend the ropes, going slowly in small steps for the first five steps (Fig. 9–10). The friend shows impressive progress on these five easy steps. Encouraged by this flawless progress and excited by the possibility of having the friend enter a major race on the weekend, the pro talks the friend into entering the event—the big step number 6 in Figure 9–10. The novice may be frightened by the race's intensity, experience several failures (by losing control at the unexpected high speeds), and suffer injury (perhaps a broken leg). In frustration, the friend says "I quit," and both people have lost a great chance to develop an activity they could have shared if they had stuck to the small steps shown in Figure 9–9.

FIGURE 9–9   **Small and easy steps of successive approximation. Each + indicates positive reinforcement.**

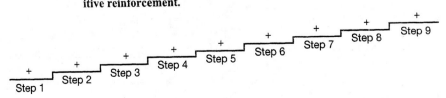

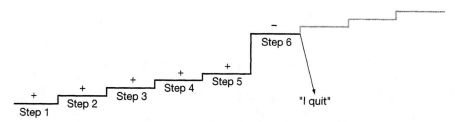

FIGURE 9–10   **One big step can create problems. After steady progress under positive reinforcement (+ signs), the big jump to step 6 led to failure (– sign) and quitting.**

Haphazard shaping with big steps may produce such punishing results that the student finds the activity aversive and avoids further shaping. Parents are committing the same error if they expect rapid progress in their child's musical skills and volunteer the child for a public recital (a big step) before the child is ready. The husband who is eager to have his wife share rock climbing or scuba diving—and rushes her to reach his level of proficiency—often creates an aversive learning situation and finds she no longer wants to learn new activities from him.

When an individual's behavior is being shaped by social feedback from two or more people with dissimilar values and goals, the individual's behavior may be shaped in multiple, and sometimes conflicting, directions. For years, Jenny's parents have been shaping her behavior to create a daughter who is demure, tactful, and quiet. At work, however, Jenny's peers may be shaping her skills for asserting herself, speaking up for women's rights, and becoming politically active. Each step Jenny takes in learning to be more assertive and socially active earns her more respect and admiration from her peers. Yet each evening when she comes home from work, her behavior is shaped in another direction. Jenny may learn two repertoires of social behavior under the S^D control of different social contexts. She may be assertive at work and demure at home. Having one's behavior shaped in two different directions can be very stressful and aversive for a person if the two behavioral repertoires contain incompatible responses. How can Jenny be demure and assertive at the same time? Jenny may feel torn, confused, pulled in opposite directions. Her inner feelings result from the incompatible patterns of shaping that operate at home and at work.[21]

Even if Jenny decides to move to an apartment of her own, she may not totally escape conflicting shaping effects. Because her friends have different personalities, interests, and goals in life, Jenny's behavior may continue to be shaped in multiple directions. If one of Jenny's roommates is excited about modern dance, Jenny may join her for lessons and practice, being shaped several steps up the ladder of learning to dance. But when the dance novelty wears off—and the effort involved in developing good skills becomes more apparent—Jenny may no longer receive enough reinforcement to progress further in improving her dance skills. Dance practice may drop to zero when Jenny's other roommate invites her to go jogging in the evening after work. They start with short jogs at first, and novelty effects are maximal. They progress in small, easy steps, running only a little bit further each day. When someone at work invites Jenny to try the 10-kilometer race on Saturday, Jenny takes too big a shaping step and ends up pulling a tendon, which stops her running. During the following weeks, Jenny's behavior may be shaped through several steps in an evening art class, a business finance class, and in other contexts. Looking back, we see that Jenny's behavior has been shaped a few steps one way, a few steps another way, and so forth, in a variety of directions; but there has not been any single, stable target. As a result, Jenny has made quite a few steps of behavior change, but not attained any single goal. This process may be judged as either good or bad: Jenny has explored a variety of activities and may continue to do so until she finds one that suits her well; but after several years of dabbling briefly in numerous activities, she may regret never having learned any one skill thoroughly.

People often give reinforcers or punishers to others because they (the givers) are happy or sad, and not because the other people have exhibited good or bad behavior. This can produce haphazard shaping. For example, parents may punish their child because they, the parents, are unhappy or in a bad mood, even though the child was not doing anything unusual or bad.[22] Later, the parents may be in a good mood and not punish or extinguish some undesirable aspect of their child's behavior, even though they should. A husband may criticize his wife—not because she was unkind, but because he got in a bad mood during a golf game he lost. Whenever we are influenced by people who indiscriminately give off reinforcement and punishment based on their feelings—not our behavior—we are exposed to haphazard shaping.

Much of the literature concerning the wise use of behavior principles in everyday life stresses the following:[23] *We should not give reinforcers and punishers in response to our own emotions. Instead, we should give reinforcers for desirable behavior—whether the behavior is our own or that of others—and put undesirable behaviors on extinction (or punishment, if rapid change is needed).* Parents should resist the tendency to criticize, snap at, or otherwise punish their child simply because they (the parents) are angry. The desirable or undesirable qualities of the child's behavior should dictate when parents give reinforcers or punishers. Lovers should avoid "dumping" any emotion they might have—good or bad—on their partner, independent of their partner's behavior.

BEHAVIOR MODIFICATION

Shaping is often part of behavior modification. It is almost second nature for behavior modifiers to reward the most desirable and creative variations in behavior, then shift their criteria of reinforcement as new and better variations emerge through response generalization.

A classic study in behavior modification shows how Patient Z made dramatic improvement with shaping. At age 21, Z was admitted to a mental hospital diagnosed as a catatonic schizophrenic patient. Records show that Z "became completely mute almost immediately upon commitment."[24] For 19 years, he did not say a word. He was completely withdrawn into a world of passivity and silence. None of the psychologists, nurses, or staff had ever succeeded in coaxing even one word from him. He made no eye contact. In group therapy, Z sat wherever he was placed and stared ahead with a fixed gaze, being unresponsive—even when people waved their hands or cigarettes in front of his eyes. Z was in a different world.

One day a psychologist at the hospital noticed a tiny feature of Z's behavior that would serve as the starting point for shaping Z's behavior through a series of stages of successive approximation toward normal speech. The psychologist accidentally dropped a pack of chewing gum. Z's eyes briefly turned to focus on the gum and then returned to their fixed gaze. The psychologist noticed this first small sign of responsiveness. Z could respond to something! Perhaps gum was a reinforcer for him. If so, gum might be used to reinforce and shape higher levels of social responsiveness. The psychologist met with Z about three times per week for shaping. During weeks 1 and 2, the psychologist held up a stick of gum within Z's range of vision and waited until Z's eyes moved toward it. As soon as Z showed this first approximation of social responsiveness, he was given the gum. Change was slow at first, but by the end of the second week, Z's eyes turned to the gum as soon as it was presented. Because eye movement occasionally causes movements in other facial muscles, the psychologist changed the criteria of differential reinforcement in week 3 and gave the gum only if Z moved both his eyes and lips. This occurred toward the end of the first session in week 3, and was reinforced to a higher frequency by the end of the week. Next, the psychologist raised the criteria again: Z needed to move his lips and make some sound—any sound—to receive the gum. By the end of week 4, seeing a piece of gum caused Z to look, move his lips, and make a croaking sound—which was rewarded by receiving gum. In weeks 5 and 6, the psychologist said, "Say gum, gum" while holding up the gum. Each time Z made his croaking sound, the psychologist repeated his prompt, "Say gum, gum." Z made different variations on his croaking sound, and the psychologist rewarded any vocalizations that approximated the sound of "gum." At the end of week 6, Z suddenly broke out and said, "Gum, please." Nineteen years of silence were broken.

Soon Z answered questions about his name and age, being rewarded with gum and social attention from the psychologist, and each week talked more and more with the psychologist. But he was still silent with other people. So the next step of successive approximation was to bring in other people and reward Z for looking at and talking with them. Within a month of working with a nurse, Z learned to talk with her. Later, Z brought his coat to a hospital volunteer, and she took him out for a walk. The psychologist instructed her and other staff members to give Z what he wanted only when he spoke, and not when he was mute. Gradually, Z learned to ask for walks outside and other things, rather than use nonverbal gestures.

A year earlier, Z had looked like an unresponsive catatonic schizophrenic. But shaping allowed him to gain major improvements in his quality of life in only a few months.

CONCLUSION

Differential reinforcement modifies the frequencies of responses that already exist in a person's behavior repertoire. It can come from the social or nonsocial environment as an individual has successes or failures in dealing with people, animals, plants, or objects.

Differential reinforcement often leads to the production of new responses, via the process of response generalization, and these new responses are the raw material for further behavioral change. Once new responses are produced through response generalization, they may be strengthened or weakened by subsequent differential reinforcement. When the criteria for differential reinforcement go through a series of changes, behavior can be shaped into forms that are quite different from the initial patterns. Systematic shaping involves a series of well-designed steps of successive approximation toward a clearly defined final performance, and it is an effective means of producing behavior change. It can be done so that failures and punishers are kept to a minimum and the learner experiences high rates of positive reinforcement while making steady progress in gaining skills. This, in turn, helps build the learner's self-confidence in approaching future learning opportunities.

In everyday life, some teachers, trainers, and coaches become quite skillful in shaping the behavior of their students. As students observe how expert shaping is done, they can learn how to shape their own behavior, giving themselves immediate self-reinforcement for desirable behavior. Self-shaping allows people to mold their own behavior without needing a coach or teacher. Unfortunately, in everyday life, shaping is not always conducted systematically or efficiently. As a consequence, people's behavior often changes in haphazard ways that involve unnecessary amounts of aversive experience. Knowledge of the principles of differential reinforcement and shaping can help people minimize the problems resulting from haphazard conditioning.

QUESTIONS

1. What is differential reinforcement? How does it affect the variations in commonly seen behavior?
2. How do some behavioral variations come under S^D control and others under S^Δ control?
3. Why do some behaviors show continuous response variability? How does the bell-shaped curve of response variation change under differential reinforcement?
4. Explain the change from undifferentiated to differentiated responses in baseball throwing. In being a door-to-door salesperson.
5. How can having practice dates help a person learn better social skills?
6. What is response generalization? What produces it?
7. How does response generalization make possible the emergence of new operants?
8. How does response generalization make possible the shaping of behavior?
9. What is the definition of systematic shaping? Give an example that clearly shows it.
10. Explain the shaping of high-jump skills. Use this example to clarify response generalization, differential reinforcement, and steps of changing criteria.
11. How can an art teacher use systematic shaping to help a student?
12. How can an art student learn to do self-shaping? Exactly what does the student do to alter his or her own behavior via shaping?
13. What benefits and reinforcers can a student obtain by learning self-shaping?
14. What is haphazard shaping? Why is it common in everyday life? What problems can it create?
15. Why do some people use indiscriminant social reinforcers and punishers based on their personal emotions rather than the quality of target behaviors?
16. Explain the behavior modification used with patient Z, who had been mute for 19 years.

NOTES

1. Bartlett (1980, p. 69, n. 24).

2. Gena, Krantz, McClannahan, and Poulson (1996).

3. Donahoe (1998).

4. Although there is no food reinforcement, there is novel sensory stimulation in playing with a spoon and propelling food in many different directions; hence there is some reinforcement for food play at first, until the novelty wears off (pp. 165–166).

5. Catania (1971); Nevin (1971a); Rescorla (1991, 1993); Lattal (1995).

6. Behaviorists object to the term "trial and error" learning because (1) a person need not be "trying to learn something" in order to be influenced by differential reinforcement, and (2) the term "error" focuses on failures without stressing the greater importance of successes and reinforcement in strengthening the nonerroneous behaviors.

7. Fox, Hopkins, and Anger (1987); Tudor and Bostow (1991); Goldstein et al. (1992); Bay-Hinitz, Peterson, and Quilitch (1994); Flor et al. (1995); Sharpe, Brown, and Crider (1995); Tudor (1995); Ervin, Miller, and Friman (1996).

8. Ericsson, Krampe, and Tesch-Römer (1993).

9. Mischel and Peake (1982).

10. Simpson et al. (1995).

11. Response generalization—also called induction or transfer—is discussed by Skinner (1938, 1953, pp. 93–94), Catania (1971), and Balsam et al. (1998).

12. Balsam et al. (1998).

13. Schulman (1973); Ruggiero (1984).

14. Skinner (1953); Staats (1963); Catania (1971); Lovass (1977); Michael and Bernstein (1991); Wagaman, Miltenberger, and Arndorfer (1993).

15. Balsam et al. (1998).

16. Bandura (1986).

17. Ericsson et al. (1993).

18. Cavanaugh (1998).

19. Bandura (1971) and Mahoney (1974) summarize the literature on the observational learning of self-evaluation and self-reinforcement skills.

20. Baker (1979).

21. Skinner (1974, pp. 149–150) explains that the internal conflicts a person feels should be traced to the conflicting contingencies of reinforcement.

22. McIntire (1970).

23. Skinner (1971); Mahoney (1974).

24. Isaacs, Thomas, and Goldiamond (1960). Also see Rye and Ullman (1999).

Chapter

10 Modeling and Observational Learning

DO AS THE ROMANS

When in Rome, do as the Romans. When in New York City, do as the New Yorkers. When in Santa Barbara, do as the Santa Barbarians (a pun we are allowed to make because we live in Santa Barbara). When we do not know how people behave in a certain situation, we are often well advised to observe the behavior of people who are familiar with the situation. If you are visiting a small kingdom high in the Himalayas and all the locals bow deeply when Xuhinzau enters the room, there may be reinforcers for doing the act—or punishers for not doing it—and you might benefit from imitating.

Observing others is often a fast way to learn new behaviors—or to learn which of our preexisting behaviors is most appropriate in a new situation. In many cases, observational learning is faster than shaping. Have you ever gone to an upscale restaurant where the tables are set with far more knives, forks, and spoons than most people use? There is a tendency to watch other people, hoping to see which utensils they use and learn from them—without having to open your mouth and say, "Wow, I've never seen so many forks and stuff. Which ones are we supposed to use first?" If you are encouraged to order the lobster or crab, you may wonder, when it finally arrives, how best to eat it. Again, watching the locals may provide the quickest and easiest clues. Throughout much of history, observational learning has been the central way that culture and knowledge have been transmitted to the next generation. Some of the earliest written wisdom was advice to an ancient Egyptian king, more than 4000 years ago: "Copy your forefathers, for work is carried out through knowledge."[1] Copying may seem uncreative, but it actually helps keep the creative knowledge of prior generations alive and moving on to the next generation.

When someone copies *your* behavior, how do you feel? Flattered? People often say, "Imitation is the sincerest form of flattery." People tend to imitate behavior that they see is valuable in reaching reinforcers or avoiding punishers. The fact that someone picked your behavior to copy shows that he or she thought you had done something impressive, creative, or good. The positive and rewarding feelings that emerge during the flattery of imitation tend to build positive social bonds and warm relations.[2]

In this chapter, you will discover how people learn by observing the behavior of others. You will also see why they imitate others from time to time, while not imitating most behavior and occasionally doing just the opposite of what they see others do. Much of the original research on observational learning was done by Rotter, Bandura, and Walters.[3]

MODELS

When one person observes the actions of another, the experience may change the observer's future behavior. While leaving a crowded theater, someone may try an unused exit that had been closed. If the door opens, the person's explorative behavior is reinforced by a rapid exit and escape from slow lines. When nearby people see the first person leave, several may follow, and eventually this new exit is as crowded as the rest. *People are influenced by observing the behavior of others. The people who first display a behavior are called* **models**. *Observers who see, hear, or read about a model's behavior (1) gain information about the model's behavior, and (2) may use this information to guide their own behavior.*[4]

Because we are frequently in situations where we can observe other people's behavior, we can be influenced by social models countless times each day. The effects of social modeling can be subtle or conspicuously obvious. We have to be quite attentive to see how quickly 2-year-old children learn new words when adults model their use with novel and previously nameless objects.[5] Children who grow up with very verbal parents can learn vocabularies that are four times larger than vocabularies of children with quiet parents.[6] In adulthood, one person may use a generous number of intellectually sophisticated words during a conversation. If the second person likes the speaker, the second person may show a slight increase in the use of erudite, polysyllabic words. The effects may be so subtle that neither the model nor the observer notices the effect. In sharp contrast, models can produce powerful effects on hundreds or thousands of people. During a mass gathering, the actions of a few salient individuals can influence large numbers of people to do the same thing all at once. When several people suddenly begin to shout and rush at the police, nearby observers who previously had no intention of participating in a mass protest may find themselves irresistibly attracted to joining those who are modeling aggressive action.[7] Mob behavior, mass panics, and fads all reflect modeling effects, when large numbers of observers imitate the behavior of those around them.

*Models can be **real** (bodily present) or **symbolic** (presented via books, movies, TV, or verbal descriptions).* Real models tend to be easier to observe and learn from, if we can be close with them. Symbolic models may impress us more if they are famous or very competent at any given behavior. Even a modest videotape of mothers being sensitive with their infants can provide symbolic models who produce a significant improvement in the skills of new mothers—as revealed by their increased vocal exchanges with, looking at, and physically contacting their infants.[8]

An observer may show behavior changes *immediately* after seeing a model's behavior, *after a delay,* or *never.* Observers who copy a model's behavior either immediately or later are *imitating* the behavior. Observers tend to imitate modeled behavior if they like or respect the model, see the model receive reinforcement, see the model give off signs of pleasure, or are in an environment where imitating the model's performance is reinforced. *There are times when an observer does the opposite from the model.* This *inverse imitation* is common when an observer does not like the model, sees the model get punished, or is in an environment where conformity or imitation is being punished.

Three Types of Modeling Effects

There are three main types of modeling effects: (1) observational learning, (2) inhibitory and disinhibitory effects, and (3) response facilitation effects.[9]

*1. **Observational learning** involves the learning of new behavior. When an observer sees a model do a behavior that the observer has never done, the observer may learn how to do the behavior merely by watching.* Five-year-old Stacie watches mother planting the spring garden, then picks up a tool and imitates mother's behavior. A new member in a teenage street gang sees a few of the older members chugalugging whole cans of beer at once, so the observer picks up a can, snaps it open in the same nonchalant manner that was just modeled, and pours it down in one long gulp. A business school graduate applying for an executive job in a bank watches how the executives dress, walk, talk, and smile. Soon the graduate is acting in a way that closely resembles the models' mannerisms. This does not mean that Stacie will become proficient at planting a garden after watching mother one time, and the new gang member may half choke while pouring down a can of beer. Nor does the green business school graduate become a polished executive overnight. Much additional modeling, shaping, prompting, and rule use may be involved in polishing the observer's behavior. Nevertheless, people can learn a great deal about new activities merely by observing others.

When a model's behavior is only one or two steps ahead of the observer's present level of competence, the observer may satisfactorily replicate the new behavior after the first exposure to the model's behavior. When an athletic young mountain climber sees how a pro prepares the ropes and rappels down a sheer cliff, the youth may need no more information to learn the needed skills. The visitor to a foreign culture may only need one exposure to a new hand gesture to learn the cultural practice. It is only when a model's behavior is several steps ahead of the observer's present skills that the observer is less likely to imitate the behavior skillfully and successfully without practice.[10]

New behavior can usually be learned much more rapidly and efficiently by observational learning than by shaping alone.[11] Life would be quite short if we had to learn how to deal with the hazards of exposed electrical wiring, guns, poisonous snakes, automobile driving, or machine operation via differential reinforcement alone. The presence of skillful social models speeds our learning and minimizes our risk of potentially lethal accidents. In addition, it is unlikely that complex cultural behavior—such as eloquent speech, subtle dance movements, or advanced computer skills—could be learned by shaping alone; yet, these activities are often acquired quickly by observing real or symbolic models. In preliterate societies, observational learning of cultural practices is obtained from real models and from symbolic models whose behavior is described by word of mouth. In our society, models portray cultural practices in many more formats—such as pictures, books, and electronic media—which only facilitate the dissemination of cultural information, though we may never know the symbolic models in the flesh. Whereas observational learning involves the learning of a new behavior, the next two types of modeling effects do not involve new learning.

2. Inhibitory and disinhibitory effects *occur when observing a model reduces or increases the chances that an observer will do a behavior at some later time.* No new behavior is learned. Instead, the probability of an already existing behavior is merely decreased or increased. If a model's behavior is clearly followed by punishment, not only will the model be less likely to repeat the behavior in the future, the observer will also be less likely to do the behavior. This is the *inhibitory effect.* If a model's behavior clearly leads to reinforcement, not only will the model be more likely to repeat the behavior in the future, the observer will be more likely to do the behavior, too. This is a *disinhibitory effect.*

When a high school graduate arrives at college and sees that all the people she likes wear faded jeans, it is a disinhibitory effect for wearing her old jeans frequently. If she also sees her new college friends belittle a student who pursues some activity she used to enjoy in high school, the observation has inhibitory effects, leading her to avoid the activity even though no one had ever criticized *her* for doing the behavior. She might even laugh with her new friends at the childishness of the activity she was doing only 2 months ago.

3. Response facilitation *occurs when a model's behavior serves as an S^D for a similar response by the observer.* Josh lights up a cigarette, and within 60 seconds, Delia does, too. Delia tells Josh that she wishes she could stop smoking, and this is an S^D for Josh to say, "I've tried to quit five times." In both cases, the model's behavior facilitates the observer's doing something similar shortly thereafter. Facilitative effects do not involve new learning (modeling effect 1), nor do they produce lasting effects that increase or decrease the frequency of future performances of old behavior (modeling effect 2). Facilitation effects are relatively fleeting, occurring shortly after the model's behavior serves as an S^D for a similar response from the observer. For example, if Delia has already learned to smoke one and only one pack of cigarettes a day, she has learned a stable frequency of responding—20 smokes a day. When she sees Josh pull out a cigarette and light up, Josh's behavior is part of her S^D collage that increases the chances Delia will light up at the same time, via response facilitation. Delia has not had any new learning experiences and she does not change the number of cigarettes she smokes per day: She is a one-pack-a-day woman. Social facilitation occurs only because a model's behavior has provided S^Ds that help set the occasion for the observer's making a similar response.

If you are walking down the street and see ten people watching something happening in a department store window, the ten models provide S^Ds that increase the likelihood that you too will feel the inclination to stop and have a look. "What are they looking at?" If you are exposed to other S^Ds—perhaps a stimulating conversation with a friend—that produce competing responses, the S^Ds from the ten people at the store window may not produce much effect on your behavior. But if there are few S^Ds for competing responses, and the ten people seem to be particularly interested in the events in the store window, social facilitation effects may be quite noticeable and you may stop to look, too. Social facilitation can be very strong when an observer sees a crowd of people gathering and staring at some person or object. Perhaps someone is injured? Maybe there was an accident? What's that guy doing on the ground? Seeing a crowd gathering and looking can provide strong S^D control for stopping and looking. The effects of social facilitation on observers is often seen when models do altruistic acts, volunteer their services, donate money to a cause, or pick up a new conversational topic after someone else takes the lead.

In the remainder of the chapter, we focus primarily on observational learning, the first of the three types of modeling effects just discussed. However, many of the factors that influence observational learning can also produce inhibitory or disinhibitory effects and influence social facilitation.

PAVLOVIAN CONDITIONING

When a person observes a model, various aspects of the model and the model's behavior may serve as CSs for the observer. First, the ability of social cues to serve as CSs is traced to Pavlovian conditioning. Among the most important responses elicited by CSs from models are conditioned emotional responses, which are called *vicarious emotional responses*. Second, when new stimuli are paired with the CSs from a model, the new stimuli become CSs, too, through a process known as *vicarious Pavlovian conditioning*. Third, all of the CSs derived from a model can function as secondary reinforcers and punishers, called *vicarious reinforcers and punishers*.

Vicarious Emotional Responses

Models give off many social cues that can function as CSs for the observer, and many CSs elicit conditioned emotional responses in the observer.[12] When an observer sees someone else smiling, the smiles are likely to serve as CSs that elicit pleasurable emotional responses, and perhaps even a smile, in the observer. When an observer sees someone in tears, the crying may serve as a CS that elicits sadness, perhaps even tears, in the observer. When people are watching a soap opera on TV, they often experience emotions similar to those portrayed by the actors. *These conditioned emotional responses are called vicarious emotional responses,* to indicate that the observer is taking part in the feelings and emotions of other people.

The ability to have vicarious emotional responses is learned through Pavlovian conditioning in situations where the model's behavior is paired with USs or CSs that elicit emotional responses in the model and observer. Starting in infancy, a large number of social cues—such as laughter, twinkling eyes, frowns, tears, and words—become CSs, and the conditioning continues all through life. For example, the smiles of friendly people usually become CSs for vicarious pleasant emotions in the observer. From the early months of life, smiles from the parents are predictive stimuli that frequently precede events that are pleasurable for the infant. The mother smiles when she picks up and plays with the child. The father smiles as he feeds and bathes the child. Eventually, just seeing the mother or father smile elicits pleasure in the infant—including a smile in return—even if the parents do not play with, feed, or do anything else with the child. The child is learning to respond with vicarious pleasure to signs of other people's pleasure. As the years pass, the child continues to learn that the smiles of friendly people usually precede pleasurable experiences, which adds power for the CSs to elicit vicarious pleasurable emotions in the child.

The Pavlovian conditioning of smiles continues long after childhood. When friends greet us with a big smile, the smiles are predictive stimuli usually associated with pleasurable interactions, which further conditions their smiles as CSs for our vicarious pleasurable emotions. People often smile when telling jokes or engaging us in friendly banter, which also adds to the conditioning of smiles as CSs for our vicarious pleasurable emotions. Just seeing a friend smile before starting to tell a joke elicits pleasant feelings that help us enjoy the joke long before we hear the punch line. These vicarious emotional responses allow us to enjoy our friend's pleasure even before we learn why our friend finds the joke funny.

The conditioning of smiles and other social cues is influenced by numerous cues in the stimulus collage, often allowing us to learn subtle discriminations. Although the smiles of friends usually elicit pleasurable feelings, the smiles of people who deceive or manipulate us come to elicit quite different feelings, due to the following type of Pavlovian conditioning. When devious people smile at us just before taking advantage of us, their smiles become associated with aversive situations, and we learn to discriminate between different uses of smiles. Thereafter, smiles used by people who might hurt us elicit uncomfortable feelings—feelings of uneasiness—even though we may not be able to verbalize precisely why we feel uncomfortable about the way a person is smiling at us. *After years of experience, most people respond to numerous social cues, such as people's facial expressions, words, tones of voice, and body postures as CSs that elicit vicarious emotions.*

Empathy for the feelings of others is based largely on vicarious emotional responses. When we see a child wide-eyed with excitement while opening birthday presents, the child's bright eyes, smiles, and laughter are likely to be CSs that elicit pleasant feelings in us. We cannot share exactly the same emotional responses the child is having, but our vicarious emotional responses are pleasurable and somewhat akin to the child's emotions. Seeing a friend crying at her mother's funeral may make us feel sad, even though we never met her mother. Naturally, the observer does not feel the exact same emotional responses that the model feels. However, there is often a similarity in emotional responses if the observer has had enough emotional conditioning in situations similar to the one the model is experiencing. For example, a young child who is present at the funeral of your friend's mother may feel sad, in response to social cues such as tears, hushed voices, and somber colors. However, the child's ability to empathize with your friend and her family is quite limited compared with that of adults who have lost someone very close.

The more similar the past social learning experiences of a model and observer, the more likely it is that the observer can empathize with the model (and vice versa). If several women are talking and one tells how she was attacked and raped several months ago, her words, gestures, and trembling tone of voice serve as CSs that elicit vicarious emotional responses in the listeners. The other people in the room will be able to empathize with her feelings to varying degrees, depending on their prior experiences with rape. A listener who has been raped herself is more likely to feel strong vicarious emotional responses than is a second listener who has never been raped and never been sensitized to the fear and anxiety associated with rape. People who have had similar past experiences—hence similar emotional conditioning—are most likely to feel vicarious emotional responses that allow them to empathize sensitively with each other's feelings. Strong empathetic responses are most likely when the similarities of the model and listeners are salient, the model vividly and emotionally describes the shared similar experiences, and the listeners try to imagine themselves in the model's role.[13]

When an observer has strong emotional responses to a model, the observer may *feel* an empathetic bond with the model, but the observer's feelings may be quite different from the model's feelings. For example, men and women who have been raised with a double standard of sexuality sometimes make mistakes in responding to the feelings of the other sex. When men and women meet in a bar and exchange smiles and pleasant words, these social cues often elicit pleasurable emotions and sexual feelings in the men, and the men feel as if the women are more sexually interested than most women really are.[14] Women are often surprised that men feel a smile in a bar means more than friendly attraction. Different gender socializations can cause males and females to have quite different emotional feelings in a situation where they think they are communicating—only to discover that they misjudged the other person's feelings. Such cases of misunderstood feelings can occur whenever two people—regardless of gender—have had past emotional conditioning that is quite different.

Vicarious Pavlovian Conditioning

When models provide CSs that elicit vicarious emotional responses in an observer, neutral stimuli paired with these CSs can also become CSs due to higher order Pavlovian conditioning. This is the observational learning of new conditioned emotional responses (CERs) via **vicarious Pavlovian conditioning.**[15] For instance, if your best friend is becoming skillful at playing the banjo and is visibly enthusiastic about her newest music, there is a strong likelihood you will find yourself beginning to respond to her banjo music as a CS for pleasurable CERs. Her signs of enthusiasm (which are positive CSs) will elicit positive vicarious emotions in you while you hear the banjo music. The stronger her signs of enthusiasm, the sooner the banjo music will become a positive CS for you, due to vicarious Pavlovian conditioning. Naturally, the background variables must also be correct: If your friend did not have enough skill to create listenable music or if she only played one song—"Turkey in the Straw"—over and over again, these aversive stimuli could outweigh the positive effects of her enthusiasm. However, if the background variables are neutral or positive, your friend's unbridled enthusiasm will produce positive vicarious Pavlovian conditioning of banjo music. The next time you hear a banjo on TV, you may smile and feel good.

Having friends, teachers, or other models who truly enjoy the things they are doing—and show it—brings an abundance of vicarious pleasures into our lives and causes the vicarious conditioning of many new positive CSs. Enthusiasm is contagious: Due to your friend's enthusiasm for her banjo, you have come to enjoy the banjo, too. People who surround themselves with enthusiastic models learn, through vicarious Pavlovian conditioning, to enjoy many of the things those models enjoy, whether it be psychology, music, jogging, political activism, motorcycling, or anything else.

Seeing sad or unhappy models can cause neutral stimuli to become CSs for sad feelings due to vicarious Pavlovian conditioning. Seeing movies that show people suffering and crying in some poor country can provide many CSs that elicit painful CERs, perhaps sadness or tears. The words paired with these pictures of sad, hungry people—such as *overpopulation* and *poverty*—may become CSs for unpleasant emotions because they are paired with such painful pictures. After seeing several documentaries on undeveloped countries, this conditioning may cause you to feel strong emotional responses when you hear someone mention overpopulation or poverty.

Vicarious Reinforcement and Punishment

The CERs we learn from a model (via vicarious Pavlovian conditioning) can function as secondary reinforcers and punishers in our lives, even if the model is not present. Once we have learned to respond to banjo music or poverty as CSs that elicit emotions in us, those CSs can provide **vicarious reinforcement or punishment** for our operant behavior. Vicarious reinforcers and vicarious punishers can come either directly from the model's social cues (such as smiles) or indirectly from stimuli (such as banjo music) that have been paired with the model's signs of pleasure or pain. Vicarious reinforcement and punishment play an important role in the observational learning of operant behavior.

Vicarious reinforcement occurs when a behavior is followed by CSs that are secondary reinforcers due to vicarious Pavlovian conditioning. Because your friend truly enjoys playing the banjo, you may pick up the instrument when she is not playing. If your friend smiles approvingly as you explore the strings, her smile provides vicarious reinforcement for your attempting to play. Even if your friend is not in the room, you will obtain vicarious reinforcement for plucking the strings because the banjo sounds themselves are now reinforcing, due to earlier vicarious Pavlovian conditioning when you heard your friend play.

Vicarious punishment occurs when a behavior is followed by CSs that are secondary punishers due to vicarious Pavlovian conditioning. Seeing other people's pain, suffering, and sadness both elicits vicarious emotions in the observer and provides vicarious punishment that can stop activities that cause pain. For example, if several people are playing a rough game, and one person is badly injured, the signs of pain are likely to serve as CSs that are vicarious punishers for others. Suddenly the game seems less fun, and you may suggest stopping the game and doing something else. Vicarious punishment stopped the game, even if the injured person never asked people to stop playing. Some of us cannot bring ourselves to criticize sensitive people because in the past our criticisms of sensitive people have been followed by signs of sadness from the sensitive people, and this vicarious sadness is the CS that inhibits our giving them further criticism.

OPERANT BEHAVIOR

Bandura and Walters identified two quite different phases—acquisition and performance—in the observational learning of operant behavior.[16] *Acquisition involves perceiving and remembering information about a model's behavior.* *Performance involves using that information to carry out some relevant behavior.* For example, a child may watch father take coins out of a piggy bank and instantly acquire the knowledge about how the trick is done, but it may be days or weeks before the child performs an imitative response. Because acquisition and performance are affected by different variables and performance can occur seconds, weeks, or even years after acquisition, these two aspects of observational learning are quite distinct and best analyzed separately.

Acquisition of modeled information is a prerequisite for behavior performance that uses that information. But the acquisition of information does not mean the information will ever be used. Much information that is acquired never affects performance. TV provides dozens of models of violence, killing, and crime each day. Most of us have acquired the information for doing these operants, but few of us will ever perform the acts of violence we learned from TV models. Thus, acquisition and performance are two quite separate issues.

Acquisition

Why do we acquire information from some models, but not learn much from others? Several factors influence the degree to which we acquire information about a model's behavior.[17]

1. The model's behavior has practical value and produces reinforcing consequences.
2. The observer feels closely akin or similar to the model.
3. The model and observer are engaged in similar activities.
4. There are reinforcers for watching the model.
5. The model's behavior is salient and easily visible.
6. The model's behavior is not far beyond the observer's present level of skill.

1. The Model's Behavior Is Reinforced. *If an observer sees that a model's behavior has practical value because it produces reinforcing consequences, the observer is likely to acquire information about the behavior.* The rewards associated with the model's behavior may not be consciously evaluated by the observer, but observers do respond to three kinds of cues that facilitate the acquisition of information about useful behavior.

1a. Seeing the Consequences of a Model's Behavior. *Seeing a model receive reinforcers or escape punishers is obvious evidence of the usefulness of a behavior.* When TV ads show how popular, attractive, or sexy people become when they use Product X, the advertising psychologists are capitalizing on the fact that the positive consequences will facilitate the acquisition of the advertised message by the TV observers. When a high school student sees another student escape detention by making excuses, the negative reinforcement increases the likelihood that the excuses will be remembered by the observer, even though acquisition alone does not determine whether the observer will ever use such excuses. Children who grow up in homes where one or both parents have prolonged illnesses are more likely than other people their same age to report symptoms of illness.[18] Seeing how nicely people treat their ill parent provides vicarious reinforcement for noticing symptoms and helps an observer learn illness behavior.

When a model and observer respond to different reinforcers, a model may be doing something that produces reinforcing consequences for the model, and yet not be noticed by observers who do not respond to the consequences as reinforcers. A stamp collector may receive frequent reinforcers for systematically checking through the office's incoming mail for interesting foreign stamps, yet observers who do not respond to foreign stamps as reinforcers are unlikely to notice how many rewards the collector derives from a rare foreign find. Hence they are not likely to pay attention to, acquire information about, or remember details of the behavior. Thus, a modeled behavior is likely to be acquired only if it has utility "in the eyes of the beholder," that is, functions as a reinforcer for the observer.

1b. Seeing a Model's Emotional Responses. *Even though an observer may not notice a model's behavior lead to any detectable reinforcers, the model's smiles, happy explications, and other emotional cues can be powerful CSs that indicate the behavior is reinforcing—because they elicit pleasurable vicarious emotions in the observer.* The observer is likely to pay attention to the model's behavior and acquire information about it because these activities lead to the vicarious reinforcement of seeing CSs associated with pleasure. If a model is smiling, and chuckling while reading a magazine, a passerby may note the name of the magazine as something worth looking into, even though it is not clear what reinforcers had caused the model so much pleasure. If you see a group of people laughing and clearly enjoying a game of badminton, you may feel positive vicarious emotions and pause to watch. While watching, you acquire information about the game, its rules, and ways to have fun playing it. If the people had been playing badminton without showing signs of enjoying themselves, you would have been less likely to stop and watch, since there were no signs of pleasure to indicate that playing the game was reinforcing. If the badminton players had grumbled and griped all through the game, most of us would have found them to be unattractive models, and we might have been turned off to badminton—even though we might have enjoyed learning about it from a group of jovial players.

Some people smile a lot, even when engaged in boring tasks, whereas others rarely smile, even when doing a favorite activity. People who show signs of pleasure are more likely to attract attention and cause the acquisition of modeled information than their un-smiling counterparts. *Differences in the emotional expressiveness of models can mislead an observer.* Leigh has been thinking about becoming either a doctor or a lawyer. She meets a doctor who seems to be constantly cheerful and happy, and a lawyer who has a deadpan facial expression. The positive social cues given off by the doctor attract Leigh's attention and increase the likelihood that she will acquire information about the doctor's job. The fact that the lawyer does not give off positive cues makes it likely that Leigh will acquire less information from the lawyer. Leigh may be misled by the social cues, how-ever. The doctor might have smiled just as much if she had been a lawyer or an accoun-tant, and her enthusiasm would have caused Leigh to learn about law or accounting rather than medicine. In addition, the deadpan lawyer might love the law as much as the smiling doctor loves medicine, but the absence of visible social cues makes it difficult for others to appreciate this.

1c. Respecting or Admiring a Model. Acquisition of information about a modeled behavior can occur even though an observer may not see a model receive reinforcers (1a) or show signs of pleasure (1b). *Observers will often attend to and acquire information from a model's behavior if the observers respect, admire, or like the model.* When we see many positive things in another person, we may find the person to be a very attractive model—even if we do not understand how their behavior is linked with rewards or posi-tive emotions; and, almost anything the model does may take on positive associations that attract our attention and promote our acquiring information about their behavior. Merely seeing a respected or admired model provides us with positive feelings for paying atten-tion to and acquiring information about the model's actions. Young children usually ac-quire a great deal of information by observing their parents' behavior because Mom and Dad are associated with many positive and loving experiences.[19] If Mom is a realtor, her children are likely to imitate realtor behavior during play because they love her. Dad may not enjoy driving a truck for his livelihood, but his children may attend to and acquire all sorts of information related to trucks because they love him. Simply thinking about mother and father—and their behavior—provides vicarious pleasure for the children; hence they find vicarious reinforcement in attending to and learning information from their parents. (For the same reason, children find vicarious reinforcement for doing role play that imitates their parents' behavior.)

All through life, we tend to acquire information about behavior from people we re-spect or admire. A 5-year-old child may want to be a firefighter or law officer because these people's uniforms and heroic work elicit respect and admiration in children. A 10-year-old's models may include movie stars, athletes, detectives, doctors, teachers, and so forth. A 15-year-old may be influenced by rock stars, fashion models, athletes, entrepre-neurs, or race car drivers. The models who have status in our eyes keep changing as we grow up, change social settings, and take new roles in life.

Behavior performed by models who are loved and respected is often well worth learning. Such people seem to be doing something right, given how good we feel about them. Somehow their behavior is compatible with good things in life, with reinforcement, even if we do not fully understand why. We often attend to and learn about many overt activities of a respected model without knowing which of these is actually associated with the model's success or happiness. Perhaps a respected model owes his or her happiness to self-discipline, but on the surface appears to be undisciplined and carefree. An observer may learn the hang-loose behavioral style of the model and never pick up on the actual behaviors that make the model happy and successful.

2. Similarity of the Observer and the Model.   *If an observer sees two models doing two different things, the observer usually learns more from the model who is more similar to the observer (assuming all other variables are equal).* At a doctors' convention, surgeons tend to pay attention to and learn from other surgeons, rather than from psychiatrists, gynecologists, or pediatricians. Of course, other factors can outweigh similarity: Doctors from many different specialties may pay special attention to a highly respected dermatologist who has recently won world fame.

Similarity is a powerful attractant in many situations. People with similar interests, ages, and jobs have things in common, which makes it easy to locate mutually interesting—hence mutually rewarding—topics about which to exchange information. Similar people can serve as models for each other as each one shows his or her personal take on their shared interests. At a resort, golfers may end up in one group, new mothers in another group, and tennis lovers elsewhere. There is so much we can learn from models who have interests similar to ours; hence people tend to interact longer with individuals who share common interests. A golfer may not learn much from a tennis pro who models a beautiful swing, but she pays close attention and learns from a golf pro who models golf swings suited to different distances. Thus, similarity increases the likelihood that people will acquire modeled information through observational learning.

3. Similarity of Behavior.   *When two people are engaged in similar tasks, they tend to be more observant of the other person's behavior than when they are doing different tasks.* "Follow the leader" comes close to being a pure example of modeling effects due to similar behavior. The eighth person to climb into a lifeboat is likely to use the same method of climbing in that the seventh person used. If person 7 holds onto the rigging to climb in, the eighth person is likely to do the same without considering the utility of the behavior or the similarities of their personalities: It may not be the most efficient way to enter the boat (relevant to point 1), and the two people may have little in common (point 2). People standing in line often attend to and copy each other's behavior as if they were playing follow the leader. You may not see an additional checkout station open in a store, but when some nearby people move to it and you see their behavior, you may follow their lead. In crowds, mobs, and mass happenings, people often observe and copy each other simply because they are engaged in similar activities. If a conspicuous member of a crowd begins to shout over and over, "Down with the dictator!" others may copy the chant, and the slogan may spread to a thousand mouths in a matter of minutes.

An interesting variation on follow the leader is "the blind leading the blind." During an avant-garde concert, the musicians may come to a long pause, and the audience may not know whether or not to clap, but everyone is influenced by the behavior of others. If enough people begin clapping, the entire audience may break into applause, even though the composer designed the pause to allow a solo violinist to quietly build the next theme of the piece. Rumors and fads sometimes result from the blind leading the blind.

All of the factors that influence the acquisition of modeled behavior can operate at the same time. For example, when a novice is learning from an experienced friend how to paddle a canoe, the novice can see the practical value of the model's skillful use of the paddle. The practical value is usually even more salient once the novice tries paddling and finds that canoeing skills are not acquired instantly: Now the observer looks twice to see how the model holds and uses the paddle. If the novice likes and respects the model, there will be even more reinforcement for acquiring information about the model's behavior. Similar interests in being in nature also aid acquisition. Finally, the effect of doing similar behavior is present, too. After the two canoeists have pushed off from shore, the novice picks up the pace and style of the model's paddling patterns. As the experienced canoeist changes techniques to deal with different situations, the novice watches and imitates in a follow-the-leader style.

4. Reinforcement for Vigilance and Attention.   An observer's degree of attentiveness to a model can lie anywhere on a continuum from paying no attention to the model to focusing very close attention to the model's behavior. Clearly, there can be no acquisition when there is no attention. *Increasing vigilance increases the likelihood that the observer will acquire information about the model's behavior.* Vigilance and attention can be modified by (a) differential reinforcement, (b) observational learning, (c) prompts, and (d) rules.

4a. Differential Reinforcement. *Observers learn to be more attentive when there are reinforcers for paying attention.* Teachers and shapers often reinforce good attention skills when they want an observer to benefit maximally from observational learning. For example, parents may reward a child for paying close attention when the stewards explain the proper use of life preservers at the start of a cruise. On the other hand, natural patterns of reinforcement are often quite effective in training people to observe models, especially in situations where both reinforcement and punishment are possible. When climbing in the Rockies, a novice may pay close attention to the behavior of others in hopes of learning skills that reduce the risks of falling and increase the joys of reaching great vistas. Even when no one is telling us to pay attention, we often learn to be attentive to the behavior of others in times of danger or emergency, in uneasy social situations, when new behavior is demanded, and when new skills are needed. Paying attention can help us reach good outcomes, and inattentiveness can lead to disasters.

4b. Observational Learning. *People also learn when to be vigilant or lax by observing others.* Seeing other people pay close attention to a snake, or fire, or a department store window increases the likelihood that the observer will pay attention and acquire information. In contrast, when we see that everyone in a group is relaxed and inattentive to details, we may be inclined to relax and monitor the situation less closely.

4c. Prompts. *Vigilance and attention can be prompted by turning a person's head or body toward the model who is to be attended.* Little children are often bodily picked up and aimed at a model whom the parents would like the children to observe. Pointing a finger toward a model is another prompt that can focus a person's attention on a model and increase the likelihood that information is acquired.

4d. Rules. *Rules and verbal commands are quick and easy ways of focusing people's attention.* Explicit rules, such as "Watch how those people do it if you want to learn how to do it right," clearly point to modeled behavior and indicate the practical value of observing others. Less explicit rules can also direct attention to models: "Wow, those people are fantastic." "That's worth seeing."

5. The Visibility of the Modeled Behavior. *The more visible a model's behavior is for an observer, the easier it is for the observer to learn from watching.* It is easiest for us to acquire information from a model when we are close enough to see and hear the model, have good eyes and ears, and are on the correct side of the model to see the most important actions. Also, some behavior is inherently more visible than others: External responses such as body movements and facial expressions are more visible than internal responses—such as using the glottis to roll "r's" in a foreign language. Anyone who has tried to imitate yodeling, whistling, ventriloquy, or voice impersonations knows that not being able to see the model's complex internal muscle movements creates major problems in acquiring the information needed to replicate a model's behavior. Thus, modeled behavior can lie anywhere on a continuum from total invisibility to total visibility, and the acquisition of information usually improves as visibility improves.

6. The Easiness of the Modeled Behavior. The easiness of modeled behavior can best be understood by locating the behavior of both the model and the observer on relevant steps of increasing skill. *If a modeled behavior is too many steps ahead of an observer's skills, the observer may not be able to acquire much useful information from the model.* For example, an experienced guitarist may show a friend how to play advanced classical music (at step 10 in Fig. 10–1), yet the friend may not learn much at all if he or she is at step 1, still learning the first three chords. The observer sees a flurry of rapid finger movements, but the information is too complex to be of much use. The model could help the observer more by coming down to the lower steps and showing the observer the best methods for playing the basic chords. As the novice advances to higher steps of improved skills, the model could demonstrate progressively more complex motor patterns and expect the observer to learn from them.

In everyday life, the fifth and sixth factors—visibility and easiness of modeled behavior—often hinder the observational learning of complex, advanced skills. Models frequently do not know that observers are interested in learning from them; thus, they do not make their behavior more visible and easy to imitate. Models may not know how to do an effective job of demonstrating behavior of the appropriate step of complexity even if they are aware of their role.

Most models fall into one of two main categories: mastery models or coping models.[20] **Mastery models** demonstrate only the final steps of mastering a skill (steps 9 and

FIGURE 10–1 If your behavior is at step 1 or 2, a model's behavior may be only a few steps ahead of yours (at step 4), or many steps away (at step 10—which means having complete mastery of the behavior).

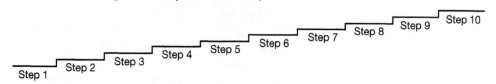

10); hence they deprive observers of the information needed to traverse the early steps. **Coping models** *demonstrate the skills that an observer needs to cope with the problems of moving up the next one or two steps.* Coping models have the skills needed to model behavior that is only a step or two ahead of the observer's skills. A person who is only one or two steps ahead of you could be a good coping model for you. Mastery models with advanced skills can serve as coping models for a beginner by showing and emphasizing the most basic aspects of their performance. A world-class surfer may place a surf board on a sandy beach and show observers how to hop onto the board from a lying position.[21] Observers can do practice imitations while on the safety of their sandy beach.

While coping models are valued for their helpfulness in advancing up the next steps of learning, mastery models are often valued for the inspiration and expertise they bring. When people see or read about a mastery model they greatly admire—perhaps an athlete, politician, or scientist—they usually see very advanced behavior (step 10) that is the product of years of learning. A master athlete's behavior is amazing in its perfection; however, many elements of the mastery model's behavior—especially all the prior years of practice—are likely to be invisible. The master has skills that are ultracomplex and difficult for us to comprehend. Both the complexity and poor visibility of all the details of a mastery model's behavior are impediments to observational learning, and they can create problems when observers see mastery models they would like to emulate. However excited and eager the observer may be to acquire the master's athletic skills, he or she may not even know where to begin: The master's advanced behavior does not provide the information the beginner needs.

For instance, after hearing a world famous novelist discuss the exhilaration of creative writing, a student may become very enthusiastic about writing. The writer's open face, sparkling eyes, gentle humor, wise tone of voice, and skillful ways with words are all CSs that elicit positive emotional responses for the student and provide vicarious reinforcement for listening to the novelist's advice. However, the writer's behavior gives no clue about the years of practice, study, rejections from publishers, and rewrites that went before. Thus, the student does not have access to information about all the steps involved in becoming a master of writing. The enthusiastic student may resolve to try writing, too, and get a chapter or two onto paper before realizing the story line is simplistic and uninteresting. Because the young writer saw step 10 behavior from the mastery model—rather than steps 1 and 2—the student writer may not realize that the mastery model went through similar struggles in the beginning.

Most of us have had experiences in which we saw a mastery model and felt a burst of vicarious enthusiasm for becoming a doctor, athlete, lawyer, musician, or artist; but the absence of modeled information about the skills needed to progress from step 1 to step 10 left us frustrated, not knowing how to begin. Mastery models usually do not provide all the information that beginners need.

Nevertheless, seeing mastery models is beneficial for beginners. A master's spectacular performance provides CSs that elicit positive emotional responses in the observer, which adds to the vicarious Pavlovian conditioning that makes the modeled behavior serve as a secondary reinforcer for the observer. After hearing a master guitarist, a novice guitarist may feel so ecstatic—with vicarious emotions about guitar music—that it is easy to practice longer, at least for a few days or weeks. In addition, mastery models help observers learn to set high standards of performance for themselves.[22] However, if beginners are actually to acquire advanced levels of skill, they often need coping models who provide useful information about the skills that beginners need to learn first.

Performance

After information has been acquired by observation, several factors determine when and how observers might use that behavioral information and perform similar behavior. *There are two key determinants of behavioral performance.*

1. There are S^Ds present that signal that imitating certain models and behaviors has been rewarded in the past.
2. There are S^Ds that signal that imitating certain models and behaviors will be rewarded now.

Observers are most likely to perform imitative behavior when models have been and still are rewarded for that behavior in S^D situations similar to the observer's present situation.

But first a small digression. The word *imitation* has negative connotations to some people because it may suggest that the observer is a "copycat" rather than a creative genius. Although creativity is wonderful, imitation has incredible "survival value," and we could not live long without it. First, if we watch the person ahead of us climb into the lifeboat successfully as our ship sinks beneath our feet, we may be wise to imitate, even if our behavior is not creative. Much valuable behavior can be acquired and performed more quickly by observational learning than any other way.

Second, studies on creativity show that imitation is a part of the learning that fosters creativity. Observational learning does not usually lead to exact imitations of modeled behavior: When we imitate a model's creative performance, we always introduce novel features into the replication, reflecting the unique features of our behavior repertoire and personality. In addition, we typically learn information about any given behavior from numerous models, and then piece together fragments of information about each model's performance into our own rendition of the behavior—that differs from the behavior of any given model.[23] Having exposure to numerous real and symbolic models is in fact a major source of creativity. Art students who study the styles of many famous painters are more likely to arrive at a creative style than art students who never study the works of others, or who study only one artist. When you realize that most imitative behavior is also influenced by differential reinforcement, shaping, rules, and prompts, it becomes clear that imitation is not usually done at the copycat level at which copy machines operate.

When TV reports news on some bizarre or novel crime, there is always a worry that the symbolic models shown on TV could trigger "copycat crimes." Seeing shootings in one high school may cause students in other schools to do something similar. Many TV producers are reluctant to give vivid details of crimes that could trigger copycat effects—even if the "copy" were somewhat different from the original crime. Criminals and pranksters are sometimes punished harshly by the legal system so that no one will want to imitate their deeds. As a prank, three young people removed stop signs from a Florida rural intersection; three teens died when they drove through the intersection and their car collided with an eight-ton truck.[24] The pranksters were convicted of three counts of manslaughter and sentenced to each serve 15 years in prison. This news was covered in the media for other potential pranksters to see. In the early days of movies, actors sometimes mentioned phone numbers in the movies, and some observers went home and did copycat dialing. To avoid having their customers bothered by people calling phone numbers mentioned in the movies, the phone companies had Hollywood use a 555 prefix on all movie phone calls because this prefix is not assigned to any location in the United States.

Once an observer has acquired behavioral information from a model, what factors influence when and where that information will be used? *S^Ds and S^Δs control the performance of imitative acts, and this stimulus control is influenced by both past and present patterns of reinforcement.*

1. Past Reinforcement. *Past reinforcement for imitating a certain model or a certain type of behavior increases the probability of performing the modeled behavior in S^D contexts similar to those in which reinforcement occurred in the past.* Beginning early in life, people learn to discriminate which kinds of models and behaviors to imitate and which contexts are appropriate for imitation. As is true of all discrimination, the discriminations about who, what, when, and where to perform a modeled behavior are the result of differential reinforcement. *Cues about behavior, models, or contexts that precede reinforcement for imitation become S^Ds for performing the modeled behavior. Any cues that precede nonreinforcement or punishment for imitation become S^Δs for not performing the modeled behavior.*

1a. Behavior. *Due to differential reinforcement, people learn that imitating certain kinds of behavior brings rewards but that imitating other kinds of behavior brings punishment. We learn to be sensitive to the S^Ds and S^Δs that predict reinforcement and punishment.* Drivers often receive reinforcers for imitating the driving speed of others. If everyone else on the road slows down, we tend to slow down. This imitative performance is often reinforced by our not hitting slower cars, avoiding police traps, or getting a better view of a roadside accident. Thus, the speed of the general traffic flow becomes an S^D for imitation. In contrast, imitating behavior that may produce an automobile accident is likely to be punished or extinguished. Hence other drivers' accident-prone behavior becomes an S^Δ for not imitating. As we gain experience, many modeled behaviors become S^Ds or S^Δs that increase or decrease the likelihood of imitation.

A child is more likely to receive reinforcers for imitating same-sex behavior than behavior typical of the other sex. This differential reinforcement causes children to discriminate and perform same-sex behavior more readily than other-sex behavior. Boys are more strongly punished than girls for imitating the behavior unique to the other sex, and boys do less of this cross-sex imitation.[25] If a little boy imitates some of his mother's or sister's behavior, the imitation may be punished with a comment such as, "Little boys don't do that." The neighbor boys might mock, "Andy is a sissy. Andy is a sissy." These punishments suppress the imitation of behavior seen only in females, and make feminine behavior an S^Δ for not imitating. If the boy imitates the masculine behavior of his father or brother, these imitative responses are more likely to be reinforced. This makes same-sex behavior an S^D for future imitation. Thus, the boy's imitativeness comes under S^D

control for performing male behavior and under S^Δ control for not performing female behavior. Little boys often acquire the information about how females apply makeup or put on stockings, but they would not perform the behavior! Little girls receive less punishment for cross-sex imitation and are more likely to do cross-sex imitation than boys are—wearing sports gear, swearing, and affecting male bravado.

1b. Models. After imitating the behavior of various models, we learn that imitating successful people is more reinforcing than imitating failures. *Imitating competent and well-liked people is usually more reinforcing than imitating incompetent and unpopular people; thus, many features of a model become S^Ds for imitation and others become S^Δs for not imitating.* We may watch both good and bad skiers and acquire information about their different styles, yet we are more likely to attempt to perform the responses shown by the competent models than those shown by the incompetent ones. Movie and TV stars often become S^Ds for imitation: People may pick up mannerisms, styles of dress, or idioms from performers they like, and if this produces reinforcing results, the stars become S^Ds for further imitative performances. Leaders, popular people, and friends may become S^Ds for imitation for similar reasons. One of the reasons these individuals are leaders or stars, popular, or liked is that they have certain desirable social skills; thus, imitating these people is likely to add a social skill that brings reinforcers to the person who imitates.

Naturally, people learn to discriminate that a certain subset of the behavior shown by any model can be reinforcing to imitate, whereas other subsets of behavior are not. An observer may imitate the way an attractive model dresses, but not imitate the harsh way the model treats other people. A little girl may imitate her father's use of complex words, but not imitate his shaving and perusal of automobile magazines. An athlete may imitate the running style of a champion without imitating any of the rest of the champion's behavior. This is one more reason why imitation does not make us copycats: We pick up bits and pieces of information from so many different sources that our performances are uniquely "us."

1c. Contexts. *Because a behavior may be reinforced in one context but not in others, context cues become important S^Ds or S^Δs that influence the performance of imitative behavior.* For example, if a child imitates some of father's profanity while at home, the child may be punished and thus learn that the home is a context for not imitating father's profanity. Yet the child may receive numerous reinforcers for using profanity in interacting with peers. Thus, interaction with peers becomes an S^D for imitative swearing, and the home is an S^Δ that inhibits imitating. If a deeply respected friend likes to talk about serious philosophical topics—death, religion, truth, the purpose of life—an observer may learn to talk about these topics, too. Yet imitation will come under stimulus control of context cues. Serious conversation may be very reinforcing in certain S^D situations, but in those situations where it puts a damper on fun or destroys a light mood, serious talk may evoke critical or derogatory comments from others—making those contexts S^Δs that inhibit serious topics.

2. Present Reinforcement.   *Performance is also influenced by present patterns of reinforcement and punishment.* Seeing other people receiving immediate rewards for a behavior increases the probability of imitation. If an observer sees someone repeatedly winning big payoffs while playing some 25-cent slot machines, the immediate reinforcers to the model increase the probability of the observer's trying the slots, too. Punishment has the opposite effect. Seeing someone get a ticket for speeding decreases our tendency to imitate the speeders who pass us.

Often we cannot see people receiving reinforcers or punishers, but their positive or negative emotional cues communicate their pleasure or pain to us. Seeing people smiling as they leave an ice cream store increases the probability of our going in for a cone, too. In contrast, seeing people sitting inside a restaurant and looking bored decreases the chances that we will imitate their choice of restaurants.

Sometimes we can watch what happens to other people when they imitate a given model's behavior. If their imitation leads to reinforcement or punishment, the outcomes they experience often indicate the type of consequences we might expect for imitating. If the first person who jumps into a beautiful stream appears to enjoy rollicking in the current, you may be somewhat inclined to get in the water, too. If several other people imitate the model and all show signs of enjoying themselves, it is even clearer that imitation is reinforcing, and you will be even more inclined to follow suit. But imitation is not always reinforced. The first person in the water may be an excellent swimmer who can handle the strong current. The people who imitate and get into the water next may not fare so well in the water. They may be thrown down or dunked by the strong current and come out of the water with facial expressions that communicate the aversiveness of the situation and serve as vicarious punishers for you. The consequences experienced by these imitators will influence your decision about imitating.

Inverse Imitation

Up to this point we have considered imitation in which the observer performs a response similar to a model's behavior. *When an observer performs a response that is opposite from a model's behavior, the observer is doing **inverse imitation**.*[26] *People learn to do inverse imitation when there is reinforcement for behavior that complements or differs in other ways from the model's performance.* When a student is learning how to waltz by taking lessons from a good dancer, the student must imitate the teacher but must invert the information. When the teacher puts her left foot forward, the student must pull his right foot back. If the teacher steps one step to the right, the student must step one step to the left. The student is acquiring information from the model, much as in regular imitation. However, performance is an inverted version of the modeled behavior because only the inverse action produces positive reinforcement.

Situations in which inverse imitation is reinforced often involve punishment for regular imitation. If a dance student performed precisely the same waltz steps that the model did—stepping forward at the same time the teacher did—the two dancers would collide or step on each other's feet. Thus, regular imitation is punished in this situation. When inverse imitation helps avoid these collisions and aversive consequences, there is negative reinforcement for inverse imitation. When it produces a beautiful dance and a happy couple, there is also positive reinforcement for inverting the information.

There are two main types of inverse imitation. The first occurs when an observer's behavior must complement the model's. The movements of the two waltzers must complement each other to produce reinforcing results. When two people are cutting down a large tree with a lumberjack's saw, one must push the saw while the other pulls in order for each behavior to complement the other and produce effective results. Thus, each person watches the other and coordinates with an inverse imitation of the other's behavior. Many tasks with a push-pull or give-take structure involve inverse imitation to synchronize the complementary roles.

A second type of inverse imitation is only reinforced when the observer is being different from the model. For example, members of a tough juvenile gang often hate the police. Any behavior that looks like the "straight" behavior modeled by the cops is likely to be punished by other gang members. Behavior that differs from the straight behavior is negatively reinforced by escape from social criticism from peers, and it may also be positively reinforced by peers who approve of rebellion—that is, doing anything different from straight behavior. The gang members see that the police walk with straight posture and maintain a neat appearance, so they learn to avoid similar behavior by slouching, sliding down in chairs, and wearing sloppy clothing.

Inverse imitation for "being different" often occurs when observers dislike a model, see negative consequences follow the model's behavior, or receive strong reinforcers for demonstrating to others (or to themselves) that they are not conformists.

Dislike. People often go out of their way to refrain from doing activities or wearing things that are customarily associated with ethnic, religious, political, or social groups they dislike. Many Catholics and Protestants in Northern Ireland show inverse imitation of aspects of each other's behavior. Each group gives reinforcers to its members for being different from the other group, thus exacerbating their differences. When people interact with a disliked group, they often find their own mannerisms, vocabulary, and conversation topics are chosen to be opposite from those of the disliked group.

Negative Consequences to Model. When a motorcyclist sees a close friend get killed because the friend did not wear a helmet, the negative consequences to the model will increase the likelihood the observer will use a helmet more. When parents see how sick a neighbor child became from eating under-cooked hamburger meat, they may decide to grill their child's burgers extra long.

Children sometimes do inverse imitation of their parents' behavior. If a girl watches her parents spend money recklessly and waste all their wealth on frivolous purchases, she may decide to avoid their cycle into poverty and homelessness by vowing to shun wasteful purchases. As with all avoidance responses, we know what she will avoid, but we do not know what actions she might take to solve the problem. Will she decide to invest in real estate, play the stock market, or start her own company? A boy may see his parents create a living nightmare for each other by bickering and picking on each other almost every waking hour. Seeing how much unhappiness they create for each other, he may decide to avoid such self-inflicted pain in his relationships. We do not know exactly what kind of relations he will be able to create during his life, but the motivation to avoid painful relationships sets the stage for inverse imitation and the creation of some form of respectful and rewarding relationships. *Notice that people who do inverse imitation do not reject all the behavior of relevant models. They are most likely to avoid the behaviors which they see leading to aversive consequences!* As each generation seeks creative ways to avoid the problems that plagued the prior generation, successful innovations add to their culture's repository of knowledge and skills for making life better. Inverse imitation is one of the reasons why cultures tend to develop better behavioral practices over time.

Nonconformists.   Some people do inverse imitation because they have been rewarded for being "different" or have been punished for being conformists. When men start wearing long hair and beards, the nonconformist shaves off his. When the skirt length goes up, the nonconformist gives her short skirts to the Salvation Army and buys long skirts. If a nonconformist was once a strong supporter of ideology A but now finds that others are also switching to espouse A, the nonconformist might begin to preach the dangers of A. The game of "devil's advocate" is well suited to people who like to obtain social attention for taking arguments that run counter to the opinions of others.

BEHAVIOR MODIFICATION

Observational learning is often used in behavior modification. Models have been used to help others learn assertiveness, language skills, sexual skills, socializing skills, better health practices, ways to overcome phobias, prosocial ways to deal with frustration, teaching styles, industrial and management skills, and much more.[27] People with behavioral deficits can learn many types of behavior merely by interacting with skilled peers in situations that are likely to bring reinforcement for attention, information acquisition, and imitation. Having access to multiple models reduces the chances that the observer's behavior will seem like a copycat version of one single model's behavior.

Observational learning may take place quickly or need many repeated sessions, depending on the complexity of the behavior being learned, the observer's initial level of skill, and many other factors. It can take a 5-year-old Japanese child a year of observational learning—while playing with English-speaking children—to learn the complex skills needed to talk as rapidly in English as his playmates do.[28] In one month, children with disabilities can learn numerous simple activities that other children their age can do if they are helped by peers who are trained to model those activities for them. Werts, Caldwell, and Wolery (1996) trained 12 elementary school students with no diagnosed disabilities to interact with and serve as peer models for three classmates with significant disabilities. The 12 peer models were taught how to model five specific skills, such as using a calculator for addition, and then directed to model the five behaviors with the disabled children. Not only did the challenged children learn the modeled behaviors, they also learned numerous social skills that allowed them to increase social interactions in the classroom and develop friendships. This helped the disabled children become "a part of the class" (p. 63) and have a higher quality of life. Children with challenges and disabilities can fall behind their peers in social development if they do not have opportunities for frequent social interactions. Once they have fallen behind socially, they can have an especially difficult time in making the complex adjustments of adolescence.[29] Hence repeated use of peer models from an early age is invaluable for any child who might not interact much with his or her peer group and gradually fall behind in social development.

Sometimes observational learning creates successful behavior modification within a few hours. Öst (1989) worked with 20 phobic patients who had fears of dogs, cats, rats, spiders, birds, or hypodermic needles. Over 10% of Americans have a phobia and many never overcome it. Öst arranged for each of his patients to live through their feared experiences in natural settings in the presence of a coping model who showed how to deal with any possible problems. The goal was to create "a large amount of 'overlearning'" (p. 2) in a one-session treatment lasting about 2 hours. Follow-up studies, which were done about 4 years later (on average), showed that 90% of the people remained much improved over the entire period. By condensing the therapy into one session, Öst solved a problem common in therapy, of having dropouts—people who fail to return for second and later sessions. And only 3 out of 23 patients to whom he offered this therapy "did not accept the offer of a one-session treatment" (p. 6).

All of us can use observational learning in self-modification. Focus on the best one or two behaviors that you see in each of your friends and acquaintances. If that behavior serves them well, could you also benefit from learning it? If the answer is yes, watch how others do the behavior and see what you can learn.

CONCLUSION

Much of the behavior seen in everyday life is learned or modified by observing other people. When we observe a model, we often learn enough information about the model's behavior that we can imitate the behavior—immediately or at a later time. Models can influence an observer in three ways: (1) by allowing the observer to *learn new responses,* (2) by *inhibiting or disinhibiting old responses* in the observer's behavior repertoire, or (3) by *providing S^Ds that set the occasion for an old response* that the observer normally does from time to time. Emotional signs that models display can serve as CSs that elicit vicarious emotional responses in observers, and these can cause vicarious Pavlovian conditioning in which an observer learns to associate emotional responses to new CSs. Finally, CSs given off by models or stimuli associated with the model's emotion can function as vicarious reinforcers and vicarious punishers for observers who imitate the models' behaviors.

The operant learning from models occurs in two phases: the acquisition of information about the modeled behavior and the performance of imitative responses. Both acquisition and performance are influenced by a variety of factors, including reinforcement and punishment, the competence and likeability of the model, the nature and complexity of the modeled behavior, and context cues. Mastery models have all the skills needed for doing certain behaviors at outstanding levels, often eliciting awe and enthusiasm in observers. Hence they can be inspirational and lead observers to set goals of mastery, too. However mastery models often have such advanced skills that beginners can also benefit from observing coping models—who model simpler forms of behavior and help beginners advance to the next level of skills. Various contingencies of reinforcement cause inverse imitation, in which an observer makes a response that complements or is opposite from a model's response. Sometimes we do inverse imitation to attain the rewards of co-operative interaction (as in dancing) and sometimes inverse imitation is motivated by avoiding pain (as in avoiding our parents' mistakes). Behavior modification often involves the use of models who show the "right way" to cope with situations and obtain rewarding results.

QUESTIONS

1. Why are we told to act like Romans when in Rome?
2. What are the differences between real and symbolic models?
3. Why is observational learning sometimes much faster than response differentiation and shaping?
4. What are the three main ways in which the behavior of models affects observers?
5. Explain how models create inhibitory effects, giving an example. Explain how models create disinhibitory effects, giving an example.
6. How do models provide S^Ds that set the occasion for imitative responses, without the observer's actually showing any lasting changes of behavior?
7. How do models serve as sources of CSs that elicit vicarious emotions in observers? Give an example.
8. How can models cause observers to learn new emotional responses via Pavlovian conditioning? Give an example.
9. How can vicarious emotions function as vicarious reinforcers or punishers that modify an observer's operant behavior? Give an example.
10. What are the two main phases of observational learning? Why are they separate and distinct?
11. What are the six main determinants of the acquisition phase of observational learning?
12. Why is the reinforcement value—or practical value—of an operant so crucial in influencing the acquisition phase? What three cues do observers use to assess the reinforcement value of a modeled behavior?
13. How is the acquisition phase influenced by similarities of the observer and model? How is the acquisition phase influenced by similarities of their behaviors?
14. How is the acquisition phase influenced by reinforcers for vigilance and attention?
15. How is the acquisition phase influenced by the visibility of the modeled behavior? How is the acquisition phase influenced by the easiness of the modeled behavior?
16. What are mastery models? How do they affect an observer's behavior? What are coping models? How do they affect an observer's behavior?
17. What are the two factors that affect the performance of an imitative response?
18. What are the two types of inverse imitation? Why do people do each one?
19. How is observational learning used in behavior modification? Give an example.

NOTES

1. Bartlett (1980, p. 3; n. 13).
2. Chartrand and Bargh (1999).
3. Rotter (1954); Bandura and Walters (1959, 1963); Bandura (1969, 1977). Bandura's work is not without its critics (Masia & Chase, 1997).
4. Rotter (1954); Bandura and Walters (1963); Bandura (1969, 1986); Öst (1989); Eckerman and Stein (1990); Young et al. (1994); Theeboom et al. (1995).
5. Akhtar, Carpenter, and Tomasello (1996).
6. Wickelgren (1999).
7. Bandura (1973, 1986).
8. Wendland-Carro, Piccinini, and Millar (1999).

9. Experimental evidence related to the three modeling effects is presented by Bandura and Walters (1963), Bandura (1969, 1977, 1986), Eckerman and Stein (1990), Young et al. (1994), and Theeboom et al. (1995).

10. Practice may involve either overt replications of the behavior or cognitive rehearsal (Bandura, 1977; Mahoney, 1974). Learning is much faster when a person does both overt and covert practice (Kazdin, 1982; Mize & Ladd, 1990).

11. Bandura (1969, 1986); Quinn, Sherman, Sheldon, Quinn, and Harchick (1992).

12. Bandura (1969, pp. 167–168); Mineka and Hamida (1998).

13. Bandura (1969, 1986).

14. Abbey (1982).

15. See Berger (1962), Craig and Weinstein (1965), Bandura and Rosenthal (1966), Bandura, Blanchard, and Ritter (1969), Öst (1989), Menzies and Clarke (1993), Rapee and Hayman (1996), and Mineka and Hamida (1998) for studies on vicarious Pavlovian conditioning.

16. The distinction between acquisition and performance is central to theories of observational learning (Bandura & Walters, 1963, pp. 52–60).

17. This is only a partial list of the factors known to affect the acquisition of information about modeled behavior (Bandura, 1969, pp. 128–143; Bandura & Walters, 1963; Dinsmoor, 1995b; Eckerman & Stein, 1990; Quinn et al. 1992; Rapee & Hayman, 1996).

18. Schwartz, Gramling, and Mancini (1994).

19. Bandura, Ross, and Ross (1963); Bandura (1986).

20. Meichenbaum (1971); Bandura and Barab (1973).

21. Beyette (1999).

22. Skinner (1980, p. 283); Theeboom et al. (1995).

23. Bandura et al. (1963); Bandura (1977, 1986); Eckerman and Stein (1990).

24. Clary (1997a,b).

25. Bandura et al. (1963); Lynn (1969).

26. Skinner (1953, p. 121).

27. Bandura (1969, 1986); Öst (1989); Mize and Ladd (1990); Lombard, Neubauer, Canfield, and Winett (1991); Goldstein and Cisar (1992); Elliott and Gresham (1993); Pierce and Schreibman (1995); Öst, Ferebee, and Furmark (1997).

28. Personal observation. Also see Kymissis and Poulson (1990).

29. Mize and Ladd (1990); Christopher, Nangle, and Hansen (1993).

Prompts
and Fading

LIFE IS A STAGE

It is the third rehearsal, with 2 months still to go before a new play opens. The stage is bare and the set crew is noisily constructing props in the wings. On stage the performers are practicing the second scene. Their spoken lines, gestures, and movements are far from well mastered. As the actors work through their lines, they often pause and glance at the director for help. A brief prompt—such as giving the first 3 words of the next line—is usually enough to start the performers on the right track again. The prompting is frequent and freely given in order that the actors can keep moving through their lines and learn the broad outlines of the entire scene. The director knows that after a few more practice sessions, the performers will speak their lines much more naturally, and the prompting can be gradually phased out—or faded. If the actors are good, the prompts will be reduced to zero well before opening night.

All through life we are like actors on a stage, learning new actions and ways of explaining things, moving on to new scenes.[1] Prompts are among the aids people give each other to hasten the learning process. A teacher's uplifted hands prompt us to speak louder in class so others can better hear our words. Lights and sounds in our car prompt us to buckle up and check the gas gauge. As learning progresses and prompts are no longer needed, most people naturally fade out the prompts they give to others and decrease their attention to prompts given to them by others. Prompts are such a simple and basic part of social life that we often do not notice how much they contribute to our everyday learning. Prompting is most obvious in childhood social learning, but most people give and receive prompts all through life.

PROMPTS AND FADING

Learning from prompts usually occurs in three phases: prompting, reinforcement, and fading. *First, a target behavior is* **prompted** *by words, gestures, physical nudges, or other stimuli that help start the behavior.* When actors cannot recall the next line of a new play, the first three words of the next line can serve as a verbal prompt. Prompts are special stimuli that are introduced to initiate the target behavior during early learning, although they are not wanted or needed once the behavior is learned.[2] Many prompts can be given almost effortlessly once we have learned how to give them.

Second, prompted behavior is generally learned most rapidly when it is followed by **reinforcement.** Thus, when helping their child learn new behaviors, parents often use prompts to start the behavior, then give enthusiastic praise to reinforce its frequency. Actors whose careers and reputations depend on learning a complex set of lines usually respond quickly to the director's prompts, because they know how rewarding it is to master their lines. A person picked randomly from the street might not learn the lines of a play—even after a thousand prompts—if there were no reinforcers for learning. Reinforcement is crucial for strengthening the prompted behavior. All operant behavior depends on reinforcement. Sometimes the natural reinforcers for doing a prompted behavior are sufficient for effective learning, but most of us benefit from extra reinforcement—such as genuine approval from others—if our goal is rapid learning.

Third, as learning proceeds, prompts are gradually faded until the target behavior occurs without prompts.[3] **Fading** *is the gradual removal of any prompting stimulus so the prompted response comes under stimulus control of naturally occurring stimuli.*[4] In everyday life, the fading process is usually a natural aftereffect of successful prompting. As actors learn their lines, their director gradually phases out the prompts because prompting is no longer needed. Fading is a very natural process: When actors no longer pause and wait for prompts, they cease giving the directors the S^Ds that evoke more prompting. Gradually, the target behavior comes under the control of natural reinforcers, and the director can also fade out any special social reinforcers that were used in the early phases of prompting.

New behavior is learned most efficiently if fading is done neither too rapidly nor too slowly, but is systematically paced according to each learner's rate of progress. In everyday life, some people are more skillful than others at providing prompts, giving reinforcement, and fading their help in a sensitive and efficient manner. In behavior modification, the prompting and fading are usually done more systematically than in everyday life.

Physical Guidance

People frequently use physical guidance as a prompt when helping children learn new behavior.[5] Adults often discover that moving a child's arms, legs, or body through the desired behavior sequence may be easier than telling the child what to do. Physical prompting is especially effective with preverbal children, since they do not respond much to verbal rules and social modeling is not always effective.

When a child first begins to walk, the parents may support and move the child's body in ways that promote walking and prevent falling. Shifting the child's weight from foot to foot helps the child take the first steps. Continued physical prompts facilitate prolonged walking. Most parents give generous reinforcement in the form of attention, cheerful encouragement, and affection as the prompted behavior appears with greater skill—and this speeds the learning process. Next, the fading process is a very natural aftereffect of successful prompting: Because parents find it rewarding to see their child walk unaided, they receive reinforcers for fading out their assistance as soon as they can.

A child may be physically prompted to play with a new toy when the parents manually guide the child's hands to touch, hold, pull, or shake the toy in a manner that produces noise, lights, or other effects. After being prompted several times to pull the string connected to a toy duck, the child's pulling the string is rewarded by sensory stimulation—hearing the duck go "Quack-quack" and seeing the colorful wheels go around. As the child learns to pull the toy here and there, the parents fade their prompts.

Physical prompts often help in learning various athletic activities, musical instruments, and dances. A teacher may put a bow and arrow in a student's hands, and then physically move the student's arms into the correct position for accurate shooting. Swimming teachers often support their beginner students in the water and physically move the students' arms or legs to produce swimming movements. These movements are then reinforced by praise and positive feedback. As the students learn the proper stroking patterns, the teachers can remove the prompts and supports.

Children are often prompted into social interactions by physical guidance. The first time a young child confronts Santa Claus in a department store, the child may be reluctant to climb onto Santa's knee. The parent may physically lift the child into place to start the interaction. A friendly greeting from Santa and some candy usually reinforce the prompted behavior, and future trips to see Santa require less prompting.[6] When a distant relative comes to visit, the child may be physically pushed toward Uncle Max to encourage interaction. If a child shows reluctance about approaching a new teacher, a doctor, a barber, or a neighbor's dog, prompting may be used to create first approximations of the desired behavior. The ensuing consequences—reinforcement or punishment—determine whether the prompted behavior becomes more or less frequent.

Prompting is often used for teaching people to abstain from certain responses. A parent may prompt a child to be quiet at a religious service by gently touching the child's wiggling leg and holding it still. A gentle prompt alone would not be expected to produce lasting effects in stopping the wiggling: Prompts only start a learning process. Parents who give loving rewards to their child for sitting quietly can expect more long-lasting effects.

Physical prompting is not as common in adulthood as in the early years. Physical prompts are often replaced by verbal rules as children gain more language skills and respond more quickly and accurately to verbal instructions—both written and spoken. However, even adults respond better to the physical prompting of a guiding hand than to verbal instruction, in certain situations. For example, during sexual activities, a gentle hand can often communicate and guide the movements of the partner much better than words could ever do. A prompting hand shows exactly what needs to be done to provide the stimuli each person desires.[7]

Physical prompting also occurs during the learning and rehearsal of theater performances. Both choreographers and fellow dancers may use physical prompts to help dancers move their bodies in certain patterns. Likewise, actors may learn various gestures in this manner. Football players, karate students, and other athletes also find that a guiding hand often communicates the desired information more efficiently than words can.

In old age, prompts can help teach new behavior or maintain old behavior that might be forgotten.[8] Some old people gradually lose their mental faculties and act more like children, needing to be fed, helped into their clothing, and so forth. As this happens, caregivers often begin to use physical prompts more and more, though excess prompting can be less beneficial than rewarding their continued use of every skillful behavior they still have.

Mechanical Prompts

Metronomes are a form of mechanical prompt that provides stimuli to help musicians learn the timing of music. As students master the speed and rhythm of a given passage, they can fade out the prompt until they can play without the metronome.

Television performers, announcers, and newscasters occasionally fall back on mechanical TelePrompTers, which provide a large, easily read script. If speakers come to a section they remember, they can let their eyes wander from the screen and talk without prompts until they hit the next rough spot.

In order to help their child learn to ride a two-wheeler, parents sometimes attach two training wheels to the sides of the bike to prevent the bike from falling over. The two side wheels serve as mechanical prompts that help teach basic bike-riding skills while preventing falls. By adjusting the training wheels so that both touch the ground simultaneously, the bike can be kept in the vertical position, and the child can learn the basics of pedaling, turning, and stopping, without having to deal with balance problems. Once these basic skills are mastered, the training wheels can be adjusted upward a bit, so the bike can tip slightly from side to side. Now the child can begin to learn how to balance. When the child makes mistakes, the bike does not fall over because the training wheels keep it up. As the child's skills for balancing improve, the training wheels can be lifted further off the ground. This gradual removal of mechanical support is the fading process. During each step in which support is faded out, the child can lean the bike over further and learn from the consequences.[9]

Modern cars are built with buzzers, lights, and speech synthesizers that prompt people to fasten their seatbelts, check the emergency brake, notice a low fuel supply, and so forth. Computers programmed to teach reading, mathematics, or other subjects to children often use prompting procedures. Easy problems—filled with hints, *italicized words,* informative diagrams—are used at the beginning of each lesson, and as the student learns to answer questions correctly, the computer automatically fades the hints associated with questions that are of equal difficulty to those the student has already answered correctly.

Pictures

When children first learn to read, they are often given books that contain many pictures related to the words. The simplest books may have one word per picture. The word *apple* appears in bold print under a picture of an apple. The word *rabbit* appears under a picture of a cottontail. Seeing the word and picture together assists the child in saying the correct word. Later, as the child has more experience with printed words, the pictures are faded out: Smaller or sketchier pictures may be used, and the number of words per picture increases. As the pictures are faded, the child learns to rely more and more on the printed words as the S^Ds that control the verbal responses. Studies have shown that fading the prompts is crucial for efficient learning: Children who always see the picture of an apple above the word *apple* do not learn to respond to the word alone as rapidly as children who have the picture prompts gradually faded until only the word is visible.[10]

The control knobs on the dashboards of some automobiles have pictures that show a horn, lights, wipers, fan, and other features. When you first drive the car, you may rely on the pictures to determine which knob to turn for air or music. After learning the placement of the controls, you do not need to look at the pictures to reach the correct knob; hence you automatically fade out the use of the pictorial prompts as your learning progresses.

Gestures

With a few gestures, a conductor can prompt an orchestra to modify the tempo, volume, or tone quality of each passage of music. After several rehearsals, the musicians learn how the conductor expects them to play each piece, and the conductor can fade the more exaggerated gestures. By the time of the concert, much of the conductor's hard work is complete and is no longer reflected in the less exaggerated gestures that now keep the musicians coordinated.

Actors and dancers also learn from gesture prompts. When an actor speaks too quietly, the director may give arm gestures, emphasizing the upward movements, in order to encourage more vigor and volume from the speaker's voice. A turning motion made with the hands can prompt a dancer to face further toward the right or the left. When a director creates new gestures that succeed in prompting a desired behavior, the successful effects reinforce the director's creative prompting.

Teachers and lecturers frequently use prompts to guide the attention of their listeners. A lecturer who points a finger to guide your eyes to one part of a diagram or chart is prompting attention to the correct target. At first, your attention is under S^D control of the pointing finger, but as you learn more about the diagram, stimulus control shifts to the diagram, and the lecturer can fade the use of finger gestures. All through life, people rely on pointing to direct other people's eyes and attention. Because pedestrians and automobile drivers usually cannot hear each other, they often resort to numerous gestures to prompt each other to turn, slow down, stop, advance, and so forth. Workers at a noisy construction site do the same. Athletes use gestures on the playing field to prompt their teammates to run or wait, turn or move.

Words

When a person is learning new patterns of verbal behavior, words are often effective prompts. An actor learning a new script is in the same type of position as a child trying to learn a poem or a prayer. When the last words that a person speaks do not have enough S^D control to bring up the next phrase, it helps to have someone prompt the next word or two. Parents frequently use verbal prompts to teach their children to say "Hello, Mrs. Garcia," "Thank you," "Goodbye," and other polite phrases.

When people cannot remember an important detail while telling a story, they may look to a friend who knows what they need to say, waiting for a prompt. They may even prompt their friend to give the verbal prompt by looking helpless or speechless or by gesturing with empty hands. After the friend fills in the missing word or words, the original speaker can continue the story. For example, when two people try to tell about the places they went on a trip together, they may often turn to each other for help in filling in the names of various cities, shops, museums, or restaurants. After telling their vacation story several times with prompts, storytellers often learn their lines well enough that they cease to need prompts.

BEHAVIOR MODIFICATION

Prompting and fading are a common part of behavior modification. For example, signs are often used in natural environments as prompts to modify behavior such as recycling, using condoms, and eating healthy foods. Posting a 19-by-28-inch sign marked RECY-CLABLE MATERIALS above a recycle bin was enough of a prompt to increase recycling 29% and 54% above baseline measures in two departments of a large university.[11] Prompts in the form of signs and pictures have been used successfully to increase the number of free condoms taken at bars.[12] Signs and fliers in national brand fast-food restaurants are effective in prompting customers to shift from less healthy selections to salads and low-fat, high-fiber foods.[13]

Prompts and fading are often used in dealing with childhood problems. One of the most common difficulties that parents have arises when children do not comply with parental requests.[14] For example, some children refuse to eat enough, and their parents may be unable to change their children's behavior. The problem can become serious if not resolved because chronic food refusal can lead to extreme weight loss, malnutrition, and delayed development.[15] Werle, Murphy, and Budd (1993) developed a simple prompting program that mothers could use in their homes to resolve the problems of chronic food refusal. They studied three children and their mothers who had been referred to them by an outpatient psychology clinic: All three mothers reported long-standing problems with food refusal—persisting for 15 to 50 months—and all the mothers had virtually given up on overcoming their children's problems. The mothers were trained to use very clear verbal prompts, such as "Open your mouth" and "Take a bite"—instead of using vague prompts (such as "Let's eat," "Want some rice?" or "Get going"). They were also trained to use positive attention, approval, and rewards immediately after their child ate the prompted foods, but not after food refusals.

Werle and her coworkers used a TV camera mounted on a tripod to collect behavioral data on the parents and children in their own homes, scoring the videotapes at a later time. The children were 1 3/4, 2 1/2, and 4 1/2 years old, with long histories of food refusal. Baseline video data collected before the onset of behavior modification revealed that the mothers sometimes responded inappropriately to their children. For example, when Bob refused to eat one type of food, his mother offered him other foods, which inadvertently rewarded Bob for refusing some foods by giving him access to other foods he might like more.

After the parents shifted from baseline to the use of clear prompts and social rewards, it only took five to seven sessions before the children's food refusals dropped to low levels. The authors note that making videos in the home is a useful tool for identifying some of the parents' activities that maintained the problematic behaviors.

Generous and frequent prompting can facilitiate "errorless learning," when people receive enough prompts that they never have to experience the frustration of failure.[16] If you try to learn a new poem or Lincoln's Gettysburg Address without prompts, you may experience numerous failures and frustrations. Failures feel bad and punish your attempts to learn your lines. You may quit practicing before learning much of the speech. By using prompts and reinforcing each step of successive approximation, you can enjoy errorless learning without failures and pain. If you are learning to recite some beautiful lines, you can benefit from having a coach or friend give you generous prompts and positive support, so each word and phrase in the poem takes on S^D control that calls up the next words. If prompts are given well and correct responses are rewarded genuinely, you can learn with the minimum of errors, and this minimizes the aversiveness of the task—and your frustration. Behavioral techniques that foster errorless learning create high ratios of reinforcement to punishment and make learning rewarding and fun, which increases the chances we will want to learn more in the future.

CONCLUSION

Prompts are physical, mechanical, verbal, or other assists that help a person perform a behavior that would have been unlikely without this assistance. Prompts help make learning easy and fun. After a behavior has been emitted due to prompting, reinforcement further increases the probability of the behavior. Generous prompts and reinforcers can facilitate errorless learning. After sufficient reinforcement, prompts can be removed through the process of fading.

QUESTIONS

1. What is prompting? What three phases are usually present when learning from prompts?
2. Define the word *prompt.*
3. Why is it important that reinforcement follow prompted behavior?
4. What is fading? Why do people fade out prompts?
5. Give examples of prompting and fading via (a) physical guidance, (b) mechanical prompts, (c) pictures, (d) gestures, and (e) words.
6. How are prompts and fading used in behavior modification?

NOTES

1. Shakespeare, *As You Like It,* II, vii; Goffman (1959).
2. Touchette and Howard (1984); Krantz and McClannahan (1993); Dinsmoor (1995b).
3. Skinner (1953), Bandura (1969), Kanfer and Phillips (1970), Reese (1972), Deitz and Malone (1985), and Dinsmoor (1995b) discuss various ways in which prompting and fading are used in conditioning. Goldstein and Wickstrom (1986), Honnen and Kleinke (1990), and Werle, Murphy, and Budd (1995) show its continued usefulness in behavior modification. Although prompting is less important than differential reinforcement, modeling, and rules, it is a distinctive method of learning that occurs often enough in everyday life to deserve separate attention.
4. Deitz and Malone (1985); Dinsmoor (1995b).
5. Gelfand and Hartmann (1975).
6. The role of social learning, including prompts, in establishing social spacing patterns has been discussed by Hall (1959), and Baldwin and Baldwin (1974).
7. Masters and Johnnson (1970).
8. Stock and Milan (1993); Barinaga (1998).
9. Pace, Iwata, Edwards, and McCosh (1986) show the value of using mechanical prompts with children who do self-injurious behavior.
10. Corey and Shamow (1972). Too much prompting can also retard progress in behavior modification (Zarcone et al., 1993).
11. Austin, Hatfield, Grindle, and Bailey (1993).
12. Honnen and Kleinke (1990).
13. Wagner and Winett (1988).
14. Houlihan, Sloane, and Jones (1992); Ducharme (1996).
15. Howard and Winter (1984); Bithoney and Dubowitz (1985).
16. Ducharme (1996).

Rules

THE POWER OF WORDS

Rule use begins in childhood when toddlers learn enough words that they can respond to verbal instructions: "Wave good-by to Daddy!" At first children are not good at rule following and a toddler may not wave until Daddy has already left the room. But children who receive generous, loving rewards for responding to rules gradually learn how to respond correctly to ever-more complex rules.

After several years, many children are capable of giving rules to themselves: "I should tell Mommy that I'm going outside." Skinner, Vygotsky, and others have noted that children's early rule use begins with words said out loud, then they may mouth the words silently, and finally they think the rules silently inside their brains.[1] The internal use of rules is one of the features of behavior that once seemed like a mystery, but is now yielding to scientific analysis: Rule use begins with the social exchanges that are easily observed in our external environment, then individuals gradually learn the skills for giving themselves rules in the privacy of their own brains, without uttering a word to others.

What does it feel like when children learn to give themselves rules silently inside their brains? Can you hear "little voices" inside your head? When no one is talking to you, do you "hear" a stream of words in your brain? Stop reading and "listen" to them. What are they saying? Often they are rules that tell you to do things such as "Flip ahead and see how long this chapter is." "Keep on reading and see what the point is." Words that tell us what to do are rules. They are instructions. Self-given rules and self-instructions are the words we give ourselves to guide our own behavior. These inner words allow us to be much more than a passive ball of clay that is being shaped by a sculptor's hands. If we do not like the way our lives are being molded, we can create rules and use self-instructions for directing our behavior in new and different directions.

Some people are more effective than others at using self-given rules for guiding their own behavior. Why? Some people learn more powerful and useful rules than others if they have parents, teachers, books, and media sources that provide valuable verbal information. In addition, people who understand how rules work have an extra advantage because they see how to use rules most effectively for modifying their own thoughts, emotions, and actions. Knowledge is power. The more useful knowledge we have about behavior and rule use, the more power we have to guide our own lives via rules. This chapter will help you learn useful information about rules that you can use for directing your own life—transforming your ball of clay—and creating it as *you* want it to be.

SYMBOLIC INFORMATION

Chapter 10, on modeling and observational learning, showed how the information we obtain from watching others can influence our behavior. Models whose behavior shows how to do some action provide us with raw, uncoded information about behavior, and this helps us do imitative responses. Thousands of years ago, the inventions of language, and later writing, allowed the creation of a new kind of information that is symbolically encoded in words and numbers. When symbolic information is presented as spoken or written rules, it can be used to direct behavior. The words, "Turn to p. 282 if you want to see how rules are used in behavior modification," can direct your behavior if you find the topic of behavior modification especially rewarding.

Advances in technology are now creating an information revolution that makes valuable symbolic information more accessible than ever in the past—via fax, TV, computers, the Internet, cell phones, satellite communication, and more. Simultaneously, advances in behavior science are giving us ever-more symbolic knowledge about human behavior and ways we can guide, control, and improve it. Knowledge is power, and never before have humans had access to so much symbolic knowledge relevant to understanding and improving our own behavior.

Rules are verbally encoded guidelines—such as instructions, suggestions, or hints—that tell us how to respond in various situations. Instructions for coping with multitudes of situations can be stated as rules for helping people learn new behavior patterns rapidly and efficiently.[2] After worrying about their child's frequent pouting and sulking, parents may read the following instructions: "Whenever your child pouts, avoid paying attention to the child, but pay generous attention when your child does desirable alternative behaviors. You can make pouting decline by removing the social reinforcement for pouting and directing it to more desirable alternatives." In two sentences, parents learn a powerful technique of behavior modification for coping with a problem that some parents, without access to good rules, never learn to solve.

Rules generally describe some aspect of the contingencies of reinforcement—the ABC relationship among antecedent stimuli, behavior, and consequences.[3] The behavioral guidelines for helping parents deal with a pouting child specified all three elements of the desirable contingencies of reinforcement: If the S^Ds of your child's pouting are present, your *behavior* of not showing attention will produce the rewarding *consequences* of a gradual decline in pouting. The ABCs of the second rule for rewarding alternative behavior are completely described, too. When you see the S^Ds of desirable behavior from your child, your *behaviors* that show genuine appreciation will serve as *consequences* that reward behavior that is free of pouting.

All three elements of the contingencies of reinforcement are not always made explicit because people's prior learning often allows them to fill in the missing elements. The instructions on a fire alarm—"In case of fire, break glass and pull handle"—describe only the relevant S^Ds (the presence of fire) and operants (break glass and pull handle). The instructions on the fire alarm do not need to describe the reinforcer—alarm bells and the arrival of fire trucks—because most people know this, even if they have never used an alarm. "Push button to cross street" describes the operant to be performed and the reinforcement that will follow. The sign does not need to specify that the S^Ds for pressing the button are the presence of DON'T WALK signs or busy traffic. No one would need to push the button if the S^Ds of DON'T WALK signals or heavy traffic were nonexistent. A big poster on the wall saying SMILE only indicates the behavior to be done—with no hint about the best S^D context or consequences; but some people find that even this vague rule will increase the frequency of smiles, which in turn improves their social interactions and boosts their mood.[4]

Sometimes rules need to be spelled out completely in order to maximize their effectiveness or minimize misunderstandings. Stating a complete rule, "If you clean up your room (the behavior) before dinner (the S^D), you can watch TV tonight (the reward)," is much more likely to generate the desired behavior than is stating an abbreviated rule, such as "Clean up your room."

Each one of us is barraged by an incredibly large number of rules every day: "Buy this product now," "Save at our friendly bank," "Seek and ye shall find," "Fight pollution," "Help stamp out everything that needs stamping out," "Join the millions who. . . ." There is no way we could obey all the rules. In fact, we do not even pay much attention to many of them. Clearly there is more to rule use than meets the eye. People do not automatically follow rules they are given. Sometimes they do the opposite of what they are told to do. What determines how a rule will modify a person's behavior? How does a person discriminate among the countless rules and follow a select few while neglecting most of them?

RULE USE IS LEARNED

Rules are meaningless to newborn infants. One obvious prerequisite for rule use is knowledge of language, and it takes years for children to learn sophisticated language skills. A second prerequisite that is especially visible when working in a specialized area—such as learning new skills for rock climbing, emergency first aid, or psychological counseling—is prior experience with the specialized jargon, equipment, and relevant skills.

Normally, children can begin learning to use rules as they learn the language.[5] The learning of rule use begins as preverbal behavior gradually comes under the S^D control of verbal rules. When Betsy first begins to crawl, before she can respond to rules, she learned to go to Daddy when he was smiling and his arms were open to give her a big hug. The S^Ds for approach were his smiles and open arms; the reinforcers were social attention and affection. As Betsy now gains an understanding of the language, her father may say, "Come here, Betsy" while Betsy is toddling toward him, and the spoken rule becomes part of the S^D collage associated with going to Daddy and receiving reinforcers. After several repetitions, the rule becomes a well-established part of the stimulus collage and may be enough to cause Betsy to approach even if her father forgets the smile or open-arm gesture. When Betsy follows simple rules and her parents show affection, their reinforcer increases the likelihood that Betsy will follow the rules in the future. Rewards for following rules cause rules to become S^Ds for following rules in the future. Naturally, if her parents did not reinforce rule use, Betsy would be less likely to follow rules. In addition, parents who say, "Come here, Freddie," so they can *punish* their child often find that the child *goes away* when they say *come*, due to negative reinforcement for escape and avoidance. Punishers can cause rules to become S^Δs that inhibit the behavior specified by the rule.

People learn to follow rules when rule use leads to reinforcement.[6] *Nonreinforcement decreases rule use, due to extinction. Rule use is suppressed—and people may even learn to do the opposite of a rule—when following a given rule leads to punishment.* People are most likely to learn a generalized tendency to follow rules in many situations if they have received reinforcers for following many kinds of rules, given by a large number of people in many different contexts in the past.[7]

Sometimes young children go through a cute period of *overgeneralized rule use* when they are first learning to use rules. This is most likely to occur if their parents, brothers, and sisters are consistent in giving reasonable rules and then reinforcing rule use. "Come to Mommy," "Go to Daddy," "Don't touch the hot skillet!" "Stay out of the street." If the parents and siblings follow through with reinforcement for obeying and punishment for not obeying, the child may learn to comply with almost all rules.

Little Laura is playing on the living room floor with her older brother and sister, Timmy and Lindsey. While Timmy is stacking blocks to make a complex tower, Laura keeps pushing off the top blocks and watching them fall to the floor. Crash, crash—sensory stimulation—what fun! But Laura's brother is less than happy with his little sister's behavior and says, "Stop that! You'll knock down my tower." Laura obeys and turns to the model ranch Lindsey has created. In short order, Laura receives sensory stimulation reinforcers from playing with the little plastic horses and tiny people. Soon she has eight people stacked on one horse. This clearly perturbs her sister, who is taking her ranchers' lives more seriously. So Lindsey says, "Go see Daddy, Laura."

Off Laura goes to the garage to see Daddy. But her father is working busily at his potter's wheel, and he has little time to pay attention to Laura. After Laura squashes a freshly thrown pot by accidentally stepping on it, Father tells her to go play with Timmy and Lindsey. Firmly pushed in the direction of the living room, Laura goes back to her brother and sister. Timmy's tower is taller and tottering now. When he sees Laura about ready to reach for the tower, Timmy interjects, "Hey, Laura! Don't touch that. Why don't you go play with some of Lindsey's things?" However, as Laura goes through the sequence the second time, she begins to learn an important discrimination: She is getting "the run-around." People are telling her to go see someone else just to make her go away.

In one sense, it is cute to watch a little child go from one person to the next, so trustingly, so obediently while getting the run-around. Laura may even receive enough sensory stimulation in the game of following the rule of "Go see so-and-so" to reinforce compliance for several repetitions. But as the novelty dies off and sensory reinforcers disappear, Laura may learn an important new discrimination: *Not all rules need to be followed.* She may ask, "Why should I go see Daddy? He said I should stay here and play with you." Laura is learning that rules can be questioned and challenged.[8] At an early age, most of us begin to ask "Why?" when we are given rules that require behavior that is not rewarding.

Children also learn that one person's rule can be counteracted with another person's rule. If Timmy begrudgingly gives in and allows Laura to play with some blocks, the reinforcers of play hasten Laura's learning to discriminate that not all family rules must be obeyed. Laura may even learn to invent rules: "Lindsey, Daddy said you should share some of your toys with me!" If Lindsey shares, Laura is rewarded for inventing a rule. Rules give her power to control her older brother and sister!

Over the years, children increasingly learn to counter many rules and instructions with the question, "Why?" "Why should I go play in my own room?" In different homes, these "Why?" questions may lead to varied consequences. Some parents take authoritarian roles and threaten to use force to get their child to obey. "You'll do it because *I* told you so." Other parents use reasoning: "You should leave the kitchen because I'm very tired and cannot make dinner with constant distractions." Yet others might add the promise of special reinforcers: "If you'll go play in your room, I'll let you lick the cake mix bowl and beaters when I'm done."

It takes many years to learn the thousands of rules people state and use in everyday life; hence it is understandable that 5-to-6-year-old children do not know as many rules as they will know by age 15 or 20. When asked to complete the following rule, "A penny saved is . . . ," 5-year-old children may say, "A penny saved is not much" (instead of "a penny earned"). What comes after, "Strike while the . . ."? A 6-year-old child said, "Strike while the bug is close" (instead of "while the iron is hot"). "Better be safe than . . ."? ". . . punch a fifth grader." "You can't teach an old dog . . ."? ". . . new math." It takes a long time to learn all the everyday rules most 20-year-old adults know.

THE S^Ds FOR FOLLOWING RULES

People are bombarded by more rules than they can follow, and many rules do not lead to reinforcement; consequently, people learn to disregard most rules. Most adults do not even pay attention to all the rules they hear or read each day. People are likely to follow rules only when S^Ds are present in (1) the *rule* and (2) the *context,* indicating that there has been past reinforcement for using similar rules in similar contexts.

1. The Rule. If following a certain rule has been reinforced, the rule itself becomes an S^D for following that rule in the future. If following another rule has resulted in nonrein-

forcement or punishment, this second rule becomes an S^Δ that inhibits following the second rule in the future.   People learn to discriminate. Coming from a poor family, Louie learned to value the rule: "A penny saved is a penny earned," but he never believed the rule about old dogs, because his grandparents loved learning new things. People tend to follow those types of rules that have paid off in the past and to disregard those types of rules that have led to nonreinforcement or punishment. There are two general kinds of rules that often lead to reinforcement: *Commands* and *good advice* (see below).

2. The Context. *However, things are more complex.*   Following a given rule may be reinforced in one context but not in another context. As a result, *various context cues in the stimulus collage can become S^Ds or S^Δs that help determine whether a person will follow any given rule.*[9] If your best friend were to shout hysterically, "Get out of here, there's a fire!" the tone of voice would provide S^Ds for doing as told immediately; but your friend's saying "Get out of here!" while laughing and giving you a big smile would not cause you to do as told. Countless stimuli from the rule giver, the audience, and the surrounding environment can become *context cues*—S^Ds or S^Δs—that help people discriminate when and where to follow or disregard any given rule. If you tell a child *not* to open the cookie jar—or not to do some other forbidden (but rewarding) behavior—your rule is not only an S^Δ that inhibits the child's following the rule, it may have an effect opposite from the rule's literal verbal content.

Commands and Good Advice

A **command** *is a rule enforced by consequences that the rule giver controls.* **Good advice** *is a rule whose use is reinforced by the natural consequences of following the rule (without enforcement from the rule giver).*[10] A command takes the following form: "An authority tells you to do a certain behavior, and the person in authority will make sure compliance is rewarded and noncompliance is punished." Good advice takes a very different form: "Try a certain activity, and I think you will find it rewarding." Commands can have a stronger effect on behavior than advice, especially if the person who gives the commands actually has the power to reinforce or punish. Good advice lacks the extra social enforcement associated with commands. Advice is backed up by reinforcement only to the degree that it is *good* advice that actually helps people attain rewarding experiences. Commands can contain good advice: "Thou shalt not kill" is a commandment, and it is backed up by legal sanctions. In addition, it is good advice for anyone who values living in a civilized society.

Because children lack experience with rule use, they often need commands—backed up by extra social sanctions (reinforcers or punishers)—in order to follow rules well. Merely advising a 2-year-old that it is somewhat risky to play in the street will have less effect than the command, "Do not go in the street or else you have to stay inside for the rest of the afternoon." As the years pass and people gain experience with rule use, many learn the value of good advice. As they learn to discriminate good advice from poor advice, they also learn to recall the good advice that pertains to their lives.

There are problems with advice. In many areas of life, commands are superior to advice, for both children and adults. *A listener may not follow a good rule unless com-*

manded to do so if (1) the rule is not obviously true, or (2) the rewards of rule following are in the distant future, or (3) the rule demands that the follower do something aversive (because it is uncomfortable, unusual, strange, or socially unacceptable). Friends may advise Uncle George to stop drinking so much, yet George may not be able to appreciate the future health benefits of stopping or see how he can possibly get along without the pleasures of the bottle. But when George's boss commands George to stop drinking or lose his job, the command form of the rule may have a powerful effect.

Often rule givers who want to change someone else's behavior will start out with *hints of advice,* casually suggesting: "You shouldn't drink so much, George." Then, if hints fail to change George's behavior, they may try something more powerful and offer *explicit advice:* "George, I've got some important advice for you." Next, they may restate their advice in the form of a *simple command*—"George, stop drinking"—even though no consequences are stated. Finally, the rule givers may escalate to a *full command,* with the *promises of reward* or *threats of punishment* that are needed to give commands full strength. The boss says, "You're fired if you don't quit boozing."

People do not pay much attention to most of the advice they hear. Why? Advice is cheap and easy to give; hence people hear more advice than they can possibly follow. Because it is often difficult to discriminate between good advice and bad advice, people may not respond to good advice unless clear S^Ds are present which indicate that "this advice really works." If it takes special effort to discriminate between good advice and bad advice, the effort serves as a punisher that decreases the likelihood people will try to find out which advice is actually valuable.

Even when people need rules or advice, they may first try to get along without seeking the verbal information. It sometimes takes effort to locate good advice and figure out how to use it—and effort can function as a punisher; hence people may not seek out advice until they have exhausted easier methods of solving their problems. A person who cannot make a new VCR function properly may try adjusting various controls in search of a quick, low-effort solution. If the low-effort behavior fails, the individual may eventually pull out the instruction manual or ask an expert for advice. When faced with a new problem, people frequently begin with their old skills before turning to the potentially more effortful behavior of locating and applying effective rules. Naturally, people learn to discriminate that some activities are much more likely to require instructions than others. A cook who has had misfortune with French dishes may turn to a cookbook or advice from a friend for help with *coquilles Saint-Jacques,* even though the cook seldom uses rules when cooking other recipes. Once we discriminate that certain kinds of problems are beyond our skills, we often turn to rules and expert advice to cope with them if rule use has been reinforced by successes in the past.

When people have problems running their own lives, they may seek out or invent rules to use as *self-instruction* for solving their problems. After being bothered by obsessive thoughts, a person may formulate a self-instruction such as, "I've got to stop thinking about that topic." Many repetitions of rule use may be necessary to overcome difficult problems. People often engage in extended internal monologues as they work at mastering problems and combating unhappy moods.[11] "Quit thinking such negative thoughts. You'll only drag yourself into depression." If these snippets of good advice help reduce a person's worries even temporarily, each success due to self-instruction reinforces the habits of continuing such rule use in the future.

Context Cues

Rules always appear in a context, and various cues from the rule giver, audience, and surrounding environment serve as S^Ds or S^Δs that can increase or decrease the likelihood of rule use.[12] If a close and respected friend suggests we do something, we are more likely to respond than if a distant or less respected acquaintance made the same suggestion. If some distinctive individual—a beloved mayor, relative, or TV personality—gave advice that proved very useful and rewarding in the past, the reinforcers increase our chances of following future rules from that person. A serious tone of voice is often an S^D that increases the likelihood of rule use. If a rule is presented in a logical or sensible manner, listeners are more likely to follow the rule than if it were stated in a trivial, flip, or joking manner. Of course, we can make mistakes, and mistakes help us learn discriminations. Some rules are presented as if entirely logical and reasonable, yet are punished when we follow them. A con artist uses beautiful logic to convince us to invest in a pyramid scheme, and within 2 days of paying $100 for the project we realize we have been conned. Through such experiences, many people learn to become cautious and discriminating about "logical-sounding ideas:" Some scheme that sounds "too good to be true" may be a disaster waiting to happen.

Also, the authoritativeness of the source of rules is important, along with the rule user's past experience with authority. A recent authoritative book—such as a famous cookbook or well-known manual on engine repair—is much more likely to lead to rule use than an old or cheaply printed text, especially for people who have learned to discriminate that not all sources are equally reliable. Authoritative advice from a doctor—"Your lung X-ray indicates that you had better stop smoking!"—is much more likely to affect a smoker's behavior than similar pleas from a friend or spouse. Of course, any given authority may not be respected by all people. People who distrust all doctors may not be concerned by their physician's advice about not smoking. A law officer's advice about abstaining from drugs may cause some students to avoid drugs, but have the opposite effect among the more rebellious and antiestablishment students.

Thus, many elements of the context that surrounds a rule can serve as S^Ds and S^Δs which determine how a person will respond to the rule. Because each individual has a unique prior socialization, different people may respond to any given rule and its context differently—each in a manner consistent with his or her unique history of learning experiences.

EXPLICIT VERSUS IMPLICIT RULES

There is a continuum from explicit rules to implicit rules—from fully formulated rules to sketchy abbreviations. Children usually need explicit rules that are rather clear and detailed if they are to succeed in following them. They may not find enough useful information in a vague rule—such as "Set the table, Billy"—to get the job done well. But children can master complex tasks (and reap the rewards of success) when given more explicit rules, such as "Put napkins on the left side of each plate; then come back and I'll tell you what to do next."

As the years pass, most teens and adults learn to do rule-governed behavior in response to increasingly vague and sketchy rules. "The table, Joe," may be enough of an S^D to get an adult to set the table when guests are expected. *Some people learn to do rule-governed behavior when given information in which a rule is only implicit, but not directly stated.* After enough experience with rules, some people advance to the point where they can extract rules from verbal statements that are not in rule format. During a conversation, one person may mention that "Investment properties yielded a higher annual income than any other type of investment in Pogwash County last year, and the same is predicted for next year." Many listeners would not respond to that statement as a rule. But some may respond to the sentence as if it were a rule to invest in Pogwash property for good monetary returns. The rule is *implicit* in the sentence, but extracting and following such unspoken rules require skills that come only with experience. (Most people become skillful in locating implicit rules in certain areas of life, while remaining insensitive to implicit rules in other areas, depending on prior learning experience and conditioning in each area. A real estate investor may put money into Pogwash properties, but fail to detect implicit rules in conversations about the importance of exercise and good diet for a long and healthy life.)

ON RULE GIVING

People learn to give rules to others because rules often provide a rapid way of helping—or forcing—another person to do specific acts that are reinforcing to the rule giver.[13] The practice of giving rules to others is reinforced if it is successful in modifying their behavior in the desired direction. Parents usually find that giving 3-year-old toddlers rules, such as "Don't go in the street or you'll have to stay in the house," speeds the children's learning considerably. Rules help children discriminate which behaviors are forbidden. Rules also help them do self-instructed, rule-governed behavior the next time they are about to dash into the street. "Mommy said, 'Don't go in the street.'" When children follow the rules, the parents' practice of giving rules is reinforced.

In many situations where shaping, observational learning, or prompting may take a long time to produce the desired behavior, a rule can take effect immediately. If your chubby friend is on the way to the kitchen to get some snacks, you may modify your friend's behavior with a tactfully worded rule such as, "Hey, I thought your new diet didn't allow you to eat snacks." Hearing the rule again may help your friend avoid snacking for several hours, whereas shaping and modeling would not have worked nearly so quickly. Rules coupled with rewards for compliance produce even better effects, and your friend may thank you for your help when unwanted pounds begin to disappear.

Rules can also help people see that behavior they learned in one context can be useful in other situations—helping these behaviors to generalize to appropriate contexts.[14] Useful rules help explain when, where, and why a behavior is valuable—and when it is not. If a child learns to "fix" broken toys by banging them on the floor until the parts move freely again, this technology may yield rewards in some situations, but not others. Mom may offer a rule: "Limit your banging to large, crude things, and try a gentle bang before a hard bang. Please bring fragile things to me for fixing."

Rules are especially important in facilitating learning and behavioral change in the following circumstances:

1. *When reinforcers are few and far between, rules can build "behavioral persistence" and keep a person going.*[15] Your pudgy friend may find it easier to stick to his diet if he hears the rule, "It can take several weeks before you get rewarded by seeing significant weight loss, but stick to your diet and good things will happen." A door-to-door salesperson may sell an expensive product only once in 15 houses, yet the rule—"Keep going and you may sell another one today"—helps link the rewards to the needed behavior.

2. *When the reinforcers associated with a target behavior are too distant in the future to allow differential reinforcement to modify behavior, rules can guide a behavior and show its connection with future reinforcers.*[16] A college student may receive few immediate reinforcers for diligent studying. But by creating and repeatedly stating a rule—"I've got to study hard so I can have an interesting career"—the student makes the future rewards more vivid and more logically linked with studying, so they can have more influence over current behavior.

3. *When there is a risk of punishment, rules for avoiding problems can help people learn without having to make mistakes—hence without punishment.* Advice from a coworker—"Never leave the extension cords plugged in overnight because the night watchman could trip and get hurt"—can help a person benefit from "errorless learning"—without ever having to make a mistake.

Sharing Firsthand Experience

In some circumstances, rules sum up years of firsthand experience with some task and pass it on to another person who has no firsthand experience with the task. A woman who has owned and run a shop for half her life has learned many skills for treating customers nicely, maintaining all items in stock, keeping the books accurately, and so forth. *Much of firsthand experience is based on differential reinforcement, shaping, observational learning, and prompts as countless successes and failures gradually mold a repertoire of advanced knowledge and skills.* When a storekeeper hires new assistants, the easiest way to orient the assistants to the routine of the shop is to formulate rules. "Remember, the customer is always right." "When you leave the front room, lock the cash register." Things the shopkeeper learned the slow way can be formulated in a few words and can prevent the assistants' having to learn the slow way, too. The shopkeeper may have learned not to criticize or challenge customers by losing sales, but her assistants learn by hearing the relevant rule *and* by being commended when they follow it or corrected when they do not.

Learning from firsthand experience (the way the shopkeeper did) differs from learning by rules in several ways:[17]

1. When rules are used correctly, they usually produce more rapid learning than shaping during firsthand experience.

2. If rules are formulated well, they can help a rule user avoid many of the mistakes and aversive consequences that are often experienced during success and failure learning (differential reinforcement) in everyday life.

3. Rule-governed behavior often has a mechanical quality not found in behavior acquired by firsthand experience. The linear structure of language imposes a linear structure on rules: "Do A, then B, then C, and D." The resulting behavior is often performed in more rigid steps than similar behavior learned by firsthand experience.
4. Learning from rules often involves different reinforcers and punishers than learning from firsthand experience. Gain or loss of customers taught the shopkeeper, whereas positive and negative comments from the shopkeeper teach her assistants.
5. All of these differences contribute to the fact that the person who was taught by rules knows different things than the person whose behavior was learned by other means. The shopkeeper knows the whole history of her running of the business, and she has a "feel" for the countless complexities involved. Her apprentices know the rules—a list of do's and don'ts—but lack the shopkeeper's "feel" for whether or not to bend a rule in a unique situation.

A person who used firsthand experience to create rules is often disappointed with a rule users' failure to understand unique situations as well as the rule giver does. Even if the rule giver expands on the rule with several auxiliary rules, the less experienced rule user simply will not show all the finesse of the person who learned from firsthand experience. "I told my assistants a dozen times how to deal with grouchy old Mr. Wurtzelkopf, but they never seem to handle him the way I want them to." One solution to the problem is to let the rule users gain increasing amounts of firsthand experience—the kind that shaped the shopkeeper's behavior—in order to supplement the learning begun with rules alone.

Rules Plus Firsthand Experience

If a rule is simple and the behavior to be performed is not difficult, a listener may perform the operant flawlessly the first time, after hearing the rule only once. But much of life is not so simple. *When rules are complex and require operant performances beyond a person's present level of skills, the rule user may need extra, firsthand experience (involving differential reinforcement, shaping, observational learning, or prompts) in order to learn the behavior.* "Just follow the on-screen instructions and the computer will do all the work for you," is an easy rule for people to follow if they have successfully operated computers in the past. However, the same instruction may be quite inadequate for a person who has never used a computer. While trying to follow these instructions, a novice might misunderstand several of the computer's instructions, enter an improper command, and cause the system to malfunction. However, with extra instruction and several hours of firsthand experience at the computer keyboard, many a novice can gradually gain the skills needed for successfully operating a variety of simple computer programs.

As a person gains firsthand experience with any new activity, early rule-governed behavior—which tends to be clumsy and mechanical at first—usually undergoes important changes. *As people repeat rule-governed behavior and gain firsthand experience with it, the clumsy and mechanical early performances usually are smoothed out under the influence of differential reinforcement, shaping, observational learning, and prompting.* As people follow a rule, they gain firsthand experience that conditions more "natural," coordinated, and subtle behavior. The early clumsiness and mechanicalness disappear as smoother and more polished behavior is learned.

For example, Amy, who is taking tennis lessons, hears numerous rules for how to swing the racket, move across the court, use her backhand, and so on. At first, Amy's rule-governed behavior looks much more rigid and mechanical than her teacher's. Seeing the ball coming to her left side is an S^D that brings up the following rule: "Put both hands on the racket and prepare for a backhand." The next S^Ds lead to the thought: "Put your whole body into the swing, as if throwing a medicine ball." Amy's response is somewhat awkward. It lacks spontaneity. In a moment of hesitation, you can almost hear her thinking, "What should I do now?"

However, if Amy sticks with the game, her ability to apply and follow the rules will improve with practice and firsthand experience. She will learn to discriminate among ever finer subtleties of rule information. In addition, repeated differential reinforcement shapes more advanced skills than those that can be learned from verbal rules alone: A fortunate twist of her wrist may put a nice spin on the ball and win a volley (positive reinforcement), but a clumsy move may produce the opposite result. Watching good role models serve the ball provides additional learning experience, as does receiving physical prompts on how to hold her arms. This extra learning helps smooth out the clumsiness of Amy's early rule-governed behavior, decrease some of the mechanicalness of early rule use, and shape smooth behavioral chains that flow with ease.

Because most rules are not entirely accurate, firsthand experience helps correct for the errors or inadequacies traced to crude rules. Few behavior patterns are so simple that the behavior can be described completely by 20 or 200 word rules; hence the extra firsthand experience gained after learning new rules is crucial to correct for the limits of rules. Also, a rule may include some wrong advice or omit some important steps in explaining a behavior. Amy's tennis coach may think that breathing is crucial and teach students many unnecessary rules about breathing. While focusing on breathing, the coach may forget to mention some important points on footwork. Although the coach's advice may partially mislead Amy during the early weeks, firsthand experience on tennis courts will help her learn many correct responses and thereby partially compensate for the imperfect rules.

Not everyone gets a chance to have the firsthand experience needed to correct for inadequate rules. In some cases, rule givers become impatient when they observe that a rule receiver cannot perform some specified behavior, and they may intercede in order to finish the task themselves—rather than allow the rule user to struggle with the problem and gain firsthand experience. If a mother tells her young son how to prepare some beans for dinner, she may get a bit perturbed as the son fumbles along slowly and delays the casserole. If she takes over the task herself, however, she only prevents the child from learning the needed skills from direct experience with differential reinforcement. A perfectionist father may tell his high-school-age daughter how to use woodworking tools, then not let her help him build some garden chairs for fear her work will be less than perfect. The father may be amazed at how little his daughter learns from him: "I've taught her all I know about carpentry, but the chair legs she made will never do. This just proves that you can't teach females to do a male's job." Over the next 10 years, the daughter may finally have the opportunity to do enough woodwork projects that she can learn advanced skills via firsthand experience. Ten years later, when looking at a beautiful coffee table she built, her father says, "I taught her all I knew, and you can see that she turned out to be a darn good craftsperson, just like her dad." When his daughter was younger, the father failed to see the need for giving his daughter something more than rules; 10 years later, he failed to see how much her refined skills were due to her years of firsthand experience beyond his early rule giving.

TACIT AND EXPLICIT KNOWLEDGE

When we compare two people who have learned similar behavior—but one learned from rules and the other without rules—we find they know different things.[18] The so-called "natural" tennis player who never took lessons but learned from firsthand experience knows different things than the equally competent player who originally learned from rules and then mastered further skills during firsthand experience.

People who have learned a behavior from rules usually find it much easier to talk about the behavior than do people who learned similar behavior from firsthand experience alone. Rule users learned the behavior by hearing others talk about it, so doing the behavior and talking about it go hand in hand. At first, their talk may be heavily influenced by the rules and words that were given to them when they learned the activity, but as learning continues they may add their own words based on personal observations. Even when no one is asking them to verbalize about their behavior, they are likely to be thinking relevant words while doing the behavior—especially in the early period before the behavior becomes well learned. Whenever you ask them about the behavior, they are likely to "explain" their actions in words that seem logical.

In most cases, naturals—who did not learn a given behavior by rules—are less likely than rule learners to talk or verbally think about how they perform that behavior. If someone asks them how they manage such a powerful and accurate backhand, naturals are likely to give a vague response such as, "You just swing and you know it's right when it feels right." Naturals can describe the conspicuous parts of the behavior, "You just swing," but a rule user might have added, "keeping your center of gravity in front of your feet so you can fall toward the stroke." Naturals are more likely to say, "You just have to get the *feel* for the right way." They are discriminating among countless external and internal CSs, various S^Ds and S^Δs that feel right or wrong, but many of these feelings are very hard to describe in words. How do you describe subtle differences in the inner feelings of balance, muscle tension, knee bend, or arm stretching as you dash to hit a tennis ball that rushes at you only to bounce with an odd spin?

Note that people who are naturals at one behavior may be rule users when doing another behavior. When we identify people as naturals in regard to a specific behavior, we are merely noting that this particular behavior was learned without rules, instructions, or lessons. Thus, being labeled a natural for one behavior does not indicate the existence of some universal personality trait that affects all other behavior.[19]

*The person who learned a behavior from rules and thinks about the behavior in terms of rules has **explicit knowledge** about the behavior. The person who learned from firsthand experience, without rules, is less likely to think about the behavior in terms of rules and has **tacit knowledge**—or unspoken knowledge—about the behavior.*[20] Rules provide people with explicit knowledge that is easy to verbalize and easy to share with others because the knowledge was verbally encoded from the start, when the person first heard the rules. Explicit knowledge is readily made public knowledge because it is easy to communicate to others. Explicit knowledge makes people feel they are consciously and verbally aware of the reasons for their behavior. "My coach says I should increase my running to 10 miles per day, four times a week, to build up my endurance."

In contrast, the natural is playing it by feel, often without verbal awareness of the causes of behavior. A person who is a natural at athletics exercises at a level that feels right. Naturals clearly know something about the behavior they do, but it is *tacit knowledge,* unspoken knowledge. It is personal knowledge as opposed to public knowledge, and it has an *intuitive*[21] quality because it is guided more by nonverbal sensations than by verbal instructions.

Because a person's tacit knowledge is private knowledge, based on firsthand experience, all this unique, personal knowledge dies when the person dies. In contrast, explicit knowledge that is encoded in rules is public knowledge, and it can be passed from person to person—or through symbolic media—with the potential for outliving the rule formulator.[22] *Even though public knowledge is secondhand and sometimes crude, culturally accumulated rules help people learn more than any single person could learn in a lifetime from firsthand, personal experience alone.* Many people have tried jogging and injured themselves before learning the basic information contained in simple books for the novice jogger.

Because naturals may not be skilled at explaining how they perform their behavior or how they acquired the behavior, their behavior may appear more mysterious and more inexplicable than the behavior of rule users. People who had guitar lessons can tell you the rules for learning to play; hence there is no mystery to the behavior. But, a natural guitarist may tell you that playing the guitar just came naturally: "I just developed a feel for the instrument." Because the causes for the behavior are less apparent to people who do not understand behavior principles, there is more room for wonder. "Beth plays so beautifully and she's never had lessons! She must have a special musical talent!" In fact, she may have no more talent than a person who relied on rules to learn the guitar.

It is not at all uncommon to see people receive more attention, respect, and admiration for a behavior that was not learned via rules. The natural athlete or artist tends to enthrall people's imaginations more than the athlete or artist who obviously studied rules of technique and practiced prescribed exercises. Many people have realized this fact and learned to keep quiet about how much they have practiced rule-governed behavior, pretending they are naturals when they are not. They are likely to receive extra social attention, interest, and reinforcement for doing this.[23]

Actually, natural behavior is no more mysterious than rule-governed behavior. Both are learned; only the method of learning differs. When we understand how naturals learn via observational learning, prompting, and shaping—coupled with thousands of hours of practice—their behavior does not appear any more mysterious or difficult to explain than does rule-governed behavior. And people who learned from rules are far better off than people who were not lucky enough to learn from rules or natural firsthand experience:

Think of all the people who never learned to play tennis or guitar because no one ever gave them useful rules and they gave up after a few feeble attempts.

People Know More Than They Can Tell[24]

It is clear that *naturals* know when their behavior *feels* right or wrong. *These inner feelings are the subjective experiences created by S^Ds, S^Δs, and CSs that have been conditioned while the natural learned from models, prompts, differential reinforcement, and shaping.* Tacit knowledge is clearly demonstrated when naturals are producing highly skilled behavior, but this knowledge is hard for them to describe verbally. Naturals know more than they can tell. They know more than they can explain.

Even rule users are likely to know more than they can tell, especially when they gain enough firsthand experience to polish their behavior beyond the early phases of mechanical rule use. Rules may be helpful for starting beginners in learning a new behavior, but rules are rarely detailed enough to explain all the minute features of a behavior chain. As rule users gain additional firsthand experience, they also develop tacit knowledge—hunches and intuitions—that goes beyond the original rules. Eventually, they too know more than they can tell.

How can we know who has the best tacit knowledge about any given behavior—since people cannot explain their tacit data? People whose behavior leads to high levels of success and rewarding results show us *through their behavior* that they have good mixtures of tacit and explicit wisdom, based on years of experience. Successful people with behavioral expertise are recognized as having valuable resources, even if they cannot make all their knowledge explicit.[25] Often we can learn from observing their behavior and listening to their "hunches" and "intuitions."

Because people cannot tell all they know about complex behavior, communication concerning many intricate details of life tends to be rather sketchy. There is so much we cannot explain. In trying to describe their tacit knowledge, people often use phrases such as: "You just get the feel for it." "You know what I mean?" "Sort of like this." "You know?" "Right?" When they are finished explaining their feel for tennis, you may not be sure you know exactly what they meant. You know what we mean?

Sketchy explanations are both commonplace and widely accepted in most everyday interactions. Being totally explicit is rarely demanded. As a result, people often become quite irritated if too many "whys" are asked. "Why did you do this? Why did you do that?" It is true that many children go through a period in which they ask their parents a million whys, but eventually the behavior is suppressed by punishment or extinction. People cannot tell all they know, and most children learn to live with incomplete information.

People often describe social life as if it were guided by "social norms"—or "societal rules"—and some seem quite surprised when people cannot describe the norms or rules that were presumed to be controlling their behavior. According to the behavioral analysis, much of everyday behavior is based on tacit knowledge gained through firsthand experience, without much assistance from norms and rules. Thus, it is no wonder that people have little explicit verbal awareness about the exact procedures they use to negotiate their way through much of everyday life.

The Reinforcers for Inventing Rules

When people are put in situations where they have to explain their actions, some tend to explain their behavior *as if* it were rule governed. If a woman is asked why she was so polite when dealing with a man who was stealing from her company, her answer may sound like a rule: "We must always be as considerate as possible in order to minimize unnecessary hostility toward the company." The woman has provided a *verbal account* of her behavior and this account *sounds like* it might be a rule that guides her behavior. However, in many cases it is difficult to determine whether such verbal accounts are ad hoc descriptions of behavior after it occurred or accurate summations of rules that were used to guide rule-governed behavior.

If naturals receive reinforcers for creating verbal descriptions and accounts of their behavior, they usually learn to formulate, talk, and think about the details of their behavior. However, their *verbal accounts*—which appear *after* behavior has been learned by firsthand experience—should not be confused with *rules,* which guide rule-governed behavior *before* it has been mastered. Naturals may claim that deep breathing exercises they read about in a book on yoga are the key to their success—even though we suspect there is more to the story. Thus, we need to always be aware that people's verbal accounts about their behavior may accurately reflect rules they used to guide their behavior or they may be an ad hoc invention that does not really explain their behavior.

Because most behavior is the product of many influences besides rules, it is often unwise to infer that behavior is strictly rule governed—even when people allude to rules to "explain" their activities. All too often verbal explanations do not reflect the real causes of behavior. People are especially handicapped in describing natural behavior because (1) it was learned without verbal instruction, and (2) most people are not aware of how differential reinforcement, shaping, models, and prompts affect their behavior. Hence they find it hard to explain the real causes of the aspects of their behavior that are not captured in terms of rules.

Even when people do not know why they did a certain behavior, there are contingencies of reinforcement that lead most people to create *verbal justifications* for their actions. *Creating credible accounts for our behavior—especially if they sound intelligent—often leads to more reinforcement than not saying anything, thereby appearing to be ignorant about our own actions.* When Dave is asked why he double-parked, he might answer, "I don't know—I just did it." Or he might say, "I was in a hurry and I figured that I would be in and out of the shop so fast that I'd never get a ticket." The second explanation sounds like Dave rationally planned the behavior, and it is more likely to avoid criticism because it sounds more intelligent than the first answer. Explaining something like double parking with words such as "I don't know—I just did it" is virtually asking for a critical rejoinder: "The next time you ought to think before you do something silly like that." By making behavior sound like it was rational and rule guided, people avoid some of this criticism. *As a result, most of us learn to talk as if our behavior were rational, planned, and rule governed, because this helps us avoid criticism.* The more skillful people become at inventing reasonable and intelligent-sounding accounts, the more likely they are to escape aversive consequences—and even be admired and rewarded for their intelligence.

Much of everyday behavior is influenced by complex mixtures of differential reinforcement, shaping, models, and prompts; hence verbal accounts that "explain" behavior in terms of rules alone often mask the actual determinants of behavior with a simplistic cover story. Even if rules were used in the initial learning of a behavior, all the extra first-hand experience that refines the early rule-governed behavior into smoothly polished performances is rarely captured by restating the rules as simple verbal accounts. We should be wary whenever we hear someone try to explain behavior as if it were the product of rules or norms alone. The mere fact that people say they did something because of such and such a rule or norm does not necessarily justify the assumption that the rule or norm was a key controlling factor of the behavior. Behavioral science can help us see through the biases in people's verbal accounts of their own actions and focus on the broader range of behavioral determinants: differential reinforcement, shaping, models, prompts, *and* rules. This broader view of behavior helps us gain a better understanding of ourselves and others, which is useful in coping effectively with the complexities of everyday life.

BEHAVIOR MODIFICATION

Rules are often used in behavior modification.[26] Therapists give clients instructions on how to do various activities needed to overcome deficits, control excesses, and improve the quality of their lives. Clients may be given books or pamphlets about the behaviors they need to learn, and these reading materials often contain very explicit rules for arranging behavioral changes. Large bookstores often contain many shelves full of self-help books for people with social deficits, sexual problems, drug dependency, marital difficulties, and other problems.[27] There are books to help people develop their skills in parenting, sales and management, leadership, public speaking, dating, exercise, tennis, golf, and other sports. This list goes on and on, and many of these books use behavior principles as the source of their rules for starting a self-help program.

People can expect the best success in guiding their own behavior when they use scientifically tested rules for self-instruction. Knowledge is power. Knowing the behavior principles of rule use greatly increases our power to organize and direct our own lives: It is wise to clarify all three elements of the behavioral ABCs and then reinforce all behaviors that successfully approximate the desired goals. Learning how to modify our own behavior frees us from being in the passive role of a lump of clay that is molded by some sculptor or potter—without our consent. One of the main goals of behavior modification is to clarify the means by which behavior is changed so people can take a more active role in their own self-direction.[28]

At what age can children begin to learn to do self-instruction? It usually begins in the first 5 years of life. Berk (1994) studied children from various types of homes and found that the children who knew how to give themselves many rules and self-guiding comments made the fastest progress in learning new activities. Their skills at self-instruction could be traced back to their home environments. In some subcultures, parents do not converse much with their children, relying on gestures more than words. Children from such taciturn homes do not engage in much verbal self-instruction, and they are slow in mastering new skills. In other subcultures, parents talk frequently with their children, interacting in a warm and responsive manner. Parents who generously share practical advice and useful rules—and serve as role models for using rules to talk oneself through problems—are giving their children precious gifts.[29] Children from such loving, verbal homes can tackle new problems with optimism and a large repertoire of practical rules for confronting difficulties and solving problems.

Berk observed that the youngest children talked audibly to themselves as they learned, but the self-talk and self-instruction gradually faded into inaudible muttering, and finally the child thought the words silently—as inner speech. Can you hear your inner words? The processes by which your audible self-instructions faded into muttering and finally into silent self-talk happened to you so many years ago that you probably cannot recall its happening. Now you are gaining knowledge about rule-use skills that can help you become even more skillful at self-instruction via self-spoken rules or silent words of wisdom.

Many children do not receive the best start in learning how to verbalize about their own behavior—describing their numerous options in life, the possible consequences of each option, and rules that could guide them toward the best outcomes. Behavior modification provides useful information—and clear rules—for improving each and every step in chains of behavior—describing options, consequences, rules. We can help the next generation of young people learn how to guide their own behavior more effectively by explaining how to carefully design the self-talk and rules for reaching great goals. Behavior modification has proven that this can be done with individuals with "mild intellectual disabilities,"[30] so there is no reason why many others cannot benefit more from this approach to life.

CONCLUSION

Some rules are very explicit statements of the contingencies of reinforcement (the ABCs): "When you first set up your new computer (A), make sure the wires are connected as shown in the picture (B), and you should have no difficulties (C). All three elements of the ABC equation are present. In contrast, many rules are only vaguely stated: "Smile, my friend." It can take considerable learning experience and skill for a rule user to extract information from statements that are not even presented as rules and then respond with the rule-governed behavior—investing in Pogwash county. Rules have the ability to guide behavior only because following rules has been reinforced in the past. Children have to learn how to use rules—and discriminate when and where not to do so. Depending on each individual's unique history of prior reinforcement, various rules and context cues become S^Ds or S^Δs for following or not following any given rule in various contexts.

People learn to create and give rules to others because rules often produce reinforcing results. Merely saying, "Open the windows, please" can lead to rewarding consequences, if the room is too hot and stuffy. However, rules about complex activities may not suffice to guide behavior to successful outcomes; and rule users often need additional firsthand learning experience—gained from differential reinforcement, shaping, models, and prompts—before their behavior is fully polished. The more that rule-governed behavior is coupled with firsthand experience, the more it begins to look like the types of "natural" behavior that are learned without rules. Even when people describe their behavior *as if* it were completely directed by rules, it is likely that other types of learning were involved, although these other types of learning are more difficult to describe because they are less likely to be mediated by words. Thus, people know more than they can tell. It is sometimes easy to explain the explicit knowledge that rules encode, but all the tacit knowledge that comes from firsthand experience is often difficult to explain. It just "feels" right to do the behavior in ways that have been reinforced in the past. Rules are used in various ways in behavior modification. By helping people learn to use rules for problem solving and self-guidance, behavior modification increases their autonomy and ability to direct their own lives.

QUESTIONS

1. How can knowledge about rules help you formulate clearer ABC rules that could be useful in gaining greater control over your own life?
2. Why can vague rules—such as "The table, Vince"—come to be effective? How does this show the importance of learning in being skillful at rule use? Could a 4-year-old follow that rule?
3. Why do S^Ds from both the rule and context cues influence rule use?
4. Can you imagine a case where a friend says "Do X" and context cues lead you to do the opposite of X? Why would you do the opposite?
5. What is the difference between commands and good advice? How do they both influence us?
6. What is the difference between explicit and implicit rules? If you had $100,000 to invest, would you invest in Pogwash county after hearing an implicit rule about the payoffs?
7. Why do we learn to give rules to others?
8. Why are rule givers sometimes disappointed by the errors they see in the behavior of people who attempt to follow their rules?
9. How does firsthand experience help a rule follower polish behavior first learned from rules? What kind of learning is going on during firsthand experience?
10. Which produces tacit and explicit knowledge: rules or firsthand experience? Why?
11. Why do people know more than they can tell? Why does this tell us that few people learn from rules alone?
12. What reinforcers are there for talking *as if* our behavior were rule governed, even when that is not usually 100% true?
13. How can rules be used in behavior modification?
14. What happens in homes that produce children who can use self-given rules to solve problems and guide their own behavior effectively?

NOTES

1. Vygotsky (1962, 1978); Blanck (1990); Skinner (1991); Berk (1994); Catania (1998); Shimoff and Catania (1998).
2. Skinner (1988); Reese (1989); Vaughan (1989); Danforth, Chase, Dolan, and Joyce (1990); Baum (1995); Hayes and Ju (1998).
3. Skinner (1969); Keller (1991).
4. Abbreviated rules—such as "Smile" or "Stop"—are much the same as prompts (Chapter 11).
5. Skinner (1957, 1989a,b); Hayes, Zettle, and Rosenfarb (1989).
6. Staats (1968); Skinner (1969, 1989a,b); Schutte and Hopkins (1970); Ferster, Culbertson, and Boren (1975); Nau, Van Houten, Rolider, and Jonah (1993); Horne and Lowe (1996).
7. Karen (1974, p. 123); Stokes, Osnes, and Guevremont (1987); Schlinger (1993).

8. Olinger and Epstein (1991).

9. Ferster et al. (1975); Stokes et al. (1987); Schlinger (1993).

10. Skinner (1969, pp. 148–149).

11. Mahoney and Thoresen (1974); Meichenbaum and Cameron (1974); Poppen (1989); Kazdin (1994); Martin and Pear (1996); Watson and Tharp (1997); Parkinson and Totterdell (1999).

12. Kohlenberg et al. (1991); Schmitt (1998).

13. Skinner (1969, pp. 157–159).

14. Crowley and Siegler (1999).

15. Martens, Bradley, and Eckert (1997).

16. Skinner (1969, p. 168).

17. Skinner (1969, pp. 139–171); Hineline and Wanchisen (1989); Michael and Bernstein (1991).

18. Skinner (1967, pp. 166–171); Reese (1989).

19. Mischel (1968, 1981).

20. Skinner (1969); Baldwin and Baldwin (1978); Reese (1989).

21. Intuitive knowledge is not always correct (McCloskey, 1983). Of course, explicit knowledge is not always correct either (Wulfert, Dougher, & Greenway, 1991); but it is easier to locate and correct errors in explicit knowledge than in intuitive (that is, tacit) knowledge (Skinner, 1969, p. 167).

22. Polanyi (1960).

23. Goffman (1959) and Skinner (1969, p. 152) have observed that people will go to great lengths to cover up the fact that deliberate planning (rules) and extensive practice were involved in polishing a given behavior. Potter's (1948, 1951) advice clearly reflects that people who can hide their prior rule use and practice are likely to be "one up" on the person who cannot.

24. Polanyi (1960); Skinner (1969, p. 150); Lieberman (2000).

25. Bower (1998); Klein (1998).

26. Horner et al. (1991); Keller (1991); Hayes and Ju (1998).

27. Heiman and LoPiccolo (1988); Hayes, Kohlenberg, and Melancon (1989); Poppen (1989); Zilbergeld (1992); Greenspan (1995); Latham (1996).

28. Logue (1995); Watson and Tharp (1997).

29. Bloom (1985); Brigham (1989); Berk (1994).

30. Taylor and O'Reilly (1997).

Schedules

LUCK CAN CHANGE YOUR LIFE

You put a dollar bill in a change-making machine and four quarters come out. Behavior is quickly followed by the reinforcer and you are happy to have the change. Some machines produce very predictable schedules of reinforcement—one buck in and four quarters out—and these are easy to live with because they allow us to plan ahead and predict the consequences of our actions. But not all aspects of life and schedules of reinforcement are so clear-cut. Some schedules involve random events that can toss our behavior toward good or bad.

Ms. V is a compulsive gambler. It wrecked her marriage and drained her wallet long ago. Her kids don't like her because she is always out of money—and borrowing money from them—waiting for the next big win that she hopes will give her all the cash she needs to escape her current mess. Ms. V is one of 1.8 million U.S. adults who is a pathological gambler.[1]

How did Ms. V become a compulsive gambler? The answers lie in the schedules of reinforcement located in her past learning environments. In high school, one of V's boyfriends liked to bet the ponies and she went along one day for the heck of it. She bet $20 on a filly named "Flo" and won $480. What a rush! Luck brought her a giant reinforcer without much effort—with no "downside" in sight. Her boyfriend was excited, too. V saved the money and went back to the track several times over the next weeks—

sometimes alone, sometimes with her boyfriend—making more $20 bets. Most lost. A few made small wins. But V found that betting was exciting, and she liked the rush of sensory stimulation when her horse took one of the front positions. Especially exciting was the high of seeing her favorite filly forging into first place.

When V's $480 was about half gone, she bet five times more than usual on a long shot with big odds. No one expected "High Fives" to win, but V put down $100 on a hunch. "High Fives" started slowly but gradually picked up the pace, passed horse after horse, and won by a nose. What a fantastic race! V walked away with $6,100 in her wallet! Racetracks and other gambling places are noisy and exciting environments that contain schedules of reinforcement that can hook some people on betting: When people have several big wins during the early months of gambling, they can be drawn powerfully toward gambling. Some people—such as Ms. V—stay hooked on the ponies even when they have fewer big wins than in the early "lucky" period.[2] Early periods of generous reinforcement can have major effects on our later behavioral decisions.[3]

Our physical and social environments are the sources of the schedules of reinforcement that affect our behavior. You put a dollar in a change-making machine and four quarters come out—most of the time. If the machine fails to give you enough change, you complain and your critical feedback helps assure that defective machines get repaired or disappear from our environment. Thus, we can affect our environments and the schedules of reinforcement and punishment they impose on us. Knowledge about behavior principles can help us understand how schedules work and how we can fix schedules that rob us of optimal outcomes.

THE EVER-PRESENT EFFECTS OF SCHEDULES

Although we have seen in earlier chapters that consequences modify behavior, we now focus on an important subtlety: Behavior is not always followed by reinforcement or punishment. *The timing, spacing, and randomness of consequences can have dramatic effects on behavior.*

Schedules of reinforcement describe the timing, spacing, and variability of the reinforcers that follow operant behavior. Most schedules of reinforcement lie somewhere in our environment. On Monday a salesman may give his presentation to ten customers and be reinforced by having three people buy his product. However, the next day he may give a slightly different pitch to ten different customers and make only one sale. The schedule of reinforcement on Monday was three times more rewarding than that on Tuesday, and this affects behavior—inclining the salesman to return to Monday's presentation on Wednesday. There are schedules of punishment, too. *Schedules of punishment* describe the timing, spacing, and variability of the punishers that follow operant behavior. Most schedules of punishment lie somewhere in the external environment. In some towns, speeders are picked up each and every time they exceed the speed limits; but in other towns, arrests are made less frequently, and speeders may be punished only 1 time in 20 that they break the law. In which town would you risk breaking the speed limits?

Many schedules are determined by our physical and social environments. Change-making machines reward you every time you put in money (if they are in good working order); but slot machines may reward you only once each 5 to 15 times you play. The police determine whether drivers are arrested every time they speed or merely one time in 20. *Some schedules are determined by our own behavior.* Jake rewards himself every time he makes a good tennis play by thinking words such as "Nice job!" but Jenn rarely rewards herself by thinking such positive words.

Schedules are among the most powerful determinants of behavior.[4] *All reinforcers and punishers are embedded in one schedule or another; therefore, schedule effects are ever present.* There are many types of schedules, and each one has its own characteristic effects on behavior. In addition, any behavior can be under the control of several schedules, and the effects of these schedules can interact and influence each other. Schedule effects also interact with the effects created by differential reinforcement, shaping, models, prompts, and rules—contributing to the complexity, variety, and interest of the behavior we see in everyday life.

This chapter describes the major types of schedules that have been systematically studied, along with their characteristic effects on behavior.

Acquisition and Maintenance

The two broadest and most general types of schedules relate to the acquistion and maintenance of behavior. *When we are learning a behavior, it is on* **acquisition schedules.** *As the behavior becomes well learned, it gradually shifts to* **maintenance schedules,** *or it extinguishes if not adequately reinforced.* Reinforcement is needed for both the acquisition of new behavior and the maintenance of old behavior. Generally, a higher frequency of reinforcement is required to produce the acquisition of new responses than to maintain old responses. Parents give children generous rewards for speaking their early words (in the acquisition phase), but then give fewer rewards for their 5-year-old's fluent speech (in the maintenance phase). Thus, reinforcement is often more conspicuous during acquisition than maintenance. As a result, it sometimes *appears* that well-learned old responses do not even need reinforcement, although this is not true: *Reinforcement is needed during both acquisition and maintenance; otherwise, behavior extinguishes.*

The fact that reinforcement is often less frequent and conspicuous during maintenance misleads some to believe that the maintenance of old behavior is automatic, and not dependent on reinforcement. It is common to hear people say that so-and-so "learned his lesson" or "internalized the values of the group"—as if getting the lesson or the values into the person (the acquisition phase) is the only process needed to explain learned behavior. However, behavior does not remain in a person's active behavior repertoire unless there continue to be reinforcers that maintain the frequency of the response. Without reinforcement, behavior extinguishes.

Consider the example of personal hygiene—a behavior we acquire early in life. Once learned, does it require reinforcement to be maintained? During childhood toilet training, we all learn (or "internalize") hygienic practices. The praise and punishment that parents use in toilet training make it quite obvious that acquiring toilet control depends on reinforcement and punishment. Once a child acquires hygienic habits, they *appear* to be rather automatic. But are they? What would happen to behavioral maintenance if all social reinforcers were removed?

A study of college students during their summer jobs demonstrates what can happen to hygienic behavior when maintenance schedules are changed to have no social rewards for toilet control.[5] The students were working as fish wardens—watching for illegal fishing—along the rivers of Alaska. Each warden was dropped at an inlet to live and work alone for the summer. When the wardens first made camp, they usually set up a latrine at a respectable distance from their tent, so that the latrine was out of sight and private. For the first several days or weeks, the wardens went to the latrines to relieve themselves, much as one would expect from people who had learned good hygienic practices. However, walking to the latrine took effort, and no one was around to provide social reinforcement for maintaining hygienic practices. By the end of summer, the fish wardens no longer left camp to relieve themselves, even though the buildup of excrement near their tents resulted in strong odors and poor hygiene. One of the first civilized habits we acquire in childhood can be lost in short order if social reinforcement is removed. Upon returning to civilization, the fish wardens resumed good hygienic practices, due to the return of maintenance schedules of social reinforcement.

People living in mental hospitals and old age homes sometimes begin to urinate and defecate in their clothing.[6] When staff members give them more social attention—a powerful reinforcer—for this behavior than for practicing good hygienic control, the elderly lose toilet skills faster than when the staff rewards good elimination control. Again it is the maintenance schedules that affect the continuation of behaviors learned years ago. *Clearly, maintenance schedules are as important as the more obvious schedules of reinforcement seen in the acquisition of new behavior.* All the remaining schedules discussed in this chapter can be seen during both acquisition and maintenance.

RATIO SCHEDULES

There are two types of ratio schedules in which *a certain number of responses* must occur before the last response produces one reinforcer or one punisher. Both *fixed ratio* and *variable ratio* schedules are common in everyday life.

Fixed Ratio Schedules[7]

*Whenever a behavior is reinforced after a fixed number of repetitions, the schedule is called a **fixed ratio (FR) schedule.*** If every single response is reinforced, the behavior is on an FR 1 schedule, indicating that the fixed ratio is one response per reinforcer. When there must be two responses before reinforcement, the behavior is on an FR 2 schedule. FR 10 indicates that ten responses must occur before reinforcement. The ratio number can be any number, but different ratios have different effects on behavior.

FR 1 schedules are also called **continuous reinforcement (CRF) schedules,** because rewards are continuously available every time the target behavior appears. People learn quickly when each correct response is reinforced, which makes FR 1 a powerful tool for speeding the acquisition of new behavior. If parents want their child to learn to be polite, they will model politeness and then reward the child every time the child is polite. Young children who receive loving words, caring smiles, or tender touches each time they are polite or considerate acquire these skills much faster than children who are rewarded less frequently or less consistently. Parents who value seeing their children make rapid progress often learn to use the continuous reinforcement of FR 1 schedules because they—the parents—are rewarded by seeing the rapid progress their children make with continuous reinforcement.

Skillful teachers also learn the importance of giving continuous reinforcement during the early phases of behavioral acquisition. The continuous use of positive words and enthusiastic smiles makes learning maximally reinforcing. When flight instructors watch new students use the controls in the cockpit, they can help their students learn quickly by using continuous reinforcement—"That's right," "Good," "Well done"—for every correct response. A tennis coach who gives positive feedback to novices for each and every good play is also providing the best schedule of reinforcement for producing rapid learning.

In addition, FR 1 schedules continue to produce high and constant rates of responding even after a behavior is established. Some factories use an FR 1 schedule called "piecework," in which employees are paid for each piece of work that they finish. Thus, employees working for a dollar per piece of work can earn $140 on the day that they finish 140 pieces, but earn only $125 on a day in which they finish 125 pieces. Most people respond by working rapidly on this type of FR 1 schedule:[8] After all, they can increase their salary by 10% by increasing their speed by 10%. Speeding up the pace of activity sometimes makes the work more stimulating, challenging, and exciting,[9] but it can also create considerable strain. Unions and labor groups usually oppose the use of FR 1 schedules because they fear that once workers increase their output, management will cut the amount paid per piece, which would leave the employees working harder for less.[10]

FR 1 schedules of punishment produce rapid response suppression and maintain low rates of responding. Parents who punish their child every time the child runs into the street are more likely to suppress the behavior quickly than if they punished the response once every fifth time (FR 5) or once every tenth time (FR 10). A flight instructor who criticizes a student for each error is more likely to suppress these sloppy and dangerous responses quickly than if punishment were less frequent.

Many nonsocial reinforcers and punishers also appear on FR 1 schedules. Every time children balance their bikes correctly, they are rewarded by the fun of riding, and each time they lose balance, they are punished by a fall. Every time people get their fingers too close to fire, they get burned. Learning proceeds rapidly! Many skills learned from nonsocial FR 1 schedules are acquired quickly and maintained all through life due to the strong control these schedules have over behavior.

Although FR 1 schedules are the most common fixed ratio schedule in everyday life, we also encounter FR schedules with ratios higher than one. Whenever two or more responses are needed to complete an activity, behavior is on an FR schedule that is not FR 1. "Mix six eggs and three cups of flour" involves an FR 6 schedule and an FR 3 schedule. When changing a wheel on a car, we have to remove the wheel's five lug bolts, which involves an FR 5 schedule. Work on assembly lines often involves repeating the same number of responses over and over—such as connecting nine leads to each automatic transmission (FR 9), sewing six buttons onto each blouse (FR 6), welding four seams on each casing (FR 4).

    *FR schedules with high ratio numbers tend to produce high rates of responding until the reinforcer is reached, at which time there is often a pause, called a **postreinforcement pause.*** For example, a precision drill press operator may have to finish drilling 10 accurately placed holes in a custom engine block to earn each $10. The master machinist is on an FR 10 schedule where every 10th accurate response is reinforced by $10 earned. On this FR 10 schedule, workers will usually drill all 10 holes at a steady pace, then stop for a postreinforcement pause at the completion of the 10th response. *Generally, the higher the ratio, the longer the postreinforcement pause.* If a worker had to drill 50 precision holes to finish one piece of work, the FR 50 schedule would tend to produce a steady rate of responding while drilling all 50 holes, then a long pause at the end, before beginning the next piece. Figure 13–1 shows that the postreinforcement pause after the 50th response on an FR 50 schedule is longer than the postreinforcement pause after the 10th response on an FR 10 schedule. Once the post reinforcement pause is over, people tend to return to a high and constant rate of behavior. This produces cumulative records like those seen in Figure 13–1, steep and steady rises interspersed with pauses that are longer when FR numbers are higher. (Fig. 13–1 also shows behavior on an FR 2 schedule, which shows very steady behavioral output since postreinforcement pauses are minimal.)

    As the ratio number on FR schedules increases, a person has to work longer to earn one reinforcement. *Increasing the ratio number is called **stretching** or **thinning the schedule of reinforcement,*** *since there are fewer rewards as ratio numbers rise.* After be-

FIGURE 13–1   **The cumulative record of responses on FR 2, FR 10, and FR 50 schedules. Each reinforcement is marked by a slash. Note that the postreinforcement pauses become longer on the thinner schedules (with higher FR numbers).**

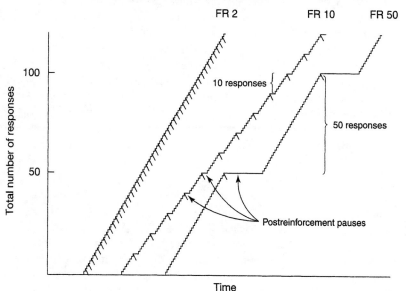

havior modifiers start behavioral acquisition with generous schedules of reinforcement, such as FR 1 or FR 2, they may systematically "fade out" the reinforcers as learning advances; and this involves stretching or thinning the schedule of reinforcement. Typically, as FR schedules become thinner and contain fewer rewards, people work less diligently and take longer postreinforcement pauses. *When FR ratios become so high that the costs of doing the behavior exceed the rewards, people pause and do not resume the activity— unless enough new rewards are added to tip the cost-reward ratio so rewards exceed costs.* You can ask a child to count to 20 and expect 20 responses as the child completes the entire FR 20 schedule, but what if you ask the child to count to 200, or 2000? As the FR number rises, larger numbers of responses must be made to earn one reward. An FR 2000 schedule that rewards a person for counting to 2000 without errors is a thin schedule of reinforcement and may not produce much behavior—unless the reward were large, perhaps $200 in cash.

Punishment can also occur on FR schedules other than FR 1. One person may get a "second chance" (FR 2) before receiving punishment. Another person may get "three strikes and you're out" (FR 3). *In general, punishment becomes less effective in suppressing behavior as the ratio number increases.*[11] If you could make 2000 errors before being fired from a good job, you might not pay much attention to errors until your boss reported that you had reached 1900.

Variable Ratio Schedules

*Whenever a behavior is reinforced after a variable number of responses, the schedule is called a **variable ratio (VR) schedule.*** It may take an average of three twists to unscrew bottle caps, but some come off with one twist and others take five. Bottle-cap-twisting is on a VR 3 schedule, averaging three turns per bottle, but varying from bottle to bottle. Variability is a common feature of everyday life, thus variable ratio schedules are more common than fixed ratio schedules. It may take 20 swings with an ax to fell one tree and 60 swings to fell the next. Twenty sentences may convince one listener to sign your petition for political action, but 60 sentences may be needed to persuade the next person. Parents usually do not reinforce each and every desired behavior that their child does (FR 1); nor do they keep precise counts and reinforce only one behavior in six (FR 6). Instead, their patterns of reinforcement may vary considerably, although they may *average* one reinforcer for every four desired responses (VR 4).

When one person is teaching another a new skill, it is common to see the "teacher" begin with FR 1 schedules of reinforcement to produce rapid early learning, then switch to variable ratio (VR) schedules as the "student" gains competence. A flight instructor may give continuous reinforcement (FR 1) as a beginning student learns early flying skills. However, as the new pilot begins to master the essential skills, the instructor is likely to stop using FR 1 schedules and shift to VR schedules, giving a reinforcer for every second, third, or fifth correct response. The instructor is "stretching the schedule" in a variable manner, thinning the number of reinforcers given for correct responses to VR 3. Next, the flight instructor might stretch the schedule to VR 10 in which the number of responses needed to produce reinforcement might vary from 5 to 15, but it can be any other number—as long as it averages 10. Why does the instructor thin the schedule? It takes less effort to give intermittent reinforcement than to give continuous reinforcement. Naturally, the teacher only thins the schedule once it is obvious that the student is learning how to fly without making major errors.

VR schedules are quite adequate for reinforcing behavior once a person moves from the acquisition phase to the maintenance phase. In fact, we will see that VR schedules are better than FR 1 for producing behavioral persistence and resistance to extinction. However, people stop doing many kinds of behavior if VR schedules are thinned too quickly or too far.

In social interaction, we do not always tell other people when they have chosen their words well, but every once in a while someone says, "That's a colorful choice of words, Marcie." This intermittent use of reinforcement may not provide enough reinforcers to produce rapid acquisition of colorful word use, but it is adequate to maintain the response in the behavior repertoire of people who have already developed advanced verbal skills. Friendly compliments on any of a person's skills—how they dress, dance, treat others—help maintain the skills, even if the reinforcers are few and far between.

VR schedules usually produce more variable response patterns than FR schedules do. An FR 10 schedule tends to produce ten rapid responses followed by a postreinforcement pause.[12] A VR 10 schedule also produces behavior patterns that contain pauses, but the pauses are briefer and more randomly interspersed among the responses. If a movie reviewer has to write 5, 10, or 15 pages before having a one page movie review accepted by a magazine, the writer is on a VR 10 schedule. The next reinforcer is somewhat unpredictable, but never too far way. During February, the writer may have great luck and have several articles published after writing only 6, 8, or 9 pages, and the generous burst of rewards may lead to a very different pattern of pausing than in April. On variable schedules, the frequency of reinforcement can change over time. During April, the writer may have to write 11, 13, or 15 pages before the next one page review is accepted, and the writer may slow down during these thinner variations on the VR 10 schedule.

As shown in Figure 13–2, response rates are usually quite high and there are few postreinforcement pauses when the variable reinforcers come frequently (e.g., VR 10), but the responding can drop off to sporadic low rates when the variable schedule becomes too stretched out—too thin (e.g., VR 75). If a writer hears encouraging feedback on a VR 75 schedule, in which positive feedback comes only after writing perhaps 70 or 80 pages, the rate of writing may become quite irregular, and the writer may produce only a few pages at a time on a very unpredictable basis. The writer's low productivity results from the high ratio of costs to rewards.

Numerous other activities are on VR schedules of reinforcement—such as hunting, fishing, sales, begging, card games, gambling, and scientific research. There is no fixed relationship between the number of responses and reinforcement. A salesperson may have to talk to 2, 4, 10, or 20 customers before making the next sale. A gambler may have to make 3, 5, or 9 bets before getting a winner. In all VR schedules, people with the skills to keep the ratio numbers low will earn more reinforcers and show higher rates of responding than people with fewer skills. People with the skills needed to pick winning horses are usually much more devoted to betting on the horses than people who lose almost all the

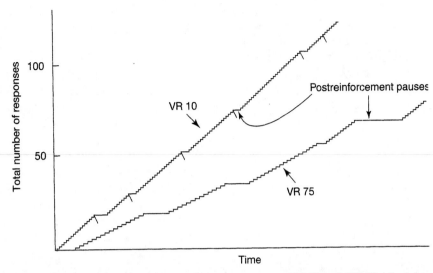

FIGURE 13–2   **The cumulative record of responses on VR 10 and VR 75 schedules. Each reinforcement is marked by a slash. Note the long postreinforcement pause and slow rate of responding on the thinner VR 75 schedule.**

time (unless the losers are finding other rewards in betting, such as being with friends or avoiding work).[13] In contrast, many of us develop "risk aversion" for those activities where the costs outweigh the rewards—such as gambling—because the risk of failure and loss is too great.[14] But when a state's lottery jackpot exceeds several million dollars, even some risk-averse people take a gamble.[15]

Punishment often appears on VR schedules. You may be stung once in a while when you try to shoo bees out of your car, making it something like a VR 25 or VR 50 schedule, depending on how lucky or skillful you are. VR punishment is less effective than FR 1 punishment of the same intensity, but it can still suppress behavior. A study on preschool children showed that VR 4 punishment was almost as effective as FR 1 punishment, and it had the advantages of (1) requiring less effort by the teachers and (2) being less aversive for the students (who were punished only one fourth as often as on FR 1).[16] Speeders do not get arrested every time they exceed the speed limit; but a speeder who got a series of hefty traffic tickets on a VR 20 schedule might eventually stop speeding. In general, a high cost-benefit ratio—with many punishments per reward—tends to inhibit behavior more than lower ratios of cost to benefits.[17]

INTERVAL SCHEDULES

Two main types of schedules are based on time intervals. Both fixed interval and variable interval schedules are common in everyday life.[18]

Fixed Interval Schedules

*There are many circumstances in which behavior cannot be reinforced or punished until a fixed interval of time has elapsed. After that fixed interval, the first response is reinforced, or punished. These are **fixed interval (FI) schedules**.*[19] If the interval is 1 minute, the schedule is designated as FI 1 minute. If the interval is 1 day, the schedule is designated as FI 1 day. The interval can be any length—years or fractions of a second. The person who finds a nightly game show on TV to be very exciting and reinforcing is on an FI 1 day schedule. Every 24 hours, turning on the TV after the fixed interval has elapsed is reinforced by seeing the show.

Not unexpectedly, the game-show lover learns to turn on the TV at about the same time each night. Fixed interval schedules are often coupled with a **limited hold,** *a limited period in which reinforcers are available.* The first appropriate response after the interval has elapsed is reinforced, but if the appropriate response does not occur during the limited hold period, reinforcement ceases to be available. If a game-show lover's favorite game comes on at 7:00 P.M. and ends at 7:30, there is a 30-minute limited hold. After the limited hold has ended, turning on the TV is no longer reinforced by seeing the game show. The limited hold usually conditions people to turn on the TV during the hold period because the rewards are available only during the hold period.

Fixed interval schedules tend to produce patterns of responding in which responses are timed to occur near the point where reinforcement first becomes available. When two lovers—C and D—live in different cities and C phones D precisely each night at 9 P.M., D may notice that as 9 o'clock rolls around, there is a tendency to hang around the phone, make sure roommates are not on the phone, and pick up after the first ring. When important reinforcers are timed precisely, our behavior becomes timed, too. Obviously, clocks and watches help people time responses closer to the crucial fixed interval than would be possible without these mechanical aids.

Because the first appropriate response after a fixed time interval is reinforced on fixed interval (FI) schedules, increasing the interval length usually increases the time gap between clusters of responses and lowers the total number of responses. Halley's comet returns once each 76 years, and few people look for it between its rare visits.

When we do not have clocks or calendars to measure time intervals precisely, we often cannot time our behavior precisely. If your roommate "R" never wears a watch or bothers with clocks, R may not know precisely when a nightly 9 P.M. phone call will come from his girlfriend, with the rewards of an amorous conversation. People who ignore clocks—and animals, too—tend to show a unique form of behavior described as *scalloped-shaped curves* in their cumulative records, as is seen in the J-shaped curve in Figure 13–3. R starts to look at the phone around 8 P.M. and glances with increased frequency at the phone during the next hour. Figure 13–3 shows R making some glances toward the phone around 8 P.M., and the number of glances becomes more frequent over the hour before 9 P.M., creating one scallop-shaped curve on each evening. In contrast, people who regularly use clocks need not glance toward the phone much before 9 P.M. since they can rely on the S^Ds of their timepiece to regulate their behavior precisely.

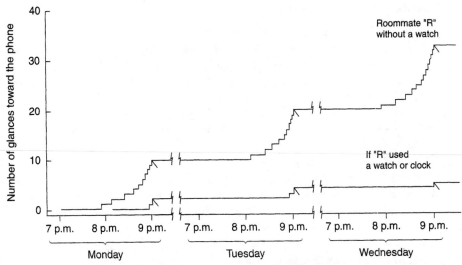

FIGURE 13–3   The cumulative record shows how many times roommate "R" (who does not use watches) glanced at the phone on three evenings while waiting for a 9 P.M. phone call from his girlfriend. Note the "scalloped-shaped" curves. If "R" regulated his behavior with a watch, his glances would have been timed more closely to 9 P.M. (and fewer in number). The slash marks show when a glance was rewarded by the arrival of the 9 P.M. phone call.

Variable Interval Schedules

In everyday life, many interval schedules are not as perfectly fixed as the schedules of TV programs, election days, or the return of Halley's comet. Life is filled with variability. *On variable interval (VI) schedules, the first appropriate response after a variable time interval has elapsed is reinforced.* Mrs. Q's mail carrier usually comes around 10 A.M., but the timing may vary from 9 to 11 A.M. This is a VI 24-hour schedule—with intervals averaging 24 hours, and some variations being an hour shorter or longer than the average.

Variable interval schedules produce more variable behavior and higher rates of responding than FI schedules do. If the mail came precisely at 10 o'clock each morning (an FI 24-hour schedule), Mrs. Q would never go to the box before 10 A.M., and would make only one trip after 10:00. If Mrs. Q is elderly and finds her mail to be one of her big rewards of the day, she would probably look for and bring in her mail at 10 A.M. or shortly thereafter on most days. A VI 24-hour schedule produces quite different effects. People like Mrs. Q. may start looking out the window for signs of the mail carrier by 9 A.M., because the mail sometimes comes that soon, providing rewards for early looking. Some retired people check the mailbox two or three times before the mail carrier arrives, especially if the mail comes after 10 A.M. Their behavior is less predictable than if the mail came precisely at 10 A.M., because "any time" might be "mail time." In the past, elderly mailbox watchers may have received reinforcers for checking the mail at 9:15, 9:45,

10:30, 10:45, 11:30, and various other times; hence box checking has been rewarded at many different times of day. Because variable responding has been reinforced, VI schedules can produce quite variable and unpredictable behavior. Some parents reward and punish their child on VI schedules, timed according to daily variations in the parents' multiple tasks and free time, rather than contingent on the child's misbehavior. Not surprisingly, this method of child rearing produces variable results.

When intervals are short, VI schedules can produce high rates of responding, because just about any time can be reward time. Thus, VI schedules can be effective for maintaining behavior (top of Fig. 13–4). If buses ran at frequent but variable intervals (VI 5-min), people might look several times a minute to see if a bus was coming. However, if the buses only came every 1 or 1.5 hours (VI 75-min), few people would look for the bus during the half hour after the last bus, and looking would only gradually increase in frequency as the time passed (bottom of Fig. 13–4).

FIGURE 13–4   The cumulative record of responses on VI 5-minute and VI 75-minute schedules. Each reinforcement is marked by a slash. Notice the high and steady rate of responding on the VI 5-minute schedule. In contrast, the long VI 75-minute schedule produces a slow initial rate of responding with a gradual acceleration as the variable interval reward is ever more likely to arrive.

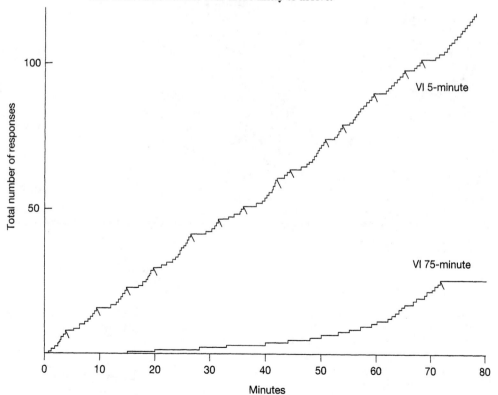

A variable interval schedule may be linked with a ***limited hold,*** *a limited period in which reinforcers are available.* An elderly couple may like to chat with the neighbor children when the children are outside. The children may come out on variable schedules and be around for only a few minutes before heading down the street. If the elderly people peek out the window frequently, they may see when the children are around and be able to initiate a rewarding interaction. Because the children usually leave after being outside for a few minutes, the seniors have to check more often and respond more quickly when the children are present than if the children stayed in their yard. Thus, combining variable interval with limited hold schedules increases the rate of responding compared with either (1) a fixed interval or (2) a condition without limited hold.

When refugees are escaping a war-torn city or disaster area, it is hard to know when the next boat or plane will arrive. Each boat or plane is on limited hold because it fills up rapidly and leaves no room for additional passengers. Most refugees learn quickly to be alert and check frequently to see if a new boat or plane has arrived—and to approach it quickly when it does.

SCHEDULE EFFECTS

Figure 13–5 shows the typical cumulative records produced on the four types of schedules we discussed in the preceding sections. All the cumulative records show examples where the schedules have not been stretched so far that behavior is declining due to extinction. *It is clear that variable schedules (VR and VI) tend to produce faster responding—with fewer pauses—than do fixed schedules.* Fixed schedules are interrupted with longer

FIGURE 13–5   These five cumulative records show typical response patterns on VR, VI, FR, and FI schedules (if they have not been stretched too far). Each reinforcement is marked by a slash. On FI schedules, people can make many fewer responses if they use watches or clocks.

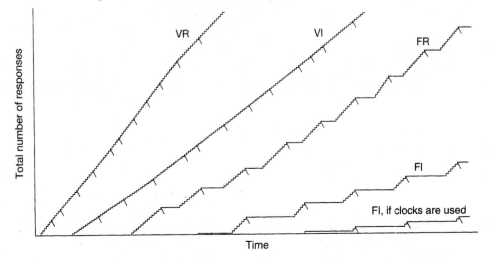

postreinforcement pauses that reduce overall rates of responding. On variable schedules that have not been overly thinned, there are numerous occasions in which a few fast responses produce several reinforcers in rapid succession, and these periods of frequent reinforcement for fast responding cause people to respond at high rates. After several wins in a row on the slot machines, people learn that fast responding can be very rewarding, and they continue rapid responding, even if the last 15 plays have not produced a single win.

In addition, ratio schedules usually produce more rapid responding than interval schedules, as you can see from their steeper slopes. On all ratio schedules, the faster you respond, the more rewards you obtain. This is not true of interval schedules, where time intervals determine when reinforcement next becomes possible. Turning on the TV set six times a day does not make a 7 P.M. game show come any sooner; therefore, rapid responding is extinguished on long interval schedules. People who use clocks can minimize their responding to a few accurately timed behaviors.

Behavioral Contrast

Behavioral contrast describes the increased or decreased response rates that occur when people shift from one reinforcement schedule to another one with more or less rewards.[20] There are two main types of behavioral contrast. *First, when people switch from a thin schedule of rewards to a highly reinforcing one, they often show* **positive contrast:** *They increase their total output and work harder than people who have been on the highly reinforcing schedule for a long time.* For example, when poor immigrants arrive in the United States—where their labors often earn much greater wealth than was possible in the old country—they usually work much harder than they did before. *By contrast,* wages seem very high in the United States, compared with the old country; and doing extra work is rewarded with surprising wealth. The extra work now—as compared with lower levels of work done in the old country a couple years before—is the *behavioral contrast.* In any job, where the work and pay schedules are identical for both immigrants and people born in the United States, immigrants tend to work harder because the rewards are so much greater than in the old country, where they had been on a thin schedule. (After enough time in the United States, many immigrants slow down and work at the same speed as the people born in the United States.)

Second, when people are suddenly shifted from a very generous schedule to a very thin one, they often show **negative contrast:** *They often slow their behavioral output and do less than people who have been on a thin schedule for a long time.* When well-paid workers are forced to take a big cut in salary or forced to switch to unrewarding jobs, they often stop working or slow down significantly. If the workers cannot negotiate pay increases or find better jobs, they may eventually accommodate to working on thin schedules of reinforcement, but they have more bad feelings about this than people who were always on thin schedules (such as workers in poor nations often are).

Both positive and negative behavioral contrast are seen most clearly in the time period when people are first shifted to more or less generous schedules. If they continue on the new schedules, the frequency of their behavior usually begins to approach the rate shown by other people who have been on that schedule for a long time.

Behavioral Momentum

It has been hypothesized that behavior can be thought of as having momentum, much as moving objects have momentum and tend to keep going once started in motion.[21] Once an operant behavior has been reinforced for a long time and become a high probability response in certain S^D contexts, the behavior tends to stay strong, even if schedules change.

Behavioral momentum *is the tendency for behavior to continue, unchanged, when environmental conditions change.* If Fred grows up in a house where his dad and two brothers shout at the TV during sports events, he sees TV shouting modeled over and over. When he learns to join in, he gets happy grins from three people he loves. After years, his TV shouting develops so much behavioral momentum that his college girlfriend is amazed that she cannot convince him to stop TV shouting—or at least tone it down. Even if she tries to punish the behavior or put it on extinction, Fred's TV shouting continues. In common parlance, Fred has learned a habit he cannot easily change. For him, shouting at the TV seems so natural that he cannot imagine doing anything else.

Behavior with momentum is resistant to change, even when environmental conditions change. Sometimes lovers get into the habit of teasing and picking on each other. At first it is fun and exhilarating because it generates sensory stimulation: The other person responds in unpredictable ways. As their teasing gains behavioral momentum, they may find it harder and harder to stop the momentum of behaviors, even though too much teasing can hurt their friendship with a thousand small cuts and barbs. If their natural pestering has too much behavioral momentum, they may keep on teasing long after it ceases being fun.

Behavioral momentum has positive forms, too. Some children learn to be polite and thoughtful early in life, if these behaviors are associated with generous levels of reinforcement over long periods of time. By age 15 such young people feel that it is only natural to be kind to others, ask questions of them, and show concern. Even if they take jobs that would anger others, their politeness has so much behavioral momentum that they find it easy to be kind and considerate during tough and painful times.

When we see people persist at any given behavior—even when they fail to obtain rewarding results—we see the power of behavioral momentum to keep people going in face of extinction (the absence of rewards). Some children show amazing behavioral persistence—or stick-to-itiveness—when working on jigsaw puzzles. Why? Perhaps they began with simple puzzles where it is easy to put each piece in the correct location after one, two, or three attempts: This is a VR 2 schedule that provides rather high levels of reinforcement for early learning. Over time, parents may bring their child puzzles of *gradually* increasing difficulty. As the puzzles become more complex, Timmy may have to make 5, 10, or 15 attempts at placing a piece before finding the correct position (VR 10). As Timmy gradually accommodates to these schedules of partial reinforcement, he learns to keep working at a puzzle even when the last 5, 10, or 15 attempts at placing a piece have failed. After months of puzzle play, Timmy learns that eventually each piece will fit in somewhere. "Sticking to the task inevitably leads to reinforcement, if you just keep trying." Sometimes it only takes one or two tries; sometimes it takes 20 or 25 tries. But in the end, there is always success: Persistence pays off. After children have learned to enjoy the sensory stimulation of hunting for solutions to each step of solving puzzles, they often show an amazing persistence in working puzzles, trying dozens of pieces in every possible location, even though most of their moves result in failure. Variable schedules help people learn **behavioral persistence**—or stick-to-itiveness—how to persevere in the face of failure. Their behavior shows strong behavioral momentum, continuing even though successes are few and far between.[22]

Sometimes behavioral momentum, stick-to-itiveness, and persistence are admirable; sometimes they are nuisances. It depends on whether the behavior in question is desirable or undesirable. We usually consider it admirable when a person is persistent at desirable behavior. A child who does not give up on difficult homework problems may eventually solve the problems, thereby learning more than another child who gave up before finding the solution. The minority group leader who keeps fighting for the rights of his or her people—in spite of frequent failure or only limited success—is admired for dedication and determination. The diplomat who keeps working to reach a peaceful settlement between hostile nations—and does not give up in spite of countless failures—may eventually negotiate a peace treaty that averts war and saves countless lives. In all areas of life, there are many admirable people who have the behavioral persistence to withstand long periods of failure and eventually accomplish important tasks, when others would have quit trying long before.

When people learn persistence in doing undesirable behavior, others may lament. A little boy who whimpers and whines for hours at a time shows behavioral momentum that may seem incomprehensible to his parents, driving them to frustration. Many people retain "childish behaviors"—such as whining, pouting, crying, doing self-pity, being a nuisance—well into adulthood: Behaviors that received strong reinforcement for many years during childhood can develop so much behavioral momentum that they are hard to stop even years later. Although childish behaviors often cause parents to give their child abundant social attention and social reinforcers, immature behavior often prevents people from developing high quality relationships in their teens and adult years. After several evenings out with a guy who throws tantrums and anger fits, Paula decides to look for a more mature partner. Her next companion engages in hours of self-pity. She is so happy when she finally discovers a lover who can communicate and relate without doing childish behaviors.

DIFFERENTIAL REINFORCEMENT SCHEDULES

Several types of schedules are based on differential reinforcement. In all cases, actions that are rewarded increase in frequency, and the unrewarded behaviors decrease in frequency.

Differential Reinforcement of High Rates of Responding

*When a behavior must be done rapidly to produce reinforcement, the behavior is on a schedule of **differential reinforcement for high rates of responding (DRH)**.*[23] Sprinters and racing bicyclists are on DRH schedules to run or pedal as fast as they can, if they are to be rewarded by victory. Lawyers who race against the clock to document a case before court convenes are on DRH schedules. Police, fire, and other emergency workers often must work fast in order to be rewarded by success.

All DRH schedules modify behavior by reinforcing high rates of responding while either extinguishing or punishing slow rates. For example, various fast-drying paints, cements, and glues impose DRH schedules on their users. When people first work with a fast-drying cement, their original response rates may show considerable variability, with some slow and some fast actions (shown by the broken line in Fig. 13–6). However, response rates slower than rate X are punished, because the cement sets before it has been worked into the correct shape. Hence, these slow rates are suppressed (downward arrows in Fig. 13–6). High response rates, on the other hand, are reinforced because they allow the user to shape the cement into suitable forms before the material becomes unworkable. These rapid rates are reinforced (upward arrows in Fig. 13–6). Thus, after experience with DRH, people learn to respond quickly (the solid curve in Fig. 13–6).

Differential Reinforcement of Low Rates of Responding

When a behavior must be performed slowly to produce reinforcement, the behavior is on a schedule of **differential reinforcement for low rates of responding (DRL).**[24] Creating fine art or beautifully finished wood work often requires slow performance rates in order to avoid errors and produce rewarding results. People who drink alcohol too fast at parties may come under DRL schedules: If they drink too fast (the broken line in Fig. 13–7), they get drunk and sometimes do things they later regret. If drinking faster than rate X is frequently punished, high rates of drinking become suppressed (downward arrows in Fig. 13–7). Slow rates of drinking allow the person to enjoy social drinking without getting into trouble. Hence slow rates of sipping are reinforced and become more frequent (upward arrows). If the differential reinforcement of low rates is strong enough (and is not opposed by social rewards for rapid drinking), the person who used to drink too fast will learn to drink more slowly (solid line in Fig. 13–7).

FIGURE 13–6   **DRH schedules cause an increase in behaviors that are faster than rate "X."**

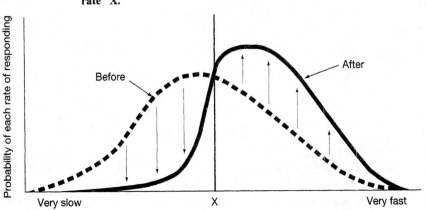

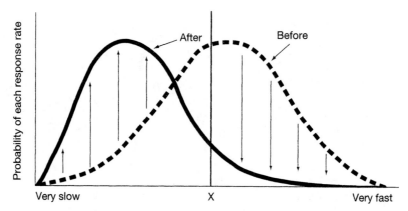

FIGURE 13-7   **DRL schedules cause an increase in behaviors that are slower than rate "X."**

A helpful strategy for weight watchers is to impose a DRL schedule on eating activities.[25] Instead of shoveling in food at a high rate, weight watchers learn to slow down and pause between each bite of food. A sip of water between bites also helps decrease eating rates while filling the stomach with noncaloric intake. By slowing the intake of food, an overweight person avoids cleaning the plate too soon, and thus avoids the S^Ds for taking seconds or thirds.

Pacing Schedules

Pacing schedules are related to DRH and DRL schedules. *On **pacing schedules**, responses must be neither too fast nor too slow: They must be paced at a certain speed in order to be reinforced.* A child who plays jump rope must pace each jump with the rhythm of the rope in order to continue the game. Musicians must pace their playing with the conductor—or with each other—in order to produce beautiful music. Whatever the pace, responding at the specified rate is necessary for reinforcement. Other rates are either punished or not reinforced. Novice music students often play passages too rapidly or too slowly. At first, their teachers reward correct pacing and criticize wrong pacing. Later the sounds of good music reinforce correct pacing and bad sounds punish incorrect pacing. Eventually, music students learn the skills for precise pacing. Punishment suppresses poor pacing (downward arrows in Fig. 13–8), and reinforcement increases the probability of correct pacing (upward arrows).

Differential Reinforcement of Other Behavior

*Whenever a person must abstain from some target behavior in order to attain reinforcers, the schedule is called **differential reinforcement of other behavior (DRO)**.*[26] Doing *anything other* than the target behavior—even sitting quietly—will bring reinforcement. If their teenager continues to show childish behavior, such as whining and pouting, parents

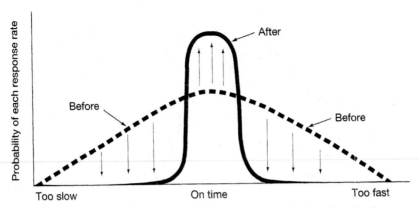

FIGURE 13–8   Pacing schedules lead people to get "in synch" with the pace that is "on time."

can help by using DRO and rewarding *any other* response class besides childish behavior. As long as their teen abstains from childish behavior, the parents are friendly and cheerful. This is DRO, the reinforcement of any behavior *other* than the undesirable behavior, including aggressive and destructive behavior.[27] Even children who do self-injurious behavior (SIB), frequent "habit coughs," or muscular tics can be effectively treated with DRO.[28] Any child who does "strange," "different," or "unusual" behavior is at risk of being teased or shunned by peers. This can have life-long negative effects on the person's development and socialization.

DRO schedules are useful in reducing the frequency of problematic behaviors. If frequent trips to the kitchen result in snacking and gaining unwanted weight, a person might set up rewards for doing any other behavior besides visiting the kitchen. When Aaron feels hungry, he makes a phone call or gets a glass of water from the bathroom. This distracts him from thoughts of snacking, and he is rewarded by his successful avoidance of food because he knows he may see a lower reading on the scale the next day.

There is a subset of DRO, called DRI, that is important because it is especially powerful in suppressing undesirable behaviors. *The **differential reinforcement of incompatible behavior (DRI)** is remarkably powerful in causing target behaviors to disappear.*[29] For example, aggression and bullying are childhood behaviors that many parents and teachers find undesirable. The logic of DRI suggests that we should find alternative behaviors that are incompatible with aggression and bullying: If we reward such incompatible behaviors as cooperative play, sharing and helping others, the reinforcement of prosocial behavior should drive down the frequency of antisocial behavior, since the two response classes are incompatible. Studies show that DRI is very effective at changing bullies and aggressive children into more friendly and cooperative individuals.[30]

In order to reduce his excess weight, Aaron might decide to participate in more athletic activities that keep him outside and away from the kitchen, while completely distracting him from thoughts of eating. Whenever a person has a problematic behavior, it is wise to ask, "What would be some healthy alternatives to that activity?" The more a person fills his or her days with healthy, active, creative, and prosocial behaviors—and rewards these (DRI)—the less time there is for all incompatible behaviors.

Alcoholics Anonymous uses DRI to help alcoholics stay sober. During AA meetings, former drinkers reward each other for learning any new activities or skills that help them avoid drinking. Various drug rehabilitation centers, smoking clinics, and weight-watching groups reward the acquisition and maintenance of competing activities that are incompatible with the unwanted behavior. For example, the Delancey Street drug rehabilitation center in San Francisco rewards its members for doing volunteer work in the community, learning new job skills, teaching the police how to deal with drug addicts, and so forth. These DRI schedules give each person freedom to select whatever competing responses he or she finds most rewarding.

In general, DRI schedules are better than punishment for reducing the frequency of unwanted behavior: DRI gives people positive new alternatives to enjoy instead of merely suppressing undesirable old activities. DRI behaviors tend to distract us from problematic behaviors because they are so different from and incompatible with them.

COMPOUND SCHEDULES

When two or more different schedules are linked together or intermixed, they are called **compound schedules.** Everyday life contains complex and frequently changing patterns of compound schedules that fit in three main categories: *chained, multiple,* and *concurrent schedules.*

Chained schedules *consist of a linear series of schedules, and the end of each link in the chain serves as the S^D that signals the onset of the next schedule.* Cooking often involves chains of schedules. A recipe may specify a chain of three schedules: Add 3 egg whites (FR 3), 5 tablespoons of sugar (FR 5), and beat at high speed (DRH) until they form stiff white peaks. The completion of each schedule in the chain is the S^D to move to the next schedule, chaining all the activities in a linear flow. All the steps lead toward a final reinforcer: something delicious to eat.

Multiple schedules *consist of two or more schedules that appear in cycles or randomized alternations, each cued by a distinctive S^D.* Multiple schedules cause people to alternate between two or more activities. Preparing a dinner often requires the cook to alternate among multiple different tasks. After putting the dessert in the oven, the cook shifts to salad preparation. Ten minutes later the timer on the oven rings, serving as an S^D for removing the dessert and pouring chocolate sauce on it. When this is done, it is time to return to finishing the salad. When we are working under multiple schedules, only one of the multiple schedules is operating at any point in time, and we deal with each one, one at a time.

Concurrent schedules *consist of two or more separate schedules that operate at the same time, allowing a person to switch back and forth at any time.* The person chooses when to alternate activities, rather than having the sequence of activities imposed by the nature of the task—as in chained and multiple schedules. Concurrent schedules leave us room for choices among activities. While painting a canvas, an artist is free to leave any feature of the picture and switch over to work on others at any time. Erin is becoming frustrated with the way the foreground of her self-portrait is developing, so she decides to return to developing the face in greater detail. Maybe she will be able to improve the foreground if she returns to it "fresh" at a later time.

Concurrent Schedules and Choice

People are on concurrent schedules whenever two or more schedules of reinforcement are available at all times, and they can choose how much time they wish to devote to two or more activities that have different patterns of reinforcement. Concurrent schedules—which allow people to switch back and forth freely between different activities—are quite common in everyday life. If you are tired of watching sitcoms, you can switch to CNN for the news or to a sports channel. These and many other choices are open to you all the time. Modern industrialized societies offer us far more choices each day than people in pre-industrial societies could imagine!

An amusement park provides a large number of concurrent schedules of reinforcement: There are many rides and activities from which you can choose. Each activity has its own distinctive kinds of rewards that are separate and independent from the others. For example, the shooting gallery provides a VR 3 schedule if you hit the target about every third time you shoot. The haunted house provides a VR 12 schedule if there is a new surprising experience about every 12 steps. The roller coaster provides almost continuous reinforcement (CRF) once it starts moving. You can alternate back and forth among the activities in any order you want. Do you want to go first to the roller coaster, then the haunted house, then back to another roller coaster? The choice is yours.

The study of concurrent schedules has greatly improved our knowledge about choice and the way people make their choices.[31] *The first thing to notice about choice is that choice is relative.* The choice of any activity X depends on all concurrently available alternatives—X, Y, and Z. If activity Z becomes more attractive, it affects people's choices of all three activities—X, Y, and Z—even though only Z has changed: Why? If people choose Z more, they have less time to devote to X or Y. If Club X is always exciting and a couple has been going there one night per week, their choice may be changed if one of their alternative activities (Y or Z) becomes more or less attractive, even though Club X itself remains unchanged. If "Z Film Festival" (Z) comes to town for two weeks, the couple may choose to see several great movies in a row and skip Club X for two weeks. Club X may be equally exciting every night, but the attractiveness of choices X and Y is influenced by an increase in the rewards of schedule Z. *On concurrent schedules, changes in the attractiveness of one schedule of reinforcement can affect a person's choices of both this and the other available schedules.*

A world-class long-distance runner may use pacing schedules when training for major competitions. The runner chooses to practice with one of three fellow athletes who set three different running paces. If one of these three athletes has a minor sprain and has to run at a slower pace, the long-distance runner may decide to spend less time running with the injured athlete and more with the other two athletes, even though these two have not changed their pace in the least.

Because choice is influenced by the alternatives, we cannot understand people's choices without knowing what alternatives are available to them. Just knowing that a couple loves music and has a new CD by a favorite artist does not tell us enough to predict they will stay home and listen to music. Their choice depends on the alternatives: Has "Z Film Festival" brought an exciting new movie to town? Was the couple called to the hospital because of an emergency in the family?

Research on concurrent schedules has identified three variables that have crucial impacts on choice.[32] *People's choices among different concurrent schedules are influenced by the **frequency (F), magnitude (M), and delay (D) of reinforcement** associated with each schedule.* Increases in the frequency and magnitude of reinforcement increase the attractiveness of any given schedule. In contrast, increases in the delays of reinforcement cause a schedule to be less attractive. Therefore, the *general attractiveness of any given choice* is captured by the following simple equation:

$$\frac{F \times M}{D} \quad \text{(also written as } F \times M \div D\text{)}$$

Generally, schedules of reinforcement are very attractive if they provide frequent reinforcers of high magnitude—with minimal time delay.[33]

If we want to evaluate the attractiveness of various video games that simulate spaceship battles, we need to look at all three aspects of their reinforcement schedules: F, M, and D. A video game that schedules *frequent* opportunities to shoot enemy spaceships should be more attractive than a game that schedules only rare opportunities to blast alien adversaries. The *magnitude* of the audiovisual effects is also important. Seeing an enemy spaceship explode in a brilliant star burst of colorful fragments—with stunning sound effects—provides a greater magnitude of sensory stimulation than merely seeing the enemy ship slowly fade from the screen, and games with high-magnitude audiovisual displays are usually an attractive choice. Finally, *time delays* that are scheduled between the player's action and the events on the screen have an inverse effect on attractiveness: Short delays keep the total attractiveness high. Increasing the delay between action and reinforcement causes a decrease in the attractiveness of the game. It is no wonder that video-game designers program their games to have nearly instant responsiveness. It is much more exciting to shoot a laser beam and score an instant hit on the enemy spaceship than to fire a "slow ball" weapon with a projectile that may not reach the target for 30 seconds. Increasing the delay of reinforcement reduces the attractiveness of an activity. A 2-minute "slow ball" is an even bigger yawn.

The three part equation—F × M ÷ D—tells us something about the attractiveness of any given schedule of reinforcement, but we must remember that people compare the attractiveness of all their alternatives before making choices. The values of F, M, and D for each schedule of reinforcement help predict which choice is the most attractive. If we want to know which of two space war games would be more popular, we must compare the F × M ÷ D equations for the two games. We might find that (1) Game A allowed a player to score 20 hits per minute on enemy targets (F = 20 per min.), (2) hits caused a fireball 2 inches in diameter on the video screen (M = 2 in.), and (3) the delay between shooting and seeing the explosion was 10 milliseconds (D = 10 msec.). Game B might allow 50 hits per minute (F = 50), with smaller explosions that were 1 inch in diameter (M = 1), and longer delays of 50 milliseconds (D = 50).

Game A

$F = 20, M = 2$

$D = 10$

$$\frac{F \times M}{D} = \frac{20 \times 2}{10} = 4$$

Game B

$F = 50, M = 1$

$D = 50$

$$\frac{F \times M}{D} = \frac{50 \times 1}{50} = 1$$

When the correct numbers are multiplied and divided, they yield answers of 4 and 1, which indicate the relative attractiveness of each game: The schedules of reinforcement in game A are 4 times more attractive than those in Game B.

The **matching law** describes how the attractiveness of different concurrent schedules affects choice: People tend to match the frequency of their behavior to the relative attractiveness of the available concurrent schedules.[34] If two schedules are equally attractive, people usually alternate back and forth between the two, spending equal amounts of time on each. If one choice is twice as attractive as a second, people usually spend twice as much time on the more attractive alternative. A couple that enjoys a night at the club twice as much as a night at the movies would go to clubs about twice as often as to the movies. If video game A is 4 times more attractive than game B, most people would play game A 4 times more often than game B. The frequency of each choice matches the attractiveness of each choice, compared with the alternatives.

The matching law cannot predict all choices, because there are other variables besides F, M, and D that influence choice, but this simple law is surprisingly successful in explaining patterns of choice.[35] (To understand choices based on "reasoning" and "rules," see Chapter 15.)

In order to know how much time a person will spend on any given schedule, we must compare its attractiveness to the total attractiveness of all the available schedules. In the simplest case of two activities—A and B—the amount of time devoted to schedule A is proportional to the attractiveness of A divided by the total attractiveness of A plus B.

$$\text{Time doing choice A} = \frac{\text{attractiveness of A}}{(\text{attractiveness of A}) + (\text{attractiveness of B})}$$

This equation merely shows that the portion of time a person chooses to devote to A is based on the attractiveness of A compared with the total attractiveness of A and B. If two schedules A and B are equally attractive, with each scored as +1, then the calculation is as follows:

$$\text{Time doing choice A} = \frac{\text{attractiveness of A}}{(\text{attractiveness of A}) + (\text{attractiveness of B})} = \frac{1}{1 + 1} = \frac{1}{2}$$

which means that half the time people will do activity A (and the other half the time they will do B). If someone liked chocolate and vanilla ice cream just the same (and couldn't buy any other flavor), the person would choose chocolate about half the time and vanilla about half the time.

If video game A has an attractiveness of +4 and game B an attractiveness of +1, the calculation is as follows:

$$\text{Time doing choice A} = \frac{\text{attractiveness of A}}{(\text{attractiveness of A}) + (\text{attractiveness of B})} = \frac{4}{4+1} = \frac{4}{5}$$

which means that four times out of five, people will play game A (and the remaining one time out of five they will play game B).

Because we know that attractiveness is proportional to $F \times M \div D$, we can write the equation for the *matching law* of choice as follows:

$$\text{Time doing choice A} = \frac{F \times M \div D \text{ for } A}{(F \times M \div D \text{ for } A) + (F \times M \div D \text{ for } B)}$$

This is the same as writing the equation as follows:

$$\text{Time doing choice A} = \frac{\dfrac{F_A \times M_A}{D_A}}{\dfrac{F_A \times M_A}{D_A} + \dfrac{F_B \times M_B}{D_B}}$$

This equation is the formal expression of the matching law of choice. In everyday parlance it merely states that the amount of the time that a person chooses schedule A equals the attractiveness of A divided by the total attractiveness of A + B (where attractiveness of each is determined by the frequency, magnitude, and delay of reinforcement).

Let us examine some everyday examples of the matching law of choice.[36] If a person has to choose between e-mailing letters to a friend who lives in a distant city or interacting with an equally good friend who lives nearby, the matching law predicts that the person will prefer to communicate most often with the nearby friend. Why? Because the strength (or magnitude) of both friendships is the same, M is the same in both equations—for the e-mail friend (E) and the nearby friend (N).

E-mail writing	Face-to-face interaction
$\dfrac{F_E \times M_E}{D_E}$	$\dfrac{F_N \times M_N}{D_N}$

Therefore, the choice depends on F and D—the frequency and delay of reinforcement associated with e-mail and face-to-face interaction. Because writing e-mail is slower and more laborious than talking, most people exchange fewer words by e-mail than they do in a face-to-face interaction. Thus, the frequency (F) of rewarding words is lower in e-mail exchanges than in face-to-face interactions. Because the distant friend may not respond to an e-mail for hours or days, the time delay (D) is longer in e-mail communications than in face-to-face interactions. Even if we do not put exact numbers into the equations, we can see that the schedule of reinforcement for interacting with nearby friends is more reinforc-ing and attractive: F is larger and D is smaller. Although we often promise to e-mail or write old friends when we split up and move to different cities, those promises usually are hard to keep if we have good nearby friends with whom we can enjoy frequent reinforce-ment with little delay.

Naturally, things change considerably if the distant friend is a very special person. Lovers who live in different cities sometimes e-mail or write every day, taking time away from nearby friends to exchange lengthy messages. Love makes the magnitude (M) of gratification so high that it can override the delays (D) and limited frequency (F) of words exchanged by typing. Nevertheless, exchanging e-mail or letters is not as attractive as ac-tually being with one's partner.

When choosing careers, people are also influenced by the relationship of F, M, and D. The frequency, magnitude, and delay of reinforcement differ from career to career, and careers that offer frequent rewards of generous magnitude and minimal delay tend to be the most appealing. Teenagers sometimes dream of hitchhiking to Hollywood, walking into a studio, and being instantly recognized as hot new talent that deserves frequent at-tention (F) and contracts of great monetary magnitude (M). The ideal career offers high values of F and M, with minimal D.

In choosing between concurrent schedules that provide immediate rewards and those that involve delayed rewards, *immediate rewards are often quite tempting, unless the frequency and/or magnitude of the delayed rewards make delayed gratification worth the wait.*[37] College students often have to struggle with the choice of (1) working hard for many years to enter law, medicine, clinical psychology, or other professions (hoping the future rewards will outweigh the costs of the delay), or (2) having fun now, without delay-ing gratification (hoping that rewarding choices will come their way after college). If a hard-working student receives a few bad grades that endanger long-term plans for a pro-fessional career, turning to immediate gratification becomes especially tempting.

People are often aware that the temptations of immediate gratification can lead them to unwise decisions. The brief delay (low value of D) associated with the immediate gratification of perpetual partying might seduce a hard-working student away from a much superior option (with high F and M of reinforcement) that requires longer delays (high values of D). But people who can vividly imagine the great values of the delayed choice may resist the lure of immediate gratification and persevere toward valued long-term goals.

The seductive power of immediate reinforcement (with low delays, D) can lead some people to become "happy slaves," to use B.F. Skinner's (1971) words. *It can be so rewarding to select immediate gratification—happiness now—that some people become enslaved to habits that are not good for their long-term health and well being.* The person who needs the next "fix" of drugs is trapped in the role of a happy slave—enslaved to a drug because of the immediate gratification of each "fix." Concurrent schedules of rein-forcement make it hard for some people to avoid overeating. If they choose to eat, they are on an FR 1 schedule that produces immediate taste rewards for each bite of food. If they choose to diet, they can expect to lose weight, but there may be a 7-day delay before they even begin to notice a rewarding change on the bathroom scales. Many overweight people say they would like to diet; but they are happy slaves of fattening foods: The delayed reinforcement of weight loss is often less attractive than the immediate pleasures of eating the next piece of fudge.

How can a person escape the seductive power of immediate reinforcement when it endangers valuable, long-term goals? One solution is to *proact:* Make choices about valuable goals *before* tempting situations arise—while the time delay before the next reinforcers are still long.[38] People who are overweight often cannot resist eating when they have fudge, ice cream, cake, and other sweets in the house. When the food is nearby, the choice of eating is very attractive and hard to resist: It may take only 30 seconds to walk to the kitchen and find something fattening to eat, hence impulsive eating is rewarded immediately. It is much easier to diet if there are no fattening foods in the house, since there are no S^Ds that tempt us into impulsive actions based on immediate rewards.

By planning ahead at the grocery store, people can proact and minimize the temptations caused by having fattening food in the house. If they decide—while at the grocery—to buy fruit, vegetables, lean meat, and no sweets, their proactive behavior will reduce later temptations to eat fattening foods. Once they get home and stock the kitchen with healthy, low-calorie food instead of sweets, they have less difficulty making health-smart choices than if they had come home with fudge, ice cream, and cake.

Overweight people find it easier to make wise diet decisions in the grocery than in their own kitchen—if it is stocked with rich foods—because there is a longer time delay between food choices and food reinforcers. The longer delay reduces temptations for immediate gratification. The following table of delay times shows why proacting is useful. If the decision to be a "happy fudge slave" or a "healthy veggie eater" is made in a fudge lovers kitchen, the delay until reinforcement is 30 seconds for eating fudge (because the food is nearby) and 7 days for abstaining (because it takes 7 days before the scales show rewarding progress for skipping rich foods). When standing in the grocery store, the choice of fudge or veggies and fruit involves a 30-minute delay for eating fudge (because it takes time to check out, get home, and eat) and a 7-day delay for seeing rewarding results on the scales. People have a much better chance of choosing a healthy diet while in the grocery than in the kitchen. The numbers in the table show that the attractiveness of fattening foods is 60 times lower in the grocery than in their own home, because the 30-minute delay until eating is 60 times longer than 30 seconds. That does not mean that all people can decide to resist fattening foods while in the grocery, but the chances are much better when there is less temptation for immediate gratification. By making wise decisions in the grocery and purchasing healthy foods, people help ensure that they will have minimal temptations to eat fattening foods when they are at home.

	Eat fudge	*Eat healthy food*
HOME	30-sec delay	7-day delay
GROCERY	30-min delay	7-day delay

NONCONTINGENT SCHEDULES

Ever since introducing FR 1 schedules, we have been discussing contingent schedules in which rewards and punishments do not occur unless people do something that earns them. *In schedules of contingent reinforcement, people must do one or more operants to produce reinforcement or punishment.* On an FR 10 schedule, reinforcement depends upon the appearance of the tenth response. On an FI 24-hour schedule, reinforcement is contingent on the appearance of the first response after a 24-hour period. Reinforcement is contingent on the response occurring: No response means no reinforcement.

What happens if reinforcement appears independent of behavior? *When reinforcers occur irrespective of the actions preceding them, the reinforcers are called noncontingent.* These reinforcers are sometimes called "windfall" rewards or "response-independent reinforcers" to indicate that they come without anyone doing anything to earn them. Your boss approaches you at the soft drink machine and gives you a check for $741.37, explaining that the accountant found your payroll deductions had been too large. Is $741.37 fun to receive? Yes. You can buy some nice things with it. But it will not reinforce such operants as spending more time at the soft drink machine. As we explained at the end of Chapter 3 on operant conditioning, noncontingent reinforcement is usually much less effective than contingent reinforcement in modifying operant behavior.

There are, however, some situations in which noncontingent consequences produce unusual and dramatic effects. A variety of different effects have been observed, depending on the frequency and magnitude of the noncontingent events, whether reinforcement or punishment is involved, and other variables.

Superstitious Behavior

When noncontingent reinforcement accidentally follows an operant, it may cause the operant to occur more frequently. *Behavior produced by this random, noncontingent reinforcement is called* **superstitious behavior.**[39]

Athletes often develop superstitious behaviors based on the reinforcers of scoring and winning. If a baseball pitcher accidentally fingers the ball in an unusual way before throwing three strikes in a row, some irrelevant fingering response may become a learned superstitious ritual. If a quarterback mumbles the name of the pass receiver before throwing the ball, and if this is accidentally followed by several good passes, the noncontingent reinforcement may create a verbal superstition.

Because noncontingent reinforcement has less effect on behavior than does contingent reinforcement, superstitious behavior usually develops when the costs of doing the behavior are low and the rewards are high.[40] Mumbling a name is a low-cost behavior, and winning an important game is very rewarding. Also, the more there *appears* to be a possible connection between a behavior and reinforcement, the more likely a superstition is to develop. The appearance of a contingent relationship can mask the accidental, noncontingent sequence of events. For example, what happens if a swimmer chances to sample some of her roommate's fad diet supplement at breakfast and then breaks her own personal record and wins a swim meet that afternoon? The chance association between the unusual breakfast and the big win could lead to the learning of the superstitious habit of eating the fad diet supplement whenever the swimmer was preparing for her event.[41] Even if the roommate gave up the fad diet, the swimmer might continue using it, in part because she feared she might lose her next competition if she did not use the diet.

Whenever people have highly rewarding experiences, just about any preceding operant that stands out as unusual and correlated with the rewards may be reinforced and become a superstitious practice. A history student who happened to study in the physics library before earning the highest grade in the class on a history final might learn the superstitious practice of studying history in the physics library. The unusualness of both the behavior and the reward creates conditions conducive to superstitious learning, especially if the behavior is not costly to perform and the rewards are high.

Valued rewards that are not completely under our own control—not completely assured by skill alone—often cause the learning of superstitions. Athletes learn more superstitions for their sport than for driving cars or ordering at restaurants: Cars and eateries are much more under their own personal control than is the outcome of the next game. In situations where skill alone does not always produce success—because there are too many uncontrollable variables—success is much more capricious, and any unusual activity associated with success can be reinforced and become a superstitious behavior.

After a superstition has been acquired via noncontingent reinforcement, the behavior may be maintained by contingent reinforcement, if the behavior attracts social attention—a reinforcer. When superstitious behavior is unusual and colorful, it often attracts attention. "Hey, Carla, do you still think that green powder you put on your cereal really helps you swim any better?" Of course, social criticism can have the opposite effect, punishing and suppressing the frequency of a superstition, in public at least. A second way superstitious behavior can produce reinforcement is by creating an illusion of being in control or feeling that one has a special edge in dealing with difficult situations. These positive thoughts can reduce anxiety in the face of uncertainty and reinforce the continued use of superstitions.

Superstitions can be passed on to others by observational learning or rules.[42] Thus, superstitions can spread through a culture once one individual acquires the response. There are many culturally transmitted superstitions: dropping coins in wishing wells, crossing your fingers, knocking on wood, avoiding paths crossed by black cats, praying to rain gods, not walking under ladders, and so forth. Americans are so superstitious about not accepting $2 bills that the government is stuck with 4 million $2 bills that people will not use.

Passivity

Noncontingent consequences that occur at high frequency can condition passivity.[43] This has been best demonstrated with noncontingent punishment, but it appears to occur with noncontingent reinforcement, too.

People who receive frequent noncontingent punishment can develop **learned helplessness,** *involving passivity, apathy, and depression.*[44] When people are first exposed to noncontingent punishment, they try to avoid it or stop it. However, if the punishment is truly noncontingent, then there is no relationship between it and the person's behavior;

hence there may be nothing the person can do to stop it. Gradually, attempts to avoid punishment extinguish (if they all fail), and the victim learns to accept the pain passively. Victims of noncontingent punishment often feel helpless, hopeless, and depressed.

Children raised in highly abusive homes sometimes develop learned helplessness. When parents take out *their* anger on the children—independent of the children's behavior—the children are punished noncontingently. Because children are weaker than and dependent on the adults, there is not much young children can do to avoid the physical and verbal abuse. Unavoidable punishment can induce passivity, depression, and feelings of helplessness.

Once people develop learned helplessness, they often learn to accept later contingent punishment—even when they *could* avoid it by merely taking a more active role. Women who were raised in abusive homes are often quite fatalistic if they get married to men who beat them: They tolerate abuses that other women would resist. Once people become passive due to learned helplessness, the passivity interferes with their learning to actively resist punishment in later situations—unless a friend, counselor, therapist, or social worker helps them learn to be more active and assertive.

One study of street prostitutes found that many of the women had come from violent homes, been victims of incest at home, been abused and beaten up by their pimps and customers, and been robbed and raped while on the streets.[45] After a long history of victimization, many were "psychologically paralyzed." They believed there was little or nothing they could do to avoid further abuse. They felt powerless to change their lives, and their habits of passivity biased them not to explore active means for avoiding aversive experiences.

People who receive generous and frequent noncontingent reinforcement can acquire **learned laziness.**[46] Large amounts of free rewards can create apathy, passivity, and lack of motivation. It is not surprising that free reinforcers promote passivity. If you could do absolutely nothing and still receive frequent and ample reinforcers, why do anything? There is not much incentive—or motivation—to exert the effort to do much other than lounge around, goof off, waste time. "It's like they pay me for doing nothing, so I do nothing."

Children who are showered with attention, toys, and treats by doting parents often become "spoiled."[47] They may refuse to do anything that takes effort—such as doing homework, chores, yard work, or cleaning their room—and still they receive free reinforcers. Some spoiled children, although not all, become rather lazy. (Those spoiled children who receive generous parental attention contingent upon whining, screaming, asking for things, or complaining can learn some high activity behaviors that also fit the label of "spoiled.")

Very attractive people sometimes become spoiled, too. They receive all sorts of attention because they are beautiful or handsome, even if they do nothing special. If they become increasingly unmotivated and passive, they still receive attention and flattery. Reinforcement is not contingent upon behavior: It merely comes for being handsome or beautiful.

Elderly people who are pampered with overly generous care in nursing homes sometimes become more passive than they need to be. This can cause them to lose skills faster than people who are less pampered. Too many noncontingent rewards can also make people feel "useless," since they do not need to do much of value any more. We can help retirees avoid deskilling and feeling useless by avoiding the use of noncontingent rewards: Rewards for maintaining skills and being useful help keep the senior years good.[48] The behavioral decline of Alzheimer's patients can be slowed by prompting them to use as many of their skills as possible and then giving them rewards contingent on doing for themselves rather than becoming dependent on others.[49]

LOOSELY DEFINED CONTINGENCIES OF REINFORCEMENT

Loosely defined contingencies of reinforcement allow people to attain rewarding outcomes from any of a variety of behaviors that lie within broad and loosely defined limits. These lie between the two extremes of (1) the strictly defined contingencies that produce precisely specified behavior, and (2) the random, noncontingent reinforcement that produces superstitious or passive behavior. *Compared with strictly defined contingencies, loosely defined contingencies allow a large amount of variability in behavior by only loosely specifying which behavior may be reinforced.* But loosely defined contingencies do require some kind of behavior to occur; hence they are not noncontingent producers of passivity. Two important products of loosely defined contingencies are personal style and behavior drift, and both allow people to develop unique patterns of responses that contribute to their individuality.

Personal style usually arises in instrumental tasks that can be performed in a variety of ways. For instance, legible handwriting is a broad operant response class that contains millions of different styles, and all styles that successfully communicate are reinforced. One person writes backhand, another with flourishes, and yet another with italic strokes. There are countless variations that are readable. As long as a style has good effects—that is, it brings reinforcement because it communicates—it does not matter which style is used. After years of writing and countless reinforcers, each of us develops a unique style.

The difference between style and superstitious behavior is traced to the size of the response class that is reinforced. Superstitious behavior arises when *any* possible response can be reinforced. Reinforcers come no matter what. Style arises when any variation *within* a specific but broad response class can be reinforced. Handwriting consists of making marks on the page. There is nothing superstitious about making the letters; some kind of style is necessary. A quarterback can throw a pass without mumbling the name of a pass receiver, but a person cannot do handwriting without using some style of writing. Because the response class of readable writing is very broad, countless different writing patterns are possible, and each person can learn his or her own unique style.

There is some looseness in the definition of most response classes, hence some room for style to appear. As a result, each of us learns personal styles of dress, speech, posture, hand gestures, eye contact, walking, greetings, and so forth. Modern societies that emphasize "freedom" and "individuality" have greatly broadened the definition of many response classes and opened more room for our learning unique personal styles.

Behavior drift appears when behavior that is under loosely defined contingencies of reinforcement changes over time.[50] A person's handwriting style can drift over the years, perhaps tilting more to the right or the left, perhaps becoming larger or smaller, sometimes becoming more sloppy or illegible. Behavior that is rewarded in a large, loosely defined response class can drift around and take many forms, yet still be reinforced; so drift often involves unpredictable changes. How has your handwriting changed in the past decade?

Many behaviors are acquired under strictly defined contingencies of reinforcement, then ever-larger and more loosely defined response classes are accepted and reinforced under maintenance schedules. In the early grades, children practice making their handwriting conform to models in books or on classroom walls. Once children can write moderately well, teachers move on to teach other topics and accept any readable writing. Hence behavior drift often becomes more visible after the early strict contingencies are loosened.

Consider the example of succinct speech. Children often use complicated and confusing sentences when telling stories or explaining complex events. Because adults may become irritated when their time is wasted by a youngster who cannot express an idea succinctly, young people are often required to learn to explain themselves clearly, simply, and efficiently. Under such contingencies most young people learn to get to the point and minimize redundancy. However, as the years go by and people gain seniority, status, or advanced age, there are fewer people who criticize irrelevant or redundant ramblings. When 70-year-olds are rambling on and on about their past, younger people may abstain from criticizing out of kindness or respect. This means that speech can shift to loosely defined contingencies with increasing age, and it is common to find older people talking and thinking less clearly than they did in prior decades. Long before senility or physical impairment hampers their abilities, some adults have their verbal behavior—both their speech and verbal thoughts—drifting away from succinctness. Eventually some older people become inattentive to detail, absentminded, repetitive, and confused about simple points. The senior citizens who speak most succinctly and show the least behavior drift are often those who continue to apply high standards of logic and clarity to their own verbal behavior—and request honest friends to comment on their slipups.

Behavior drift is not a result of biological aging. It can occur in young people, too. Verbal behavior seems especially prone to drift, which can lead to large discrepancies between what people say and what they actually do. When a person first begins to drift away from habits of punctuality or living up to promises, it may be laughed off or forgotten because "everyone slips up once in awhile." But when a person's behavior drifts further, there may be an increasing frequency of promising one thing—"I'll be there at 8 o'clock for sure"—and doing something else. This drift may be prevented if the person is criticized: "You caused 12 people to sit around and waste 45 minutes waiting for you this morning." But without critical feedback, the drift can continue. The less critical feedback people receive, the easier it is for their verbal and actual behavior to drift apart. Eventually everybody begins to accept Lyle as irresponsible, a person who promises much, but—in the end—does whatever he wants to do.

Behavior drift is one source of behavioral variability that contributes to the colorfulness and fun of everyday life—unless you were depending on Lyle for a lift home tonight. Behavior drift, along with superstitious behavior and style, produce unpredictable variations in people's behavior, which may strike others as interesting, funny, imaginative, or creative. However, if behavior drifts beyond certain limits, it may appear inconsiderate, pathetic, deviant, or even dysfunctional.

CONCLUSION

There are many different kinds of schedules of reinforcement and punishment. Schedule effects are superimposed on all the types of conditioning effects described in the previous chapters. Schedules have ever-present effects on behavior because reinforcement always appears on some type of schedule, and most types of schedules have their own distinctive effects on behavior. Some people think learning theory applies only to behavioral acquisition. But the maintenance of behavior depends on reinforcement, too—hence depends on the schedules of reinforcement.

The first phase of behavioral acquisition may involve FR 1 (or CRF) schedules of continuous reinforcement, but once a behavior begins to be acquired, there is often a shift to partial (or intermittent) reinforcement, such as FR 4 or FR 10. Variable schedules are more common than fixed schedules in everyday life, and they contribute to the amount of behavioral variability and "color" seen in natural settings. They also help people learn behavioral persistence. When under FI, VI, DRH, DRL, and pacing schedules, people learn to time their responses to synchronize with the cycles and rhythms of daily events. In everyday life, numerous schedules often interlock, as chained, multiple, or concurrent schedules. Concurrent schedules allow people to choose among two or more alternative schedules. The matching law describes how choices are related to the attractiveness of the alternative schedules. Noncontingent reinforcement and punishment can produce superstitious or passive behavior. Loosely defined contingencies of reinforcement foster the idiosyncratic response variations seen in behavioral style and drift. A certain amount of variability is accepted as normal and even welcomed because "variety is the spice of life." However, when behavior drifts beyond certain limits, people usually begin to define variations as inappropriate, deviant, or even dysfunctional.

QUESTIONS

1. Why are schedule effects ever present?
2. Why are schedules often different during acquisition and maintenance?
3. What are fixed ratio schedules? How does an FR 1 schedule differ from an FR 5 or FR 500 schedule?
4. What are variable ratio schedules? How do they differ from FR schedules?
5. What are interval schedules? How do fixed interval schedules differ from variable interval schedules?
6. What are the schedule effects that produce behavioral contrast?
7. What are the four schedules based on differential reinforcement? Can you explain DRO, DRH, DRL, and pacing?
8. Why is DRO so important? How can it be used to decrease unwanted behavior? Why is DRI (a subset of DRO) especially powerful at doing this?
9. What are compound schedules? What are the three types?

10. How do concurrent schedules allow choice? How has research on concurrent schedules helped us understand the role of the frequency, magnitude, and delay of reinforcement?
11. What is the matching law? Give an example of it.
12. What are noncontingent schedules? When can they produce superstitious behavior? When can they produce passivity?
13. What are loosely defined schedules? Why can they produce personal style? Why can they produce behavior drift?

NOTES

1. Wellford (1999).
2. Weiner (1965, 1969); Rosecrance (1985).
3. Lattal and Neef (1996); Plaud and Gaither (1996).
4. Ferster and Skinner (1957); Dews (1963, p. 148); Morse and Kelleher (1970, 1977); Zeiler (1977); Foltin and Schuster (1982); Shull and Lawrence (1998).
5. Scott (1971, p. 180).
6. Schwartz and Stanton (1950, pp. 404–416); Walen, Hauserman, and Lavin (1977, pp. 65–105).
7. For more information on specific schedules, see Ferster and Skinner (1957); Nevin (1971b); Williams (1973, pp. 43–44).
8. Lincoln (1946).
9. Roy (1953).
10. Homans (1974, p. 99).
11. Walters and Grusec (1977, pp. 71–72).
12. Schlinger, Blakely, and Kaczor (1990).
13. Rosecrance (1985).
14. Hastjarjo, Silberberg, and Hursh (1990).
15. Lyons and Ghezzi (1995).
16. Clark, Rowbury, Baer, and Baer (1973).
17. Lehrman, Iwata, Shore, and Kahng (1996).
18. Catania (1991).
19. In the laboratory, the next interval does not begin until the behavior is emitted. In everyday life, intervals often begin at a fixed length of time from the start of the previous interval, independent of the occurrence or timing of the behavior involved.
20. Reynolds (1961); Koegel, Egel, and Williams (1980); Flora (1990); Freeman and Lattal (1992); Perone and Courtney (1992); Maurer, Palmer, and Ashe (1993); Hantula and Crowell (1994); Weatherly, Melville, and Swindell (1997).
21. Nevin (1974, 1979, 1992, 1995, 1996, 1998); Nevin, Mandell, and Atak (1983); Plaud, Gaither, and Lawrence (1997); Cohen (1998). This concept of behavioral momentum is not without its critics (Houlihan & Brandon, 1996).
22. Behavioral persistence used to be explained in terms of "partial reinforcement effects in extinction"—or PREE—(Kimble, 1961). But PREE has been called into question by recent research; Nevin (1988); Lerman et al. (1996) suggest that behavioral persistence may result more from abundant prior reinforcement than from partial reinforcement.
23. Catania (1991).
24. Catania (1991); Iversen (1991).
25. Lennox, Miltenberger, and Donnelly (1987).
26. Barton, Brulle, and Repp (1986); Mazaleski et al. (1993); Hoyert and Zeiler (1995).
27. Luiselli (1996).
28. Wagaman et al. (1995); Lindberg, Iwata, Kahng, and DeLeon (1999).
29. Sharenow, Fuqua, and Miltenberger (1989); Stark et al. (1989); Lalli, Browder, Mace, and Brown (1993); Wagaman, Miltenberger, and Arndorfer (1993); Jones, Swearer, and Friman (1997); Woods and Wright (1998).
30. Richman et al. (1997); Kellam et al. (1999).
31. Herrnstein (1961); Sakagami, Hursh, Christensen, and Silberberg (1989); Shurtleff and Silberberg (1990); Mazur (1991); Silberberg, Thomas, and Berendzen (1991); Piazza, Fisher, Hagopian, Bowman, and Tolle (1996); Fisher and Mazur (1997); Nevin (1998).

32. Herrnstein (1961, 1970); de Villiers (1977).

33. Rachlin (1989); Killeen and Fantino (1990); Christensen, Parker, Silberberg, and Hursh (1998); Williams and Bell (1999).

34. Herrnstein (1961); de Villiers (1977); Logue (1983); Epling and Pierce (1988); Luco (1990); Bickel, Green, and Vuchinich (1995). Choice behavior has been analyzed in terms of both matching and maximizing, and the relative merits of the two theories are still being debated (Rachlin, 1989; Rachlin, Battalio, Kagel, & Green, 1981). Matching is presented here, and maximizing in Chapter 15.

35. de Villiers (1977); Baum (1979); Wearden (1983); Zeiler and Blakely (1983); Spetch, Belke, Barnet, Dunn, and Pierce (1990); Williams (1991); Davison and Jones (1995); Mazur (1995); Rachlin (1995).

36. Beardsley and McDowell (1992); Pierce and Epling (1995); Mace and Neef (1996).

37. Rachlin et al. (1991); Myerson and Green (1995); Green, Myerson, and Ostaszewski (1999).

38. Logue (1988, 1995); Grace (1999); Loeb, Wilson, Gilbert, and Labouvie (2000).

39. Superstitious learning was the first effect of noncontingent reinforcement to be studied (Skinner, 1948b, 1957), but other work shows it is much more complex than was originally thought (Hammond, 1980; Killeen, 1978; Matute & Miller, 1998; Schwartz, 1984, pp. 154–173; Staddon, 1977).

40. Gmelch and Felson (1980).

41. The long time lag between behavior and consequences in some cases of superstitious learning suggests that conditioning results during cognitive rehearsal (Bandura, 1977; Klatzky, 1980) as people ruminate over the unusual and rewarding events of the past several hours or days (Klinger, 1977, 1978).

42. Subbotsky (1993).

43. When reinforcement and punishment are large and infrequent, people are open to learning superstitions; when they are large and frequent, passivity may be learned (Peterson et al. 1993).

44. Seligman (1975); Garber and Seligman (1980); Peterson et al. (1993); Rodd, Rosellini, Stock, and Gallup (1997); Overmier and LoLordo (1998).

45. Silbert and Pines (1981). Also see Farley and Barkan (1998).

46. Seligman (1975); Peterson et al. (1993).

47. Skinner (1980, p. 100).

48. Thomas (1999).

49. Barinaga (1998).

50. Behavior drift, along with superstitious learning, is analyzed by Skinner (1948b, 1957).

Chapter

14

Positive and Negative Control

DRAGONS AND DUNGEONS

If we could climb into a time machine and cruise back to everyday scenes in most of the great empires and civilizations of the past, we would find an abundance of dungeons, torture chambers, chains, whips, knives, and other devices of coercive control. Most of the largest societies of the past were like police states, ruled by kings, emperors, or sultans who relied heavily on corporal punishment to control the masses.[1] The leaders of these societies had wealth and luxury, but they often used harsh punishment to terrify the masses into compliance with their dictates. Many common people suffered countless pains and had nightmares about dragons and dungeons, if not torture and death.

Only as our time machine cruises back toward the present day would we see a gradual revolution against heartless tyrants, coupled with a demand for increasing democracy. We land our time machine in the present and appreciate our place in history—where millions of people are concerned for human rights for all people, working diligently to reduce the use of pain, torture, and coercive control in social life. Knowledge of the behavior principles is proving to be extremely valuable in understanding punishment and coercive control, along with ways to replace them with positive reinforcement so people can minimize pain and attain higher levels of satisfaction in life.

Positive control consists of all conditioning and stimulus control that is based on positive reinforcement. People love positive reinforcement—be it genuine thanks for a job well done or a sincere smile of appreciation. Positive reinforcement increases the frequency of operants, and it causes predictive stimuli to become CSs that elicit pleasurable emotions. Under positive control, learning new knowledge and skills is enjoyable; hence people are eager to continue developing their human potential. *Negative control consists of all conditioning and stimulus control that is based on punishment and negative reinforcement.* Punishment suppresses the frequency of operants and causes predictive stimuli to become CSs that elicit fear, anxiety, and other aversive emotions. Negative control also motivates escape and avoidance—because these responses are often followed by negative reinforcement.

Behavioral research has shown that almost any activity can be learned under either positive or negative control. There are, however, important emotional and motivational differences in the behavior produced by positive reinforcement and punitive control. Pedro is learning to play the piano under positive control. Because his parents play the piano and show their love of music, Pedro experiences vicarious reinforcement when he sees how much his parents enjoy music. Pedro is given generous encouragement and positive feedback for his playing because his parents are happy to see him showing an interest in music. He obtains sensory stimulation reinforcers from the music he is learning to create for himself. As a result of all this positive conditioning, Pedro comes to love the piano, squeezes in extra time here and there to play, and looks forward to learning more difficult music in the future. Noah, in contrast, is learning to play the piano under negative control. His family and friends do not play, and some of his peers make fun of him for having to practice. Noah's parents give sharp reprimands for errors but seldom comment on well-played passages. Any failure to advance as rapidly as possible is criticized. His teacher often compares Noah with other students who are excelling, and tells him that his playing is dull and uninspired. Noah's parents tell him how disappointed they are. Everyone nags him to practice harder. As a result of this negative control, Noah learns to hate the piano, hate the nagging about practice, avoid playing, and fear whatever future learning his parents may demand of him. Learning under positive control, Pedro came to love the piano and persisted until he mastered difficult material.[2] Learning under negative control, Noah came to hate and avoid the piano.

In this chapter you will learn the various problems associated with negative control—punishment and negative reinforcement—along with techniques for replacing negative control with more positive alternatives. After thousands of years of coercive control and human suffering, we are finally discovering methods for replacing negative control with positive control.[3]

HUMANISTIC APPLICATIONS

Much of modern technology and culture functions to decrease our exposure to aversive stimuli and increase our access to positive stimuli. Technologies for coping with the physical environment provide clear examples. Medicine has given us countless drugs and procedures to protect or cure us from disease—helping us to have healthier and happier lives. Architecture and technology have made our living spaces safer—free of aversive climatic extremes—and more pleasant. Mechanical and electronic inventions have greatly reduced the need for back-breaking and mind-numbing work—helping us find work easier and play more fun. Democracy and the rule of law have also developed over the centuries to help us avoid tyranny and injustices so that we can focus on creating social conditions conducive to life, liberty, and the pursuit of happiness.

However, our current technologies and cultures are far from perfect. Aversive stimuli are still with us, generating a great deal of unhappiness and misery in many people's lives. There is much room for improvement in making the world a more positive place in which to live. Behavior science is one of the younger sciences, but it promises many important scientific and humanistic breakthroughs for making life more positive. *Behavior science is the first discipline to analyze positive and negative control, develop better methods of positive control, devise alternatives to aversive control, and give people the information they need to switch from negative to positive methods of social interaction.*

These discoveries are new. Most people have never learned how to make use of behavior principles for this end. Yet the positive approach of behavior science has already been successfully implemented in many realms of behavior modification—interpersonal relations, marital counseling, sexual therapies, child-rearing practices, educational programs, self-control strategies, self-actualization programs, special educational programs for mentally and physically challenged people, and more.[4] Considering how young behavior science is, it is reasonable to assume that many more behavioral situations will be analyzed and converted to positive control as the science advances.

A major goal of behavior science is to help people learn ways to minimize "aversives"—the pains of negative control—and replace them with practices that increase positive reinforcers in everyone's lives.[5] Almost all behavior can be brought under positive control. As more people acquire the skills for using positive control—and avoiding aversives—we will create a much happier society, free of guilt, fear, anxiety, hatred, and numerous other ugly side effects of aversive control.

How does one increase the use of positive control and decrease negative control? The answer depends somewhat on the situation. If other people are engaging in *desirable* behavior, it is easier to use positive control than if they are engaging in *undesirable* activities. The remainder of the chapter explains the positive ways of responding to desirable and undesirable behavior.

DESIRABLE BEHAVIOR

When a person is learning or doing any desirable behavior—kindness, honesty, improving their skills or creativity—the advantages of positive control are obvious. *Positive control increases the frequency of the behavior and makes the person eager to learn more. Positive control also conditions the behavior itself into a secondary reinforcer, so merely doing the behavior elicits positive emotional responses and becomes intrinsically rewarding.*

The disadvantages of using negative control and aversives with desirable behavior are also clear. *Negative control tends to lower the frequency of behavior and condition the behavior into a secondary punisher.* Desirable activities that could have been enjoyable become aversive. Noah hates playing the piano after learning under negative control. Under most circumstances, people try to escape or avoid aversive control and the behavior conditioned by it. When parents, teachers, friends, spouse, or others rely on aversive control while attempting to teach valuable skills, they can create avoidance responses that interfere with or prevent the acquisition of the desirable behavior.

The obvious advantages of positive control for desirable behavior help many people avoid putting such behavior under aversive control. But other people lack skill in being as positive as they could be, and if their positive approaches fail, they may turn to negative control. Megan suggests to Cliff that it would be great fun to go water skiing this week-end, and he mumbles, "I'm busy." Then she gives another positive line, "You remember how much fun we used to have skiing at the lake. I know you'll love it once you get there." Showing irritation, Cliff repeats, "I'm *biizzy!*" This time Megan turns to the aver-sive mode and snaps, "Cliff, you never want to do anything anymore except watch those stupid games on TV. If you won't get up, I'll just go with José and Dave." Now Megan may get some action, but she had to use negative control to get it. Even if Cliff agrees to go, the aversive control may make the weekend trip less pleasant than it could have been if both Megan and Cliff were more skillful at and appreciative of positive interaction styles.

The research on behavior acquisition and maintenance indicates that virtually all de-sirable operant behavior can be learned and maintained under positive control. Merely teaching Megan a few more positive phrases may not resolve all the problems between Cliff and her. However, real progress can be expected if *both* people learn a larger reper-toire of positive skills that make him more rewarding to talk with, her more rewarding to ski with, and both of them more positive about learning mutually rewarding patterns of interaction. When people succeed in coupling their shared activities with high levels of positive stimuli, it does not take a lot of coaxing by one to convince the other to interact further. Activities that have been under positive reinforcement in the past become high probability responses that people love doing and are eager to repeat.

Becoming more positive involves learning skills for increasing the use of positive reinforcers with desirable behaviors while avoiding the use of aversives—punishers or negative reinforcers—for these behaviors. There are two ways people can increase their use of positive control of desirable behavior and three ways to decrease negative control.

Increasing Positive Control.   *People benefit enormously by learning how to increase the use of positive reinforcement for their own behavior and the behavior of others.* The two ways to do this involve the use of primary and secondary reinforcers.

1. Primary Reinforcers.   Parents with young children are the main sources of primary positive reinforcers in their children's lives. The parents provide the food, fluids, warmth, clothes, bed, and optimal sensory stimulation that children cannot yet provide for them-selves. Some parents scratch, rub, and tickle their children, providing reinforcers via the tactile senses. Parents provide toys for and play with their children, giving them sensory stimulation reinforcers. With this tremendous supply of primary positive reinforcers com-ing from the parents, it is not surprising that most young children love their parents im-mensely. Parents who make sure that their powerful primary rewards follow their children's desirable behavior—but not undesirable behavior—are helping their children get an especially strong start in life.

Two lovers can also provide a generous supply of primary positive reinforcers for each other. Conversations and shared activities provide optimal sensory stimulation. Intimacy provides reinforcing tactile and sexual stimulation. By synchronizing their lives, two people can enjoy food together, sleeping together, keeping each other warm on cold winter nights, and so forth. As lovers learn how much their relationship benefits from frequent exchanges of positive reinforcers, they can focus on increasing the quality and quantity of reinforcers they bring to each other. This helps focus both lovers on building the best relationship they can create.

In nonsexual interactions, the most commonly exchanged primary positive reinforcer is optimal sensory stimulation. People are creating sensory stimulation for each other when they talk together, play together, watch or participate in sports, make cheerful banter, engage in horseplay at a dull job, or share activities together. It takes skill to generate behavior that brings optimal levels of sensory stimulation to oneself and others. Luckily, there are many responses that increase or reduce sensory stimulation (pp. 175–176), and each of us can develop the skills that best suit our own personality. *Most people prefer to be with and learn from individuals who bring reinforcers into their lives, and optimal sensory stimulation is a major primary reinforcer in most social exchanges.*

2. Secondary Reinforcers.   It is possible to follow desirable behavior with large numbers of secondary reinforcers. Almost everyone responds to smiles, kindness, and consideration as secondary reinforcers, and once we learn how to give these generously, it seems almost effortless to use positive reinforcers with everyone who does desirable behavior. Another way to bring secondary positive reinforcers to others is to show an interest in their lives. This involves a willingness to listen to people and respond supportively to the desirable and healthy aspects of their lives. Our showing enthusiasm about their prosocial goals, interests, and behavior also provides positive reinforcement. Our smiles, laughter, positive words, and signs of happiness provide vicarious positive reinforcers for others. By learning to show our love for and enjoyment of the desirable things in life—art, kindness, sports, creativity—we are generating positive vicarious reinforcers that help others learn to love those things, too.

Helping people enjoy their favorite activities is another way to increase their secondary positive reinforcers. If you know your best friend loves art posters or poetry books, it might be easy to bring a poster back the next time you visit a bookstore. You can be confident that things related to people's favorite activities are secondary reinforcers for them. If Tricia's favorite sport is golf, your suggesting a game of golf may be a positive thing to do. But if you hate golf, you may not be able to enjoy playing with Tricia, and she may soon learn that playing with you is not as rewarding as playing with someone who really likes golf. *In general, people with similar values and behavior repertoires bring more reinforcers into each other's lives than do people with dissimilar values and behavior repertoires.*[6] Two people's values and behavior repertoires do not have to be identical for maximal reward: A certain number of differences add interest. However, too many differences can prevent both people from both enjoying their shared activities. Thus, you are most likely to be able to help others develop desirable behaviors if you love and enjoy those activities yourself.

Decreasing Negative Control. In everyday life, desirable behavior is sometimes at least partially under negative control. *There are three ways to reduce the aversives, and each one can shift the cost/reward ratio of the behavior more toward the positive side.*

1. Reducing Aversives: "Lightening Others' Loads." The behavior of parents with young children provides an archetypal example of the positive value of pain reduction. When their children cry, parents remove diaper pins, soiled diapers, and splinters. They often medicate and soothe colds, cuts, wounds, and bee stings. Their caresses and assuring words dispel the fears elicited by nightmares, thunderstorms, ghost stories, and sirens. Children love and approach their parents not only because the parents provide many positive reinforcers, but also because parents can make aversives disappear.

All through life, we value a true friend or loving companion who helps us avoid or escape painful experiences. By providing security and emotional support in times of distress, a friend can help us find relief from anguish or suffering. A friend can help by listening carefully, suggesting solutions to our problems, and assisting in times of need. This reinforces our love and respect for the person who helps us. Helpers who care about advancing desirable behavior—rather than selfish or antisocial behavior—can have numerous beneficial effects on the people they aid.

People need not be friends or lovers to reduce negative stimuli by "lightening each other's loads." When one person has *skills* or *strengths* that a second person does not, the first person can often help the second with little effort. The skills and strengths can be mental, physical, or emotional. By volunteering to carry the heavier backpack, the strong person ensures that the weaker one will not find the hike painful, which helps person two enjoy the experience more. The person who has learned to cope with death may be able to take some of the burden off other family members by arranging for the funeral, the legal concerns, and other details. An expert can make life easier for others—and advance their learning of desirable behavior—by sharing advanced skills and knowledge with others. An accomplished tennis player can give a few tips to a novice, helping the beginner avoid many mistakes and learn faster. A skillful mechanic can quickly identify a carburetor problem and save a novice hours of frustration in fixing it. Helping is often rewarded with thanks, appreciation, and better friendship.

2. Not Adding Aversives: "No Nagging, Please." People who nag, nag, nag are creating aversives for others. These negative stimuli—such as "Don't do this," "Stop doing that"—may be used as rules to suppress behavior that someone else found rewarding. Words such as "Take out the trash," "Hang up your clothes" are rules that tell others to do tasks they do not enjoy. Repeated nagging is a form of negative control that makes social interaction less rewarding and generates bad feelings about the nagger.

Nagging, needling, harping, criticizing, and fighting are unfortunately all too common in many people's lives. People are most likely to learn to nag others if their harping has often succeeded in controlling the behavior of others, hence been reinforced. *If our goal is to help others do desirable behavior, we are wise to avoid nagging and other types of negative control. Aversive words condition desirable target behaviors into CSs that elicit aversive feelings for the recipients of the nagging.* As a result, the people who were nagged come to dislike a desirable behavior and avoid doing the behavior—unless nagged some more!

Many of the positive practices in the prior sections can be used instead of negative control. Instead of nagging, a person can try polite requests before the desired behavior, coupled with positive reinforcement during and after the behavior. Naturally, people who have used negative control for a long time cannot expect prior victims to respond instantly to their new positive methods—because of the prior history of nagging and negative control. Reformed naggers may require some practice to master positive skills completely, and their prior victims will need time for all the stimuli associated with both the ex-naggers and the previously nagged behaviors to be counterconditioned into CSs that elicit positive feelings.

Other types of negative control that can usually be avoided are sarcasm, snide remarks, one-upmanship, insults, irritability, rudeness, hostility, domination, dogmatism, pulling rank, and using guilt trips. These all add aversive stimuli to other people's lives and condition both desirable behaviors and social relations in negative ways; hence they are worth avoiding. By the way, criticism need not be a form of negative control if it is clearly done constructively, with genuine signs of caring and friendship.

3. Not Removing Positive Stimuli: "No Withholding of Love, Please." People often punish undesirable behavior by removing positive rewards, but this should not be done with desirable behavior. When he does not get his way, Cliff pouts. He becomes silent and will not talk to Megan for hours, and sometimes for days. By terminating interaction, Cliff has removed the reinforcers he and Megan normally enjoy together. The loss of reinforcers is aversive for both Cliff and Megan, but Cliff can hold out longer, and Megan usually comes around. "Cliff, I'm sorry we couldn't go to the football game last weekend. How about going this weekend?" This reinforces Cliff's pouting—the behavior that removes positive stimuli that could have strengthened desirable behaviors that would have improved their relationship.

Pouting, sulking, withdrawal, and withholding love are all common ways of controlling others by removing positive stimuli. People often learn such behavior in childhood. The sullen child who will not talk because her parents refused to let her watch TV may be allowed to watch TV after her parents find the sulking aversive enough. If people do not have opportunities to learn more mature social skills, they continue to apply their childish skills well into adulthood. This is unfortunate: People who do desirable behavior should never be punished with pouting or sulking. And even people who do undesirable behavior deserve more carefully designed responses—as the rest of the chapter shows.

UNDESIRABLE BEHAVIOR

It may seem obvious that desirable behavior should always be under positive control, with the minimum of negative control. But what about undesirable behavior? If a child lies or steals, is positive control possible? Doesn't undesirable behavior deserve negative control rather than positive control? How should one respond to selfishness, rudeness, or inconsiderateness? Can juvenile delinquency and adult crime be dealt with via positive control? If a person is killing himself or herself with alcohol, cigarette smoke, or dangerous drugs, how can one suppress the undesirable behavior except with aversive control?

Undesirable behavior is behavior that people would like to stop, and most people rely on punishment for suppressing such behavior. However, there are problems with the use of punishment. In the next section, we review the disadvantages of using aversive control to suppress undesirable behavior. In the final section, we examine the alternatives that allow us to minimize negative control even when dealing with undesirable behavior.

The Problems with Punishment

There are six main problems with using punishment. After examining these, we will present several positive ways to stop undesirable behavior—and show why they work better than punishment in many situations. Although it is possible to minimize the use of punishment, it is probably unrealistic to think that punishment can be totally avoided when dealing with highly undesirable behavior. Many believe that punishment will have to be used in certain cases, although it should be employed as sparingly as possible.[7]

1. Punishment Often Teaches Aggression.   When parents, teachers, military leaders, or prison guards use punishment, they may inadvertently provide models for aggression, violence, or the use of force in dealing with others.[8] The recipient of the punishment—and any onlookers—may quickly learn that physical or verbal aggression is an effective means of dealing with others. *Thus, punishment often teaches aggression via modeling effects. The observers may not perform aggressive acts in the presence of the punitive model, but they may use the modeled aggression on others at a later time.*

Studies on boys raised by punitive parents in middle-class homes show the principles clearly.[9] When Jeremy misbehaves, his parents try to suppress his undesirable behavior with verbal and physical punishment. They raise their voices and shout harsh words. "You idiot! Why did you do such a dumb thing?" They may push Jeremy around roughly, then spank or hit him. Most children learn not to fight back because punitive parents usually apply *more* punishment if the child responds with violence. Many children who experience verbal and physical punishment at home do not imitate the violent behavior at home, but they tend to use verbal and physical aggression when interacting with their peers. On the playground, Jeremy uses harsh words and hits other children more than other boys do.

Violence often begets violence, via observational learning. While one person is punishing another, the immediate success of punishment is visible, but the problems of acting as aggressive role models are not as visible. As a result, observers may be inclined to use aggressive behavior on others in the future. People who have never had much chance to learn more positive skills for dealing with social problems may find aggressive behavior to be one of their more successful means of dealing with others, and this reinforces their use of aggression. Of course, people who do aggressive behavior are not always raging and fighting: Their behavior is under S^D control. For example, as Jeremy grows up, he learns to be polite and friendly as long as everyone else is friendly. But any type of disagreement or conflict provides the S^Ds for raising his voice, using strong language, yelling, and making aggressive gestures. If others do not give in, the S^Ds for hitting are present.

Fortunately, violence does not always beget violence. Not everyone gets caught in a "cycle of violence."[10] Some children from physically abusive homes become withdrawn, inhibited, or depressed, rarely using aggression on others. Others become well-adjusted adults, if they have enough positive role models, friends, and reinforcement for overcoming their early pains and learning more positive social skills.[11]

2. Punishment Causes More Vigorous Responding.   *When a person receives intense punishment—be it harsh criticism or physical blows—the person is likely to show a general increase in muscle tension and increase in vigor of responding.*[12] Whatever responses the person emits next—crying, talking, hitting back—are likely to be more intense than they would otherwise have been. The increased vigor and intensity can convert talking into shouting and threatening gestures into physical blows. In these cases, punishment has increased the response vigor of the person who received aversive stimulation, making that person's behavior seem increasingly angry and aggressive to others.

It is true that some people have learned not to shout at or threaten people who punish them. They may have learned to plead for forgiveness, to count to 20, to turn the other cheek, or to seek a more rational solution to the problems at hand. However, individuals who have learned to talk back or threaten may find that punishment from others only increases the vigor of their aggressive responses. On the playground, Jeremy frequently uses aggression, and intense responses from others only increase Jeremy's own violence. Later, in marriage, when Jeremy threatens his wife and she shouts back at him, her shouting is an aversive stimulus that causes Jeremy's responses to become increasingly vigorous until he actually hits her and knocks her to the floor. Domestic violence is the leading cause of injuries to women aged 15–44 years old.[13]

3. Punishment Produces Only Temporary Response Suppression.   *If an undesired behavior is punished, the rate of responding will be suppressed, but in most cases response suppression is only temporary.*[14] Thus, punishment is only a temporary solution to the problem of undesirable behavior, unless the person wielding punishment is able to continuously monitor and frequently punish the unwanted responses. One of the reasons we learn relatively well-suppressed responses from the nonsocial environment is that the physical environment imposes strict contingencies of punishment. When we are clumsy with the butcher knife and cut a finger, the punishment is both immediate and on an FR 1 schedule. This is the most efficient mode of punishment, and it suppresses the clumsy use of knives to a low level. Social punishment is rarely as immediate as a painful cut, and is rarely on an FR 1 schedule; thus, social punishment tends to be less effective. A child may be punished for lying on the average of once for every eighth lie (VR 8 schedule), and the punishment may follow the lie by several hours or days. Delayed and intermittent punishment are not as effective as immediate FR 1 punishment in suppressing behavior; hence people who rely on social punishment as the *primary* method of socialization often fail to achieve results they desire.

4. The Punished Person Learns to Avoid Both Punishment and the People Who Punish.   Whenever people use punishment, they set up conditions that negatively reinforce any responses the punished person can find to avoid punishment. *Socializing agents must realize that if they opt to use punishment in order to suppress someone else's behavior, they will motivate the punished person to avoid detection and/or the people who punish.*[15] First, a child who is punished for lying may learn how to tell more sophisticated lies—lies that are harder to detect—rather than learning not to lie. A juvenile delinquent who is punished for stealing cars may learn to be more skillful in avoiding detection rather than learning not to steal. Second, if socializing agents rely too heavily on punishment, their victims eventually learn to avoid the people who punish them. Once this happens, the socializing agents lose golden opportunities to exert either positive or negative control. This is a double loss: Punitive agents can no longer control undesirable behavior and can no longer teach desirable alternatives. Because avoidance responses are often resistant to extinction, their victims may never stop avoiding the socializing agents. Once their child runs away from home, parents can no longer guide the child's development. Any beneficial influences the parents might have to offer can no longer help the child.

People who are punished can avoid punishment either physically or psychologically. Runaways physically distance themselves from excessively aversive parents. Juvenile delinquents and criminals go underground and learn to live in a world not easily monitored by the police. If physical escape is not possible, some people learn to withdraw psychologically, spending increasing time in fantasy worlds; or they become preoccupied with reading, TV, hobbies, or individual sports; or they turn to alcohol, drugs, or suicide. After the Communists established an extremely brutal, death-dealing police state in Cambodia in 1975, many people risked their lives crossing minefields and deadly booby traps to flee the country.[16] Others retreated into total silence or suffered emotional breakdowns. Some committed suicide, the ultimate means for avoiding aversive experience.

5. Punishment Conditions Negative Emotions.

Negative control is based on aversives, and these aversive stimuli condition many other features of the punished person's life into CSs that elicit painful emotions. Some of the negative emotions created by this Pavlovian conditioning may be adaptive, but others are often maladaptive. Parents who punish their child for running into the street may condition the child to fear playing near traffic (which is adaptive), but they may also condition the child to fear the parents (which is not adaptive). A music student who is frequently criticized for sloppy performances may have sloppy playing conditioned into an aversive CS (which is adaptive), but too much criticism can cause music *in general* to be conditioned into an aversive CS (which is not adaptive).

People who have received relatively frequent punishment often learn to respond to a large number of stimuli as CSs for aversive emotional responses such as fear, anxiety, shame, guilt, or bad feelings about themselves. In most societies, females receive more aversive control than males. As a result, girls and women often learn more negative emotional responses than do males. Females have significantly more nightmares, depression, insomnia, nervousness, and irrational fears than males.[17] Negative emotions can make people fearful of engaging in many activities associated with criticism and punishment. Some people become so sensitized to punishment that even small criticisms or warnings are enough to cause anxiety. Such negative emotions are not conducive to a happy life.

6. Punishment Can Lead to Generalized Response Suppression.

When some behavior, X, is punished, we may note that behavior X, and only X, becomes suppressed. *In contrast, when behavior X and numerous other activities are punished, we may see generalized response suppression.* When people are punished for a large number of different activities, punishment can produce generalized inhibitions that affect much of their entire behavior repertoires. *Generalized punishment can produce highly inhibited people—people who are afraid to speak up, who never take the lead, who fear aversive consequences at every turn.* Heavy doses of negative control often give inhibited people excessively negative emotional responses (item 5) and a strong propensity for physical or psychological avoidance (item 4). Extreme cases of generalized response suppression are not too common, but milder forms such as shyness are. A study of high school and college students showed that about 40% of the students reported feeling shy.[18]

ALTERNATIVES TO PUNISHMENT

Punishment can be brutal and dehumanizing. It can produce many undesirable side effects. There are five major positive alternatives to punishment that have the effect of suppressing undesirable behavior without the undesirable side effects of punishment. It is frequently possible to use two or more of these methods at once—which further minimizes the need for punishment.

1. Differential Reinforcement of Other Behavior—Especially Incompatible Behavior. An effective nonpunitive method for decreasing the frequency of a behavior is the use of differential reinforcement of other behavior, DRO (see pp. 303–304).[19] If Mark is hooked on TV and Nina wants to help him kick the habit, she can use DRO. By rewarding Mark for *other* responses except watching TV, she may get Mark into bowling, dining out, dancing, movies, or visiting with friends in the evening. The more positive reinforcement Nina can bring to these other activities, the better. If both she and Mark enjoy some common friends, the extra social reinforcement may help lure Mark away from the tube and into alternatives that both he and Nina find more gratifying.

Differential reinforcement of other behavior works best when the *other* behavior is *incompatible* with the undesired behavior. These schedules are called *differential reinforcement of incompatible behavior, DRI* (see p. 304). If Nina had used DRO, she might have rewarded Mark for going out with some common friends, but this could eventually lead to his watching TV at the friends' house. DRI is more precise and more focused: Only those activities that are incompatible with TV viewing—such as dancing, doing outdoor sports, going to museums, or shopping—would qualify for DRI, since they make TV viewing unlikely. If your best friend worries a lot, DRO for *any other* behavior besides worry would be less efficient than DRI for *incompatible* responses—which interfere with or distract your friend from worry. Differential reinforcement for *any* behavior other than worry might include reinforcement for reading the newspaper or watching the news on TV; however, the media might expose your friend to news about disasters, epidemics, crime, or other things that trigger new worries. But DRI would distract your friend from worry by reinforcing attention to positive alternatives, such as learning stimulating new pastimes like computers, artistic hobbies, jogging, skating, and traveling with cheerful friends. Each additional hour that your friend devotes to rewarding and nonworrisome activities leaves fewer hours for worry.

DRO and DRI can have long-lasting positive effects. Once a person taps into a new source of reinforcers, the person may never go back to the earlier problematic behavior.

Once your friend gets excited about joining a ball team or volunteering for a charity group, these new activities may leave little time for worrying. After a couple of years, your friend may find it hard to believe there once was a time in which worry used to fill the day. If Bart had been selfish in preschool, DRI could be used to reinforce all non-selfish behaviors. After Bart learns to be kind, thoughtful, and concerned about others, this new style of social interaction makes it very unlikely that he could revert to previous habits of inconsiderate and selfish behavior.

All methods for avoiding the use of punishment can be used in combination. When it is imperative that a problematic behavior never be emitted again, threats of punishment can be made more effective when combined with DRO and DRI. Ms. L had gotten hooked on cocaine in college but has been abstinent for the last year. Now Ms. L has a stimulating new job that occupies many hours of the day and keeps her away from drugs (DRI), but the threat of losing her job if she is caught using drugs adds an extra incentive to stay off them. The mere threat of punishment can motivate Ms. L to avoid drugs and stay oriented toward her new, healthier, and more rewarding lifestyle; and these nondrug behaviors can be so rewarding that Ms. L need never experience the actual punisher of being fired.

2. Observational Learning.   *Models can provide information and vicarious reinforcement that increases desirable behavior, which often suppresses undesirable behavior.* When a model we like or respect is in an S^D context where we might do an undesirable behavior, the model may abstain from the undesirable behavior and respond in ways that help us, as observers, resist the "temptation" (or S^D control) to do the behavior. We observers may learn to abstain and to do some of the behaviors used by the model without having to be punished.[20]

What if we, as children, had heard our parents get into heated discussions, and then heard one or both parents say wise words that brought a peaceful resolution? "Hey, we can't fight about this. We're both mature adults. We've got to calm down and figure out a reasonable solution." This type of behavior provides an excellent model of techniques for avoiding undesirable behavior and switching to more positive alternatives. If the alternatives succeed and our parents show signs of being happy with their new solutions, their skills for avoiding a painful fight—and our vicarious reinforcement from seeing them solve their problems and become happy again—would help us learn skills for coping with heated arguments in a civilized manner. Did you have this observational learning in your childhood? Would you wish it for your children? What do you have to learn before you can give that gift to your children? People who learn how to avoid arguments are likely to miss many punishing social exchanges that less skillful people experience in close relationships, while also serving as models who help others learn these skills.

Coping models provide more useful information than mastery models and usually help observers gain positive skills faster. Mastery models demonstrate perfect mastery without revealing many of the steps needed to attain the mastery of positive control. Coping models reveal the methods they apply to any given problem as they struggle to cope with it.[21] Parents who have completely mastered the problem of resolving disagreements may resolve their infrequent conflicts with only a few words. The onlooking child has little opportunity to learn the dozens of skills that the parents may have mastered in earlier years. Another set of parents may reveal much more of their repertoire of coping skills. After seeing the parents show anger, the child may hear a dialogue full of self-instruction for coping with anger. "I don't want to say harsh words; I want to let you see I love you." "I feel the same. Let's try to work out a compromise." "Fine, but first let me be sure I understand your complaint." As the dialogue continues, the child will observe many of the specific skills the parents use to cope with their problems. Because the coping models give the child more information, they increase the chances that the child will be able to imitate their interpersonal skills successfully.

3. Reasoning and Rules.   One of the most effective ways of decreasing the frequency of undesirable behavior is the use of reasoning and rules. *Instead of punishing people for undesirable behavior, it is often possible to have a gentle but firm conversation with them about the consequences of both the undesirable behavior and several more positive alternatives.* This type of loving and logic-filled conversation helps people learn skills for rationally evaluating the problems or dangers of undesirable behavior, along with the advantages of more desirable alternatives. Undesirable behavior is often deemed undesirable because it damages something—people, animals, plants, places, or things—and learning to talk about problematic behavior gives us reasons to avoid both undesirable behavior and its aversive consequences. Learning to talk about more valuable alternatives gives us reasons and rules for directing our behavior in more positive directions.

One type of reasoning is called **humanistic reasoning** because it emphasizes the human happiness or suffering produced by many of our actions. Humanistic reasoning has been shown to be far superior to physical punishment in all aspects of life. *First, when used in child rearing, reasoning helps children understand how their emotions and actions affect both others and themselves.*[22] What if 5-year-old Shane is playing with several of his toys on the steps of the house and his father trips on them, falling down two steps? Rather than spank Shane, Dad winces with pain, then calmly sits down and extends his arm for Shane to come and sit, gently embraced by his Dad's arm. In this loving context, reasoning and rules can have a positive and dramatic effect. Dad says softly:

> I love you Shane, but I need you to think about having all those toys on the steps where everyone has to walk. Mom and I can't always check to see where your toys are, and a fall down some stairs can lead to serious injuries. I'm OK—I think (chuckling); but you need to think about this thing of toys on the steps. Is there any place safer that you could play with them?

When done gently and lovingly, humanistic reasoning may lead to long conversations that involve both individuals. Shane can suggest other places to play and Dad can reward him by saying, "Good idea." The goal is to help Shane learn to use his brain and think through complex situations in terms of the consequences that they have for himself and others. Humanistic reasoning should not be confused with a "guilt trip," since it focuses loving and logical words on the links between behavior and consequences—including the feelings of all people involved.

Humanistic reasoning lets a child see how many good things come from considerate and prosocial behavior. A parent who uses reasoning does not attack the child and undermine his or her self-concept by saying, "You're stupid and inconsiderate." Because humanistic reasoning is done in a loving way, the parent is *not* saying, "I don't love you." In addition, the parent provides a role model for self-control and humanistic concern rather than a model of verbal or physical aggression.

Humanistic reasoning gives the child rules for avoiding both undesirable behavior and the unhappiness it causes. "So please, don't leave your toys on the steps." Humanistic discussions of the pros and cons of various behaviors generate verbal CSs for positive and negative conditioned emotional responses so the child feels good about considerate behavior and feels sad about harmful behavior.[23] Humanistic reasoning also helps produce generalized prosocial behavior because it gives a child general principles—broad, humanistic rules of considerate conduct—which aid in building self-control. Rather than getting spanked for having toys on the stairs, Shane received a broad lesson in concern for others and the use of reason. By using reasoning, parents teach their child valuable verbal skills for talking and thinking about the positive and negative consequences of all kinds of behavior. Later, if Shane brings a Frisbee or butterfly net into the house, reasoning skills and the generalized rules for considerate conduct will help him be careful not to hurt someone or damage something—a valuable effect that would not have occurred if Shane had merely been spanked after Dad fell over his toys on the steps.

Reasoning helps children learn to avoid hurting others—and therefore avoid being targeted for punishment. It helps them learn to think ahead, evaluate the consequences of various actions, and select good options that minimize bad consequences. Reasoning is best when both people can participate democratically, since everyone who helped create wise rules for future behavior knows why those rules are wise.

Reasoning can be useful at any age. A man and woman may be on the verge of an argument—each ready to angrily criticize the other's shortcomings. If they can reason together, they may be able to avoid starting an argument and punishing each other with harsh words. "I'm angry, but I don't want us to fight. Let's try to reason our way through this." If the two people can talk with the other about their problems and possible solutions, both can use reasoning to create a list of all the advantages and disadvantages associated with each possible solution to their problems. Eventually, the solutions with most advantages for both individuals will begin to stand out as attractive options, without either person's having to punish the other for suggesting one of the poorer options that is eventually dropped from their discussions. Once they have seen the reasons why one option is most desirable, both people will understand the rationale for working toward that most promising solution to their problem.[24]

Once people are used to reasoning, lengthy discussions can be faded to a few brief sentences: "That's not appropriate in this context. Let's keep it polite." There is a small hint about the unwanted behavior and a positive rule for staying polite.

Reasoning can be used in many contexts. People on the board of directors may use reasoning when trying to resolve differences of opinion and to decide how best to steer the future of their corporation. Again, reasoning can avert fights and harsh words. A supervisor may use reasoning in discussions with workers about possible improvements in factory procedures. If the supervisor can present enough positive reasons for adopting the new procedures, the workers will see the benefits of switching to the new activity. If the workers cannot be convinced of the positive value of the new practices, they may convince the supervisor that some other alternative would work better. *Reasoning tends to facilitate democratic decision making, engage many brains in decision making, and allow the most rewarding options to be selected from the available alternatives. It breeds mutual respect and minimizes the need for fights and punishing exchanges. Less desirable choices do not need to be punished; they merely lose their attractiveness as more positive alternatives are suggested and discussed democratically.*

4. Extinction.   The frequency of operants can be decreased by removing the reinforcers that maintain them, but it takes skill to use extinction well. If Jeremy is whining, his parents may have to work hard to avoid rewarding him with their attention. Extinction may require days or weeks to reduce an unwanted behavior to zero. Extinction is even slower if the undesirable behavior has strong behavioral momentum due to a long history of generous reinforcement. Because extinction does not produce an immediate and rapid decline in response rates, many people find it difficult to learn how to use extinction effectively. However, there are advantages for using extinction rather than punishment. *Because extinction does not involve the application of aversive stimuli, it does not condition aversive emotional responses. Also, it does not provide models for verbal or physical attacks on others.*

As we saw in Chapter 8 (Secondary Reinforcers and Punishers), children may learn a variety of attention-getting behaviors. Some forms of attention getting are undesirable: throwing tantrums, starting fights, shouting, being insolent, whining, and so forth. If attention from adults is the main source of reinforcement for the behavior, adults can terminate the behavior successfully by ceasing to pay attention. To make extinction work, it is important to know what reinforcers are maintaining the undesirable response and be able to remove a large portion of these. If it is not possible to remove most of the reinforcers, then some other method besides extinction may need to be used. For example, if a child's peer group is the key source of reinforcement for aggressive behavior that is used to attract social attention, adults may not be able to stop the behavior by cutting off adult attention alone. Reasoning and DRI might work better in this case.

Nevertheless, extinction is well suited for dealing with many of the undesirable actions in everyday life. Because parents are the major source of reinforcers for young children, they can often terminate unwanted behavior by extinction. A child who wakes the parents and demands a glass of water in the middle of the night will cease demanding after the parents cease giving reinforcement. A child who keeps pestering mother and father with inconsiderate behavior will stop pestering after parental attention is no longer forthcoming. Extinction can be combined effectively with any of the other methods in this section. For example, while pestering and inconsiderate behaviors are being extinguished, the parents could make special efforts to model thoughtful and considerate behavior, then quickly reward all imitative responses the child makes.

People in intimate relationships often control many of the reinforcers that condition or maintain each other's behavior. She may yell at him because yelling is the only way she can make him listen, and her yelling is reinforced by his paying attention to her complaints and complying with some of her demands. In contrast, he pouts when he does not get his way, and his pouting is reinforced when she eventually comes over to him, says nice things, and tries to make up. These, and many other behavior problems that blemish intimate relations, can often be removed by extinction. In advance, the two lovers agree to do this for each other: He promises to stop reinforcing her yelling by *not* paying attention to her when she yells, and she promises to stop reinforcing his pouting by *not* paying attention when he sulks. This method works especially well in conjunction with DRO and DRI: He pays special attention to her when she is not yelling, and she is especially friendly and considerate when he is not pouting. The extinction of undesirable behavior is hastened by the rewards of social attention for incompatible behavior.[25]

People need not be parents or lovers to be major sources of reinforcers for each other. Friends, coworkers, neighbors, and acquaintances often exchange many reinforcers. Whenever people are dependent on one another for many rewarding events—such as fun and games, mutual support, sympathy, or team effort—they need each others' reinforcers; hence the removal of reinforcers can decrease the frequency of undesirable behavior via extinction. For example, if several coworkers all depend on each others' joking and horseplay to combat the boredom of a tedious job, stopping the fun and games after one person offends another will help stop the offensive behavior.

5. Gentle Punishment.   There are two very gentle but effective and nonviolent forms of punishment—timeout and response cost. They are often advocated because they emphasize the desirability of good behavior and its positive consequences without modeling anger or aggression. They help people value positive reinforcement by showing that reinforcers can be lost when undesirable behavior occurs.

Timeout is a period of time during which a person cannot enjoy normal reinforcement schedules because some undesirable behavior has occurred. If your books are overdue, the library may cut off your borrowing privileges as long as the books are unreturned. You are on a "timeout" and cannot enjoy the rewards of library use until you show that you can follow the library's rules. When little April cannot behave nicely during her family's evening TV and popcorn party, her parents take her to the most boring room in the house where she must stay for a predetermined period of time. Wise parents make sure April sees the contingent link between her behavior and the timeout, so she can think about the links between acting up and losing rewards. April's parents model calm and poise as they take April to the timeout area, and this helps calm her down. (Screaming parents and physical punishment would have modeled agitation and aggression—and would have been the opposite of calming.) After April regains her composure and appreciates that misbehaving hurts herself and others, she can come back to the family fun and be treated in a friendly manner by others.

Timeout has proven to be very effective in dealing with many problem behaviors.[26] When people use timeout, they need to have a timeout area that contains very few reinforcers. If April had been sent to her room and it was full of toys, a TV and VCR, a computer full of games and her own on-line Internet service, being sent to her room would not be very punishing. Timeout is most likely to work if April is sent to the most boring part of the house where she can think about her behavior. In larger groups, such as classrooms, timeout can be done by having a person move to a distant seat or wear a timeout ribbon after misbehaving. These timeout cues let others know that person is on timeout and must be excluded from rewarding activities until the timeout period is over.[27]

How does timeout feel? Our students told us: "I really hated the loss of my rights to play outside, and it made me aware that I did not want to mess up again," said Cagnie. "I got 15 minutes of timeout if I accepted it quietly, but 20 or 30 minutes if I mouthed off, so I learned to accept the consequences of my behavior," said Catherine. "Loss of access to privileges was good because it made me aware that they all were *privileges,* and this is an introduction to adulthood—where speeding and other things can lead to loss of driver's license, etc.," said Erik. "My parents talked with me democratically and asked me what timeout period I thought would be fair for each misdemeanor. It helped me see that they were struggling to figure out what was best and fair; and I was impressed that they trusted me to participate in their system of 'justice,'" said Brett.

Response cost *attaches some extra cost to an undesirable behavior, without taking away reinforcers—the way timeout does.*[28] If you write a bad check, the bank adds a charge to your checking account. There is no timeout period in which your checking account is frozen so you cannot write checks. Response costs make us aware that we cannot take our checking account for granted. Others experience costs and inconveniences when we write checks that bounce, and our having to pay a response cost punishes us and makes us aware of our mistakes. Response costs can easily be used in token economies, when a person is docked a few tokens for errors or misbehavior. When we abuse our library privileges, monetary fines for overdue and lost books are response costs: They punish our errors and make us aware that the library provides free services that should not be taken for granted. Monetary fines punish via response cost, whereas loss of library privileges punishes by timeout. Both work.

In essence, response cost is punishment by addition (or positive punishment), since extra costs are added. In contrast, timeout is punishment by subtraction (or negative punishment), since rewards are lost during the timeout. Both forms of gentle punishment heighten our awareness of the positive rewards, behaviors, or services we have taken for granted—and abused; hence they have the beneficial effects of helping us value good things more—be they family fun, library privileges, or the convenience of a checkbook. Most other forms of punishment do not have these positive side effects.

CONCLUSION

People usually use combinations of positive and negative control in their interactions with others. Centuries ago, people used punishment much more than today, but there is still room for improvement in helping people minimize punishment and shift to positive control. Positive reinforcers make life much more pleasant than punishment. Guilt, anxiety, and worry become things of the past.[29] Under positive control, each person can learn constructive, creative behavior and feel good about his or her contributions. There are six main problems with punishment, which give us reason to avoid using it—even with undesirable behavior. Fortunately, there are five ways to reduce unwanted behavior without resorting to physical punishment or verbal abuse. Although punishment may never be totally abolished, it can be minimized. It is needed only as a backup, a stopgap for those situations in which more positive practices do not work quickly enough.[30] Singer, Gert, and Koegel (1999, p. 88) summarize: "Nonaversive alternatives are available and can replace aversive procedures in all but a very small number of highly unusual cases."

As people gain skill in using positive models, rules, prompts, and reinforcement, they can make sure desirable behavior is acquired and maintained under positive control without aversive associations. The sooner that children learn to regulate their lives by humanistic reasoning and use positive interaction styles with others, the more likely they are to approach their entire lives in a positive manner.

QUESTIONS

1. Can you define positive control and negative control?
2. What are the broad historical trends in the use of positive and negative control?
3. How do science and technology allow us to shift from negative to positive control?
4. Why is it wise to use positive control with desirable behavior? Why is it unwise to use negative control with desirable behavior?
5. How can people increase their use of positive control? How does this apply to primary reinforcers? To secondary reinforcers?
6. Give three ways to decrease the use of negative control in everyday life.
7. List six problems with punishment. Explain each one clearly.
8. Give five ways to reduce undesirable behavior without resorting to punishment.

NOTES

1. Harris (1977); Adams (1994).

2. Bloom (1985); Gottfried et al. (1998)

3. Horner et al. (1990); Koegel et al. (1992); Koegel, Koegel, and Dunlap (1996); Latham (1996); Seligman (1998); Gillham and Seligman (1999); Gottman (1999); Baldwin and Baldwin (2000); Seligman and Csikszentmihalyi (2000).

4. Bandura (1969); Mahoney and Thoresen (1974); Bellack and Hersen (1977); Redd, Porterfield, and Anderson (1979); Goldstein and Cisar (1992); Ducharme and Popynick (1993); Gottman (1994, 1999); Kazdin (1994); Cautela and Ishaq (1996); Martin and Pear (1996); Watson and Tharp (1997); Loeb et al. (2000).

5. Skinner (1953, 1971); Bandura (1973, 1986); Repp and Singh (1990); Maccoby (1992); Berryman, Evans, and Kalbag (1994); Snyder and Patterson (1995). However, there are times when punishment is desirable (Fisher et al., 1993; Newsom, Favell, & Rincover, 1983; O'Neill & Reichle, 1993).

6. Homans (1974); Hatfield and Rapson (1993).

7. Walters and Grusec (1977); Axelrod and Apsche (1983); Maccoby (1992).

8. Bandura (1973, 1986).

9. Bandura and Walters (1959); Hoffman (1960). Girls usually receive so much more conditioning against the use of violence that they do not readily imitate aggressive parents (Baldwin, 1983; Bandura, 1973).

10. Widom (1989); Dodge, Bates, and Pettit (1990).

11. Werner (1989).

12. Bandura (1973); Walters and Grusec (1977); Nilsson and Archer (1989).

13. Novello, Rosenberg, Saltzman, and Shosky (1992); Dutton (1995).

14. The effects of reinforcement are temporary, too, but intermittent reinforcement can maintain high rates of responding more effectively than intermittent punishment can suppress behavior (Walters & Grusec, 1977).

15. Staats (1963, pp. 51–52); Cressey (1978, p. 45).

16. Dirge of the Kampucheans (1978).

17. Chesler (1971); Tavris and Wade (1984); Boggiano and Barrett (1991).

18. Zimbardo, Pilkonis, and Norwood (1975); Zimbardo and Radl (1981); Carducci and Zimbardo (1995).

19. Wagaman et al. (1993); Wagaman et al. (1995); Luiselli (1996); Richman et al. (1997); Kellam et al. (1998); Woods and Wright (1998); Zanolli, Daggett, Ortiz, and Mullins (1999).

20. Gena et al. (1996).

21. Meichenbaum (1971, pp. 298–307); Bandura and Barab (1973); Bandura (1986).

22. Hoffman (1970); La Voie (1974); Rottschaefer (1991); Eisenberg et al. (1999).

23. Cheyne and Walters (1970); Öhman and Soares (1998).

24. Marital partners can avoid inflicting unnecessary pain on each other by reasoning with each other on an equal basis rather than fighting (Gottman, 1994, 1999).

25. Woods and Miltenberger (1995).

26. Van Houten (1983); Sisson, VanHasselt, Hersen, and Aurand (1988); Handen, Parrish, McClung, Kerwin, and Evans (1992).

27. Foxx and Shapiro (1978).

28. Rapport, Murphy, and Bailey (1982); Little and Kelley (1989); Kelley and McCain (1995); Reynolds and Kelley (1997); Zhou et al. (2000).

29. Kaufmann (1973); Seligman and Csikszentmihalyi (2000).

30. Walters and Grusec (1977); Newsom et al. (1983).

Chapter

15

Thinking, the Self, and Self-Control

SELF-CONFIDENCE

Ben is afraid to try new things. He is certain that he will mess up, be a big failure, embarrass himself in front of others, and be criticized. As a result, Ben stays home and watches a lot of TV. But outside his living room window, other guys his age are playing, socializing, doing things, having a good time. Ben feels that something is terribly wrong with him. But what?

Ms. W—who is his next-door neighbor—is a high school counselor and has noticed Ben's absence from the outdoor activities around her house. Ms. W is quite familiar with Ben's problem: Learned helplessness can lead to passivity and depression. She gives him a book about this problem and its solution—*Learned Optimism,* by Martin Seligman (1998).

As Ben starts reading the book, he quickly sees himself in the examples of men and women with learned helplessness. They have often failed at important activities or received more criticism than a person should. They fear that they will not succeed at new challenges and activities—expecting more failures and criticisms. As he reads, Ben notices his head filling up with new thoughts he has never had before. He can understand and empathize with the childhoods of people who now feel helpless, passive, and depressed. Then he marvels at the positive learning experiences that some people have, and the way they developed learned optimism and self-confidence. The book is full of words that are spilling into his head and helping him think in new ways about himself. Ben is happy that there are three chapters about behavior modification that tell him to do many of the things he had already guessed might help him.

Armed with new words that serve as rules to guide behavior, Ben decides to increase his positive feelings about himself and his sense of optimism: He should try to learn an activity that he had always wanted to do, but had avoided for fear of failure. He should learn to talk to himself in an optimistic way about learning the new behavior and taking practical steps to be certain that he succeeds at it. It might be good to find a coach or teacher to help him learn the new skill in a safe and rewarding environment, without risk of failure. With useful rules and positive reinforcement, he could begin to master the basics, confident that practice and rewards would bring improved skills. He needs to find a teacher who models the behavior, gives generous positive reinforcement, and asks Ben to try the next more challenging step—when and only when—Ben is ready. As Ben makes real progress at gaining skill, without the failures he had so feared, his fear of failure disappears, counterconditioned by a history of new successes. Ben gains increased optimism and self-confidence, feels better about himself, and is motivated to approach other new challenges.

Ben always liked watching martial arts on TV, so he went to four places in town that offered such training and interviewed four trainers, in search of one who seemed like the best model of self-confidence and happiness. Mr. Miyagi was perfect, always optimistic and self-disciplined. After several months of rewarding progress toward a valued goal, Ben became a new person, with a growing sense of self-confidence. Reading had given him words that allowed him to think in new ways and learn behaviors that freed him from the narrow life he had had just months before.

THINKING IS BEHAVIOR[1]

Early behaviorists focused their attention mostly on *overt* behavior—the external behavior that is easy to see and hear, measure objectively with laboratory instruments, and analyze scientifically. *As behavior theory and research have advanced, increasing attention has been given to **covert behavior**—such as thinking, feeling, reasoning, awareness of meaning, awareness of self and identity, perceived self-efficacy, and self-control. Scientific studies indicate that covert behavior can be explained by the same principles that explain overt behavior.[2] Thinking is a form of behavior.* The things we think about are learned from models, rules, prompts, and reinforcement. The person who finds surfing very rewarding learns from peers and practice, and thinks about surfing when in and out of the water. Our self-concept and identity depend on the words we learn to describe our own behavior. "I am a surfer. It's a big part of my life."

Thinking is the behavior of the brain. Cognitive behaviorists focus primarily on the thought processes of which we are aware.[3] *Our awareness is mostly occupied with sense perceptions of our body and the current environment along with an **internal dialogue**—or inner conversation—that we carry on with ourselves inside our heads.* The sense perceptions are given to us through the five external senses and the internal sense receptors. The inner conversation of thought emerges in childhood when we begin to talk with others and learn how to keep on talking to ourselves with our lips closed.[4] The inner conversation consists of the silent words we "hear" inside our heads when everyone stops talking and we "listen" to our thoughts. Thinking is sometimes called "subvocal speech," because the words we hear during thought are similar to spoken words except that they are below the vocally spoken level—hence subvocal.

Our "minds" and "inner words" often seem so deep inside us that we think them to be very private and personal. But this is only partially true. *The internal words of our thoughts are a gift to us from society—from the verbal community that talks to us, asks us to describe our behavior, and reinforces self-descriptive verbal responses.*[5] This is most obvious when you realize that you think in English rather than in Russian or Swahili. During your socialization, the verbal community provided *models* of the English language. You heard the *rules* of English grammar and syntax: "Don't use double negatives." *Differential reinforcement* was given for correct and incorrect use of English phrases and idioms: When you used word patterns that were comprehensible to other English speakers, you reaped the rewards of successful communication; but gibberish led to extinction or punishment.[6] Through this process, you not only learned to speak English but also to think—carry out subvocal speech—in English. But not all children receive the gift of language equally well. Research by Hart and Risley (1995) shows that children are most likely to develop verbal skills when their parents and teachers model large vocabularies and reward the children for using a large range of words, keeping punishment to a minimum.[7]

In addition, the *contents* of your thoughts are largely a gift of the society in which you live. We do not worry about witch-hunts, as people did in Salem, Massachusetts, in 1692. Our thoughts are filled with the issues of the current historical moment—tonight's TV programs, the latest political events, current job opportunities, whether to buy a car. Much of our thought content depends on the subculture in which we live. Motorcycle enthusiasts learn how to talk about carburetors and camshafts, the performance of different bikes, and the advantages of various equipment. Artists may speak a very different language, discussing trends in modern art, new exhibits at local museums, and the galleries where one's work will get good exposure. Most motorcyclists and artists live in different subcultures, hear different verbal inputs, and learn to think about different things.

If your closest friends frequently discuss sex, birth control, and overpopulation, you are likely to talk—and think—about these topics, too. If you hear a news item relevant to these topics, you are likely to both think about the information and communicate it to your friends, because these verbal behaviors are often reinforced in your circle of friends. Because your history of learning experience is unique, your thoughts will never be the same as anyone else's; hence your rethinking of any topic will usually introduce novel variations—your "personal perspective" on the topic. Because variety is a source of sensory stimulation reinforcement, the "spice of life," each individual's personal variations make interaction more reinforcing than if we all had identical thoughts and said precisely the same things.

We learn the ability to think conscious verbal thoughts from symbolic social interaction. Words and verbal thoughts are gifts given to us by all those people who helped us learn to speak and think with words. They began outside our bodies and came inside via learning. *Our thoughts are closely related to verbal patterns common in our historical period and subculture. But each individual's unique history of learning experience introduces unique variations into that individual's thoughts and words.*[8]

OPERANT CONDITIONING OF THOUGHTS

Speaking and thinking are both verbal behavior. One is overt (outward), the other is covert (inward). Homme labeled thoughts as **coverants** *to designate their status as covert operants.*[9] *The research on coverants indicates that these "operants of the mind" are acquired and maintained in much the same manner as overt operants are.*[10] We learn the language that will become our inner words from *models, rules,* and *verbal prompts*—which give us exposure to spoken and written words. It is then the patterns of *differential reinforcement* that follow each coverant which modify the frequency of the numerous coverants in a person's inner conversation.[11]

Models. *People learn many coverants from observing and listening to others.*[12] An admired friend who talks at length about working in the Peace Corps serves as a positive model for your learning similar verbal thoughts. Later, you may find yourself thinking that perhaps you should consider the Peace Corps, with its opportunities for international travel and helping people in distant nations. Because you like your friend and feel good about the conversation, you experience vicarious reinforcement as you rethink the coverants your friend gave you. The novelty of thinking about yourself in a Peace Corps job will provide sensory stimulation reinforcers, too—until the novelty of the topic "wears off," due to habituation. If you have no urgent competing responses to distract you, you may have hours to think about the Peace Corps, enjoying the vicarious and sensory reinforcement that makes these coverants become more frequent.

Later you may share your new ideas with someone else who spent two years in the Peace Corps. What if this person had suffered unbelievable hardships, contracted a serious disease, and felt the work was futile? Each enthusiastic thought you voice is likely to be followed by a pessimistic rebuttal based on this person's negative experiences. The pessimist is simultaneously punishing your thinking of idealistic thoughts and modeling a new set of bleaker verbal descriptions of Peace Corps work. If you like this second person, this negative description of Peace Corps work will affect you more than if you dislike the person. In any case, you may find that you now have both positive and negative verbal thoughts about the Peace Corps, which might lead you to think, "I'd need to get some more data about the Peace Corps before I'd join."

Rules. *Rules also affect the acquisition and maintenance of coverants.* If you have often heard people say, "Never trust politicians; always be critical of what they say," the rules may influence your internal words. After hearing a political speech full of generous campaign promises, you may recall the rule and begin to think of possible criticisms of the politician's promises. The campaign promises serve as S^Ds for recalling the rule—"be critical"—and the rule serves as an S^D for thinking of various possible critiques.

While at a formal party, you may recall a rule of etiquette stating that one should graciously thank the hosts before leaving. The rule then serves as an S^D for silently rehearsing several things you might say. This cognitive rehearsal gives you practice in wording your comments tactfully and allows you to identify the phrasing that sounds most positive—and most "you."[13] After you approach the hosts and thank them, your carefully chosen words are likely to create good effects that reinforce both the rule use and your cognitive rehearsal skills.

Verbal Prompts. *Thoughts are sometimes influenced by verbal prompts.* Verbal prompts are most often used when one person cannot think of a crucial word or phrase and a second person suggests the word or phrase that is needed. Later, the person may recall the words more easily than before the prompting occurred.

Reinforcement and Punishment. Thoughts can be modified by any type of reinforcement or punishment that seems to have a contingent connection to them.[14] *First, a thought can be modified by primary reinforcers or punishers when the coverant leads to overt actions that produce reinforcement or punishment.* The thought of popping some popcorn may begin a chain of responses that ends in a delicious snack and the primary reinforcer of food. Thinking of a way to stop the house from losing its heat on windy winter nights is negatively reinforced by the avoidance of being too cold. What happens when thoughts lead to primary punishers? A child who thinks that honeybees are pretty little creatures and reaches out to touch one usually gets stung. Because external punishment suppresses thoughts and behavior, the thought of touching bees will become less frequent.

Although all primary reinforcers and punishers can affect the frequency of coverants, sensory stimulation can influence the frequency of thoughts without their having to lead to overt behavior first. Thinking produces sensory stimulation. If a person is not overstimulated, novel and complex thoughts are usually more reinforcing than familiar and simple thoughts. When a young person first imagines being a movie star, a doctor, or a professional athlete, much of the reinforcement for the thought comes from imagining oneself in a new and exciting role. Children can spend hours at a time in *fantasy role play,* as they think about the careers and roles they have seen modeled by adults, TV performers, and their peers. This mental play is reinforced by the sensory stimulation it brings, and it gives the child practice for playing a variety of social roles. Once the novelty of the fantasy of being a TV news anchor wears off, a child may latch onto a new fantasy. Other examples of thought patterns reinforced by the novel sensory stimulation they produce include problem solving, playing with new ideas, daydreaming, and drug trips. Since sensory stimulation is only one of the many reinforcers in life, not all our thoughts are shaped by sensory rewards.

Second, thoughts can be modified by secondary reinforcers and punishers from either inside or outside the body. A clever thought about how to earn more money may be reinforced by the internal secondary reinforcers of thinking about spending all the money. It may also be reinforced by the external secondary reinforcers of carrying out the plan and actually earning a sizable chunk of cash. The thought of driving to the country may be reinforced by pleasurable thoughts about the beauty of the countryside. The decision to take the drive is reinforced by seeing the lovely views. For people who find the thought of going to jail aversive enough, thoughts of robbing a bank are usually punished and suppressed by the unpleasant thoughts of being caught and imprisoned.

People can learn to use positive and negative thoughts to modify other aspects of their behavior. After noticing and commenting on a friend's generous actions, we can reward ourself with positive thoughts such as "I'm happy I noticed that." This type of cognitive self-reinforcement can even be used to reinforce other patterns of thought.[15] If we wish to increase our production of creative thoughts, we should notice each clever or creative idea and make positive self-comments—"That's beautiful!"—either aloud or silently to ourself. Even silent and subvocal self-reward helps reinforce and build the skills for creative thinking. After thinking undesirable thoughts, we can help decrease the frequency of those thoughts with self-punishment: "John, don't waste your precious time thinking about junk like that." Self-punishment works best when we couple it with a rule to think about some new, more positive, and beneficial topics.

PAVLOVIAN CONDITIONING OF THOUGHTS

Although thinking is a behavior, thoughts also function as stimuli. Through Pavlovian conditioning, thoughts can become conditioned stimuli (CSs) that can, in turn, elicit conditioned responses, including emotional responses. Merely thinking about someone you find sexually attractive can elicit sexual responses such as vaginal lubrication or penile erection and erotic feelings.[16] Thinking about a recent embarrassing experience can elicit feelings of discomfort, along with blushing, nervous sweating, and trembling.[17]

Positive Thoughts

Thoughts associated with positive and rewarding events can become CSs that (1) elicit pleasurable emotional responses and (2) function as secondary positive reinforcers. As young children learn that birthdays are associated with parties and presents, the mere thought that their birthday is coming soon becomes a CS that elicits pleasurable feelings and reinforces frequent thoughts of the party. The closer the big day comes, the more a child thinks about all the ice cream, cake, and presents. Merely thinking these thoughts generates the pleasurable cognitive CSs that reinforce continued thinking about the birthday. Teenagers who love to think about distant places may find that their daydreams about travel are longer and more frequent than daydreams about other, less rewarding activities. Adults often find their thoughts turning to the new furniture or car they plan to buy, to memories their last vacation, or other positive events. Thinking optimistic thoughts and daydreaming about wonderful experiences are reinforced by the positive stimuli they produce. A person may also receive social reinforcement for positive thinking—because other people usually find interaction with a cheerful, optimistic individual to be rewarding.

Negative Thoughts

If optimistic thoughts are so rewarding, why is it that people do not think positive thoughts all the time? If a person has often experienced trauma, failure, disappointment, or other punishers after optimistically planning for future events, the punishment can suppress optimistic thinking. Also, people who have experienced horrible events or have many things to worry about often find that worry is a competing response which decreases optimism.[18]

Thoughts associated with pain and punishment can become CSs that (1) elicit aversive emotional responses and (2) function as conditioned punishers.[19] Painful thoughts can suppress the frequency of chains of thoughts that lead to them. Many people find the thought of their own death to be aversive, and after a while they stop thinking about it. Some students hate taking exams: They hate thinking about finals and all the work they have to do. Even though they know final exams are coming up in a few weeks, they avoid thinking about them because the thoughts are aversive. Some students cannot bring themselves to think seriously about studying until shortly before finals when fears of failing their courses negatively reinforce their thinking about cramming for the tests.

Worry and Self-Torment.   If thoughts and worries about aversive things are CSs that function as conditioned punishers, why do some people end up worrying all the time? Why is it that they cannot stop thinking about the problems, heartaches, torments, regrets, uncertainties, and fears that all function as CSs for painful emotions? *There are several patterns of conditioning that reinforce worrying more strongly than the pain of the negative thoughts can punish and suppress worry habits.*[20]

First, worry is often negatively reinforced by the escape from or avoidance of major problems. A student who worries about not passing a course may plan ahead, study hard, and eventually be rewarded by a good grade. A person who worries about vacation plans for months ahead may succeed in getting everything arranged so the vacation goes well. Thus, worry can be a type of problem-solving behavior, and it can be negatively reinforced because it allows people to avoid various problems. However, while people are thinking about possible future problems, they may be exposing themselves to numerous worrisome issues that are cognitive CSs for aversive feelings, and these can distort problem-solving processes.[21] Fortunately, other kinds of problem-solving skills are more rewarding (see the section on reasoning, pp. 349–354).

Second, positive social reinforcement can strengthen habits of worrying. People who worry often receive sympathy from others, and this social reinforcement can condition worry into a high frequency response. People who worry out loud about their medical problems may receive lots of social attention, and they may learn to worry about any strange sensation in their bodies. People who criticize or belittle themselves often find that other people respond with sympathy—perhaps enumerating all their good points. The social attention given to worry and self-criticism can condition these coverants into high-frequency responses, even though worry and self-censure are CSs that elicit aversive emotions.

Third, negative social reinforcement can heighten worries. Beginning in the early years of life, some children learn to be self-critical and self-punitive because this behavior often reduces the likelihood that other people will punish them. For example, parents are more likely to punish their daughter's transgressions if she shows no self-punishment than if she is blaming herself for breaking a valuable vase, criticizing her own clumsiness, and saying how bad she feels. If she cries and says how sorry she is, she might even receive comfort, "It's OK, dear. We'll be able to replace it." Thus, some children learn to escape social punishment by engaging in self-punishment. Because escape and avoidance behavior can be very resistant to extinction, these individuals may continue to engage in self-punishing thoughts long after there is any reason to do so. This can lead to a lifelong habit of excessive self-castigation for even tiny errors.

Fourth, once any of these three patterns of reinforcement causes a person to begin worrying, the worries may be further reinforced by sensory stimulation. If a person begins to worry about being shy or unattractive, dozens of new worries can follow: "Will I ever meet someone who loves me?" "Will I ever get married?" "Will I be lonely all my life?" The more novel problems and "worst case scenarios" a person discovers to worry about, the more sensory stimulation reinforcement there is for worrying.[22] Some people who worry a great deal are especially skilled at locating problems to worry about, and the more things they can find to fret over, the more sensory stimulation reinforcement they receive for their problem-finding skills. Eventually flashbacks to prior traumas can be embellished with more terror images than they originally reported. Even when things are going right, fear-focused people think about things that could go wrong, and many discover—or invent—numerous problems that would have never occurred to other people. Sadly, the more problems they envision, the more painful worries they bring into their lives.

Thoughts Condition Thoughts

Through Pavlovian conditioning, the CSs in one train of thoughts can condition other thoughts. If thoughts about topic X function as CSs for pleasurable emotions, other thoughts that precede and predict positive thoughts about X will also become increasingly pleasurable.[23] When you fall in love with someone, you often find that many of the things that person likes also become more appealing to you. If the person you love is an avid sailor, you may find yourself—for the first time in your life—fantasizing about sailing in the Caribbean. Each time the fantasies of sailing are paired with the positive thoughts of sharing the experience with your lover, the thoughts of sailing become more strongly conditioned into CSs that elicit pleasure. Eventually, sailing may become such a strong CS for pleasurable feelings that you notice yourself lingering over magazine pictures of sailboats (indicating that the CSs of sailboat pictures reinforce your prolonged attention), and smiling as you picture yourself on the boat (indicating that the CSs of sailboats have elicited positive emotional responses).

A person who loves money and financial security may find that thoughts which were once neutral become positive if they are linked with financial success. An entrepreneur may have never cared much for Florida vacations, but when she gets a good buy on a resort hotel on the beach near Miami, thinking about Florida vacations will become more positive due to Pavlovian conditioning. When the entrepreneur thinks about people flying to Miami for the sun and surf, for the night life, for a leisurely stay in a resort hotel on the beach, she may also think about the monetary success of her new investment. Soon, the investor's thoughts of Florida beaches become such positive CSs that they reinforce the purchase of Florida posters for her office walls—and elicit her smiles as she imagines the palm-lined shores.

If thoughts about topic Y function as CSs for painful emotions, other thoughts that precede and predict negative thoughts about Y will become increasingly painful. Some people who live in cities near nuclear power plants have relatively neutral opinions about nuclear power. However, if their local nuclear plant malfunctions and releases radioactive isotopes into the environment, they may find their thoughts and feelings about nuclear power changing, as the thoughts become CSs for aversive feelings. The more the people think about meltdowns, radiation poisoning, and radiation-induced cancers, the more frightened they become, and the more the thought of nuclear power becomes a fear-eliciting CS. (After the nuclear accident at Three Mile Island, many people who lived nearby experienced prolonged aversive mental conditioning and some developed a chronic form of stress that lasted for years.[24])

People who worry a great deal may inadvertently condition a large number of once-neutral thoughts into fear-eliciting CSs. After a person has learned to be afraid of dying in an airplane accident, the person may pair other thoughts with the first fear and thereby condition new fears. While worrying about flying home for a vacation, the person may imagine being in an airplane crash, being helplessly trapped in the burning plane, and dying a horrible death. While worrying about these gory details, the person may happen to think about driving to the airport and suddenly imagine there could be an automobile accident: The car could crash, trap the passengers, then catch on fire. In a panic, the person thinks, "Is there anything that's safe? Even walking is dangerous. A car could run out of control, come careening across the sidewalk and kill you at any moment." What began with worrying about dying in an air accident has become worry about other kinds of travel, and the person has created several new conditioned fears by pairing thoughts of driving and walking with thoughts of a frightening death. Continuing these types of fear-producing worries can condition fear of any kind of travel, and eventually make the person afraid to leave the house—a condition known as agoraphobia.[25]

S^{D}s AND THOUGHTS

Because thoughts are operants, they come under S^D control. Stimuli that regularly precede a reinforced thought become S^{D}s that set the occasion for the thought in the future. Each of the following S^{D}s has strong stimulus control over people's coverants: "What is your name? Where were you born? What is your birthday? What is 2 times 2?" Other S^{D}s have less predictable S^D control: "Name a color. Name a foreign country." These S^{D}s allow more room for *free associations* because many responses can be correct and deserving of reinforcement. At any moment, the stimulus collage exposes us to multitudes of S^{D}s that set the occasion for our thoughts: Some of these have strong control for specific responses and others have looser control, allowing free associations.

Those thoughts called *memories* provide a clear example of S^D control. When a child grows up in Hometown, the people, places, and activities unique to Hometown provide the child with firsthand learning experiences; but eventually the thoughts experienced in childhood become memories only. Years later, the person may try to recall memories of childhood in Hometown and be surprised how little comes back. But note what happens when the adult gets out old photo albums or high school yearbooks. The photos of Mom and Dad at the Fourth of July picnic suddenly bring back memories of things that happened on that occasion. A picture of the person's best friend in high school triggers off a long chain of thoughts that the person may not have had in years. Each picture is a stimulus collage that contains many S^Ds for dozens of thoughts that may not have been emitted for years. Thus, S^Ds serve as *keys to memory*. Each new picture provides new S^Ds that may evoke more memories. When the person goes back to Hometown after 10 years of being away, the experiences of walking down some old familiar streets and looking at the grade school playground expose the person to multitudes of S^Ds—in three dimensions and living color—that can bring back more old memories than photo albums ever did. The more numerous and vivid the S^Ds are, the more likely they are to evoke the old coverants.

The S^Ds that call back memories do not need to be visual. *Because thoughts can function as stimuli, they can become S^Ds for other operants, covert or overt.* A person may use thoughts or reminiscences about Hometown as the S^Ds that unlock yet other memories. Many verbal descriptions that you can give of your hometown contain words that may serve as S^Ds for other memories. If you set aside time to think about your memories, you will notice that some of your memories serve as S^Ds for yet other memories. Creating more time for recall lets you bring up even more thoughts that serve as S^Ds for memories of the past.

When you learn a person's name, many stimuli in the stimulus collage may become associated with the name—for example, the person's facial expressions, hair color, clothing, the topic of the conversation, the room where you met. Later when you try to think of the name, you may reconstruct several elements of the stimulus collage before enough S^Ds are present to bring back the name. People often "search their memories" by presenting themselves with as many relevant S^Ds as possible that might bring up the desired thought. When eager to recall someone's name, you might ask yourself a series of questions: "Who introduced me to her?" "Where did we meet?" "What was she interested in?" Maybe one of these general questions will serve as an S^D that brings back enough thoughts about the person and setting to serve as S^Ds for her name.

Another strategy for name recall is to slowly say the letters of the alphabet—"A . . . B . . . C . . . D . . ."—trying to begin several names with each letter: "Aisha, Alexa, Angela, Ashley, Becky, Benita, Bridget. . . ." This systematic review of relevant S^Ds is often useful in bringing up the right name: "Becky." Mnemonics help us remember words by providing the first letters or phrases of the correct words. Roy G. Biv is not a person, but a mnemonic that can help you remember the colors of the spectrum in the correct order: red, orange, yellow, green, blue, indigo, violet. If knowing the spectrum allows you to earn points on science tests, you will find it rewarding to remember Roy G. Biv. Acronyms serve the same function: MADD is the acronym for Mothers Against Drunk Driving.

THE STREAM OF CONSCIOUSNESS

Thinking has been described as a "stream of consciousness"—a constant flow of images, ideas, flashbacks, fantasies, and other thoughts. The stream of ideas does not necessarily follow a rational order or pattern, though it can. Many of the novels and movies that are done with a stream-of-consciousness style allow scenes to be spliced together as if they were appearing as free associations. Bits and pieces of the main character's past and present life are joined together as if the person were living a complex present and frequently flashing back to past memories in a semirandom order. Human thought often follows this pattern, in response to the constant flux and flow of S^Ds in the external and internal stimulus collage. Sometimes the stream of consciousness is highly organized and rational, but often it is not. *The stream of consciousness is actually a long chain of perceptions and thoughts.* Perceptions of incoming stimuli from all external and internal sense organs serve as S^Ds for thoughts. These thoughts, in turn, can function as S^Ds for more thoughts and for overt behavior.

Most thought patterns contain both rational sequences and jumps to irrelevant or only partially pertinent ideas. Although some people compare human thought with the logical operations of computers, this computer analogy—which emphasizes rationally programmed data processing and information storage—suggests that human mental activity is more rational and machinelike than it actually is.[26] It is more accurate to portray human thought in terms of a stream of consciousness—or a long chain of coverants—with some links being fairly logical while others are irrational. Each new link in the chain serves as S^Ds for even more thoughts and actions. And so the chains go on, and on, getting longer and longer.

Humans are not innately rational so the stream of thoughts does not always flow in a systematic and logical pattern. *There are two situations that tend to produce rational chains of thought.* First, the stream of consciousness may be rational when the S^Ds from sense perceptions appear in a rational order—for example, while listening to someone develop a clear, logical argument—especially if we are listening closely, and succeed in following the reasoning. Reading a book or magazine with a logically developed thesis helps entrain our thoughts in a rational order, too. Second, people who have been rewarded for speaking and writing with well-reasoned words may learn how to think rationally. Once people learn the skills for organizing complex and confusing material into rational verbal accounts, the stream of consciousness and words may be rational, even when the perceived S^Ds are not in logical order.

No one has a stream of consciousness that is completely rational all the time. First, our environments often contain a jumble of multiple S^Ds that do not fit into simple, logical patterns. Second, it is impossible to learn enough rational skills to make sense of *all* the complexities of life.

Everyone learns some skills for reasoning and rational thinking, but it takes special conditions for people to learn to use reasoning frequently and systematically in a wide variety of circumstances. People who have had ample contact with models, rules, and prompts for rational thinking have a good chance of *acquiring* these cognitive skills. However, the frequency of their *utilizing* and *honing* rational skills depends on reinforcement. Social reinforcement from parents, teachers, friends, and coworkers can help a person learn to use logical, well-reasoned thought and speech. Vicarious reinforcement from seeing respected models demonstrate the power and elegance of rational thought and speech also increases the chances that the observer will acquire, utilize, and hone similar skills. Once a person applies reason to daily problems, rational thinking automatically comes under differential reinforcement: Skillful reasoning is reinforced (because it solves problems), but sloppy reasoning is not reinforced. It may even be punished. Once the natural reinforcement of effective problem solving becomes frequent enough, social reinforcement from parents, teachers, and other sources can be faded out, and the person will continue to use and hone the skills for rational thinking.

Rationality is not a personality trait or global skill that automatically generalizes to work in all facets of life.[27] Quite often, people who seem highly rational and logical when dealing with some things may not apply logic and reason to other areas of their lives. For example, a surgeon must think clearly and rationally while performing a long series of precise steps needed during a complex operation. Sloppy thoughts and actions could lead to fatal consequences. To master the precise and rationally ordered steps for performing surgery, it takes years of learning from models, rules, prompts, and differential reinforcement. Long after a surgeon has acquired the essential skills, the continued demands of the task provide differential reinforcement that continues to polish precise patterns of thought and action. However, rational cognitive skills may not generalize to all S^D contexts. Some surgeons seem absentminded, scatterbrained, and less than rational when they are in the office—where the staff handles all the appointments, records, billing, broken equipment and other day-to-day problems. The surgeon's attention to billing and appointments is not under strict contingencies of reinforcement in the office—because other people are responsible for those tasks. Even people who are world famous—due to their intelligent and rational contributions in art, literature, politics, or science—sometimes make quite irrational pronouncements about topics outside their area of expertise.

Although some tasks require logical, rational thought and action for success, not all do. There are many circumstances in which reason is not needed to attain reinforcement. Sometimes being crazy, corny, and wild makes us the life of the party and we get social attention for developing quirky free associations. Thought patterns that are not rational are not necessarily wrong or invaluable. As we saw in Chapter 12 on rules, *naturals* who learn a behavior without the use of rules often perform quite well even though they are unable to verbalize rationally about their behavior (pp. 278–280). Instead, they have a *feel* for how to do the behavior: Although they have *tacit* and *intuitive* knowledge, they may not be able to think or verbalize about the behavior in a rational manner. *Rational thoughts and words are not essential for the performance of many skillful and useful behaviors.*

When a person with tacit knowledge gets an idea or thinks of a solution to a problem without the help of a rational series of mental steps, the thought may be described as an *intuition.* Because the person cannot identify where the thought came from or what S^Ds triggered it, the intuitive thought may seem more mysterious than a rational thought that was developed at a conscious, verbal level through a highly ordered series of logical steps. If the problems of child rearing or machine repair cause a person to "check twice" even when—or especially when—everything seems to have worked out nicely on the first try, a person may learn an intuitive thought that does not seem rationally defensible. "Things have been going without a glitch. I'd better check twice because something is bound to be wrong." The S^Ds of everything-going-right bring up the thought of checking twice. If the person cannot remember the prior occasions on which he or she learned to have this thought, the intuitive thought may seem especially mysterious, perhaps suggesting ESP or a premonition. If checking twice does reveal a problem, the person's belief in ESP or premonitions may be reinforced. Intuitive thoughts sometimes appear to be irrational, and they may be hard to defend when challenged by someone who demands to see the logic behind them. However, they may work often enough to reinforce their continued use—even if they are criticized as being irrational.

Naturally, not all nonrational, intuitive thinking is correct, but neither is all rational thinking. *Both intuitive and rational thinking can be either right or wrong. However, intuitive thinking has several limitations not found in rational thinking.*[28] First, even though it is possible to determine *if* intuitive thinking is correct or useful, it is difficult to evaluate *why,*—because the causes for intuitive thoughts are not easily identified and evaluated. Therefore, even if an intuitive thought seems to be true in one situation, it is hard to assess whether or not it will hold true in other situations. Second, if one individual frequently has very good intuitive thoughts, it is difficult for others to learn how to think in a similar manner because the intuitive thinker cannot easily verbalize the mental steps needed for others to arrive at equally accurate intuitive thoughts.

Rational thought does not suffer these limitations. First, because the logic behind rational thought can be put into words, it is possible for others to check the logic, test crucial assumptions against the facts, and correct any errors or weaknesses. This type of critical evaluation not only allows rational thoughts to be checked and improved, but also helps assess the range of situations in which the ideas are useful. Second, the skills for accurate rational thinking can be communicated to others, so that many people can learn to benefit from this form of thinking. Because steps of rational thinking can be verbalized and made public, they can be shared with others via modeling, rules, and verbal prompts. In addition, rational skills can be improved by differential reinforcement and shaping, because knowledgeable people can give positive and negative feedback when others display accurate versus inaccurate reasoning.

Rational Choice

In Chapter 13 on the schedules of reinforcement, we saw that choice is often well explained by the matching law (pp. 308–311). In many situations, people tend to match the ratio of their choices of different alternatives to the relative amount of reinforcement associated with each choice. A person who likes chocolate and vanilla ice cream equally will choose each flavor about equally, but someone who likes chocolate five times more than vanilla will tend to choose chocolate five times more often than vanilla. Because rational choice can have goals other than matching the frequency of choices to the relative reinforcement of each alternative, the matching law does not always predict or explain rational choice.[29]

Many families and social groups provide models and rules that help young people learn to use reason when making decisions. *Rational choice involves (1) listing all the alternative behaviors that we might do in a choice situation, (2) assembling accurate information on the immediate and delayed consequences (reinforcers and punishers) associated with each of these behaviors, then (3) carefully evaluating all the pros and cons of each alternative, trying to avoid biases.*[30] At any given choice point, a person considers all the possible alternatives along with both the short-term and long-term consequences associated with each alternative. This process allows the person to compare the pros and cons of each alternative and evaluate which alternative is most likely to produce the best consequences, based on prior experience with such situations.

When a college student is faced with difficult decisions about choosing a major, deciding what kind of summer job to take, or selecting a future career, reasoning is a valuable decision-making tool. Jerry may think of all the summer jobs that are available both near campus and in Hometown. While imagining all the alternatives, he begins to think of the pros and cons of each job. One job pays far more than the others. An internship pays poorly but it is quite interesting and provides important work experience that could build toward an exciting career. The jobs in Hometown would allow Jerry to renew close contacts with old high school friends; but he has several new college friends who plan to work near campus during the summer, and it would be fun to spend the summer getting to know them better. At times Jerry may systematically think through all the pros and cons of each job, *but free associations can actually be quite useful.* Jerry free-associates to hypothetical questions such as "Could I get a summer job in Jamaica or Hawaii?" Such free associations help expand the lists of possible choices. Hence free associations are not antithetical to the reasoning process: They can improve it by broadening and diversifying the number of choices being considered. What is most important for a well-reasoned choice is that we (1) consider as many alternative choices as feasible, (2) seek as much accurate information as possible on the short-term and long-term consequences of each choice, and (3) honestly evaluate all the pros and cons of each choice, without bias.

As we think about all the short-term and long-term *consequences* of all our choices, we are allowing each choice to be influenced by the numerous reinforcers and punishers that might result from it. Reasoning allows memories of various types of pleasant or unpleasant consequences to reinforce or punish our thoughts about each option. For example, if we have six alternatives to choose from (behaviors 1 through 6 in the figure), a rational decision would be based on an analysis of all the pros and cons of each behavior. As we review the positive and negative aspects of each choice (the + and − signs in the figure), the positive and negative thoughts serve as secondary reinforcers and punishers that modify and shape our preferences for each behavior until a stable preference is reached. After careful evaluation, we would realize that behavior 2 was the best choice (with behavior 3 being next best) because it was associated with the best consequences. The more accurately we identify all the important short-term and long-term consequences of each behavioral option, the more likely we are to select the option that will have the most rewarding outcomes.

The Alternatives	The Consequences short term								long term		
behavior 1	(+)	(+)	(−)		(+)	(−)	(+)		(−)		(−)
behavior 2	(−)	(+)		(−)	(+)			(+)	(+)	(+)	(+)
behavior 3	(+)	(−)	(−)	(+)		(+)	(+)	(+)	(−)		
behavior 4	(−)		(+)	(+)	(+)	(−)		(+)	(−)	(−)	(−)
behavior 5	(+)	(−)			(+)	(+)	(−)		(+)		(−)
behavior 6		(+)	(−)	(+)		(−)	(+)			(+)	(−)

When people do not follow the guidelines for making rational choices, they often focus on the immediate consequences of the most conspicuous choices. This narrows their range of choices to include only the most obvious options. It also biases their selection in favor of immediate gratification rather than long-term planning.

Knowing all the short- and long-term reasons why each alternative is good or bad is useful when carrying out any choices that may involve sacrificing immediate gratification in the pursuit of a better but more distant reward. When people evaluate the pros and cons of all their behavioral alternatives—by talking with others and/or thinking it through by themselves—they are actually learning the *reasons* why they need to select or reject each option. If a premed student decides to take a summer job doing library work in a medical library rather than returning to a fun job as a lifeguard, there might be times when the library work seemed tedious or boring. But instead of feeling bad about researching some dry medical texts, the student could mentally review the reasons for making the job choice: The long-term rewards of gaining medical experience are worth certain sacrifices in immediate rewards. These rational thoughts not only help combat the aversive experience of doing a difficult library task, they also orient the student toward doing a good job now in order to attain the distant future goal.

When making very complex or momentous decisions, people may spend days, weeks, or months mulling over the pros and cons of all their possible options, imagining what it would be like to carry out each one. People who have not been reinforced for reasoning may find this task so effortful and unpleasant that they skip through the rational evaluation process and fail to reach a well-reasoned decision based on a careful appraisal of all the data. However, some people learn to enjoy the mental processes of working through complex decisions and seeing carefully reasoned choices emerge—if rational thinking has led to rewarding results in the past.

Rational decision methods do not guarantee that people will always make the best choices.[31] The method is based on a careful assessment of the known consequences of the known alternatives. *When little is known about all the alternatives and all their consequences, rational methods may not lead to the best possible choice—although no other method can guarantee better decisions.* When people have limited knowledge about their alternatives, they need to seek information from other people, newspapers, magazines, books, or the Internet—or obtain it via personal experience. Naturally, the more complete and accurate the information, the more likely a person is to arrive at a good choice.

Rational Therapy. When people do not have adequate reasoning skills, they sometimes flounder when facing daily problems that could be solved by reasoning. Lacking a rational view of their situation, they may plague themselves with irrational thoughts and fears that magnify their problems rather than resolving them.[32] For example, some people become preoccupied with irrational fears about dirt, germs, and cleanliness while their marriage and family relations are falling apart due to their not taking a more responsible role in resolving family problems. Perfectionists can become so obsessed getting every behavioral detail under total control that they check their work over and over, feeling bad about any imperfections. Trauma victims, including survivors of sexual abuse, sometimes become preoccupied with negative self-talk that causes anxiety, depression, and behavioral inhibition. Other people become obsessed with gambling—as their family funds disappear. Fortunately, cognitive behavioral interventions have been developed to help people reach rational resolutions to their problems.[33]

Behavior therapists have developed techniques for helping people cope with their problems more rationally by teaching them to relax and think rationally—using logical and scientifically defensible internal conversations—when confronting problematic situations.[34] This can be done in many ways. A therapist listens carefully to a person's discussion of his or her life, recording any irrational or self-defeating words. Next, the therapist helps the person devise rational rebuttals to any irrational thoughts he or she might have. The therapist serves as a model for rational thinking and talking, saying things such as, "When things don't go right in my life, I say to myself: 'OK. What's my problem? What are all the possible solutions? What are the consequences of each possible solution? Which is the best solution? What steps should I plan to follow? Who can I ask to help me with my plans?'" The therapist may spend hours talking with a person, customizing these general rational guidelines to each client's unique needs. The therapist also shares accurate scientific information about the problems and shows how to use that information to create useful rules for effective problem solving: "Break large problems into small pieces. Attack one piece at a time. What are the realistic probabilities of good and bad things happening? How can you make things better? What alternative activities would be rewarding? And never forget to give yourself words of encouragement about your progress in working toward a more positive future."

Many people who used to give up when they faced problems learn to cope better after acquiring skills for rational problem solving from good models and rules. People are most likely to practice and develop these rational skills if their use of reasoning is reinforced. To facilitate that process, behavioral therapists provide generous positive feedback for all the early steps of acquiring and using reasoning techniques. Gradually, as each client gains skill at applying reasoning to daily problems, the natural reinforcement that comes from solving problems via rational thinking will replace the therapist's social reinforcement, and the therapist's reinforcement can gradually be faded out.

What about people whose problem is that they already spend excess time thinking and making rational decisions about every detail of life? Some people waste hours each day on trivial choices. Rational people can usually convince themselves that it is unwise to spend too much time struggling with the choice of today's shoes or belt. If trivial decisions take too much time, it is rational to force the decision with the flip of a coin and positive advice—"Well, we'll see how the 'brown shoe' experiment goes today"—then move on.

ATTACHING MEANING

B.F. Skinner, G.H. Mead, and other behaviorists have emphasized the importance of showing how behaviorism deals with meaning—since some critics claim that a science of behavior cannot explain something as subjective as "meaning."[35] Behaviorists rebut the criticism by showing how people learn to find some things meaningful—how they learn to attach meaning to some things. Note we do not learn to find everything meaningful.

There are many foreign languages that each contain tens of thousands of words that are meaningless to us.

How does a person learn to attach meaning to certain things, but not to others? *Any element in our stimulus collage can become an S^D or CS for meaningful responses via operant or Pavlovian conditioning.*[36] *These stimuli—be they S^{D}s or CSs—are called **referents** (the "things being referred to"), and the meaningful responses include (1) verbal operants, (2) nonverbal operants, and (3) conditioned emotional responses.* As a child learns the meaning of "a house is on fire," a burning house becomes a referent for meaningful responses. When seeing the referent—a burning house—the child may respond (1) by shouting "Fire," (2) by pointing to the house, and (3) with emotional responses such as fear and a pounding heart. The child has shown that the burning house is a meaningful referent in three different ways. The burning house is the referent that functions as an S^D for the verbal operant of shouting "Fire" and the nonverbal operant of pointing. It also functions as a CS for emotional responses.

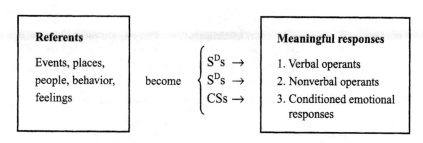

Referents	become		Meaningful responses
Events, places, people, behavior, feelings		S^{D}s → S^{D}s → CSs →	1. Verbal operants 2. Nonverbal operants 3. Conditioned emotional responses

The meanings we attach to any given referent—be it an object, behavior, or thought—are conditioned by the consequences linked with the referent. If our house is on fire, the consequences are disastrous: We could lose everything, including our lives. A hammer is meaningful because the consequences of using it is driving nails. A phone has meaning because of its consequences of facilitating communication at a distance. Meaning is not arbitrary. You cannot use a hammer to call a friend in a distant city. Only a phone can do that, and that fact gives meaning to the word "phone"—or *Telephon* in German, or *téléphone* in French, or *teléfono* in Spanish.

In order to understand how a stimulus becomes a meaningful referent for a person, let us consider some of the ways a child can learn to use the word "love" in a meaningful way. When Janie is very young, her parents may say, "Who do you love, Janie?" Janie may look back in silence. The child has not yet learned the referent for the word "love." The parents may prompt, "Do you *love* Mommy, Janie?" After hearing this verbal prompt, Janie may echo the word "Mommy" from her mother's last sentence. (Saying Mommy is already under partial S^D control of seeing mother.) Mother may hug the child (reinforcing the child's response) and again ask the first question, "Who do you *love*?" The chances are that the child will again say, "Mommy."

Both mother and father may play this verbal game with little Janie in a variety of contexts until the child has learned to answer either "Mommy" or "Daddy." It is true that the child does not have a very deep understanding of the concept of *love* at this time, but the learning process has begun. Later, as the father snuggles Janie into his arms, he may say, "I love you, Janie." If she imitates the first three words, "I love you," she is likely to receive reinforcers. In contrast, if Janie says "I love you" while being angry or selfish, her parents may give a more critical answer, such as, "That's not the way to behave when you love someone." Over time, through imitation and differential reinforcement, Janie learns how to use the word "love" in S^D contexts associated with correct usage, but not in S^Δ contexts associated with incorrect usage. When Janie is happy and her parents are being affectionate, the S^Ds are present for her to say "I love you." When she is angry or her parents have been punitive, there are S^Δs that inhibit saying, "I love you." Her parents may use rules, too, to help Janie learn the meaning of love. They may say, "You should tell your grandmother that you love her." This helps Janie attach the word to new referents, in this case, her grandmother. Even though a 2-year-old child cannot give a good definition of the word "love," most onlookers would agree that Janie knows *something* about the meaning of the word—because she has learned to use the word "love" in a large number of correct S^D contexts.[37]

Whenever a person learns to respond to the referents of a word with appropriate responses of all three types—verbal, nonverbal, and emotional—other people are likely to agree that the person has learned the "true" meaning of the concept. If Janie only makes verbal responses such as "I love you," but does not show loving behavior and loving emotional responses, onlookers may judge that she has not yet learned the "full" meaning of the word, even though she only uses the word in the correct S^D contexts. If Janie is raised in a loving home, she will eventually learn all three types of appropriate responses—verbal, nonverbal, and emotional—and onlookers will conclude that she has learned the fuller awareness of the meaning of the word "love."

As the years go by, we are exposed to countless learning experiences in which we can acquire one, two or all three types of meaningful responses.[38] We hear *models* defining "love" and see them showing consideration for the people they love. We hear *rules* stating that if you truly love someone, you treat them in special ways. A person we love may physically *prompt* us to touch in a certain way when we are expressing our love. There is *differential reinforcement* for the verbal and nonverbal components of the response class called "loving behavior." If we experience many reinforcers and few punishers from those dear to us, we undergo the *Pavlovian conditioning* that causes them to become CSs that elicit emotional responses of love and security.

Naturally, some people are given more opportunities to learn a large repertoire of loving responses than others. With good models, rules, prompts, differential reinforcement, and Pavlovian conditioning, a person will acquire a large repertoire of loving verbal, nonverbal, and emotional responses. The person will be able to say loving things to his or her partner, treat the partner in a gentle, considerate manner, and feel positive emotional responses of love and security. Onlookers will conclude that this person has learned to attach a great deal of meaning to love and knows the deeper significance of the concept. Children raised in homes where love and affection were limited—and fights were frequent—may be slower to learn the skills and warm feelings of love and security, but fortunately even they can learn all three components of love as teens and adults if they find friends and lovers who are caring and affectionate.

Numerous experiences can allow people to learn inappropriate responses to a given referent. We would not conclude that a man knew the true meaning of love if we saw him treat someone he said he loved in a cruel and selfish manner, even if he claimed to attach a great deal of meaning to love. *Because the verbal and nonverbal components of behavior can be relatively independent, they can be modified in different directions by diverse models, rules, prompts, differential reinforcement, and Pavlovian conditioning. Therefore, it is possible for people to learn incongruous, even hypocritical response patterns to any given word or concept.*[39] For example, when there are rewards for saying one thing and doing another—professing enduring love, then cashing in on one-night stands—discrepancies can appear between the verbal and nonverbal meanings a person attaches to a given referent. If person Q has obtained sexual rewards for saying "I'll love you forever" at night, then experienced reinforcers of freedom for moving on the next morning, Q may learn behavior that seems hypocritical. In addition, the emotions attached to the referents in the hypocritical lover's life can be quite different from those of less hypocritical people. If Q has received reinforcers for saying "Love forever" and moving on the next day, both the talk and the action will be CSs that elicit positive emotions. Q may feel warm, romantic feelings while speaking of enduring love one night and may also enjoy the feelings of freedom while hitting the road the next morning.

Because we all have unique histories of learning experience, we learn to attach somewhat different meanings to the referents in our lives. Yet each of us attaches meanings that overlap with those of the people we are close to because (1) we have been raised in the same culture, (2) we learn from each other, and (3) the rewards of social interaction depend on sharing sufficiently similar meanings that we can communicate and coordinate efficiently. If two lovers have radically different definitions of love, they are likely to have many misunderstandings. But each success they have in communicating about love helps them learn a bit more from the other about the meaning of this word for the other person.

THE SELF

Many people think of their "self" as something that originates from inside and guides the rest of their behavior—as in, "I composed that e-mail message all by myself." However, both psychologists and sociologists agree that the self has its origins in society.[40] A baby does not have a sense or awareness of self, nor can it compose an e-mail by itself. But children learn to think that they have a "self" when their parents, brothers, sisters, and others begin to teach them to think of people as having personalities or selves that explain behavior. After hearing father say, "Your brother drew this picture all by himself," it is easy for Britt to learn that her brother is a person and a "self" who does certain kinds of drawings. Then father turns to Britt and asks, "What about yourself? What did you draw today?" She learns to respond, "I drew this today." Britt is learning to describe herself with words such as "I," "me," and "myself." When others approve of her picture, they are giving Britt reinforcers for both her picture and for her self-description. Implicit in the language is the notion that her behavior is a product of her self. "I drew this all by myself," Britt says.

When a person learns to do self-observation and self-description—describing his or her own body and behavior in terms of "I," "me," and "myself"—the person comes to develop a self-concept. The skills for self-description are learned from models, rules, prompts, and differential reinforcement during social interaction. Parents provide simple models for the young child: "Britt, did you draw that pretty house?" The child quickly learns to substitute a few words and create a self-descriptive phrase that is likely to be reinforced: "I like to draw pretty houses." Rules are often used to encourage self-observation and self-description. "Britt, watch that you don't spill your milk." "Britt, watch that you don't break your brother's toys." These rules focus the child's attention on watching her own behavior, and often the child receives reinforcers for responding: "I'm watching. I won't break anything." All these processes reinforce self-observation and self-description: Britt is a person with a self—the self she can discover through self-observation and self-reports, if she is rewarded for doing so (and most of us are rewarded for learning about our self). "I'm watching myself, so don't worry about my breaking things."

Toward a Sense of Identity

Our "description of self"—our "self-concept"—becomes more complex with age and experience. A young child learns to describe his or her own actions as "mine," done by "me," or something "I" created. As the years pass, Britt will learn improved skills of self-description that allow her to identify patterns in her own behavior. "I often promise to do things, but then forget." As she gains these self-descriptive skills, she will be able to make increasingly complex observations about her "self," perhaps labeling herself as "forgetful" or "busy" or "unreliable" (depending on the models, rules, prompts, and reinforcers associated with the use of each label).

Naturally, not everyone learns advanced self-descriptive skills or learns them equally rapidly. A person surrounded with many models and rules for advanced, sensitive, and subtle self-description skills will have a good chance for learning these skills quickly. The more reinforcers people receive for using the skills, the more polished and practiced they become. A person with a simple life and consistent behavior patterns can learn accurate self-description more easily than a person with a complex life and highly variable behavior. The first person merely has an easier task because simple behavior patterns are easier to learn to describe.

*A person acquires a sense of **identity** when he or she learns self-descriptions that (1) hold true over a broad range of situations and (2) reveal consistent patterns of interests and behaviors.* By the time Britt is in college, her life is much more complex than it was at age 4, and she has learned to describe her behavior in a more detailed manner. If Britt's past socialization has pointed her toward one goal—becoming an architect—she may have a strong sense of identity as a future architect, especially if she has been generously reinforced for learning vocabulary and drawing skills related to architecture. If several family members or close family friends are architects, she will have seen enough of the professional role models to easily describe the things that happen in architectural school and later in professional life. This allows her to have a clear picture of her identity as a future architect. Because many elements of her self-descriptions fit one relatively consistent pattern, she may feel a strong sense of having an identity.

People whose socializations have not provided clear and simple patterns of life objectives may find it difficult to discover their "identity." Pamela has toyed with dozens of different interests including law, dance, art, and being a good mother. She is no stranger to haphazard shaping (pp. 228–230). She has received a little support and encouragement for each interest, but no strong and consistent reinforcement for any single one. She has been popular in some circles but unpopular in others. Some days she feels happy about life; other days, rather sad. Her self-descriptions are inconsistent. There is no simple, unifying pattern. When other people ask her what she plans to be doing in two years, she answers, honestly, "Who knows." Her self-descriptions do not reveal a consistent pattern, and she lacks a sense of identity. Her self-descriptions suggest a fragmented person who lacks a unified sense of direction.[41] If no one criticizes Pamela about her lack of direction, her lack of identity may not be aversive to her. If all her friends say they feel equally confused about life—and her favorite rock stars say the world is mixed up—she may feel normal. But if people criticize her for not knowing what to do with her life, her lack of identity can become aversive. Her mother says, "Why don't you do like Britt and make something with your life?" Her father says, "You'll never amount to anything." This kind of negative conditioning can make her lack of an identity so aversive she feels an *identity crisis*. Thinking about her lack of identity has become a CS that elicits aversive emotions, due to negative social control.

Identity crises can come at any time in life. If Britt fails in architectural school and has to drop out, she will lose the single theme that once gave her a sense of identity. In addition, all her old self-descriptions about being a successful architect will now be linked with painful thoughts about her inadequacies. Her failure at her life's goal may cause her to have as painful an identity crisis as Pamela had a couple of years earlier.

A person's self-concept and sense of identity will be positive if many of the person's self-descriptions are CSs for pleasant emotions, due to a history of positive experiences. People who have succeeded at many things and received generous social reinforcement tend to find that many elements of their self-descriptions are CSs that elicit good feelings about themselves. They develop a strong positive sense of *perceived self-efficacy.*[42] They can clearly perceive that their behavior is effective at creating rewarding consequences. In contrast, people who have failed frequently, received more criticism than praise, or received reinforcers for frequent self-criticism tend to have a more negative self-concept and low perceived self-efficacy.

Learning to have a positive self-concept and high perceived self-efficacy makes life pleasant, if not thoroughly exciting. It allows people to feel good when they think about themselves, their lives, their plans, their futures. Having a strong sense of perceived self-efficacy also helps people be more enthusiastic about *doing* things in life, rather than being passive. The people who think of themselves as good athletes or good musicians, for example, have this positive conditioning due to past positive reinforcement, and they can enjoy looking forward to running harder or playing more complex music tomorrow—because these future-oriented thoughts are CSs that elicit good feelings. They look forward to life with pleasure, whereas people who have received too much punishment fear what pains life may bring next. When people have been criticized repeatedly for not being good enough in the past, thoughts about themselves are CSs that bring up bad feelings and thinking about future tasks and obligations elicits more fears of failure and being criticized *yet again.*

People can change a negative self-concept into a positive self-concept—and low perceived self-efficacy into high.[43] This is what Ben did at the beginning of the chapter. First, Ben learned new skills that increased his successes—and decreased his failures—at coping successfully with his social and physical world.[44] As he observed himself *succeeding* at more things and enjoyed receiving more reinforcers, these positive experiences conditioned his self-descriptions into CSs that elicited positive emotions, strengthening his growing sense of self-efficacy.

SELF-CONTROL

Self-control *consists of any proactive behavior—either overt or covert—that we do at one time to control our later behaviors and increase our chances of success in those later behaviors.*[45] At 4 P.M. a person may remember, "I've got to phone Fabio tonight." That moment of recall may not assure that the call is made; but proactive responses—such as writing a big note, PHONE FABIO AT 8 and taping it on the refrigerator door—may do the job nicely. Self-control behavior at 4 P.M. helps increase the likelihood of phoning at 8 P.M. Self-control skills are merely a subset of our total behavior repertoire. As we learn an increasing number of effective self-control skills, we gain greater ability to proact and direct our own behavior to accomplish things that otherwise we might have failed to do. This can help us reach positive goals that enrich our lives and make us happier.

Self-control involves a chain of five basic response classes: self-observation, self-description, self-evaluation in terms of valued goals, goal-oriented self-instruction, and reinforcement.[46] For example, Mr. G's self-observation (1) may lead to the covert self-description (2), "I'm not spending much time with my children." These words may serve as S^Ds to do self-evaluation in terms of family values (3). If Mr. G values quality time with family, the self-evaluation may serve as an S^D for his constructing appropriate self-instructions (4), "I have to spend at least two hours each evening with the kids." Reinforcement (5) is the last link in the chain of self-control behavior, and it either directly or indirectly strengthens each of the prior links in the five-link chain. If Mr. G has received enough reinforcement in the past for following his own self-instructions, these self-generated rules may actually lead to behavioral change—such as setting aside more time for being with the children. If spending time with his children is rewarding, Mr. G will tend to do more child-oriented self-control behavior in the future. Mr. G could also use verbal self-reinforcement to strengthen his self-control habits: "I'm glad I resolved to be with the kids more."

Self-control skills are learned from models, rules, prompts, and reinforcement. This learning begins early in life, and additional skills can be added at any age. Why do parents teach self-control skills to young children? Parents of young children spend a great deal of time and effort cleaning up spilled food and milk, changing dirty clothing, and fixing things that children break. If parents teach children to regulate and manage their own behavior via self-control, child rearing and family interaction are much less effortful for the parents. Not all parents are equally skillful at teaching self-control; but early in childhood, most parents give children rules for doing self-observation (1), "Watch your elbow; it's about to knock over your milk glass." They also try to train self-description (2), "What's your elbow going to do to that glass of milk?" Some parents are good at teaching skills for self-evaluation (3), "If the milk spills, will someone have to clean up the mess? Is that fun?" Some parents encourage children to create rules for doing self-instruction (4), "What should you tell yourself to avoid knocking over the milk?" Reinforcement (5) can come from two different sources. Parents often reward children for making progress in learning self-control and/or punish the lack of self-control. Children also learn from the immediate consequences of their acts: A spilled glass of milk can make one's clothing wet and uncomfortable, while self-control and no spills avoid these aversive consequences. Even children with developmental disabilities can have relatively normal lives when they learn self-control skills.[47]

After childhood, we are all exposed to different combinations of models, rules, prompts, and reinforcement for self-control. Naturally, some people learn more self-control skills than others. There are times when most of us wish that we had more self-control—so we could better manage our moods and thoughts, eating and exercise habits, behaviors that accidentally hurt people we love, and so forth. Knowledge about behavior principles makes it possible for us to learn advanced levels of self-control and proact to guide our own lives more effectively.[48] The more you learn about behavior modification, the more you can use behavior principles to design and modify your own life. People who do not know the principles by which behavior is acquired, maintained, and modified usually find it more difficult to control their own lives than those who know the principles—and have been rewarded for applying those principles to their own lives.

The following paragraphs briefly demonstrate how people can increase their self-control by employing some of the principles presented earlier in the book.

Chapter 1: Science and Human Behavior.   The scientific approach to the study of behavior is based on careful observation. Self-control begins with careful self-observation. The use of diaries or graphs to keep written records helps us collect data on the *ABCs* of behavior: the antecedents, behaviors, and consequences. This, in turn, helps us create objective behavioral definitions of our target behaviors. It is wise to keep records on both desirable and undesirable behavior, along with information on the events that occur before and after each behavior. The more careful, objective, and scientific we can be in our self-observations, the better our chances of linking our observations with the behavior principles discussed in the other chapters of this book.

Chapter 2: Pavlovian Conditioning.   People can create new CSs through Pavlovian conditioning. If you would like to increase the number of things you enjoy in life, you can set up pleasurable learning experiences that will create new pleasure-eliciting CSs for you. For example, if you see that other people really enjoy jazz or opera, it is likely these types of music are CSs that elicit pleasurable emotions for them. If you wanted to learn to enjoy jazz—i.e., find jazz a CS for pleasure—you would pair jazz with pleasurable events. You might arrange your next special date to include a jazz concert or drinks at a jazz bar. You could ask a friend who loves jazz to play some favorite CDs and give you pointers. The jazz lover's smiles and enthusiasm for the music would cause you to experience vicarious positive emotional responses. The pointers would be rules to focus your attention on the musical details that others enjoy. "Yow, dig that wild sax!" Due to positive conditioning, jazz will become a pleasure-eliciting CS for you, and you will feel good when you tune into a radio station that is playing jazz.

Pavlovian conditioning can also be used to countercondition CSs that elicit aversive emotions. If thinking about going to graduate school makes you anxious and fearful, you could talk with graduate students who are genuinely excited about advancing their education, and their positive responses will help countercondition some of your fears and apprehensions. (Avoid the graduate students who are sulkers or pessimists, because they could create conditioned aversions to advanced education.)

Chapter 3: Operant Conditioning.   The consequences that follow a behavior are crucial determinants of its frequency. If you want to *increase* the frequency of operants—such as creative writing, exercising, thinking rationally, being considerate—either positive or negative reinforcement will work. Positive reinforcement is usually more pleasant than negative reinforcement: It is fun to treat yourself to a new CD (positive reinforcement) each time you increase your weekly jogging distance by a specified amount. If you want to decrease the frequency of operants—such as overeating, wasting time, or having temper outbursts—punishment, extinction, and DRO may be useful. If a boy tells his girlfriend that she should simply walk out and go home whenever he loses his temper, he is attempting to suppress his temper outbursts by extinction and punishment: Her leaving removes social reinforcement (extinction), and being left alone may be aversive enough to be a punisher.

People can use either *external* or *internal* reinforcers and punishers. If you ask a friend to give you an encouraging word every time you do something that shows sensitivity to others, this reinforcement (of external origin) will help you gain greater sensitivity. After you have observed which features of your behavior your friend is reinforcing, you will learn to better identify when you are being sensitive and learn to give yourself internal self-reinforcement for those behaviors.[49] Whenever you think positive or negative things to yourself because of an operant you performed, the positive or negative inner words will reinforce or punish the operant. Thus, the following type of internal dialogue can be quite useful in modifying behavior: "I'm glad I remembered to thank Sherri for her help. But it was inconsiderate of me not to say 'Hi' to her roommate."

Chapter 4: Pavlovian and Operant Conditioning Together.   Because Pavlovian conditioning often occurs as a natural by-product of operant conditioning, you might decide to overcome certain conditioned fears by learning the relevant operant skills—knowing that the desired emotional conditioning will occur as a by-product. For example, you could overcome fear of skiing by taking lessons from an expert. Choose a skillful and cheerful instructor: Acquiring good skills will minimize the fears of risk or danger while skiing, and the instructor's cheerful behavior will guarantee that skiing will be paired with positive social stimuli that will make skiing a CS for pleasurable emotions. While you are learning the operant skills in a reinforcing social context, the positive experiences will automatically countercondition your old fears. As people receive positive reinforcers for learning any skills—public speaking, dancing, swimming, mountain climbing, self-defense—old fears about these activities disappear.

Chapter 5: The Stimulus Collage.   As you keep diaries and records about the stimuli that precede and predict your behavior, you will learn about both your S^Ds and CSs. Using this information, you can arrange the best antecedent stimuli to produce the behavior you want. If you want to stop thinking about a lover who broke your heart, remove all his or her photos and belongings (because they are S^Ds that bring up thoughts of the person) and immerse yourself in other friendships and activities. If you want to remember to phone your parents more often, put their photo next to the phone to serve as an S^D for the desired response.

Self-observation can help you discover which CSs elicit desirable and undesirable emotions. For example, some music albums may cause you to become sad or blue, whereas other music elicits cheerful moods and makes you smile. Still other music may elicit romantic moods. As you learn the power of music to serve as CSs for various emotions, you can select your musical CSs more wisely and gain increasing control over your moods.

Chapter 6: Behavior Modification.   People can take the role of behavior modifiers who modify their own behavior. Careful observations of one's own behavior can lead to multiple hypotheses about the ABCs of behavior. We face both advantages and disadvantages in applying behavior modification to ourselves. On the positive side, we can see many details of our behavior that others cannot—such as our thoughts, emotions, and any private actions we hide from the view of others. This allows us to give instant reinforcement and punishment to target behaviors that others might not notice. On the negative side, we may be more biased in studying ourselves than another person would be. Here is where a friend can be of help. We can discuss our goals for self-modification with a friend, then ask the friend to give us feedback on our successes and failures. We can encourage our friend to give us constructive tips and suggestions about things we could do to improve our plans and behavior. In some forms of self-modification, we might want to experiment with ABAB reversal designs or multiple baselines across several different behaviors.

Chapters 7 and 8: Reinforcers and Punishers.   Because reinforcers and punishers are the prime movers of operant conditioning—and can produce Pavlovian conditioning as a by-product—it is wise to learn how to use these stimuli effectively. First, know your reinforcers and punishers. Use self-observation to find out which reinforcers and punishers are most powerful in modifying and maintaining your behavior so you can use these effectively in your own self-control. Second, plan to use reinforcers more than punishers: This makes self-control more rewarding, and it increases the chances that you will continue your efforts to guide your own life—rather than letting your life be controlled by factors beyond your control. Some people keep a long list of all the rewards they enjoy receiving and all the things they most enjoy doing in order to have lots of reinforcers to choose from when deciding how to reward progress in self-modification.

You can use your reinforcers to increase or decrease the frequency of desirable or undesirable operants. If you want to *increase* the frequency of exercising regularly, you could reward yourself for each step of progress with reinforcers such as a movie, a new CD, some new clothes, or anything else you like. If you can find a friend who likes to jog, the social reinforcers you obtain while exercising will increase the likelihood of jogging and condition exercise into a CS that elicits pleasurable feelings (rather than aversive ones). You can *decrease* unwanted behaviors by reinforcing incompatible responses (DRI). Negative thoughts will gradually disappear if you reinforce positive and optimistic thoughts, perhaps thinking about upbeat conversations with cheerful friends. The frequency of temper outbursts will decrease automatically if you reinforce yourself for your gentle and considerate behavior. You may have to punish yourself from time to time for having temper flareups with a good friend—"Crazy me! How could I say something so inconsiderate to my best friend?"—but generous use of positive reinforcement for considerate behavior will allow you to keep self-punishment to a minimum. The more skillful you become at applying your reinforcers, the more effective you can be at conditioning your own operants and obtaining the desirable Pavlovian effects that occur as natural by-products of operant conditioning (see Chapter 4).

Chapter 9: Differential Reinforcement and Shaping. Differential reinforcement allows you to increase or decrease the frequency of responses you already have in your behavior repertoire. If your singing is sometimes good and sometimes not so good, you can obtain differential reinforcement that will help you by singing along with your favorite recordings that are easy to imitate. When you sing well, your voice will blend well with the recording (providing reinforcement for your musical skills), but poor singing will not sound good (providing punishment for your errors). These differential consequences will gradually increase your ability to sing well.

Shaping allows you to go beyond simple differential reinforcement and reach entirely new levels of performance. Shaping generally proceeds most rapidly and smoothly if it is done in small steps of successive approximation. If you want to improve your writing, you would not start by deciding to write a novel as your first project. Practice first on vignettes and short stories. As you gain the skills for writing and the self-control to sit for longer periods of time at a word processor, you will find it easier to produce longer and better works. Trying to advance too rapidly to longer written pieces increases the likelihood you will experience setbacks and other aversive consequences that punish you and make you stop working toward your long-term goal. Life can be seen as a long series of easy steps towards mastering many valuable skills, and the goal is not to arrive at the end of life, but rather to make every step as rewarding as possible—so we look forward to each new step.

Chapter 10: Modeling and Observational Learning. A rapid way to learn new behavior is to find models who already do the behavior and visibly enjoy it. Coping models usually provide more useful information than mastery models, because the coping models are only a step or two ahead of you and they can share much that you need to know to make your next steps of progress. You may learn more about playing guitar by watching a friend who is only a few steps better than you than by attending a concert and watching a mastery model with highly advanced skills. On the other hand, mastery models are valuable if they inspire you to set high goals and keep practicing. If the models you select clearly enjoy their activities and are people you like, you can benefit by the vicarious reinforcement they generate for you. If you want to learn to surf, find a friendly, competent surfer. If you want to help yourself move toward a professional career, seek out friends who are enthusiastic about becoming professionals, or volunteer in an internship where you can be close to real-life models and see the excitement and rewards they experience.

Chapter 11: Prompts.　　The acquisition of many physical skills can be hastened by prompts. In learning how to hold and comfort a baby, you could ask someone with years of experience to adjust your arms and hands into the best positions. A good archer can help you learn to hold the bow correctly by standing behind you and moving your arms into the proper geometry. You can ask anyone with good skills to guide your performances: Many people are happy to share their skills with someone who values and wants to learn those skills.

Chapter 12: Rules.　　Clear and accurate rules can help you learn many operants you want to master. "To stop yourself from thinking negative and depressing thoughts, ask yourself to list all the good things you have in life. Ask yourself to elaborate on each one in a thoughtful way." You can obtain useful rules from other people, books, and the Internet. Experts are often better than novices in giving rules—if they can communicate their knowledge clearly and enthusiastically. Once you have heard several knowledgeable psychologists or personal trainers share the rules they have found most valuable for living life, you will be able to give yourself self-instructions that will steer your behavior in desirable directions. You can carry these rules in your head and use them over and over whenever you need. Although rule use may seem a bit mechanical at first, it becomes smoother and more natural as people combine rule use with learning from firsthand experience. People with good coping skills often carry on a rational internal conversation with themselves when they confront new challenges—asking themselves questions about the situation, how many solutions can they imagine, what would be the consequences of each alternative, and then using this information to verbally direct each new step of activity toward the best outcome.

Chapter 13: Schedules.　　Behavior acquisition is most rapid when it is on a schedule of continuous reinforcement (CRF). Be generous with yourself when you are first learning a new activity, give yourself abundant reinforcement via self-talk—"Hey, that is a nice improvement over yesterday"—and promise yourself some special reinforcer for reaching your next big goal. As you master a behavior, it is wise to gradually thin the schedule, because intermittent reinforcement trains behavioral persistence. After several years of jogging, writing songs, or developing social skills, it is only natural not to make a big deal out of each small step of accomplishment, and only reward the behavior from time to time. Strictly defined contingencies of reinforcement produce more clearly guided behavioral change than do loosely defined contingencies. That is why it is better to set precise goals (such as "I will run 2 miles, four times each week"), rather than loose goals (such as "I'll run some each week").

Chapter 14: Positive and Negative Control.   The more you can rely on positive control, the more you will enjoy learning new activities, and the longer you are likely to continue your self-improvement programs. People who try to control their tempers by punishing each outburst may not continue doing self-control as long as people who reward themselves every time they can remain calm and courteous in emotional situations (DRI). People enjoy themselves—and their self-control skills—much more when they reward their progress more than punish their shortcomings. Although some punishment is appropriate for serious errors, it can be minimized by focusing more on rewarding error-free behavior. It is wise to center our social lives around happy and well-adjusted people who model behaviors and personality styles we respect and admire: We benefit from having positive models and being involved in conversations that contain rules for increasing the quality of both our thoughts and actions.

Chapter 15: Thinking, the Self, and Self-Control.   Because our thoughts are influenced every day by countless social learning experiences, it is wise to ensure that our thoughts about improving self-control receive ample social support on a regular basis. Spending time with other people who value self-improvement gives you good positive models, along with vicarious reinforcement for talking and thinking about self-betterment. As you talk with others about attaining your life goals, their feedback—if it is positive and supportive—will help reinforce your commitment to achieving those goals. Naturally, if you interact with people who do not value your goals, you run the risk of having your goals undermined, confused, and negated—unless you have already learned considerable behavioral persistence in pursuing your goals in the face of adversity. By thinking encouraging thoughts and giving yourself generous positive feedback for self-guidance, you can retain strong self-direction even when other people are nonsupportive. Having a clearly defined, positive sense of "self" and "identity" helps give you a well-learned internal conversation that allows you to defend your values to yourself. It gives you someone positive to talk with—your "self"—even when those around you are being negative. Your internal dialogue with yourself can give you a positive set of goals and positive philosophy of life to guide you in both easy and difficult times.

These brief recaps of the chapters only hint at a few items from each chapter that you can use to increase your self-control. If you reread the preceding chapters, you will see many items in each one that can increase your self-control and reduce the chances that your behavior will be a ball of clay, sculpted and molded by forces beyond your control.

CONCLUSION

Thinking is behavior. Sometimes it is described as "subvocal speech" or an "internal conversation" of silent words. Thinking with words is learned much as any other behavior is learned. We tend to think about things that we see or hear modeled by others, especially if there is reinforcement for using those thoughts. Rules and advice can also affect the direction of our thoughts. Through Pavlovian conditioning, thoughts can become CSs that elicit positive or negative emotions—and these emotion-laden thoughts can condition other stimuli (including other thoughts) to become CSs that elicit similar emotions.

As we learn to observe and describe ourselves, we gain a self-concept, and eventually a sense of identity. All of us can mold our behavior and identity toward higher goals via self-control. The combination of self-observation, self-description, self-evaluation, and self-instruction allows us to give ourselves rules that can control our behavior. If we are successful in following these self-given rules, the reinforcement of success helps us learn and become quite skillful at directing our own behavior. Knowledge of the behavior principles can greatly increase our skills at guiding our behavior, and information in each chapter of this book can be used to develop greater self-control.

Behavior science has come a long way since Pavlov's early experiments with dogs. At present, there is a growing interest in the study of human behavior in natural environments—how skills are learned, maintained, and sometimes lost. As we gain increasing knowledge about our own behavior in everyday life, we can come closer to achieving the goal set by the ancient Greeks: "Know then thyself." We can also come closer to attaining the goal of freedom through wise self-control.

QUESTIONS

1. Explain how thinking can be seen as behavior. Do you think in English or Swahili? Why is that the case?
2. How do we learn the inner words of our thoughts from models, rules, and prompts? How do reinforcers and punishers affect the frequencies of various thoughts?
3. Why do we enjoy having many thoughts that are CSs for positive emotions? How does a person attain such a positive internal conversation? What role does positive reinforcement play?
4. If positive thoughts are pleasant to have, why do some people worry so much? Explain the four reasons for worrying.
5. How can one thought with emotional associations affect preceding thoughts through Pavlovian conditioning? Give an example.
6. Because thoughts can function as S^Ds, explain how one thought can set the occasion for other thoughts. Give an example of people using certain thought patterns to bring back memories. Do you recall Roy G. Biv?
7. Why is thinking sometimes likened to a "stream of consciousness"? Is this analogy better or worse than the analogy that thinking is akin to a computer's processing data? Is most of the stream of thought rational? What is needed to produce rational thought?
8. Why is the stream of thought sometimes punctuated with intuitions? Are hunches and intuitons good or bad? Wise or foolish?
9. How does a person make rational choices? What basic steps should a person use for reasoning through complex choices?
10. How can behavioral therapy help people learn to replace irrational thoughts with more accurate ones?
11. How do we come to attach meaning to the stimuli in our stimulus collage? Why do children often have fewer and less complex meanings attached to the word *love* than adults do? How can the hypocrite learn to have contradictory meanings attached to the word *love*?
12. How does a child begin to learn a verbal awareness of "self"? How can our growing self-concept lead to a sense of identity—or to an identity crisis?
13. What are the five basic steps needed for self-control? Why are parents motivated to teach their children the skills of self-control?
14. Do we all learn equal amounts of self-control? What can a person learn from each chapter of this book that will help increase self-control?

NOTES

1. "The simplest and most satisfactory view is that thought is simply behavior—verbal or nonverbal, covert or overt" (Skinner, 1957, p. 449). Forty years later Fantino (1998, p. 355) could say: "Behavior analysts have developed powerful methodologies to assess central phenomena in areas that have been dominated by cognitive psychologists." Also see Skinner (1989a), Stemmer (1992), Hauser (1994), J. Moore (1995), Hawkins and Forsyth (1997); and Reitman and Drabman (1997).

2. This analysis can be done "without abandoning the basic position of behaviorism" (Skinner, 1969, p. 228) because it treats thinking and other covert processes as behavior rather than spiritual or otherwise dualistically conceived processes (Skinner, 1957, p. 449). For further development of the behavioral position, see Mead (1934, pp. 38, 40, 47, 105, 260), Skinner (1957, 1969, 1974, 1989a, 1990), Staats (1968, 1975), Bandura (1969, 1971, 1977), Mahoney (1970, 1974), Meichenbaum (1977), Rachlin (1980), Mischel (1981), Baldwin and Baldwin (1981, 1982); Baldwin (1985, 1986b, 1988), Mace and Lalli (1991), Delprato and Midgley (1992), Goldstein and Cisar (1992), Donahoe and Palmer (1994), Corrigan (1995), and Cautela (1996). Also see the journals *Behavior and Philosophy* and *The Behavior Analyst.*

3. Much of the brain's activites are not done at the aware level. Skinner (1969, p. 246) stressed that "all behavior is basically unconscious," unless "well established practices of self-description generate consciousness." Behaviorists view the unconscious as all those brain processes needed to process habits, reflexes, balance, and our countless bodily functions. Behaviorists do not assume that the unconscious is filled with selfish wishes or lustful drives, as Freud did (Kobes, 1991; Maddi, 1980).

4. Hart and Risley (1995); Flavell, Green, Flavell, and Grossman (1997).

5. Skinner (1957, 1969, 1974); Cullen (1988); Wulfert et al. (1991); Koegel et al. (1998).

6. Skinner (1957); MacCorquodale (1970); Baer and Detrich (1990); Stemmer (1990).

7. Franz and Gross (1996); Sulzer-Azaroff (1997); Wickelgren (1999).

8. Mead (1934); Baldwin (1986b). Thinking should not be conceived of as the action of an isolated, self-contained individual, but as the action of a person enmeshed in ongoing social and historical processes (Lamal, 1991).

9. Homme (1965).

10. Staats (1968, 1975); Mahoney (1974); Bandura (1977); Rosenthal and Zimmerman (1978); Mischel (1981).

11. Verbal conditioning need not involve awareness. Our thoughts and speech can be modified without conscious awareness (Rosenfeld & Baer, 1969). However, rules that make a person aware of patterns of reinforcement and punishment facilitate verbal conditioning (Mahoney, 1974, pp. 41–42).

12. Bandura (1986). Watching puppets or videos of themselves allows similar learning (Gronna, Serna, Kennedy & Prater, 1999; Rapee & Hayman, 1996).

13. Rosenthal and Zimmerman (1978, pp. 260–261).

14. Newman, Hofmann, Trabert, Roth, and Taylor (1994); Garven, Wood and Malpass (2000).

15. Bandura (1977, 1986).

16. Masters and Johnson (1966, 1979); Baldwin and Baldwin (1997b); Crooks and Baur (1999).

17. Scholing and Emmelkamp (1993).

18. Warda and Bryant (1998); Breitholtz, Johansson, and Öst (1999).

19. Miller (1951); Barber and Hahn (1964); Kent and Jambunathan (1989); Bernstein (1990); McNeil and Brunetti (1992); Shafran et al. (1993); Bower (1996).

20. Bandura (1971, 1977, 1986); Clark (1999).

21. de Jong, Mayer, and van den Hout (1997); Gotlib and Krasnoperova (1998); Öhman and Soares (1998); Stöber (1998).

22. Merckelbach, Muris, Horselenberg, and Rassin (1998).

23. Osgood and Tannenbaum (1955); Staats (1968, 1975); Mahoney (1974); Bandura (1977); Schwartz (1984).

24. Herbert (1982).

25. Hoffart (1995); Rachman (1997).

26. Skinner (1974, p. 110); Subbotsky (1993); Damasio (1994); Fantino (1995).

27. Mischel (1968, 1981); Mischel and Peake (1982); Henderson (1991); Subbotsky (1993); Hantula and Crowell (1994).

28. Skinner (1969, p. 167).

29. Rachlin et al. (1981); Rachlin (1989); Hantula and Crowell (1994); Green and Freed (1998); Mazur (1998).

30. Mead (1934); Skinner (1953); Kaufmann (1973); Staats (1975); Rachlin (1989); Fantino (1998).

31. Stolarz-Fantino and Fantino (1995); Schachtman and Reed (1998).

32. de Jong et al. (1997); Gotlib and Krasnoperova (1998); Öhman and Soares (1998); Stöber (1998). Bouchard, Rhéaume, and Ladouceur (1999).

33. Bujold et al. (1994); Craske, Maidenberg, and Bystritsky (1995); Johnston, Ward, and Hudson (1997); Abramowitz (1998); Farrell, Hains, and Davies (1998); Ladouceur, Sylvain, Letarte, Giroux, and Jacques (1998); Slade and Owens (1998); Bouchard et al. (1999); Saboonchi, Lundh, and Öst (1999); Salkovskis (1999); de Silva and Marks (1999).

34. Ellis (1962); Mahoney (1974); Meichenbaum (1976, 1977); Kendall and Hollon (1979); Rachlin (1989); Bujold et al. (1994); Chadwick, Lowe, Horne, and Higson (1994); Woods and Miltenberger (1995); Martin and Pear (1996); Taylor (1996); Öst, Brandberg, and Alm (1997); Taylor et al. (1997); Watson and Tharp (1997); Westbrook and Hill (1998).

35. Skinner (1953, 1968; 1974); Baldwin (1986b).

36. Skinner (1957, 1974, pp. 90–91, 1989a); Horne and Lowe (1996); Astley and Wasserman (1998).

37. The behavioral analysis of meaning concurs with Wittgenstein's (1953) position that "the meaning of a word is its use in the language." See Day (1970).

38. The behavioral analysis is thoroughly sociological because it traces the causes of attached meaning back to the social environment in which the person learned to attach and use meaning. Learning theory provides an ideal tool for people who seek to link social behavior to social causes (Baldwin, 1985; Baldwin & Baldwin, 1978, Burgess & Bushell, 1969; Kunkel, 1975; Scott, 1971).

39. Bryan (1969); Scott (1971); Bandura (1986); Stokes et al. (1987).

40. Mead (1934); Staats (1963, 1975); Bem (1967); Mischel (1968, 1981); Skinner (1969, p. 244f; 1974, pp. 149f, 167f); Greenwood (1991); Green and Myerson (1993); Watson and Tharp (1997).

41. Skinner (1974, p. 149).

42. Bandura (1986).

43. Van Hout, Emmelkamp, and Scholing (1994); Seligman (1998).

44. Bandura (1986).

45. Seibert, Crant, and Kraimer (1999).

46. Many other elements and variations on these elements may be present, too, such as rehearsal, practice, keeping written records, making contracts, and self reinforcement. Several sources provide detailed information on behavioral self-control: Goldfried and Merbaum (1973); Mahoney and Thoresen (1974); Rudestam (1980); Bandura (1986); Perone, Galizio, and Baron (1988); Rachlin (1989); Skinner (1989a); Green and Myerson (1993); Wolko et al. (1993); Kahle and Kelley (1994); Logue (1995, 1998); Workman and Katz (1995); Rapee and Hayman (1997); Watson and Tharp (1997); Aspinwall (1998); Ninness, Ellis, and Ninness (1999).

47. Koegel, Harrower, and Koegel (1999).

48. Rosenbaum, (1990a,b); Koegel et al. (1992); Epstein (1997); Roberts and Neuringer (1998).

49. See Bandura (1971, 1977, 1986) for further information on self-reinforcement and self-punishment.

References

Abbey, A. (1982). Sex differences in attributions for friendly behavior: Do males misperceive females' friendliness? *Journal of Personality and Social Psychology, 42,* 830–838.

Abe, J.A.A., & Izard, C.E. (1999). The developmental functions of emotions: An analysis in terms of differential emotions theory. *Cognition and Emotion, 13,* 523–549.

Abramowitz, J.S. (1998). Does cognitive-behavioral therapy cure obsessive-cumpulsive disorder? A meta-analytic evaluation of clinical significance. *Behavior Therapy, 29,* 339–355.

Adams, C. (1994). *For good and evil: The impact of taxes on the course of civilization.* New York: Madison.

Ainsworth, M.D.S., Blehar, M.C., Waters, E., & Wall, S. (1978). *Patterns of attachment: A psychological study of the strange situation.* Hillsdale, NJ: Erlbaum.

Akers, R.L. (1973). *Deviant behavior: A social learning approach.* Belmont, CA: Wadsworth.

Akhtar, N., Carpenter, M., & Tomasello, M. (1996). The role of discourse novelty in early word learning. *Child Development, 67,* 635–645.

Allan, R.W. (1998). Operant-respondent interactions. In W. O'Donohue (Ed.), *Learning and behavior therapy* (pp. 146–168). Boston: Allyn and Bacon.

Alling, K., & Poling, A. (1995). The effects of differing response-force requirements on fixed-ratio responding of rats. *Journal of the Experimental Analysis of Behavior, 63,* 331–346.

Antonuccio, D.O., Boutilier, L.R., Ward, C.H., Morrill, G.B., & Graybar, S.R. (1992). The behavioral treatment of cigarette smoking. In M. Hersen, R.M. Eisler, & P.M. Miller (Eds.), *Progress in behavior modification* (Vol. 28, pp. 119–181). Sycamore, IL: Sycamore Publishing.

Appel, J.B. (1961). Punishment in the squirrel monkey *Saimiri sciurea. Science, 133,* 36–37.

Arafat, I.S., & Cotton, W.L. (1974). Masturbation practices of males and females. *The Journal of Sex Research, 10,* 293–307.

Arcediano, F., Matute, H., & Miller, R.R. (1997). Blocking of Pavlovian conditioning in humans. *Learning and Motivation, 28,* 188–199.

Aspinwall, L.G. (1998). Rethinking the role of positive affect in self-regulation. *Motivation and Emotion, 22,* 1–32.

Astley, S.L., & Wasserman, E.A. (1998). Object concepts: Behavioral research with animals and young children. In W. O'Donohue (Ed.), *Learning and behavior therapy* (pp. 440–463). Boston: Allyn and Bacon.

Austin, J., Hatfield, D.B., Grindle, A.C., & Bailey, J.S. (1993). Increasing recycling in office environments: The effects of specific, informative cues. *Journal of Applied Behavior Analysis, 26,* 247–253.

Axelrod, S. (1977). *Behavior modification for the classroom teacher.* New York: McGraw-Hill.

Axelrod, S. (1991). Smoking cessation through functional analysis. *Journal of Applied Behavior Analysis, 24,* 717–718.

Axelrod, S., & Apsche, J. (Eds.). (1983). *The effects of punishment on human behavior.* New York: Academic Press.

Ayllon, T., & Haughton, E. (1964). Modification of symptomatic verbal behavior of mental patients. *Behaviour Research and Therapy, 2,* 87–97.

Ayllon, T., & Michael, J. (1959). The psychiatric nurse as a behavioral engineer. *Journal of the Experimental Analysis of Behavior, 2,* 323–334.

Ayres, J.J.B. (1998). Fear conditioning and avoidance. In W. O'Donohue (Ed.), *Learning and behavior therapy* (pp. 122–145). Boston: Allyn and Bacon.

Baer, D. M. (1962). Laboratory control of thumbsucking by withdrawal and representation of reinforcement. *Journal of the Experimental Analysis of Behavior, 5,* 525–528.

Baer, R.A., & Detrich, R. (1990). Tacting and manding in correspondence training: Effects of child selection of verbalization. *Journal of the Experimental Analysis of Behavior, 54,* 23–30.

Baeyens, F., Hermans, D., & Eelen, P. (1993). The role of CS–US contingency in human evaluative conditioning. *Behaviour Research and Therapy, 31,* 731–737.

Baker, A.T. (1979). 41 survivors. *Time, 114*(1), 68.

Baldwin, J.D. (1985). Social behaviorism on emotions: Mead and modern behaviorism compared. *Symbolic Interaction, 8,* 263–289.

Baldwin, J.D. (1986a). Behavior in infancy: Exploration and play. In G. Mitchell & J. Erwin (Eds.), *Comparative primate biology* (Vol, 2, Part A): *Behavior, conservation, and ecology* (pp. 295–326). New York: Alan R. Liss.

Baldwin, J.D. (1986b). *George Herbert Mead: A unifying theory.* Beverly Hills, CA: Sage.

Baldwin, J.D. (1988). Mead and Skinner: Agency and determinism. *Behaviorism, 16,* 109–127.

Baldwin, J.D., & Baldwin, J.I. (1974). The dynamics of interpersonal spacing in monkeys and man. *American Journal of Orthopsychiatry, 44,* 790–806.

Baldwin, J.D., & Baldwin, J.I. (1978). Behaviorism on verstehen and erklären. *American Sociological Review, 43,* 335–347.

Baldwin, J.D., & Baldwin, J.I. (1981). *Beyond sociobiology.* New York: Elsevier.

Baldwin, J.D., & Baldwin, J.I. (1982). Sociobiology or balanced biosocial theory. In T.C. Wiegele (Ed.), *Biology and the social sciences* (pp. 311–317). Boulder, CO: Westview Press.

Baldwin, J.D., & Baldwin, J.I. (1997a). Gender differences in sexual interest. *Archives of Sexual Behavior, 26,* 181–210.

Baldwin, J.D., & Baldwin, J.I. (1997b). Sexual behavior, human. In *Encyclopedia of human biology* (2nd ed., Vol. 4). New York: Academic Press.

Baldwin, J.D., & Baldwin, J.I. (2000). Some winning combinations. *Journal of Positive Behavior Interventions, 2,* 59–64.

Baldwin, J.I. (1983). The effects of women's liberation and socialization on delinquency and crime. *Humboldt Journal of Social Relations, 10,* 90–111.

Balsam, P.D., Deich, J.D., Ohyama, T., & Stokes, P.D. (1998). Origins of new behavior. In W. O'Donohue (Ed.), *Learning and behavior therapy* (pp. 403–420). Boston: Allyn and Bacon.

Bandura, A. (1969). *Principles of behavior modification.* New York: Holt.

Bandura, A. (1971). Vicarious and self-reinforcement processes. In R. Glaser (Ed.), *The nature of reinforcement* (pp. 228–278). New York: Academic Press.

Bandura, A. (1973). *Aggression: A social learning analysis.* Englewood Cliffs, NJ: Prentice Hall.

Bandura, A. (1977). *Social learning theory.* Englewood Cliffs, NJ: Prentice Hall.

Bandura, A. (1986). *Social foundations of thought and action: A social cognitive theory.* Englewood Cliffs, NJ: Prentice Hall.

Bandura, A., & Barab, P. (1973). Processes governing disinhibitory effects through symbolic modeling. *Journal of Abnormal Psychology, 82,* 1–9.

Bandura, A., & Walters, R.H. (1963). *Social learning and personality development.* New York: Holt.

Bandura, A., Blanchard, E.B., & Ritter, B. (1969). The relative efficacy of desensitization and modeling approaches for inducing behavioral, affective, and attitudinal changes. *Journal of Personality and Social Psychology, 13,* 173–199.

Bandura, A., Grusec, J.E., & Menlove, F.L. (1967). Vicarious extinction of avoidance behavior. *Journal of Personality and Social Psychology, 5,* 16–23.

Bandura, A., & Rosenthal, T.L. (1966). Vicarious classical conditioning as a function of arousal level. *Journal of Personality and Social Psychology, 3,* 54–62.

Bandura, A., Ross, D., & Ross, S.A. (1963). A comparative test of the status envy, social power, and secondary reinforcement theories of identificatory learning. *Journal of Abnormal and Social Psychology, 67,* 527–534.

Bandura, A., & Walters, R.H. (1959). *Adolescent aggression.* New York: Ronald.

Bannerman, D.J., Sheldon, J.B., & Sherman, J.A. (1991). Teaching adults with severe and profound retardation to exit their home upon hearing the fire alarm. *Journal of Applied Behavior Analysis, 24,* 571–577.

Barber, T.X., & Hahn, K.W., Jr. (1964). Experimental studies in "hypnotic" behavior: Physiological and subjective effects of imagined pain. *Journal of Nervous and Mental Disease, 139,* 416–425.

Barinaga, M. (1998). Alzheimer's treatments that work now. *Science, 282,* 1030–1032.

Barlow, D.H., Agras, W.S., Leitenberg, H., Callahan, E.J., & Moore, R.C. (1972). The contribution of the therapeutic instructions to covert sensitization. *Behaviour Research and Therapy, 10,* 411–415.

Barlow, D.H., Agras, W.S., Leitenberg, H., & Wincze, J.P. (1970). An experimental analysis of the effectiveness of "shaping" in reducing maladaptive avoidance behavior: An analogue study. *Behaviour Research and Therapy, 8,* 165–173.

Barlow, D.H., & Hersen, M. (1984). *Single case experimental designs: Strategies for studying behavior change.* New York: Pergamon Press.

Barnet, R.C., Grahame, N.J., & Miller, R.R. (1993). Local time horizons in Pavlovian learning. *Journal of Experimental Psychology: Animal Behavior Processes, 19,* 215–230.

Barnett, O.W., Miller-Perrin, C.L., & Perrin, R.D. (1997). *Family violence across the life span: An introduction.* Thousand Oaks, CA: Sage.

Baron, A. (1991). Avoidance and punishment. In I.H. Iversen & K.A. Lattal (Eds.), *Experimental analysis of behavior: Part 1* (pp. 173–217). New York: Elsevier.

Barrett, J.E., & Glowa, J.R. (1977). Reinforcement and punishment of behavior by the same consequent event. *Psychological Reports, 40,* 1015–1021.

Bartlett, J. (1980). *Familiar quotations* (15th ed.). Boston: Little, Brown.

Barton, L.E., Brulle, A.R., & Repp, A.C. (1986). Maintenance of therapeutic change by momentary DRO. *Journal of Applied Behavior, 19,* 277–282.

Baum, W.M. (1979). Matching, undermatching, and overmatching in studies of choice. *Journal of the Experimental Analysis of Behavior, 32,* 269–281.

Baum, W.M. (1995). Rules, culture, and fitness. *The Behavior Analyst, 18,* 1–21.

Bay-Hinitz, A.K., Peterson, R.F., & Quilitch, H.R. (1994). Cooperative games: A way to modify aggressive and cooperative behaviors in young children. *Journal of Applied Behavior Analysis, 27,* 435–446.

Beardsley, S.D., & McDowell, J.J. (1992). Application of Herrnstein's hyperbola to time allocation of naturalistic human behavior maintained by naturalistic social reinforcement. *Journal of the Experimental Analysis of Behavior, 57,* 177–185.

Beck, J.G., & Zebb, B.J. (1994). Behavioral assessment and treatment of panic disorder: Current status, future directions. *Behavior Therapy, 25,* 581–611.

Becker, H.S. (1963). *Outsiders: Studies in the sociology of deviance.* New York: Free Press.

Becker, H.S. (1964). *The other side.* New York: Free Press.

Bellack, A.S., & Hersen, M. (1977). *Behavior modification: An introductory textbook.* Baltimore: Williams and Wilkins.

Bellack, A.S., Hersen, M., & Kazdin, A.E. (Eds.). (1982). *International handbook of behavior modification and therapy.* New York: Plenum Press.

Bem, D.J. (1967). Self-perception: An alternative interpretation of cognitive dissonance phenomena. *Psychological Review, 74,* 183–200.

Bem, D.J. (1970). *Beliefs, attitudes, and human affairs.* Monterey, CA: Brooks/Cole.

Berger, S.M. (1962). Conditioning through vicarious instigation. *Psychological Review, 69,* 450–466.

Berk, L.E. (1994). Why children talk to themselves. *Scientific American, 271*(5), 78–83.

Bernstein, D.J. (1990). Of carrots and sticks: A review of Deci and Ryan's intrinsic motivation and self-determination in human behavior. *Journal of the Experimental Analysis of Behavior, 54,* 323–332.

Bernstein, I.L., Webster, M.M., & Bernstein, I.D. (1982). Food aversions in children receiving chemotherapy for cancer. *Cancer, 50,* 2961–2963.

Berryman, J., Evans, I.M., & Kalbag, A. (1994). The effects of training in nonaversive behavior management on the attitudes and understanding of direct care staff. *Journal of Behavior Therapy and Experimental Psychiatry, 25,* 241–250.

Bevins, R.A., & Ayres, J.J.B. (1992). One-trial backward excitatory fear conditioning transfers across context. *Behaviour Research and Therapy, 30,* 551–554.

Beyette, B. (1999, July 19). Have swimsuit, will learn. *Los Angeles Times,* p. E2.

Bickel, W.K., Green, L., & Vuchinich, R.E. (1995). Behavioral economics. *Journal of the Experimental Analysis of Behavior, 64,* 257–262.

Bijou, S.W., & Baer, D.M. (1965). *Child development: Vol. 2. The universal stage of infancy.* New York: Appleton-Century-Crofts.

Birchler, G., Weiss, R., & Vincent, J. (1975). Multimethod analysis of social reinforcement exchange between maritally distressed and nondistressed spouse and stranger dyads. *Journal of Personality and Social Psychology, 31,* 349–360.

Birnbrauer, J.S. (1976). Mental retardation. In H. Leitenberg (Ed.), *Handbook of behavior modification and behavior therapy* (pp. 361–404). Englewood Cliffs, NJ: Prentice Hall.

Bithoney, W.G., & Dubowitz, H. (1985). Organic concomitants of nonorganic failure to thrive: Implications for research. In D. Drotar (Ed.), *New directions in failure to thrive: Implications for research and practice* (pp. 47–68). New York: Plenum Press.

Bitterman, M.E., & Woodard, W.T. (1976). Vertebrate learning: Common processes. In R.B. Masterton, C.B.G. Campbell, M.E. Bitterman, & N. Hotton (Eds.), *Evolution of brain and behavior in vertebrates* (pp. 169–189). Hillsdale, NJ: Erlbaum.

Bivens, M. (1994, January 27). New facts point up horror of Nazi siege of Leningrad. *Los Angeles Times,* pp. A1, A6.

Blaisdell, A.P., Denniston, J.C., & Miller, R.R. (1999). Posttraining shifts in the overshadowing stimulus—unconditioned stimulus interval alleviates the overshadowing deficit. *Journal of Experimental Psychology: Animal Behavior Processes, 25,* 18–27.

Blanchard, E.B., Hickling, E.J., Taylor, A.E., Loos, W.R., & Gerardi, R.J. (1994). The psychophysiology of motor vehicle accident related posttraumatic stress disorder. *Behavior Therapy, 25,* 453–467.

Blanck, G. (1990). The man and his cause. In L.C. Moll (Ed.), *Vygotsky and education: Instructional implications and applications of sociohistorical psychology* (pp. 31–58). New York: Cambridge University Press.

Bloom, B.S. (Ed.). (1985). *Developing talent in young people.* New York: Ballantine.

Boakes, R. (1984). *From Darwin to behaviourism: Psychology and the minds of animals.* New York: Cambridge University Press.

Boggiano, A.X. & Barrett, M. (1991). Gender differences in depression in college students. *Sex Roles, 25,* 595–605.

Bonuses for executives in 1997? Guess again. (1998, April 3). *Los Angeles Times,* p. D2.

Booth, R., & Rachman, S. (1992). The reduction of claustrophobia—I. *Behaviour Research and Therapy, 30,* 207–221.

Botella, C., Baños, R.M., Perpiñá, C., Villa, H., Alcañiz, M., & Rey, A. (1998). Virtual reality treatment of claustrophobia: A case report. *Behaviour Research and Therapy, 36,* 239–246.

Bouchard, C., Rhéaume, J., & Ladouceur, R. (1999). Responsibility and perfectionism in OCD: An experimental study. *Behaviour Research and Therapy, 37,* 239–248.

Boudewyns, P.A., & Shipley, R.H. (1983). *Flooding and implosive therapy.* New York: Plenum Press.

Bouton, M.E., & Nelson, J.B. (1998). The role of context in classical conditioning: Some implications for cognitive behavior therapy. In W. O'Donohue (Ed.), *Learning and behavior therapy* (pp. 59–84). Boston: Allyn and Bacon.

Bower, B. (1996). Introspection, for better or worse. *Science News, 150,* 123.

Bower, B. (1998, July 18). Seeing through expert eyes: Ace decision makers may perceive distinctive worlds. *Science News, 154,* pp. 44–46.

Brackbill, Y. (1960). Experimental research with children in the Soviet Union: A report of a visit. *American Psychologist, 15,* 226–233.

Brand, P., & Yancey, P. (1993). *Pain: The gift nobody wants.* New York: HarperCollins.

Breitholtz, E., Johansson, B., & Öst, L.-G. (1999). Cognitions in generalized anxiety disorder and panic disorder patients. A prospective approach. *Behaviour Research and Therapy, 37,* 533–544.

Brewer, D.D. (1992). Hip hop grafitti writers' evaluations of strategies to control illegal graffiti. *Human Organization, 51,* 188–196.

Brigham, T.A. (1989). *Self-management for adolescents.* New York: Guilford Press.

Brigham, T.A., Meier, S.M., & Goodner, V. (1995). Increasing designated driving with a program of prompts and incentives. *Journal of Applied Behavior Analysis, 28,* 83–84.

Broad, W.J. (1980). Use of killer weed grows in third world. *Science, 208,* 474–475.

Bronowski, J. (1965). *Science and human values* (Rev. ed.). New York: Harper & Row.

Bronowski, J. (1977). *A sense of the future: Essays in natural philosophy.* Cambridge, MA: MIT Press.

Bryan, J.H. (1969). How adults teach hypocrisy. *Psychology Today 3*(7), 50–52, 65.

Budney, A.J., Higgins, S.T., Delaney, D.D., Kent, L., & Bickel, W.K. (1991). Contingent reinforcement of abstinence with individuals abusing cocaine and marijuana. *Journal of Applied Behavior Analysis, 24,* 657–665.

Bujold, A., Ladouceur, R., Sylvain, C., & Boisvert, J.-M. (1994). Treatment of pathological gamblers: An experimental study. *Journal of Behavior Therapy and Experimental Psychiatry, 25,* 275–282.

Burgess, R.L., & Bushell, D. (1969). *Behavioral sociology.* New York: Columbia University Press.

Burgess, R.L., & Huston, T.L. (Eds.). (1979). *Social exchange in developing relationships.* New York: Academic Press.

Candland, D.K. (1993). *Feral children and clever animals: Reflections on human nature.* New York: Oxford University Press.

Cantor, J., Ziemke, D., & Sparks, G. (1984). Effect of forewarning on emotional responses to a horror film. *Journal of Broadcasting, 28*(1), 21–31.

Carducci, B.J., & Zimbardo, P.G. (1995). Are you shy? *Psychology Today, 28*(6), 34–48.

Carlin, A.S., Hoffman, H.G., & Weghorst, S. (1997). Virtual reality and tactile augmentation in the treatment of spider phobia: A case report. *Behaviour Research and Therapy, 35,* 153–158.

Carr, E.G. (1994). Emerging themes in the functional analysis of problem behavior. *Journal of Applied Behavior Analysis, 27,* 393–399.

Carton, J.S., Kessler, E.A., & Pape, C.L. (1999). Nonverbal decoding skills and relationship well-being in adults. *Journal of Nonverbal Behavior, 23,* 91–100.

Carton, J.S., & Nowicki, S. (1998). Should behavior therapists stop using reinforcement? A re-examination of the undermining effect of reinforcement on intrinsic motivation. *Behavior Therapy, 29,* 65–86.

Carton, J.S., & Schweitzer, J.B. (1996). Use of a token economy to increase compliance during hemodialysis. *Journal of Applied Behavior Analysis, 29,* 111–113.

Case, D.A., Ploog, B.O., & Fantino, E. (1990). Observing behavior in a computer game. *Journal of the Experimental Analysis of Behavior, 54,* 185–199.

Catania, A.C. (1971). The nature of learning. In J.A. Nevin & G.S. Reynolds (Eds.), *The study of behavior* (pp. 31–68). Glenview, IL: Scott, Foresman.

Catania, A.C. (1991). Time as a variable in behavior analysis. In I.H. Iversen & K.A. Lattal (Eds.), *Experimental analysis of behavior: Part 2* (pp. 1–19). New York: Elsevier.

Catania, A.C. (1998). The taxonomy of verbal behavior. In K.A. Lattal & M. Perone (Eds.), *Handbook of research methods in human operant behavior* (pp. 405–433). New York: Plenum Press.

Cautela, J.R. (1967). Covert sensitization. *Psychological Reports, 20,* 459–468.

Cautela, J.R. (1996). Training the client to be empathetic. In J.R. Cautela & W. Ishag (Eds.), *Contemporary issues in behavior: Improving the human condition* (pp. 337–353). New York: Plenum Press.

Cautela, J.R., & Ishaq, W. (Eds.). (1996). *Contemporary issues in behavior: Improving the human condition.* New York: Plenum Press.

Cavanaugh, J.P. (1998, September). Sylvan's fast learners. *Johns Hopkins Magazine,* pp. 35–39.

Centers, R. (1963). A laboratory adaptation of the conversational procedure for the conditioning of verbal operants. *Journal of Abnormal and Social Psychology, 67,* 334–339.

Chadwick, P.D.J., Lowe, C.F., Horne, P.J., & Higson, P.J. (1994). Modifying delusions: The role of empirical testing. *Behavior Therapy, 25,* 35–49.

Chandler, L.K., Lubeck, R.C., & Fowler, S.A. (1992). Generalization and maintenance of preschool children's social skills: A critical review and analysis. *Journal of Applied Behavior Analysis, 25,* 415–428.

Chartrand, T., & Bargh, J. (1999). The chameleon effect: The perception-behavior link and social interaction. *Journal of Personality and Social Psychology, 76,* 893–910.

Chesler, P. (1971). Women as psychiatric and psychotherapeutic patients. *Journal of Marriage and the Family, 33,* 746–759.

Cheyne, J.A., & Walters, R.H. (1970). Punishment and prohibition: Some origins of self-control. In T.M. Newcomb (Ed.), *New directions in psychology.* New York: Holt.

Christensen, J., Parker, S., Silberberg, A., & Hursh, S. (1998). Trade-offs in choice between risk and delay depend on monetary amounts. *Journal of the Experimental Analysis of Behavior, 69,* 123–139.

Christopher, J.S., Nangle, D.W., & Hansen, D.J. (1993). Social-skills intervention with adolescents: Current issues and procedures. *Behavior Modification, 17,* 314–338.

Clark, D.M. (1999). Anxiety disorders: Why they persist and how to treat them. *Behaviour Research and Therapy, 37,* S5–S27.

Clark, H.B., Rowbury, T., Baer, A.M., & Baer, D.M. (1973). Timeout as a punishing stimulus in continuous and intermittent schedules. *Journal of Applied Behavior Analysis, 6,* 443–453.

Clary, M. (1997a, June 11). For fallen stop sign, vandals face life. *Los Angeles Times,* pp. A1, A13.

Clary, M. (1997b, June 21). Deadly sign prank sends 3 to prison. *Los Angeles Times,* p. A16.

Coates, T.J., & Collins, C. (1998). Altering behavior is still the primary way to control the epidemic. *Scientific American, 279*(1), 96–97.

Cobb, S., & Rose, R.M. (1973). Hypertension, peptic ulcer, and diabetes in air traffic controllers. *Journal of the American Medical Association, 224,* 489–492.

Cohen, R., DeJames, P., Nocera, B., & Ramberger, M. (1980). Application of a simple self-instruction procedure on adult exercise and studying: Two case reports. *Psychological Reports, 46,* 443–451.

Cohen, S.L. (1998). Behavioral momentum: The effects of the temporal separation of rates of reinforcement. *Journal of the Experimental Analysis of Behavior, 69,* 29–47.

Cole, R.P., & Miller, R.R. (1999). Conditioned excitation and conditioned inhibition acquired through backward conditioning. *Learning and Motivation, 30,* 129–156.

Comfort, A. (1976). *The good age.* New York: Crown.

Cook, S., Peterson, L., & DiLillo, D. (1999). Fear and exhilaration in response to risk: An extension of a model of injury risk in a real-world context. *Behavior Therapy, 30,* 5–15.

Cope, J.G., & Allred, L.J. (1991). Community intervention to deter illegal parking in spaces reserved for the physically disabled. *Journal of Applied Behavior Analysis, 24,* 687–693.

Corey, J.R., & Shamow, J. (1972). The effects of fading on the acquisition and retention of oral reading. *Journal of Applied Behavior Analysis, 5,* 311–315.

Correa, E.I., & Sutker, P. B. (1986). Assessment of alcohol and drug behaviors. In A.R. Ciminero, K.S. Calhoun, & H.E. Adams (Eds.), *Handbook of behavioral assessment* (2nd ed., pp. 446–495). New York: Wiley.

Corrigan, P.W. (1995). On the battle between behavior and cognition: Lessons from physicists and pragmatists. *Journal of Behavior Therapy and Experimental Psychiatry, 26,* 209–214.

Costello, J.M. (1983). Generalization across settings: Language intervention with children. In J. Miller, D.E. Yoder, & R.L. Schiefelbusch (Eds.), *Contemporary issues in language intervention* (pp. 275–297). Rockville, MD: ASHA.

Craig, K.D., & Weinstein, M.S. (1965). Conditioning vicarious affective arousal. *Psychological Reports, 17,* 955–963.

Craighead, L.W., Stunkard, A.J., & O'Brien, R. (1981). Behavior therapy and pharmacotherapy of obesity. *Archives of General Psychiatry, 38,* 763–768.

Craske, M.G., Maidenberg, E., & Bystritsky, A. (1995). Brief cognitive-behavioral versus nondirective therapy for panic disorder. *Journal of Behavior Therapy and Experimental Psychiatry, 26,* 113–120.

Cressey, D.R. (1978). White collar subversives. *The Center Magazine, 11*(6), 44–49.

Crolley, J., Roys, D., Thyer, B.A., & Bordnick, P.S. (1998). Evaluating outpatient behavior therapy of sex offenders: A pretest-posttest study. *Behavior Modification, 22,* 485–501.

Crombez, G., Eccleston, C., Baeyens, F., & Eelen, P. (1998). Attentional disruption is enhanced by the threat of pain. *Behaviour Research and Therapy, 36,* 195–204.

Crooks, R., & Baur, K. (1999). *Our sexuality,* 7th ed. Pacific Grove, CA: Brooks/Cole.

Crosbie, J. (1998). Negative reinforcement and punishment. In K.A. Lattal & M. Perone (Eds.), *Handbook of research methods in human operant behavior* (pp. 163–189). New York: Plenum Press.

Crowley, K., & Siegler, R.S. (1999). Explanation and generalization in young children's strategy learning. *Child Development, 70,* 304–316.

Csikszentmihalyi, M. (1975). *Beyond boredom and anxiety.* San Francisco: Jossey-Bass.

Csikszentmihalyi, M. (1993). *The evolving self: A psychology for the third millennium.* New York: HarperCollins.

Csikszentmihalyi, M., & Csikszentmihalyi, I.S. (Eds.). (1988). *Optimal experience: Psychological studies of flow in consciousness.* New York: Cambridge University Press.

Cullen, C. (1988). Applied behavior analysis: Contemporary and prospective agenda. In G. Davey & C. Cullen (Eds.), *Human operant conditioning and behavior modification* (pp. 15–25). New York: Wiley.

Curtiss, S. (1977). *Genie: A psycholinguistic study of a modern day "wild child."* New York: Academic Press.

Damasio, A.R. (1994). *Descartes' error: Emotion, reason, and the human brain.* New York: Putnam.

Damianopoulos, E.N. (1989). Biological constraints revisited: A critique. *Animal Learning & Behavior, 17,* 234–242.

Danaher, B. G. (1974). Theoretical foundations and clinical applications of the Premack principle: Review and critique. *Behavior Therapy, 5,* 307–324.

Danforth, J.S., Chase, P.N., Dolan, M., & Joyce, J.H. (1990). The establishment of stimulus control by instructions and by differential reinforcement. *Journal of the Experimental Analysis of Behavior, 54,* 97–112.

Darby, R.J., & Pearce, J.M. (1997). The effect of stimulus preexposure on responding during a compound stimulus. *The Quarterly Journal of Experimental Psychology, 50B,* 203–216.

Davey, G. (Ed.). (1987). *Cognitive processes and Pavlovian conditioning in humans.* New York: Wiley.

Davey, G., (1988). Trends in human operant theory. In G. Davey & C. Cullen (Eds.), *Human operant conditioning and behavior modification* (pp. 1–14). New York: Wiley.

Davey, G., (1994). Defining the important theoretical questions to ask about evaluative conditioning: A reply to Martin and Levey (1994). *Behaviour Research and Therapy, 32,* 307–310.

Davidson, T.L., & Benoit, S.C. (1998). Learning and eating. In W. O'Donohue (Ed.), *Learning and behavior therapy* (pp. 498–517). Boston: Allyn and Bacon.

Davis, K. (1940). Extreme social isolation of a child. *American Journal of Sociology, 45,* 554–565.

Davis, K. (1947). Final note on a case of extreme isolation. *American Journal of Sociology, 52,* 432–437.

Davison, M., & Jones, B.M. (1995). A quantitative analysis of extreme choice. *Journal of the Experimental Analysis of Behavior, 64,* 147–162.

Day, H.M., Horner, R.H., & O'Neill, R.E. (1994). Multiple functions of problem behaviors: Assessment and intervention. *Journal of Applied Behavior Analysis, 27,* 279–289.

Day, W.F. (1970). On certain similarities between the philosophical investigations of Ludwig Wittgenstein and the operationism of B.F. Skinner. In P.B. Dews (Ed.), *Festschrift for B. F. Skinner* (pp. 359–376). New York: Appleton-Century-Crofts.

de Jong, P.J. (1999). Communicative and remedial effects of social blushing. *Journal of Nonverbal Behavior, 23,* 197–217.

de Jong, P.J., Mayer, B., & van den Hout, M. (1997). Conditional reasoning and phobic fear: Evidence for a fear-confirming reasoning pattern. *Behaviour Research and Therapy, 35,* 507–516.

Deci, E.L., & Ryan, R.M. (1985). *Intrinsic motivation and self-determination in human behavior.* New York: Plenum Press.

Deitz, S.M., & Malone, L.W. (1985). Stimulus control terminology. *The Behavior Analyst, 8,* 259–264.

Dekker, E., & Groen, J. (1956). Reproducible psychogenic attacks of asthma: A laboratory study. *Journal of Psychosomatic Research, 1,* 58–67.

Delprato, D.J., & Midgley, B.D. (1992). Some fundamentals of B.F. Skinner's behaviorism. *American Psychologist, 47,* 1507–1520.

De Luca, R.V., & Holborn, S.W. (1992). Effects of a variable-ratio reinforcement schedule with changing criteria on exercise in obese and nonobese boys. *Journal of Applied Behavior Analysis, 25,* 671–679.

Demasio, A.R. (1994). *Descartes' error: Emotion, reason and the human brain.* New York: Putnam.

Derby, K.M., Fisher, W.W., & Piazza, C.C. (1996). The effects of contingent and noncontingent attention on self-injury and self-restraint. *Journal of Applied Behavior Analysis, 29,* 107–110.

Derby, K.M., Wacker, D.P., Berg, W., DeRaad, A., Ulrich, S., Asmus, J., Harding. J., Prouty, A., Laffey, P., & Stoner, E.A. (1997). The long-term effects of functional communication training in home settings. *Journal of Applied Behavior Analysis, 30,* 507–531.

de Silva, P., & Marks, M. (1999). The role of traumatic experiences in the genesis of obsessive-compulsive disorder. *Behaviour Research and Therapy, 37,* 941–951.

de Villiers, P. (1977). Choice in concurrent schedules and a quantitative formulation of the law of effect. In W.K. Honig & J.E.R. Staddon (Eds.), *Handbook of operant behavior* (pp. 233–287). Englewood Cliffs, NJ: Prentice Hall.

Dews, P.B. (1963). Behavioral effects of drugs. In S.M. Farber & R.H.L. Wilson (Eds.), *Conflict and creativity* (pp. 699–798). New York: McGraw-Hill.

DiCara, L.V. (1970). Learning in the autonomic nervous system. *Scientific American, 222*(1), 30–39.

Dinsmoor, J.A. (1995a). Stimulus control: Part I. *The Behavior Analyst, 18,* 51–68.

Dinsmoor, J.A. (1995b). Stimulus control: Part II. *The Behavior Analyst, 18,* 253–269.

Dinsmoor, J.A. (1998). Punishment. In W. O'Donohue (Ed.), *Learning and behavior therapy* (pp. 188–204). Boston: Allyn and Bacon.

Dirge of the Kampucheans. (1978). *Time 112*(14), 45.

Dodge, K., Bates, J., & Pettit, G. (1990). Mechanisms in the cycle of violence. *Science, 250,* 1678–1683.

Donahoe, J.W. (1998). Positive reinforcement: The selection of behavior. In W. O'Donohue (Ed.), *Learning and behavior therapy* (pp. 169–187). Boston: Allyn and Bacon.

Donahoe, J.W., & Palmer, D.C. (1994). Learning and complex behavior. Boston: Allyn and Bacon.

Donohue, B., Acierno, R., Van Hasselt, V.B., & Hersen, M. (1995). Social skills training in a depressed visually impaired older adult. *Journal of Behavior Therapy and Experimental Psychiatry, 26,* 65–75.

Doogan, S., & Thomas, G. V. (1992). Origins of fear of dogs in adults and children: The role of conditioning processes and prior familiarity with dogs. *Behaviour Research and Therapy, 30,* 387–394.

Ducharme, D.E., & Holborn, S.W. (1997). Programming generalization of social skills in preschool children with hearing impairments. *Journal of Applied Behavior Analysis, 30,* 639–651.

Ducharme, J.M. (1996). Errorless compliance training: Optimizing clinical efficacy. *Behavior Modification, 20,* 259–280.

Ducharme, J.M., & Popynick, M. (1993). Errorless compliance to parental requests: Treatment effects and generalization. *Behavior Therapy, 24,* 209–226.

Ducharme, J.M., & Van Houten, R. (1994). Operant extinction in the treatment of severe maladaptive behavior. *Behavior Modification, 18,* 139–170.

Dukas, H., & Hoffmann, B. (1979). *Albert Einstein: The human side.* Princeton, NJ: Princeton University Press.

Dunham, P. (1977). The nature of reinforcing stimuli. In W.K. Honig & J.E.R. Staddon (Eds.), *Handbook of oper-*

ant behavior (pp. 98–124). Englewood Cliffs, NJ: Prentice Hall.

Dunlap, G., Kern-Dunlap, L., Clarke, S., & Robbins, F.R. (1991). Functional assessment, curricular revision, and severe behavior problems. *Journal of Applied Behavior Analysis, 24,* 387–397.

Dutton, D.G. (1995). *The domestic assault of women: Psychological and criminal justice perspectives.* Vancouver, BC: UBC Press.

Dworkin, B.R., & Dworkin, S. (1995). Learning of physiological responses: II. Classical conditioning of the baroreflex. *Behavioral Neuroscience, 109,* 1119–1136.

Dysinger, W.S., & Ruckmick, C.A. (1933). *The emotional responses of children to the motion-picture situation.* New York: Macmillan.

Eckerman, C.O., & Stein, M.R. (1990). How imitation begets imitation and toddlers' generation of games. *Developmental Psychology, 26,* 370–378.

Egeland, B. (1993). A history of abuse is a major risk factor for abusing the next generation. In R.J. Gelles & D.R. Loseke (Eds.), *Current controversies on family violence* (pp. 197–208). Newbury Park, CA: Sage.

Egger, M.D., & Miller, N.E. (1962). Secondary reinforcement in rats as a function of information value and reliability of the stimulus. *Journal of Experimental Psychology, 64,* 97–104.

Egger, M.D., & Miller, N.E. (1963). When is a reward reinforcing? An experimental study of the information hypothesis. *Journal of Comparative and Physiological Psychology, 56,* 132–137.

Eifert, G.H., Forsyth, J.P., Zvolensky, M.J., & Lejuez, C.W. (1999). Moving from the laboratory to the real world and back again: Increasing the relevance of laboratory examinations of anxiety sensitivity. *Behavior Therapy, 30,* 273–283.

Eisenberg, N., Fabes, R.A., Shepard, S.A., Guthrie, I.K., Murphy, B.C., & Reiser, M. (1999). Parental reactions to children's negative emotions: Longitudinal relations to quality of children's social functioning. *Child Development, 70,* 513–534.

Eisenberger, R., Karpman, M., & Trattner, J. (1967). What is the necessary and sufficient condition for reinforcement in the contingency situation? *Journal of Experimental Psychology, 74,* 342–350.

Eisenberger, R., & Selbst, M. (1994). Does reward increase or decrease creativity? *Journal of Personality and Social Psychology, 66,* 1116–1128.

Ekman, P. (1972). Universal and cultural differences in facial expressions of emotions. In J.K. Cold (Ed.), *Nebraska symposium on motivation* (Vol. 19, pp. 207–283). Lincoln: University of Nebraska Press.

Ekman, P. (1980). *The face of man: Expressions of universal emotions in a New Guinea village.* New York: Garland STPM Press.

Ekman, P. (1984). Expression and the nature of emotion. In K. Scherer & P. Ekman (Eds.), *Approaches to emotion* (pp. 319–344). Hillsdale, NJ: Erlbaum.

Ekman, P. (1993). Facial expression and emotion. *American Psychologist, 48,* 384–392.

Ekman, P., & Keltner, D. (1997). Universal facial expressions of emotion: An old controversy and new findings. In C. Ullicia, E. Segerstrale, & P. Molnar (Eds.), *Nonverbal communication: Where nature meets culture* (pp. 27–46). Mahwah, NJ: Erlbaum.

Ekman, P., Roper, G., & Hager, J.C. (1980). Deliberate facial movement. *Child Development, 51,* 886–891.

Elias, J., & Gebhard, P. (1969). Sexuality and sexual learning in childhood. *Phi Delta Kappan, 50,* 401–405.

Elkins, R.L. (1991). An appraisal of chemical aversion (emetic therapy) approaches to alcoholism treatment. *Behaviour Research and Therapy, 29,* 387–413.

Elliott, S.N., & Gresham, F.M. (1993). Social skills interventions for children. *Behavior Modification, 17,* 287–313.

Ellis, A. (1962). *Reason and emotion in psychotherapy.* New York: Stuart.

Ellis, H. (1942). *Studies in the psychology of sex* (Vols. 1–2). New York: Random House. (Original work published in seven parts, 1896–1928.)

Ellis, M.J. (1973). *Why people play.* Englewood Cliffs, NJ: Prentice Hall.

Emmelkamp, P.M.G. (1982). Anxiety and fear. In A.S. Bellack, M. Hersen, & A.E. Kazdin (Eds.), *International handbook of behavior modification and therapy* (pp. 349–395). New York: Plenum Press.

Epling, W.F., & Pierce, W.D. (1988). Applied behavior analysis: New directions from the laboratory. In G. Davey & C. Cullen (Eds.), *Human operant conditioning and behavior modification* (pp. 43–58). New York: Wiley.

Epstein, R. (1997). Skinner as self-manager. *Journal of Applied Behavior Analysis, 30,* 545–568.

Ericsson, K.A., Krampe, R.T., & Tesch-Römer, C. (1993). The role of deliberate practice in the acquisition of expert performance. *Psychological Review, 100,* 363–406.

Ervin, R.A., Miller, P.M., & Friman, P.C. (1996). Feed the hungry bee: Using positive peer reports to improve the social interactions and acceptance of a socially rejected girl in residential care. *Journal of Applied Behavior Analysis, 29,* 251–253.

Espinosa, J.M. (1992). Probability and radical behaviorism. *The Behavior Analyst, 15,* 51–60.

Evans, I.M., & Matthews, A.K. (1992). A behavioral approach to the prevention of school dropout: Conceptual and empirical strategies for children and youth. In M. Hersen, R.M. Eisler, & P.M. Miller (Eds.), *Progress in behavior modification: Vol. 28* (pp. 219–249). Sycamore, IL: Sycamore Publishing.

Falls, W.A. (1998). Extinction: A review of theory and the evidence suggesting that memories are not erased with nonreinforcement. In W. O'Donohue (Ed.), *Learning and behavior therapy* (pp. 205–229). Boston: Allyn and Bacon.

Fantino, E. (1977). Conditioned reinforcement: Choice and information. In W.K. Honig & J.E.R. Staddon (Eds.), *Handbook of operant behavior* (pp. 313–339). Englewood Cliffs, NJ: Prentice Hall.

Fantino, E. (1995). To err is human: A case for a behavioral approach. *Behavior and Philosophy, 23*(1), 49–51.

Fantino, E. (1998). Behavior analysis and decision making. *Journal of the Experimental Analysis of Behavior, 69,* 355–364.

Fantino, E., & Logan, C.A. (1979). *The experimental analysis of behavior: A biological perspective.* San Francisco: W. H. Freeman.

Fantino, E., & Moore, J. (1980). Uncertainty reduction, conditioned reinforcement, and observing. *Journal of the Experimental Analysis of Behavior, 33,* 3–13.

Farley, M., & Barkan, H. (1998). Prostitution, violence, and posttraumatic stress disorder. *Women and Health, 27*(3), 37–49.

Farrell, S.P., Hains, A.A., & Davies, W.H. (1998). Cognitive behavioral interventions for sexually abused children exhibiting PTSD symptomatology. *Behavior Therapy, 29,* 241–255.

Fawcett, S.B. (1991). Some values guiding community research and action. *Journal of Applied Behavior Analysis, 24,* 621–636.

Feinberg, R.A. (1990). The social nature of the classical conditioning phenomena in people: A comment on Hunt, Florsheim, Chatterjee, and Kernan. *Psychological Reports, 67,* 331–334.

Ferster, C.B., Culbertson, S., & Boren, M.C.P. (1975). *Behavior principles* (2nd ed.). Englewood Cliffs, NJ: Prentice Hall.

Ferster, C.B., & Skinner, B.F. (1957). *Schedules of reinforcement.* Englewood Cliffs, NJ: Prentice Hall.

Finney, J.W. (1991). On further development of the concept of social validity. *Journal of Applied Behavior Analysis, 24,* 245–249.

Fischer, C.S. (1981a). *To dwell among friends: Personal networks in town and city.* Chicago: University of Chicago Press.

Fischer, C.S. (1981b). The public and private worlds of city life. *American Sociological Review, 46,* 306–316.

Fisher, W.W., Grace, N.C., & Murphy, C. (1996). Further analysis of the relationship between self-injury and self-restraint. *Journal of Applied Behavior Analysis, 29,* 103–106.

Fisher, W.W., & Mazur, J.E. (1997). Basic and applied research on choice responding. *Journal of Applied Behavior Analysis, 30,* 387–410.

Fisher, W.W., Ninness, H.A.C., Piazza, C.C., & Owen-DeSchryver, J.S. (1996). On the reinforcing effects of the content of verbal attention. *Journal of Applied Behavior Analysis, 29,* 235–238.

Fisher, W.W., Piazza, C., Cataldo, M., Harrell, R., Jefferson, G., & Conner, R. (1993). Functional communication training with and without extinction and punishment. *Journal of Applied Behavior Analysis, 26,* 23–36.

Flavell, J.H., Green, F.L., Flavell, E.R., & Grossman, J.B. (1997). The development of children's knowledge about inner speech. *Child Development, 68,* 39–47.

Flor, H., Breitenstein, C., Birbaumer, N., & Fürst, M. (1995). A psychophysiological analysis of spouse solicitousness towards pain behaviors, spouse interaction, and pain perception. *Behavior Therapy, 26,* 255–272.

Flora, S.R. (1990). Undermining intrinsic interest from the standpoint of a behaviorist. *The Psychological Record, 40,* 323–346.

Follette, W.C., Bach, P.A., & Follette, V.M. (1993). A behavior-analytic view of psychological health. *The Behavior Analyst, 16,* 303–316.

Foltin, R.W., & Schuster, C.R. (1982). Effects of extinction on responding maintained under a second-order schedule of food presentation in rhesus monkeys. *The Psychological Record, 32,* 519–528.

Foreyt, J.P., & Goodrick, G.K. (1984). Health maintenance: Exercise and nutrition. In E. A. Blechman (Ed.), *Behavior modification with women* (pp. 221–244). New York: Guilford Press.

Fox, D.K., Hopkins, B.L., & Anger, W.K. (1987). The long-term effects of a token economy on safety performance in open-pit mining. *Journal of Applied Behavior Analysis, 20,* 215–224.

Foxx, R.M., & Shapiro, S.T. (1978). The timeout ribbon: A nonexclusionary timeout procedure. *Journal of Applied Behavior Analysis, 11,* 125–136.

Francoeur, R.T. (1991). *Becoming a sexual person* (2nd ed.). New York: Macmillan.

Franz, D.Z., & Gross, A.M. (1996). Parental correlates of socially neglected, rejected and average children. *Behavior Modification, 20,* 170–182.

Freeman, T.J., & Lattal, K.A. (1992). Stimulus control of behavioral history. *Journal of the Experimental Analysis of Behavior, 57,* 5–15.

Freiheit, S.R., & Overholser, J.C. (1997). Training issues in cognitive-behavioral psychotherapy. *Journal of Behavior Therapy and Experimental Psychiatry, 28,* 79–86.

Friman, P.C., Hayes, S.C., & Wilson, K.G. (1998). Why behavior analysts should study emotion: The example of anxiety. *Journal of Applied Behavior Analysis, 31,* 137–156.

Friman, P.C., & Poling, A. (1995). Making life easier with effort: Basic findings and applied research on response effort. *Journal of Applied Behavior Analysis, 28,* 583–590.

Fulcher, E.P., & Cocks, R.P. (1997). Dissociative storage systems in human evaluative conditioning. *Behaviour Research and Therapy, 35,* 1–10.

Galizio, M. (1999). Extinction of responding maintained by timeout from avoidance. *Journal of the Experimental Analysis of Behavior, 71,* 1–11.

Garber, J., & Seligman, M.E.P. (1980). *Human helplessness: Theory and applications.* New York: Academic Press.

Garcia, J., Brett, L.P., & Rusiniak, K.W. (1989). Limits of Darwinian conditioning. In S.B. Klein & R.R. Mowrer (Eds.), *Contemporary learning theories: Instrumental conditioning theory and the impact of biological constraints on learning* (pp. 181–203). Hillsdale, NJ: Erlbaum.

Garcia, J., & Riley, A.L. (1998). Conditioned taste aversions. In G. Greenberg & M.M. Haraway (Eds.), *Comparative psychology: A handbook* (pp, 549–561). New York: Garland Publishing.

Garven, S., Wood, J.M., & Malpass, R.S. (2000). Allegations of wrongdoing: The effects of reinforcement on children's mundane and fantastic claims. *Journal of Applied Psychology, 85,* 38–49.

Gelfand, D.M., & Hartmann, D.P. (1975). *Child behavior analysis and therapy.* New York: Pergamon Press.

Gena, A., Krantz, P.J., McClannahan, L.E., & Poulson, C.L. (1996). Training and generalization of affective behavior displayed by youth with autism. *Journal of Applied Behavior Analysis, 29,* 291–304.

Gil, K.M., Phillips, G., Webster, D.A., Martin, N.J., Abrams, M., Grant, M., Clark, W.C., & Janal, M.N. (1995). Experimental pain sensitivity and reports of negative thoughts in adults with sickle cell disease. *Behavior Therapy, 26,* 273–293.

Gillham, J.E., & Seligman, M.E.P. (1999). Footsteps on the road to a positive psychology. *Behaviour Research and Therapy, 37,* S163–S173.

Ginsburg, E.H. (1990). *Effective interventions: Applying learning theory to school social work.* New York: Greenwood Press.

Glover, J.A., & Gary, A.L. (1975). *Behavior modification: Enhancing creativity and other good behaviors.* Pacific Grove, CA: Boxwood Press.

Gmelch, G., & Felson, R. (1980). Can a lucky charm get you through organic chemistry? *Psychology Today* 14(7), 75–76, 78.

Goddard, M.J. (1997). Spontaneous recovery in US extinction. *Learning and Motivation, 28,* 118–128.

Goetz, E.M., & Baer, D.M. (1973). Social control of form diversity and the emergence of new forms in children's block building. *Journal of Applied Behavior Analysis, 6,* 209–217.

Goetz, E.M., & Salmonson, M.M. (1972). The effect of general and descriptive reinforcement on "creativity" in easel painting. In G. Semb (Ed.), *Behavior analysis and education* (pp. 53–61). Lawrence: University of Kansas Press.

Goetz, L., Schuler, A., & Sailor, W. (1979). Teaching functional speech to the severely handicapped: Current issues. *Journal of Autism and Development Disorders, 9,* 325–343.

Goetz, L., Schuler, A.L., & Sailor, W. (1981). Functional competence as a factor in communication instruction. *Exceptional Education Quarterly, 2,* 51–60.

Goffman, E. (1959). *The presentation of self in everyday life.* Garden City, NY: Doubleday Anchor.

Goldfried, M.R., & Merbaum, M. (1973). *Behavior change through self-control.* New York: Holt.

Goldstein, A.P., & Kanfer, F.H. (1979). *Maximizing treatment gains.* New York: Academic Press.

Goldstein, H., & Cisar, C.L. (1992). Promoting interaction during sociodramatic play: Teaching scripts to typical preschoolers and classmates with disabilities. *Journal of Applied Behavior Analysis, 25,* 265–280.

Goldstein, H., Kaczmarek, L., Pennington, R., & Shafer, K. (1992). Peer-mediated intervention: Attending to, commenting on, and acknowledging the behavior of preschoolers with autism. *Journal of Applied Behavior Analysis, 25,* 289–305.

Goldstein, H., & Wickstrom, S. (1986). Peer intervention effects on communicative interaction among handicapped and nonhandicapped preschoolers. *Journal of Applied Behavior Analysis, 19,* 209–214.

Gollub, L. (1977). Conditioned reinforcement: Schedule effects. In W.K. Honig & J.E.R. Staddon (Eds.), *Handbook of operant behavior* (pp. 288–312). Englewood Cliffs, NJ: Prentice Hall.

Gorman, T. (1996, June 17). Deaths on tracks take heavy toll on engineers. *Los Angeles Times,* pp. A3, A15.

Gormezano, I., Prokasy, W.F., & Thompson, R.F. (1987). *Classical conditioning* (3rd ed.). Hillsdale, NJ: Erlbaum.

Götestam, B., Götestam, K.G., & Melin, L. (1983). Anxiety and coping behavior during an emergency landing. *Behavior Modification, 7,* 569–575.

Gotlib, I.H., & Krasnopervona, E. (1998). Biased information processing as a vulnerability factor for depression. *Behavior Therapy, 22,* 603–617.

Gottfried, A.E. (1985). Academic intrinsic motivation in elementary and junior school students. *Journal of Educational Psychology, 77,* 631–645.

Gottfried, A.E., Fleming, J.S., & Gottfried, A.W. (1998). Role of cognitively stimulating home environment in children's academic intrinsic motivation: A longitudinal study. *Child Development, 69,* 1448–1460.

Gottman, J.M. (1994). *Why marriages succeed or fail.* New York: Simon & Schuster.

Gottman, J.M. (1999). *The marriage clinic.* New York: W.W. Norton & Co.

Gould, R.A., & Clum, G.A. (1995). Self-help plus minimal therapist contact in the treatment of panic disorder: A replication and extension. *Behavior Therapy, 26,* 533–546.

Grabowski, J., Stitzer, M.L., & Henningfield, J.E. (Eds.). (1984). *Behavioral intervention techniques in drug abuse treatment.* Health and Human Services, Public Health Service, Alcohol, Drug Abuse, and Mental Health Administration, National Institute of Drug Abuse. Washington, DC: U.S. Government Printing Office.

Grace, N.C., Thompson, R., & Fisher, W.W. (1996). The treatment of covert self-injury through contingencies on response products. *Journal of Applied Behavior Analysis, 29,* 239–242.

Grace, R.C. (1999). The matching law and amount-dependent exponential discounting as accounts of self-control choice. *Journal of the Experimental Analysis of Behavior, 71,* 27–44.

Green, C.W., & Reid, D.H. (1996). Defining, validating, and increasing indices of happiness among people with profound multiple disabilities. *Journal of Applied Behavior Analysis, 29,* 67–78.

Green, L., & Freed, D.E. (1998). Behavioral economics. In W. O'Donohue (Ed.), *Learning and behavior therapy* (pp. 274–300). Boston: Allyn and Bacon.

Green, L., & Myerson, J. (1993). Alternative frameworks for the analysis of self control. *Behavior and Philosophy, 21*(2), 37–47.

Green, L., Myerson, J., & Ostaszewski, P. (1999). Amount of reward has opposite effects on the discounting of delayed and probabilistic outcomes. *Journal of Experimental Psychology: Learning, Memory, and Cognition, 25,* 418–427.

Green, P.C. (1972). Masochism in the laboratory rat: An experimental demonstration. *Psychonomic Science, 27,* 41–44.

Greenspan, S.I. (1995). *The challenging child.* New York: Addison-Wesley.

Greenwood, C.R., Delquadri, J.C., & Hall, R.V. (1984). Opportunity to respond and student academic performance. In W. Heward, T. Heron, D. Hill, & J. Trap-Porter (Eds.), *Focus on behavior analysis in education* (pp. 58–88). Columbus, OH: Bell and Howell.

Greenwood, J.D. (1991). Self-knowledge: Looking in the wrong direction. *Behavior and Philosophy, 19*(2), 35–47.

Griffiths, D., Feldman, M.A., & Tough, S. (1997). Programming generalization of social skills in adults with developmental disabilities: Effect on generalization and social validity. *Behavior Therapy, 28,* 253–269.

Gronna, S.S., Serna, L.A., Kennedy, C.H., & Prater, M.A. (1999). Promoting generalized social interactions using puppets and script training in an integrated preschool: A single case study using multiple baseline design. *Behavior Modification, 23,* 419–440.

Guerin, B. (1992). Social behavior as discriminative stimulus and consequence in social anthropology. *The Behavior Analyst, 1,* 31–41.

Hagopian, L.P., Fisher, W.W., Thompson, R.H., Owen-DeSchryver, J., Iwata, B.A., & Wacker, D.P. (1997). Toward the development of structured criteria for interpretation of functional analysis data. *Journal of Applied Behavior Analysis, 30,* 313–326.

Haider, H., & Frensch, P.A. (1999). Eye movement during skill acquisition: More evidence for the information-reduction hypothesis. *Journal of Experimental Psychology: Learning, Memory, and Cognition, 25,* 172–190.

Hall, E. (1959). *The silent language.* New York: Fawcett.

Hall, R.V., Axelrod, S., Tyler, L., Grief, E., Jones, F.C., & Robertson, R. (1972). Modification of behavior problems in the home with a parent as observer and experimenter. *Journal of Applied Behavior Analysis, 5,* 53–64.

Halle, J.W., & Holt, B. (1991). Assessing stimulus control in natural settings: An analysis of stimuli that acquire control during training. *Journal of Applied Behavior Analysis, 24,* 579–589.

Hammond, L.J. (1980). The effect of contingency upon the appetitive conditioning of free operant behavior. *Journal of the Experimental Analysis of Behavior, 34,* 297–304.

Handen, B.L., Parrish, J.M., McClung, T.J., Kerwin, M.E., & Evans, L.D. (1992). Using guided compliance versus time-out to promote child compliance: A preliminary comparative analysis in an analogue setting. *Research in Developmental Disabilities, 13,* 157–170.

Hantula, D.A., & Crowell, C.R. (1994). Behavioral contrast on a two-option analogue task of financial decision making. *Journal of Applied Behavior Analysis, 27,* 607–616.

Harding, J., Wacker, D.P., Cooper, L.J., Asmus, J., Jensen-Kovalan, P., & Grisolano, L.A. (1999). Combining descriptive and experimental analyses of young children with behavior problems in preschool settings. *Behavior Modification, 32,* 316–333.

Harrigan, J.A., & Taing, K.T. (1997). Fooled by a smile: Detecting anxiety in others. *Journal of Nonverbal Behavior, 21,* 203–221.

Harris, M. (1977). *Cannibals and kings: The origins of cultures.* New York: Vintage Books/Random House.

Harrison, J.M. (1990). Simultaneous auditory discrimination. *Journal of the Experimental Analysis of Behavior, 54,* 45–51.

Harrison, J.M. (1991). Stimulus control. In I.H. Iversen & K.A. Lattal (Eds.), *Experimental analysis of behavior: Part 1* (pp. 251–299). New York: Elsevier.

Hart, B., & Risley, T.R. (1995). *Meaningful differences in the everyday experience of young American children.* Baltimore, MD: Paul H. Brooks Publishing.

Hastjarjo, T., Silberberg, A., & Hursh, S.R. (1990). Risky choice as a function of amount and variance in food supply. *Journal of the Experimental Analysis of Behavior, 53,* 155–161.

Hatfield, E., & Rapson, R.L. (1993). *Love, sex, and intimacy: Their psychology, biology and history.* New York: HarperCollins.

Hauser, L. (1994). Acting, intending and artificial intelligence. *Behavior and Philosophy, 22*(1), 23–28.

Hawkins, R.P. (1991). Is social validity what we are interested in? Argument for a functional approach. *Journal of Applied Behavior Analysis, 24,* 205–213.

Hawkins, R.P. & Forsyth, J.P. (1997). Bridging barriers between paradigms: Making cognitive concepts relevant for behavior analysis. *Journal of Behavior Therapy and Experimental Psychiatry, 28,* 3–6.

Hawthorne, N. (1850). *The scarlet letter.* Boston: Ticknor & Fields.

Hayek, F.A. (1988). *The fatal conceit: The errors of socialism.* Chicago: University of Chicago Press.

Hayes, S.C., & Ju, W. (1998). The applied implications of rule-governed behavior. In W. O'Donohue (Ed.), *Learning and behavior therapy* (pp. 374–391). Boston: Allyn and Bacon.

Hayes, S.C., Kohlenberg, B.S., & Melancon, S.M. (1989). Avoiding and altering rule-control as a strategy of clinical intervention. In S.C. Hayes (Ed.), *Rule-governed behavior: Cognition, contingencies, and instructional control* (pp. 359–385). New York: Plenum Press.

Hayes, S.C., Zettle, R.D., & Rosenfarb, I. (1989). Rule-following. In S.C. Hayes (Ed.), *Rule-governed behavior: Cognition, contingencies, and instructional control* (pp. 191–220). New York: Plenum Press.

Haynes, S.N., & O'Brien, W.H. (1990). Functional analysis in behavior therapy. *Clinical Psychology Review, 10,* 649–668.

Hebb, D.O. (1972). *Textbook of psychology (3rd ed.).* Philadelphia: Saunders.

Heiman, J., & LoPiccolo, J. (1988). *Becoming orgasmic: A sexual and personal growth program for women*. New York: Prentice Hall.

Henderson, D.K. (1991). Rationalizing explanation, normative principles, and descriptive generalizations. *Behavior and Philosophy, 19*(1), 1–20.

Hendrick, S.S., & Hendrick, C. (1992). *Liking, loving and relating* (2nd ed.). Pacific Grove, CA: Brooks/Cole.

Herbert, W. (1982). TMI: Uncertainty is causing chronic stress. *Science News, 121*, 308.

Hermann, J.A., de Montes, A.I., Dominguez, B., Montes, F., & Hopkins, B.L. (1973). Effects of bonuses for punctuality on the tardiness of industrial workers. *Journal of Applied Behavior Analysis, 6*, 563–570.

Herrnstein, R.J. (1961). Relative and absolute strength of response as a function of frequency of reinforcement. *Journal of the Experimental Analysis of Behavior, 4*, 267–272.

Herrnstein, R.J. (1970). On the law of effect. *Journal of the Experimental Analysis of Behavior, 13*, 243–266.

Hersen, M., & Barlow, D.H. (1976). *Single-case experimental designs: Strategies for studying behavior change*. New York: Pergamon Press.

Hersen, M., & Bellack, A.S. (Eds.). (1985). *Handbook of clinical behavior therapy with adults*. New York: Plenum Press.

Hester, R.K. (1995). Behavioral self-control training. In R.K. Hester & W.R. Miller (Eds.), *Handbook of alcoholism treatment approaches: Effective alternatives* (2nd ed., pp. 148–159). Boston: Allyn and Bacon.

Heward, W.L., & Malott, R.W. (1995). Introduction: How the happy few might become the competent many. *The Behavior Analyst, 18*, 69–71.

Hilberg, R. (1961). *The destruction of the European Jews*. Chicago: Quadrangle.

Hill, R.D., Rigdon, M., & Johnson, S. (1993). Behavioral smoking cessation treatment for older chronic smokers. *Behavior Therapy, 24*, 321–329.

Hiltzik, M.A. (1996, June 15). More firms giving a stake to employees. *Los Angeles Times*, pp. A1, A22–A23.

Hineline, P.N., & Wanchisen, B.A. (1989). Correlated hypothesizing and the distinction between contingency-shaped and rule-governed behavior. In S.C. Hayes (Ed.), *Rule-governed behavior: Cognition, contingencies, and instructional control* (pp. 221–268). New York: Plenum Press.

Hoffart, A. (1995). Cognitive mediators of situational fear in agoraphobia. *Journal of Behavior Therapy and Experimental Psychiatry, 26*, 313–320.

Hoffman, M.L. (1960). Power assertion by the parent and its impact on the child. *Child Development, 31*, 129–143.

Hoffman, M.L. (1970). Moral development. In P.H. Mussen (Ed.), *Manual of child psychology*. New York: Wiley.

Holland, P.C. (1977). Conditioned stimulus as a determinant of the form of the Pavlovian conditioned response. *Journal of Psychology: Animal Behavior Processes, 3*, 77–104.

Holland, P.C. (1999). Overshadowing and blocking as acquisition deficits: No recovery after extinction of blocking and overshadowing cues. *The Quarterly Journal of Experimental Psychology, 52B*, 307–333.

Homans, G.C. (1974). *Social behavior: Its elementary forms*. New York: Harcourt Brace Jovanovich.

Homme, L.E. (1965). Perspectives in psychology: XXIV. Control of coverants, the operants of the mind. *The Psychological Record, 15*, 501–511.

Honey, R.C. (2000). The Experimental Psychology Society Prize Lecture: Associative priming in Pavlovian conditioning. *The Quarterly Journal of Experimental Psychology, 53B*, 1–23.

Honig, W.K., & Staddon, J.E.R. (1977). *Handbook of operant behavior*. Englewood Cliffs, NJ: Prentice Hall.

Honig, W.K., & Urcuioli, P.J. (1981). The legacy of Guttman and Kalish (1956): Twenty-five years of research on stimulus generalization. *Journal of the Experimental Analysis of Behavior, 36*, 405–445.

Honnen, T.J., & Kleinke, C.L. (1990). Prompting bar patrons with signs to take free condoms. *Journal of Applied Behavior Analysis, 23*, 215–217.

Horne, P.J., & Lowe, C.F. (1996). On the origins of naming and other symbolic behavior. *Journal of the Experimental Analysis of Behavior, 65*, 185–241.

Horner, R.H. (1994). Functional assessment: Contributions and future directions. *Journal of Applied Behavior Analysis, 27*, 401–404.

Horner, R.H., & Day, H.M. (1991). The effects of response efficiency on functionally equivalent competing behaviors. *Journal of Applied Behavior Analysis, 24*, 719–732.

Horner, R.H., Day, H.M., Sprague, J.R., O'Brien, M., & Heathfield, L.T. (1991). Interspersed requests: A nonaversive procedure for reducing aggression and self-injury during instruction. *Journal of Applied Behavior Analysis, 24*, 265–278.

Horner, R.H., Dunlap, G., Koegel, R.L., Carr, E.G., Sailor, W., Anderson, J., Albin, R.W., & O'Neill, R.E. (1990). Toward a technology of "nonaversive" behavioral support. *Journal of the Association for Persons with Severe Handicaps, 15*, 125–132.

Houlihan, D., & Brandon, P.K. (1996). Compliant in a moment: A commentary on Nevin. *Journal of Applied Behavior Analysis, 29*, 549–555.

Houlihan, D., Sloane, H.N., & Jones, R.N. (1992). A review of behavioral conceptualizations and treatments of child noncompliance. *Education and Treatment of Children, 15*, 56–77.

Houston, J.P. (1976). *Fundamentals of learning*. New York: Academic Press.

Howard, R.B., & Winter, H.S. (1984). *Nutrition and feeding of infants and toddlers*. Boston: Little, Brown.

Hoyert, M.S., & Zeiler, M.D. (1995). Stimulus properties of the differential-reinforcement-of-not-responding schedule. *The Psychological Record, 45*, 73–93.

Huang, W., & Cuvo, A.J. (1997). Social skills training for adults with mental retardation in job-related settings. *Behavior Modification, 21*, 3–44.

Hull, J. (1994). Running scared. *Time, 144*(21), 92–99.

Hume, K.M., & Crossman, J. (1992). Musical reinforcement of practice behaviors among competitive swimmers. *Journal of Applied Behavior Analysis, 25,* 665–670.

Hursh, S.R. (1977). The conditioned reinforcement of repeated acquisition. *Journal of the Experimental Analysis of Behavior, 27,* 315–326.

Isaacs, W., Thomas, J., & Goldiamond, I. (1960). Application of operant conditioning to reinstate verbal behavior in psychotics. *Journal of Speech and Hearing Disorders, 25,* 8–12.

Ishaq, W. (1996). The social relevance of applied behavior analysis and psychological intervention strategies. In J.R. Cautela & W. Ishaq (Eds.), *Contemporary issues in behavior therapy: Improving the human condition,* (pp. 235–259). New York: Plenum Press.

Istvan, J., Griffitt, W., & Weidner, G. (1983). Sexual arousal and the polarization of perceived sexual attractiveness. *Basic and Applied Social Psychology, 4,* 307–318.

Iversen, I.H. (1991). Methods of analyzing behavior patterns. In I.H. Iversen & K.A. Lattal (Eds.), *Experimental analysis of behavior: Part 1* (pp. 193–241). New York: Elsevier.

Iwata, B.A. (1987). Negative reinforcement in applied behavior analysis: An emerging technology. *Journal of Applied Behavior Analysis, 20,* 361–378.

Iwata, B.A., Pace, G.M., Dorsey, M.F., Zarcone, J.R., Vollmer, T.R., Smith, R.G., Rodgers, T.A., Lerman, D.C., Shore, B.A., Mazaleski, J.L., Goh, H.-L., Cowdery, G.E., Kalsher, M.J., McCosh, K.C., & Willis, K.D. (1994). The functions of self-injurious behavior: An experimental-epidemiological analysis. *Journal of Applied Behavior Analysis, 27,* 215–240.

Izard, C.E. (1977). *Human emotions.* New York: Plenum Press.

Jacobsen, P.B., Bovbjerg, D.H., Schwartz, M.D., Andrykowski, M.A., Futterman, A.D., Gilewski, T., Norton, L., & Redd, W.H. (1993). Formation of food aversions in cancer patients receiving repeated infusions of chemotherapy. *Behaviour Research and Therapy, 31,* 739–748.

Jakobs, E., Manstead, A.S.R., and Fischer, A.H. (1999). Social motives, emotional feelings, and smiling. *Cognition and Emotion, 13,* 321–345.

Jansen, A., Broekmate, J., & Heymans, M. (1992). Cue-exposure vs. self-control in the treatment of binge eating: A pilot study. *Behaviour Research and Therapy, 30,* 235–241.

Janzen, W., & Cousins, S.O. (1995). "I do" or don't: Marriage, women, and physical activity throughout the lifespan. *Journal of Women and Aging, 7,* 55–70.

Jason, L.A., McMahon, S.D., Salina, D., Hedeker, D., Stockton, M., Dunson, K., & Kimball, P. (1995). Assessing a smoking cessation intervention involving groups, incentive, and self-help manuals. *Behavior Therapy, 26,* 393–408.

Johnson, M.D., & Fawcett, S.B. (1994). Courteous service: Its assessment and modification in a human service organization. *Journal of Applied Behavior Analysis, 27,* 145–152.

Johnston, L., Ward, T., & Hudson, S.M. (1997). Deviant sexual thoughts: Mental control and the treatment of sexual offenders. *The Journal of Sex Research, 34,* 121–130.

Jones, K.M., Swearer, S.M., & Friman, P.C. (1997). Relax and try this instead: Abbreviated habit reversal for maladaptive self-biting. *Journal of Applied Behavior Analysis, 30,* 697–699.

Kagan, J. (1997). Temperament and the reactions of unfamiliarity. *Child Development, 68,* 139–143.

Kagan, J., Snidman, N., & Arcus, D. (1998). Childhood derivatives of high and low reactivity in infancy. *Child Development, 69,* 1483–1493.

Kahle, A.L., & Kelley, M.L. (1994). Children's homework problems: A comparison of goal setting and parent training. *Behavior Therapy, 25,* 275–290.

Kahng, S.W., & Iwata, B.A. (1999). Correspondence between outcomes of brief and extended functional analyses. *Journal of Applied Behavior Analysis, 32,* 149–159.

Kalish, H. (1981). *From behavioral science to behavior modification.* New York: McGraw-Hill.

Kamin, L.J. (1968). "Attention-like" processes in classical conditioning. In M.R. Jones (Ed.), *Miami symposium on the predicting of behavior, 1967. Aversive stimulation* (pp. 9–31). Coral Gables, FL: University of Miami Press.

Kamin, L.J. (1969). Predictability, surprise, attention, and conditioning. In B.A. Campbell & R.M. Church (Eds.), *Punishment and aversive behavior.* New York: Appleton-Century-Crofts.

Kamps, D.M., Barbetta, P.M., Leonard, B.R., & Delquadri, J. (1994). Classwide peer tutoring: An integration strategy to improve reading skills and promote peer interactions among students with autism and general education peers. *Journal of Applied Behavior Analysis, 27,* 49–61.

Kanfer, F.H., & Phillips, J.S. (1970). *Learning foundations of behavior therapy.* New York: Wiley.

Karen, R.L. (1974). *An introduction to behavior theory and its applications.* New York: Harper & Row.

Katahn, M., Pleas, J., Thackrey, M., & Wallston, K.A. (1982). Relationship of eating and activity self-reports to follow-up maintenance in the massively obese. *Behavior Therapy, 13,* 521–528.

Kaufmann, W. (1973). *Without guilt and justice.* New York: Wyden.

Kawachi, I., Sparrow, D., Vokonas, P.S., & Weiss, S.T. (1994). Symptoms of anxiety and risk of coronary heart disease: The normative aging study. *Circulation, 90,* 2225–2229.

Kazdin, A.E. (1980). *Research design in clinical psychology.* New York: Harper & Row.

Kazdin, A.E. (1982). The separate and combined effects of covert and overt rehearsal in developing assertive behavior. *Journal of Behaviour Research and Therapy, 20,* 17–25.

Kazdin, A.E. (1988). The token economy: A decade later. In G. Davey & C. Cullen (Eds.), *Human operant condi-*

tioning and behavior modification (pp. 119–137). New York: Wiley.

Kazdin, A.E. (1993). Evaluation in clinical practice: Clinically sensitive and systematic methods of treatment delivery. *Behavior Therapy, 24,* 11–45.

Kazdin, A.E. (1994). *Behavior modification in applied settings* (5th ed.). Pacific Grove, CA: Brooks/Cole.

Kehoe, E.J., & Macrae, M. (1998). Classical conditioning. In W. O'Donohue (Ed.), *Learning and behavior therapy* (pp. 36–58). Boston: Allyn and Bacon.

Kellam, S.G., Ling, X., Meriaca, R., Brown, C.H., & Ialongo, N. (1998). "The effect of the level of aggression on the first grade classroom on the course and malleability of aggressive behavior into middle school. *Development & Psychology, 10,* 165–185.

Keller, J.J. (1991). The recycling solution: How I increased recycling on Dilworth Road. *Journal of Applied Behavior Analysis, 24,* 617–619.

Kelley, M.L., & McCain, A.P. (1995). Promoting academic performance in inattentive children. *Behavior Modification, 19,* 357–375.

Keltner, D., & Gross, J.J. (1999). Functional accounts of emotions. *Cognition and Emotion, 13,* 467–480.

Keltner, D., & Haidt, J. (1999). Social functions of emotions at four levels of analysis. *Cognition and Emotion, 13,* 505–521.

Keltner, D., & Kring, A.M. (1998). Emotion, social function, and psychopathy. *Review of General Psychology, 2,* 320–342.

Kendall, P.C., & Hollon, S.D. (1979). Cognitive-behavioral interventions. New York: Academic Press.

Kent, G., & Jambunathan, P. (1989). A longitudinal study of the intrusiveness of cognitions in test anxiety. *Behaviour Research and Therapy, 27,* 43–50.

Kern, L., Childs, K.E., Dunlap, G., Clarke, S., & Falk, G.D. (1994). Using assessment-based curricular intervention to improve the classroom behavior of a student with emotional and behavioral challenges. *Journal of Applied Behavior Analysis, 27,* 7–19.

Kheriaty, E., Kleinknecht, R.A., Hyman, I.E., Jr. (1999). Recall and validation of phobia origins as a function of a structured interview versus the phobia origins questionnaire. *Behavior Modification, 23,* 61–78.

Killeen, P. (1978). Superstition: A matter of bias, not detectability. *Science, 199,* 88–90.

Killeen, P., & Fantino, E. (1990). Unification of models for choice between delayed reinforcers. *Journal of the Experimental Analysis of Behavior, 53,* 189–200.

Kimble, G.A. (1961). *Hilgard and Marquis' conditioning and learning.* New York: Appleton-Century-Crofts.

King, G.R., & Logue, A.W. (1990). Humans' sensitivity to variation in reinforcer amount: Effects of the method of reinforcer delivery. *Journal of the Experimental Analysis of Behavior, 53,* 33–45.

King, N.J., Clowes-Hollins, V., & Ollendick, T.H. (1997). The etiology of childhood dog phobia. *Behaviour Research and Therapy, 35,* 77.

Kinsey, A.C., Pomeroy, W.B., & Martin, C.E. (1948). *Sexual behavior in the human male.* Philadelphia: Saunders.

Kinsey, A.C., Pomeroy, W.B., Martin, C.E., & Gebhard, P.H. (1953). *Sexual behavior in the human female.* Philadelphia: Saunders.

Klatzky, R. (1980). *Human memory: Structures and processes* (2nd ed.). San Francisco: Freeman.

Klein, G. (1998). Sources of power: How people make decisions. Cambridge, MA: MIT Press.

Klein, S.B., & Mowrer, R.R. (Eds.). (1989). *Contemporary learning theories: Pavlovian conditioning and the status of traditional learning theory.* Hillsdale, NJ: Erlbaum.

Kleitman, N. (1949). Biological rhythms and cycles. *Physiological Review, 29,* 1–30.

Klinger, E. (1977). *Meaning and void: Inner experience and the incentives in people's lives.* Minneapolis: University of Minnesota Press.

Klinger, E. (1978). Modes of normal conscious flow. In K.S. Pope & J.L. Singer (Eds.), *The stream of consciousness* (pp. 226–258). New York: Plenum Press.

Knight, M.F., & McKenzie, H.S. (1974). Elimination of bedtime thumbsucking in home settings through contingent reading. *Journal of Applied Behavior Analysis, 7,* 33–38.

Kobes, B.W. (1991). On a model for psycho-neural coevolution. *Behavior and Philosophy, 19*(2), 1–17.

Koegel, L.K., Camarata, S.M., Valdez-Menchaca, M., & Koegel, R.L. (1998). Setting generalization of question-asking by children with autism. *American Journal of Mental Retardation, 102,* 346–357.

Koegel, L.K., Harrower, J.K., & Koegel, R.L. (1999). Support for children with developmental disabilities in full inclusion classrooms through self-management. *Journal of Positive Behavior Interventions, 1,* 26–34.

Koegel, L.K., Koegel, R.L., & Dunlap, G. (Eds.). (1996). *Positive behavioral support: Including people with difficult behavior in the community.* Baltimore: Paul H. Brookes Publishing.

Koegel, L.K., Koegel, R.L., Hurley, C., & Frea, W.D. (1992). Improving social skills and disruptive behavior in children with autism through self-management. *Journal of Applied Behavior Analysis, 25,* 341–354.

Koegel, R.L., Bimbela, A., & Schreibman, L. (1996). Collateral effects of parent training on family interactions. *Journal of Autism and Developmental Disorders, 26,* 347–359.

Koegel, R.L., Camarata, S., Koegel, L.K., Ben-Tall, A., & Smith, A.E.. (1998). Increasing speech intelligibility in children with autism. *Journal of Autism and Developmental Disorders, 28,* 241–251.

Koegel, R.L., Egel, A.L., & Williams, J.A. (1980). Behavioral contrast and generalization across settings in the treatment of autistic children. *Journal of Experimental Child Psychology, 30,* 422–437.

Koegel, R.L., & Frea, W.D. (1993). Treatment of social behavior in autism through the modification of pivotal social skills. *Journal of Applied Behavior Analysis, 26,* 369–377.

Koegel, R.L., Koegel, L.K., & Schreibman, L. (1991). Assessing and training parents in teaching pivotal behaviors. In R.J. Prinz (Ed.), *Advances in behavioral assessment of children and families* (Vol. 5, pp. 65–82). London: Jessica Kingsley.

Kohlenberg, B.S., Hayes, S.C., & Hayes, L.J. (1991). The transfer of contextual control over equivalence classes through equivalence classes: A possible model of social stereotyping. *Journal of the Experimental Analysis of Behavior, 56,* 505–518.

Kohn, A. (1992). *No contest: The case against competition* (rev. ed.). Boston: Houghton Mifflin.

Korner, A. (1974). The effect of the infant's state, level of arousal, sex, and ontogenetic stage on the caregiver. In M. Lewis & L.A. Rosenblum (Eds.), *The effect of the infant on its caregiver* (pp. 105–121). New York: Wiley.

Krantz, P.J., & McClannahan, L.E. (1993). Teaching children with autism to initiate to peers: Effects of a script-fading procedure. *Journal of Applied Behavior Analysis, 26,* 121–132.

Kunkel, J.H. (1975). *Behavior, social problems, and change: A social learning approach.* Englewood Cliffs, NJ: Prentice Hall.

Kymissis, E., & Poulson, C.L. (1990). The history of imitation in learning theory: The language acquisition process. *Journal of the Experimental Analysis of Behavior, 54,* 113–127.

Ladouceur, R., Sylvain, C., Letarte, H., Giroux, I., & Jacques, C. (1998). Cognitive treatment of pathological gamblers. *Behaviour Research and Therapy, 36,* 1111–1119.

Lalli, J.S., Browder, D.M., Mace, F.C., & Brown, D.K. (1993). Teacher use of descriptive analysis data to implement interventions to decrease students' problem behaviors. *Journal of Applied Behavior Analysis, 26,* 227–239.

Lalli, J.S., & Kates, K. (1998). The effect of reinforcer preference on functional analysis outcomes. *Journal of Applied Behavior Analysis, 31,* 79–90.

Lalli, J.S., Mace, F.C., Livezey, K., & Kates, K. (1998). Assessment of stimulus generalization gradients in the treatment of self-injurious behavior. *Journal of Applied Behavior Analysis, 31,* 479–483.

Lamal, P.A. (Ed.). (1991). *Behavioral analysis of societies and cultural practices.* New York: Hemisphere Publishing Corp.

LaMere, J.M., Dickinson, A.M., Henry, M., Henry, G., & Poling, A. (1996). Effects of a multicomponent monetary incentive program on the performance of truck drivers: A longitudinal study. *Behavior Modification, 20,* 385–405.

Lance, M. (1996). A battle with no victors. *Time, 147*(22), 33.

Larson, R. (1988). Flow and writing. In M. Csikszentmihalyi, & I.S. Csikszentmihalyi (Eds.), *Optimal experience: Psychological studies of flow in consciousness* (pp. 150–171). New York: Cambridge University Press.

Latham, G.I. (1996). The making of a stable family. In J.R. Cautela & W. Ishaq, *Contemporary issues in behavior therapy: Improving the human condition* (pp. 357–382). New York: Plenum Press.

Lattal, K.A. (1995). Contingency and behavior analysis. *The Behavior Analyst, 18,* 209–224.

Lattal, K.A., & Neef, N.A. (1996). Recent reinforcement-schedule research and applied behavior analysis. *Journal of Applied Behavior Analysis, 29,* 213–230.

Laumann, E.O, Gagnon, J.H., Michael, R.T., & Michaels, S. (1994). *The social organization of sexuality: Sexual practices in the United States.* Chicago: University of Chicago Press.

La Voie, J.C. (1974). Aversive, cognitive, and parental determinants of punishment generalization in adolescent males. *Journal of Genetic Psychology, 124,* 29–39.

Lazarus, A.A. (1997). Disenchantment and hope: Will we ever occupy center stage? A personal odyssey. *Behavior Therapy, 28,* 363–370.

Leiblum, S.R, & Rosen, R.C. (1988). *Sexual desire disorders.* New York: Guilford Press.

Leiblum, S.R, & Rosen, R.C. (Eds.). (1989). *Principles and practice of sex therapy: Update for the 1990s* (2nd ed.) New York: Guilford Press.

Leitenberg, H., Agras, S., Butz, R., & Wincze, J. (1971). Relationship between heart rate and behavioral change during the treatment of phobias. *Journal of Abnormal Psychology, 78,* 59–68.

Lennox, D.B., Miltenberger, R.G., & Donnelly, D.R. (1987). Response interruption and DRI for the reduction of rapid eating. *Journal of Applied Behavior Analysis, 20,* 279–284.

Lepper, M.R., & Greene, D. (1975). Turning play into work: Effects of adult surveillance and extrinsic rewards on children's intrinsic motivation. *Journal of Personality and Social Psychology, 31,* 479–486.

Lerman, D.C., & Iwata, B.A. (1996). Developing a technology for the use of operant extinction in clinical settings: An examination of basic and applied research. *Journal of Applied Behavior Analysis, 29,* 345–382.

Lerman, D.C., Iwata, B.A., Shore, B.A., & Kahng, S.W. (1996). Responding maintained by intermittent reinforcement: Implications for the use of extinction with problem behavior in clinical settings. *Journal of Applied Behavior Analysis, 29,* 153–171.

Levenson, R.W. (1999). The intrapersonal functions of emotion. *Cognition and Emotion, 13,* 481–504.

Lieberman, D.A., Cathro, J.S., Nichol, K. & Watson, E. (1997). The role of S^Δ in human observing behavior: Bad news is sometimes better than no news. *Learning and Motivation, 28,* 20–42.

Lieberman, M.D. (2000). Intuition: A social cognitive neuroscience approach. *Psychological Bulletin, 126,* 109–137.

Lincoln, J.F. (1946). *Lincoln's incentive system.* New York: McGraw-Hill.

Lindberg, J.S., Iwata, B.A., Kahng, S.W., & DeLeon, I.G. (1999). DRO contingencies: An analysis of variable-momentary schedules. *Journal of Applied Behavior Analysis, 32,* 123–136.

Little, J.C., & James, B. (1964). Abreaction of conditioned fear reaction after eighteen years. *Behaviour Research and Therapy, 2,* 59–63.

Little, L.M., & Kelley, M.L. (1989). The efficacy of response cost procedures for reducing children's noncompliance to parental instructions. *Behavior Therapy, 20,* 525–534.

Loeb, K.L., Wilson, G.T., Gilbert, J.S., & Labouvie, E. (2000). Guided and unguided self-help for binge eating. *Behaviour Research and Therapy, 38,* 259–272.

Logue, A.W. (1983). Signal detection and matching: Analyzing choice on concurrent variable-interval schedules. *Journal of the Experimental Analysis of Behavior, 39,* 107–127.

Logue, A.W. (1988). Research on self-control: An integrating framework. *Behavioral and Brain Sciences, 11,* 665–679.

Logue, A.W. (1995). *Self-control: Waiting until tomorrow for what you want today.* Englewood Cliffs, NJ: Prentice Hall.

Logue, A.W. (1998). Self-control. In W. O'Donohue (Ed.), *Learning and behavior therapy* (pp. 252–273). Boston: Allyn and Bacon.

Logue, A.W., Ophir, I., & Strauss, K.E. (1981). The acquisition of taste aversions in humans. *Behaviour Research and Therapy, 19,* 319–333.

Lombard, D., Neubauer, T.E., Canfield, D., & Winett, R.A. (1991). Behavioral community intervention to reduce the risk of skin cancer. *Journal of Applied Behavior Analysis, 24,* 677–686.

Lovaas, O.I. (1977). *The autistic child: Language development through behavior modification.* New York: Irvington.

Lovaas, O.I., & Simmons, J.Q. (1969). Manipulation of self-destruction in three retarded children. *Journal of Applied Behavior Analysis, 2,* 143–157.

Luco, J.E. (1990). Matching, delay-reduction, and maximizing models for choice in concurrent-chains schedules. *Journal of the Experimental Analysis of Behavior, 54,* 53–67.

Luiselli, J.K. (1996). Functional assessment and treatment of aggressive and destructive behaviors in a child victim of physical abuse. *Journal of Behavior Therapy and Experimental Psychiatry, 27,* 41–49.

Lynch, D.C., & Green, G. (1991). Development and cross-modal transfer of contextual control of emergent stimulus relations. *Journal of the Experimental Analysis of Behavior, 56,* 139–154.

Lynn, D.B. (1969). *Parental and sex role identification: A theoretical formulation.* Berkeley, CA: McCutchan.

Lyons, C.A., & Ghezzi, P.M. (1995). Wagering on a large scale: Relationships between public gambling and game manipulations in two state lotteries. *Journal of Applied Behavior Analysis, 28,* 127–137.

Lyubomirsky, S., & Tucker, K.I. (1998). Implications of individual differences in subjective happiness for perceiving, interpreting, and thinking about life events. *Motivaton and Emotion, 22,* 155–186.

Maccoby, E.E. (1992). The role of parents in the socialization of children: An historical overview. *Developmental Psychology, 28,* 1006–1017.

MacCorquodale, K. (1970). On Chomsky's review of Skinner's Verbal Behavior. *Journal of the Experimental Analysis of Behavior, 13,* 83–99.

Mace, F.C., & Lalli, J.S. (1991). Linking descriptive and experimental analyses in the treatment of bizarre speech. *Journal of Applied Behavior Analysis, 24,* 553–562.

Mace, F.C., & Neef, N.A. (1996). Effects of problem difficulty and reinforcer quality on time allocated to concurrent arithmetic problems. *Journal of Applied Behavior Analysis, 29,* 11–24.

Mackintosh, N.J. (1975). A theory of attention. *Psychological Review, 82,* 276–298.

Mackintosh, N.J. (1977). Stimulus control: Attentional factors. In W.K. Honig & J.E.R. Staddon (Eds.), *Handbook of operant behavior* (pp. 481–513). Englewood Cliffs, NJ: Prentice Hall.

Maddi, S.R. (1980). *Personality theories: A comparative analysis* (4th ed.). Homewood, IL: Dorsey Press.

Mahoney, M.J. (1970). Toward an experimental analysis of coverant control. *Behavior Therapy, 1,* 510–521.

Mahoney, M.J. (1974). *Cognition and behavior modification.* Cambridge, MA: Ballinger.

Mahoney, M.J. (1975). The sensitive scientist and empirical humanism. *American Psychologist, 30,* 864–867.

Mahoney, M.J., & Thoresen, C.E. (Eds.). (1974). *Self-control: Power to the person.* Monterey, CA: Brooks/Cole.

Maloney, K.B., & Hopkins, B.L. (1973). The modification of sentence structure and its relationship to subjective judgements of creative writing. *Journal of Applied Behavior Analysis, 6,* 425–433.

Malott, R.W. (1998). Operant conditioning. In G. Greenberg & M.M. Haraway (Eds.), *Comparative psychology: A handbook* (pp. 576–585). New York: Garland Publishing.

Mansell, W., & Clark, D.M. (1999). How do I appear to others? Social anxiety and processing of the observable self. *Behaviour Research and Therapy, 37,* 419–434.

Marks, I.M., & Gelder, M.G. (1967). Transvestism and fetishism: Clinical and psychological changes during faradic aversion. *British Journal of Psychiatry, 113,* 711–729.

Marks, I.M., Rachman, S., & Gelder, M.G. (1965). Methods for assessment of aversion treatment in fetishism with masturbation. *Behaviour Research and Therapy, 3,* 253–258.

Marshall, W.L. (1999). Current status of North American assessment and treatment programs for sexual offenders. *Journal of Interpersonal Violence, 14,* 221–239.

Marshall, W.L., Bristol, D., & Barbaree, H.E. (1992). Cognitions and courage in the avoidance behavior of acrophobics. *Behaviour Research and Therapy, 30,* 463–470.

Martens, B.K., Bradley, T.A., & Eckert, T.L. (1997). Effects of reinforcement history and instructions on the persistence of student engagement. *Journal of Applied Behavior Analysis, 30,* 569–572.

Martin, G., & Pear, J. (1996). *Behavior modification: What it is and how to do it* (5th ed.). Upper Saddle River, NJ: Prentice Hall.

Martin, I., & Levey, A. (1994). The evaluative response: Primitive but necessary. *Behaviour Research and Therapy, 32,* 301–305.

Martin, L.L., & Davies, B. (1998). Beyond hedonism and associationism: A configural view of the role of affect in evaluation, processing, and self-regulation. *Motivation and Emotion, 22,* 33–51.

Martindale, D. (1977). Sweaty palms in the control tower. *Psychology Today, 10*(9), 70–72, 75.

Martinson, F.M. (1994). *The sexual life of children.* Westport, CT: Bergin & Garvey.

Masia, C.L., & Chase, P.N. (1997). Vicarious learning revisited: A contemporary behavior analytic interpretation. *Journal of Behavior Therapy and Experimental Psychiatry, 28,* 41–51.

Masters, J.C., Burish, T.G., Hollon, S.D., & Rimm, D.C. (1987). *Behavior therapy* (3rd ed.). New York: Harcourt Brace Jovanovich.

Masters, W.H., & Johnson, V.E. (1966). *Human sexual response.* Boston: Little, Brown.

Masters, W.H., & Johnson, V.E. (1970). *Human sexual inadequacy.* Boston: Little, Brown.

Masters, W.H., & Johnson, V.E. (1979). *Homosexuality in perspective.* Boston: Little, Brown.

Masters, W.H., Johnson, V.E., & Kolodny, R.C. (1995). *Human sexuality* (5th ed.). New York: HarperCollins.

Mathis, C.E., Johnson, D.F., & Collier, G.H. (1995). Procurement time as a determinant of meal frequency and meal duration. *Journal of the Experimental Analysis of Behavior, 63,* 295–311.

Matson, J.L., Bamburg, J., Smalls, Y., & Smiroldo, B.B. (1997). Evaluating behavioral techniques in training individuals with severe and profound mental retardation to use functional independent living skills. *Behavior Modification, 21,* 533–544.

Matson, J.L., Smalls, Y., Hampff, A., Smiroldo, B.B., & Anderson, S.J. (1998). A comparison of behavioral techniques to teach functional independent-living skills to individuals with severe and profound mental retardation. *Behavior Modification, 22,* 298–306.

Matute, H., & Miller, R.R. (1998). Detecting causal relations. In W. O'Donohue (Ed.), *Learning and behavior therapy* (pp. 483–497). Boston: Allyn and Bacon.

Maurer, T.J., Palmer, J.K., & Ashe, D.K. (1993). Diaries, checklists, evaluations, and contrast effects in measurement of behavior. *Journal of Applied Psychology, 78,* 226–231.

May, J.L., & Hamilton, P.A. (1980). Effects of musically evoked affect on women's interpersonal attraction toward and perceptual judgment of physical attractiveness of men. *Motivation and Emotion, 4,* 217–228.

Mazaleski, J.I., Iwata, B.A., Vollmer, T.R., Zarcone, J.R., & Smith, R.G. (1993). Analysis of the reinforcement and extinction components in DRO contingencies with self-injury. *Journal of Applied Behavior Analysis, 26,* 143–156.

Mazur, J.E. (1991). Choice. In I.H. Iversen & K.A. Lattal (Eds.), *Experimental analysis of behavior: Part 1* (pp. 219–250). New York: Elsevier.

Mazur, J.E. (1993). Predicting the strength of a conditioned reinforcer: Effects of delay and uncertainty. *Current Directions in Psychological Science, 2,* 70–74.

Mazur, J.E. (1995). Conditioned reinforcement and choice with delayed and uncertain primary reinforcers. *Journal of the Experimental Analysis of Behavior, 63,* 139–150.

Mazur, J.E. (1998). Choice and self-control. In K.A. Lattal & M. Perone (Eds.), *Handbook of research methods in human operant behavior,* pp. 131–161). New York: Plenum Press.

McCarthy, D.C., & Davison, M. (1991). The interaction between stimulus and reinforcer control on remembering. *Journal of the Experimental Analysis of Behavior, 56,* 51–66.

McClanahan, T.M. (1995). Operant learning (R-S) principles applied to nail-biting. *Psychological Reports, 77,* 507–514.

McCloskey, M. (1983). Intuitive physics. *Scientific American, 248*(4), 122–130.

McEwan, K.L., & Devins, G.A. (1983). Is increased arousal in social anxiety noticed by others? *Journal of Abnormal Psychology, 92,* 417–421.

McGonigle, J.J., Rojahn, J., Dixon, J., & Strain, P.S. (1987). Multiple treatment interference in the alternating treatments design as a function of the intercomponent interval length. *Journal of Applied Behavior Analysis, 20,* 171–178.

McIntire, R.W. (1970). *For love of children.* Del Mar, CA: CRM.

McNeil, D.W., & Brunetti, D.G. (1992). Pain and fear: A bioinformational perspective on responsivity to imagery. *Behaviour Research and Therapy, 30,* 513–520.

Mead, G.H. (1934). *Mind, self and society.* Chicago: University of Chicago Press.

Mechner, F. (1994). The revealed operant: A way to study the characteristics of individual occurrences of operant responses (3rd ed.). In S.S. Glenn (Ed.), *Progress in behavioral studies* (Monograph no. 3, pp. 1–78). Cambridge, MA: Cambridge Center for Behavioral Studies.

Mees, H.L. (1966). Sadistic fantasies modified by aversive conditioning and substitution: A case study. *Behaviour Research and Therapy, 4,* 317–320.

Meichenbaum, D. (1971). Examination of model characteristics in reducing avoidance behavior. *Journal of Personality and Social Psychology, 17,* 298–307.

Meichenbaum, D. (1976). A cognitive-behavior modification approach to assessment. In M. Hersen & A.S. Bellack (Eds.), *Behavior assessment: A practical handbook* (pp. 299–398). New York: Pergamon Press.

Meichenbaum, D. (1977). *Cognitive behavior modification.* New York: Plenum Press.

Meichenbaum, D., & Cameron, R. (1974). The clinical potential of modifying what clients say to themselves. In M.J. Mahoney & C.E. Thoresen (Eds.), *Self-control: Power to the person* (pp. 263–290). Monterey, CA: Brooks/Cole.

Mental health: Does therapy help? (1995, November). *Consumer Reports,* pp. 734–739.

Menzies, R.G., & Clarke, J.C. (1993). A comparison of in vivo and vicarious exposure in the treatment of childhood water phobia. *Behaviour Research and Therapy, 31,* 9–15.

Merckelbach, H., Muris, P., Horselenberg, R., & Rassin, E. (1998). Traumatic intrusions as 'worse case scenario's.' *Behaviour Research and Therapy, 36,* 1075–1079.

Mersch, P.P.A., Emmelkamp, P.M.G., Bögels, S.M., & van der Sleen, J. (1989). Social phobia: Individual response patterns and the effects of behavioral and cognitive interventions. *Behaviour Research and Therapy, 27,* 421–434.

Michael, R.L., & Bernstein, D. J. (1991). Transient effects of acquisition history on generalization in a matching-to-sample task. *Journal of the Experimental Analysis of Behavior, 56,* 155–166.

Millenson, J.R., & Leslie, J.C. (1979). *Principles of behavioral analysis* (2nd ed.). New York: Macmillan.

Miller, D.L., & Kelley, M.L. (1994). The use of goal setting and contingency contracting for improving children's homework performance. *Journal of Applied Behavior Analysis, 27,* 73–84.

Miller, L., & Ackley, R. (1970). Summation of responding maintained by fixed-interval schedules. *Journal of the Experimental Analysis of Behavior, 13,* 199–203.

Miller, N.E. (1951). Learnable drives and rewards. In S.S. Stevens (Ed.), *Handbook of experimental psychology* (pp. 435–472). New York: Wiley.

Miller, N.E. (1969). Learning of visceral and glandular responses. *Science, 163,* 434–445.

Miller, N.E. (1978). Biofeedback and visceral learning. *Annual Review of Psychology, 29,* 373–404.

Mineka, S., & Hamida, S.B. (1998). Observational and nonconscious learning. In W. O'Donohue (Ed.), *Learning and behavior therapy* (pp. 421–439). Boston: Allyn and Bacon.

Mischel, W. (1968). *Personality and assessment.* New York: Wiley.

Mischel, W. (1981). *Introduction to personality* (3rd ed.). New York: Holt.

Mischel, W., & Peake, P.K. (1982). Beyond deja vu in the search for cross-situational consistency. *Psychological Review, 89,* 730–755.

Mize, J., & Ladd, G. W. (1990). A cognitive-social learning approach to social skill training with low-status preschool children. *Developmental Psychology, 26,* 388–397.

Montagu, A. (1981). *Growing young.* New York: McGraw-Hill.

Montgomery, R.W., & Ayllon, T. (1995). Matching verbal repertoires: Understanding the contingencies of practice in order to functionally communicate with clinicians. *Journal of Behavior Therapy and Experimental Psychiatry, 26,* 99–105.

Monti, P.M., Rohsenow, D.J., Colby, S.M., & Abrams, D.B. (1995). Coping and social skills training. In R.K. Hester & W.R. Miller (Eds.), *Handbook of alcoholism treatment approaches: Effective alternatives* (2nd ed., pp. 221–241). Boston: Allyn and Bacon.

Moore, D.W. (1995, December). Three million children victims of physical abuse last year. *Gallup Poll Monthly, 363,* 4–16.

Moore, J. (1995). Radical behaviorism and the subjective-objective distinction. *The Behavior Analyst, 18,* 33–49.

Morrow, G.R., & Morrell, C. (1982). Behavioral treatment for the anticipatory nausea and vomiting induced by cancer chemotherapy. *New England Journal of Medicine, 307,* 1476–1480.

Morse, W.H., & Kelleher, R.T. (1970). Schedules as fundamental determinants of behavior. In W.N. Schoenfeld (Ed.), *The theory of reinforcement schedules* (pp. 139–185). Englewood Cliffs, NJ: Prentice Hall.

Morse, W.H., & Kelleher, R.T. (1977). Determinants of reinforcement and punishment. In W.K. Honig & J.E.R. Staddon (Eds.), *Handbook of operant behavior* (pp. 174–200). Englewood Cliffs, NJ: Prentice Hall.

Myerson, J., & Green, L. (1995). Discounting of delayed rewards: Models of individual choice. *Journal of the Experimental Analysis of Behavior, 64,* 263–276.

Nathanson, L.W. (1996). *The portable pediatrician's guide to kids.* New York: Harper Perennial/Harper Collins.

Nau, P.A., Van Houten, R., Rolider, A., & Jonah, B.A. (1993). The failure of feedback on alcohol impairment to reduce impaired driving. *Journal of Applied Behavior Analysis, 26,* 361–367.

Nevin, J.A. (1971a). Stimulus control. In J.A. Nevin & G.S. Reynolds (Eds.), *The study of behavior* (pp. 115–149). Glenview, IL: Scott, Foresman.

Nevin, J.A. (1971b). Conditioned reinforcement. In J.A. Nevin & G.S. Reynolds (Eds.), *The study of behavior* (pp. 155–198). Glenview, IL: Scott, Foresman.

Nevin, J.A. (1974). Response strength in multiple schedules. *Journal of the Experimental Analysis of Behavior, 21,* 389–408.

Nevin, J.A. (1979). Reinforcement schedules and response strength. In M.D. Zeiler & P. Harzen (Eds.), *Advances in analysis of behaviour: 1. Reinforcement and the organization of behaviour* (pp. 117–158). Chichester, England: Wiley.

Nevin, J.A. (1988). Behavioral momentum and the partial reinforcement effect. *Psychological Bulletin, 103,* 44–56.

Nevin, J.A. (1992). An integrative model for the study of behavioral momentum. *Journal of the Experimental Analysis of Behavior, 57,* 301–316.

Nevin, J.A. (1994). The discriminated operant revealed in pigeon multiple schedule performance: Effects of reinforcement rate and extinction. (The revealed operant: A way to study the characteristics of individual occurrences of operant responses, 3rd ed.) In S.S. Glenn (Ed.), *Progress in behavioral studies* (Monograph no. 3, pp. 93–99). Cambridge, MA: Cambridge Center for Behavioral Studies.

Nevin, J.A. (1995). Behavioral economics and behavioral momentum. *Journal of the Experimental Analysis of Behavior, 64,* 385–395.

Nevin, J.A. (1996). The momentum of compliance. *Journal of Applied Behavior Analysis, 29,* 535–547.

Nevin, J.A. (1998). Choice and momentum. In W. O'Donohue (Ed.), *Learning and behavior therapy* (pp. 230–251). Boston: Allyn and Bacon.

Nevin, J.A., Mandell, C., & Atak, J.R. (1983). The analysis of behavioral momentum. *Journal of the Experimental Analysis of Behavior, 39,* 49–59.

Newman, M.G., Consoli, A.J., & Taylor, C.B. (1999). A palmtop computer program for the treatment of generalized anxiety disorder. *Behavior Modification, 23,* 597–619.

Newman, M.G., Hofmann, S.G., Trabert, W., Roth, W.T., & Taylor, C.B. (1994). Does behavioral treatment of social phobia lead to cognitive changes? *Behavior Therapy, 25,* 503–517.

Newsom, C., Favell, J.E., & Rincover, A. (1983). The side effects of punishment. In S. Axelrod & J. Apsche (Eds.), *The effects of punishment on human behavior* (pp. 285–316). New York: Academic Press.

Nilsson, L.-G., & Archer, T. (1989). Aversively motivated behavior: Which are the perspectives? In T. Archer & L.-G. Nilsson (Eds.), *Aversion, avoidance and anxiety.* Hillsdale, NJ: Erlbaum.

Ninness, H.A.C., Ellis, J., & Ninness, S.K. (1999). Self-assessment as a learned reinforcer during computer interactive math performance: An experimental analaysis. *Behavior Modification, 23,* 403–418.

Novello, A.C., Rosenberg, M., Saltzman, L., & Shosky, J. (1992). From the Surgeon General, U.S. Public Health Service. *Journal of the American Medical Association, 267,* 3132.

Öhman, A., & Soares, J.J.F. (1998). Emotional conditioning to masked stimuli: Expectancies for aversive outcomes following nonrecognized fear-relevant stimuli. *Journal of Experimental Psychology: General, 127,* 69–82.

O'Leary, K.D., Kaufman, K.F., Kass, R.E., & Drabman, R. (1970). The effects of loud and soft reprimands on the behavior of disruptive students. *Exceptional Children, 37,* 145–155.

Olinger, E., & Epstein, M.H. (1991). The behavorial model and adolescents with behavior disorders: A review of selected treatment studies. In M. Hersen, R. Eisler, & P. Miller (Eds.), *Progress in behavior modification.* Newbury Park, CA: Sage.

O'Neill, A.W. (1995, Sept. 16). Child molester who posed as space alien gets 20 years. *Los Angeles Times,* p. B3.

O'Neill, R.E., Horner, R.H., Albin, R.W., Storey, K., & Sprague, J. (1990). *Functional analysis of problem behavior: A practical guide.* Sycamore, IL: Sycamore Publishing.

O'Neill, R.E., & Reichle, J. (1993). Addressing socially motivated challenging behaviors by establishing communication alternatives: Basics of a general-case approach. In J. Reichle & D.P. Wacker (Eds.), *Communicative alternatives to challenging behavior: Integrating functional assessment and intervention strategies* (Vol. 3, pp. 205–235). Baltimore: Paul H. Brookes.

Osgood, C.E., & Tannenbaum, P.H. (1955). The principle of congruity in the prediction of attitude change. *Psychological Review, 62,* 42–55.

Öst, L.-G. (1989). One-session treatment for specific phobias. *Behaviour Research and Therapy, 27,* 1–7.

Öst, L.-G., Brandberg, M., & Alm, T. (1997). One versus five sessions of exposure in the treatment of flying phobia. *Behaviour Research and Therapy, 35,* 987–996.

Öst, L.-G., Ferebee, I., & Furmark, T. (1997). One-session group therapy of spider phobia: Direct versus indirect treatments. *Behaviour Research and Therapy, 35,* 721–732.

Öst, L.-G., & Hugdahl, K. (1981). Acquisition of phobias and anxiety response patterns in clinical patients. *Behaviour Research and Therapy, 19,* 439–447.

Oswald, I. (1962). Induction of illusory and mental voices with considerations of behavior therapy. *Journal of Mental Science, 108,* 196–212.

Overmier, J.B., & LoLordo, V.M. (1998). Learned helplessness. In W. O'Donohue (Ed.), *Learning and behavior therapy* (pp. 352–373). Boston: Allyn and Bacon.

Pace, G.M., Iwata, B.A., Edwards, G.L., & McCosh, K.C. (1986). Stimulus fading and transfer in the treatment of self-restraint and self-injurious behavior. *Journal of Applied Behavior Analysis, 19,* 381–389.

Papini, M.R. (1998). Classical conditioning. In G. Greenberg & M.M. Haraway (Eds.), *Comparative Psychology: A Handbook* (pp, 523–530). New York: Garland Publishing.

Parkinson, B., & Totterdell, P. (1999). Classifying affect-regulation strategies, *Cognition and Emotion, 13,* 277–303.

Paul, R.H., Marx, B.P., & Orsillo, S.M. (1999). Acceptance-based psychotherapy in the treatment of an adjudicated exhibitionist: A case example. *Behavior Therapy, 30,* 149–162.

Pavlov, I.P. (1927). *Conditioned reflexes.* Oxford: Oxford University Press.

Perone, M. (1991). Experimental design in the analysis of free-operant behavior. In I.H. Iversen & K.A. Lattal (Eds.), *Experimental analysis of behavior: Part 1* (pp. 135–171). New York: Elsevier.

Perone, M., & Courtney, K. (1992). Fixed-ratio pausing: Joint effects of past reinforcer magnitude and stimuli correlated with upcoming magnitude. *Journal of the Experimental Analysis of Behavior, 57,* 33–46.

Perone, M., Galizio, M., & Baron, A. (1988). Human operant conditioning and behavior modification. In G. Davey & C. Cullen (Eds.), *Human operant conditioning and behavior modification* (pp. 59–85). New York: Wiley.

Peterson, A.L., & Halstead, T.S. (1998). Group cognitive behavior therapy for depression in a community setting: A clinical replication series. *Behavior Therapy, 29,* 3–18.

Peterson, C., Maier, S.F., & Seligman, M.E.P. (1993). *Learned helplessness: A theory for the age of personal control.* New York: Oxford University Press.

Petroski, H. (1992). *The evolution of useful things.* New York: Knopf.

Piazza, C.C., Adelinis, J.D., Hanley, G.P., Goh, H.L., & Delia, M.D. (2000). An evaluation of the effects of matched stimuli on behaviors maintained by automatic reinforcement. *Journal of Applied Behavior Analysis, 33,* 13–27.

Piazza, C.C., Fisher, W.W., Hagopian, L.P., Bowman, L.G., & Tolle, L. (1996). Using a choice assessment to predict reinforcer effectiveness. *Journal of Applied Behavior Analysis, 29,* 1–9.

Pierce, K., & Schreibman, L. (1995). Increasing complex social behaviors in children with autism: Effects of peer-implemented pivotal response training. *Journal of Applied Behavior Analysis, 28,* 285–295.

Pierce, W.D., & Epling, W.F. (1995). The applied importance of research on the matching law. *Journal of Applied Behavior Analysis, 28,* 237–241.

Plaud, J.J., & Gaither, G.A. (1996). Behavioral momentum: Implications and development from reinforcement theories. *Behavior Modification, 20,* 183–201.

Plaud, J.J., Gaither, G.A., & Lawrence, J.B. (1997). Operant schedule transformations and human behavioral momentum. *Journal of Behavior Therapy and Experimental Psychiatry, 28,* 169–179.

Polanyi, M. (1960). *Personal knowledge.* Chicago: University of Chicago Press.

Polanyi, M. (1966). *The tacit dimension.* Garden City, NY: Doubleday.

Poppen, R.L. (1989). Some clinical implications of rule-governed behavior. In S.C. Hayes (Ed.), *Rule-governed behavior: Cognition, contingencies, and instructional control* (pp. 325–357). New York: Plenum Press.

Potter, S. (1948). *The theory and practice of gamesmanship.* New York: Holt.

Potter, S. (1951). *One-upmanship.* New York: Holt.

Premack, D. (1965). Reinforcement theory. In D. Levine (Ed.), *Nebraska symposium on motivation* (pp. 123–180). Lincoln: University of Nebraska Press.

Premack, D. (1971). Catching up with common sense, or two sides of a generalization: Reinforcement and punishment. In R. Glaser (Ed.), *The nature of reinforcement* (pp. 121–150). New York: Academic Press.

Puca, R.M., & Schmalt, H.-D. (1999). Task enjoyment: A mediator between achievement motives and performance. *Motivation and Emotion, 23,* 15–29.

Quinn, J.M., Sherman, J.A., Sheldon, J.B., Quinn, L.M., & Harchik, A.E. (1992). Social validation of component behaviors of following instructions, accepting criticism, and negotiating. *Journal of Applied Behavior Analysis, 25,* 401–413.

Rachlin, H. (1980). *Behaviorism in everyday life.* Englewood Cliffs, NJ: Prentice Hall.

Rachlin, H. (1989). *Judgement, decision, and choice: A cognitive/behavioral synthesis.* New York: Freeman.

Rachlin, H. (1995). Behavioral economics without anomalies. *Journal of the Experimental Analysis of Behavior, 64,* 397–404.

Rachlin, H., Battalio, R.C., Kagel, J.H., & Green, L. (1981). Maximization theory in behavioral psychology. *The Behavioral and Brain Sciences, 4,* 371–388.

Rachlin, H., Raineri, A., & Cross, D. (1991). Subjective probability and delay. *Journal of the Experimental Analysis of Behavior, 55,* 233–244.

Rachman, S. (1997). A cognitive theory of obsessions. *Behaviour Research and Therapy, 35,* 793–802.

Rapee, R.M., & Hayman, K. (1996). The effects of video feedback on the self-evaluation of performance in socially anxious subjects. *Behaviour Research and Therapy, 34,* 315–322.

Rapport, M.D., Murphy, H.A., & Bailey, J.S. (1982). Ritalin versus response cost in the control of hyperactive children: A within-subject comparison. *Journal of Applied Behavior Analysis, 15,* 205–216.

Rauhut, A.S., McPhee, J.E., & Ayres, J.J.B. (1999). Blocked and overshadowed stimuli are weakened in their ability to serve as blockers and second-order reinforcers in Pavlovian fear conditioning. *Journal of Experimental Psychology: Animal Behavior Processes, 25,* 45–67.

Read, P.P. (1974). *Alive: The story of the Andes survivors.* New York: Lippincott.

Redd, W.H., Porterfield, A.L., & Anderson, B.L. (1979). *Behavior modification: Behavioral approaches to human problems.* New York: Random House.

Reese, E. (1972). *The analysis of human operant behavior.* Dubuque, IA: Wm. C. Brown.

Reese, H.W. (1989). Rules and rule-governance: Cognitive and behavioristic views. In S.C. Hayes (Ed.), *Rule-governed behavior: Cognition, contingencies, and instructional control* (pp. 3–84). New York: Plenum Press.

Reitman, D. (1998). The real and imagined harmful effects of rewards: Implicatons for clinical practice. *Behavior Therapy and Experimental Psychiatry, 29,* 110–111

Reitman, D., & Drabman, R.S. (1997). The value of recognizing our differences and promoting healthy competition: The cognitive behavioral debate. *Behavior Therapy, 28,* 419–429.

Repp, A.C., & Singh, N.N. (Eds.). (1990). *Perspectives on the use of nonaversive and aversive interventions for persons with developmental disabilities.* Sycamore, IL: Sycamore Publishing.

Rescorla, R.A. (1967). Pavlovian conditioning and its proper control procedures. *Psychological Review, 74,* 1–80.

Rescorla, R.A. (1969). Pavlovian conditioned inhibition. *Psychological Bulletin, 72,* 77–94.

Rescorla, R.A. (1980). *Pavlovian second-order conditioning: Studies in associative learning.* Hillsdale, NJ: Erlbaum.

Rescorla, R.A. (1988). Pavlovian conditioning: It's not what you think it is. *American Psychologist, 43,* 151–160.

Rescorla, R.A. (1991). Associative relations in instrumental learning: The Eighteenth Bartlett Memorial Lecture. *Quarterly Journal of Experimental Psychology, 43B,* 1–23.

Rescorla, R.A. (1993). Inhibitory associations between S and R in extinction. *Animal Learning & Behavior, 21,* 327–336.

Rescorla, R.A. (1997). Response-inhibition in extinction. *The Quarterly Journal of Experimental Psychology, 50B,* 238–252.

Rescorla, R.A. (1999a). Associative changes in elements and compounds when the other is reinforced. *Journal of Experimental Psychology: Animal Behavior Processes, 25,* 247–255.

Rescorla, R.A. (1999b). Summation and overexpectation with qualitatively different outcomes. *Animal Learning & Behavior, 21,* 50–62.

Rescorla, R.A., & Wagner, A.R. (1972). A theory of Pavlovian conditioning: Variations in the effectiveness of reinforcement and non-reinforcement. In A.H. Black & W.F. Prokasy (Eds.), *Classical conditioning II: Current theory and research* (pp. 64–99). New York: Appleton-Century-Crofts.

Reynolds, G.S. (1961). Behavioral contrast. *Journal of the Experimental Analysis of Behavior, 4,* 57–71.

Reynolds, L.K. & Kelley, M.L. (1997). The efficacy of a response cost-based treatment package for managing aggressive behavior in preschoolers. *Behavior Modification, 21,* 216–230.

Rhodes, R. (1973). *The ungodly.* New York: McKay.

Richman, D.M., Berg, W.K., Wacker, D.P., Stephens, T., Rankin, B., & Kilroy, J. (1997). Using pretreatment and posttreatment assessments to enhance and evaluate existing treatment packages. *Journal of Applied Behavior Analysis, 30,* 709–712.

Rilling, M. (1977). Stimulus control and inhibitory processes. In W.K. Honig & J.E.R. Staddon (Eds.), *Handbook of operant behavior* (pp. 432–480). Englewood Cliffs, NJ: Prentice Hall.

Roberts, S., & Neuringer, A. (1998). Self-experimentation. In K.A. Lattal & M. Perone (Eds.), *Handbook of research methods* (pp. 619–655). New York: Plenum Press.

Rodd, Z.A., Rosellini, R.A., Stock, H.S., & Gallup, G.G. Jr. (1997). Learned helplessness in chickens (*Gallus gallus*): Evidence for attentional bias. *Learning and Motivation, 28,* 43–55.

Rodewald, H.K. (1979). *Stimulus control of behavior.* Baltimore: University Park Press.

Rosales-Ruiz, J., & Baer, D.M. (1997). Behavioral cusps: A developmental and pragmatic concept for behavior analysis. *Journal of Applied Behavior Analysis, 30,* 533–544.

Rosas, J.M., & Bouton, M.E. (1997). Renewal of a conditioned taste aversion upon return to the conditioning context after extinction in another one. *Learning and Motivation, 28,* 216–229.

Rosecrance, J. (1985). *The degenerates of Lake Tahoe: A study of persistence in the social world of horse race gambling.* New York: P. Lang.

Rosenbaum, M. (1990a). Introduction: From helplessness to resourcefulness. In M. Rosenbaum (Ed.), *Learned resourcefulness* (pp. xxv–xxxv). New York: Springer Publishing.

Rosenbaum, M. (1990b). The role of learned resourcefulness in the self-control of health behavior. In M. Rosenbaum (Ed.), *Learned resourcefulness* (pp. 3–30). New York: Springer Publishing.

Rosenfeld, H.M., & Baer, D.M. (1969). Unnoticed verbal conditioning of an aware experimenter by a more aware subject: The double-agent effect. *Psychological Review, 76,* 425–432.

Rosenhan, D.L. (1973). On being sane in insane places. *Science, 179,* 250–258.

Rosenthal, T.L., & Zimmerman, B.J. (1978). *Social learning and cognition.* New York: Academic Press.

Rothbaum, B.O., & Hodges, L.F. (1999). The use of virtual reality exposure in the treatment of anxiety disorders. *Behavior Modifiation, 23,* 507–525.

Rothbaum, B.O., Hodges, L.F., Kooper, R., Opdyke, D., Williford, J.S., & North, M. (1995). Virtual reality graded exposure in the treatment of acrophobia: A case report. *Behavior Therapy, 26,* 547–554.

Rottschaefer, W.A. (1991). Social learning theories of moral agency. *Behavior and Philosophy, 19*(1), 61–76.

Rotter, J.B. (1954). *Social learning and clinical psychology.* Englewood Cliffs, NJ: Prentice Hall.

Roy, D.F. (1953). Work satisfaction and social reward in quota achievement: An analysis of piecework incentive. *American Sociological Review, 18,* 507–514.

Rudestam, K.E. (1980). *Methods of self-change.* Monterey, CA: Brooks/Cole.

Ruggiero, V.R. (1984). *The art of thinking: A guide to critical and creative thought.* New York: Harper & Row.

Rutter, D.R., & Stephenson, G.M. (1979). The functions of looking: Effects of friendship on gaze. *British Journal of Social and Clinical Psychology, 18,* 203–205.

Ryder, R.G. (1968). Husband-wife dyads versus married strangers. *Family Process, 7,* 233–238.

Rye, M.S., & Ullman, D. (1999). The successful treatment of long-term selective mutism: A case study. *Journal of Behavior Therapy and Experimental Psychiatry, 30,* 313–323.

Saar, M. (1996, February 1). Cardboard crime fighter. *Los Angeles Times,* p. B4.

Saboonchi, F., Lundh, L.-G., Öst, L.-G. (1999). Perfectionism and self-consciousness in social phobia and panic disorder with agoraphobia. *Behaviour Research and Therapy, 37,* 799–808.

Sakagami, T., Hursh, S.R., Christensen, J., & Silberberg, A. (1989). Income maximizing in concurrent interval-ratio schedules. *Journal of the Experimental Analysis of Behavior, 52,* 41–46.

Salkovskis, P.M. (1999). Understanding and treating obsessive-compulsive disorder. *Behaviour Research and Therapy, 37,* S29–S52.

Saunders, K.J., & Spradlin, J.E. (1990). Conditional discrimination in mentally retarded adults: The development of generalized skills. *Journal of the Experimental Analysis of Behavior, 54,* 239–250.

Saunders, K.J., & Williams, D.C. (1998). Stimulus-control procedures. In K.A. Lattal & M. Perone (Eds.), *Handbook of research methods in human operant behavior,* pp. 193–228. New York: Plenum Press.

Saunders, R.R., Drake, K.M., & Spradlin, J.E. (1999). Equivalence class establishment, expansion, and modification in preschool children. *Journal of the Experimental Analysis of Behavior, 71,* 195–214.

Schachter, S. (1967). Cognitive effects on bodily functioning: Studies on obesity and eating. In D. G. Glass (Ed.), *Neurophysiology and emotion* (pp. 117–144). New York: Rockefeller University Press.

Schachter, S., & Singer, J.F. (1962). Cognitive, social and physiological determinants of emotional state. *Psychological Review, 69,* 379–399.

Schachtman, T.R., & Reed, P. (1998). Optimization: Some factors that facilitate and hinder optimal performance in animals and humans. In W. O'Donohue (Ed.), *Learning and behavior therapy* (pp. 301–333). Boston: Allyn and Bacon.

Schafe, G.E., Sollars, S.I., & Bernstein, I.L. (1995). The CS–US interval and taste aversion learning: A brief look. *Behavioral Neuroscience, 109,* 799–802.

Schlinger, H.D., Blakely, E., & Kaczor, T. (1990). Pausing under variable-ratio schedules: Interaction of reinforcer magnitude, variable-ratio size, and lowest ratio. *Journal of the Experimental Analysis of Behavior, 53,* 133–139.

Schlinger, H.D. (1993). Separating discriminative and function-altering effects of verbal stimuli. *The Behavior Analyst, 16,* 9–23.

Schmitt, D.R. (1998). Effects of consequences of advice on patterns of rule control and rule choice. *Journal of the Experimental Analysis of Behavior, 70,* 1–21.

Schneier, F.R., Martin, L.Y., Liebowitz, M.R., Gorman, J.M., & Fyer, A.J. (1989). Alcohol abuse in social phobia. *Journal of Anxiety Disorders, 3,* 15–23.

Schoenfeld, W.N. (1995). "Reinforcement" in behavior theory. *The Behavior Analyst, 18,* 173–185.

Scholing, A., & Emmelkamp, P.M.G. (1993). Cognitive and behavioural treatments of fear of blushing, sweating or trembling. *Behaviour Research and Therapy, 31,* 155–170.

Schulman, M. (1973). Backstage behaviorism. *Psychology Today, 7*(1), 51–88.

Schultz, D.D. (1965). *Sensory restriction: Effects on behavior.* New York: Academic Press.

Schur, E.M. (1965). *Crimes without victims.* Englewood Cliffs, NJ: Prentice Hall.

Schutte, R.C., & Hopkins, B.L. (1970). The effects of teacher attention on following instructions in a kindergarten class. *Journal of Applied Behavior Analysis, 3,* 117–122.

Schwartz, B. (1984). *Psychology of learning and behavior.* New York: Norton.

Schwartz, B., & Gamzu, E. (1977). Pavlovian control of operant behavior. In W.K. Honig & J.E.R. Staddon (Eds.), *Handbook of operant behavior* (pp. 53–97). Englewood Cliffs, NJ: Prentice Hall.

Schwartz, I.S., & Baer, D.M. (1991). Social validity assessments: Is current practice state of the art? *Journal of Applied Behavior Analysis, 24,* 189–204.

Schwartz, M., & Stanton, A.H. (1950). A social psychological study of incontinence. *Psychiatry, 13,* 399–416.

Schwartz, S.M., Gramling, S.E., & Mancini, T. (1994). The influence of life stress, personality, and learning history on illness behavior. *Journal of Behavior Therapy and Experimental Psychiatry, 25,* 135–142.

Scott, D.S., Scott, L.M., & Goldwater, B. (1997). A performance improvement program for an international-level track and field athlete. *Journal of Applied Behavior Analysis, 30,* 573–575.

Scott, J.F. (1971). *Internalization of norms: A sociological theory of moral commitment.* Englewood Cliffs, NJ: Prentice Hall.

Scruggs, T.E., & Mastropieri, M.A. (1998). Summarizing single-subject research: Issues and applications. *Behavior Modification, 22,* 221–242.

Seibert, S.E., Crant, J.M., & Kraimer, M.L. (1999). Proactive personality and career success. *Journal of Applied Psychology, 84,* 416–427.

Seligman, M.E.P. (1966). CS redundancy and secondary punishment. *Journal of Experimental Psychology, 72,* 546–550.

Seligman, M.E.P. (1975). *Helplessness.* San Francisco: Freeman.

Seligman, M.E.P. (1998) *Learned optimism.* New York: Simon & Schuster.

Seligman, M.E.P., & Csikszentmihalyi, M. (2000). Positive psychology: An introduction. *American Psychologist, 55,* 5–14.

Seligman, M.E.P., & Hager, J. (1972). *The biological boundaries of learning.* New York: Appleton-Century-Crofts.

Selye, H. (1956). *The stress of life.* New York: McGraw-Hill.

Shafran, R., Booth, R., & Rachman, S. (1993). The reduction of claustrophobia—II: Cognitive analyses. *Behaviour Research and Therapy, 31,* 75–85.

Sharenow, E.L., Fuqua, R.W., & Miltenberger, R.G. (1989). The treatment of muscle tics with dissimilar competing response practice. *Journal of Applied Behavior Analysis, 22,* 35–42.

Sharpe, T., Brown, M., & Crider, K. (1995). The effects of a sportsmanship curriculum intervention on generalized positive social behavior of urban elementary school students. *Journal of Applied Behavior Analysis, 28,* 401–416.

Sheeber, L., Hops, H., Andrews, J., Alpert, T., & Davis, B. (1998). Interactional processes in families with depressed and nondepressed adolescents: Reinforcement of depressive behavior. *Behaviour Research and Therapy, 36,* 417–427.

Sherman, A.R. (1972). Real-life exposure as a primary therapeutic factor in the desensitization treatment for fear. *Journal of Abnormal Psychology, 79,* 19–28.

Shimoff, E., & Catania, A.C. (1998). The verbal governance of behavior. In K.A. Lattal & M. Perone (Eds.), *Handbook of research methods in human operant behavior* (pp. 371–404). New York: Plenum Press.

Shore, B.A., Iwata, B.A., Lerman, D.C., & Shirley, M.J. (1994). Assessing and programming generalized behavioral reduction across multiple stimulus parameters. *Journal of Applied Behavior Analysis, 27,* 371–384.

Shull, R. L., & Lawrence, P.S. (1998). Reinforcement: Schedule performance. In K.A. Lattal & M. Perone (Eds.), *Handbook of research methods in human operant behavior* (pp. 95–129). New York: Plenum Press.

Shurtleff, D., & Silberberg, A. (1990). Income maximizing on concurrent ratio-interval schedules of reinforcement. *Journal of the Experimental Analysis of Behavior, 53,* 273–284.

Sieder, J.J. (1996). The latest head trip: Virtual reality technology may be a cost-effective therapy. *U.S. News & World Report, 120*(6), 55.

Sigmundi, R.A., & Bolles, R.C. (1983). CS modality, context conditioning, and conditioned freezing. *Animal Learning & Behavior, 11,* 205–212.

Silber, K.P., & Haynes, C.E. (1992). Treating nailbiting: A comparative analysis of mild aversion and competing response therapies. *Behaviour Research and Therapy, 30,* 15–22.

Silberberg, A., Thomas, J.R., & Berendzen, N. (1991). Human choice on concurrent variable-interval variable-ratio schedules. *Journal of the Experimental Analysis of Behavior, 56,* 575–584.

Silbert, M.H., & Pines, A.M. (1981). Occupational hazards of street prostitutes. *Criminal Justice and Behavior, 8,* 395–399.

Silva, F.J., & Timberlake, W. (2000). A clarification of the nature of backward excitatory conditioning. *Learning and Motivation, 31,* 67–80.

Silva, K.M., & Timberlake, W. (1997). A behavior systems view of conditioned states during long and short CS–US intervals. *Learning and Motivation 28,* 465–490.

Simpson, J.A., Ickes, W., & Blackstone, T. (1995). When the head protects the heart. *Journal of Personality and Social Psychology, 69,* 629–641.

Singer, G.H.S., Gert, B., & Koegel, R.L. (1999). A moral framework for analyzing the controversy over aversive behavioral interventions for people with severe mental retardation. *Journal of Positive Behavior Interventions, 1,* 88–100.

Singh, N.N., & Solman, R.T. (1990). A stimulus control analysis of the picture-word problem in children who are mentally retarded: The blocking effect. *Journal of Applied Behavior Analysis, 23,* 525–532.

Sisson, L.A., Van Hasselt, V.B., Hersen, M., & Aurand, J.C. (1988). Tripartite behavioral intervention to reduce stereotypic and disruptive behaviors in young multihand-icapped children. *Behavior Therapy, 19,* 503–527.

Skinner, B.F. (1938). *The behavior of organisms: An experimental analysis.* New York: Appleton-Century.

Skinner, B.F. (1948a). *Walden two.* New York: Macmillan.

Skinner, B.F. (1948b). Superstition in the pigeon. *Journal of Experimental Psychology, 38,* 168–172.

Skinner, B.F. (1953). *Science and human behavior.* New York: Macmillan.

Skinner, B.F. (1957). *Verbal behavior.* New York: Appleton-Century-Crofts.

Skinner, B.F. (1966). The phylogeny and ontogeny of behavior. *Science, 153,* 1205–1213.

Skinner, B.F. (1968). *The technology of teaching.* Englewood Cliffs, NJ: Prentice Hall.

Skinner, B.F. (1969). *Contingencies of reinforcement.* New York: Appleton-Century-Crofts.

Skinner, B.F. (1971). *Beyond freedom and dignity.* New York: Knopf.

Skinner, B.F. (1974). *About behaviorism.* New York: Knopf.

Skinner, B.F. (1980). *Notebooks.* Englewood Cliffs, NJ: Prentice Hall.

Skinner, B.F. (1988). The operant side of behavior therapy. *Journal of Behavior Therapy and Experimental Psychiatry, 19,* 171–179.

Skinner, B.F. (1989a). *Recent issues in the analysis of behavior.* Columbus, OH: Merrill Publishing.

Skinner, B.F. (1989b). The origins of cognitive thought. *American Psychologist, 44,* 13–18.

Skinner, B.F. (1990). Can psychology be a science of mind? *American Psychologist, 45,* 1206–1210.

Skinner, B.F. (1991). The originating self. In W. Grove & D. Cicchetti (Eds.), *Thinking clearly about psychology: Vol. 2: Personality and psychopathology. Essays in honor of Paul E. Meehl* (pp. 3–9). Minneapolis: University of Minnesota Press.

Slade, P.D., & Owens, R.G. (1998). A dual process model of perfectionism based on reinforcement theory. *Behavior Modification, 22,* 372–390.

Sloan, D.M., & Mizes, J.C. (1996). The use of contingency management in the treatment of a geriatric nursing home patient with psychogenic vomiting. *Journal of Behavior Therapy and Experimental Psychiatry, 27,* 57–65.

Smith, J.E., & Meyers, R.J. (1995). The community reinforcement approach. In R.K. Hester & W.R. Miller (Eds.), *Handbook of alcoholism treatment approaches: Effective alternatives* (2nd ed., pp. 251–266). Boston: Allyn and Bacon.

Smith, R.E., Smoll, F.L., & Christensen, D.S. (1996). Behavioral assessment and interventions in youth sports. *Behavior Modification, 20,* 3–44.

Smith, R.G., & Iwata, B.A. (1997). Antecedent influences on behavior disorders. *Journal of Applied Behavior Analysis, 30,* 343–375.

Smith, R.G., Iwata, B.A., Goh, H.-L., & Shore, B.A. (1995). Analysis of establishing operations for self-injury maintained by escape. *Journal of Applied Behavior Analysis, 28,* 515–535.

Smith, S.G., Rothbaum, B.O., & Hodges, L. (1999). Treatment of fear of flying using virtual reality exposure therapy: A single case study. *The Behavior Therapist, 22*(8), 154–158.

Snyder, J.J., & Patterson, G.R. (1995). Individual differences in social aggression: A test of a reinforcement model of socialization in the natural environment. *Behavior Therapy, 26,* 371–391.

Spaulding, W. (1986). Assessment of adult-onset pervasive behavior disorders. In A.R. Ciminero, K.S. Calhoun, & H.E. Adams (Eds.), *Handbook of behavioral assessment* (2nd ed., pp. 631–669). New York: Wiley.

Spetch, M.L., Belke, T.W., Barnet, R.C., Dunn, R., & Pierce, W.D. (1990). Suboptimal choice in a percentage-reinforcement procedure: Effects of signal condition and terminal-link length. *Journal of the Experimental Analysis of Behavior, 53,* 219–234.

Staats, A.W. (1963). *Complex human behavior.* New York: Holt.

Staats, A.W. (1968). *Learning, language, and cognition.* New York: Holt.

Staats, A.W. (1975). *Social behaviorism.* Homewood, IL: Dorsey.

Staats, A.W. (1999). Valuable, but not maximal: It's time behavior therapy attend to its behaviorism. *Behaviour Research and Therapy, 37,* 369–378.

Staddon, J.E.R. (1977). Schedule-induced behavior. In W.K. Honig & J. E. R. Staddon (Eds.), *Handbook of operant behavior* (pp. 125–152). Englewood Cliffs, NJ: Prentice Hall.

Stark, L.J., Allen, K.D., Hurst, M., Nash, D.A., Rigney, B., & Stokes, T.F. (1989). Distraction: Its utilization and efficacy with children undergoing dental treatment. *Journal of Applied Behavior Analysis, 22,* 297–307.

Stein, B.E., & Meredith, M.A. (1993). *The merging of the senses.* Cambridge, MA: MIT Press.

Stein, L. (1958). Secondary reinforcement established with subcortical stimulation. *Science, 127,* 466–467.

Steketee, G. (1994). Behavioral assessment and treatment planning with obsessive compulsive disorder: A review emphasizing clinical application. *Behavior Therapy, 25,* 613–633.

Stemmer, N. (1990). Skinner's verbal behavior, Chomsky's review, and metalism. *Journal of the Experimental Analysis of Behavior, 54*, 307–315.

Stemmer, N. (1992). Skinner and a solution to the problem of inner events. *The Behavior Analyst, 15*, 115–128.

Stepanek, M. (1999, December 13). Using the net for brainstorming. *BusinessWeek*, pp. EB55–EB59.

Steriade, M. (1996). Arousal: Revisiting the reticular activating system. *Science, 272*, 225–226.

Stern, D. (1977). *The first relationship: Mother and infant.* Cambridge, MA: Harvard University Press.

Stix, G. (1995). Putting the man back in transit. *Scientific American, 272*(5), 32–33.

Stöber, J. (1998). Worry, problem elaboration and suppression of imagery: The role of concreteness. *Behaviour Research and Therapy, 36*, 751–756.

Stock, L.Z., & Milan, M.A. (1993). Improving dietary practices of elderly individuals: The power of prompting, feedback, and social reinforcement. *Journal of Applied Behavior Analysis, 26*, 379–387.

Stokes, T.F., Osnes, P.G., & Guevremont, D.C. (1987). Saying and doing: A commentary on a contingency-space analysis. *Journal of Applied Behavior Analysis, 20*, 161–164.

Stolarz-Fantino, S., & Fantino, E. (1995). The experimental analysis of reasoning: A review of Gilovich's how we know what isn't so! *Journal of the Experimental Analysis of Behavior, 64*, 111–116.

Storms, L.H., Boroczi, G., & Broen, W.E., Jr. (1962). Punishment inhibits an instrumental response in hooded rats. *Science, 135*, 1133–1134.

Strauss, M.A., & Gelles, R.J. (1990). *Physical violence in American families.* New Brunswick, NJ: Transaction Books.

Subbotsky, E.V. (1993). *Foundations of the mind.* Cambridge, MA: Harvard University Press.

Sulzer, B., & Mayer, G.R. (1972). *Behavior modification procedures for school personnel.* Hinsdale, IL: Dryden Press.

Sulzer-Azaroff, B. (1997). Why should I talk to my baby? A review of *Meaningful differences in the everyday experience of young American children* by Hart and Risley. *Journal of Applied Behavior Analysis, 30*, 599–600.

Tavris, C., & Wade, C. (1984). *The longest war: Sex differences in perspective* (2nd ed.). New York: Harcourt Brace Jovanovich.

Taylor, I., & O'Reilly, M.F. (1997). Toward a functional analysis of private verbal self-regulation. *Journal of Applied Behavior Analysis, 30*, 43–58.

Taylor, J.E., Deane, F.P., & Podd, J.V. (1999). Stability of driving fear acquisition pathways over one year. *Behaviour Research and Therapy, 37*, 927–939.

Taylor, S. (1996). Meta-analysis of cognitive-behavioral treatments for social phobia. *Journal of Behavior Therapy and Experimental Psychiatry, 27*, 1–9.

Taylor, S., Woody, S., Koch, W.J., McLean, P., Paterson, R.J., & Anderson, K.W. (1997). Cognitive restructuring in the treatment of social phobia. *Behavior Modification, 21*, 487–511.

Teitelbaum, P. (1977). Levels of integration of the operant. In W.K. Honig & J.E.R. Staddon (Eds.), *Handbook of operant behavior* (pp. 7–27). Englewood Cliffs, NJ: Prentice Hall.

Telch, M.J., Lucas, J.A., Schmidt, N.B., Hanna, H.H., Jaimez, T.L., & Lucas, R.A. (1993). Group cognitive-behavioral treatment of panic disorder. *Behaviour Research and Therapy, 31*, 279–287.

Terrace, H.S. (1971). Classical conditioning. In J.A. Nevin, & G.S. Reynolds (Eds.), *The study of behavior.* Glenview, IL: Scott, Foresman.

Theeboom, M., De Knop, P., & Weiss, M.R. (1995). Motivational climate, psychological responses, and motor skill development in children's sport: A field-based intervention study. *Journal of Sport & Exercise Psychology, 17*, 294–311.

Thibaut, J.W., & Kelley, H.H. (1959). *The social psychology of groups.* New York: Wiley.

Thomas, K. (Ed.). (1999). *The Oxford book of work.* New York: Oxford University Press.

Thompson, J.K. (1992). Body image: Extent of disturbance, associated features, theoretical models, assessment methodologies, intervention strategies, and a proposal for a new DSM IV diagnostic category—body image disorder. In M. Hersen, R.M. Eisler, & P.M. Miller (Eds.), *Progress in behavior modification* (Vol. 28, pp. 3–54). Sycamore, IL: Sycamore Publishing.

Thorpe, S.J., & Salkovskis, P.M. (1998). Selective attention to real phobic and safety stimuli. *Behaviour Research and Therapy, 36*, 471–481.

Thyer, B.A. (1995). Promoting an empiricist agenda within the human services: An ethical and humanistic imperative. *Journal of Behavior Therapy and Experimental Psychiatry, 26*, 93–98.

Tolin, D.F., Lohr, J.M., Lee T.C., & Sawchuk, C.N. (1999). Visual avoidance in specific phobia. *Behaviour Research and Therapy, 37*, 63–70.

Tollison, C.D., & Adams, H.E. (1979). *Sexual disorders: Treatment, theory and research.* New York: Gardner Press.

Touchette, P.E., & Howard, J.S. (1984). Errorless learning: Reinforcement contingencies and stimulus control transfer in delayed prompting. *Journal of Applied Behavior Analysis, 17*, 175–188.

Tsukamoto, M., Iwanaga, M., & Seiwa, H. (1997). A facilitator in self-reported perception of physical symptoms: The role of contingency between physical symptom and aversive event. *Perceptual and Motor Skills, 85*, 787–799.

Tudor, R.M. (1995). Isolating the effects of active responding in computer-based instruction. *Journal of Applied Behavior Analysis, 28*, 343–344.

Tudor, R.M., & Bostow, D.E. (1991). Computer-programmed instruction: The relation of required interaction to practical application. *Journal of Applied Behavior Analysis, 24*, 361–368.

van Dijk, W.W., Zeelenberg, M., & van der Pligt, J. (1999). Not having what you want versus having what you do not want: The impact of negative outcome on the experience of disappointment and related emotions. *Cognition and Emotion, 13,* 129–148.

Van Hout, W.J.P.J., Emmelkamp, P.M.G., & Scholing, A. (1994). The role of negative self-statements during exposure in vivo: A process study of eight panic disorder patients with agoraphobia. *Behavior Modification, 18,* 389–410.

Van Houten, R. (1983). Punishment: From the animal laboratory to the applied setting. In S. Axelrod & J. Apsche (Eds.), *The effects of punishment on human behavior.* New York: Academic Press.

Van Houten, R., & Rolider, A. (1988). Recreating the scene: An effective way to provide delayed punishment for inappropriate motor behavior. *Journal of Applied Behavior Analysis, 21,* 187–192.

Vaughan, M. (1989). Rule-governed behavior in behavior analysis: A theoretical and experimental history. In S.C. Hayes (Ed.), *Rule-governed behavior: Cognition, contingencies, and instructional control* (pp. 97–118). New York: Plenum Press.

Veljaca, K.-A., & Rapee, R.M. (1998). Detection of negative and positive audience behaviours by socially anxious subjects. *Behaviour Research and Therapy, 36,* 311–321.

Vollmer, T.R., Iwata, B.A., Zarcone, J.R., Smith, R.G., & Mazaleski, J.L. (1993). The role of attention in the treatment of attention-maintained self-injurious behavior: Noncontingent reinforcement and differential reinforcement of other behavior. *Journal of Applied Behavior Analysis, 26,* 9–21.

Vollmer, T.R., Marcus, B.A., Ringdahl, J.E., & Roane, H.S. (1995). Progression from brief assessments to extended experimental analyses in the evaluation of aberrant behavior. *Journal of Applied Behavior Analysis, 28,* 561–576.

Vygotsky, L.S. (1962). *Thought and language* (E. Hanfmann & G. Vakar, Eds. & Trans.). Cambridge, MA: MIT Press. (Original work published 1934.)

Vygotsky, L.S. (1978). *Mind in society: The development of higher psychological processes* (M. Cole, V. John-Steiner, S. Scribner, & E. Soubermand, Eds.). Cambridge, MA: Harvard University Press.

Wagaman, J.R., Miltenberger, R.G., & Arndorfer, R.E. (1993). Analysis of a simplified treatment for stuttering in children. *Journal of Applied Behavior Analysis, 26,* 53–61.

Wagaman, J.R., Miltenberger, R.G., & Williams, D.E. (1995). Treatment of a vocal tic by differential reinforcement. *Journal of Behavior Therapy and Experimental Psychiatry, 26,* 35–39.

Wagner, A.R., & Brandon, S.E. (1989). Evolution of a structured connectionist model of Pavlovian conditioning (AESOP). In S.B. Klein & R.R. Mowrer (Eds.), *Contemporary learning theories: Pavlovian conditioning and the status of traditional learning theory.* Hillsdale, NJ: Erlbaum.

Wagner, J.L, & Winett, R.A. (1988). Prompting one low-fat, high-fiber selection in a fast-food restaurant. *Journal of Applied Behavior Analysis, 21,* 179–185.

Walen, S.R., Hauserman, N.M., & Lavin, P.J. (1977). *Clinical guide to behavior therapy.* Baltimore: Williams & Wilkins.

Walters, G.C., & Grusec, J.E. (1977). *Punishment.* San Francisco: Freeman.

Warda, G., & Bryant, R.A. (1998). Thought control strategies in acute stress disorder. *Behaviour Research and Therapy, 36,* 1171–1175.

Ward-Robinson, J. & Hall, G. (1999). The role of mediated conditioning in acquired equivalence. *The Quarterly Journal of Experimental Psychology, 52B,* 335–350.

Watson, D.L., & Tharp, R.G. (1997). *Self-directed behavior: Self-modification for personal adjustment* (7th ed.). Pacific Grove, CA: Brooks/Cole.

Watson, T.S. (1996). A prompt plus delayed contingency procedure for reducing bathroom graffiti. *Journal of Applied Behavior Analysis, 29,* 121–124.

Watson, T.S., & Sterling, H.E. (1998). Brief functional analysis and treatment of a vocal tic. *Journal of Applied Behavior Analysis, 31,* 471–474.

Wearden, J.H. (1983). Undermatching and overmatching as deviations from the matching law. *Journal of the Experimental Analysis of Behavior, 40,* 332–340.

Weatherly, J.N., Melville, C.L., & Swindell, S. (1997). Behavioral contrast using a percentage reinforcement procedure. *Learning and Motivation, 28,* 368–381.

Webb, E.J. (1966). *Unobtrusive measures: Nonreactive research in the social sciences.* Chicago: Rand McNally.

Webster-Stratton, C., & Herbert, M. (1994). Strategies for helping parents of children with conduct disorders. In M. Hersen, R.M. Eisler, & P.M. Miller (Eds.), *Progress in behavior modification* (Vol. 29, pp. 121–142). Pacific Grove, CA: Brooks/Cole.

Weinberg, M.S., Williams, C.J., & Calhan, C. (1995). "If the shoe fits . . .": Exploring male homosexual foot fetishism. *The Journal of Sex Research, 32,* 17–27.

Weiner, H. (1965). Conditioning history and maladaptive human operant behavior. *Psychological Reports, 17,* 935–942.

Weiner, H. (1969). Controlling human fixed-interval performance. *Journal of the Experimental Analysis of Behavior, 12,* 349–373.

Weisberg, P., & Rovee-Collier, O. (1998). Behavioral processes of infants and young children. In K.A. Lattal & M. Perone (Eds.), *Handbook of research methods in human operant behavior* (pp. 355–370). New York: Plenum Press.

Weiss, S.J. (1972). Stimulus compounding in free-operant and classical conditioning: A review and analysis. *Psychological Bulletin, 78,* 189–208.

Weiss, S.J., & Panlilio, L.V. (1999). Blocking a selective association in pigeons. *Journal of the Experimental Analysis of Behavior, 71,* 13–24.

Weiss, S.J., & Weissman, R.D. (1992). Generalization peak shift for autoshaped and operant key pecks. *Journal of the Experimental Analysis of Behavior, 57,* 127–143.

Welch, J. (1998). *Jack Welch speaks: Wisdom from the world's greatest business leader.* New York: Wiley.

Welker, W.I. (1961). An analysis of exploratory and play behavior in animals. In D.W. Fiske & S.R. Maddi (Eds.), *Functions of varied experience* (pp. 175–226). Homewood, IL: Dorsey Press.

Welker, W.I. (1971). Ontogeny of play and exploratory behaviors: A definition of problems and a search for new conceptual solutions. In H. Moltz (Ed.), *The ontogeny of vertebrate behavior* (pp. 171–228). New York: Academic Press.

Wells, A., & Papageorgiou, C. (1998). Social phobia: Effects of external attention on anxiety, negative beliefs, and perspective taking. *Behavior Therapy, 29*, 357–370.

Welsh, T.M., Miller, L.K., & Altus, D.E. (1994). Programming for survival: A meeting system that survives 8 years later. *Journal of Applied Behavior Analysis, 27*, 423–433.

Wendland-Carro, J., Piccinini, C.A., & Millar, W.S. (1999). The role of an early intervention on enhancing the quality of mother-infant interaction. *Child Development, 70*, 713–721.

Werle, M.A., Murphy, T.B., & Budd, K.S. (1993). Treating chronic food refusal in young children: Home-based parent training. *Journal of Applied Behavior Analysis, 26*, 421–433.

Werner, E.E. (1989). Children of the garden island. *Scientific American, 260*(4), 106–108, 108D, 110–111.

Werts, M.G., Caldwell, N.K., & Wolery, M. (1996). Peer modeling of response chains: Observational learning by students with disabilities. *Journal of Applied Behavior Analysis, 29*, 53–66.

Westbrook, D., & Hill, L. (1998). The long-term outcome of cognitive behaviour therapy for adults in routine clinical practice. *Behaviour Research and Therapy, 36*, 635–643.

White, C.T., & Schlosberg, H. (1952). Degree of conditioning of the GSR as a function of the period of delay. *Journal of Experimental Psychology, 43*, 357–362.

White, G.L., Fishbein, S., & Rutstein, J. (1981). Passionate love and the misattribution of arousal. *Journal of Personality and Social Psychology, 41*, 56–62.

White, T.H. (1978). *In search of history: A personal adventure.* New York: Harper & Row.

Wickelgren, I. (1999). Nurture helps mold able minds. *Science, 283*, 1832–1834.

Widom, C. (1989). The cycle of violence. *Science, 244*, 160–166.

Wiertelak, E.P., Watkins, L.R., & Maier, S.F. (1992). Conditioned inhibition of analgesia. *Animal Learning & Behavior, 20*, 339–349.

Wilkie, D.M., & Willson, R.J. (1992). Time-place learning by pigeons, *Columba livia. Journal of the Experimental Analysis of Behavior, 57*, 145–158.

Williams, B.A. (1991). Choices as a function of local versus molar reinforcement contingencies. *Journal of the Experimental Analysis of Behavior, 56*, 455–473.

Williams, B.A. (1994). Conditioned reinforcement: Experimental and theoretical issues. *The Behavior Analyst, 17*, 261–285.

Williams, B.A., & Bell, M.C. (1999). Preference after training with differential changeover delays. *Journal of the Experimental Analysis of Behavior, 71*, 45–55.

Williams, C.D. (1959). The elimination of tantrum behavior by extinction procedures. *Journal of Abnormal and Social Psychology, 59*, 269.

Williams, D.A. (1995). Forms of inhibition in animal and human learning. *Journal of Experimental Psychology: Animal Behavior Processes, 21*, 129–142.

Williams, J.L. (1973). *Operant learning: Procedures for changing behavior.* Monterey, CA: Brooks/Cole.

Winter, F., Ferreira, A., & Bowers, N. (1973). Decision-making in married and unrelated couples. *Family Process, 12*, 83–94.

Wittgenstein, L. (1953). *Philosophical investigations.* New York: Macmillan.

Wixted, J.T. (1998). Remembering and forgetting. In K.A. Lattal & M. Perone (Eds.), *Handbook of research methods in human operant behavior,* pp. 263–289. New York: Plenum Press.

Wolko, K.L., Hrycaiko, D.W., & Martin, G.L. (1993). A comparison of two self-management packages to standard coaching for improving practice performance of gymnasts. *Behavior Modification, 17*, 209–223.

Woods, D.W., & Miltenberger, R.G. (1995). Habit reversal: A review of applications and variations. *Journal of Behavior Therapy and Experimental Psychiatry, 26*, 123–131.

Woods, D.W., & Wright, L.W., Jr. (1998). Dismantling simplified regulated breathing: A case of a bilingual stutterer. *Journal of Behavior Therapy and Experimental Psychiatry, 29*, 179–186.

Workman, E.A., & Katz, A.M. (1995). *Teaching behavioral self-control to students.* Austin, TX: pro•ed.

Wulfert, E., Dougher, M.J., & Greenway, D.E. (1991). Protocol analysis of the correspondence of verbal behavior and equivalence class formation. *Journal of the Experimental Analysis of Behavior, 56*, 489–504.

Wyckoff, L.B. (1969). The role of observing response in discrimination learning. In D.P. Hendry (Ed.), *Conditioned reinforcement* (pp. 237–260). Homewood, IL: Dorsey Press.

Yerkes, R.M., & Dodson, J.D. (1908). The relation of strength of stimulus to rapidity of habit formation. *Journal of Comparative Neurology and Psychology, 18*, 459–482.

Young, J.M., Krantz, P.J., McClannahan, L.E., & Poulson, C.L. (1994). Generalized imitation and response-class formation in children with autism. *Journal of Applied Behavior Analysis, 27*, 685–697.

Zanolli, K., Daggett, J., Ortiz, K., & Mullins, J. (1999). Using rapidly alternating multiple schedules to assess and treat aberrant behavior in natural settings. *Behavior Modification, 23*, 358–378.

Zarcone, J.R., Iwata, B.A., Vollmer, T.R., Jagtiani, S., Smith, R.G., & Mazaleski, J.L. (1993). Extinction of self-injurious escape behavior with and without instructional fading. *Journal of Applied Behavior Analysis, 26*, 353–360.

Zeiler, M. (1977). Schedules of reinforcement: The controlling variables. In W.K. Honig & J.E.R. Staddon (Eds.), *Handbook of operant behavior* (pp. 201–232). Englewood Cliffs, NJ: Prentice Hall.

Zeiler, M.D. (1992). On immediate function. *Journal of the Experimental Analysis of Behavior, 57,* 417–427.

Zeiler, M.D., & Blakely, T.F. (1983). Choice between response units: The rate constancy model. *Journal of the Experimental Analysis of Behavior, 39,* 275–291.

Zeiler, M.D., & Harzem, P. (1979). *Reinforcement and the organization of behavior.* New York: Wiley.

Zhou, L., Goff, G.A., & Iwata, B. (2000). Effects of increased response effort on self-injury and object manipulation as competing responses. *Journal of Applied Behavior Analysis, 33,* 29–40.

Zilbergeld, B. (1992). *The new male sexuality.* New York: Bantam.

Zimbardo, P.G., Pilkonis, P.A., & Norwood, R.M. (1975). The social disease called shyness. *Psychology Today, 8*(12), 68–70, 72.

Zimbardo, P.G., & Radl, S. (1981). *The shy child.* New York: McGraw-Hill.

Zimmerman, E.H., & Zimmerman, J. (1962). The alteration of behavior in a special classroom situation. *Journal of the Experimental Analysis of Behavior, 5,* 59–60.

Zuckerman, M. (1974). The sensation seeking motive. In B.A. Maher (Ed.), *Progress in experimental personality research* (Vol. 7, pp. 79–148). New York: Academic Press.

Zuckerman, M. (1984). Sensation seeking: A comparative approach to a human trait. *The Behavioral and Brain Sciences, 7,* 413–434.

Zuckerman, M. (1994). *Behavioral expressions and biosocial bases of sensation seeking.* New York: Cambridge University Press.

Zvolensky, M.J., Lejuez, C.W., & Eifert, G.H. (2000). Prediction and control: Operational definitions for the experimental analysis of anxiety. *Behaviour Research and Therapy, 38,* 653–663.

Name Index

Subject Index

401